Beneath The Shroud

James Joseph Jacks

Beneath The Shroud

By James Joseph Jacks

Published By
Positive Imaging, LLC
http://positive-imaging.com
bill@positive-imaging.com

All Right Reserved

This book or any portion thereof may not be reproduced or used in any manner whatsoever without the express written permission of the publisher except for the use of brief quotations in a book review.

Copyright © 2019   James Joseph Jacks
ISBN: 9781944071929

Life inside two secret companies funded by the United States to do their bidding in hot war zones during the Cold War. This shows a close-up view of the suffering they played a part in while supporting what history has clearly shown to be the misguided foreign policies of the United States in the Congo and Cambodia.

I have tried to recreate events, locales and conversations from my memories of them. In order to maintain their anonymity in some instances I have changed the names of individuals and places, I may have changed some identifying characteristics and details such as physical properties, occupations and places of residence.

The portrayal of certain individuals whose names and other details have been changed to conceal their true identities are solely based on my opinions.

Table of Contents

Dedication	5
Prologue	6
Hamilton—My Mayberry	9
Journey To Nod	31
Anchor's Away	37
Soaring On The Wings of the Wind	79
Descending Into The Heart of Darkness	113
Cambodia—Trail of Tears	375
Epilogue	511
Index	517

Dedication

Beneath The Shroud is dedicated to all those we left behind. Those Cambodians who trusted us to keep our word and not abandon them if they followed us into the Vietnam War effort. Very specifically it is dedicated to my wife's family members of whom she is the sole survivor: her father, HRH Prince Norodom Phurissara, her brother Prince Sisowath Doung Khara, her brother Prince Sisowath Ritharavong, her sister Princess Norodom Ronida, her sister's husband and three precious little children, her brother Prince Norodom Vondera, his wife and two children, her brother Prince Norodom Vinsady, and her brother Prince Norodom Thanarath . . . all murdered or allowed to starve by the Khmer Rouge.

It is dedicated to my children who over the years never ceased urging me to "write it down." Finally, to my wife Princess Norodom Danine who patiently tolerated immeasurable hours of absence as I stayed locked up in my study at my computer while recording this. Also, I thank my classmate Michal Jones Bagley for her numerous hours spent proofing in a valiant effort to save me from myself.

Prologue

To grasp the full impact of Beneath The Shroud, it is necessary to experience the story through the worldview of a young boy who grew up in rural Texas during the 1950s. While such a blessed childhood instilled much intrinsic worth, it left most, if not all of us, significantly unprepared to experience the destruction and carnage the United States was sowing either in places like Vietnam where the entire world was watching, or the equally horrific but, for the most part invisible, "secret wars." These secret wars were being carried out by what was known in the trade as "proprietary airlines," as well as numerous agents in parts of the world, that for the most part, nobody ever heard of.

Beneath The Shroud is not the story of life inside two of the many special airlines (proprietary companies) whose sole customer was the Central Intelligence Agency. Rather it is the story of life inside these proprietary companies for one of Hamilton's sons. Many of Hamilton's brave young men have served . . . WWI, WWII, Korea, Vietnam, Afghanistan, Iraq. While they can never be fully appreciated, at least they are recognized. May we never forget to thank them for their service and in the case of those who served in Vietnam, remember to *welcome them home*.

For years the story behind Beneath The Shroud could not be told. However recently the CIA released over 10,000 pages of declassified documents many dealing with the proprietary companies operating in Vietnam, Laos, Cambodia, and Thailand. Often referred to as "The Secret War." These documents are now housed at Texas Tech University Vietnam Center and Archive.

A very bright side of this often heavy book is that by default the reader will gain insight into life in Hamilton and Hamilton County Texas during this period. In many instances, it will be possible to walk the streets of Hamilton, fish the rivers and streams, and meet some of the residents.

While the injustice and carnage rising like smoke from a military burn pit worked tirelessly to reshape boundaries and dull my conscience, somehow, remarkably, the vast majority of who I was emerged intact at the other end, although not without a few skirmishes with PTSD and some other minor social adjustments.

The Prodigal Son

Jimmy Joe Jacks was the archetypical prodigal son of Hamilton. Despite some significant outwardly divergent appearances, he was deeply rooted in his Christian faith. This undoubtedly was thanks to his God-fearing parents and the tireless work of Sunday school teachers from the First Baptist Church of Hamilton and the unceasing prayers of a few saints who refused to give up on him when all others had. To those hand full of saints, even to this day, I remain eternally grateful.

Once again, the key to understanding the true meaning of Beneath the Shroud is to realize you are viewing it through the eyes of a 1950s era prodigal son of Hamilton Texas. It's not a history of Hamilton Texas; it's not a biography; it's not an expose of CIA Proprietary Companies.

Hamilton – My Mayberry

*Beulah Land, I'm longing for you and some day on thee I'll stand.
There my home shall be eternal. Beulah Land -- Sweet Beulah Land*[1]

Carpe Diem

Hamilton was Mayberry; the perfect microcosm in which to learn about life, love, role models, right and wrong; it was all there. School began with the Pledge of Allegiance, life centered on the church; banks and other businesses closed on Sundays and for General Robert E. Lee's birthday...homes were never locked. Important issues from politics to Friday night's Hamilton Bulldogs football game were all on the open agenda at Fred Fetty's *Fred's Café* on the South side of the square. Land sold for $60 an acre; it cost 3 cents to mail a first-class letter. When you picked up the phone to make a call, the operator said, "number please," and you gave her the three-digit phone number you wanted to call. Many people were on "party lines" which meant you could pick up the phone to make a call and find your neighbor talking to somebody. The August night skies glowed red from Hamilton's three cotton gins burning the hulls extracted from the cotton. A light left burning on the front porch of Riley's Funeral Home meant someone had died. For a young boy, Hamilton was a close-to-perfect place in time.

Somehow, via some enigmatic subliminal process, some of those ethics and tenets were inscribed in my value system. However, I must reluctantly be the first of many to proclaim it was some significant time afterward before any of these values perceivably influenced my behavior.

My father, Jimmie Jacks, was the manager for the Lone Star Gas Company, a large corporation responsible for all the natural gas distribution in our part of Texas. In 1952, my mother Lois, my younger sister Camille and I followed my father, Jimmie to his new assignment as manager of the Hamilton district of Lone Star Gas.

With few exceptions, most of the articulated memories I have of childhood occur in Hamilton County Texas, the place I shall always call home. The banks of the Leon River and Hamilton County's various creeks and ponds provided an exceptional opportunity to learn the ways of the outdoors. It was a wonderful opportunity to learn to hunt, trap, fish, swim, and camp. For many of us, our fathers had grown up in a like manner. This offered priceless opportunities to learn from them as they had learned from their fathers.

---

[1] *Beulah Land* by Squire Parsons – 1973, inspired by song of same title by Edgar Page Stites circa 1875

My East Ward Elementary School Playground

Hamilton of the early 1950s was a safe environment. We roamed all over the East Hill *afoot* (in summertime literally shoeless) and on our bicycles. There was little traffic and little danger and no drugs. Our sheriff didn't even wear a gun.

One particular forbidden and alluring danger was the old East Ward Elementary School. This was an old abandoned two-story brick school building. We kids all were strictly warned not to go inside. Not only was it forbidden, it was scary inside there as well. My best memories of the old East Ward School were sliding down its fire escape slides. Today East Ward School is gone; Hamilton County General Hospital stands on the site. But my memories remain.

Life in Hamilton was full of joy and I was determined to get my share. Early in adolescence, I recall my beloved cousin James McDonald (*Little Jimmy* named for my father) telling me about the ancient Roman expression "*carpe diem*" meaning seize the moment or more literally…seize the day. While my childhood years were indisputably barren with respect to academia, I'm sure I understood this carpe diem factor well prior to puberty. It unquestionably was one of my driving forces for several decades.

A Man And His Mules

His name was Benjamin Linton; most folks just called him Ben. I called him "Mr. Linton." He lived in a house that reminded me of old houses in the Saturday matinée western movies at the Strand Theater. His house had no paint and no evidence of paint. It was down an old unpaved caliche road which is now Nicholson Street, just by where St. Thomas Catholic Church is located today. Ben Linton was old. He told me he had lived 84 years. He said he was born in 1870. He wore denim overalls and white long sleeve shirts, buttoned at the neck. His only transportation was a wooden wagon. I always figured his wagon was older than he was. He had two white mules he would hitch to his wagon. Mr. Linton would pick up extra money plowing people's gardens. He had an old plow that also reminded me of the ones in the matinée movies. He would put the plow in the back of his wagon and head out looking for gardens to plow. I never wondered at the time how he managed to get the heavy plow up in the back of his old wagon; but the fact that he did attested to his pioneer character.

He would always stop and talk with me when he saw me playing in my front yard. He would let me climb up in the seat of the wagon with him and he would hand me the reins. I'm quite sure I controlled nothing. The mules knew where they were, where they lived, and were probably anxious to get home. No doubt Ben Linton found humor in my naiveté and excitement.

So much did I enjoy his company that I would often ride all the way to his house. He would frequently stop the wagon and point out various spots. Ben Linton had grown up in his house. He related stories about the Tonkawa Indian tribe that lived not far from his house. He told me about how when he was a young boy, he slipped into his mother's kitchen and stole an iron pot so he could go trade the pot to the Indians for a real bow and some arrows. I asked him if he got a whipping; he replied yes. The village was only a few hundred yards from his house. He showed me the very spot.

One day, just after a hard rain, I was perched up in the seat of Mr. Linton's wagon. As we got about halfway down the road to his house, he stopped the wagon and pointed to an open field on the right side of the road. He told me if I walked around in that field and looked closely after a rain, I could probably find some arrowheads. I didn't wait another second. I hopped out of the wagon, slipped between the barbed wire of the fence and started looking closely at the ground. It wasn't long before, just as Mr. Linton had said, I spotted my first arrowhead. I found many nice points and plenty of chips in that same field while I was growing up. The field was located not far from what today is Bert and Fay Schrank's back yard. It was many years later, before the housing edition and Navajo Trail were built. He also showed me another place which today is behind St. Thomas Catholic Church. There was no church there at that time. I found an almost perfect spear point and a bird arrow point on that location. Both were rare finds.

I remember in 1955; it was a cold day in February. We were just returning from enjoying our recess on the dirt playground of Ann Whitney Elementary School (named after a Hamilton County pioneer school teacher killed by a roving band of Comanche Indians July 9, 1867). As we took our seats, our teacher announced that Mr. Ben Linton had just died. My heart was sad. I had lost a friend. Benjamin W. Linton: February 27, 1870 – February 28, 1955. Most were thinking about the old man who drove around Hamilton in a wooden wagon pulled by two white mules. I was thinking about my friend who let me drive his wagon and told me wonderful stories about the Indians. I was blessed to have had Ben Linton as my friend.

The Queen In My Living Room

One of my first vivid memories from Hamilton childhood was the coronation of Queen Elizabeth II on 2 June, 1953. She looked so young and beautiful. I was sitting in our living room on East Boynton Street gazing intently at our new RCA black and white television set. It was a gift from my beloved cousin, *Little Jimmy,* to my mother and father. The kindest thing I could say about the image was that it tended to appear "snowy" and the set required somebody to get up frequently and adjust the vertical hold control to keep the picture from scrolling. But that was the nature of the beast back then; a small inconvenience indeed for such a wonderful entertainment device. Not to mention the status, irrespective of how transitory, of having one of the first TV sets in Hamilton.

A King Far Away

On 9 September 1953, more than 9,000 miles from Hamilton, while my family was still learning to adjust their new RCA television, Cambodia was gaining its independence from France. King Norodom Sihanouk, at age 31, became head of state. He had been King of Cambodia since 1941 but Cambodia until 9 September, 1953, had been part of French Indochina. Threads of this multifarious tapestry were continuing to be woven into place by the Master Weaver but few were watching and far fewer were able to conceptualize its far-reaching pattern, a pattern that would someday reach into my father's living room in Hamilton.

King Of The Hill

We lived on what was then called the "East Hill." The town square lay at the foot of the hill. As far as I know, the term "East Hill" is no longer in common use. But, living on the hill had some definite advantages. For one thing, it meant we had the best TV reception in town. Hamilton was far from any TV station so to pull in any kind of watchable signal, a tower of considerable height was required. While "rabbit ears" worked for those living in the big cities like Dallas and Ft. Worth, we Hamiltonians needed a tower. I remember our neighbors Bert and Fay Schrank got a television set about the time we did. Bert, with his background in electronics and radio from his US Air Force service had purchased and rigged a motorized, rotating device so he could select, via a little command module sitting on top of his TV set, the direction he wanted the antenna to point. Ours required a much greater physical input. TV stations were not numerous then. I can remember KCEN TV in Temple, KWTX in Waco, and on good days WFAA in the Dallas – Ft. Worth area.

1954: The bulk of the French army is defeated at Dien Bien Phu. This is the first time in history a colonial power is militarily defeated; a massive decolonization follows worldwide. At the Geneva conference, the country is partitioned at the 17th parallel as an interim stage. The North becomes the Democratic Republic of Vietnam, a communist state supported by China and the USSR. The French colonial area was known as French Indochina and today in Vietnam, Cambodia, and Laos. This defeat gave birth to communism exported from China and Russia into the entire region which was French Into China.[2]

The King of Kings

Life for our family, as it was for most families in Hamilton back then, was centered around the church. For my family it was the First Baptist Church. Everybody went to church on Sunday. If, on rare occasions, someone decided instead to go fishing or do some other non-church activity, it was

---

[2] Timeline of Vietnam History By Quang-Tuan Luong © 2001

necessary to leave town via the most sparsely-traveled streets in order to avoid being the object of wagging tongues. I recall doing this more than once.

Sometimes a local businessman named Thomas Addis Emmett would take me fishing on Sundays. Everybody just called him "Add." I, of course, called him Mr. Emmett. He was a super fisherman and knew how to land some huge bass. He was also getting old enough that he appreciated having somebody to jump out and open all the pasture gates for him. We would be scheduled to leave about 7:00 a.m. and when I would wake up at 6:45 I would see his car parked out in front of our house patiently waiting for me. While he never said, I could tell he was a bit disappointed that I did not share his enthusiasm for getting an early start on things. Add Emmett didn't believe in taking all the back streets, and I can remember slinking down in his front seat a bit until we were well out of town for fear of being seen by some of the First Baptist Church's devout brothers and sisters. Looking back now it seems ludicrous, but at the time it was a very real sense of guilt. Fishing with Mr. Emmett taught me some excellent techniques for bass that I've employed throughout the years with considerable success.

But in spite of my semi-regular Sunday morning backsliding, under the gentle nurturing of my mother, I placed my faith in Jesus as my redeemer, made my public confession of faith in front of the full congregation one Sunday morning, and in obedience, was Baptized on Sunday April 12 1953, nine days before my tenth birthday.

The music of my First Baptist Church years remains with me today. Sometimes it was years later before the depth of some of the lyrics finally reached home. A specific lyric from Amazing Grace used to perplex me. It went:

> *When we've been here ten thousand years*
> *Bright shining as the sun.*
> *We've no less days to sing God's praise*
> *Than when we've first begun.*

It was decades later before I fully understood what a wonderful way to spend eternity that would be. Today, so many decades later, I can still hear the deep bass voice of Brad Corrigan, Sr., and Otto Lengefeld's beautiful tenor singing those timeless hymns from our church choir.

The "King" In My Living Room

Another TV moment for me came a couple of years later when Elvis Presley made his famous Sunday, 9 September, 1956, appearance on The Ed Sullivan Show. For me and all my 13-year-old Hamiltonian friends, this was the event of the century…and we almost missed it. How…because, it was a Sunday and we were supposed to go to church! Over 60 million people watched that Sunday evening…82.6% of the nation's television audience. I wouldn't be surprised if over 90% of the parents watching thought we were all going to hell. While our parents weren't yet ready for Elvis, all my Ann Whitney Elementary School 8th grade friends were. We were ready to rock & roll![3]

King Of The Wild Frontier[4]

Getting back to my first days in Hamilton, I was blessed to have Randy Hays as a neighbor. She was tall, beautiful, and just my age. Within days of our family moving to Hamilton, Randy and I were best of friends. We would ride our bicycles all over the East Hill. We were never "boyfriend and girlfriend," just close friends.

Randy was a good listener and somehow tolerated my endless Daniel Boone, Jim Bowie, and Davy Crockett male chauvinistic personas. It seems each time a movie framed in the frontier setting would come out, I'd appropriate various character traits exhibited by my movie heroes. They just seemed to fit what I was certain I was destined to become. I even learned to play "The Ballad of Davy Crockett," the theme song from the Walt Disney movie, on our piano. I must have played it a million times. Back then with no air conditioning and everybody's windows up in the summer, this must have thrilled Bert and Fay Schrank, our next-door neighbors on East Boynton Street.

At the time, East Boynton Street had no other street to the north. What is now East Gentry was then, north and east of N. Wieser, a seldom-used two rut car trail through an open field just across the street from our house. I'm unable to remember now if there had ever been any asphalt on it but when I lived there East Gentry marked the beginning of my *wild frontier*.

I shot my first rabbit with my Crossman .22 caliber pellet gun between Boynton and Gentry. Pecan Creek ran about half a mile north of my front door, through fields and wooded areas. After crossing Gentry (if I counted that as a street), there were no more streets or roads to cross. To a boy of about 11, half a mile seemed like five miles. What a great adventure wandering about in that "wild frontier." It was also the perfect place to learn to shoot my trusty frontier rifle, aka Crossman pellet gun.

Dr. Robert A. Kooken's home was off to the northwest just a bit but never visible and Ben Linton's house lay to the northeast where St. Thomas Catholic Church is today, also not visible. There were no houses to destroy the illusion of wilderness. Randy and I would wander through these vast stretches of "wild frontier" together. Our friend Cindy Robinson would sometimes join us as we explored the *wilderness*. I proudly wore my Montgomery Ward mail

---

[3] Edgerton, Gary R. The Columbia History of American Television p187. Columbia University Press; 2007. ISBN 0-231-12165-2.

[4] Davy Crockett, King of the Wild Frontier a 1955 Walt Disney adventure film starring Fess Parker as Davy Crockett

order hunting knife at my side just in case I needed to protect them with something other than my pellet gun. Jim Bowie could not have possibly been any prouder of his famous namesake than was I of my trusty "Monkey-Ward" knife with embossed leather sheath. I was king-of-cool.

Another piece of my great outdoors paraphernalia was a Montgomery Ward mail order casting rod and reel. I would spend countless hours practicing learning to drop a plug inside an old tire placed at the end of the driveway while my little sister Camille rode her tricycle over my fishing line. Initially, I also spent countless hours undoing backlashes so prevalent in those old open-face reels. The unusual casting accuracy I had as a teenager, without doubt, came from those endless hours of casting a plug at that old tire in the driveway. My real fishing skill was developed from fishing trips to the Hamilton City Lake either on my bicycle or with my father in his pickup, followed later by trips with friends to the Leon River.

My friend Travis Cozby lived "out in the country" as we used to say. His place was ideal for hunting and camping. His mom Reba and dad Pete (always Mr. & Mrs. Cozby to me) were super parents and always helped us out with some of the camping gear (especially iron skillets, pots, etc.) Alton (Pete) Cozby was an outstanding outdoorsman and I learned as much from him as I did my own father who was an expert fisherman and trapper.

Before we would go camping, I would go to A.G. Thompson's grocery store or Otto Lengefeld's grocery store and carefully select items in cans that were easy to cook, or in reality, heat on a campfire. Pork and beans, and Vienna sausage were top favorites. I'd buy a couple of large potatoes to bake in the ashes as well. I'd pay partly from my allowance and partly with contributions from my mother and father. I would then carefully save the S&H Green Stamps to give to my mother. I envisioned myself as a genuine campfire culinary master chef.

While we were learning to camp, fish, and hunt, in addition to exploring the subtle nuances of being attracted to members of the opposite gender, halfway around the world, in 1955, the pro-American Ngo Dinh Diem became President of South Vietnam in October. America agreed to train Diem's army. For the most part, this distant event went unnoticed.

Garage Dances, Friends, and Feelings

Elvis was King and the airwaves were starting to come alive with something besides Hank Williams. When our parents went shopping outside Hamilton (an almost treasonous act at the time) we would send our saved-up allowances and promises of best behavior along with them so they would buy and bring home to us the very latest 45 rpm recordings. I so clearly remember my mother and father bringing back from Waco Elvis's *"Love Me Tender."*[5] I found the flip side, *"Any Way You Want Me"* equally attractive as both sides were slow and romantic and even a moron could grasp the potential this

---
[5] *#1 on the Billboard charts the week ending November 3, 1956*

offered. I also remember my mother saying, "that's not even correct…it's Love Me Tenderly." But I wasn't going to let a minor thing like an incorrect adverb misdirect my focus, which was firmly fixed on Randy's upcoming "garage dance." Her parents were letting her have a party…a "boy and girl party"…a real dance. I remember getting my father to drive me out to Travis Cozby's house just east of town on Highway 36 to tell him Randy wanted him to come to her party. Travis, as many back then who did not live in town, did not have a telephone. He was so excited. Heck… we were all excited. Randy's girl friends were coming. We were going to get to dance with girls. But the problem was…the girls were all better dancers than we were. They practiced. They practiced dancing with other girls. That certainly wasn't an option for us. We were just going to have to try not to step on their toes. To further complicate the situation, for the most part, they were all taller than we were. Travis was probably the only exception.

This special occasion called for a new shirt. After all, image was everything. I negotiated with my parents for the shirt purchase. I'd pay half from my allowance and the money I made working at odd jobs. I won their approval. They were probably as excited for me as I was excited about the dance. Anyway, I made a quick trip down to Harelik's dry goods store on the square. Milton Harelik helped me find something my size that I was sure all the girls would like. Milton was so cool. He assured me they would all like my new shirt. I remember seeing Milton's dad, Mr. Haskell Harelik, in the store. He didn't do too much anymore, he just more or less left it all to Milton, but Mr. Haskell was a living legend in Hamilton. He had started as a Jewish immigrant with nothing, just after the turn of the century, selling vegetables from a wagon. I never went in that store without thinking I was probably looking at the most respected man in Hamilton.

The night of the dance came. Randy's parents, A.C. and Cleo Hays, had helped decorate the garage. We had a record player. Everybody brought their best, records and we danced, and we danced, and we danced. But for sure, the most played record was my just-arrived "Love Me Tender" by Elvis. It was slow; it was romantic; I'm sure I fell in love. I must have. The songs were so full of meaning. We were living our lives in four-quarter time. We were blessed.

A year or so later, the most beloved of all my teachers, Leila Craddock, the foremost individual responsible for my understanding of grammatical structure, declamation and debate, playfully announced to the class that the song's title was grammatically incorrect…that it is "Love Me Tenderly"…that tenderly was an adverb. That made twice I got the adverb lecture…my mother and later Mrs. Craddock. Thank you Leila Craddock; the lessons you taught me have served me well.

Puppy Love

By the sixth grade I was sure I had found "true love." Her name was Gloria Ann Keller (pseudonym). The extent of our relationship was long romantic gazes across the classroom and the exchange of pencil and notebook paper "love letters" (I think we used words like "really like") via trusted third-party girlfriends. On occasional instances, with my heart pounding so loudly that was all I could hear, I would pass the note directly to her. The relationship was complicated by the fact that she lived out in Blue Ridge and rode the school bus every day. She did get to come to town with her parents on Saturday while they did their shopping around the square. Back then, almost everyone came to Hamilton on Saturday to buy supplies. The parents would use this time to visit and exchange information as well as buy needed items. In those days you didn't run to the grocery store every time you needed something. While the parents were doing their shopping, the children were allowed to attend the 10 cent matinée at the Strand Theater located on the north side of the square roughly where the Hamilton County Appraisal District is now. Later, when the Strand closed, we went to the Texan Theater. There we could sit together with our friends and if you had a girlfriend, and you were really in serious love, you might on rare occasions, hold each other's nervous, sweaty hand. We watched old black and white movies, like Abbott and Costello, Lash LaRue, and The Lone Ranger.

Meanwhile, in Vietnam, Diem started to arrest anyone suspected of being in the Vietminh.

Teenager In Love

The complexities and nuances of adolescence soon found the focus of my romantic energies centered on another classmate, Michal Jones. Our romantic relationship included going to movies together, attending church-sponsored hayrides, and occasional dances hosted by the parents of some of our group. Michal's parents Bob & Evelyn Jones, like A.C. & Cleo Hays, and Cindy Robinson's parents, Bill and Lydia helped nurture and channel our neophyte ventures into the uncharted waters of teen social interaction.

Also, by this time, Michal and I had graduated to the teenage preoccupation with talking on the phone for hours on end. This practice was far more annoying to adults then than it is today because we were all on party-lines and our telephone line was shared by one or more telephone subscribers. Sharing the party-line with a teenager back then was akin to the plague. These poor souls would pick up the handset and rather than hear the standard "number please" or later, a dial tone, would hear two teenage voices chatting away.

A good friend and classmate, Hardy Morgan's parents John and Blanch, were others who took an active interest in polishing our newly acquired social acumen. One of the earliest parties Hardy hosted was a "sit-down dinner" in their formal dining room. The girls were, of course, better at this kind of stuff, the boys had to concentrate on not holding their knife like they were about to skin a rabbit, a deer, or something, while also trying to remember it was not necessary to strangle our fork. Following dinner, there were "dance lessons" in the kitchen and den. John and Blanch Morgan did a wonderful job of placing us in a learning environment and keeping it fun, so no one felt self-conscious. A significant task considering fifty percent of the group was composed of adolescent country boys.

I don't now recall exactly when, but as is the usual way of teen love, the romance Michal and I shared turned back to friendship and we each moved on. I have been blessed as I approach my seventh decade of life, with many of those years spent in foreign countries, to be once again close friends with Michal.

Elvis In My Bed Room

Ours was a blessed generation. We watched as country western and southern gospel music gave birth to rock & roll. Elvis, Little Richard, Buddy Holley, The Platters, Chuck Berry, The Drifters, Jerry Lee Lewis, Roy Orbison; the list goes on and on. Our records came to us mostly on 45 rpm "singles" followed soon afterward by 33 rpm "LP (long play)" albums. But record collections were expensive, around $0.89 to $1 a pop for a hot new 45, and Hamilton had no record shops. Once again, my beloved cousin *"Little Jimmy"*, made me the envy of Hamilton, at least for a few weeks, with the gift of a brand-new RCA Victor Portable 45 rpm Auto Change Record Player. I proudly carried it to our increasingly popular dances. Its sound quality was reminiscent of a beetle pooting in a can, but when you were dancing close (as close as we dared) becoming an amateur audiophile was not an option for any sensible red-blooded Hamilton County country boy. We would stack as many of the most romantic records we could make fit on the spindle, gently take the center of our affection for the moment in our arms and become lost in time. Our parents were more likely than not to believe the lyrics accompanied by the on-stage gyrations of our heroes were tickets straight to hell. Most of us committed the lyrics to memory without really giving a thought to the meanings. Looking back now, quite a few of those lyrics were a little more than a bit risqué.

"KCLW, 900 on your radio dial," our local radio station, broadcast from 7:30 a.m. till 6:15 p.m. They were still playing what their advertising customers liked, "Hillbilly"… Tennessee Ernie Ford, Eddy Arnold, Webb Pierce, Ernest Tubb (The Texas Troubadour) and Hank Snow…Plus still, plenty of Hank Williams although he died on New Year's Day 1953. Bobby Swinson, our most prominent local DJ, would read the news, read the local grocery store and dry good store advertisements for that week, and announce all the deaths and funeral times. The station had a very local flavor to put it kindly. The station got its call sign KCLW from its first owner Clyde L. Weatherby, who also for a time was the local Ford Motor Company dealer. It was great for the adult community but totally boring for a rock and roll-starved teen.

But by the mid-1950s top 40 radio pioneer Gordon McLendon took his radio station KLIF in Dallas to the rock and roll format and from then on there was no turning back. Our music was here to stay…And we could hear it on the radio without coughing up a dollar for a 45. Probably even more significant, we could hear it in our cars, which, as soon as we had reached 14 and old enough to get our driver's license, became the center of all our lives.

At night many of us tuned to the high power "clear channel" AM stations like KOMA 1520 in Oklahoma City, and WNOE 1060 New Orleans, both operating at 50,000 watts. Under ideal conditions, their signals could cover half the United States. Well, "clear channel" really meant "almost clear." I can still remember radio preachers like Oral Roberts selling "prayer handkerchiefs" or some other "holy object" drifting in on top of the song I was listening to. Normally this would only last a few seconds. But even that was too long when we were hanging on every word and note. I spent literally countless hours under the sheets with my AM radio trying to muffle the sound so my parents wouldn't come in and tell me to turn it off and go to sleep. Looking back now, I'm sure they could hear it and were just giving me "my space." At that time, I didn't yet have a transistor radio as they were still rather pricy. So, I drug the whole radio, electric cord and all, under the sheets. I can still feel the warm, surreal cocoon created by my radio and the sheets. Amazing how you recall some things so clearly. I was blessed.

My Father And My Evening Prayers

Each night before my music under the sheets routine, my father would come into the bedroom and say my prayers with me. This lasted until I left home for Loco Hills and the Navy. I can still today, some sixty years later, close my eyes and see him right there. I can feel his strong hand resting on my chest as he sat on the edge of my bed beside my head.

> *"Now I Lay Me Down To Sleep*
> *I pray the LORD my soul to keep*
> *Watch and guard me through the night*
> *And wake me with the morning light*
> *Amen"*

The Wolf Man In My Living Room

After having mentioned the parental social nurturing of Randy, Cindy, Michal and Hardy's parents, I would be seriously remiss if I left out my own parents, Jimmie and Lois Jacks. They had a costume party, along with a dance for our group. My beloved cousin James McDonald (*Little Jimmy*) who was an actor in New York had come to visit for a few days. He somewhere, I can't remember where now, came up with all this fuzzy black hair…real honest to goodness human hair… and spent hours somehow gluing it to his face, neck and hands. He looked more like a "wolf-man" than anything I'd ever seen in any movie.

Little Jimmy stayed out of sight and none of my friends knew he was there. Then, about midway through the party, he suddenly lifted the living room window which we had purposefully left ajar, and thrust himself, all the way up to his waist, into the room letting out a bloodcurdling growl. Travis Cozby was sitting closest the window and it literally scared the daylights out of him. Parents were ready with the camera and we got a priceless shot of all the kids jumping out of their seats and Travis's expression of mortal fear. Next week's Hamilton Herald News ran the photo. Little Jimmy's stage name was Jacks McDonald and although it would be five or six more years before Wolfman Jack would burst into national prominence propelled by the 250,000-watt Mexican border station XERF, for all practical purposes, "Wolfman Jacks" visited our living room in Hamilton Texas that night.

Living Contradictions

During this period, my personality was being molded like some abstract figure in the hands of a sculptor with a significant case of bipolar disorder. Not as in manic-depressive but rather as in the opposing influences, of culture versus agriculture, country western versus Broadway and classical, Hank Williams versus Tennessee Williams, *Classics Illustrated Comic Books* and Chaucer. I could leave my room where my record player would be playing something like *Faded Love* by Bob Wills and The Texas Playboys and walk into the living room where my mother would be listening to Judy Garland or one of Frédéric Chopin's Polonaises. I could even "hum along" on some of her favorites like *Polonaise in A-flat Major*. She had an old 78 rpm recording of Paderewski playing it in concert somewhere. That old recording must have had grooves worn as deep as the Grand Canyon. So, I grew up quite happily in a world of opposing yet not colliding forces. I was blessed.

High School – Driver's License and Girls

Just before graduating from the 8th grade at Ann Whitney Elementary School, immediately after my 14th birthday, I took advantage of a loophole in Texas law allowing fourteen-year-olds, with the consent of their parents, to acquire a driver's license under what was called a "hardship" condition. The regular minimum age for getting a driver's license in Texas was sixteen. So, as fate would have it, I had a driver's license at age 14, before I graduated from the 8th grade. My friend Randy Hays did too.

It was in the summer of the 8th grade that I seriously noticed Paula James (pseudonym). She was a year younger than I. It seemed she was the total center of my life. I could think of nothing else…my homework, my job delivering the Waco Times Herald…nothing. It was as if I'd lost my mind. I was sure every song I heard on the radio was about her. Jimmy Joe was in love. For real this time!

Meanwhile a group of North Vietnamese, known as the Vietminh, started a campaign of guerrilla warfare in South Vietnam. They later would become known as "Viet Cong." I'm sure neither Paula nor I ever gave a serious thought to who this group was and what they were trying to achieve. Much less likely could we have imagined how they would someday soon, tear that part of the world apart entangling an entire generation of America's finest young men.

At about this time, barely visible paths winding through the jungles of Vietnam, Laos, and Cambodia, were just beginning to be used by the Viet Cong to move men and supplies from the north into South Vietnam. These narrow winding paths would later be referred to as the "Ho Chi Minh Trail." Who would have thought these barely visible traces through the jungle would someday impact my life.

In a year or so, the romance Paula and I shared had dwindled. That was the path such things were preordained to follow. After Paula came the typical high school boy-girl dating scenario. There were several micro-romances as we all groped in the dim dawning light of our adolescence to discover ourselves. These were bewildering yet beautiful times. Nevertheless, even today, Paula remains an indelible memory.

Life was a turbulent mixture of music, hormones, highs and broken hearts; so profoundly complex that only another teenager in a transit moment of sanity could possibly comprehend. I was blessed.

281 Drive In
The Back Seat of My 48 Chevy

Along with getting my driver's license came the admission to another elite group…those who had the means to attend the drive-in movie just south of town on Highway 281. Sometimes I would only take my girlfriend of the moment but on other occasions, the penny-pinching in all of us would prevail and we would ditch the girls and all the boys would pile into one car to take advantage of the $1.00 per carload specials. Six people in the car was not uncommon. But the evening would not be entirely without the company of the feminine gender…the girls would be doing the same thing. The drive-in had just installed a new swimming pool so we would all sit around the pool or swim and watch the movie (go figure). These were magical summer nights. It was always sad when they were pushed aside by fall and the start of school.

Joe Ruben Register
When Death Comes Before Its Time

I have heard of a land on the faraway strand,
'Tis a beautiful home of the soul;

Built by Jesus on high, where we never shall die,
'Tis a land where we never grow old.[6]

Tuesday, December 3rd, 1957, dawned cold in the old wooden house in Littleville where my classmate Joe Ruben Register lived with his family. The temperature was about 35 degrees. It was 7:00 a.m. Joe got out of bed and went to restart the fire that had burned almost completely out during the night. He put a few pieces of wood into the stove and then doused some kerosene from a tin can onto the wood. Nothing happened. Joe then went to the kitchen and brought a five-gallon gas can filled with kerosene used by the family for cooking. He opened the wood stove's door and sloshed more kerosene on the smoldering wood. The stove immediately exploded unleashing an inferno. Joe was instantly covered in flames. According to Joe's sister Betty, also my classmate, Joe ran from the house…a human torch. Joe's mother and Betty frantically tried to put out the flames. Both Betty and her father were badly burned. In a matter of seconds, the old wooden structure was totally engulfed. Joe's mother raced back in the house barely managing to save her infant child. The house burned to the ground. Joe was rushed to the nearest hospital, in Hico, by Riley Funeral Home's hearse where they tried desperately but in vain to save Joe's life.

Later, the family theorized the stove's damper had vibrated closed from family members walking on the house's old floorboards. With the damper closed, the exploding flames had nowhere else to go but out the opening provided by the stove's open door.

Many classmates attended the funeral. I remember "Pop" Jordan's deep bass voice as they sang the typical funeral songs. I remember the open casket. In addition to being very sad, the funeral was a bit unsettling. Old people were supposed to die. But Joe was just shy of his sixteenth birthday. His sister Betty and I were only fourteen. I found it very unsettling. Sixty years later, as Betty recounted the details, she clearly carried both the physical and emotional scars of the tragedy.

Later in the Congo and especially in Cambodia while facing the carnage, the savage senseless acts of war, I would realize how poorly equipped my previous experiences had left me to process what I was seeing. Joe Ruben Register, while awakening the realization of life's unpredictability and seeming unfairness, would fall far short of providing an adequate shield for what I would later experience…far short.

Daring Love

I was a sophomore and she a senior. I wasn't particularly distinguishing myself in any of my subjects in high school, but Algebra II was proving far more than I was able to deal with. Looking back now, it would have been so simple. All I had to do was exactly what my teacher was telling me to do.

[6] *Where We'll Never Grow Old - James C. Moore, 1914*

"Quit trying to understand it and just memorize and properly apply the formulas." But to me, that was selling out. I was determined to understand it…just like I did everything. As a result, I was falling farther and farther behind the class. If something didn't happen soon, I was going to fail that six-week period.

But something did happen. My teacher decided he was going to get me some help. He appointed Kalie Brown (pseudonym) to give me special after-class instructions. I proved to be a quick learner. Somehow, I passed Algebra II but, in the process, I found myself hopelessly in love with an older girl. She was extremely popular, and my worst nightmare was that the senior boys would discover us and hand out a little retribution for daring to enter their turf. Fortunately, this never came about. Paul Anka's song, Diana, even today, brings back her memory so clearly. Just like it was yesterday. "I'm so young and you're so old…This, my darling, I've been told."[7]

Sundays Fishing On The Cowhouse Creek
Just like Peter, James, and John

Although this was a time when many of us were trading our fishing rods and hunting rifles in for cars and girls, my good friend Jerry Drake and I still managed to hunt and fish. I can see as clearly as if it were yesterday, Jerry and me along with his younger brother Bobby, sitting at their kitchen table, Sunday afternoons after church, enjoying Vivian Drake's incredible, made from scratch, rolls and perfectly fried chicken, potatoes and gravy. It was so good. After a huge meal, Jerry's dad Owen, (always Mr. Drake to me) would retire to his favorite armchair in the living room and doze. Jerry, Bobby, and I would then go fishing or dove hunting. Those were wonderful times. When Jerry and I get together now, we still remember those incredible meals and Sunday afternoons even though they occurred more than fifty years ago.

Rock House Baptist Church—Beer—And Pledge Cards
And Don't Forget The Church Key

While I attended the First Baptist Church of Hamilton every Sunday morning, a group of us boys would often attend Sunday evening services at the Rock House Baptist Church out near the Leon River east of Hamilton. Travis Cozby, his parents and his grandparents were all members there. I believe his grandparents may have been founding members. The church was tiny, and, in the summer they held revivals in an old brush arbor just behind the church. Because the church congregation was poor and could ill afford to present much of a "love offering" they usually could only find young seminary students to come and preach. Such was the case one summer night when a group of us decided to attend. While I can't remember now, I'm

---

[7] "Diana" by Paul Anka 1957

pretty sure we were there as a result of Travis's God-fearing mother, Reba, who always kept an eye on our souls.

Well, had the truth been known, some of us let Mrs. Cozby down seriously. We had a couple of six-packs of beer iced down in the trunk of my car and the plan was to leave the revival and go imbibe. The sermon was finished, and the call to accept the Lord was behind us...the sole element of the service remaining was a pledge of abstinence to alcohol. That was all that was standing in the way for us to be out of there. Unfortunately for us, this young seminary student had come with some primitively-printed pledge cards for all to sign saying we would never drink alcohol. Admirable enough I suppose for most of those in attendance. However, we were soon faced with a dilemma. All the adults and the young ladies in the congregation had signed the cards as soon as they were handed out. Our little group was the only holdout. All eyes were on us. We were as nervous as the preverbal *whore in church*. In those days, it was customary for the young people to sit on the front row close to some of the church elders so our behavior would remain above reproach or at the very least under scrutiny. None of us wanted to be duplicitous but simultaneously none of us wanted the ice packed around our beer to melt. We faced a dilemma. My logical mind soon began to see the advantages of compromise. I honestly don't remember who was the first of us to sign but sign we all did. Decades later, sitting around a campfire on a deer lease on Morgan Creek in Burnet County, Texas, several of us who had been in the group, now married with children of our own, confessed our transgressions to Mr. and Mrs. Cozby.

Aunts In The Dirt

The "Uranium Sitting Houses" Craze

My beloved cousin Little Jimmy was coming from New York where he lived and pursued his acting career. When he called, he said he would be bringing his mother, my father's sister Aunt Una Lee and her sister, my Aunt Ruth.

When they arrived we learned the rest of the story. My Aunt Una Lee was still a beautiful lady, for someone in her mid-sixties. But it was a family joke that she was a certifiable hypochondriac...something was always wrong with her. The high point of her week was her vitamin B12 injections. Aunt Una Lee had run across one of the hundreds of news and magazine articles about this wonder cure people were experiencing by sitting in dirt that contained traces of radioactivity from uranium. The epicenter of this Uranium Sitting craze was just next door in Comanche County, mostly around a little spot on the road nobody had ever heard of called Newberg, with a population of 35 according to official figures in 1968. It was only 27 miles if you went out the "Pottsville highway" and took a left toward Energy not far after the Country Club.

So my cousin Little Jimmy, shaking his head in disbelief at his mother's gullibility, persuaded me to go along with him. Little Jimmy and I sat in the front of his new rental car and his mother and my Aunt Ruth sat in the back. All the way there they were chattering like magpies about the miraculous cure they were both sure they were going to receive.

Apparently, some dairy farmer named Jesse Reese "discovered" the "healing" properties of the dirt on his farm. According to the story in Life Magazine's October 24, 1955 issue, thousands were flocking to receive these radio-active dirt energized cures. People were sitting on crowded benches with their bare feet in the dirt. Some people were lying in it while one of the "attendants" shoveled the dirt on them. Aunt Una Lee had brought along the copy of the specific Life Magazine to share with us. Upon our arrival, she decided to select the white cotton sock filled with the radioactive dirt draped around her neck and resting on her shoulders. Aunt Ruth went for the "feet in the sandbox" cure. It was hot as hell as we were in what appeared to be a converted chicken coup. As I remember, there were probably 50 or 60 people there at the time. It didn't take long for everybody to start perspiring. The reddish dirt was passing through the loosely woven cotton sock and soon was making a horrible looking reddish mud mess on Aunt Una Lee's neck. It was funny as hell but neither Little Jimmy or I dared laugh. However, that incident provided many a laugh in the years to come.

Snake Bit

It was on one of our Sunday-afternoon-after-church-outings that Jerry had what could have been a close call and I, for some still unknown reason, completely failed him. One of our favorite things to do after eating all the wonderful fried chicken, mashed potatoes, and heavenly hot rolls his mom, Vivian Drake, would fix for Sunday dinner, was to go fly fishing in Cowhouse Creek.

The weather was perfect. The creek level was perfect. The bass were biting. The technique was to wade the shallows with our fly rods using ultra-light jigs or spinner baits. We would generally split up. We'd been fishing for about thirty minutes and I thought I heard Jerry calling. Something very unusual for any of us to do. I made my way back up to the high ground of the bridge so I could hear better and hopefully see Jerry. When I reached the bridge, I was able to see him. He was standing in the shallows shouting he'd been bitten by a snake. To this day I still have no idea why I didn't believe him but for whatever the reason, I thought he was joking. I started to laugh and told him to cut the funny business. I left a perfectly good fishing spot to see what he was shouting about. His younger brother Bobby reached him about that time and confirmed he did in fact have two small puncture wounds. This could only mean water moccasin. Bobby & I loaded Jerry up in the car and we headed for Hamilton County General Hospital.

When we arrived, of course there was no doctor on duty. They had to call one. The nurses had some experience with snake bite (usually rattlesnake). They said that so far it was not showing any signs of venom having been injected with the bite. Jerry seemed to be doing OK except for being a little nervous. I suppose being bitten by a snake and being in the hospital could be considered just cause for being a little nervous. However, he was more than a little unhappy with me for not believing him when he said he'd been bitten by a snake. I suppose he had just cause for that as well. At any rate, I knew I had a date and it probably would be a good idea from her parents' point of view for me not to show up late again. I also thought he'd get over being upset with me for not believing him. So I headed home to get a bath and dressed up for my date. I was wrong about his getting over my not believing him. Now, more than fifty years later, he still shakes his huge fist at me and mumbles not very nice things about that day.

When I returned to the hospital with my date, Jerry had been admitted. He was in a hospital gown about which he emphatically warned me I would be in more pain than he was in if I even looked like I was going to laugh. He had a suction machine hooked to the spot of the two little punctures. They now appeared to have been enlarged by the hospital. There were hoses leading from the site of the bite to a large glass jar under his bed. The contents of the jar didn't look too good. But Jerry was now back to normal. After a few minutes, I grabbed my date and headed out the door before he started thinking about my laughing and not believing him again. Probably at one or both of our funerals, this story will be retold.

Asleep At The Wheel

On 8 July, 1959 the Viet Cong killed two U.S. Military advisors at Biên Hòa, the first American dead of the Vietnam War.

1 November 1959, Patrice Lumumba was arrested in the Belgium Congo. Congo's Mobutu became an asset of the US CIA during a meeting in Brussels approximately the same time.

My junior year at Hamilton High School (1959/1960) saw my grades continue gradually moving downward. It was like nobody was steering my ship. My parents quite understandably were becoming more anxious about me. Life had somehow evolved into one continuous search for adrenalin. I knew the path I was on was not only non-productive, but catastrophe-ladened as well. Yet it seemed I was somehow powerless to decelerate or at the very least, make some minor course adjustment. And in retrospect, at that time, I don't think there was much motivation for directional change. I was truly asleep at the wheel. *"I am slow of study."*[8]

---

[8] William Shakespeare - A Midsummer Night's Dream

The Best Laid Plans

As if all this weren't enough for my poor mother and father, a friend and I decided our classroom routine needed a little injection of excitement. We decided a well-crafted sulfur-based stink bomb should adequately ratchet things up a notch or two. Mrs. Hattie Newman's speech class was selected. Why Hattie Newman? I have no idea. She was the mother of my friend Bobby Newman, she was very nice, and we sometimes hung out over at her house. In retrospect, rationality was seldom applied to anything during that period in my life.

Phase one of our operation went according to design plan. We (my good friend Hardy Morgan…now Dr. Morgan, MD) took some of the solid-propellant rocket fuel we had been using in several earlier amateur rocket experiments and downgraded the oxidization agent to keep it from deflagrating too quickly. We then adjusted its sulfur component upward to insure the gas it produced would be especially noxious. We ignited a representative sample to check that we had the burn down correctly (a proof of concept exercise so to speak). It was essential for this mix to burn slowly, producing a generous quantity of "smoke." We had our proportions down correctly. The burn was just what we needed. The ignited mixture would remain confined in our primitive burn chamber and it would generate a decent amount of offensive sulfur-smelling smoke.

We still had to design and fabricate an igniter, a triggering device, and find a suitable power source for the igniter. I believe we settled on three or four D-cells hooked in parallel as our power source. The igniter was a simple thin strand of copper wire wrapped to form a coil. We placed the igniter in the little can of powder. We rigged an open/close circuit switch designed spring-loaded closed. The spring-loaded closed switch was held open by a thin, easily breakable thread which we attached to the outward opening classroom door. When Hattie Newman opened the door Monday morning, the thread would break, the spring-loaded circuit would close, the current would flow, heating our igniter, setting off our powder, and a sulfur smelling smoke would slowly be produced. At least that was the plan.

Our operation then entered the execution phase. Friday during speech class, I wedged a small piece of notebook paper in the window to insure it would not close securely. That night, we returned, climbed through the unlatched window and placed our device, set the triggering mechanism and supporting batteries, attached the thread to the door and left via the same window. I don't think I had a second thought about the episode the entire weekend.

As Monday morning came, I was set for what I was sure would be a great laugh…first period speech class students pouring out of the classroom complaining about the stink. But alas, *"The best laid schemes of mice and men go often awry, and leave us nothing but grief and pain, for promised joy!"* [9] Somehow over the weekend, as best as we could later tell from our subsequent analysis, the batteries had drained to a point too low to heat the igniter coil to a degree required to achieve sustained combustion of our powder. Had this been our regular rocket fuel, it would easily have ignited but we had choked down this mixture to retard the burn rate as well as increase the sulfur smell. Sustainable combustion required a lot more heat than we generated that morning. It just fizzled and went out. Years later, I'm sure I could fill a sizable mission debrief report on things we could have done better, including not doing it at all.

The Fizzle That Lead To Our Dismissal

"Just fizzled" hardly does justice to the last act of this comedy of errors in which after 60 years, the final curtain still refuses to close. As Hattie Newman and her students entered the classroom, rather than being greeted by a slowly developing cloud of foul-smelling smoke, they spotted our admittedly somewhat sinister looking device sitting on the floor. It had powder and batteries...superficially it did look menacing. Then Mrs. Newman lost it. She went running down the hall screaming "Mr. Love, Mr. Love...somebody's trying to kill me!" "Mr. Love" was Prof. Rodney Love...the high school principal. At this point, it certainly did not require a rocket scientist to figure out our little plan was careening wildly off course. And we had no self-destruct button to push allowing it to vanish harmlessly from sight. Our harmless "little prank" was now in the spotlight and appeared to bask in the attention it was getting. Hardy and I were wishing for a rock to crawl under, but alas there was none. By normal policy, the sheriff was called. Everybody was still thinking this thing was a bomb. Someone found one of the science teachers and our little "bomb" was taken over to the high school lab where it was pronounced harmless. But by that time the genie was out of the bottle. The sheriff didn't have a clue what to do with a "bomb" (something entirely new for Hamilton) so he called the Texas Rangers. One was immediately dispatched to Hamilton (from Stephenville I believe). My first period class seemed like it would never end. The entire school was humming with the news and of course, with speculation. It seems everybody in the entire school knew we had done it. Or at least it seemed that way to me.

While sitting in our second period class I heard the clomp, clomp, clomp, of what was obviously a large person wearing cowboy boots walking down the hall. A few minutes later I was called out of class. I was soon asked by the superintendent what I knew about the "bomb" that was put in the speech class. For whatever reason, my courage seemed to immediately return and I answered..."I know everything about it!" That defiant response would soon bring me face to face with the source of the "clomp, clomp, clomp"...a real, honest to goodness, Texas Ranger.

---

[9] *To A Mouse - Robert Burns*

He was tall and seemed to me to look exactly like what Texas Rangers were supposed to look like. He asked me a few questions and I told him the complete truth. Before too long I could see he was having to work at keeping a stern look on his face. Finally he said, "Son, I realize this was supposed to be a joke...but *blank blank* it, you just can't go around doing *expletive* like this." To which I uttered the sincerest "yes sir" that had ever crossed my lips...before or since. The superintendent suspended us both for 3 days, which took several points off our six weeks average. I suspected my accomplice's grades could withstand that hit much better than mine. Miraculously I somehow had enough points not to fail anything. That or some sympathetic teachers gave me a point or two here and there. I sincerely would not rule this out. I had some exceptional teachers. It's too bad I never fully took advantage of all they had to offer. And even more regrettable is the fact that I never got to tell most of them that.

In retrospect, examining the execution of our plan, we had focused too narrowly on the fuel burn at the expense of the power source for our igniter. That, and we had completely failed to carry out any risk/benefit ratio calculations. No risk/benefit analysis...no exit strategy...no backup plan...no nothing. What were we thinking?

But life goes on. While the incident was over, the exploit still lives. As a matter of fact, at our 50th class reunion, the subject was still alive and well. As a modern country song so profoundly expressed it, *"you're always seventeen in your home town."*[10] My accomplice was truly gifted in science. He later became a physician. I became a pilot.

Pilgrimages To Priddy

The *"Priddy Stomp"* was as far from Randy Hays' garage dance as the East was from the West. The "Texas Schottisch," the Polka, the "two-step," boots scuffing along rough wooden dance hall floors, to the very Texas flavored music of Curtis Troutt' and his band. We'd all pile in somebody's car and head west. Past the Perry Country Club, through Pottsville, and 25 miles later pull into the relatively crowded dirt parking lot (an adjoining field) of the dance hall. Somewhere over the years, Curtis Troutt's venue changed. He is now regionally well known for writing and performing Christian music.

Once in the parking lot we'd begin the critical operation of finding someone to buy a six-pack for us. I was barely seventeen and didn't shave yet. I probably looked about fourteen. Looking back now, we must have been a ridiculous sight. We would open a beer and pass it around. After a few sips, our neophyte neurons would be buzzing. Then we would go in and stand around the wall and watch folks dance. I had no idea at the time that I was experiencing a vanishing part of Texas history. Priceless!

---

[10] *You're always seventeen in your home town."* - Cross Canadian Ragweed

Occasionally some of the older girls or married ladies would feel sorry for us and invite us to dance with them. The innocence of such community social events has long since vanished. If replaced at all, it has been by modern "red dirt" music venues with $20 - $40 admission fees. Gone are the Nocona and Justin boots made in Texas and purchased on the square in Hamilton from Robert Williams, the manager of Garner Alvis. Many are now made in China. In the place of the real Texas boots, are $500 and up Lucchese and Black Jack boots. I've seen some approaching $3000. An era has passed. I was blessed to have been a part it.

Lavender Blue

A beautiful spring was coming to an end and summer rapidly approaching. My father arranged a summer job for me in Loco Hills New Mexico. I would be working in an oil field and living with a former Lone Star Gas employee and longtime friend of my father. I was truly excited about the change of environment.

Far from Hamilton, on 3 April 1960 King Norodom Suramarit died, provoking a constitutional crisis over the successor to the late King. King Suramarit was the father of King Norodom Sihanouk. When King Sihanouk abdicated the throne on 2 Mar 1955 his father succeeded him as king of Cambodia. Sihanouk abdicated in order to become prime minister.

On 11 April Cambodian Prime Minister Prince Sihanouk and his entire cabinet resigned. Cambodia was without a government. On June 14, 1960, after winning a national referendum Prince Sihanouk became head of state. It's doubtful that anyone in Hamilton even noticed.

Just before I left, I became close friends with "Kalie's" younger sister Katie Brown (pseudonym). I liked her so much. I will always remember listening with her to the radio in my 1950 Ford as [11]Sammy Turner sang "Lavender Blue."[12] Each April the 1st, her birthday, wherever I am in the world, I remember her and wish her health and happiness. Katie was a very special beautiful memory, un très beau souvenir

While Katie and I listened as Sammy Turner sang Lavender Blue, 7,800 miles from Hamilton, in the darkest part of Africa, the Congo was gaining its independence from Belgium. Patrice Lumumba became its first prime minister and Joseph Kasavubu the first president. One month later the Congolese army mutinied; Moise Tshombe declares Katanga independent; Belgium immediately sends troops to Katanga province, supposedly to protect Belgium citizens and the sizable Belgium mining interests in Katanga. The UN Security Council voted almost immediately to send in troops to help establish order, but the troops were prohibited from interfering in internal affairs.

---

[11] *By Sammy Turner 1959 – an old English love song from circa 1672*
[12] *Lavender-Blue (Dilly Dilly) Sammy Turner Charted at # 3 in 1959*

Journey To Nod

And Cain went out from the presence of the LORD[13], and dwelt in the land of Nod, On the East of Eden[14]

Hamilton In My Rear-View Mirror

My bags were packed. My black 1950 flathead Ford was full of gas for probably the first time since I'd owned it. I was as ready as I would ever be. This was almost certainly something strategically arranged by my mother and father to give me (and them) some breathing space. I knew I was ready. I never had a questioning thought. Yet there was that little tug of uncertainty which any sane teenager would have as they leave home for the first time. Their physical presence in my life, every day since I entered this world, was an unseen but subliminally felt security blanket. Our family friend with whom I would be staying was waiting for me in Loco Hills New Mexico. It was time. It was my last night in town. I stopped by my friend Michal's house for just a few minutes. We sat out in my car and talked. The entire visit was probably about 15 minutes. I went straight home and tried to sleep.

The next morning, I pointed my "50 Ford" west and drove out of Hamilton on Highway 36 toward Comanche. I planned to drive west through Abilene, Sweetwater, Big Spring, Andrews, Hobbs, and finally Loco Hills. As I left the Hamilton city limits, I remember thinking of countless people whom I should have called or stopped by to say goodbye. Friends, saints who prayed for me constantly…it was a long list. But heck…I'd be back in less than three months. At least that was my loose, very loose, plan. My car was running well, and loved the long level stretches of West Texas highways.

Around Colorado City I stopped for the night. The name of the motel was "States Motel." It had 48 rooms and of course they didn't have numbers but state names. I thought that was so cool. It was a dump, even back then, but I was too naïve to realize it at the time. This was my first stay in a motel other than a fishing lodge. And of course…I asked for the "Texas" room. I remember the manager told me how lucky I was that that room was not yet taken. I'll bet he said that to everybody who got the room they first requested.

I had departed Hamilton that morning at a reasonable hour, stopped and piddled a bit, then had a hamburger at a drive-in someplace around Abilene. I stopped for the night in Colorado City after about only four hours of driving.

---

[13] Holy Bible Genesis 4:16

[14] Nod" (נוד) is the Hebrew root of the verb "to wander"

That was a long hard day to me then. Looking back now, everything seemed to be on such a grand scale. Yet, in today's reality, in accordance with our much faster life styles, everything was almost laughably microscopic. Just before my retirement I regularly flew non-stop flights of over 7700 miles (London to Los Angeles non-stop for example.) But I'm so glad it was like it was. We were blessed.

Colorado City was just about the mid-point of my trip. I planned to do the same thing again the following day, arriving in Loco Hills well before dark. I called home collect and told my mother and father where and how I was. It was good to hear their voices. For the first time I realized I would also be missing Camille. I had a hard time getting to sleep that night. It was the first time I could ever remember spending the night away from home and being completely alone. It certainly would not be the last.

Loco Hills

I was up early the next morning and headed west again. I arrived in Loco Hills in the early afternoon. Loco Hills had to have been the original "spot on the road." Situated on Highway 82, also known as the Lovington Highway, 25 miles west of Artesia. It couldn't have had more than 30 houses, most of which were built and owned by oil companies. The houses all looked just alike. There was nothing around Loco Hills but desert and oil wells; miles and miles of oil wells. Oil wells, sidewinder rattlesnakes, an occasional cougar, and without any doubt, the biggest jackrabbits I'd ever seen. And, oh yes, there were coyotes. That was new to me. Back then, Hamilton County had no coyotes. The oil wells would provide a significant income for me that summer. I loved the desert. I loved its look, its smell, and I didn't even mind the heat. This would be a summer close to nature and close to hard work. Loco Hills was a marvelous place in time. It's as vivid in my mind today, fifty plus years later, as it was in the summer of 1960.

Within a couple of days I was part of the crew of what is called in oil field parlance, a "pullin unit." A "pullin unit" is really a "pulling unit"...a large vehicle mounted rig which arrives at the site of an oil well, is subsequently positioned over the actual wellbore, and from this position, is used to pull the rods, pumps, and casing to the surface where they can be repaired or replaced. I loved this work from the very first second. It had lots of action and the pay was, by Hamilton County Texas standards, exceptional.

However, I could also see the trap. It was an exceptionally high paying dead-end job which would rob men of the best years of their life and then cast them aside. I knew I could not remain too long as the paramour of this enticing enchantress of devastation. The fruit of her allure was all around me in the oil fields. Weather-beaten men of fifty who looked and moved as though they were seventy. I gave lots of thought to this. I knew if I returned to Hamilton, the only "home" I had ever known, I'd soon be back in my old rut leading to certain self-ruin. I knew equally well that to remain here working would produce an equally ruinous result.

Nonetheless, it was not yet my custom, at that point in my life, to dwell too long on probable outcomes. I had met a couple of young guys my age at the First Baptist Church of Loco Hills, and we soon started hanging out together. We would go hunting in the wide-open deserts. Or, sometimes, just sit on one of our front steps talking and watching the traffic drive down the highway. These too were good times…no girls…just guys hanging out. I wrote letters to a couple of girls back home in Hamilton but for the first time in a very long time, there were no girls in my life. This would become the norm for the next couple of years.

In June of 1960 the CIA began training a group of Cuban exiles from Miami for an invasion of Cuba.[15]

Jackrabbits Sidewinders and Cougars

The deserts around Loco Hills provided a wonderful opportunity to learn about a completely foreign ecosystem. I'd grown up around rattlesnakes. Hamilton County had some huge ones. But they were the western diamondbacks. While the folks around Loco Hills told me they had diamondbacks, I never saw one that summer. But I saw countless sidewinders. They were small, averaging between two to three feet, but could move lightning fast. I remember the first one I saw was while driving down one of the dirt roads in the pulling unit truck. We were headed to an oil well site. It was my first day on the job and I wanted them to stop the truck so I could look at its tracks, but they just laughed and told me I'd have plenty of chances to see sidewinder tracks. It didn't take me long to understand what they were saying. I can't remember how many I saw on that first day of work. I do remember I was counting though. And I do remember it was some horrendous number. They were hard as hell to spot. A sidewinder could blend into the color of the sand perfectly. They did leave that telltale signature though. It was a little "j" looking track in the loose desert sand. The first time I came upon one of those tracks was while out hunting. It was fascinating. We decided to follow the track as it appeared fresh. The ever-drifting sand had not yet moved over the path, filling in the details. It's hard to describe that feeling as I knelt to look at the track. That feeling would bind with many more that summer creating an extra-special memory.

One of our favorite but totally non-productive after-work activities was strolling through the desert hunting. Really, it could hardly be called "hunting." The shameful reality was we were out shooting just about anything that moved. Jackrabbits, coyotes, sidewinders, while always hoping for a crack at the elusive but nevertheless not so uncommon, cougar. And

---

[15] Dr. Jack B. Pfeiffer - The Taylor (Gen. Maxwell B.) Committee Investigation of the Bay of Pigs -declassified

everywhere there were enormous birds of prey. Mostly hawks feeding on the numerous rodents that called the New Mexico desert home. But at least I can say we declared them off limits. They were safe.

Naked In The Desert

Naked I came from my mother's womb, and naked I will leave this life.[16]
And naked did I wander in the desert with a borrowed Savage .243[17]

Some of my most memorable moments from that summer of 1960 were while walking alone in the desert. The air seemed cleaner and fresher, and around thirty minutes prior to sunset the colors of the desert took on an almost magic tonality. Bushes, flowers, distant mountains, the sand, they were all transformed. I used to ponder as I walked out away from any evidence of "civilization," except the ever-present oil wells and an occasional shimmering contrail from a jet passing high overhead in the sky, how it was possible for anyone not to believe in a Supreme Architect, some Master Builder. All this breathtaking beauty could not possibly be an accident…the result of *random chance*. All this beauty could *randomly* assemble itself? Unlikely…no matter how long you gave it to happen.

Another memorable aspect of the desert was the smell in the air as the first drops from a rain shower arrived. Probably the change in elevation from Hamilton's 1300 feet above sea level to Loco Hills' 3700 feet enhanced this sensation. The perception of freshness was so vivid. All those desert plants and flowers poised to release their own special essence when kissed by one of the first drops of the shower. Unforgettable.

It was during one of my late afternoon stroll/half-hearted hunting outings that one of these desert showers happened. As is so often the case in the desert, the rain cloud wasn't that large and only produced a very light shower. This left the sun still shining and coating everything in beautiful golden light. Golden light was now being mirrored about by the gleaming reflective coating of fresh rain on all the leaves. To crown the event, slightly above the horizon, was a breathtaking rainbow.

I had borrowed a Savage .243 hunting rifle from my father's friend with whom I was staying. I was easily a mile from where I'd left my 1950 Ford (almost certainly with its windows rolled down) when the shower started. Allowing this borrowed gun to get wet was not an option. I first removed my shirt and tried wrapping the rifle in my shirt. A white t-shirt was not nearly large enough. So, I steadied myself by leaning on the rifle while I removed my boots and got out of my pants. It wasn't long before I realized my undershorts were needed in this operation as well. When the entire wrapping process was completed, all I was wearing was a baseball cap, my socks, and my boots. But the .243 Savage was protected. I was miles from any human,

---
[16] Job 1:21 Holman Christian Standard Bible (CSB)
[17] Jimmy Joe Jacks circa July 1960

so I enjoyed the walk back to the car. That was probably the closest to nature I've ever been before or since. The walk did require a significant amount of focus to avoid critical area contact with any of the abrasive desert vegetation. I arrived back at the car unscratched.

On 30 June 1960, while I was becoming one with nature in the deserts surrounding Loco Hills, the Congo won its independence from Belgium.[18] Shortly thereafter, the United States began sending weapons and CIA personnel to aid forces allied with Kasavubu and combat the emergence of a Soviet presence in the Congo.[19] Perhaps some in Hamilton had seen this in the Dallas, Ft. Worth, or Waco papers. But then the world was not yet small. Even those in our primitive intelligence agencies were connecting few dots.

From Boots to Boot Camp

A few weeks earlier I'd seen a Navy recruiting sign. I found myself wondering about what life in the Navy would be like. And of course "join the Navy...see the world" kept flashing through my mind. I wrote home to my parents to see what their reaction would be. I was only seventeen and needed their written permission. I soon got a call from them. With some reservations, they thought the idea had merit. Probably, they as did I, recognized the high risk of returning and falling back into my old routine. They wanted to know if I was sure this was what I wanted to do. Once I signed on the dotted line, there was no turning back. I'd be in the Navy. I took a deep breath and said yes.

Mother and Daddy drove from Hamilton to Loco Hills to see me for one last time, sign the Navy forms and say good bye. Boy that was heavy. I was so excited and so ready to go do this but inside I was trembling. This was a commitment of almost four years of my life. My talks with the recruiter had ignited a fire of excitement when I looked at the long list of schools they offered. I never dreamed there were so many things I could become. They had given me a battery of tests and to my utter amazement I scored in the upper ten percent. I remember saying a silent "thank you" to so many of my teachers who had, despite my nonchalant attitude, often bordering on total disregard, somehow managed to slip something into my largely dormant neurons.

Because of my test scores, I could select and be guaranteed the school of my choice as long as it did not fall outside the fields I scored the highest in. I selected the Hospital Corp. When I told my parents they were pleased. It felt so nice to be pleasing them for the first time in a very long time. I vowed at that time it would not be the last. I felt this was possibly a turning point in my life. Retrospection clearly confirms this.

---

[18] The Guardian - Friday 1 July 1960
[19] Heart of Darkness: the Tragedy of the Congo, 1960-67-By Dr. Robert Craig Johnson

Anchors Away

When you're between any sort of devil and the deep blue sea, the deep blue sea sometimes looks very inviting. (Sir Terence Rattigan)[20]

I finished another couple of weeks working on the pulling unit and waiting for my Navy report date. I was full of anticipation and yet I enjoyed every second of my work in the oil field. Hard, hot, and yet somehow strangely rewarding.

I asked the owner of the well service company where I worked to send my last paycheck home to my parents as the Navy gave strict instructions not to come with much money. I don't remember the amount now, but they were making it very clear that we were now charges of the United States Navy and that they would provide what we needed. I left my car in Loco Hills for our family friend to sell and hopped a bus to Albuquerque where I met up with the recruiter again. A small group of recruits had assembled there. We were to travel together on the train to San Diego where the United States Naval Training Center was located. I was on my way to boot camp. USNTC San Diego would be my home for the next three months. I was excited, I was a little nervous, and most of all I was so ready to see what life held just over the horizon.

All the new Navy recruits were seated together. It would be an overnight train ride and we all had berthing compartments. Most of the guys passed the time playing poker and talking trash. I found most of them about as interesting as dirt, so I spent most of my time looking out the wide picture windows of our compartment. I'd only been that far from Texas once before when Herald Stroud took us on a Boy Scout trip to Philmont Scout Ranch in northern New Mexico. Then we were traveling in an old pickup pulling a small trailer. Two could ride up front, all the rest of us rode in the back of the pickup. The Navy's traveling accommodations were a vast improvement.

His Name Was "Sally"

What is straight? A line can be straight, or a street, but the human heart, oh, no, it's curved like a road through mountains.[21]

As we rocked and click-clacked along on the rails (a quite pleasant sensation), one of my fellow recruits, who had been appointed by the Navy recruiter upon departure to be "in charge" of the group due the fact he was a little older than the rest of us and already had a couple of years college, became the group comedian. His name was Bill Sanders (pseudonym). Bill had a persona

---
[20] Sir Terrence Rattigan - The Deep Blue Sea
[21] Tennessee Williams A Streetcar Named Desire

he called Sally and *she* would drive everybody into insane laughter. Perhaps others in the group realized it right away but we were several weeks into boot camp before I understood that Sally was not so much a persona as I had initially, innocently, imagined. My naïveté in the lesser mainstream ways of life was deeply rooted in Hamiltonian culture. I was clueless. But Sally's little not so secret secret did not stop us from becoming friends. "Sally" always seemed more caring than any of the others and earned my trust and friendship. I never saw *her* again after our basic training, but *she* is one of the very few from boot camp I even remember.

E Pluribus Unum[22]
James J. Jacks, SR
Company 60-372
USNTC
San Diego 33, California

As far as I was ever able to tell, the purpose of "boot camp" was extremely basic. For some, an important factor was to increase physical stamina. However, in my case, just having come from a summer in the oil fields, the endless physical drills did nothing for my physical fitness. It was a walk in the park. But when one looks beyond the unrelenting physical drills, an underlying thread becomes visible. Woven into the fabric of everything we did, every task we were assigned, every waking moment, was the obligation to function as a member of a group; every individual action being interdependent upon the accurately executed actions of others. A more palpable objective was to push each recruit to the boundaries of their physical limitations. Something many had never experienced. I was amazed at the number who wanted to quit because it was hard. When I signed my name on those enlistment papers, I committed to a way of life, for a given period. Quitting was not an option. Failing was not an option. Finishing in the lower part of my class was not an option. Virtually every aspect of my life up until entering the United States Navy was no longer an option. My mother would be worried for me…my father extremely proud. I remember being very proud of them as I would sit at night and listen to the stories some of the members of Company 60-372 would tell while sitting on their bunks just before "taps" and "lights out." Some had come from pretty messed up upbringings. Many, while hating the ordeal of boot camp, were without a doubt very glad to be there. I knew I had been blessed. Now I had to make my mother and father proud. God knows I'd caused them enough grief.

> *Most Holy spirit! Who didst brood*
> *Upon the chaos dark and rude,*
> *And bid its angry tumult cease,*
> *And give, for wild confusion, peace;*
> *Oh, hear us when we cry to Thee*
> *For those in peril on the sea!*[23]

---

[22] Out of many, one

We drilled and marched. We fought fires and fired rifles. We drilled and marched more. We learned to wear gas masks and tried them out in "the gas chamber" filled with tear gas. We took countless aptitude tests. We were fed like kings in the Navy's "mess hall." We drilled and marched. We washed our clothes by hand and hung them out to dry. We shined our shoes and scrubbed the floors (decks). We drilled and marched.

And as we were drilling and marching, Colonel Joseph Desiré Mobutu was meeting covertly with CIA agents. Subsequently, on 14 September 1960, Mobutu, with support from the CIA, overthrew the government of the Congo and arrested Patrice Lumumba the new country's first Prime Minister.

On yet another front, in late September, the CIA sent one of its scientists, Dr. Sidney Gottlieb, to the Congo carrying "lethal biological material" (a virus) specifically intended for use in Lumumba's assassination. The virus, which was supposed to produce a fatal disease indigenous to the Congo area of Africa, was transported via diplomatic pouch... As matters evolved in the Congo, the virus was never used, for the CIA's Congo station was unable to come up with "a secure enough agent with the right access" to Lumumba before the potency of the biological material was no longer reliable.[24]

After ten weeks at the United States Naval Training Center, Company 60-372 passed in final review. Boot camp was over. I now wore two stripes instead of one and had a caduceus resting on top of them. I was now a Hospitalman Apprentice or HA. The same day I opened a large brown envelope containing my orders. After two weeks of home leave I would be stationed on the USS Los Angeles, CA 135, a heavy cruiser class ship presently in port in Long Beach California. But of significantly greater importance, was notification that I would report after less than six months on the USS Los Angeles to the US Naval Hospital in San Diego for Hospital Corp School. I was equally excited about both.

A Heavy Cruiser and Homecoming

I suppose the bus ride from San Diego to Hamilton was long. But to me it flashed by as though in some mental fast-forward mode. I missed my mother and father. I missed Camille. But the heavy cruiser class navy ship waiting in Long Beach dominated my thoughts. Suddenly horizons beyond anything I'd ever contemplated were coming into view. It was a strange sensation. I was heading toward the only home I'd ever known. The only real classmates I'd ever known. The only girls I'd ever loved or thought I'd loved...and all I could think about was this 674-foot-long steel boat tied to a pier at the naval facility at Terminal Island (Long Beach). While passing unrecognized at the time, in retrospect, this was the awakening of a facet of my personality approaching obsessive–compulsive disorder...the determination never again to fail and never again cause my parents embarrassment. To repay the

[23] The Navy Hymn - Eternal Father, Strong to Save - Rev. William Whiting. 1825-1878
[24] Killing Hope by William Blum

handful of saints who had believed in me and faithfully prayed daily for me. And, with genuine humor, disappoint those who believed I'd soon be in jail or in the grave yard.

Home

When I walked into the house, although I'd only been gone for four months, I recall everything looked "strange." While it was all familiar, it looked somehow smaller. Mother had spent lots of time making everything just perfect for my return. I was very glad to be home.

Homecoming

I had arrived just as Hamilton High School was having its homecoming. I attended the Thursday pep rally and Friday night game. I was peppered with questions about what the Navy was like and why I'd left. My classmates were just the same as when I'd left. I had changed. Boot camp's regiments had silently achieved their intended purpose. As for me, I took significant silent pride in boot camp's success.

The Highway

Two days later, I tenderly told my mother I needed to leave for Long Beach and my new assignment. I told her I wanted to get there early so I'd have plenty of time to familiarize myself with what life on a ship was going to be like. I would be working as a trainee in the ship's medical department. I wanted to get settled in early, so I'd be ready for my new assignments. At first, I had to convince her that she had done nothing wrong. That "home" could not have been any more perfect. As I held her, and her eyes filled with tears I realized this new-found drive came at a price. I could see resolve taking control in my life. Failure was no longer an option…nor was mediocrity. The following day I boarded the bus in front of Jordan's Pharmacy. I was dressed in my Navy uniform; I had my sea-bag on my shoulder. I looked like a sailor…I was a sailor. Our goodbyes were hard. In my heart I knew I should have stayed longer. "If Only."

On 16 September 1960, while I was in Hamilton, a Cablegram from Elbridge Durbrow, United States Ambassador in Saigon, was being transmitted to Secretary of State Christian A. Herter in Washington.[25] Its contents were highly secret and sensitive. Ambassador Durbrow was trying to help President Eisenhower and his cabinet understand how fragile the US backed Vietnamese government was both to external and internal forces.

Heavy Cruisers

From the bus station in Long Beach I took a cab for the short ride to Terminal Island. I presented my ID card at the gate and was directed to where the USS Los Angeles was tied to the pier. It was mid-morning; the

---

[25] The Pentagon Papers, Gravel Edition, Volume 2, pp. 633-635

weather was typical California pleasant. As soon as saw it I knew this was going to be fun. It was like the first time you see a Corvette. The thing was 674 feet long, was home to 1,142 sailors and marines in peacetime and up to 1700 in combat conditions. And the guns…those huge 8-inch guns…I could only vaguely imagine what kind of impression they could make on an enemy. I walked up the gangplank and saluted the flag and then the officer of the deck. I recited the statement learned in boot camp and practiced subsequently on the bus and cab ride to the ship, "request permission to come aboard sir." To which the OOD replied "permission granted." The OOD directed me to a senior petty officer standing on duty nearby who requested to see my orders. He took a couple of minutes going over them and muttering to himself, and then escorted me below deck to the ship's hospital quarters known as "H Section." I was introduced to a first class petty officer named McCanless. He was the ranking enlisted man in the ship's medical division. "Mac" was friendly and would later prove a mentor (of sorts). I was assigned a "rack" (navy parlance of a bed), a locker, and told to unpack my sea bag, and secure my locker then report to Sick Bay where I'd be introduced to everybody and start indoctrination. My "rack" was third from the floor. I would have to learn to climb carefully up to it in the dark. The focus was not on my falling but rather how not to step on somebody's fingers. The fall would probably be the preferable of the two possibilities.

Shots–Sheets–And Scrubbing The Ward's Decks

My indoctrination didn't take long, probably no more than two hours. Once completed, my hands-on training began. From changing sheets to recording temperatures, pulses, and respirations, I was learning the basics. The days turned rapidly into weeks. Everything I was learning would soon become a significant advantage when I arrived back in San Diego to attend the Navy's Hospital Corps School. Most attending the school had never been exposed to anything vaguely close to the course's curriculum. But by a twist of fate, my boot camp completion date did not correspond to the commencement of any Corps School class dates, so I was sent "to sea" to await my class. I could have been sent instead to work in the mess hall of a large nearby Navy facility peeling potatoes until my class date. There certainly was no shortage of nearby potato pealing places. When I did arrive at school, I found out that indeed some had done just that…worked in a mess hall or galley.

While learning was exciting, equally exciting was life onboard ship for a not yet 18-year-old. My entire experience while onboard the USS Los Angeles was good. We would go to sea for a week or so at a time. Just shaking down the ship making sure everything still worked. This not only served to keep the equipment exercised, but the crew as well. They would fire the guns and occasionally launch a missile. By today's standards, the Regulus 1 wouldn't be considered much of a missile. It had a tiny little jet engine, enabling it to deliver a thermonuclear warhead within a range of 500 nautical miles. But in 1960 it was pretty much state of the art.

Beyond The Sea

I was a bit worried about going to sea for the first time. I was worried about getting seasick. Thus far I had been an exemplary sailor. I didn't need to mess up at this point. But the undeniable fact was that I got sick riding in the back of a car. What was a country boy from Hamilton Texas going to do when this 34-million-pound boat, the length of more than two football fields, started rocking and rolling out there in the Pacific? I'd heard plenty of stories about guys who spent the first week embracing the toilet. Luckily for me, one of the senior corpsmen named Charlie took me to the pharmacy and gave me several meclizine hydrochloride tablets and told me to break them in half and start taking one in the morning and one at bedtime the day before we left port. The pharmacy tech laughed and said "well, *little doc*, you are just about the last of the new hands to come asking for some pills. What took you so long?" That was a good question. My approach to this potential problem had been completely wrong. I should have consulted with the many in my own hospital division who had been to sea numerous times.

A day later we left the port of Long Beach and headed for the open sea. The deck of this huge ship gently vibrated underneath my feet. This vibration was emanating from the General Electric geared engines capable of generating 120,000 SHP (shaft horsepower). The exhilaration I experienced as we entered open water remains vivid today. For the first time in my life I was completely out of sight of land. The water was indescribably beautiful…several shades of blue, silver, white. I'd never seen anything that looked like this. The Hamilton City Lake didn't…Lake Buchanan didn't…the Gulf of Mexico didn't. It was inconceivably beautiful. I can still see it so clearly in my mind's eye.

Late that afternoon the sea went from smooth to light chop and by meal time we were in sea conditions that were causing some to become a bit uncomfortable gastro-intestinally speaking. I recall sitting in the mess hall and watching the salt and pepper shakers slide around the table. Our meals were served on trays and you needed to keep one hand on your tray to keep it in front of you. I did not have to get up and go throw up but I sure as heck did not feel very well at all. I must have said a few hundred silent "thank you Charlies" and I'm sure a couple of face to face ones as well. Without those meclizine tablets I'd have been one very sick puppy.

Anyway, the rough seas passed, and I went up on the main deck "topside" as often as I could to look at the beautiful ocean. The "old salts" were very understanding. Many of the newer sailors took their cameras topside and were takings lots of photos. I did not yet have a camera. I wanted one badly and I certainly had the money, and in the Base Exchange, they were much cheaper than in downtown Long Beach. But I did not know what lay ahead when I reported for school in San Diego and I decided to keep saving my pay in the event something arose that I had not anticipated. However, I must give the Navy credit; they generally did not allow situations to arise that could cause a sailor to lose his ability to function. They would always provide you with shelter and meals. There were plenty of sailors all around me who hadn't a clue how to manage their paycheck. They were the ones who very soon become enslaved to the loan sharks onboard ship who ran illegal but highly profitable "slush funds." These loan sharks would make short term loans of $5 to sailors who would have to repay $7 on the next twice monthly payday. The term was "five for seven." For those who had purchased cameras, watches, jewelry, and other items that could easily be stored in one's locker, the onshore pawn shops were a frequent ensnarement. Many would buy a new camera at the Base Exchange for perhaps $50 (about half a month's pay) and within three or four months, would have lost it to a pawn broker for failure to repay a loan. I was truly amazed at the lack of self-discipline so many of the sailors had. It made me uncomfortable. I suppose I could see my old self in them...the one I was now always running from.

My pay while on the USS Los Angeles was $88/month. We were paid in cash twice monthly. I received two $20 bills and two $2 bills each payday. I did not recall ever having seen a $2 bill until I joined the Navy, but I remembered my father mentioning them.

I Love Things That Go "Bang"

While at sea, they fired the huge 8-inch guns. Because many who will read this book never served in the Navy, I feel I should digress a moment to share what an 8-inch gun is. Of course, for the re-loaders who do their own ammunition, this is elementary. But for the others, a minor digression would probably help visualize the enormity of these guns. First, it is not a pistol with an 8-inch barrel but rather a huge cannon which fires a projectile 8 inches in diameter (20cm) and whose barrel is 55 calibers (8inx55=440in) or 36.5 feet long. Its range…over 16 miles…like from Hamilton's square to the Evant square.

Free But Not Idle

It was during my free time, despite all the reading, that I experienced the worst of my homesickness. Boot camp did not provide the time for being homesick. This was probably purposefully factored into the regimen. But onboard ship, when my eight-hour work day was over, unless I was assigned night duty on the ward, my time was free. I read a lot. I must have read every book in the hospital's collection of reference books. Reading was something new to me. What scant homework I'd done in high school that required reading was accomplished by a self-taught form of scanning. I enjoyed my new nightly reading time. This satisfaction was bolstered by the knowledge that in just a few short months, I would be assigned copious quantities of nightly compulsory reading after having spent eight hours in class. Due to my lackluster performance in high school, my reading skills were not what they should have been, and I pushed myself to improve them. A lot of what I was reading was medical technology and anatomy & physiology that I could not yet fully understand. Even so, I could tell I was at least gaining some familiarity with medical terms and procedures, as well as acquiring some measurable degree of competence in reading comprehension and speed. I was deriving gratification from pushing myself. It was fun. I'd only previously experienced this in distance running in high school, so this was truly a fascinating phenomenon. And somehow, during all this, I managed to study for my next rank advancement. A test was necessary. So when I needed a break for the medical books, I would study for my advancement (Hospitalman E-3).

I was free to leave the ship and go into the nearby city of Long Beach. The Navy referred to this as "liberty." But I found the lifestyle on liberty dangerously unhealthy. There were plenty of bars more than happy to serve underage sailors. And plenty of Navy military police called "shore patrol" going into the bars looking for their underage drinkers. An arrest, as minor an offense as this would have been, would be enough to blemish my military service record and my chance to go to school. Such lifestyles were never seriously considered. If I went ashore, which was usually every couple of weeks, I would visit museums. The town was filled with girls wanting to meet sailors, but such women were usually not of the highest caliber. Of course, there were nice women in Long Beach, just nowhere near anyplace I could afford to go. And nothing about such an arrangement could contribute to my goals. So the women of Southern California were only a part of my life in an occasional song I would hear on the radio.

Life after work was not all reading. I spent a lot of time writing home to my family as well as a couple of girls. But writing home usually triggered a feeling of loneliness. Reading medical books did not. One girl back home with whom I regularly corresponded, Sarah Ann Ellsworth (pseudonym) always sent perfumed letters. Of course this would cause a loud tumult at mail call when all the guys were gathered around to receive their newly arrived letters from home. One day I got a letter with her return address, but it was not from her. It was from her parents. They demanded our correspondence end immediately. I suppose I couldn't really blame them. I probably wouldn't want my daughter corresponding with me either. Initially I was a bit hurt and angry. But this soon passed as I realized their actions were a direct reaction to mine. Had I previously been a little more focused in the proper direction, I almost certainly would not be holding this letter. I shrugged it off as…fair enough, "for whatsoever a man soweth, that shall he also reap."[26]

The USS Los Angeles also had its own radio station. It was run by the Special Services division. Some of the DJs we heard on the ship's radio were trained by the Navy in media, radio and television, while others were just volunteers who had some related experience and would come do a shift as a DJ. When

---
[26] Holy Bible KJV Galatians 6:7

we went to sea, they became our only radio station. While in port, they rebroadcast or relayed the Long Beach and Los Angeles radio stations down below deck so we could pick them up on our little cheap personal radios. Not too many radio stations could penetrate the six-inch-thick steel armored sides and decks of our heavy cruiser. They were designed to keep torpedoes, artillery, and the like out . . . not allow radio signals in. So, without the help of the guys in Special Service, there would not have been much music. I thought these Navy DJs were pretty good. After growing up listening to KCLW in Hamilton, with its ultra-grassroots style, it was easy to like the ship's radio. They broadcast a bittersweet mix of music. So many of the songs they played reminded me of home. At least I was not alone. Sailors, when they are not on duty or ashore on liberty are probably the loneliest species on the planet. I remember listening to Ray Peterson's *Corinna Corinna*, *Save The Last Dance For Me* by The Drifters, and *He Will Break Your Heart* by Jerry Butler. Rock and Roll and Doo Wap was a powerful new style of music and a significant part of my life. Meanwhile, on shore, Senator John F. Kennedy narrowly defeated Vice President Richard M. Nixon in the U.S. Presidential election on 9 November.

Two days later, on 11 November 1960, in Saigon, 8200 miles from the USS Los Angeles, South Vietnamese paratroopers staged a failed coup d'état against President Ngo Dinh Diem. While the Vietnamese president survived the attempt, the fears of many intelligence specialists and political analysts were being substantiated. President-elect Kennedy would now shift his focus from the election campaign to a very different campaign. Vice President-elect Lyndon Baines Johnson probably took note as he unknowingly marched closer to his Vietnam destiny as well. I took note of Kennedy's election. I failed to note the coup attempt...I didn't even know exactly where Vietnam was.

A Heavy Cruiser Christmas–
No Tree–No Family–No Nobody

It was hard to realize that Christmas was here. It was not cold, palm trees were everywhere, and I was not home. For the first time in my life, I would experience a Christmas without my parents, without Camille, without anybody. The ship's radio broadcast the usual Christmas music but that just made it worse. I read more, but that just made it worse. I'd get letters from home, but that just made it worse. A Christmas package arrived in the mail from my parents. But that just made it worse as well. In the package was a very expensive Remington Rechargeable electric razor. Back in 1960 they were extremely expensive. It must have cost my parents close to a hundred dollars. One hundred dollars I knew they could not afford to spend. I could say nothing though because I realized it was their way of coping with the first Christmas I would not be home. Christmas cards arrived as well. Not just from my parents, but from people in the church, neighbors, old girlfriends, most just made me feel worse. The only very notable exceptions were the ones from old saints who continued to pray for me. I wish I had told them before they went to be with the Lord how much their prayers had meant to me. But I didn't. If Only...

The United States Navy prepared a Christmas dinner that would rival any mother's cooking. I remember when I went to the mess hall; I could hardly believe my eyes. I knew the Navy could cook. I knew their reputation for feeding better than any branch of the military service. Yet I had no idea just how good these guys were. The Navy spared no expense on the food and the Navy cooks spared no effort. Even the grumpiest of the sailors onboard were thanking the cooks. We were in port for Christmas. Many had gone ashore or gone home on leave. But for me, I didn't have any more leave on the books, at least not enough to go home for Christmas. So I was spending my first Christmas with about one third of the ship's 1142 compliment.

The number of US military personnel in Vietnam had reached approximately 900[27]

A New Year

Somehow, I survived that Christmas and by the time New Year arrived, I was already focused on my departure for Corp School a couple of months later. I was so ready. I read the medical books longer and harder. I studied the pharmacology books and the advanced first aid and trauma books, as part of our training would be to prepare us to serve in what they called independent duty. That could be in the FMF (Fleet Marine Service). The Marines were a division of the Navy and used Navy Corpsmen as their medics. The other really demanding assignment would be as the lone medic onboard a small naval vessel like a submarine. There would be no doctor and you would be responsible for handling medical emergencies until they could be medevac'd to a larger facility. That was probably the steepest learning curve I could face. The no-stress assignment would be to a large naval hospital. But any way I looked at it, failure was not an option, nor would it ever be again if I could help it. I must not only pass that school but pass it with some degree of distinction. I never again wanted to return to my chaotic high school years. While they were the most beautiful period in my entire life, they were bitter-sweet.

While I was studying onboard the USS Los Angeles, On 6 January Soviet premier Nikita Khrushchev made a speech promising support for "wars of national liberation." [28] *The implications of this would reach to the Congo and South East Asia.*

While this was happening, the CIA began supplying, training and supporting the Hmong (Meo) tribesman in Laos under Vang Pao (Operation Momentum).B

On 17 January, Patrice Lumumba was handed over to the Katanga secessionist government for certain execution. The Belgium government and CIA were suspected of engineering the move.[29]

---

[27] VietnamGear.com
[28] VietnamGear.com

Beneath The Shroud

Pickin & Grinnin

Oblivious to the Congo's situation and the spiraling-out-of-control situation in Vietnam I frequently played my 5-String banjo with Dr. Hess, the ship's medical officer and only doctor. He would invite me to his quarters, and we would play together from time to time. I'd learned to play as a teenager in Hamilton. Those little breaks from the books were good for me. I would also go to the sickbay ward and pick and grin for a while there. The patients always enjoyed an opportunity to sing along and it was an occasional break from my studies.

On 20 January, John F. Kennedy was inaugurated as the 35th President of the United States. This was a big event onboard the Los Angeles as we were receiving a new Commander In Chief. There was some type of ceremony as I remember.

A week after his inauguration, Kennedy approved the Counterinsurgency Plan (CIP) for Vietnam.

Upon assuming office, President Kennedy inherited a paramilitary contingent in training with aircraft, bombers, ground support and transports, in addition to an infantry brigade which probably had the heaviest concentration of firepower in the Caribbean basin, if not in all of Latin America.[30] *The Army Special Forces, Air Force, National Guard and CIA were all involved.*

Sea Bags & San Diego

"Beyond The Sea"[31]

Soon it was time to leave the USS Los Angeles and head 94 miles south straight down the coast to San Diego, home of the famed US Navy's Hospital Corps School. To say that I was excited would be a bit of an understatement. While I'd enjoyed almost every moment onboard the Los Angeles, all those moments were spent dreaming of Corps School. It was finally time. The moment of truth. Was I anxious…of course? Was I confident…? I was prayerfully confident. I was about to begin a curriculum more difficult and much faster paced than high school, my only previous point of reference. We would be attending eight hours of class five days a week and studying late into the night. Could I hold up to the demands…I knew I could. But could I master the curriculum? I didn't know. I had never applied myself in school. Never. I had skated, relying on my general intelligence or the kindness of various teachers to somehow get me through. I already had a mound of evidence clearly demonstrating that technique would not work here. It hadn't worked in Hamilton High School.

---

[29] Frances 24 Television
[30] Dr. Jack B. Pfeiffer - The Taylor (Gen. Maxwell B.) Committee Investigation of the Bay of Pigs - declassified
[31] Song performed by Bobby Darin in 1958 - words by Jack Lawrence

I took a bus from Terminal Island to downtown Long Beach. I hopped an express bus to San Diego and two and a half hours later, I was in a taxi headed for the Naval Hospital located just next to the famous Balboa Park. I noticed the huge San Diego High School out the window of the cab as we were nearing the Naval Hospital. A few short months later, I'd be enrolled there. I got out of the taxi at the hospital's main gate. I was in my "dress blues;" my sea bag was perched on my shoulder and my heart was pounding in my ears. I was ready. I was so ready. Just like when I ran track and was at the blocks waiting for the starting gun to fire. I was ready to run. I noticed the USS Los Angeles patch on my dress blues got me a little extra respect at the gate. First time for that. The guards pointed out a building a couple of blocks away. I was told that was the quarters for the corps school. A few short minutes later I was checking in with the senior petty officer in charge of the dormitory. I filled out a couple of short forms and was escorted to my quarters. It was Saturday afternoon and I had nothing to do 'till Monday morning when I reported for school.

Going back down to re-explore San Diego was out of the question. I had to explore the hospital facility to be sure I knew where my Monday morning reporting point was and find all the critical places like the base exchange (store) the mess hall, and just the general layout. I had been given a map when I checked in the dorm. It's interesting looking back now. There must have been other new reporting students who would be my future classmates there, but I was so focused on not screwing up that I didn't care about anything that wasn't critical to my mission of making a problem-free entry into school. I must have been so uptight. Not scared, just focused like a laser. I was starting to enjoy this newly discovered capability of focusing. There were times when I felt like throwing up…when I realized I could have been doing this all along. But at other times, when I contemplated all the incredible experiences I'd had in life to this point, I decided perhaps it might be possible that I was supposed to have reached here from there. Who is to say?

Anatomy–Physiology–Pharmacology

"I hold the care of the sick and injured to be a sacred trust"[32]

Monday morning at 8:00 am we were sitting in our indoctrination lecture. Textbooks and other study materials were issued. Most found the enormous stack of study material horrifying. I was clearly in the majority. But I kept telling myself *"the only thing to fear was fear itself."*[33] I recognized some from my reading onboard the ship. If it were as hard as I was imagining, nobody would ever graduate. I had to continually reassure myself. I knew an entire group of corpsmen back on the USS Los Angeles who had graduated. Most weren't

[32] from Hospital Corpsman's creed
[33] paraphrased from Franklin D. Roosevelt's first inaugural address

rocket scientists. "Just keep your cool and divide this mountainous pile of material into manageable blocks. If they did it...I can do it." And thus, began my first day in corps school.

In a meeting of 11 March 1961, the Agency presented its plan for the invasion of Cuba to the President, the Secretary of State, senior DOD personnel, and others, but as a result of objections from the Department of State and at the direction of the President, the Agency (CIA) was ordered to seek alternative sites and plans. [34]

School soon established its own rhythm. The days began early and ended late, but they were not unbearable. The Navy seemed to have this ability to judge exactly how far to push its people without breaking them. The material we were learning was hard but extremely interesting. I loved class and I loved to study. I found it hard to believe that I could have such a thought. Study enjoyable? Amazing. I even found a small group of guys to study with prior to exams. We would sit around and ask each other questions. Today, the memory of corps school has this one curious quirk. I can recall a few faces from boot camp and an occasional name. I can remember numerous faces and names from onboard ship. I cannot recall one single face or name for corps school. I wonder why?

I remember pharmacology had a lot of memory work. We needed to memorize entire conversion charts so we would be able to calculate quickly the various values as expressed in the apothecary's system of weights. The system was centuries old but unfortunately for us, was still being used in the early 1960s. I can remember a pound was divided into 12 ounces, an ounce into 8 drachms, and a drachm into 3 scruples or 60 grains. I made up vulgar little rhymes to help me memorize all these totally meaningless terms and values. There were not yet any hand-held calculators to quickly produce the results. You could not walk around with a textbook under your arm in order to have reference to the tables. The only reasonable solution was to have them in your head. Finally, but alas too late to save me this agony, the United States adopted the metric system in the US Pharmacopoeia in 1971. Today all these units of measure, while living on in my brain, are mere footnotes in history...useless footnotes.

While I was getting used to Corps School's daily routine on California's west coast, just off Florida's east coast, on April 17, 1961, about 1,400 exiles invaded southern Cuba at the Bahia de los Cochinos (Bay of Pigs). They were totally defeated by the Cuban army by 20 April. Most of the invaders were killed or taken prisoner. Critics of this failure blamed the last-minute withdrawal of naval air support by US president John F. Kennedy (1917-63), but closer investigation disclosed that the CIA scheme, meant to be secret but long a matter of public knowledge, had been based on faulty intelligence information, was poorly planned, and ultimately was poorly executed. The

---

[34] Dr. Jack B. Pfeiffer - The Taylor (Gen. Maxwell B.) Committee Investigation of the Bay of Pigs - declassified

failed invasion aggravated already hostile US-Cuban relations.[35] A huge part of this "naval air support" was a fleet of CIA converted B-26 aircraft piloted by US trained Cuban exiles, members of the famed Brigade 2506. This turned out to compound the U.S. embarrassment.

Blood & Pain

I had always been squeamish about getting shots. I remember some at the beginning of recruit training passed out in the shot line as their time came. This was so common that the corpsmen giving the shots always kept ammonia inhalers close at hand. There were some of us in the class who shared this trait. Now we were going to be on both ends of the needle. We were required to practice on ourselves. This was the last step before finishing this phase of our training. It was mandatory that you demonstrate practically what you had mastered in theory. I was just hoping I wouldn't embarrass myself by having to have somebody snap the ammonia inhaler for me. We paired off, prepared to practice on each other. We cleaned the neck of our 2cc sterile water ampules, snapped the specially designed neck of the ampule, and aspirated the contents into our sterile syringe. We then cleaned the injection site on our fellow corpsman's arm with an alcohol swab and gave him "our best shot." There were, to be sure, numerous pre-injection threats being exchanged between most of the pairs, but all came off well. We were now signed off to give injections. However, mercifully for our future patients, the signoff was for "initially under supervision."

While we were learning to give each other shots and struggling with pharmacology, in Stanleyville, in the Congo, those loyal to the deposed and now murdered Patrice Lumumba set up a rival government under Antoine Gizenga. During this time, the Congo, being in a state of complete anarchy had three break away governments all struggling for power. The CIA was busily and quietly at work.[36] The country was filled with CIA operatives, mercenaries, mutinous Congolese soldiers, Belgium troops, United Nations troops, rape, murder, and terror. The Congo was the darkest place on the dark continent during that time.

One day while studying at the hospital library, I ran across a brochure from San Diego High School. I went past the high school every time I left the hospital going into downtown San Diego. The brochure was advertising evening classes. These classes were designed for college bound people who wanted more than just a GED certificate. They offered a program where you could challenge the GED test and if you passed, you could enter their high school program immediately. California's educational system had many innovative programs. If you failed the GED challenge, you could take their special GED prep course and retake the test. Upon passing you would receive your GED and continue working on your regular high school diploma. I took one of the brochures and filed it away in my dorm locker. I

---
[35] Armed Conflict Events Data (ACED)
[36] Who Killed Lumumba - BBC

knew I wanted to do this as soon as possible. With the intensity of my present school hardly leaving a waking hour, I knew this would have to be something after corps school.

I had already made my application for Operating Room Technician School. If my grades were high enough and my recommendations good enough, and if they had openings in the class, I could go to that much more advanced school after completing this school. The Navy offered several such classes. X-ray Technician, Pharmacy Technician, Respiratory Technician, to name only a few. But OR Tech seemed to me the most interesting. In addition, it was located here on this facility. It was in the basement of the "Gray Ghost" (US Naval Hospital's main building) where all the operating room suites were located. The hope of being admitted to Operating Room Technician School served to push me even harder to do well in my present classes. I was running toward my goals while running from my demons. I was enjoying every second of it. I was enjoying being focused.

As it did onboard ship, time flew. The days rushed into weeks and the weeks into months. Finally, graduation day. But this time there was no marching. This time we sat in our classroom and listened to speeches by the commander of the training facility, and most of our instructors. I was proud and relieved. And, I was in the top ten percent of my class. I don't remember my exact position, I never expected to be first. I just wanted to have a respectable position and I succeeded. I was now a Hospital Corpsman.

Immediately after the ceremony we met individually with our instructors and received our next duty assignment. When my brown envelope was opened (the Navy loved these large brown envelopes) it was there. Operating Room Technician School, US Naval Hospital, San Diego three months away. My orders contained a TYD (temporary duty assignment) of US Naval Hospital, San Diego. What this really said was that I would be assigned duty on a hospital ward as a regular corpsman until my class date. This was great news as I would now get to practice all the theory that had been stuffed in my brain for 40 hours a week for the past several months. I was excited about the ward duty and I was super-excited about being selected for Operating Room Technician School. Many that applied didn't get the school.

Mr. Kelley

From Smoke Bombs To Smoking Machines

My integration onto the neurosurgery ward on the second floor in the "Gray Ghost" went painlessly. I was assigned to a nurse for the first week to work under her direct supervision until I was signed off to do patient care unsupervised. The work here wasn't hard and was at an unhurried pace. We would take every patient's vital signs (temperature, pulse, and respiration) several times daily. We would give the patient's medications, any required injections, start and monitor their IVs, and make their beds. There was a personal aspect too. Many of the older patients were veterans from WWII and some from WW1. They were old and lonely. I would sometimes spend time talking with them. They loved to tell about when they were in the service, though some stayed away from the battle stories. I found these older patients quite interesting and I enjoyed listening to them. They were bona fide heroes…I was a young pup.

This was back in the day when smoking was permitted everywhere, and everybody smoked. Somehow, during corps school, I had picked up the nasty habit myself. It was even possible back then to smoke on the wards if there was no oxygen in use nearby. Another condition was that the patients could not smoke in bed due to fire concerns. We had this old patient named Mr. Kelley. He missed his cigarettes but was unable to get out of his bed due to general weakness and IVs. He would ask me to light and hold his cigarette for him so he could have a few puffs. Often, I didn't have the time to assist him when he wanted to smoke. It required me to stand there and hold it for him. Somehow, the idea came to me to make Mr. Kelley a smoking device. I got a large upright standing ashtray (about two feet tall which was filled with sand). I took one of his cigarettes and inserted it into a four-inch-long glass tubing used in rigging rubber tubing for aspiration and draining devices. I taped the glass tubing holding his cigarette to the ashtray, so it hung over the sand in the top. I then attached about five feet of rubber drainage tubing to the other end of the glass tube and ran this up to Mr. Kelley's bed rail where I secured it again with tape. To the remaining end of the rubber tubing I inserted another four-inch glass tube and lit Mr. Kelley's cigarette perched beside his bed in the ashtray. I gave the glass tubing to Mr. Kelley and told him to puff away. I'd be back in a few minutes. I can still see the huge grin on Mr. Kelley's tired old near-death face as he lay in bed sucking on that glass tube and exhaling smoke. While I was gone, the senior nurse came by and found my device. She called the other nurses and was telling them what a fine example of patient care I had created. She later that day put a note of commendation in my records for my ingenious and caring attitude. Today they would probably give you a strong reprimand for assisting someone close to death in having a few last puffs.

A couple of days after Mr. Kelley's smoking machine, I was lying in my bed studying and listening to my little radio playing quietly after lights out. I caught a piece of a news report talking about some kind of failed invasion attempt on the island of Cuba involving the United States and the CIA.

On April 17, 1961, about 1,400 exiles invaded southern Cuba at the Bahia de los Cochinos (Bay of Pigs), but were totally defeated by the Cuban army by April 20; most of the invaders were killed or taken prisoner.[37]

---

[37] Armed Conflict Events Database

The Death Of Mr. Kelley

One generation passes away, and another generation comes: but the earth abides forever[38]

A few days later, when I reported to the ward for duty at 7:00 am, I was told Mr. Kelley had just passed away. We all had known that it would happen soon, but nevertheless I suddenly realize I was having strange feelings and thoughts. All kinds of visual images of Mr. Kelley lying in his bed talking to me went flashing through my mind. Since his death had occurred just at shift change time, the oncoming shift would be responsible for readying his body to go to the morgue. The senior corpsman and I were assigned to ready the body and take him down to the morgue.

When we entered the room Mr. Kelley's body temperature was still slightly warm. I remember his mouth was open just a little as it so often was when he slept. I was a little queasy. This was my first time to encounter a deceased person. My previous life experiences had not prepared me for this. Somehow, I got through it. We had studied all the procedures required in readying a patient's body to be transported to the morgue. There were even trays made up in advance containing all the necessary instruments, supplies, and paperwork. The senior corpsman (probably already six years in the hospital corps) told me not to worry, I'd get used to it. I don't think his encouragement did anything to improve how I was feeling. After taking Mr. Kelley down to the morgue, I piddled a little on my way back to the ward. I needed a few extra minutes to sort through some of my thoughts.

In May 1961 President Kennedy dispatched then Vice-President Lyndon Johnson to meet with South Vietnam's President Ngo Dinh Diem. Johnson assured Diem of more aid in molding a fighting force that could resist the communists. Kennedy announced a change of policy from support to partnership with Diem in defeat of communism in South Vietnam.[39]

Also in May 1961 – President Kennedy sends 400 American Green Beret 'Special Advisors' to South Vietnam to train South Vietnamese soldiers in methods of 'counter-insurgency' in the fight against Viet Cong guerrillas.

August 1961 – In the Congo, UN troops begin disarming Katangese soldiers. Fighting was heavy, many were killed. The Belgiums and the United States were almost fighting the United Nations. Moise Tshombe, with the open support of Belgium and the implied support of the United States, continued to proclaim Katanga independent. The entire country was engulfed in fighting.

After Mr. Kelley, I would watch several others answer the final summons and go the way of all flesh. This time spent on the ward was supplying, albeit insufficient, a portion of what I would need to withstand the horrors of war I

---
[38] Solomon, King of Israel - Ecclesiastes 1:4 circa 935 BC
[39] Reeves, Richard (1993). President Kennedy: Profile of Power p119

would later see in Cambodia. Years after Cambodia I would live with frequent reminders of how ill-prepared I had been.

Also during the summer of 1961, in Laos, the CIA mustered 9,000 hill tribesmen into the ranks of the Armée Clandestine. It was aided by 9 CIA agents, 9 Special Forces augmenters, and 99 Thai Special Forces troopers from the Police Aerial Resupply Unit. [40] *The conflict was now far from the borders of North and South Vietnam.*

Tijuana–"Hey Gringo"

The cities of San Diego and Tijuana could almost be called twin cities. That is if you didn't insist on the "twins" looking alike. It was only 15 miles from the hospital to the border crossing. And Tijuana was right on the border. There were always several taxis waiting to pick up sailors too inpatient to wait for the bus. Most would offer a flat rate (no meter) trip to the border at very reasonable prices. The Navy strongly discouraged going to Tijuana alone so if two or three guys decided to go, the charge was quite reasonable. I went twice before corp school started with some guys I worked with on the ward. After Operating Room Technician School started, I never went back.

This country boy from Hamilton, Texas, had never seen anything like Tijuana before. Of course, the most infamous destination was "boy's town." I think the name probably leaves little to the imagination. As we walked along the sidewalk there was a constant barrage of "Hey Gringo...you want a girl?"; "I got Spanish fly!"; "Hey Gringo, you want some marijuana?." The girl could seriously damage my health, the Spanish fly and the marijuana could seriously damage my future in the Navy and my plans for an education. The answer was always a resolute no. But that didn't stop me from sneaking a peek here and there. We would never spend the night and I did not drink alcohol at the time, so we just strolled along and looked at the shops and watched all the sidewalk hawkers. But for a country boy who had just turned eighteen, it was a real "happening."

High School Again

This Time With Distinction

The brochure from San Diego High School had not been forgotten. Once I was sure my routine on the ward would allow me to attend their classes, I walked the eight tenths of a mile from the hospital to the high school and visited their counseling office. I was scheduled the following Saturday morning to take the GED. Once again there was that little twinge of anxiety before the test. But I was starting to get used to it. It never went away, I just learned to cope with these pre-test jitters. My classmates back in Hamilton had graduated a month or so ago. This helped drive me on I suspect. Anyway, I took the test and a week later I received the results. I'd passed. Not only did I pass but I scored in the upper percentile.

[40] The Ravens: The Men Who Flew in America's Secret War in Laos. p134

21 September 1961 – The 5th Special Forces Group, 1st Special Forces is activated at Fort Bragg

The fall semester was starting, and my timing was perfect. I loaded up with the three courses the counselors said I needed to meet the graduation requirement and started back to high school. The Navy strongly supported additional education and the ward where I was working made sure I had my five weeknights free as well as my weekend days. I was subject to Saturday night duty and any shift on Sunday. All this I found easily manageable. What I was wondering about was if I could handle the Operating Room Technician School which would soon start as well as my very full high school load. The only way to find out was to try.

I started my high school full load and some very short weeks later my Operating Room Technician classes. I'd already been told this school, while an advanced school, would have less intensive classroom and homework than the corpsman school I had just finished. After the first couple of months, it would shift focus to practical application of all we had just learned. Months of intern practice followed by the more independent residency work. We would always be working beside a surgeon, but sometimes he would only have my set of hands. On other cases, heart, lung, and neuro, sometimes we had three surgeons plus another two technicians. Fun, but high stress. Our first couple of months were filled with memorizing the names of what seemed like endless numbers of surgical instruments and devices. We studied the techniques and most of the surgical procedures we would be doing ranging from simple appendectomies to complex neurosurgery. I remember wondering how a neurosurgeon ever learned all the things he was required to learn and feeling thankful all I had to do was learn what he was doing and how to do my part in assisting him. Those guys had to be smart.

My routine was tightly ordered. There was no free time. None. Class was over at 4:00pm. I'd rush back to the dorm and study what I had covered that day till 5:30pm. Then run, literally, to the cafeteria with my books for my upcoming evening class carried in a little satchel. I'd inhale my evening meal (always good) and start my brisk walk to San Diego High School. I would arrive just before class started at 6:30pm. There were lots of older people in the class due to these being night classes. There were a couple of guys from the hospital as well. I didn't really know them. They were not in any advanced Navy courses. Just working to get their high school diploma and presumably then enroll at one of the numerous colleges nearby. My class was over at 8:30pm. I'd be back at my dorm by 9:00pm where I'd study more. Taps or lights out was at 10:00pm. I'd usually study another hour or so using a small lamp then go to sleep. Many of the guys did not go to sleep at 10:00pm but the Navy was very serious about lights being out and only talking in whispers.

October 1961 – To get a first-hand look at the deteriorating military situation, top Kennedy aides, Maxwell Taylor and Walt Rostow, visit Vietnam. "If Vietnam goes, it will be exceedingly difficult to hold Southeast Asia," Taylor reports to the President and advises Kennedy to expand the number of U.S. Military advisors and to send 8000 combat soldiers.[41]

My weekends were equally regimented. Classes went from 9:00am till 3:00pm on Saturday. Sunday there was no class, but I always had duty on the ward to compensate for not working nights Monday through Friday. Many asked me how I did this with no time off for recreation. I really don't know. I just know that I didn't find it all that hard. I stayed focused on my goals (none of which were rest and recreation). The time flew by and at the end of November I graduated from San Diego High School. They had a graduation ceremony which I didn't bother to attend. I just went and picked up my diploma A nice lady that always looked after me in the admin office asked me why I didn't attend the graduation ceremony. I thoughtlessly responded that it just wasn't that important to me. She looked a little hurt and later I wished I'd been a little more socially aware. I had been attending classes for the diploma…not to walk across a stage. That diploma was my key to college. I could have cared less about some photo of me in a cap and gown. But not all people viewed it like that. I was angry at myself for not perceiving this. Especially in the case of this kind lady.

Meanwhile, in Thailand in November 1961, four RF-101C reconnaissance aircraft of the 45th Tactical Reconnaissance Squadron stationed at Misawa AB, Japan and their photo lab arrived at Don Muang. The RF-101s were sent to assist Royal Thai AF RT-33 aircraft in performing aerial recon flights over Laos .[42]

In the Congo, on 11 November 1961, thirteen Italian airmen from the United Nations taken for mercenaries are captured at Kindu by Gizengist forces of the 20th[43] Stanleyville battalion commanded by Colonel Vital Pakasa. They were killed then partially dismembered and eaten by their executioners.

Nov 18, JFK sent 18,000 military "advisors" to South Vietnam.[44]

"Too Young"

During all this, we had an approaching Navy test I was eligible to take if I wished. And of course, it required even more study. I stuffed this study time in between rounds on the ward during my weekend duty. It was almost always quiet and usually allowed plenty of time to read. This was the test for third class petty officer (HM3). If you wanted to take the test you had to go to the personnel officer and get cleared to take it. They would check all your

---

[41] Schlesinger, Robert Kennedy: His Life and Times
[42] Glasser, Jeffrey D. The Secret Vietnam War: The United States Air Force in Thailand, 1961-1975. McFarland & Company
[43] Boissonnade, 1990: 141-142
[44] Timelines Of History Database

records to be sure you had the time in rank and had completed all the requirements. I had and my name was added to the list. On the morning of the test, as was my custom, I arrived early and was waiting my turn in line to be checked off the list and be seated in the testing room. When my time came, they found my name on the list, but they looked at my enlistment date and said I hadn't been in the service long enough to take this test. The fact that I only needed to shave every two or three days probably didn't help much either. I tried to tell them I was approved by personnel and clearly, they could see my name was on the list indicating I had been screened and approved. But for whatever reason, this jerk thought he knew better. They were not going to allow me to take the test. I literally raced back upstairs to the personnel office as I was also racing against the clock. Once the room was closed nobody entered or left the room. When I got to the personnel office, they could see by the expression on my face something was clearly wrong. The Chief got up and came over and listened to my story. He then muttered somebody's name. I later found it was the "jerk's" name. The Chief surprised me in how quickly he was able to walk for a man clearly in his mid-forties. When we arrived, I was privileged to witness one of the most clearly articulated butt-chewings I'd ever not only seen, but imagined, during my Navy career. The "jerk" was only able to say, "yes sir." The Chief told me to go inside and take my test. He remained there continuing to chew this jerk out. I'll bet he didn't do that again…ever. About a month later, one of my fellow students came up to me and said congratulations. My name was on the list. I had made HM3. I could sew on my petty officer patch in about four more weeks. I didn't care about the patch as much as I did the extra money. With this promotion, I earned one of the Navy's somewhat derogatory titles…that of "rate grabber." Anyway, I didn't care. It got me a semi-private room, a lot of extra privileges, the ability to eat in the petty officer's section of the mess hall, and more money and less duty. I was happy. When I wrote home, I knew my parents would be proud as well. They made all their usual calls to those close friends and the old saints who regularly prayed for me. I was proud finally to be making them proud. Hell, based on my previous lack of distinction, I was proud to be making anybody proud.

December 1961 – Viet Cong guerrillas now control much of the countryside in South Vietnam and frequently ambush South Vietnamese troops. The cost to America of maintaining South Vietnam's sagging 200,000 man army and managing the overall conflict in Vietnam rises to a million dollars per day.[45]

On 9 December the Laos government fled to Cambodia as the capital city of Vientiane was engulfed in war.[46]

Operating Room Technician School continued its fast pace. We went through a rotation of a few weeks in each major area of surgery. We learned

---

[45] The History Place 1999
[46] Timelines Of History Database

OB-GYN, cardiovascular, neurosurgery, general surgery, ENT, and plastic surgery. Some were quite different and highly specialized, employing surgical instruments used nowhere else.

As the end of OR school approached, we were given a form to fill out listing our first and second choice of duty stations after graduation. My first choice was Saigon as I'd starting hearing little bits here and there about the conflict going on there. At that time Saigon was a civilian clothes duty assignment. My second choice was the US Naval Hospital in Corpus Christi Texas. I'm not sure why, as my homesickness was just about gone. When graduation arrived, I opened the big brown envelope once again and found Corpus Christi. I was excited. And I was glad to get finished with what was almost certain to be my last Navy school. This would leave me free to devote my energies to college. We had a little graduation ceremony presided over by the Chief of Surgery and the chief surgical nurse. The Chief of Surgery ordered a very nice cake from the cooks in the mess hall. There was a big bowl of punch. We said our goodbyes and headed to the dorm to pack.

Corpus Christi

This time I decided I'd spend more time at home. I'd also decided I would be able to spend some of my new pay increase on a car payment. It had been almost two years since I'd driven a car. I also decided to splurge and fly home rather than take the bus. I remember asking the reservation agent if my airplane would be a jet. She said of course. A new Boeing 707. Wow, I was going to fly home…not go home on a train or a bus and it would be a jet airplane. Wait 'til my parents tell the people in Hamilton that Jimmy Joe was flying home from California on a jet.

When I arrived home, Daddy told me he had already talked to the Perry National Bank and I would get a car loan. He would take me to Waco in a couple of days to look for a car. When we got to Waco, I must have looked at a hundred cars. I couldn't find anything interesting. Then over in the corner, I spotted this little MGA Roadster. I didn't have a clue what it was, but it was love at first sight. It turned out to be a 1957 model. It was white, had a little inline four-cylinder engine and was a convertible. Grossly impractical as it only had two seats, a canvas top and virtually no trunk space. But it's as if my 18 months of Navy discipline and conservative reasoning instantly vanished at the site of this cute little white critter. I bought it and drove it off the lot hoping not to get lost as I headed out of Waco toward Hamilton.

A few days later, with my civilian clothes stuffed in the tiny trunk and my sea bag filled with my navy clothes in the front seat with me, I headed toward my new duty station . . . the US Naval Hospital, Corpus Christi Texas. Once again, I was excited but by this time, I wasn't as nervous as when heading to my previous assignments. I was starting to get the hang of this.

US Naval Hospital Corpus Christi Texas

I remember the drive was so refreshing. It was exhilarating. In retrospect, probably for all the wrong reasons. The sun was giving a golden hue to the spring grass. The wind streaming over the top of the windscreen of my little MGA convertible made everything seem magical. While I didn't realize it at the time, the wind and the sun were giving my face a sunburn–windburn combo. The drive was a little over 300 miles and took just short of six hours. Basically, I was heading due south. I stayed on 281 for well over half the way.

I arrived at the US Naval Air Station Corpus Christi, just before 4:00pm. The Naval Hospital was onboard the Naval Air Station (NAS). Formalities were a minimum. I had to go into a little security building where I had to show my driver's license and auto insurance in order to get my car on base. I was given a little map showing the facility and they highlighted the way to the hospital. The entire process including some friendly small talk took less than ten minutes. A few minutes later I was walking up the steps to the dorm which would be my home for almost the next two years.

I checked in with the Master At Arms (MA) and received my sleeping quarters. I was eligible for a semi-private room with its own bath. That was nice. I had a roommate and he was in the room when I arrived. His name was Roger Williams and he was a HM2. That was one rank above me. He'd been in the service eight years. He was an X-Ray technician. He was very nice, and I liked him, but he could and did talk the ears off a brass monkey. It took three trips to get all my stuff out of my little MG. "Rog" helped me haul all my clothes in.

In my new room, we had honest-to-goodness closets. Of course, I didn't have any coat hangers, having just come from a locker environment. But that was easy enough to fix. Rog later showed me to the officer of the day's desk where I got my meal card, parking assignment, and all kinds of other indoctrination items. I elected not to report to the operating room 'til tomorrow as I was a couple of days early reporting anyway. Rog drank a lot and after we had finished a great meal at the mess hall, he insisted on showing me the enlisted men's club. I'd been in the Navy almost two years and I'd never set foot in one. I'd always been too busy studying. So, we went. They had an NCO Club (non-commissioned officers club) and we went in and looked around, but it was almost empty, so we went into the regular enlisted men's section. Decent music and cold cheap draft beer. I was just 19 but the Navy would serve you on the base. Texas laws did not apply on the base. At least that's what we were told. I had almost zero experience with drinking any kind of alcohol and so I had a small draft beer and sipped it till it was disgustingly warm. We didn't stay too long, about an hour or so, and came back to the dorm. We went in Rog's car. I was excited to have a nice room, a nice car, and a new duty station. Life was good.

A Temporary Loss Of Focus

"...sin is crouching at the door. Its desire is for you, but you must rule over it." [47] *"Runnin' from his devils, Lord, and reachin' for the stars"* [48]

The social aspect of my life, which had been so conspicuously absent for the last twenty months or so, was beginning to make its presence known via its advocate, my evil twin. Continuation of the remarkable accomplishments I'd managed to secure since joining the Navy was about to face serious challenges. The self-sacrifice and single-minded focus I'd employed in the process of obtaining these goals was about to face threats. While I couldn't accurately assess the threats then, looking back now it should have been so clear. Previously my entire work day was spent in school, either classroom, operating room, or a combination of both. Now, I was no longer a student in one of the Navy's highly accelerated and disciplined classroom environments. I was now applying the skills the Navy had taught me in a working environment. And in retrospect, that was the area where I would be facing critical exposure to non-productive forces. This new "working environment" placed me now in almost constant contact with people who were not students. Most had no intention of ever returning to any school. By this time, they had all completed the same Hospital Corps School followed by Operating Room Technician School that I had just completed. Most planned to finish out their year or so remaining in their obligation to the Navy and return to civilian life. A few planned to reenlist and make the Navy a career. Nobody I would be working with was involved in any form of college or professional training. I would be the only one going to school in the entire group and one of a tiny handful in the entire US Naval Hospital facility. This meant I would be surrounded by temptations to go to the club, go to beach parties, go to Mexico for the weekend, or go on a date. These would be new distracting factors to which I was totally unaccustomed and to a significant degree, unprepared to face. I had not been out with a girl on a date since high school. *"Yea, though I walk through the valley of the shadow of death, I will fear no evil: for thou art with me; thy rod and thy staff they comfort me."* [49] These words could have offered such strength. I was about to be walking through the "valley" but regrettably, in ignorant bliss.

While I was settling in at the Naval Hospital in Corpus Christi, more than 9,300 miles away, on *15 April 1962 Marine Helicopter squadrons arrived in Soc Trang, southwest of Saigon, as part of Operation Shufly. The Marines are to provide air support to ARVN troops fighting the Viet Cong.* [50] By this time the public was slowly becoming aware of the Vietnam issue. I can say with great certainty that I was not one of them. My attention was elsewhere.

---

[47] Genesis 4:7 Holman Christian Standard Bible
[48] The Pilgrim - Kris Kristofferson
[49] Holy Bible - Psalm 23:4 (KJV)
[50] VietnamGear.com

"Main Surgery"
As opposed to Minor Surgery I Guess

About twelve OR technicians worked in what was referred to as "Main Surgery." We had three operating rooms in the surgical suite. We did scheduled surgery five days a week. We started the surgeries around 8:00am which allowed the doctors to make preliminary rounds of critical patients before scrubbing in for their first case of the day. By the time they arrived, we would already have the rooms set up, all surgical instruments ready, the patient ready, pre-medicated, prepped, and as soon as we reported to the anesthesiologist that we saw the doctor's face, he would administer anesthesia (either spinal, epidural, etc. or general). Usually no longer than 15 minutes after the doctor arrived and changed into his "scrubs," "scrubbed in" (scrubbing hands and arms with powerful antibacterial soaps like Phisohex or hexachlorophene), the first incision was made. We were good. I soon learned each surgeon's little traits and was able to anticipate his actions and needs. This was the essence of a good operating room technician; what our school had focused on. We learned to understand the surgical procedure (what the doctor was trying to accomplish) and the surgical instruments he would need to use, and the likely reaction to his actions by the patient's body. I loved it. I was good but without doubt far from the best we had there. Some of the guys had been doing this for two or three years and they were truly awesome to watch. The teamwork was exhilarating. The hospital corp was probably, except for the corpsmen who served with the Marines, the most informal and least military group in the Navy. Our leaders were doctors, notorious for their lack of enthusiasm for the Navy's "gung-ho" attitude. Our uniforms were green pajamas with little green caps, and our shoes were canvas, loafer-like sneakers with electro-conductive soles. And oh yes…they were green too. We never shined our shoes except for big base wide inspections. We used to hear that the commanding officer of the hospital (a medical officer or doctor) would always get his butt chewed out by the admiral in command of the entire Naval facility of which we were a part, because of our continual deficiency in military comportment. The doctors never really cared though. Their promotions didn't come from that guy…they came from the Bureau of Medicine and Surgery in Washington. We were a tight group with a high degree of camaraderie between enlisted men and officers.

Lieutenant Commander Don L. McCord

One of the first doctors I met upon arrival was the highly skilled general surgeon Lieutenant Commander Don McCord. He was quiet, with a dry wit. He was probably the most intelligent person I met while serving my term in the Navy. He was both easy and enjoyable to scrub with and was always willing to teach as he performed surgery. I learned a lot from him.

Del Mar College

One of my first projects was to check in with the hospital's education officer. I did this within the first week. I had never attended college while in the Navy before, so I wanted to find out about all the programs they offered. They paid for almost all our tuition. I needed to get enrolled in that program and then enroll in college. There were two colleges there in Corpus Christi. One was the University of Corpus Christi, a small Baptist college if I remember correctly. They were not approved because their tuition was high, and their curriculum was not broad enough. That was unfortunate as they were just outside the gate of the Naval Air Station. My only choice turned out to be Del Mar College just over 10 miles from the base. I applied for the program. In about a week, the education officer called and informed me I was approved, and I needed to come get the papers I needed to present to the registrar at Del Mar. A couple of days later, with papers in hand, I was heading downtown for my first college campus experience.

Kennedy sends 5,000 Marines and 50 jet fighters to Thailand in response to the recent Communist attacks in Laos.[51]

I enrolled for the first summer session and selected the courses I would take during the second summer session. While this was my first stab at college it didn't take a rocket scientist to see that while the summer sessions were a quick way to get some credits, it was by no means an easy way to get them. It's true the professors usually cut you a little slack in the summer sessions, but you still had to cover the same material in half the time. Having a pretty good idea what was coming, I partied hard before class started. Padre Island lay just outside the base's gate. Its miles of great beaches were perfect for inexpensive, quick-to-organize parties. The female hospital corps members would join us, and we always had a great time. I would bring along my banjo. There was always a ukulele or two and of course guitars. I personally hated sand unless I could just walk barefooted in it where it was compact near the water's edge. I hated it when the wind blew and the sand got in your eyes, ears, hair, and all inside your bathing suit. I used to joke that God should have made beaches out of cement and not sand.

My Yuck Duck

"Duck"– a male urinal bedpan.

One of the functions of the Main Operating Room was that of Central Supply. The wards would come draw all their supplies, IV solutions, sterile syringes, needles, etc., from us. One day while helping stock the CSR (central supply room) inventory, I spotted this portable urinal used by bedridden male patients. It was made of stainless steel, had a flat bottom so it could rest on the bedside stand and was balanced so it would be difficult (but not impossible) to tip. It had a handle as well. To my evil twin's mind, it looked

[51] VietnamGear.com

like it would make a wonderful beer mug for beech parties. Of course, my evil twin was also advising that it would be a perfect way to keep people from grabbing a big swig of my beer. I never was a persnickety eater (or drinker) so I had no problem with the mental image that I was quite sure was going to gross almost everybody else out. I grabbed one and placed it into the autoclave (device used to sterilize surgical instruments) for double the required amount of time, took it out and took it to my room. The thought that this might be considered in some circles a misuse of government property never crossed my mind.

A couple of days later my duck and I were at the beach. Absolutely nobody asked for a sip of my beer. I was included in more photos than usual that day though. I tell you, nobody's German Hofbräuhaus mug looked as good as my evil twin's duck. I tried to impress my fellow beach party goers with some of its unique features like a narrower than normal opening to discourage sand particles and airborne critters plus its tip-over resistant design, but I found few enthusiasts.

Roy Orbison
Just Outside The Gate

Amid laparotomies, appendectomies, and beach parties, I saw a notice posted at a favorite café just outside the main gate saying Roy Orbison would be appearing at the University of Corpus Christi auditorium in about a week. Since he released *Only The Lonely* in 1960, I'd been a fan. He had such an incredible range and powerful voice. I'd only attended one concert before, that was while in OR school. I saw Louis Armstrong at the Globe Theater not far from the Naval Hospital. There was no way I was going to miss this.

The day of the concert arrived, I finished work, gave my little white MGA Roadster a wash, took a quick shower, put on my most stylish boat-neck shirt and peg-legged ultra-modern pants, and headed out the back gate and down Ocean Drive for about two miles. In five minutes I was pulling into the parking lot. I geared down my little MG just in case some nice-looking girls might be nearby. I don't recall seeing any as I got out of the MG, but by the time I ascended the steps to the auditorium, I realized this place was a bonanza. All here just like me, to see the famous Roy Orbison on stage. I had something in common with all these beautiful women, without even having to try to think of something unfoolish to use as my intro line. I continued congratulating myself on my brilliant move as I pretended to be looking for my seat while in reality, I was looking at the auditorium filled with stellar women.

And hear him we did. The place was packed. He stood meekly and humbly on center stage, his guitar in hand, wearing his signature black suit and dark glasses. As he sang, the hair on the back of my neck stood up. *Ooby Dooby*,

Only The Lonely, Crying, Running Scared, Blue Angel, Love Hurts. He totally captivated his audience. Except for brief muted polite applause during the first bar or so, you could hear a pin drop in the auditorium until he finished then the audience's reaction was thunderous. I'd never been in the presence of anyone so awe-inspiring. Obviously, everyone else thought so too. Roy Orbison went on to become one of rock and roll's greatest legends and member of The Rock And Roll Hall Of Fame. I went on to Del Mar College.

Del Mar College And Dr. Don McCord

My brief period of fun in the sun was now being eclipsed by discourses in the dark. Every Monday through Thursday from 5:30pm till 8:50pm I sat in classes at Del Mar. Because I had to stand night duty from time to time in the OR, in case we had emergency surgeries, I had to arrange for someone to swap duty with me in order to attend class. Of course, that was always easy as I was offering to swap my weekday duty for their weekend duty. A no-brainer for them. I had people standing in line to swap duty with me. When the weekend came around, I would usually find myself doing at least one if not more nights sleeping in the OR's night room. But, if we didn't have any emergency surgery, which we usually didn't, I had a quiet comfortable place to study. Nevertheless, I usually found at least one night every week or so to sing and pick my banjo in the sand or go to the NCO club for some party time and Twisting.[52]

While I was busy going to school and sometimes "Twisting The Night Away,"[53] the Soviet Union was busy shipping missiles to Cuba. The U.S. first discovered the presence of SA-2 anti-aircraft missiles. When confronted, the Soviets assured President Kennedy the only missiles in Cuba were defensive ones.[54]

While the missiles in Cuba came as a surprise to the country, a surprise at work was about to come to me. One day after we had finished up all our surgeries, Dr. McCord came up to me and asked "Jimmy, where did you tell me you were from?" When I replied "Hamilton," he smiled. "I've just completed arrangements to go there and set up my practice…it's exactly what I've been looking for." Wow, what a small world. Don McCord had completed his service obligation and was due to separate in two or three months. We spent lots of time before he left talking about life in Hamilton. I wrote home and told my parents. They were very proud to be able to say the new doctor was a friend of Jimmy Joe.

Summer quickly slipped into fall. My Del Mar routine was the same. Leave the back gate of the base, drive down Ocean Drive for about 20 minutes

---

[52] The Twist…Dance craze of the early 1960s - Hoffman, Dr. Frank. "Dance Crazes." Survey of American Popular Music
[53] Twisting The Night Away—written and recorded by Sam Cooke 1962
[54] Armed Conflict Database

dodging the potholes in the road caused by storm-driven ocean surges, turn left on Louisiana, and in a couple of more minutes, I was pulling into student parking. On the way back to the base, I'd take the slightly longer but much better road which led to the front gate. Even with my very good eyesight, dodging those potholes in the dark was a little bit too much. Especially considering the relatively small wheels and headlights of my little MG.

President Kennedy's Military Representative, General Maxwell Taylor, concluded in September 1962 that Sihanouk's (Prince Norodom) "morbid fear" of Thailand and South Vietnam had "created a situation of tension and emotionalism which might blow up at any time."[55]

On 6 Oct 1962 little-known Prince Norodom Kantol became prime minister of Cambodia. Prince Norodom Sihanouk had stepped down from the role the preceding February.

On 14 October 1962 the presence of nearly operational Soviet IRBM (intermediate-range ballistic missile) and MRBM (medium-range ballistic missile) sites were discovered in Cuba. These were clearly offensive weapons capable of reaching deep into the United States. President Kennedy instituted a selective naval blockade ("quarantine") of Cuba, demanded the removal of the missiles, and threatened further military action if the Soviets did not comply. Two days later some Soviet ships heading for Cuba changed course, although the Soviets continued work on the installations in place.[56] On 27 October the SA-2, called "Red SAM" for its trail of red smoke, was used to shoot down a U-2 reconnaissance aircraft over Cuba, almost precipitating nuclear war.[57] The Naval Air Station and Naval Hospital were rife with rumors. The Navy called this kind of talk "scuttlebutt." Many on the Naval Air Station had their leaves cancelled and some specialists were restricted to base.

Adios Amigos

I remember the day the U-2 was shot down by a Soviet missile; being in the military, incidents such as that were always an excellent source of "scuttlebutt." The base was alive with chatter. I remember coming in from school and studying a while and then going to sleep. During the night I recall hearing muffled voices outside our bedroom door. But I was dead tired and needed the sleep and Rog always slept like a dead man (except he snored). The next morning, when I opened our bedroom door, I saw three stripped beds in the general sleeping quarters adjoining our room. I wondered what was going on and if what I had heard last night might have had something to do with their disappearance. I did note that all the empty beds were Hispanic surnamed corpsmen that had grown up speaking Spanish. I learned a few

[55] U.S. Department of State 95/03/06 Foreign Relationis, 1961-63, Vol XXIII,
[56] Armed Conflict Database
[57] Steven J. Zaloga (2007). Red SAM: The SA-2 Guideline Anti-Aircraft Missile. Osprey Publishing. P11. ISBN 978-1-84603-062-8

minutes later at breakfast that special orders came in the middle of the night and they were heading for an unnamed destination highly rumored to be a Navy hospital ship off the coast of Cuba. I remember being impressed and a bit proud with how uncharacteristically fast the Navy could respond if it needed to. Many at the hospital had leaves cancelled but I don't recall them being restricted to base. I continued my nightly drives to Del Mar. A few weeks later the three guys returned with big stories of all-night airplane rides followed by days of rocking about at sea on a huge hospital ship. This time the "scuttlebutt" was accurate. Everyone was glad to see them back safe and sound.

"Ginny Come Lately"[58]

It was around 10:00pm and I was lying in the bed in our night duty quarters sleeping room. The lights were already off but the OR tech I shared duty with that night was not sleepy either. So, we were just lying in bed and listening to music from a little portable radio we kept in the duty room. We also had an old black and white TV, but the picture was so bad most people just opted for the radio unless there was a football game on. A song came on the radio I'd never heard before. "Ginny Come Lately" by Brian Hyland. It was new and moving up the charts. It was a simple song, but the lyrics captivated me. I remember thinking if I ever had a daughter, I'd want to name her Jenny…Jenny Jacks, daughter of Jimmy Jacks. I knew I wanted the name to have three Js but since I wasn't married and had yet to meet anyone of serious interest, I had plenty of time to work out all the details. But planning is always good. So, that night I made a note that someday I wanted a daughter named Jenny.

Civilian Girls

School continued to rock along. With the nights a bit chilly, beach parties were not all that popular. I'd met girls at school and would sometimes spend an occasional weekend night free from standby operating room duty taking one of them to a movie or out to eat. I was one of the few at the hospital that ever dated civilians. I never really cared for the "civilian girls" all that much as they usually required a higher expenditure and there was almost always an issue with their parents. It seems that, with few exceptions, their parents didn't want them dating "sailors." This inevitably required my meeting them someplace. Some would want to go in their car, but most wanted to ride in my little MG. I have to say that this funny-looking little four-cylinder critter paid dividends the huge gas-guzzling muscle cars never dreamed of. There was another problem with the civilian girls; they were too quick to "fall in love." And, they had a horrible habit of calling out to the public phones in our dorm in hopes of talking for hours. Hours I didn't have to waste on them. There was always homework to do and the two were incompatible. To say nothing of my fellow corpsmen that stood in line employing a repertoire

---

[58] "Ginny Come Lately"—Brian Hyland written by Gary Geld/Peter Udell

of catcalls and exaggerated sighs awaiting their turn on the phone. If a navy girl wanted to talk, she called on one of the many internal base lines. So generally, the civilian girls were simply more trouble than they were worth.

Cardiac Arrest

It was just before noon and we were in the middle of a routine general surgery procedure. Our patient was probably in her early forties, a military dependent (active duty serviceman's wife). I was "scrubbing" as opposed to "circulating." If you are scrubbed, you are part of the actual surgical team, wearing gown, and surgical gloves on top of your green PJs. If you are circulating, you are not "scrubbed in" and just wearing your surgical green PJs, mask, and cap. I've forgotten the procedure we were doing at the time, but I still clearly remember everything that followed. I'd noticed the anesthesiologist, Dr. Robert Roland (pseudonym), who was normally relaxed and slumped casually on his shiny chrome stool, sometimes even reading a magazine, now leaning forward and monitoring closely his readouts of the patient's vital signs. He then started making some rapid adjustments. The lead surgeon, who was also the "Chief of Surgery", had also noticed Robert's actions and asked…"what's going on Robert?" "Her signs are falling he replied" followed almost immediately by "she's gone into arrest." Dr. Lamar Heckman (pseudonym) called for the defibrillator; the lead surgeon started chest compressions immediately and called for the cardiac arrest cart. This was a tray of surgical instruments especially designed to allow the surgeon to open the chest cavity and massage the heart. It also contained the longest needle I'd ever seen, attached to a syringe which would enable the surgeon to inject epinephrine directly into the heart. The non-sterile part of the cart was the defibrillation machine which applied electric shock in an attempt to stimulate the heart back into beating.

The nurse, also circulating, was standing motionless with an expression of horror on her face. I immediately looked at the circulating corpsman that was, like the nurse, in a catatonic state over at the work station where the paperwork is done during surgery. He was supposed to have recorded the time from the large clock on the wall. It was obvious he'd done nothing. I felt a strange sensation come over me. It would not be the last time in my life this would happen. But the first time was quite remarkable. Like a computer had just taken over my thought process. My mind went to extreme focus and my voice dropped to a low monotone. I called out "time: 1122," and gave the circulating corpsman a glare that let him know he had better get immediately with the program. I instructed the circulating nurse to get the cardiac arrest cart. I instructed the circulating corpsman to move another "Mayo stand"[59] up by the table, in anticipation of the cardiac arrest tray's arrival (only seconds away). I instructed the circulating corpsman to get another circulating corpsman in immediately to standby for whatever Robert, the anesthesiologist, might need. I didn't have to think, at least consciously.

---
[59] Movable stand used in medical procedures

It's like I was being directed. While waiting for the cart to arrive I started moving my instruments around in anticipation of Robert lowering the head of the table so blood would naturally flow toward the brain. I didn't need my sterile instruments falling off the surgical drapes when the operating table moved.

The patient was not responding, and we were already about sixty seconds into the time callout. The cart arrived and by this time the nurse was back with the program and opened the huge sterile tray. During this time, I had also repositioned the drapes as we had been doing abdominal surgery. This would give Lamar a clear "shot" at her chest. I redirected my attention to the now opened cardiac arrest tray and began loading the scalpel. I realized Lamar was ready to make the incision while I was still attaching the blade, but he remained quiet. A couple of seconds later the blade was on and I popped the scalpel into his extended hand, I felt his fingers close on it, and I immediately pulled the huge retractor out of the tray which we would use in literally seconds, to spread her ribs so Lamar could reach her heart. It was like I was hovering above the room watching rather than participating. The part of me that was in the thick of the action was merely some kind of performer on the stage and the real "me" was in the audience. Lamar got her heart going by gently squeezing it to simulate its normal action. We then started working at "clamping and tying" all the new bleeders we had just created. Without a heartbeat, they hadn't been too enthusiastic about bleeding, but now, with a normally beating heart, they were spurting blood all over the place. I playfully looked at Lamar and said "dang…that's a pretty healthy incision." To which he equally playfully held up his larger than average hand and said…"do you see this…if that were your heart…what kind of incision would you have wanted me to make?" We laughed…both glad to edge toward normality once again.

Once the thoracic incision was closed, we redirected our attention to our original lower abdominal incision. It was like I'd forgotten all about the other significant opening we had going in her abdominal cavity. I'm reminded of the expression "when an alligator has hold of your leg, it's difficult to remember your initial intention was to drain the swamp."

When the surgery was finished, I hardly had the energy to walk or even speak. I was totally exhausted. Later, the surgeon took me aside and thanked me and told me that except for me, he felt he was alone. And he asked me "what in the *blank* happened to those people?" I had no answer. I was as amazed as he was. They just froze. This was the first time I'd ever experienced this personal phenomenon of going into auto-pilot mode. It would not be the last.

One of the sad (or perhaps good) aspects of being an OR tech is you seldom find out what happens to a patient. They arrive heavily pre-medicated and they leave still extremely groggy from the anesthesia. All you know about the patient is what was imparted by the surgeon while in the scrubbing area before entering the operating room itself. It's somewhat like a pre-operative briefing. The surgeon, of course, visits with the patient a couple of time each day till discharged. But for the OR techs, our only contact is on the table. And so it was in this case as well. Totally unlike my experience with Mr. Kelley.

Have Yourself A Merry Little Christmas[60]

For whatever reason, I decided not to go home for Christmas. Looking back now I wish I had been more sensitive to my parent's feelings. I simply didn't want to drive the five hours back home. Certainly I had leave on the books. My life has few major regrets, but unfortunately, it is littered with smaller instances of total insensitivity. I did call home but possibly that just made it worse. "If Only"

Dec 21 1962, A US and Cuba accord released Bay of Pigs captives. Dec 23, Cuba started returning US prisoners from Bay of Pigs invasion. Dec 25, The Bay of Pigs captives who were ransomed, vowed to return and topple Castro.[61]

The Navy always fed big on the family holidays. If you were stuck on base rather than going home or being invited to a meal someplace, you could always be certain of being fed a world class holiday dinner. The navy cooks combined with their civilian counterparts were incredibly talented. The holiday food was good. With school out for the holidays, all my reports and reading were done, and I just spend time basically on the base or going around downtown looking at the Christmas lights. New Year was a repeat of Christmas. What on earth was I thinking.

For many of the now 11,300 U.S. Military personnel in South Vietnam things were certainly not as good.[62]

New Year–Old Routine

With the new year came a new semester and the same old driving routine. The surgical department's senior corpsman's time in the Navy came to an end. This left me as the highest-ranking operating room technician in the department. I moved to the position of senior corpsman. This meant I spent almost no time in the OR except for emergencies that came in the night after regular hours. I spent more time now making duty rosters, approving leaves, and listening to the petty squabbles of our department members. This new position also involved ordering and maintaining our inventory as well as, to some minor extent, insuring it fell within our budget. This was an interesting new skill set. I found it enjoyable.

---

[60] From the film Meet Me In St. Louis
Hugh Martin, Ralph Blane 1943
[61] Timelines Of History Database
[62] Vietnam War Timeline—VietnamGear.com

A Baby And A Bump On The Head

It was a weekend. I was on night duty, repaying someone who had taken my weekday night duty so I could attend my Del Mar classes. It was around 2100 hours (9:00pm). There were always two of us on night standby duty. One to scrub and one to circulate. Usually nothing happened. The most common unscheduled surgeries were appendectomies, cesarean sections (C-sections) and serious car accidents. The night duty phone rang and Tyrone Black (pseudonym) picked up the phone. A natural delivery was going wrong over at OB-GYN (a different building for the Main Operating Room). While not normal, such occurrences were not exactly rare. So, for that reason a complete C-section tray was always kept over in the normal delivery room area. We were told this was critical and get there as soon as possible. We grabbed what few things we needed to take with us and dashed out to the front of the OR where we found a security pickup with lights flashing waiting for us. In less than two minutes we were at OB-GYN. The place was usually staffed by women and none were surgically trained. They were trained in natural deliveries but not C-sections. We rushed in and found Dr. Weiser (pseudonym) already scrubbing. He told us Dr. Stine (pseudonym) was in the OR already holding the baby in. This was a breech birth. They considered the baby at high risk and wanted to make the delivery by C-section. But the baby was already trying to make its arrival, feet or butt first, not head as in normal birth. The OB had people who could adequately circulate, so both Tyrone and I scrubbed. With Dr. Stine holding the baby in, we were down a set of hands. Dr. Weiser cut the scrub short and said, "let's go . . . we're out of time." Since I was the most experienced, I worked opposite Dr. Weiser and Tyrone worked the table. Normally one of us would have scrubbed and one circulated.

We had her draped and the site prepped in what I'd estimate to be under two minutes. Dr. Weiser called for "scrapple" while Tyrone and I were still trying to get setup. Tyrone understood and just dumped a handful of hemostats (little instruments used to clamp bleeding arteries) and a stack of sponges (used to absorb blood in the area of the incision) beside my hand and went back to the table. He knew what would come next and was trying to move that forward from the trays. Normally the instruments are unpacked and put on large tables in neat arrangements corresponding to their order and probability of use. There was no time for any of that here.

With what was the fastest and deepest vertical incision I'd ever seen, Dr. Weiser had cut all the way to the uterus in what could almost be described as a "slash." As could be expected blood flew everywhere. Dr. Stine's muffled voice from beneath the drapes said "hurry!" I was just trying to clamp the big bleeders, what we call the "pumpers." The little ones would just have to ooze. I called for "large Deavers" (a heavy metal instrument that was used to hold the incision open so the surgeon could work). Somehow Tyrone managed to fish two of them out of that colossal pile of unarranged instruments. I had no time to tie. I was trying to clamp with my right hand and hold the incision open with a large Deaver with my left hand. In what seemed like only seconds Dr. Weiser was ready to make the incision in the uterus. He had to see and be free to work. I took the other Deaver in my right hand and abandoned my clamping efforts. As fast as this was going, I was praying I could soon get back to clamping before she had critical blood loss. Carefully and skillfully Dr. Weiser made his incision in the uterus. If he miscalculated, he would cut the baby. His incision was perfect and within seconds we could see the baby's head. In the meantime, the patient continued to bleed at a serious rate. I could see Dr. Weiser glancing at the pumping bleeders as he was extracting the baby through his incision. Before the baby's feet cleared the uterus and while the nurse was still suctioning the baby, I dropped the Deavers and started clamping bleeders again.

A milli-second after I dropped the heavy Deavers on the drape (or what I thought was the surgical drape) I heard this terrible sound. About the only way I can describe it is to say that it sounded like what I would expect if I had dropped the heavy piece of metal on a watermelon. Unfortunately, there were no watermelons under the surgical drapes. Spontaneously the drapes began to move around, and the muffled and very unhappy voice of Dr. Stine could be heard. I was horrified. Dr. Weiser started to chuckle. Dr. Stine then said, "who in the hell did that?" To which I quickly replied, "Dr. Weiser." The ploy failed the credibility test and Dr. Stine could be heard saying "Jacks . . . I'm not going to be under these drapes much longer…you better go find a priest!" (Stine was Jewish). I felt terrible. I truly did. Soon Dr. Stine was out from under the drapes getting fresh air and showing everybody this significant lump starting to emerge on the top of his head. The anesthesiologist assured us the patients' blood loss would not require a unit of blood although we had blood standing by just in case.

As soon as the baby was out and off the mother's system, the anesthesiologist put her under a general anesthesia. We then were free to work at a normal pace, tie off all the bleeders, and suture the new mother up just like this had been a normal rather than an emergency C-section. They let the mother see her new baby for a few seconds before they put her under the general anesthesia. Dr. Stine said it looked like we had everything under control, so he sat on a stool in the corner of the room with a towel full of ice a nurse had brought him pressed against the now purple lump.

About the time of this emergency C-section, far away in Cambodia in February of 1963, a little known Cambodian Maoist named Saloth Sar (aka Pol Pot) was elected General Secretary of the Communist Party of Kampuchea (Cambodia).[63]

In March, following some public demonstrations against the government, Cambodian head of state Prince Norodom Sihanouk ordered General Lon Nol to investigate the subversives. General Lon Nol presented a list of those he considered a threat to the government to

---

[63] Brother Number One—Pol Pot by David P. Chandler

Sihanouk about two weeks later. There were thirty-four names on the list. Saloth Sar's name, along with that of Ieng Sary was on the list.[64]

Also in March 1963, an American, recently returned from Russia, named Lee Harvey Oswald purchased a 6.5 mm caliber Carcano rifle by mail-order, using the alias A. Hidell.[65]

Spring In The Air

In Corpus Christi, spring was in the air. Spring break offered a few days' relief from my four nights a week college grind. This meant I could hit the Padre Island beach a bit as well as the NCO club. A couple of us even took an overnight trip to Mexico. The drive was just less than 150 miles and took under three hours. We split the cost of gas and shared a room in Mexico to save money. Compared to Tijuana, Laredo was a sleepy little town but still it was a welcome break from night duty and night classes. It was about this time that I had my twentieth birthday. No celebration. No nothing. Just a mental note. I don't think I even told anybody. It wasn't a milestone like reaching twenty-one, but at least I was no longer a teenager. I got a birthday card from my parents.

New Faces

The chatter around the hospital was all about the new female corpsmen that were arriving. There was always a sizable number at the hospital, but this group of new faces gave everybody's conversation a refreshing new buzz. A day or so later I ran into the first group. I think it was during lunch. All the guys were hanging around them and obviously they were enjoying the attention. They mostly worked in OB-GYN, a separate division from the rest of the hospital. This meant that with my work and school I wouldn't be seeing much of them any time soon. I decided I didn't have the time to invest in that project. At least for the moment.

But it wasn't too long before I started to notice that whenever I managed to get a night off and went someplace, several of this new group of girls were always there. And eventually I got to know them. One in particular caught my eye. She was a "Yankee" from Wisconsin named Karen. Karen Ann Vermeire.

Steady Company

As summer approached, I decided I was going to take a break from school. That's all I'd done since the summer of 1960 was study and push myself. I was clearly burning out. While still passing everything, my grades had started to slump as well. For the first time, I was convinced that throwing more time and energy on this situation would not produce an improvement and it held

---
[64] Brother Number One—Pol Pot by David P. Chandler
[65] The Assassin, Warren Commission Report, pp118-119

out the possibility of producing negative results should I fail a course. I did not register for the summer semester.

Suddenly finding myself with a normal schedule, I diverted a significant amount of the energy I'd applied to school to having a good time. I started going places more often with the group from the hospital. In the process, I got to know Karen. She was witty and just nice to be with. Pretty soon we started deciding for eating out without the group. When we went to beach parties and to the enlisted club, we went together. I guess you could call this dating.

While Karen and I were exploring the beach together, the Kennedy administration was transmitting instructions via the Department of State to United States Ambassador Lodge[66] in Saigon and to General Harkins[67] indicating their support of a coup which would "remove" South Vietnam's president Ngo Dinh Diem.[68]

Also that summer, in July 1963, Pol Pot and most of the central committee of the Workers' Party of Kampuchea (WPK) left Phnom Penh to establish an insurgent base in the mountainous jungles of Rotanokiri (Ratanakiri) Province in northeastern Cambodia.[69] This group would later become the infamous Khmer Rouge. Nobody seemed to notice.

In the Congo, the United Nations was preparing to remove its troops from the country. Their mission was marred by failures and division. They accomplished little of permanent value and some harm. But Katanga's secession had been blocked.[70]

As summer turned to fall, I realized I was having serious thoughts about Karen. This was in September of 1963. I couldn't get out of my mind the thought that I'd be separating from the service in April of 1964, less than eight months away. I was very uncomfortable with the thought of leaving her behind when I left. This was truly a novel emotion for me.

But Karen was new to the Navy and I was just about to complete my tour. How could she get out and go with me? About that time, one of the corpsmen I knew had married a girl in the Navy. He was getting out and she was being discharged so she could accompany him. It was a technicality I believe they called a "hardship clause." Anyway, both Karen and I took note.

We soon began seriously discussing marriage. Believing I would get out of the service the following April, and understanding how sometimes the Navy's bureaucracy moved slowly, we decided to set a December date and press forward with plans.

---

[66] U.S. Ambassador to Vietnam Henry Cabot Lodge - 1963 to 1964
[67] Gen. Paul D. Harkins - first commander of Military Assistance Command, Vietnam (MACV)
[68] The Pentagon Papers, Gravel Edition, Volume 2, pp. 736-737
[69] Country Studies Program, formerly the Army Area Handbook Program - published by the Library of Congress
[70] The UN in the Congo: The Civilian Operations by Authur House, University Press of America

Wedding Plans

Looking back now, I must have had the sensitivity of a rock. I wanted a small wedding; small to the point of the exclusion of our parents. Karen agreed; perhaps just to please me. We planned a small affair that included only those with whom we worked. No fancy invitations…no nothing. The ceremony would be at the base chapel. Karen was Catholic and wanted to be married by a priest. While I was raised a Baptist, at that point in time, I'd acquired the pseudo-intellectual mindset so common with new college students. I labeled myself as a "gnostic Christian," which I now see was not based on anything near what Christ taught. Thank God we somehow grow out of that phony phase. The priest agreed to marry us, but I needed to go through some classes. Probably in hopes of getting through the classes quickly, I agreed with everything the priest said and proclaimed understanding of all his instruction. The priest cut the class short after I finished the second session. Mercifully, God insured there was no end of course exam.

In Washington the Kennedy administration and the US Ambassador in Saigon were busy planning and encouraging the coup that would remove from office and take the life of South Vietnamese president Diem.[71]

In November we arranged for base housing. We were fortunate there was no waiting list. Of course, we had no furniture and with service separation only a few short months away we elected to rent furniture. Within a few days we had a somewhat Spartan but cute little one-bedroom place. It was tiny but we didn't realize it at the time.

Work continued as usual for both of us. I had already begun a letter writing campaign with the aim of having a job waiting as soon as I got out of the service. Because Houston was close and certainly had the biggest economy, we decided we would move to Houston when I got out.

Meanwhile, in Dallas, Lee Harvey Oswald, was plotting the assassination of President Kennedy.[72,73,74]

On 1 November 1963, a CIA and State Department encouraged coup, lead by General Duong Van Minh began in Saigon that would take the lives of South Vietnam's President Ngo Dinh Diem and his brother.[75] *Three weeks later President Kennedy himself is assassinated. Cambodia's head of state Prince Norodom Sihanouk takes serious note.*[76]

---

[71] "Memorandom of Conference With The President" - 1 Nov 1963—Secret—Sanitized 6/21/99

[72] The Long Brown Bag - By Magen Knuth

[73] Warren Commission Hearings, Vol. I, p72-73, Testimony of Marina Oswald

[74] Warren Commission 1964, p40

[75] Vietnam War Timeline—VietnamGear.com

[76] The Tragedy of Cambodian History by David P. Chandler

Kennedy Killed

"America Mourns Camelot Dream."[77]

It was Friday 22 November 1963. It was supposed to be like any other Friday. Quite often Friday schedules were light. We had everything wrapped up by 11:30am. I was at the chief corpsman desk. Most everyone else was in the adjoining room putting surgical packs and trays together. While everyone was aware President Kennedy had come to Texas and was scheduled to visit Ft. Worth and Dallas, I don't recall anyone trying to watch the event on TV or listen on the radio. It was just a normal Friday.

Suddenly Mary Lamar (pseudonym) came rushing into CSR (central supply room). She was not shouting but very loudly announcing that someone had just shot the president. Mary was the oldest nurse we had. She was about five feet tall and appeared to be almost that wide. She was extremely excited, and I remember so clearly my first thought was that Mary might have a stroke if she didn't calm down. Everybody crowded around our little portable radio while one of the other technicians scanned the band looking for breaking news. It was just a matter of seconds before he found something. The president had been shot at 12:30 pm Texas time. It was now about 12:50. I can still see so plainly all those green pajamas huddled around the radio. Soon the doctors began to come in. They had been on the wards seeing patients. They knew we had a radio in CSR. We rushed to the tech's lounge where we had our lockers and several chairs and tried to pick up something on the old junker black and white portable TV we had. Someone brought the TV we had in our night room into CSR. The X-Ray techs started coming to CSR as well. Everybody knew we had a TV. The mood was somber; almost surreal. Some breaking news was saying the president was uninjured. Other news was saying he was in serious condition. Shortly afterwards the news was saying he could be in critical condition. All reports agreed the president was at Parkland Hospital along with Texas Governor John Connally We heard our Texas governor had been shot as well. These conflicting news reports continued to come over the radio. I remember hoping our government wasn't in this much confusion. Over the next twenty minutes or so, amidst all the conflicting stories, one could start to see an emerging consensus. This consensus was not good. At around 1:20pm the final word came. We were now starting to get coverage via the TV as well. The president was dead.

Presidential assassinations were supposed to take place in places like South Vietnam and the Congo, often with the help of American presidents and the CIA. But not here...not in the United States...not in this modern time. American presidential assassinations belonged in history books. Some of the nurses were in tears. Many of the surgical techs were hyper. I went into that disembodied spectator mode again. I remember I was more interested in the reactions of those around me and what kind of constitutional transfer of

---

[77] November 23, 1963 edition of the London Herald

power we were going to have. than the second by second conflicting barrage of confusion we were getting from the news media. But this soon passed, and I became as curious as the others about what would happen next. I imagined how President Kennedy's wife must be feeling. It was a heavy time. Unlike the cardiac arrest in the OR recently, there was nothing here for me to do. So, I just went back to my desk, put my stuff in my drawer and sat at my clean desk. I was also wondering if there were any national security concerns that would affect the Naval Air Station or the hospital.

I had duty that night and slept in the OR night duty room. The TV stations had reached the point where they were just rehashing the same news over and over. I remember things were quiet, so I put on a green top coat which we were required to wear when we left the clean environment of the operating room suites, my little green "footies" to keep my OR shoes clean and walked the probably 50 feet over to the hospital administration office. The duty officer was there as well as hospital security. I really went over to see if there was any news of increased alert status. There was a crowd around the teletype machine when I arrived. Usually they only looked at the traffic if we were among the addressees. This time everybody was watching everything. I'd been sitting around in one of the extra seats when I heard the corpsman sitting in the teletype operator's chair say "hey…take a look at this." A perfect silhouette of President Kennedy drawn with the character "X" was coming over the teletype. Normally things like this were forbidden. Sailors with too much time on their hands could tie up the teletype network sending "cute" drawings (usually slightly vulgar). But I don't think anybody said anything to anybody that night. It was very moving as line after line of Xs came over the wire marking out a perfect silhouette of the late President John F. Kennedy. It's amazing how clearly you remember things like that.

About two weeks later, on 8 December, Field Marshal Sarit Thanarat, the Thai premier died in Bangkok. He and Sihanouk had traded insults for years. The Thai government had been supporting a Cambodian insurgency group called the Khmer Serei active along the Thai-Cambodian border by providing material resources and sanctuary. In addition the Thais had supported Khmer Serei anti Sihanouk radio broadcasts. On 9 December, the day following the death of Field Marshal Sarit, Thanarat Sihanouk made a radio broadcast in Khmer in which he said "At two-week intervals our enemies have departed one after the other. The first, the one in the south (Diem), then the great boss (Kennedy), and now the one in the west (Sarit). All three have always sought to violate our neutrality and make trouble for us, to seek our misfortune. Now they are all going to meet in hell where they will be able to build military bases for SEATO. Our other enemies will join them. The gods punish all the enemies of neutral and peaceful Cambodia The spirits of our former kings protect us." [78]

---

[78] The Tragedy of Cambodian History—Politics, War, and Revolution Since 1945 by David P. Chandler

Bells–Christmas And Wedding

The wedding day finally came...23 December. A significant number of those we worked with were present. I was nervous. We had the rings. We had the license. Since I was four months away from being twenty-one, Daddy had to go to the Hamilton County Courthouse and get the license and sign granting their permission. I can't remember much about the ceremony. I do remember Karen looked very nice. I recall looking at Karen after the ceremony and saying to myself... Wow, this is my wife. I am really married. It was an interesting feeling. There was a small reception afterwards and we went "home" to our tiny little apartment located on the base. I liked it. It was "our place."

1964–A Year Of Surprise And Rapid Events

Early 1964 didn't correlate with my schedule of events. I had everything neatly planned to coincide with my mid-April scheduled separation from the service. We'd been studying Houston newspapers looking for affordable apartments. I'd made notes about various employment agencies and even corresponded with a couple. I had one interview lined up already with a medical supply company as a sales representative. We had a map of Houston. We were ready. But Karen and the Navy hadn't been studying my timeline. First Karen said the magic words "I think I may be pregnant." Wow, that's cool. So, she scheduled an appointment and sure enough...she was. A couple of weeks later, while I'm sitting at my desk in main surgery, my phone rings and it's the personnel office. "Jacks, we've just been informed we have three early out spots...are you interested?" I replied "sure...how early?" "You'll be gone in two weeks" the personnel officer said. "Let me think about it" I said. To which they replied, "you have one hour." When the word gets out, we will be swamped with people clamoring for them." I called Karen and we decided we could make it work. We were both about to become civilians.

Karen had already been arranging for her separation date to coincide with mine. Now we both had to speed it up. I called the personnel office back a few minutes later and told him I was in. Their reply was to come tomorrow morning and they'd have an out-processing packet ready for me. I realized this was going to take most of my next two weeks. I immediately spoke with the Chief of Surgery. We had already been transferring duties in anticipation of my April separation. He said to start processing now. They would manage the transition. Come in every morning and every afternoon to check on issues that may have arisen. Other than that...consider myself relieved. He liked me and I liked him. I was going to miss working with him.

Mother Gets Sick

We received a rather long letter from my mother. She always wrote in such a beautiful script. This time, while the handwriting was the same, the lines were filled with sadness. She had a lump in her stomach and was going to have surgery in Waco. At Hillcrest…where she had brought Camille and me into the world. The fear was cancer. I was stunned. I called home and they told me not to worry about coming. I should have had the sensitivity to see past that and dropped everything and gone home to be with her and my father while mother had the operation. But I didn't. "If Only".

Karen started thinking about packing up our rather meager personal and household possessions. I started writing more letters. I hardly remember the details they moved so quickly. I was already focused on Houston. Only my body was still in Corpus Christi.

The big day finally came. Karen and I loaded all our belongings into our 1958 Mercury Monterey (my cute little MGA Roadster had become too expensive to maintain) and drove out the gate of the NAS Corpus Christi and headed out of town following the signs to Victoria and then Houston. The drive was just over 200 miles and took four hours. Karen and I were excited. For the first time in my life, I was personally responsible for someone else. I wasn't afraid but I was mildly apprehensive. Karen was always reassuring and this helped a lot. She must have been apprehensive as well. Beginning a new life, away from her family with a guy she'd only known for a year. All this and being an expectant mother as well.

Meanwhile in Cambodia major dissatisfaction was growing among the increasing numbers of leftist students. The students were encouraged by the leftist section of Sihanouk's government. Massive demonstrations in front of the American and British embassies took place. Students were bussed in in government vehicles from the provinces and military personnel in civilian clothes were among the "students." Ministry of Information loudspeakers were used to encourage the students. Both embassies were damaged extensively. A significant portion of Cambodia's population was turning left following the lead of Sihanouk.[79]

In the Congo a then little known Maoist named Pierre Mulele, had returned from studies and exile in China. His armed followers were called Simbas (Swahili for Lion). Their rebellion soon controlled a large portion of the eastern Congo.[80]

A key player in suppressing the Chinese and Russian desires in the Congo came from the CIA's private air force operating under the cover of the Force Aérienne Congolaise or Congolese Air Force (which had no Congolese pilots)[81]

---

[79] The Tragedy of Cambodian History—Politics, War, and Revolution Since 1945 by David P. Chandler
[80] M. Crawford Young. Post-Independence Politics in the Congo
[81] U.S. Foreign Policy in Perspective by David Sylvan and Stephen Majeski

Soaring On The Wings Of The Wind

He rode on a cherub and flew, soaring on the wings of the wind. [82]

Houston – The Bayou City

In 1964 the population of Houston was around a million people. It was a boom town. Since 1962, NASA's Manned Spacecraft Center had been bringing people and jobs. Construction was everywhere. But this boom was not my focus. I believed I could use my hospital experience and land a job in sales and marketing for suppliers to the medical field. I already had an interview arranged. But as Karen and I drove into Houston, our priority was finding a place to live. We had been studying the apartment advertisements in the Houston paper while still in Corpus Christi. We had studied the area and had some apartments we wanted to check out.

It didn't take long at all to find an apartment. A couple of hours after we arrived in Houston, Karen and I were unpacking. Looking back now I'm sure had we been a little more experienced we would never have picked this little one-bedroom place about seven miles south of the center of Houston. But it had a swimming pool just under our balcony and lots of single and younger couples lived there. I shudder now to think we ever lived in such a place but . . . ignorance was indeed bliss. We were happy and totally focused on our little microcosm nested inside the sprawling and booming Houston Texas.

While we were unpacking our scanty belongings, on 8 March 1964 Robert McNamara (Defense Secretary) and Maxwell Taylor (JCS Chairman) began a 5-day trip to appraise the situation in Vietnam. On 16 March McNamara reported to President Johnson that the situation in Vietnam was far worse than was recognized in NSAM 273 (26 Nov 1963) (immediately after Kennedy's assassination). Approximately 40% of South Vietnamese territory was now under de facto Viet Cong control. ARVN and paramilitary desertion rates were increasing while the Viet Cong were recruiting energetically and effectively.[83]

My First Interview

The next day I put on my suit and headed off for the interview I'd arranged. It wasn't exactly as nice a place as I had envisioned but it held the potential of providing a nice income if I could land the job.

---

[82] Holy Bible—Holman Christian Standard—2 Samuel 22:11
[83] VietnameGear.com - Vietnam War Timeline: 1963-1964

I introduced myself to the secretary and she disappeared behind an office door. Soon a slightly plump white-haired man with a pleasant smile came out. He invited me into his office, and he compared the resume I'd handed him to the one I'd sent him. He asked me lots of questions and I felt I was handling everything quite well. He then proceeded to explain that every salesman had to begin working in the warehouse so he would have a thorough knowledge of all the products the company offered. He said that's how he started and that's how things worked there. I held my composure and kept the interview going but already inside I knew I did not get out of the service and come to Houston just to work in a warehouse on the promise of something better. He gave me a tour of the place. In the back I met two young men who were in training to be salesmen. One had been there over five years already. Now a voice in my head was no longer whispering but shouting No Way! They made me an offer and I told them I would need to go home and discuss it with my wife. I knew I was not coming back there. I was a little bit down but refused to think about the consequences of looking for a job until we ran out of the money we had saved while in the Navy. I went back to the apartment and started going through my notes again. Next was Snelling & Snelling. I'd corresponded with them before we left Corpus Christi but at that time, they had nothing. I went down stairs to the payphone and gave them a call. I asked for the same man with whom I'd been corresponding. Soon he was on the phone and his first words were puzzling…"well that sure didn't take long." At first, I thought he was still talking to someone else while he'd picked up the phone. But he was talking to me. He said he had just called the Naval Hospital. They told him I'd just left a couple of days previously and they didn't have a number for me. He was wondering how I got the message so quickly. To which I replied, "what message?" He said they just found the perfect job match for me and wanted me to come in right away and get setup for an interview.

Central Scientific Company
CENCO Instruments Corp.

It was a little hard to get to sleep that night, but morning finally came. Karen had my clothes all pressed, I had my notes, and out the door I went. This time I had to go into downtown Houston to the Snelling & Snelling office. I knew these recruiters got paid commissions, but I had somehow expected them to be more personnel oriented. It was all about teaching me how to get the job so they could get their commissions. Heck, I was OK with that. Welcome to the real world. They had the interview set up for the following Monday morning. It was now Friday. This gave me the weekend to try to learn about who this Central Scientific Company or CENCO Instruments was.

Snelling & Snelling had explained that CENCO manufactured scientific instruments, mostly measuring and calibration equipment, but also high school and college science lab equipment as well. By checking reference material, I was able to put together a brief profile of the company.

Also, that weekend I scouted out the location of their office so I could find it easily Monday morning. Being late was not an option. Their relatively small office in front of a large warehouse sat in an industrial area near our apartment. Just across from the CENCO office was a gas station. They were not busy at all, so I stopped and went inside. I asked the two men working there if they knew any of the people who worked in the CENCO office across the street. They said sure and remarkably provided me the names of a couple in addition to the General Manager. They were particularly familiar with the General Manager as he always had his new Chrysler company car serviced there regularly. They described him as a "Yankee" with a strong accent. I added this information to their company profile as well.

Monday morning came and I made sure I arrived early. I had the Snelling & Snelling employment application form but thought they might have their own, which it turned out they did.

When I was ushered in to the GM's office, there were two men sitting there. It turns out that the company's vice president from Chicago was in town. He occasionally spoke but allowed the GM to do most of the talking. After they had quizzed me for a while, they asked me what I knew about them. Apparently, most people fell short at this point. I recited the few facts I'd been able to come up with and then added that the GM was from Boston, drove a Chrysler, and had it serviced every two weeks at the gas station across the street. You could hear a pin drop. The two men were not looking at me but at each other. They asked me to allow them a few minutes to talk. About five minutes later I was called back in and told I was hired. Those few minutes at the gas station across the street got me the job. Maybe the book research helped a little, but ninety percent was what those two guys in the gas station told me. I reported for work the next morning. Karen and I were happy and relieved. Less than a week out of the service and I had an exceptional job. I graciously concealed my "take your warehouse and shove it" feelings as I called my first interview back and told them I wouldn't be able to take the job. When they asked who hired me and I told them CENCO they couldn't believe it. They knew the company well although it was not a direct competitor. I remember the manager saying that they all drove brand new company cars and had big expense accounts. *So I was encouraged, as the hand of the Lord my God was upon me*[84]

I would be in training working in the quotation department for a few months in order to learn the product line and then be given my own territory in Dallas. Both CENCO and my first job interview agreed it was important to learn the product line. But CENCO believed the most important part of the job was selling. They said they had engineers to explain the internal workings

---

[84] Holy Bible—New King James - Ezra 7:28

of things and warehouse people to know how many they had in stock and telex and telephones to order more. My job was to sell the stuff.

Spring and summer flew by. I loved my work learning about all the neat things CENCO sold. Stuff like single pan analytical balances, nuclear scalers (CENCO also owned Atomic Laboratories), lasers, the list was endless. I couldn't help but wish my Hamilton High School smoke bomb accomplice could see all this neat stuff that I now got paid to play with. I suppose he later got to play with the same kind of thing when he was in medical school, but he sure didn't get paid to play with it.

As I was growing in possibly wisdom and certainly knowledge, Karen was growing as well. We started thinking about Corpus Christi again. She could have the baby free if she had it at the Naval Hospital. An additional benefit would be she could be with all her old friends again. So, she finalized the arrangements we had begun before our separations from the service. The baby would be born at the Naval Hospital. The plan was to go down a couple of weeks early just in case the baby decided to come early. But we needed a reliable way to get back to Corpus Christi. Heck, we needed a reliable way to get anywhere.

Our 1964½ Ford Mustang

Back at the beginning of the summer our Mercury was starting to show serious signs of impending doom. It had a serious engine oil leak and often the oil light would come on. I knew I had to trade it in before something serious happened. I called my father who spoke with the Hamilton National Bank. They agreed to give us a new car loan. Now all I had to do was find a car we could afford and someone willing to take the Mercury. Finding the new car was the easy part.

That spring the newspapers had been full of news about this new car from Ford call the Mustang. I'd only seen pictures but there were reasonably priced and cool looking. Almost as cool as my little white MGA Roadster. With my Mercury freshly topped off with the heaviest oil I dared put in it, I drove onto the Ford dealership's lot. We went inside and looked at the cars. That Mustang was the only car I really noticed. The salesmen were like sharks and I was doing the best I could to keep them from eating me. Anyway, we walked out with a signed order for one. There was more than a month's waiting list for them. That meant I still had to drive that very fragile Mercury for four more weeks. We prayed we didn't have to go anyplace past the grocery store and work.

But finally the day came, and we picked up our new Mustang. Its paint was beautiful deep blue. It had a 289 cubic inch (4.7 L) engine, a "Rally Pac" on the steering column and an under-dash air conditioner. Wow…we had arrived.

Return To Corpus Christi

As Karen's due date started to approach we decided we had better use a weekend and drive her to Corpus. She had already arranged to stay with friends there on the base, so we planned to take the weekend and enjoy our new Mustang. Driving without the stress of possible impending breakdown was a joy. Our plan was to take a little side trip to San Antonio before going on to Corpus. We'd visit friends there first, then drive on later that day to Corpus.

Early Saturday morning we packed her small suitcase and some meager baby things in the Mustang's equally meager trunk and headed west toward San Antonio. The drive was about four hours. It was such a pleasure to be able to drive and enjoy the beautiful scenery without the worry of some mechanical breakdown. No oil leaks, no steering fluid leaks, no bald tires…it just couldn't get much better than this.

We visited with our friends in San Antonio then headed south toward the coast and Corpus Christi. This was only a three-hour drive. It felt strange as we drove through the main gate. It seemed to me like we had been gone forever. We went directly to our friends' on-base housing. Everybody looked the same. We visited for a while and I said goodbye to Karen and headed back to Houston. It was late when I arrived back at our apartment. I went straight to bed.

On May 21, 1964 a CIA telegram read: Captured Viet Cong documents reveal the importance of Cambodian and Laotian refuges: "an armed struggle should have a rear area in which to raise troops and where attack or defense is to our advantage[85]

August 1964, several thousand Simba rebels under the command of Nicholas Olenga stormed the defenses of Stanleyville, a city of 300,000 deep in the heart of the newly independent Republic of the Congo. The victorious rebels promptly took more than 1,600 European residents hostage and announced that any attempt by the Congolese government to recapture the city would precipitate the killing of the Europeans.[86] *While we were heading toward Corpus Christi, rape and murder on an enormous scale was taking place in Stanleyville at the hand of the Simbas. The Belgium and US governments were working feverishly to devise a rescue. While I'm sure this made the newspapers, it totally escaped me. I had no clue.*

In Vietnam General William Westmoreland officially becomes Commander of MACV.[87] *(May need to define or identify)*

---

[85] CIA Telegram N. 22708, to State Department, for Sullivan. May 21, 1964. 1 p. Secret/lim dis. Sanitized - Texas Tech University's Virtual Vietnam Archive
[86] Leavenworth Papers Number 14—Dragon Operations: Hostage Rescues in the Congo, 1964-1965 - by Major Thomas P. Odom - Combat Studies Institute, U.S. Army Command and General Staff College
[87] VietnamGear - Vietnam War Timeline: 1963-1964

Sunday Morning Surprise

The following morning, I woke to the sound of our recently installed telephone. As I stumbled toward the tiny kitchen to answer it, I wondered how long it had been ringing before I heard it. When I answered, it was Karen. I just left her a few hours ago. What had we forgotten? Then I heard her voice telling me we had a son. Jason Jerome Jacks. I was still in disbelief. How could this be…she just got there last night. I was still trying to get awake and simultaneously realize I was a father. She said Saturday would be fine for me to come get her. I told her I'd call her mother since she was on government or pay phones. I found the number on our telephone list inside our phone directory and called Karen's mother "Ellie" in Green Bay Wisconsin. I had expected she would be excited, but by this time "Ellie" was a grandmother numerous times. She took the news right in stride. However, I'll bet her phone line was busy calling all Karen's sisters the second I hung up.

Jason Comes Home

The week flew by. Saturday morning came and I was on the road early, headed toward Corpus to pick up Karen and see my son for the first time. This time as I drove through the main gate the place didn't feel so distant. Soon I was holding my son for the first time. So tiny, so perfect…Wow.

Karen's friends made sure she had enough formula. Like an awful lot. We put his little carrier in the back seat, the huge supply of formula in the trunk, and Karen and I were once again headed toward Houston. But this time we had a job and a new baby. Life was good. Very good.

As we were driving home in the dark, we had the radio tuned to a pop station. They played Under The Boardwalk by The Drifters. Now almost fifty years later, it's still one of my all-time favorite songs. I play it several times each week. And each time I hear it I see the inside of our 1964 ½ Ford Mustang. I see Karen sitting beside me and Jason in his little carrier in the back seat. The darkness outside highlighted the instrument panel and the rally pack. I see it as clearly as if it were yesterday.

Our little apartment got immediately smaller with Jason's arrival. His crib occupied a prominent place. But nobody cared. It was a wonderful time. And the cramped conditions would not last long.

Shortly after Jason's birth CENCO released the salesman whose territory covered almost half the state. From Dallas to El Paso. The rumor mill in the office had always been I was hired and trained as his replacement. They just failed to tell him. When I met him it was obvious he didn't care. But I'd paid little attention to any of that. I needed to learn as much as possible as quickly as possible about all the many laboratory, education, and research instruments and supplies CENCO manufactured and sold. Speculating about the guy in Dallas was simply not a priority.

Dallas
Home of the Cowboys, Jimmy Joe, Karen, And Jason

We found a very nice apartment in Irving, just west of Dallas. Irving was called a bedroom city for Dallas. Almost everyone who lived in Irving worked in Dallas. Our apartment was brand new. The bedroom and bathroom were upstairs. Karen had a nice modern kitchen with adjoining dining area. And our living room was spacious . . . well compared to anything we had previously had. The floors had nice shag carpet. The apartment complex was called The Royal Oaks. That just sounded stately. The apartment complex was located on its own short street, Haley Street. That meant your apartment number was your street address. This added to our "status" as well. Our address was 410 Haley. Just like we lived in a real house. This country boy from Hamilton, Texas, had arrived. Working for a New York Stock Exchange listed company, driving a new company car, and with an unlimited expense account. How cool was that! Looking back now, our (or my) wide-eyed naïveté was funny. But that naïveté was what made the time so special. Our lives had changed so dramatically in the past twelve months.

While Karen and I were settling into the Royal Oaks Apartments, the CIA was busy setting up a proprietary company called Anstalt Wigmo in the Principality of Liechtenstein, a tiny city state adjoining Switzerland and Austria. The purpose of the clandestine company was to manage the CIA's operations in the Congo. Basically to become its air force. Wigmo pilots and mechanics would fly and maintain the CIA's rapidly growing fleet of B-26 and T-28 attack aircraft[88]

From 23–28 November 1964 U.S. and Belgium forces carried out operations Dragon Rouge and Dragon Noir (Red Dragon – Black Dragon) to free the almost 1500 hostages held in Stanleyville, Congo. The operations were successful. However, the Simbas killed many of their hostages minutes before the para-commandos reached them. Cuban piloted CIA B26s screamed overhead trying to draw fire just 60 seconds before the C-130 aircraft arrived with the Belgium para-commandos. The hostages held for 111 days were finally freed.[89]

The nature of my new position with CENCO dictated I be gone from home Monday through Thursday of each week, only coming home on Friday night. Usually I'd allow one week per month to make my sales calls in the local Dallas–Ft. Worth area. But most of the time I was ranging from East Texas

---
[88] The Douglas Invader in Foreign Military and U.S. Clandestine Service By Dan Hagedom and Leif Hellström
[89] Leavenworth Papers Number 14 - Dragon Operations: Hostage Rescues in the Congo, 1964-1965 - By Major Thomas P. Odom - Combat Studies Institute - U.S. Army Command and General Staff College

to El Paso. I was my own boss. I made my own schedule. But the bottom line was the territory had to be covered and the only way to do it was to travel.

While I was away, Karen would make friends with the neighbor women, usually out in the courtyard watching babies or in the laundry room. They were mostly nice. I'd later meet their husbands when I returned home for the weekend. It was here that we met Tom and Nita Hafford. They lived just next to us. Tom and I would remain friends.

Many of those living in the apartment were airline pilots. The home office for American and Braniff Airlines was in the Dallas–Ft. Worth area. Dallas was a big hub for Delta as well. The Royal Oaks had a nice swimming pool and occasionally I'd go out there and sit in the sun. It was out by the pool where I got to know several of the pilots. The first thing I noticed is how they loved their work. To them, it wasn't really work. They all enjoyed flying. This observation stayed in my mind. The other thing I noticed was the pilots always seemed to be out by the pool and I always seemed to be away from home, yet we made the same money. Something was very wrong with this equation. In addition, they were all first and second year pilots…new with the airline. When I listened to what their pay scale would be as their seniority progressed year to year, I realized they would soon be making many times what I was making. My income projections were good but nothing like theirs. It wasn't long before I started asking them how they became pilots. Most came from the military with the government paying for their flight training. However, there were some who went through private flight academies.

Lois Goes Home

"I am tired and weary but I must toil on
Till the Lord come to call me away
Where the morning is bright and the Lamb is the light
And the night is fair as the day"[90]

While I was busy building sales and traveling, Mother was slowly slipping away, losing her battle with widely metastasized ovarian cancer. Daddy had called from his office and told me I should come to Hamilton. He needed to talk to me privately. I knew this was not good. I asked him if he could meet me at the old Olin Baptist Church (tiny rural church) so we could talk without being interrupted. Olin Baptist Church was 12 miles north of Hamilton on highway 281. He said that would be fine. I could tell by the sound of his voice he wasn't handling this very well.

I arrived on time. Daddy was already there waiting for me. I got into his pickup and he told me the news. Mother didn't have long. She was sad and very depressed. I'd never seen Daddy so down. Mother was not quite nineteen when they married. Daddy not quite twenty. That was in 1929.

---
[90] Peace In the Valley by Thomas A. Dorsey 1937

Now, in the spring of 1965 Mother was being taken away. I can only try to imagine his pain. I told him I would go home right away and see her. It was a long twelve-mile drive. It was still winter; the grass had not yet turned to its beautiful spring green. It was cold…the trees looked dead…the grass looked dead. I was having a hard time coming to grips with the fact that the woman who had given birth to me and always been in my life, even though I hadn't paid the attention to her that I should have, was about to die. All the missed opportunities seemed to stream before me in some endless procession. Why hadn't I spent more time with her? "If Only".

When I arrived, she was lying in bed in the back bedroom. She had combed her hair nicely and had on a little bit of makeup. Obviously, she had known I was coming. The decision of when and how to tell me had been a joint operation. I sat on the edge of the bed and held her hand. Something I hadn't done in years. Her eyes were filled with tears. Daddy was never very good with words. Mother was eloquent. She said the doctors had told her after the surgery that it didn't look good. That the cancer cells had already spread from the ovaries and were moving throughout her body. She was now experiencing constant pain and the medications they had given her didn't adequately control it. She was losing weight. They had told her she probably had less than four more months. She appeared to be slightly afraid of death but only slightly. Her Christian faith was helping her deal with it. She was worried for my sister Camille who was only fifteen. She was still in high school. Who would look after her? Who would be there for her? Mother told me that her good friend Fay Schrank had promised to help after she passed on. Fay's promise was kind, but it just wasn't the same. Camille's mother was about to leave her. Mother's grief and sorrow were indescribable. She wasn't so worried about dying as she was about how Daddy and Camille were going to make it. We visited for another hour or so, until my heart was so heavy I could hardly move. I had no strength left in my body. My mind and my body were drained by emotion. Mother's life was being poured out before her eyes and she could only helplessly watch.

I left Hamilton to drive back to Irving. I still see it all so clearly. All these forty-five years later…I can still see it like it was yesterday. I felt as though my world was filled with dark clouds, not frightening, just heavy, suffocating clouds. There was no bright shining thing anywhere. My breaths were deep and labored. I sighed frequently. My mind was a screen upon which ran a constant playback of all the times I'd failed to be there for her or the countless instances of my insensitivity. "If Only".

The following weekend Karen and I took Jason and went to Hamilton. We stayed till Sunday afternoon, and then drove back to Irving. This would be our routine until mother's condition demanded she go into the hospital. I remember sitting on the side of her bed with Jason. He was not quite one year old. He was just about to take his first steps. I'd hold him up so he wouldn't topple over and he would do a little in-place dance. Mother loved these times. I wished there had been more of them. "If Only"

The Hamilton Hospital[91]

"Mother's pain started getting worse…much worse. Dr. Don McCord began coming to the house and giving her injections to help her tolerate the pain. In her last days, she became so weak, drifting in and out of consciousness, that it became necessary to admit her to the Hamilton hospital solely to insure her last hours were as comfortable as possible. She was no longer able to tolerate any food by mouth. Hallucinations began occurring at this time too. Finally the doctors began the administration of intervenes paraldehyde rendering her almost completely unconscious. The family made the decision that she would never be left alone in the hospital. Someone sat with her the entire time. My father, Camille, Karen, close family friends Fay and Bert Schrank, and my grandmother, Grace Aldredge all kept watch over her during these last hours.

My Vision

On my night to stay with her, I sat with my chair close to her bed so I could try to hold her hand. That was difficult as she was quite restless from the hallucinations. At one time I put my head on her bed and was resting when I apparently drifted off to sleep. I would estimate the time to have been between 2:30am to 3:00am. During this sleep, I heard Mother's voice calling me. She was calling my name over and over…"Jimmy Joe…Jimmy Joe." I awoke and raised my head. There was a silver hued gentle glow above us. I could hear her calling me and the voice was coming from the light above us…not from her peacefully resting body in the bed. I said, "where are you?" And my Mother's voice replied so clearly…"I'm in the air…I'm everywhere." The light then went away, and I found myself sitting beside her bed staring into her resting face. The hair on the back of my neck and on my arms was standing up. I instantly thought she might have just died, but as I reached out and touched her hand it was warm, and she was breathing normally…something she did not always do in those last hours. She looked so at peace. For me, sleep did not return that night. I alertly watched as the sun's rays began to bring light to the darkness of that Saturday, May 8th morning, around 5:45am. As others began to arrive in her hospital room, it seemed as though all the energy in my body suddenly left. I remember being so tired I could hardly speak. I told no one about this experience. I went back to my parents' house, where I would immediately fall into an extremely deep sleep.

The End

It was while I was there sleeping, she quietly slipped away. She was surrounded by two close friends, her mother, Jimmie, and Camille. They

---

[91] No Information on this one?

would call from the hospital somehow awakening me from what was probably the deepest sleep of my life saying I needed to come to the hospital right away. She was already gone but they didn't want to tell me on the phone. As I walked in the room she was still in the bed, her face uncovered. She appeared to be sleeping. My grandmother sat stoically in the corner. Her Bible was in her lap. All others stood around quietly allowing me to have my last moments with my mother. I approached her bed, took her already cold hand in mine, kissed it, and walked out of the room. I was totally oblivious to the social obligations I owed to the others in the room. There are many moments in my life I would like the opportunity to relive differently. This is one of those. If Only.

I remember being angry with my grandmother for not showing any more emotion than she did. Just sitting there in that straight-back chair with her Bible in her lap. As my spiritual faith grew, I would come to realize that what I saw was the faith of a saint. Thank God I didn't express this anger directly toward her. I walked from Mother's hospital room, got in my new 1964 ½ Ford Mustang, pushed the gas pedal to the floor and experienced the car's full acceleration for the first time. Its 289 cubic inch (4.7 liter) V-8 engine seemed to explode. As the tires gained traction, I turned the radio to full volume. "Stop In The Name of Love" by the Supremes came blaring out at me. I hated that group and I hated that song. While I can't remember the exact stream of expletives that instantly flooded my mind, I remember clearly that they did. I did not decelerate (stop) until I reached Highway 36. There were so many good songs during that period, from the British Invasion to Sam Cooke, The Beach Boys, Marvin Gaye, The Righteous Brothers…why couldn't just one be playing on one of the small handful of stations that could be received in Hamilton's reception area. I waited at the stop sign just long enough to take advantage of a slight opening in the traffic, then turned left and pushed the accelerator to the floor once more. This time the Mustang fishtailed before finally gaining traction. Upon reaching the "Y" where Texas Highway 22 splits off from Highway 36 just by what was then Truck Town, I veered left and went out Hwy 22 as far as the City Lake. There I pulled off the road and just sat there for a while. My mind was racing as I tried to grasp what changes I might face in life with one of my parents, the woman who brought me into the world, now gone.

Lois Lynn Aldredge Jacks went to be with The Lord on Saturday, 8 May, 1965 about 11:30 am. She came into the world and she left the world on a Saturday. She was just 54 years old. Jimmie was without the only woman he had ever loved for the first time since he was twenty years old. It would be impossible to grasp the depth of his loneliness.

Lois's Funeral

Since the funeral would be a large one, and since the family was all here or very close, it was decided to hold the funeral service the following day in order to cause the least disruption to those wishing to attend. So on Sunday 9 May 1965, in the First Baptist Church, a huge portion of the town came together in the midafternoon to celebrate her life and help the family and close friends mourn. Rev. Ray Burdett, her former pastor, who came back from Austin and Rev. Mac Hargrove her present pastor conducted the service.

The casket was open; she was so remarkably beautiful and appeared to finally be resting so peacefully. At her request they were playing Claude Debussy's Clair de Lune, Liebesträume by Franz Liszt, and Take My Hand Precious Lord. And of course Amazing Grace. I can't remember if she had also requested that one, but I suppose it really didn't matter as virtually no Baptist funeral can conclude without Amazing Grace. As I recall, Clair de Lune and Liebesträum raised some eyebrows amongst some of Hamilton's church folks of 1965. Classical music was not quite what they were accustomed to hearing from the pews in Hamilton in the mid-1960s. But all realized it was in perfect character for Lois and all were graciously understanding. And she would probably have appreciated the irony…her funeral was on Mother's Day.

Afterword, at the graveside services, cars stretched southward along the east side of Highway 281 for almost half a mile It was a beautiful late spring day. There would be a tiny trace of rain with basically beautiful skies with temperatures just over 80 degrees. The cemetery plot Jimmie had selected had an oak tree on it. He knew Lois would want a spot with trees. A month later, I would purchase the lot adjoining theirs. It was important to me, then as it is now, to know I will someday rest beside my mother and father."

Karen, Jason and I returned to Irving leaving Camille and Daddy in a house without Mother. I felt so badly for them both. I was filled with a deep hurt. "If Only".

While Mother is gone, she really isn't. Almost fifty years after her death, she lives on vividly in my mind. Her parenting endures as she gently continues molding my likes and dislikes, my decisions and my actions. She liked bluebonnets, Beethoven and Broadway. She liked the Charleston, Chopin, and country roads. She loved us. We were blessed.

While Mother lay dying in the Hamilton County General Hospital, Prince Norodom Sihanouk broke off Cambodia's diplomatic relations with the United States as a reaction to a slanderous personal attack in a U.S. publication and a U.S. bombing raid inside Cambodian territory. Six months later, on 25 November 1965, General Mobutu seized power for the second time in a bloodless coup, following another power struggle between Kasavubu and Prime Minister Moise Tshombe[92]

---

[92] "Mobutu Sese Seko." Encyclopedia of African History and Culture: Independent Africa (1960 to Present), Vol. 5

New Orleans

Back in Irving, I buried myself in my work. As the weeks turned to months, I could see my hard work was making a difference. The sales for my territory were increasing and everyone was noticing. I'd received several compliments from the vice-president in Chicago.

One day I got a note from my general manager advising that we would be having a regional sales meeting in New Orleans. Karen and I were expected to attend. Neither of us had been there before and we were both excited. She scurried around finding things to wear. This wasn't a shorts and jeans occasion.

When we arrived in New Orleans, the Fontainebleau hotel was our first surprise. Only once in my life had I seen anything like that. My cousin "Little Jimmy" had invited me up to Beverly Hills where we stayed the weekend in the Beverly Hilton. So, Karen and I were wide-eyed. While the guys attended meetings, the ladies checked out New Orleans. At night the guys joined them. One night we ate in the hotel's famous Empire Room. This was after we'd had drinks in the La Chandelle Lounge. We ate the next night at Antoine's in the French Quarter and on Sunday morning before we left, we were back in the French Quarter for breakfast at Brennan's. While my mother and my father's cooking was wonderful, and Vivian Drake's cooking is still remembered today, Brennan's "Eggs Hussarde" and "Crabmeat Omelette topped with Hollandaise Sauce" defied culinary description.

A Change Of Course–My Return To School

Not long after returning to the Royal Oaks I began researching and writing to various flight academies. I even considered Purdue University and Southeastern Oklahoma State University. At the time they were just about the only aviation university programs in the country. Soon I had a pile of brochures and class schedules. I'd study them in my motel room at night. This was beginning to become a familiar routine in my thought process. I knew I could be successful at what I was doing but then what. I'd almost certainly become like my boss. He had ulcers from stress and guzzled Martinis like they were iced tea. I had known for some time I did not want to become like him. I was beginning to think I needed to make a course correction before it was too late.

I decided to take a little time off. I visited Southeastern Oklahoma State in Durant and spent the day looking at their program. They were much cheaper than Purdue but because I had a deficiency in engineering courses, I'd have to take several additional courses outside the aviation specific ones. I pretty much realized after that visit that my only option was to go to the private academies. So the next day I drove to Ardmore, Oklahoma, to visit the most famous flying school in the United States, American Flyers. I toured the flight school. They even took me up on a demonstration ride in one of their many Cessna 172 trainers. I was hooked.

It was about this time, while I was discussing my plans with some of the pilots in the apartment complex, that one of them asked me why I wasn't considering Southwest School of Aviation just thirty minutes away in Ft. Worth. I said I'd seen their listing in the phone book but hadn't contacted them yet. I was told they had an excellent reputation and he recommended I go look. The next day I called them and made an appointment.

A day or two later I drove to Ft. Worth's Meacham Field and walked into Southwest School of Aviation. I was greeted by an elegant middle-aged lady who introduced herself as Mary Wallace. Later I'd learn Mary was the wife of William (Bill) Wallace, the school's owner. The front office and a classroom I investigated resembled the United Nations. The school was full of Arabs and Europeans. It seemed like the predominate languages I heard were Arabic and French. It was a bee hive of activity with students heading for the classroom, the flight line, and Mrs. Green's little restaurant. Soon Bill Wallace came out and we went to his office to talk. He explained the courses they offered and the costs of the courses and flight training. I asked to see some of the text books. I wanted to be sure this was something I could complete should I decide to go in this direction. I left the school a couple of hours later with my head filled with visions of me enrolled in Southwest School of Aviation. I couldn't wait to get back home and share it all with Karen.

While Karen and I were evaluating the "big jump" of leaving CENCO and my going to school full time, a Top Secret report prepared by the CIA's Directorate of Intelligence was evaluating the effectiveness of our efforts in Vietnam. Part of the document stated: "So long as the U.S. Air offensive remains at present levels, it is unlikely to diminish North Vietnam's continued ability to provide material support to the war in the South."[93]

In the Congo, President Mobutu's government began seizing Belgium companies, mining interests, and property.[94]

In Phnom Penh, Cambodian head of state Norodom Sihanouk's movie "Apsara" was screened for the first time. The film was written, directed, and produced by Sihanouk. He and his wife also starred in the movie. All this, while Cambodia was fighting significant economic issues as well as problems on the diplomatic front. Some sources say the prince retreated to his movie making hobby as a way to escape some of the pressures he was facing. Several political observers mark this period as the beginning of his serious loss of control of the political machinery of Cambodia.[95]

---

[93] The Vietnamese Communists Will To Persist—CIA - Directorate of Intelligence—Top Secret - Released
[94] The Library of Congress Country Studies and the CIA World Facebook
[95] The Tragedy of Cambodian History—David P. Chandler

Karen and I took a deep breath and decided to go for it. With a wife and child, I was about to leave a very good job and enter school full time. Looking back now, I'm certain it was our youthful naïveté once again that gave us the courage to move forward.

Southwest School of Aviation
Old Cars, Old Houses, Poverty, Bean Soup

Southwest School of Aviation's tuition was not cheap. The program would cost almost four thousand dollars. Four thousand dollars we did not have. I was about to have to get a student loan for the first time in my life. At that time, the average cost at a state university for tuition was $300/year plus another $150/year for books, or about $1800 for four years. My approximately eighteen months at Southwest School of Aviation would cost double what a normal four-year degree would cost. It was a gamble. But, if I could graduate and land a job as a pilot, the rewards would make the risk well worthwhile.

My priority was to visit the Hamilton National Bank. I had to have a student loan. By this time, my friend William L. "Billy" Hamilton had worked his way from a high school student sweeping the banks floors to a loan officer. He would later become a vice president and eventually, at another bank, the president. We had an excellent payment history on our auto loans with both the 1964 ½ Ford Mustang and later the 1965 Ford Thunderbird. Billy made the loan painless with payments beginning after graduation. I was eternally grateful to Billy for this and many other favors over many years.

Next, I had to tell CENCO; that, I was not looking forward to. At first, they thought I might have been suffering from a minor case of burnout. My boss suggested I take a few days off. I told him I'd never been more focused. Then he tried to tell me that the pilots had an "air force clique" and since I wasn't ex-air force, I would never get hired by anybody. I listened politely but after a while he realized I was indeed focused, and the decision was already made. I gave them a two month notice and headed back to Irving. I was relieved to get that out of the way.

While Karen and I were preparing for the big life change, the Congo was pressing the United Nations Security Council to call a special meeting where it stated that the former Prime Minister of the Congo, Mr. Tshombe was organizing a new assault against the Congo with assistance from foreign mercenaries They accused Portugal of using its African territories to support Tshombe and the mercenaries. I failed to take notice. September & October 1966 [96]

Also in October of 1966 Prince Norodom Kantol stepped down as prime minister of Cambodia after serving for four years. He was succeeded by an army general named Lon

---
[96] United Nations document - 66-68 08-7-Complaint by the Democratic Republic of the Congo

Nol. The name Lon Nol would become well known four years later. But for now, one little-known prince was replaced by a little-known army general, in a little-known country.

Many changes in our lifestyle would be necessary. First, the new car had to go. We had equity in the car, so we sold it and bought a 10-year-old clunker. We sold our boat. We moved from the Royal Oaks in Irving to a small guest house located in the backyard (literally) of a Mexican-American family on the west side of Ft. Worth. It was near Grand Avenue and the Jacksboro Highway. But more important, it was near Meacham Field, home of Southwest School of Aviation. Not exactly a choice neighborhood. But as usual, Karen was a trooper. She was ready to do what we had to do.

Some schoolmates from Hamilton were going to school in Denton and driving to Dallas to work. They worked on a freight dock. The work was physical, but the pay was good, so, with their help, I got hired as temporary help to work from 6:00 pm till around 10:00 pm several nights a week. While the drive would be long, gasoline was cheap, and it would be enough money to keep food on the table and pay the tiny utility bill. We would do what we had to do.

Jimmy Joe–Junior Birdman

The day finally came. I turned in my company car, handed in my final expense report, and became a full-time student. There was no time to think much about it. There was an occasional flash of "what if I don't make it through school," but that thought was immediately driven from my mind. I'd read Napoleon Hill's *Think And Grow Rich* cover to cover countless times. I would not allow such thoughts to stay in my consciousness. Once again, failure was not an option. I don't say that with any arrogance or conceit. I'd burned my bridges, I'd paid my tuition, I'd resigned a significant job . . . there simply was no other way but forward.

My first visit to the school and been in my new company car. My second in my new Ford Thunderbird. My first day of school was in my very old clunker. I was issued my books and went immediately to my classroom. Most of the students were Arabs, Belgium, and French. Very few "Americans." Most of the Arabs required some getting used to but soon I was friends with all of them.

The first few weeks were filled with classroom. But, finally the day came when I'd take my first flight instruction. I'd studied the ultra-simple systems, I knew quite a bit about the little Cessna 150's Continental O-200-A engine. The engine was manufactured by Continental, had four cylinders, produced 100 horsepower and had a displacement of 3.20 liters. I met my flight instructor the first day of class. His name was "Jay" Jacobs. I liked Jay immediately. But Jay wouldn't be my instructor long. He typified why I left CENCO. He was interviewing with Trans Texas (later to become Continental Airlines). Soon after my flight training started, Jay became a

Trans Texas pilot. But for my first flight and my first solo, Jay Jacobs was my instructor.

I met Jay at the appointed time, we had a preflight briefing, he reviewed the syllabus of that day's lesson, and we walked through the terminal and out onto the ramp. I felt ten feet tall. I was about to become a pilot, even if it was a student pilot. Jay began his instruction before we even reached the airplane, pointing out features and things about the fuselage. He showed me the standard "walk-around" and told me I was to do this every time I flew the airplane. That I was to check everything, omitting nothing. And that I was to do it the very same way every time. No variations. I had the checklist attached to the ever-present clipboard. Jay spent well over thirty minutes just explaining the walk-around and demonstrating how to unlatch and latch things and pointing out fluid and fuel levels. Finally, after what seemed like an eternity, Jay finally said, "well, let's go fly."

Jay instructed me how to visually look all around the aircraft to insure no one was anywhere near the prop or the "prop wash." Then he rechecked to insure the brakes were still set, he pumped the throttle a couple of times, he opened the window and shouted "clear," and a few seconds later he turned on the ignition switch and engaged the starter. Our little Continental O-200 came alive. I can never describe adequately how exhilarating that first engine start was. With me, Jimmy Joe Jacks from Hamilton Texas, sitting in the left seat of an airplane he's about to learn how to fly. Words just can't convey it. I was truly a wide-eyed wonder.

Jay told me to take the microphone and contact the tower for taxi instructions. We had all practiced this in the classroom. Heck, I'd practiced it driving to Dallas to work on the freight dock. Taxi clearance requests, takeoff clearance requests, approach and landing clearance requests…countless people had probably curiously stared at me as I drove along the freeway to and from work talking to Meacham Ground Control and Meacham Tower from our old clunker car. They saw a twenty-two-year-old kid dressed for work on a freight dock driving an old beat-up car. But I saw Captain Jacks, piloting a gleaming jet plane. I knew I'd make it…I just had to keep believing and keep on keeping on.

When I picked up the mic, I surprised even myself. My voice became much deeper and very serious sounding. I may have not yet looked the look, or walked the walk, but I was sure as heck going to talk the talk. Looking back now it was laughable, as so many things in life are when viewed in retrospect. But the ground controller managed to conceal his almost guaranteed amusement and gave us clearance to "taxi to runway 35 via taxiway alpha." Jay told me to release the brakes, and he gently gave the aircraft some power. He positioned it on taxiway alpha and then told me to take over steering down the taxiway, giving nose wheel steering inputs with my feet via the two rudder/brake controls on the floor. He also showed me how to gently apply brake inputs by shifting my feet to the upper part of the rudder control/brakes. By applying pressure to the top of each control I could send brake pressure to either the left or right brake. By pushing forward with my feet on either the left or right control, I could give left or right rudder inputs. How cool was that? So far so good. The Hamilton County in me was pointing out the similarities to the left and right brake on a tractor.

We reached the spot on the taxiway where we would turn onto the runway, line up, and takeoff without incident. Again, so far, so good. Jay then demonstrated what's called a "mag check." Without getting too complicated, this primarily checks the condition of the engine's spark plugs and of course the magnetos. The engine rpm drop was within limits, so we were ready to line up and take off. Jay told me once again to use the aircraft radio. This time, I was to not only speak, but I first had to change frequency from ground control to tower. I'd practiced this thousands of times in my car on the way to work so I knew just what to do. I changed the radio frequency, took the microphone and in the same ridiculously deep voice, said "Meacham tower, this is N6492F ready to take off." Wow that sounded so cool. To which the tower replied "N6492F cleared for takeoff runway 35." I released the parking break, used my newly acquired taxi skills to position the aircraft on the centerline with the nose pointing straight down the runway, and under Jay's instructions slowly advanced the throttle to the full position. The engine went to full power and the little Cessna began to move down the runway. Slowly at first but quickly picking up speed. I could see the airspeed indicator start to move. I knew the rotation speed (V_R) was 48 knots so I was ready. When the speed reached about 48 kts. I applied a gentle back pressure to the control (yoke) just as I'd done in the car on my way to work countless times before. The airplane gently lifted off the ground. I, Jimmy Joe Jacks from Hamilton Texas was flying an airplane!

It wasn't long before Jay told me to be gentle on the controls. My excitement and inexperience was causing what is known as "over-controlling." The wings, rather than being steady in a given position were wobbly and jerky. It normally takes a few hours at the controls before this is overcome. We were moving skyward at around 600 feet per minute (fpm). We were traveling northward toward the designated practice area. Jay instructed me to turn to the right 45 degrees in order to be off the extended centerline of the runway. I managed to do this OK. We were now also climbing at 600fpm toward an altitude of 3500 feet above mean sea level (MSA). We should reach that altitude in about six minutes. In the mean time we were climbing at an indicated airspeed of about 67 kts. At least that was my target speed but due to my erratic flight control inputs, the speed was more like 60-70 kts. Jay assured me this was completely normal for the first few flights and before long I'd have it all nailed. I was on such a high.

When we reached the designated practice area (pastures and cultivated fields) we began practicing maneuvering the aircraft. I would first practice 360 degree turns. Then 360 degree turns holding a bank angle of 45 degrees all while trying to maintain my assigned altitude of 3500 ft. We did turns to the left and turns to the right. Before I knew it the scheduled one-hour flight was almost over, and it was time to return to Meacham. Another student and instructor would be waiting on the ramp for us to taxi in. Returning late was seriously frowned upon.

As we came within five miles of the airfield, we were required to call the tower and request landing instructions. Once again, I was an old hand at this from my drives to and from work. I picked up the mic and in my best American or Delta imitation, announced "Meacham tower, this is Cessna N6492F, five north, landing Meacham." The tower replied giving the wind, visibility, and altimeter setting. He told us to report on right downwind. I reset the altimeter just as I'd done with the classroom models. At Jay's instructions, I gently retarded the power and set up about a five hundred feet per minute (500 fpm) rate of decent and pointed the aircraft toward the airport. My stomach felt a couple of seconds of uneasiness as the engine went from cruise (around 75% of full power) to almost idle. Later in my career, as an instructor in jet aircraft, I would caution my students to move the throttles back slowly as for the passengers, "the sound of the engines is the sound of security…the absence of that sound is the sound of alarm." But as I realized the airplane would not fall out of the sky but rather entered an almost glide mode, my confidence returned. As we entered right downwind for runway 35, I once again took the mic and advised that Cessna N6492F was on right downwind. The tower cleared us to land. About 45 seconds after passing abeam the threshold of the runway, Jay told me to turn right 45 degrees to position the aircraft for right base. As we approached the centerline of the runway Jay advised me to turn final and line up with the runway. At this point he told me to fully retard the throttle. We were now at full idle and in a glide for our planned touchdown spot. Jay's hands slipped gently onto the flight controls with me and he coaxed me through the flair and onto the runway. We did bounce once, but it was a little bounce and expected for a first flight. Wow, I'd just made my first flight as a pilot. About forty years later, I'd make my last.

As I'm learning about aerodynamics, meteorology, and aircraft systems, and Boyles Law, the number of US troops in Vietnam had risen to over 385,000.[97] *In Cambodia, over 25% of its rice crop was being sold by profiteering Chinese merchants clandestinely to the pro-North Vietnamese forces operating inside South Vietnam. This seriously concerned Sihanouk who was trying desperately to walk the tightrope of neutrality after breaking relations with the United States. His goal was to keep his tiny country out of the ever-enlarging Vietnam conflict.* [98]

---

[97] Vietnam War Timelines - VietnamGear.com
[98] A History of Cambodia (second edition) by David P. Chandler

Karen and Jason Go Stay In Hamilton

Life in our little "backyard apartment" was harsh and Spartan. It was poorly heated, I was up early and at school all day, rushed home to change and then drove to Dallas to work, not getting home till almost 11:00pm. Jason was now over two years old and needed to run about and play. We had no yard. It was decided she and Jason would go stay with my father while I continued to live in our backyard apartment and come home on the weekends.

The Long Grind

Books, flight lessons, and work was my agenda day in and day out. Soon I had my private license. The commercial license was not going to be as easy. I never doubted I could get through, but at times it seemed like an endless task. I survived by focusing on one day at a time. One test at a time, getting through one cold night on the freight dock in Dallas at a time. It was a simple procedure. Just don't look up and don't look for the goal line. It was OK to dream about the end but don't look for the goal. It was out of sight.

Several months later I had passed my commercial pilot license written and flight check and had received my FAA commercial pilot's license. With no celebration or letup I moved immediately into the instrument pilot curriculum. Without any doubt this was the most difficult. Some didn't make it through the course. It required a certain mental ability involving being able to visualize where you were in relation to objects you could not see but hopefully could conceptualize based on various instrument indications. The technical term for this is called spatial visualization. An adequate definition of the process is "is the ability to mentally manipulate 2-dimensional and 3-dimensional figures." I found some of my fellow students extremely gifted in this area while others found it quite challenging. I fell someplace in the middle.

While in private pilot training, I basically maneuvered the aircraft in relation to the horizon I saw through the wind screen or the side windows. When in commercial pilot training, I used both the horizon and an instrument found in almost all airplanes called an artificial horizon. In instrument training you maneuvered the aircraft exclusive by instruments. To keep you from viewing the real horizon during simulated instrument flight on days when there were few or no clouds, your instructor put a cap like device on your head called a "hood." The device basically blocked your view of everything except the instrument panel of the aircraft. Your instructor's job was to keep you from flying into something like another aircraft, a mountain, or high-tension electrical wires, TV towers, and the like. It was demanding but fun. The months marched onward. School, work, school, work, Hamilton on the weekends, then the school work routine all over again.

While I was working on my commercial and instrument licenses, more people were leaving the government of Prince Norodom Sihanouk and joining the rapidly growing communist ideology-based resistance movement in the jungles of Cambodia. While this was happening, the Vietnamese Communists were making significant use of Cambodia's dense jungles to move supplies for their war effort across Cambodia and into South Vietnam.[99]

While the class and work regime were demanding, the course was going well. The goal was in sight. The day finally came for my instrument check ride. An FAA examiner was in the right seat. I was in the left seat. From this point on, I was required to fly the airplane via an instrument clearance I'd received from the Meacham ground controller. My air traffic control clearance was "cleared to Mineral Wells airport, climb to and maintain 3000 feet. Maintain runway heading till reaching 1000 feet then turn right heading 225 degrees. Intercept Victor 19." I had carefully written it down on the specially designed clipboard strapped to my right thigh. I then was required to read it back to the controller. My readback was correct. Controllers were not happy when they had to read your clearance to you more than once. You were expected to get it right the first time. Especially on your instrument check ride.

I made the takeoff with the hood on but tilted up so I could see the runway. As soon as we were 200 feet in the air, the examiner instructed me to tilt the hood downward till I could no longer see outside the aircraft. I then had to fly according to my clearance and control the airplane entirely by reference to instruments without looking outside. The next time I would see the ground would be on short final from an ILS approach. I'd be 200 feet above the ground and in position to land.

The air had a bit of instability that day, causing a somewhat choppy ride, but I managed to keep it within parameters. I could hear Daddy's voice back when he was teaching me how to drive on the chalky caliche roads of Hamilton County . . . "Boy, try to keep it between the bar ditches." It was his form of humor. Because of the FAA examiner sitting next to me, I didn't dare laugh. But in my heart, I was laughing.

The oral examination and the flight check had lasted a little over three hours. When the plane touched down back at Meacham Field, I had passed the flight check for an instrument rating. We walked back to the FAA's office and he examiner wrote out my temporary license. The real one would arrive in about three weeks. I was exhausted but happy. I could check off another milestone on my way to becoming a professional pilot.

By October 1967, SOG (special operations groups) teams had permission to infiltrate the entire Cambodian border area to a depth of 20 kilometers. These operations were originally called "Daniel Boone" and later renamed "Salem House".[100] Cambodia was an officially neutral country with whom we were not at war.

---

[99] The History of Cambodia - by Justin Corfield
[100] SOG: An Overview - by Lieutenant Colonel Robert L. Turkoly-Jocaik, Ph.D. (USA, Retired)

Moise Tshombe fled the Congo after being accused of treason by the Congolese government of Joseph Mobutu. He took up residence in Spain. In June of 1967, a private jet flying Tshombe was "hijacked" and forced to land in Algeria where Tshombe was imprisoned. He was later released from prison and held under house arrest in Algeria.

Jimmy Joe–Flight Instructor

I now had a commercial pilot's license which meant I could charge for my piloting services and I had an instrument pilot's rating which meant I could fly an airplane in the clouds. The problem was I had about two hundred hours of flight time. The airlines at that time were requiring a minimum of eight hundred hours. Only six months earlier they were hiring pilots with as little as 600 hours. But this was no longer the case. More pilots were coming home from Vietnam and more pilots who had seen the airline hiring boom as I had and rushed off to flight school, were now also hitting the job market. The supply of airline pilot candidates began to swell rapidly. This was allowing the airlines to be a bit more selective. Rather than requiring 600 hours, they were now requiring eight hundred flight hours. This would soon rise to 1000 and then to twelve hundred. The rules were changing beneath my feet. I had always known I would have to become a flight instructor after graduation from flight school in order to build my flight hours. This was always part of my plan. The present market situation simply meant I'd have to spend more time as an instructor. Expressed another way, I was going to have to spend a little more time than anticipated, getting paid to do something that was so much fun, I'd almost pay them to let me do. I began my flight instructor course the day after I received my instrument rating. No celebration, no nothing. I did call home and tell my father and Karen I had passed. But basically, it was just another day.

About this time, General Westmoreland told US journalists "I am absolutely certain that whereas in 1965 the enemy was winning, today he is certainly losing" (November 1967).[101]

The flight instructor classes were a drastic change from the commercial and instrument curriculum. I now spent my classroom time studying the psychology of learning. The government had lots of experience in training people. I could see where they were putting that experience to use in the material I was studying. I found this equally as interesting as the aerodynamics and meteorology courses I'd just finished. These classes lasted eight hours a day for about five weeks. Then I had to undergo some minor training in how to handle the aircraft from the right seat. I went back to the FAA office and took my written exam. I then waited another three weeks for the results to get back from the FAA's headquarters in Oklahoma City. While I was waiting, the owner of the school told me he would give me a free Advanced Ground Instructor course if I wanted. That was a no-brainer. The following day I in was taking the ground instructor course. This was always a good fallback in the event I somehow lost my FAA medical certificate. I

---

[101] Vietnam War Timeline: 1967 - VietnamGear.com

found a significant correlation between the ground instructor course and the flight instructor course I'd just finished. The course was easy, and I enjoyed it. When I finished, I again went to the FAA office and took that written examination.

Meanwhile, in Cambodia Sihanouk told U.S. Presidential Emissary Chester Bowles: ."..We are not opposed to hot pursuit in uninhabited areas. I want you to force the Viet Cong to leave Cambodia [102] But Cambodia's policies were not always straight forward. Another objective of the Salem House operations was to determine the level of Cambodian Government support for the NVA and Viet Cong.[103]

Prince Sihanouk's off-the-cuff unofficial remarks to Chester Bowles would later be used by Henry Kissinger to justify the secret bombing of Cambodia by the United States.[104]

The test results always came to the flight school. When my flight instructor results came back showing I had passed, I took the test results immediately to the FAA's local office and scheduled a check ride. I was lucky and they were able to get me on the schedule in just a few days. This check ride was not nearly as demanding as my commercial or instrument flight check had been. We were back in less than an hour. Hamilton, Texas, had a flight instructor. A week or so later my Advanced Ground Instructor rating was back. I'd passed that too. But this was the first course I'd taken that had not required a flight check. I now was not only a flight instructor but an advanced ground instructor as well.

While I was taking my courses, I'd always been happy to stop and help numerous of the foreign students who were there taking courses. Many were having their tuition paid by their governments. I enjoyed the opportunity to help them and they appreciated it as well. As soon as I got my flight instructor "ticket" I was swamped by students requesting to have me as "their" instructor. The school always tried to keep the students happy, so this was a winning situation for everybody. For the first time in my life, I was receiving a paycheck from flying. It would continue for almost forty years.

Our Ft. Worth Duplex Home

When not in the air, I was in the classroom using my new ground instructor's license. My pay rose rapidly and soon I was one of the highest paid instructors on Meacham Field. However, it still wasn't a lot. There were always junior instructors willing to give their services away just for the chance

---

[102] SOG: An Overview - by Lieutenant Colonel Robert L. Turkoly-Joczik, Ph.D. (USA, Retired)
[103] McChristian, Joseph A., The Role of Military Intelligence (Washington: U.S. Government Printing Office, 1974), page 109, - and Henry Kissinger, White House Years (Boston, Massachusetts: Little, Brown & Company, 1979), pages 250-252
[104] The Tragedy of Cambodian History—Politics, War, and Revolution Since 1945 by David P. Chandler

to get to fly and build their flight time. Flight time was key to being hired by any airline.

But the money was finally enough to afford a better apartment. Karen and I found a duplex on the north side of Ft. Worth, even closer to Meacham than our little "backyard apartment" had been. The apartment was owned by an elderly widow named Jessie who lived in the adjoining unit. It had a yard where Jason could play, was close to the grocery store, was furnished, and for the three of us…it was perfect. Karen and Jason left my father in Hamilton and came back to live in Ft. Worth. Except for my long hours at work, we almost had a normal family life once again. At least, unlike with CENCO, I was home every night. There were even times when I could play in the yard with Jason. The duplex was good. However, when the wind shifted from the north, the overpowering aroma of the Ft. Worth Stock Yards stifled every breathing creature. But for us, we were together.

Bonjour Monsieur

The students in our ground school consisted mostly of expatriates. Many were from Belgium, as well as a few from France. Most of the Belgium and French students were from Air Congo and were there to pass their FAA written examination for airline transport pilot. That was the step above the commercial license and was also the highest license any country issued. Shortly after I began teaching there, I wrote a couple of booklets that the school was using in the classroom. The subject matter of my booklets addressed areas key to passing the airline transport pilot rating or ATR written exam. The exam was quite difficult and involved numerous complex calculations used to determine the center of gravity of an aircraft in various stages of loading and fueling. I was spending a great deal of time in the classroom teaching these techniques. I couldn't help but smile internally as I recalled I was the guy who almost failed Algebra II back in Hamilton High School. If my teacher could only see me now. Heck, if my *tutor* Kalie Brown (pseudonym) could only see me now.

As I became friends with many of these French and Belgium students, they would tell me about flying in the Congo and that I could easily get hired by Air Congo if I could just go there. While their stories about life in the Congo were fascinating, I remained focused on my main goal of getting hired by a US airline.

The months of flight instructing and classroom instructing rolled on. My flight time gradually build to 1200 hours. This was the minimum requirement the FAA had established for being eligible to take the ATR written exam. (The ATR is now called an ATP for airline transport pilot license). I studied hard and passed it. By this time I also had passed the FAA flight engineer written exam. Both were virtually required by the airlines before being considered for employment as a pilot. When I began flight school two years earlier two of my instructors had been hired with just over 600 flight hours. Neither had their ATR or Flight Engineer written exam. The market was changing and while there was not yet a glut of pilots, the airlines were now getting enough applicants that their criterion had doubled. I always seemed to be just below what they were requiring. When I would reach their new level, the swollen market of pilot applicants would allow them to raise the bar even higher. The goal seemed always just outside my reach. But I never doubted for a moment. I was always sure I would soon be hired.

A Strange New Breed Of Student

Along with the French and the Belgiums, we were getting an interesting breed of pilots from Denmark, Sweden, Holland, and Columbia. This group was less polished than the Air Congo pilots. They too were coming to take our ATR ground school. Our school had an excellent international reputation and was literally filled at all times. But these guys were not cut from the same mold as the Air Congo pilots. While they studied hard, they more than once came to school in the morning with a few scratched knuckles and what they thought were hilarious stories of barroom brawls; as often as not among themselves. That part they found particularly amusing. The more "fun-loving" of the bunch seemed to be by far the Swedes and Danes. I noticed they seemed to have more money to spend than did the Air Congo pilots. These pilots all worked for a company with the strange sounding name of Anstalt Wigmo. The Air Congo pilots didn't associate with them socially at all and on more than one occasion I heard them referring in hushed voices to the Wigmo pilots as CIA.

While I found these CIA whisperings fascinating, I would only occasionally accept one of their numerous invitations to buy my dinner. My afterhours were almost exclusively focused on an extensive letter writing campaign to every US airline whose address I could find. I'd asked for their employment applications. I'd fill them out, along with the flight experience supplement used for pilots and mail them back. They would almost always respond with a letter saying I would be kept on file and to please continue to update them as my flight experience increased. I'd send updates every 200 hours or about every three months. Looking back now, it would have been so easy to give up. Several with whom I'd graduated, had already returned to non-aviation jobs. But I can honestly say the thought never crossed my mind. I didn't know where or when my break would come but I always knew it would.

As I was writing letters to airlines, Cambodia's, Prince Sihanouk, appeared to be losing his ability to keep his country on the thin tightrope of neutrality. Cambodia was sliding toward Chaos and at a time when his leadership was needed, the prince occupied himself with composing music and producing movies. The government had gradually transitioned into a reactionary mode with the military using unbridled power, including illegal arrests, harassment, and even murder against the government's rapidly growing leftist movement.[105]

While trying to keep Cambodia out of the war, Sihanouk was turning an extremely blind eye to the arms almost openly flowing through the Cambodian port of Sihanoukville from both China and Russia to the Viet Cong bases along Cambodia's border with Vietnam. Through the CIA and other intelligence sources Kissinger and Nixon were watching with growing concern and would eventually incorporate this information into their justification for invading and bombing Cambodia.[106]

In the Congo, the mysterious CIA proprietary company called Wigmo had for all practical purposes become the Congolese Air Force or Force Aérienne Congolaise with missions easily exceeding 100 per week. This largely Africanless air force consisted mostly of Cuban Americans, Danes, Swedes, Columbians, Dutch, Hungarians with British passports, Spaniards, and a few Anglo-Americans.

Daddy's Weekly Visits

My father missed having Karen and Jason living with him and missed my weekend stays in Hamilton. His emphysema had progressed to the point he was forced to medically retire from Lone Star Gas. So, now, for the first time since he was sixteen years old, he was not working full time. He seemed to rather enjoy this new phase of life and established a routine of driving up from Hamilton on Wednesday, spending the night with us and playing endless hours with Jason. On Thursday, he would return to Hamilton so he would be ready to make the Friday night Hamilton Bulldogs football game with his buddies Main Brunk, Ted Jones, Spurlin Freeman, and others. He missed my mother Lois very much, but his football and coffee drinking buddies help ease the loneliness. At least until he returned to his empty home.

A Shift In Focus

As the months of flight instructing dragged on, and the pile of airline rejection letters grew, I started to pay a little more attention to the stories told by the Wigmo pilots. They told of flying and adventures I'd never dreamed of. With this market driven shift in focus a new "airline" came to my attention. It was called Air America. I found the so-called phone number and gave them a call. This was early in 1969. I still remember the call. While today it would be considered normal, back then it was strange. After a few rings I heard an unfamiliar break in the background sound and a different ring tone started. A couple of seconds later a woman's voice answered with the words "Air America" followed by silence. I explained I'd called to request a

---

[105] The Tragedy of Cambodian History—Politics, War, and Revolution Since 1945 by David P. Chandler
[106] Good Questions—Wrong Answers, CIA's Estimates of Arms Traffic Through Sihnoukville, Cambodia During the Viewnam War—Center For The Study of Intelligence—Thomas L. Ahern, Jr.

pilot employment application. To which she politely asked for my name and address. When I'd finished giving it to her, she advised that it would be mailed today and hung up. Years later, with call forwarding now a fact of daily life, it all fits together. A call to a phone number in one part of the country was being forwarded to another undisclosed location. But in early 1969 such technology was smoke and mirrors. The Air America application arrived, and I immediately filled it out. This "airline" flew much different equipment than did the Delta and American, companies I was familiar with. Many of their aircraft were small single and twin-engine aircraft with STOL (short takeoff and landing) capability. I understood they were flying support missions in Vietnam. I had no idea about their extensive operations in Laos.

I rushed the application back to them and waited. Soon a response followed saying they were now laying off pilots but would keep my resume on file. I would later learn the layoffs were due to congressional pressure on the CIA to divest themselves of this "airline." Once again, I was just a little too late.

While congress was busy trying to force Air America and other CIA operations out of South East Asia, Henry Kissinger, was busy convincing the president to begin a secret bombing campaign in Cambodia where Viet Cong and North Vietnamese had established logistical bases. The campaign, secretly referred to as "Operation Menu," spurs the Vietnamese to move deeper into Cambodia causing US bombings to move further into "neutral" Cambodia's interior.

It was at this time that I decided I would temporarily shift my focus from the big airlines in the United States. I had been assured by the Wigmo pilots that if I just came to the Congo, they could easily get me hired. But unlike airlines who sent you a ticket, this Wigmo would not even correspond with you. They were incorporated in a tiny European principality named Liechtenstein and headed by a reputed ex-FBI agent from Coral Gables Florida named George L. Monteiro. The pilots all told me the only way is to come to Kinshasa.

A Leap In Faith

"To come" was not exactly a simple thing. It involved an expensive airline ticket. It also involved leaving my job and the paycheck associated with it. It involved sending Karen and Jason back to live with my father again. My only redeeming factor was except for my school loan, we had no debt. No car payment, no mortgage, no nothing. Karen and I talked about it and we decided to try. This was a serious gamble. Traveling to the heart of Africa on the word of pilots I'd only known for a few weeks. But it had become clear that my present strategy probably was never going to get out from behind the curve of the airline's pilot-glutted market. The decision was made…I was going to the Congo. This decision required more courage than anything I'd ever faced before. Far more courage. Bill Wallace, the school's owner told me that if things didn't work out, I could have my old job back. Most of my fellow instructors told me in so many words that I'd soon be back begging for my old job.

I contacted a local travel agent. She found a ticket on Alitalia that would route me from New York to Milano then on to Kinshasa. The ticket allowed me to stay in Milano for a few days and I decided I would use this opportunity to visit my cousin Little Jimmy. I got a passport. I then got a visa for the Congo.

I still had the problem of getting to New York but I'd heard about people wanting their cars ferried across the country and so I decided I'd see if I could use that technique to get from Ft. Worth to New York. I looked in the Fort Worth Star Telegram and found a company that specialized in making these arrangements. I gave them a call. The agency had a car coming up that needed to go to New York City. This was only a few minutes by taxi to the JFK airport. They signed me up for the trip. I had a way to New York, I had an airline ticket to the Congo, now all I needed was a job when I got there. I prayed a lot during those days of preparation. I prayed like I should have been praying all my life.

Packing My Bags

Looking back now, I can't believe how I packed. I took everything but the kitchen sink. I had aviation text books, aircraft manuals, every conceivable piece of clothing…two huge bags. I had no concept about overweight luggage. This was only my second flight on an airliner. Karen kept asking if I was sure I would need all the stuff I was trying to fit into those bags. And of course my ridiculous answer was yes.

Hit The Road Jacks

The day finally came. I'd said my goodbyes at the school, giving my sincere thanks to Bill and Mary Wallace for allowing me to come back to Southwest School of Aviation and teach if things didn't work out. I said goodbye to Bobby Wallace a fellow student and flight instructor from the most unlikely sounding place in the world…Horse Branch Kentucky. But before leaving I did manage to sell Bobby Wallace my old 1955 Buick that I'd been driving since I entered flight school. I asked $150 for it. Being an old Kentucky horse-trader Bobby offered me $75. I immediately said sold. Bobby was and still is proud of that deal. What I failed to tell him is that I'd bought the car from my father for $50. I said goodbye to my longtime friend Tom Hafford, to H.G. White my friend and CPA, and countless others. It was time to go.

I'd never been this far from Karen before and I felt uneasy about that. I truly hurt about knowing it could be months before I could play with Jason again. It would have been easy to just say the heck with it and stay home in Texas. But I was driven. Like I'd always been driven since leaving Hamilton back in the summer of 1960. Looking back now, I sacrificed many things and many people for my goals. "If Only."

I loaded my super-stuffed bags into the car I'd contracted to drive and headed north toward New York City. Once I'd been on the road for a few hours, the deep depressing feeling left me. I was now completely focused on what lay in ahead; not on my rear-view mirror. The drive was exhilarating. I'd never driven anywhere in my life except Texas and New Mexico, save one emergency trip from Hamilton to New Orleans on behalf of my friend Jerry Drake, a vacation trip in our Mustang to visit Karen's family in the Green Bay, and the CENCO trip Karen and I made to New Orleans. I loved looking at the countryside. The changing topography just heightened my excitement. By the time I saw the New York City skyline, my heart was pounding. I was so ready.

I delivered the car to the young air force couple and accepted their gracious offer to sleep on their couch. The next morning, just after sunrise, I was climbing into the back of a New York City taxi and heading for JFK. The driver was Italian with a heavy dose of that New York, New Jersey, Italian accent. He gave me the usual half helpful half threat routine about how he knew a short cut that avoided all the traffic and how his flat-rate, no meter deal would be much better for me. The unspoken but strongly implied threat was that he could wind me around taking many unnecessary turns on the meter and I'd never know it. This of course resulting in a much higher rate than his special flat rate offer. A black art they have been practicing for years. Of course I took his "special" rate.

In a few minutes I was at the Alitalia check-in. The early morning traffic had been light. I strained with my heavy bags thanking but rejecting the curbside porter's offers to help me with my bags. I needed to save every penny I could and handing out a five-dollar tip to save three minutes of very strenuous bag lugging was out of the question.

But straining with the heavy bags was easy compared to facing the unhappy Alitalia ticket agent when she weighed my luggage. I could ill afford to pay extra, and I was seriously overweight. Why hadn't I listened to Karen when I was packing? So I smiled and prayed and smiled some more. Somehow, by the grace of God, (literally) she let me slip by.

As part of my extreme austerity profile, I'd come to the airport about ten hours early. I didn't feel comfortable sitting around in the young air force couple's living room. I didn't have the money to go wandering around, especially lugging the bags. So the only logical thing to do was go to the airport. My flight didn't even have a gate assignment yet. As a matter of fact, the plane that would take me to Milano that night was still somewhere out over the Atlantic enroute to New York. It would be hours before it landed. But no longer having to drag my heavy bags around, I was free to explore JFK and look at all the duty-free shops.

I kept telling myself to relax but it didn't work. I was wound up like some spring powered device. Like the energy stored in the spring, the energy stored in me was waiting to be released. I must have checked the huge board listing the gate assignments for each flight a hundred times. Hours later, my flight finally appeared on the board. I headed for my gate.

Many sitting around the gate area were speaking Italian. This heightened my excitement even more. Finally the Alitalia gate agents arrived. A wave of confidence swept over me. I'd managed to get my overweight baggage on free, I'd managed to get to the right gate at the huge JFK airport, and now I was about to board. All that was left was to find my seat, enjoy some of the legendary Alitalia inflight service, and try to relax and get some sleep.

The Shortest Night

I found my seat and got all strapped in for takeoff. I remember starting my Breitling Navitimer's stopwatch function as the captain pushed the throttles forward and released the brakes. That was the longest takeoff roll I'd ever experienced. We were heavy. I couldn't help but speculate about my overweight bags being partly to blame. We broke ground as the Navitimer's sweep hand crossed 45 seconds. I remember wondering if the pilots ever wondered if they were going to get airborne before the end of the runway. I already knew how to do all the calculations to determine V1, VR, V2, takeoff roll distance and accelerate-stop distance. All the mathematical gymnastics associated with getting airborne. But I just couldn't help but wonder what it must have looked like sitting up there in the cockpit and watching all that runway race past. It wouldn't be long before I knew first hand, but for that moment in time, I was still not much more than a junior birdman.

"May I Have A Dr Pepper Please"

Being not only a junior birdman but a neophyte international traveler as well, when the flight attendant asked me what I would like to drink I naïvely asked if I might have a Dr Pepper. Why not. Years later I would savor my first taste of home onboard Braniff's London–Dallas flights with a DP on ice. But the Italians didn't share our Texas affinity with the Dublin Texas "nectar of the gods." Most were drinking red wine. I settled for a Coke and a condescending look.

The food was good. Italy's flagship carrier could hardly afford to defile its image. After that I watched a movie and dozed a little bit. It was just after sunset when we departed JFK. A couple of hours into my light sleep, I noticed a dim glow on the eastern horizon. I was totally surprised as it was nowhere near what I thought should be time for the sun to rise. But rising it was. I checked my Breitling, which was still set to JFK time. It was still in the middle of the night. I knew there was a six hour difference between New York and Milano, but I wasn't in Milano. What was going on? What I had failed to consider is that we were flying toward the rising sun. The sun was moving from east to west, but we were accelerating the process by flying into the sun. Soon the dim light on the horizon began to glow a faint orange and soon after that . . . we were in the daylight. I mused warmly as I thought about what my father's reaction might be when I related this experience to him upon my return home to Hamilton.

Buongiorno

I remember a light feeling of excitement in my stomach when I saw land out my window and realized I was looking at the shores of Europe. I was about to be the first in my direct Jacks family line to set foot on European soil since the patriarch of our clan, Jone Jacks, sailed from England to the American Colonies in 1667. I had many reasons to be excited.

The sun was shining brightly, and it was a beautiful almost-cloudless day over Europe. I felt my heart race again as the captain slowly pulled the throttles back and the jetliner began its decent for landing at Milano's Malpensa airport. I'd soon be visiting with my cousin Little Jimmy.

Customs and immigration were a breeze. Soon I was in a taxi handing the driver Jimmy's address which I'd prewritten on a small piece of paper for just this occasion. Jimmy shared a very nice apartment with his longtime friend Victor. Victor was both a musician and the son of the world-famous composer Victor de Sabata. I'd never met Victor but had heard much about him from Jimmy. The cab ride wasn't long at all. I didn't care about the traffic or anything. I was just enjoying looking at Italy's most sophisticated city. The traffic was chaotic. Cars jammed into hopelessly narrow, centuries old streets, accompanied by countless Vespa motorbikes weaving in and out of the traffic. And most amazing to me was how the Vespas would jump the curb and drive along the sidewalk when the traffic came to a stop. It was truly a zoo. The Vespa was made by Piaggio. Hamilton even had a Vespa in the 1950s. My cousin Jimmy later told me that vespa means wasp in Italian. These little two-wheeled devices hummed and darted about much like a wasp would.

Soon I was at Jimmy's front door. He and Victor had a beautiful apartment. Very stately. I remember the study was filled from ceiling to floor with Victor's massive collection of classical music, all on huge reels and played on his state-of-the-art Akai recorder/player. They had a bedroom all setup for me. I was tired but so excited sleep was hardly possible.

After a short rest, Jimmy took me to see the sights of Milano. I was totally unprepared for all I saw that day and the next. Growing up in Hamilton, you acquired a confined conception of old. In 1958 Hamilton celebrated its Centennial. There were Cowboys, horses, Indians; the men in town all grew beards. In Milano, most of the homes and streets were considerably older than that. It was not uncommon to see streets and buildings several hundred years old. I learned the city of Milano has been continuously inhabited since 200 BC. I was not really prepared for the things I saw that day. On many subsequent visits I realized it would take a lifetime to grasp the history and personality of Milano. But Milano had a modern side as well. It was the fashion center, financial center, and industrial center of Italy. There was plenty of glitter to accompany the historic. Jimmy would see that I experienced both. I was fortunate that Jimmy loved art and was familiar with almost every major piece in Milano.

We saw Leonardo da Vinci's "The Last Supper" in the Convent of Santa Maria della Grazie. That picture must have been in every Bible in the First Baptist Church in Hamilton. And here I was, Jimmy Joe Jacks from Hamilton, Texas, standing in front of the real thing.

We saw The Duomo, the world-famous Gothic cathedral located right in the center of Milano. I'd never seen such majestic beauty. I'd later see Notre Dame de Paris, and the Duomo in Florence but for me, this was always the most impressive. It was simultaneously delicate and imposing. The Hamilton County Courthouse would never look the same.

The following day we saw the Castello Sforzesco It was hard to believe this was once someone's home. The artwork we saw there numbed my mind. I quickly realized that this time I was ready to let all the intellectual stuff slide and just enjoy the wonderful sidewalk life and window shop at some of Milano's famous fashion houses. We then went to the area where the expensive tailors had their shops and the most elegant clothing I'd ever seen was displayed in the windows. Jimmy took me inside one, where he bought a lot of his clothing and insisted on buying me a shirt. He gave me the most beautiful shirt I'd ever seen. It was pure Italian silk. I kept it and cherished it for years. It went not only to the Congo but would later accompany me to Cambodia.

I remember the Milano sidewalks were filled with little bistro-type places, many specializing in the Italian ice cream they call gelato. Gelato is much heavier than American style ice cream. It was many years later before I learned that this was because it contains less air than American ice cream. But there's something about eating a dish of ice cream in a little Italian bistro in the heart of the old city in Milano that forever changed my view of HEB ice cream. I remember thinking how nice it would be if I could have Jason sitting on a stool beside me. He would be all smiles. "If Only."

The next day I headed back to Malpensa airport and my Alitalia flight to Kinshasa. I was sad to leave Little Jimmy, but simultaneously very ready to resume my mission. This interlude had merely been a memorable moment of pleasure before entering the heart of Africa.

Check-in went flawlessly. They didn't make near the fuss they had made at JFK about my pitifully overweight baggage. While at the check-in I noticed everybody's baggage was bulging and laboriously heavy to lift. Whites and Africans as well…everybody's baggage was stuffed. I'd soon understand why.

At the gate while waiting for boarding, I got my first up close look at Congolese. Most men were dressed in the traditional safari suits while the women wore typical long wraparound-type skirts. Most of the women had some kind of cloth wrapped around their head. Most of the men wore heavy framed, very dark expensive-looking sunglasses. With few exceptions, both men and women had a very strong, unpleasant odor. Again I would soon understand why.

As we boarded, the aircraft's cabin soon took on the unpleasant odor of most its passengers. Many of the white passengers appeared to be accustomed to the smell and seemed unaffected. Others, whom I suspected were less accustomed to the culture, seemed to be in varying degrees of distress. When the flight attendant offered me a meal, I declined. It looked pretty good, but I couldn't eat in the midst of this smell. I remember thinking I'd eaten lunch while working cows with cow pies all around me and plenty on my boots and never gave it a thought. But this smell was worse than cow pies. Much worse.

Descending Into The Heart Of Darkness

It is a land of blackness like the deepest darkness, gloomy and chaotic, where even the light is like the darkness.[107]

When Joseph Conrad wrote *The Heart of Darkness* in 1898, the evil, savagery, and pitiful condition of the Congolese people was all blamed on the Belgium Colonials. Yet when I stepped off the Alitalia flight from Milano, the evil in the air weighed heavily on every breathing creature. The Congo had been independent for almost nine years. The Belgiums had been virtually driven from their once colonial possession in a matter of a few short months following independence on 30 June 1960. During the ensuing years, the Congolese brutalized their own people, often hacking them to death with machetes. Since most of the Congolese were uneducated and had little or no understanding of political ideologies, most of the brutality was along tribal lines. Many of their perceived enemies were cannibalized. Europeans were not exempt. Missionaries, teachers, all there devoting their lives to helping the Congolese people, fell victim. The air was full of hate. I had truly come into the heart of darkness.

Erebos[108], The Land of Eternal Darkness

Beyond the Gates of The Rising Sun

It was late in the evening when our flight arrived at N'Djili airport. Congolese were asleep in every corner and on every bench. I could see some asleep under the carts used to transport the passenger baggage to the terminal. I supposed these people were on the job. It took almost an hour for our bags to get from the airplane to the customs area. The immigration police officer who examined my passport had extremely bloodshot eyes and reeked of alcohol. He knew just enough English to let me know I was going to have to pay him a little bribe if I expected to enter the country. It was useless to argue. I parted with five dollars of my very scarce funds and moved on to the customs area to collect my bags. It didn't take long to realize this was the second collection point. By the next day I would learn the word in Lingala for these bribes. It was the first word I learned, but for that moment, my goal was to get out of there. I parted with another five dollars.

---

[107] Holy Bible—Holman Christian Standard ver—Job 10:22
[108] In Greek Literature - the underworld where the dead had to pass immediately after dying.

It was now late. Only about three hours till sunrise. To take a taxi into town and look for a hotel was useless. I decided I would spend the night in the terminal at the airport and go first thing the next morning to the military end of the airport and try to find some of my former students at the Wigmo operations offices. The terminal was almost deserted, and I easily found a bench. I tucked my bags under the bench with my feet resting on top of them, so I'd feel any movement if someone tried to steal them.

I must have fallen asleep…deep asleep. I struggled to climb out of the well of my sleep in response to a blunt jabbing on my left side. As my eyes focused, I saw a Congolese military policeman banging on my ribcage with the butt of his rifle. My mind raced. My vision was now rapidly focusing, probably from a mega release of adrenaline. My eyes came to focus on his chest and abdomen. My first thought was that one quick punch to his solar plexus, and he would be totally paralyzed for maybe ten seconds, possibly more. Plenty of time to easily finish the job by grabbing his filthy and significantly rusted Belgium made FN-49 and using that same rifle butt to force his teeth down his trachea or cave his flat skull in. The first part would work easily. Even considering that the jab would have to be made without my feet being planted on the floor.

I had already scanned the immediate area and realized I was in the clear. But then reason began to rule. Was I prepared to run off and leave my bags? How far did I think my white face would get in this sea of black? Once the magazine had yielded up its ten 7.62 rounds, assuming it would fire without jamming, and assuming there were really any rounds in there, I'd be hacked to death by these savages. I sat up and acknowledged his warnings in Lingala that I was not allowed to sleep in the terminal. There was an entire airport staff sleeping all over the floors, benches, and every other conceivable place, but white people could not sleep. When I looked into his face, I saw hate. His eyes were bloodshot like those of the customs and immigration police. His breath reeked of alcohol just as theirs had done. And like those of the customs and immigration police, his eyes did not shine. They were dull black, reflecting nothing back, like looking into a pitch-black abyss. I spent the last hour of darkness sitting upright on the bench. The massive release of adrenaline assured that there was no possibility of falling back asleep. Welcome to the Congo.

As I was trying to assimilate my first encounter with Africa, U.S. B52s began carpet bombing in Eastern Cambodia, by order of President Nixon, who wanted to destroy sanctuaries for the North Vietnamese that could make remaining U.S. forces vulnerable to attack when withdrawals of U.S. forces begin. Countless innocent non-combatants were being killed. The Viet Cong always hid among the innocent locals in Cambodia as well as in Vietnam. It was an integral component of their combat strategy. While the U.S. B52s were bombing Cambodia, Cambodia's head of state, Prince Norodom Sihanouk continued to write music and direct movies. The situation had become too complex and he apparently chose not to deal with it.[109]

Wigmo—My First Look Inside

Mercifully morning came, the terminal came alive. I found a ride to the military side of the airport with a fuel truck. At first, he said he could not take me, but a dollar got me and my two huge bags onboard. I was soon lugging my bags through the military hanger and toward a sign that read "Operations." Before I could reach the door that led into operations, I heard my name being called. As I turned, I saw the smiling face of one of my Swedish students, Olaf Jansson (pseudonym). I don't believe Olaf had ever spoken an entire sentence in English that didn't contain profanity. He gave me a hearty handshake and a few more expletive-laden pronouncements, grabbed one of my bags and showed me into the dispatch area of operations. I got a brief glimpse of another door that said "Training" on it as we were walking into Operations. Olaf introduced me to everyone and then called me over to a ringed binder on the counter where he started flipping through the pages. I learned this was where flight assignments were posted. Olaf was checking his schedule for the next few days. I learned that most flights left in the early hours before sunrise so most of the pilots were already in the air. I saw a couple wearing U.S. Air Force flight suits with no insignias. I learned they were part of the flight training group. Both were Hispanics…Cuban-Americans I would later learn. Olaf jotted down his flights on a piece of paper he took from the counter and said…let's go home. You can stay with me for a few days until we can get to see George or Robert. George was George Barnes and Robert was Robert Troyes (pseudonym), both Americans. George was the number two in command and Robert was the chief.

We left operations and went out one of the back doors of the hanger. Outside was a small paved road. Cars were parked all along the back of the hanger on both sides of the little road. I would later learn these were the cars of the pilots out on flights and some of the mechanics. Many of the Wigmo people did not have cars and used the company provided Volkswagen buses. Almost everyone lived in Wigmo provided houses. Most in company compounds. Not many lived out in the community. But Olaf had his own car. An older model Peugeot 404. On the way into town I found out he also had a boat and a motorcycle. As Olaf was backing out, I noticed a huge array of antennas on the roof of the hanger with masses of coax cable neatly bound together running into a room specially built onto the back of the hanger. Access was by a steep stair. Olaf noticed me staring at the huge cluster of antennas and informed me that was the radio room. Olaf said Wigmo could talk all over the world from that little room. He said sometimes the guys would come out here and talk to their families back in Scandinavia, Europe, and South America. He said they used a military network called MARS. I was impressed. Not only was I impressed, I was starting to think I would

[109] Brother Number One, A Political Biography of Pol Pot by David P. Chandler

really enjoy working here. But first I had to get hired. Olaf seemed to take that for granted but I would not dare allow such a thought until I held a contract in my hands.

The ride from the airport was fascinating. Everywhere people walking about with bundles on their heads. I was amazed at the size of the loads they carried. Little street markets were scattered all along the road with people squatting in the dust selling small quantities of produce, cigarettes, cooking oil, and gasoline and kerosene in one-liter cold drink bottles. And every few meters there was some kind of little bar, even if they only had cane chairs and dirt floors, they had semi-cold beer. There were no regular beer bottles here. Beer came in one-liter bottles. I was starting to understand all the bloodshot eyes. On the way into the outskirts of Kinshasa, I learned Olaf's wife and children were here with him and that he lived in a large house of which his family lived on the top floor and a German Wigmo mechanic and his family lived on the bottom floor.

Soon we turned into a drive and stopped at a metal gate crowned with looped barbed wire. Olaf honked the horn. A Congolese man, perhaps in his midtwenties opened the gate. I was told he was the houseboy. After we drove in, he closed the gate. The house, like all in the area, was enclosed by a high wall. On top of the wall jagged broken glass had been embedded in the cement. Obviously security was an issue. As we got out of the car, Olaf spoke to the houseboy in Lingala. He immediately took my bags into the house. I asked Olaf how long it had taken him to learn to speak Lingala. Not long he replied. They only speak in the present tense. No past tense and no future tense. I asked him how they ever understood when the event was. He casually answered as we entered his large living room that if the Congolese tilted their head to the left it was past tense and if to the right it was in the future. If nothing…it was right now. I wasn't sure if he was joking or not, but I figured it wouldn't be long before I knew for myself.

Olaf's wife's hair was a beautiful shiny golden color. His three children's hair was even more so. They all had blue eyes. Olaf showed me to my room where my bags were already waiting. I quickly took a shower and got cleaned up. My teeth were last brushed in Milano. The water of my shower even though not heated was a very welcome feeling. I felt I had a lot to wash off. I put on fresh cloths and came out. Olaf called the family and we sat down for a lunch of sandwiches. We had iced tea with the meal. I was told the water had to be boiled and filtered before being consumed. I was hungry. I hadn't eaten since Little Jimmy's apartment. The sandwiches were loaded with cheese and butter. Very Swedish I was assured.

After lunch Olaf and I sat in the living room and talked for a while. He said later in the afternoon we would go out and explore Limete, the little suburb of Kinshasa where not only Olaf but many of the Wigmo people lived. Limete was about 17 km from the N'Djili airport when everybody worked. Olaf explained that most of the shops closed during this part of the afternoon and would reopen later.

A Journey Back In Time

Around 4 pm we got back into the Peugeot 404 and drove down Petit Boulevard de Limete heading toward the commercial center of Limete. As we drove along, I noticed many of the buildings seemed pockmarked. I'd seen plenty of bullet holes as a kid growing up in Hamilton County but none which were a direct result of war. When I asked, Olaf answered saying the bullet hole was the national emblem of the Congo. Olaf had a dry sarcasm I that I found refreshing. It appeared many of the old buildings which were obviously occupied had no windows or doors. Most appeared to have little or no furniture. Olaf's reply to that question was "yep...they used them for firewood." Many of the occupied buildings appeared to have no electrical service. In response to that he looked at me and ask, "what for?" They live here in the city just like they do in the bush." All the buildings appeared to be of the European or French Colonial style. Most could obviously lay claim to a far statelier existence once upon a time. Olaf pointed out a little plaza or square which he identified as the center of Limete.

Olaf parked the car and we headed to an old rundown hotel. This too had at one period been a far statelier place. There was a sidewalk café where we found a table and waited for service. The waiters saw us but, like at the airport the night before, appeared determined to ignore anybody white. About five minutes later, when they felt sure they had made a statement, a waiter slowly walked over. Same body odor as all those on the plane. Same glazed over eyes as those at the airport. Olaf ordered a Primus which I was told was the local beer. The waiter brought the 1-liter bottle and two less than sparkling glasses. I took my first sip of Congolese beer. It would not be my last.

As we sipped our beer, Olaf began to tell me about what had happened to the Congo after independence. He began with a long string of expletives linked to the Belgium Colonial government and how they had never prepared the Congolese for independence. When independence came unexpectedly to the Congo on 30 June 1960, just short of an armed uprising, many Belgiums and other whites left. Olaf told how immediately after their departure, the new Congolese government seized their property. Since few Congolese had any money to buy this property, the newly appointed government ministers and generals and police officials gave the property to their relatives. Houses, huge villas, businesses, even factories, overnight became the property of people, many of whom had never lived in anything other than a jungle style hut on the outskirts of Kinshasa or in the heart of the forest. Some who had previously worked in shops and factories suddenly found themselves owners or at least part owners of these businesses. Some of these new "businessmen" couldn't read or write. Often their "silent partner" was a minister or general.

I asked about the darkened walls inside so many of the houses. Olaf explained that in the bush, many of these people cooked inside their hut. He went on to explain often the huts had no means for the smoke to escape. I asked him what happens to the smoke. With his dry humor he said well some escapes out the door, but most goes in their lungs and eyes. To which he couldn't help but let out a typical deep Scandinavian chuckle. I asked why they would destroy a perfectly good door, window frame, or furniture to burn as firewood. His answer was that they had little money with which to purchase firewood; there was no firewood here in the city they could go out and chop down with their machetes like they did in the bush, and that doors, windows, and most furniture were foreign concepts to them anyway. I began to wonder if Olaf was a racist or if there had been some reverse transference of their strong hate for us. This time it was my time to laugh, though only manifested by a slight smile.

What about all the bullet holes I asked? What's the story behind that? In most cases, due to the location of the marks, there could not possibly have been a human target intended. What's the purpose of wasting perfectly good bullets damaging the walls of already deserted buildings? Olaf's reply was that bullets were the tools of the enlightened of the Congo. The less socially skilled used machetes on people then ate them. Once again that deep chuckle came out. The sun was lowering in the sky, but Olaf insisted we had time for another Primus.

As we drank our last glass, I experienced another Congo idiosyncrasy. When we began our last glass of beer the sun was still above the horizon. A few swallows later, it was dark. There was no twilight. When I commented to Olaf, he explained we were on the equator. At low latitudes like here in the Congo, the sun sets perpendicular to the horizon, while at higher latitudes, like Stockholm, the sun sets at a more oblique angle, allowing it to remain close to the horizon after sunset for a longer period. In science classes I'd viewed this as useless nonrepresentational information. It now became meaningful. He said that at home in Sweden, twilight would allow you to sit and have many more beers. But here in the Congo, we would have to get home for dinner or get in trouble. We laughed and paid for our two beers and headed back to the house.

Exploring Limete

The next morning Olaf had to fly, so I spent the day walking around the market place in Limete. There was a section for foods. There were vegetables and dried fish with flies swarming all over them. A few meters away unrecognizable cuts of beef, pork and goat meat hung from hooks, with multitudes of flies all assembled as though guests of honor. No one made any attempt to drive them away. The temperature was already approaching 32 degrees Celsius or 90 degrees Fahrenheit, yet there was no refrigeration. Absolutely none. I made a note that when I got my own place to stay, I would have somebody at the market just after sunrise. This meat had to contain bacteria modern medicine had yet to discover or name, never mind having an antibiotic that could effectively treat it. As I gazed at the putrefying meats, I wondered how I would ever learn to eat this rotting meat without becoming deathly ill. But I acknowledged there were white people all around me who were surviving. All I had to do was pay attention.

I had lunch at the same sidewalk café where Olaf and I had our two liters of Primus the previous afternoon. I ordered only a ham and cheese sandwich as I was still facing a serious cash crunch. The sandwich arrived on the classic French loaf like we had at Olaf's the day before. Thank God the Congolese didn't carry it under their armpits as so frequently the French are accused of doing. The sandwich really wasn't half bad and the price was affordable. I drank a Miranda, a locally bottled orange soft drink originating from Spain. I'd already been warned not to drink any water. If it doesn't come out of a bottle, don't drink.

Desperation Stratagem

During our drive the previous afternoon I'd seen a travel agency that was still miraculously owned by Europeans according to Olaf. They displayed a sign saying they were Alitalia agents. I had already made up my mind before leaving the States that I would have little option but to cash in my return ticket upon reaching Kinshasa…with or without employment. A bold move that would leave few options. Looking back now I can't believe I had the courage to do such a thing. Courage, or a mix of naïveté and total insanity. None the less, I'd brought my ticket with me. I walked into the Alitalia agency and walked out a few minutes later with a stack of francs, the currency of the Congo. I now had no way to get back to Texas. Not getting hired by somebody was no longer an option. I figured I had enough money to last about three weeks. I walked about looking into the mostly merchandise-devoid shops, then began the ten-minute walk to Olaf's house. Wow, nobody would ever believe I could do anything this extreme…selling my return ticket. Well, maybe Jerry Drake would. I sure didn't plan to write home telling Karen what I'd done.

Shortly after getting back to Olaf's home, he arrived from his flight. He was wearing the same gray U.S. issued flight suit with no insignia I'd seen the two pilots wearing the previous day. He told the houseboy to bring a Primus and two glasses. We went out on the back veranda to talk.

Olaf said he'd seen George Barnes after he returned from his flight. George told Olaf they did not need pilots at this moment but expected to within in a couple of months. George wanted to meet me the next morning. Olaf said he thought George was going to offer me something and I could ride to the airport with him in the morning.

A Baboon–A Red Ball–And A Colt 45

After our second liter of Primus we sat down for dinner. Olaf had a friend who had just come back from Sweden and brought a cantaloupe-size ball of cheese. It was dipped in bright red wax to preserve it. Olaf's wife had it prominently displayed right in the center of the table. There were several other items for dinner that night but obviously the bright red ball of newly arrived Swedish cheese was to be the main feature.

We had just taken our first taste of soup when I caught some rapid movement out of the corner of my eye. There was a crash on the table top, dishes were scattered, and when I had recovered enough to focus accurately, I saw two red circles. One was the red/rainbow-colored buttocks of what appeared to be a baboon. The other was the bright red, newly arrived ball of Swedish cheese tucked under the disproportionately long arm of the brown, hairy creature. The baboon had come into the dining room through the large open window leading to Olaf's back yard. All this in a matter of a couple of seconds. The baboon obviously knew that time was of essence. While still trying to grasp the situation, I heard Olaf let out of string of expletives in English but with heavy Scandinavian accent (the Swedes always seemed to prefer to swear in English). His profane thoughts and words directed toward the baboon were immediately punctuated by the deafening blast from a Colt .45 automatic (ACP) which he produced from a shoulder holster beneath his flight suit. I could see the baboon outside the window sitting on the branch of a tree. Thankfully Olaf had missed the baboon which I later learned was a family pet. But the sudden blast and probably the whistle of a 230-grain full metal jacket projectile passing in close proximity at around 850 feet per second caused the baboon to drop the prized ball of cheese. Olaf dashed outside and returned with the cheese ball. He was using his flight suit to wipe the dirt off the undamaged red ball. His wife took it and returned from the kitchen a minute later with the cheese all washed and polished and ready to eat again. Olaf was still swearing about "that worthless, lazy, "bleeping" baboon. My ears were still ringing from the sound of the 45's blast bouncing off the mostly bare plaster walls of the dining room. I could already tell, life in the Congo was going to be interesting. As I lay down that night, I found sleep difficult. I was excited about meeting George Barnes the next morning. I'd seen interesting hand-carved tourists' trinkets, vegetables and some exotic looking fruit, horrendously filthy meat, and an Alitalia agent buy my return ticket. It had in fact been a full day.

As I lay in bed in the Congo trying to get to sleep, Cambodia continued in a downward spiral. Political and economic conditions presided over by a seemingly disengaged Prince Sihanouk, had reached the point where many of his senior political and military leaders began plotting his removal from office. His cousin Prince Sisowath Sirik Matak and his Prime Minister, General Lon Nol, were in the forefront of this movement. It is not known whether the newly reopened U.S. Embassy played any role in encouraging their dissatisfaction as they had previously done in South Vietnam. 110

George Barnes

The alarm clock sounded at 3:45am. I turned on the small bedside lamp and headed for the houseboy's bathroom. Olaf had a 5:00am takeoff. There was no time to waste. Since there was no hot water in the main bathroom, it made little difference to me that this shower had no provision for hot water. To say the cold shower was invigorating was not an exaggeration. I could see my fingertips were turning blue. I was out of there in no time and back in my room getting dressed. I put on slacks and a dress shirt as Olaf had already advised not to wear a tie.

There were already a few Congolese walking or riding bicycles on the side of the road as we made our way along Boulevard Lumumba in the darkness. N'Djili airport was about a twenty-minute drive in the daylight but with no street lights working and Congolese and animals all over the road it was necessary to drive much more slowly. Most of the Congolese were walking toward small local markets scattered along the roadside with loads of firewood or produce balanced on their heads or tied to their bicycles. Before the sun climbed above the horizon, the markets would be full of people. The dim yellow glow of kerosene (pitolo) lamps were all along the road as the people were busy setting up their market stalls. It was still cool, and the people were not yet beaten down by the merciless equatorial heat.

As we pulled up to the gate leading to the air force ramp, there was an iron bar across the road. A guardhouse stood beside the gate, but it was empty. A large sign over the gate in bad need of fresh paint read *"Force Aérienne Congolaise."* Olaf honked the car's horn and after several long blasts a somnambulistic Congolese in a rumpled camouflaged MP uniform slowly emerged from a grass hut about 5 meters from the empty guardhouse. He walked slowly to the gate and raised it without ever looking inside the car. I assumed he recognized the car. Olaf was not nearly as generous mumbling a French Colonial derogatory term toward the sleepwalking Congolese. We were one of the first to arrive. I mentioned jokingly to Olaf that soon the MP would find it impossible to sleep. Olaf mumbled more expletives saying I was wrong and the (derogatory term) guy would just leave the bar up and go back to sleep in his (expletive) hut.

I went with Olaf as he picked up his first flight segment manifest and mission for the rest of the day from flight dispatch. I noticed he didn't really pay much attention to the manifest weights and loading information. I diplomatically inquired if he preferred to check them at the plane. He responded in the negative saying they were all lies anyway. He said I'll show you how to check your weight and balance when we get to the airplane. Olaf's co-pilot arrived a

---

110 A History of Cambodia—Second Edition by David Chandler

few minutes later. It was still dark. I walked with them through the hanger and out onto the flight line. Olaf spotted his plane and we headed toward it. It was one of several with groups of people all around and U.S. Air Force ground power cords attached. I soon met the Congolese loadmaster, radio operator/navigator and flight engineer. The cargo load was mostly palletized and professionally tied down. That had all been done late last night by European professional loadmasters. But crowed all around the former U.S. Air Force C-47 were its passengers. Their baggage was anything but in bags. Mostly these passengers were Armée Nationale Congolaise (ANC) and their families. When they were assigned to a new base, not only did they take their families, but also what meager household belongings and their livestock, including chickens, goats, and pigs. No special provision was made for accommodating the livestock, they flew with the passengers and bags. These aircraft were in military configuration with para-seats along the sides with the center of the aircraft for cargo. The lone toilet was in the back in a tiny 1 meter by 1-meter enclosure. Inside was the "honey-bucket." A five-gallon bucket containing (on rare occasions) what is in the aviation industry is referred to as "blue-water" which was a strong chemical solution mixed with about two gallons of water. On longer flights, it was mixed with only about one gallon of water.

I found the ANC passengers far friendlier than those I'd met to this point. We were greeted by "mbote," "mbote mingi," Lingala for "hello…a big hello." I later reasoned there were many explanations for this unexpected display of amity few of which were based on sincerity.

Olaf and his copilot both pulled powerful flashlights from their flight bags and began their walk around inspection. They were looking for unexplained oil leaks (all these old WWII aircraft leaked oil), inspection panels being left unlatched, tire condition, strut and tire inflation, prop nicks, pressure gauge readings, and countless other items listed on their walk-around inspection checklist. This was the first transport category aircraft I'd ever been around, except at an airshow. I was excited.

They finished their exterior walk-around. By this time, the loadmaster and flight engineer had herded all the passengers and animals onboard. I accompanied Olaf and his copilot to the cockpit to watch them start the number two engine. They quickly and smoothly ran their checklists and started the number two (right hand engine). I said goodbye to Olaf and the loadmaster escorted me back through the cabin, which was already starting to rapidly take on the smell of its occupants. After I hopped to the ground the loadmaster secured the huge military cargo door. I hurried out from behind the number 1 (left) engine as they started cranking it. As I got clear, it roared to life with a belch of blue-white smoke. About a minute later, they taxied out for takeoff. I could see Olaf checking things as they taxied and his copilot talking on the radio. I knew I was going to like this job if I could just get hired. I walked back through the hanger and sat down on one of the couches in the dispatch area. I watched several crews come in, pick up their papers and go out. Everyone would walk up and introduce themselves or the Dutch dispatcher would introduce me to them. It seemed the news had traveled quickly. Everybody already had heard of "the new American." Around 9:00 am the phone rang and one of the dispatchers told me George Barnes wanted to see me. He escorted me up a steep flight of metal stairs to a suite of offices which had a view of the hanger and flight line.

A Wigmo Contract

The main door lead into a large room filled with desks and administrative people. There were four women working in the office as well as men. I later learned they were the wives of some of the Wigmo people. In just a moment a rather short man with thinning hair came out to meet me. He had a genuine smile which went virtually from ear to ear. He said "Hi…I'm George." I liked him immediately. He took me into his office. He already knew all about me from Olaf. He basically wanted to know about my flight experience. While George was not a pilot, he had retired from the air force as a flight mechanic working his way from piston aircraft all the way through the B52s. And it seemed George had a funny story about every one of those aircraft.

After we had chatted for a while, he told me they would be needing more pilots in a couple of months but that in the meantime, if I'd like to join Wigmo as a dispatcher, he would put me to work this very day with the promise of a pilot contract in a couple of months.

My emotions were somewhere between laughing and crying. My huge gamble had just paid off. My thousands upon thousands of prayers had just been answered. My fellow instructors had just been proven wrong. My answer was "yes sir, I would like very much to do that." George pushed an intercom button on his desk and one of the ladies from the outer office came in. He asked me to give her my identification and write the name as I wanted it to appear on my contract and on my monthly wire transfers. About twenty minutes and forty jokes later the lady returned with a stack of papers for me to sign. The contracts all bore the Liechtenstein address. I chuckled inside as I thought about trying to explain to my father how a tiny city about a third the size of Waco could be a country and I was working for an aviation company based out of there. Never mind their only customer was the CIA. My contract for dispatcher paid $650 a month plus another $350 paid in local currency for living expenses. That was on top of a company-provided bachelor apartment and company transportation to and from the airport. Less than two weeks after leaving my job on Meacham Field in Ft. Worth Texas, I had doubled my salary and would soon be making three times my Southwest School of Aviation salary. But more than celebration, I was experiencing a deep sense of gratitude to the Lord for His answer to my prayers. Many, many prayers. Shortly after my signing, George signed for Wigmo, the lady stamped my copies and handed one to me. Countless worries and been lifted. The gamble had worked. It was now time to get to work.

George picked up the phone and dialed another number. He then resumed asking me questions about Texas and telling more jokes. Between jokes, George paused and said in a matter-of-fact tone of voice, "never let the words CIA cross your lips; we refer to them as *the customer* or *the company*." He then resumed with his enormous repertoire of jokes. The change in the tone of his voice indicated this was not a joke.

In a few minutes a tall well-built man with golden hair combed in the style of the 1950s knocked and entered. He was wearing the largest gold ring I'd ever seen. It was massive to the point of being obscene. On his arm was a matching obscene bracelet. I later learned he was referred to behind his back as "Gold Finger." George said, "Meet your new boss Stefan Szweda" (pseudonym). We exchanged a few pleasantries then Stefan took me to my new work place. In just a couple of minutes I was back in the same flight operations area I'd been before, but this time went behind the counter. I was handed over to one of the dispatchers named Ko (pseudonym). Ko was from Holland. I later learned he was the right-hand man of Stefan who was from Poland. I had almost immediately detected Stefan was not too happy about having George push this new American pilot into his department. Soon I would understand that Stefan and Ko wanted the absolute loyalty of all their people and owing them your job was one of the best ways to assure that loyalty. I just broke the mold. But I didn't really care. I'd work hard, do a good job, and soon they would appreciate me. I would soon learn that aside from a lone Britt, I was the only one professionally trained in aircraft dispatch. I would, over the next several months, gradually come to understand how all the pieces of this peculiar puzzle fit together. I was now working with a new breed of people.

Just after lunch a call came to operations concerning me. I'd just finished the butter and cheese sandwich Olaf's wife and made for me the night before. Ko was instructed to take me to the finance office. Finance was a small building just behind the hanger with a window that allowed them to make transactions without the employees going inside. It wasn't that there was anything secret inside, but rather the place was small and cramped. Plus, their cherished, cool, air-conditioned environment would get replaced by the 90-degree Fahrenheit 90% humidity equatorial air from outside. A British man, probably in his late fifties came to the window and Ko introduced us. His name was Robert Turnbow (pseudonym). Ko left and returned to dispatch. Robert had a stack of Congolese Francs waiting for me plus some papers describing housing options. Robert saw from the paperwork I filled out with George earlier that morning that my status was "family." Robert said they did not have any company provided family housing now or in the foreseeable future. He said however that he was aware of a nice two-bedroom apartment that would soon be coming up in a unit leased independently by a group of

Swedish and Danish mechanics. He recommended I contact them as they would be anxious to get someone in the unit so the cost would be divided by four again rather than by three. I assured him I was interested. He said he would call over and talk to them for me. In the meantime, he had a small unit arranged in the Wigmo bachelor's quarters. He pointed out that this would allow time for me to get my kitchen items, linen, towels, and other such things ready before my family arrived. He even suggested I immediately contact the person soon to be moving from the two-bedroom apartment and see if I could arrange to buy everything they had or at least check it out and see if I wanted to make them an offer. All Robert's advice sounded good. If it worked, it could simplify many things.

Robert handed me the keys to my new living quarters and showed me where the VW mini-bus parked. The mini-bus would be my transportation to and from work. He also told me to go introduce myself to the guys that usually drove the bus. I signed a few more papers relating to the quarters and headed back to operations with a fat wad of Congolese Zaïre in my pocket.

About an hour later, via HF (high frequency) radio transmissions from Olaf's plane and their last departure station, I learned his estimated time of arrival (ETA). Work was over at 3:30pm. Olaf was due in just before 6:00pm. I decided it would be much better for me to wait and go home with him to spend one more night. I could then bring all my belongings with me when he came out to fly the following morning. Things were starting to fall into place. I once again gave thanks in silent prayer to what was obviously The Lord's Hand in all this. *I waited patiently for the Lord, and He turned to me and heard my cry for help.*[111]

The rest of the afternoon flew by. Every task they handed me was exciting. I was no longer in the flight school environment where my job was teaching students to fly small airplanes. With a single stroke of the pen that morning, I'd graduated. I was now working with large airplanes. These were airplanes in current use by the U.S. Air Force all around the world. Almost everything I did as an instructor fell within the realm of the theoretical. Here, there were no hypothetical, suppositious, exercises. These were Congolese Air Force (*Force Aérienne Congolaise*) missions often directed by *"the customer or the company"* (slang for the CIA). Some were being flown into areas of hostility. While this was not the airline job I'd left CENCO for, it was without any doubt more exciting. I was like a small child standing before a Christmas tree. A year earlier, as I sat writing every airline I could find, it would have been impossible to even imagine doing this kind of work. God had guided me, without my knowledge, around Air Congo, and into Wigmo. *Trust in the Lord with all your heart, and do not rely on your own understanding; think about Him in all your ways, and He will guide you on the right paths.*[112]

---

[111] Holy Bible—Psalms 40:1 - Holman Christian Standard Bible (HCSB)
[112] Holy Bible—Proverbs 3:5-6 - Holman Christian Standard Bible (HCSB)

A big part of my job in dispatch would be to find the cargo listed on the manifest, which was supposedly out on the ramp somewhere, and to ascertain its weight and size. In many cases, the U.S. Military markings on the wooden cases made this easy. In some cases the pieces had to be hoisted and weighed. Once the piles and pallets were weighed or their weight was verified, we would go back into operations and decide via loading charts where the cargo had to be placed in order to keep the aircraft safely within balance. These were the same calculations I was teaching at Southwest School of Aviation. We would work out each aircraft's load (weight and balance) and put these calculations along with the standard weights for passengers found on our manifest and have it ready for the crew to inspect the following morning.

My significant proficiency in this area quickly impressed my new colleagues. However, their street smarts quickly impressed me. Many of the items appearing on the manifest were written in French. The U.S. Military markings on the cases were all in English. Some could easily be recognized. Others I found a complete mystery. But that part was the easiest. They had to stop me on more than one occasion that afternoon and point out that a particular case showed indications of having been opened. When this was observed, the weight stenciled on the box could no longer be trusted. It had to be weighed. Almost always the contents of the case far outweighed what was stenciled on the side of the box.

And then there were the mysterious locked pouches. I was told these were going to "the customer" in the field. They were always to go in the cockpit with the crew and be handed directly to the station agent by the captain or the co-pilot. We had to initial a special place on the manifest attesting to having received it. The station agent would initial as well at the destination. They always arrived via embassy vehicle the afternoon before and were locked in dispatch overnight.

As we were walking back to dispatch from the ramp, they explained how the night dispatcher had the most difficult job. The passengers and their baggage would start to arrive around 2:30am. In addition to their families, and livestock, they had contraband. Some examples of serious smuggling and some just examples of embryonic entrepreneurial endeavors. But regardless of into which category they fell, they could, if undetected, become deadly. An airplane seriously overweight or out of balance on takeoff would crash, probably resulting in the death of everyone onboard.

The passengers knew each piece of their baggage was going to be weighed. Once weighed, they would be loaded on the aircraft while the passengers and livestock remained outside. Many passengers would then wait and watch patiently for any opportunity to sneak un-weighed and un-manifested baggage onboard. They would create distractions so the dispatcher would turn his attention from the cargo door allowing them to quickly slip their un-weighed items onboard. Or more often they would simply bribe the FAC loadmaster to put it on for them. Sometimes the loadmaster would be flying on the plane, in which case they could hopefully be counted on to exercise some moderation. However, in other cases, they would not be going on the flight and God only knows how that thought process (if any) worked.

I learned most of the pilots viewed this smuggling with somewhat of a benevolent eye. Many of these *Force Aérienne Congolaise*, especially the lower ranking ones, often hadn't been paid in several months. That meant they would be forced to beg, borrow, or most likely steal, in order to feed their families. I could see it would be hard at least to some degree, not to look in the other direction.

I learned that most often their contraband was vegetables or other commodities they could buy cheaply in this area and sell at a profit at their destination. This practice was unfortunately well established among the loadmasters. I was told some had their regular schedule with regular customers waiting. They would buy a commodity in one location and sell it in another. From their first stop, they would buy something that would have a regular buyer at the next down-line station. These commodities were not always limited to harmless produce. Some traded in ivory illegally poached in the bush and had serious buyers waiting in Kinshasa. The big-ticket items like ivory, gold, and diamonds, were generally controlled by high-ranking FAC generals. Their Mercedes would be waiting for the flight and the loadmaster would go directly to his waiting car with the precious cargo. In the months to come, I'd learn plenty about all these little subtle and not-so-subtle nuances of life in the *Force Aérienne Congolaise*. I would also learn about Wigmo's *irregular missions*.

Olaf landed just about dark and taxied onto the military ramp. As the cargo door on his C-47 opened ANC started hopping out and unloading all their chickens, pigs, goats, wives and children. I saw a wounded solider being brought down on a stretcher. I did not see any waiting ambulance. Such was the Congo. I couldn't wait to share with Olaf all that had happened that day. I hardly remember the drive from the airport to his house. I was so excited. I gulped down my last meal with Olaf and his family and hurried off to my room to pack. The Wigmo van would be picking me up around 6:30 am the next morning.

High Powered Radios and Underpowered VW Vans

When the van arrived, it was already full. I was the last stop. I stuffed my bags in and found a cramped space in the back. The little VW engine strained as the now quite full van headed toward N'Djili.

There was far more bicycle and foot traffic at 6:30 am than there had been at 4:15 am when I had gone with Olaf. Drivers needed to be very cautious. Congolese were notoriously unskilled drivers with whom caution was a poorly propagated theory. Pedestrian and bicycle traffic simply seldom bothered or thought to look before entering the road or turning. The driver of our van, a

Polish mechanic with a British passport joked with me about how roads with lots of vehicle traffic like Lumumba were a Congolese version of population control. I was amazed how openly racist most of them seemed to be. But then I remembered my first night spent at the airport and the ANC MP jabbing me in the ribcage with his FN-49. While I was not yet persuaded to adopt their discriminatory attitude, my airport memory was enough to appease any thought I might have had concerning coming to their defense. Soon we were at the hanger and everybody was piling out. I waited until everybody was out of the van I before I began lugging my bags into operations.

As I glanced up on the wall at the huge map of the Congo and bordering areas, I noticed several small aluminum aircraft shapes all with their noses pointed away from Kinshasa. Every thirty minutes or so, or over discernible topographical features, the aircraft were to call in giving position reports. Their calls went to the radio room located up near the roof of the hanger. From there, the radio operator would intercom down to operations with the position reports. Ops would then update the little aircraft figures on the wall map. It was a very effective system.

The huge map consisted of meticulously stitched-together aeronautical Sectional Charts. They showed most small villages and roads. The major cities had Wigmo's code names for them displayed just below the city's name. Radio calls always came and went in code. The high-powered Collins military radios the Wigmo planes were equipped with could be heard, under the right conditions, halfway around the world. All the Wigmo base stations were equipped with state-of-the-art military issue Collins KWM-2A transceivers with an awesome 175 watts of output on SSB. The outstations all had directional antennas pointed toward Kinshasa. Kinshasa had the same radio but with a 1000-watt amplifier supported by a highly directional rotatable antenna and several other unknown and mysterious looking arrays. The roof of the radio room and its surrounding real estate reminded me of a Hamilton County porcupine. Beneath the huge wall map was a blackboard with the ETA of each flight written on it as well as little marks that indicated if there were any special messages or instructions waiting for the aircraft's next call in. When necessary, the radio room could do phone patches. Most often from operations to the aircraft when complex instructions needed to be passed. And on less frequent occasions, with various maintenance departments when the aircraft was having mechanical issues. No airline anywhere in the world had any better equipment. Most would have been envious. I was beginning to get a glimpse *beneath the shroud*.

A Cuban-American Training Pilot and A Pan Am Pilot

I had just been handed a stack of cargo manifests to find out on the ramp. The same duty routine I'd done the previous afternoon, but this time I was unsupervised. I had just stepped out of operations and into the hanger when a short, rather handsome Hispanic pilot came out of the door which led to the training department. He introduced himself as Felipe Vasquez (pseudonym). He said he'd heard there was a newly arrived American working in dispatch and that the new guy was also a pilot. We shook hands and chatted for a few minutes. As we talked, countless people walked up and spoke to him. Between interruptions he was quite interested in learning about my flight experience. I liked Felipe immediately and he appeared to like me as well. Felipe said he had to go do a maintenance flight check on a C-54 with a Congolese co-pilot flight engineer. He said he would be back in an hour or so and that he would like to visit more then.

I found the area on the ramp where my cargo was stacked and began locating the individual items and checking them off on the manifest. I had to call for the fork lift twice to weigh questionable cargo. But all in all, I thought this lot looked reasonably honest. While I was checking out the cargo, I observed Felipe doing an in-depth walk-around inspection with a white mechanic and the Congolese flight engineer and first officer (co-pilot). After about thirty minutes they went up the air stair and into the plane. I heard the C-54's onboard APU start. This was unique to military C-54s, as most civilian versions (DC-4) were not outfitted with APUs. Soon I saw them start the number three engine. Then number four was started. Soon all four engines were running, and they taxied to the run-up area. They stayed in the run-up area a long time before finally taxiing out for takeoff. Apparently, Felipe wanted to be completely sure everything was ready. I'd never flown anything with four engines, and I stood in wonder as they advanced the throttles and started the takeoff roll. I hoped I'd soon be in one myself.

I went back inside and picked up another stack of manifest papers. As I was getting my next load, I glanced up on the wall map. The planes were creeping along north and eastward toward their first destinations. Most flights were several hours from their destinations. I checked the board to see where Olaf's last position was. Then I headed out to the ramp to find my next pile of stuff. I could tell the temperature was several degrees warmer than it had been at 7:00am. It was obvious this ramp could be a brutal place to work. And, the ramp was where most work was done. The mechanics all wore shorts, and tennis shoes. Some wore t-shirts, others a type of safari shirt. Almost everyone who worked to any extent out on the ramp wore this type of dress. The pilots all wore U.S. Air Force issue flight suits. Many wore baseball-type caps.

While I was in the middle of putting together my second load of cargo, Felipe landed and taxied back in. The same white mechanic that was with him during the preflight inspection was on the ramp waiting to guide his aircraft into its parking place. The mechanic was his crew chief.

After his debrief with the crew, Felipe walked over to where I was finishing up my second load. When he saw I was heading into dispatch he asked me to stop in the training department for a moment. He said there was someone he wanted me to meet.

When we walked into the training department, I saw this huge silver-haired man sitting at a desk. He was probably at least sixty and had a jolly demeanor. His name was Lewis Holmes (pseudonym). He was retired from Pan Am and had been asked to come do some short-term training work. I later would learn that some of his Pan Am work was not directly associated with the airline business. Lewis was one of the Pan Am employees with a dual employer…the CIA. Of course Lewis did not tell me this right away but the other American I was about to meet would be quick to do so. Looking back later, I was amazed by my naiveté concerning Pan Am. Captain Holmes told me to have a seat at his desk. Unlike Felipe, he was more interested in my ground instructor and flight instructor experience. I soon realized they had been discussing me since the news broke that I had been hired.

A few minutes later, another American walked in. His name was Stanley Griffin (pseudonym). Stan wore the dark black Ray-Ban sunglasses which distinguish junior birdman from the rest of the aviation community. He wore a white long-sleeve pilot's shirt, complete with captain's epaulets, seemingly oblivious to the 32-degree Celsius (90 degree Fahrenheit) temperature just outside the door. However, I, being the most junior of birdmen present, did not dare show any recognition of his environmentally incongruent appearance. It turned out Stan was also a Texan. We all chatted for a few minutes then I excused myself and returned to dispatch before I was missed. People were pretty laid back here but with this being my second day on the job, I didn't think it the wisest of ideas to be missing for any serious length of time.

The remainder of the day flew by. Soon it was time for the morning shift to go home. I was not accustomed to any type of regular working hours…not since I was in the Navy. Even as temporary help while working on the freight dock during flight school, we stayed till the work was done. Certainly at Southwest School of Aviation there was no set go-home time. This was different and a little fun. I had a time that I could allot to something I wanted to do. But I realized I didn't know anything to do and had no transportation to go do it in.

I dragged my bags to the Wigmo van once again. While the guys in the van seemed friendly enough, it was obvious that they would not be very happy to see my bags again. Soon the van pulled into the complex where everyone in the van lived. One of the Swedish mechanics helped me with one of my bags and showed me to my little apartment. It was small and Spartan, but I was no longer imposing on anyone's hospitality. I was happy to be in my own space no matter how small and basic. I unpacked and checked out what the tiny kitchen had. Considering my noteworthy cooking disabilities, I was confident the kitchen would easily exceed my capabilities.

I immediately headed across the street to the little grocery store they had pointed out. In the Congo, like in most of Africa, these little shops or *dukas* as they were called in Swahili and Lingala were run by people of Indian descent. The Congolese referred to them as *Mhindi*. While some had Congolese wives, most only married *Mhindi*. This *duka* had few white patrons so as a result, the merchandise was quite basic. Most shops in the Congo, no matter what they sold, were owned and run by *Mhindi*. I later learned these Indians had been in Africa for generations. They reportedly were descendants of indentured laborers brought initially to East Africa when slavery was outlawed in the British Empire.

In the little *duka* I was warmly greeted in heavily Indian-accented English by the shop's owner. Immediately upon entering the shop it was impossible not to be struck by its dominant feature, a picture of President Joseph Désiré Mobutu attached to the back wall. Without fail, every shop I'd been in thus far had the very same photo usually in a gold painted wooden frame in the back of the shop. I suspected it was some kind a law. Along with the Mobutu picture was the Popular Revolutionary Movement (Mouvement Populaire de la Révolution--MPR), which Mobutu created in 1967. The MPR was the country's sole political party and Mobutu's only claim to legitimacy.

The shop owner knew I'd come from the Wigmo compound across the street. He had a decent assortment of canned meats, jams, fresh bread, and cold drinks. Everything I needed until the Wigmo van made a real grocery run down into the center of Kinshasa was right here. I bought soap, bathroom supplies, a couple of dish towels, a bath towel, and some canned sardines, and potted meat. My evening meal issue was now under control. I bought a couple of liters of cold Primus beer to finish off my food purchase. I considered myself all set for the night. Life in the Congo was beginning to come together. While light-years from anything I'd ever known, I could already tell I was going adapt well.

Resentment and Recruitment

Riding in the Wigmo van without my bags was a pleasure. I was starting to get to know some of the mechanics. As soon as I arrived in dispatch I reported to Ko for an assignment. Though polite enough, it was obvious Ko and his boss Gold Finger resented my being pushed on them by George Barnes. While this bothered me, I realized my working for them would only be temporary. As soon as a pilot position opened, they would only see my face on the flight-line side of the operations counter. I had no idea just how temporary.

Ko had just given me a telex message received from the *Armée Nationale Congolaise* (ANC) High Command in Kinshasa with a list of names of military dependents who were authorized to travel from Goma (Nectar 8 or N8) back to Kinshasa (King 1 or K1) on a *Force Aérienne Congolaise* (FAC) C-46. I was to take the list to the radio room for transmission via HF radio to our Wigmo station chief in Nectar 8. He would then pass the list to the local FAC commander. When I asked Ko why the High Command hadn't simply transmitted the message themselves, he dryly replied that most of the FAC and ANC radios hadn't worked in years.

As I was walking out the operations door heading for the radio room, I met Lewis Holmes and Felipe Vasquez on their way into operations. They asked me where I was going. As soon as I'd told them, they instructed me to hurry back. I wondered if this might have something to do with our conversations the other day about my flight and training background. I bounded up the steep steps leading to the radio room. Once inside I gave the list and instructions to Dennis Jones (pseudonym) the British radio operator on duty and scurried back down to operations.

Lewis and Felipe had gone into Stefan's office. I could hear somewhat raised voices. Then Felipe walked out followed by Lewis. Lewis turned to Stefan and said, "it really doesn't matter…he now works for the training department." Felipe told me to gather my things that I now would be working with them. I asked, "when do I start?" The towering figure of Lewis approached from behind and said, "since thirty minutes ago." I somewhat lamely said something to the effect of see you guys later and left with Lewis and Felipe. I was glad to get out of there. You could cut the tension in the air with a knife.

Lewis pointed to a desk in the corner and told me it was mine. I walked over and sat down. I was still trying to get a handle on all that had just come down in the last five minutes. I knew I was going to like training a lot more than operations.

We spent all morning talking. Felipe said he would begin checking me out as co-pilot on the C-54 right away. Lewis said he would handle my C-46 and C-47 checkouts. They said my pay would have to remain at my dispatcher's pay till I was totally checked out which might take two months. But then Lewis said I'd be making $1200 base plus overtime, plus hazardous flight pay, plus my $350/month living expense. The ink wasn't dry on my dispatcher's pay yet and I already had pilot pay in my sights. I offered virtually continuous silent micro-prayers all morning as we talked.

When lunch time came, they all had their brought from home lunches. I had mine as well. A butter and cheese sandwich like what Olaf's wife had made. But this was one different. I'd made it using ingredients purchased from the little *duka* across the street. It wasn't half bad…all things considered. Like the previous day, I bought a cold Miranda to accentuate the nuances of my self-made cheese and butter sandwich.

After lunch Felipe took me to stores. This is where all supplies except petroleum expendables and explosives were kept. He told them I needed five flight suits, flight boots, a headset, and a duffle bag. The German stores manager eyed me up and down and said he thought he had my size. Soon he was back with a stack of five new U.S. Air Force issue flight suits, battleship gray. I tried one on over my clothes. Except for being a bit long, they were just fine. The headset was again a U.S. Air Force issue. It looked like what I'd seen in the movies. I'd never worn a flight suit and I'd certainly never had a headset. I was very excited. They also brought me a microphone for use with the headset. I was slowly working my way up through the ranks of junior birdmen. Soon I was back in the training department office with my loot neatly stored in my new U.S. Air Force issue duffle bag. If Daddy could just see me now.

It was already Friday afternoon. The training department office was 7:00 am to 3:30 pm Monday through Friday. Unless there were special weekend flight training missions, this was a five day a week job. On Monday morning Lewis wanted me to begin writing training material for the Congolese student pilots they were training. He was particularly interested in some simple and practical weight and balance training material and handouts that could be used immediately in their flight training program. I knew I could have that ready by the end of the following week. Lewis was pleased.

Also, during the afternoon, I had learned that there was bad blood between Robert Troyes (Romeo Tango) and Lewis. It seemed Romeo Tango had numerous private operations going which involved the use of Wigmo aircraft. It was widely whispered that the CIA had sent Lewis to gather facts about Romeo Tango's private enterprises. Gold Finger, being Romeo Tango's right-hand man and reputedly deeply involved in the "private entreprises" had, like Romeo Tango, scarcely bothered to disguise his animosity for Lewis. As a matter of fact, they had gone out of their way to make his life there difficult. They had, however, significantly underestimated his intelligence, resourcefulness and resolve. So when Lewis walked into Romeo Tango's office and announced he was taking the new American pilot for the training department, ecstatic reactions could hardly have been expected.

Even with finding myself in the outer limits of this storm's center, I knew I was paying a small price for landing this dream job. I'd been in the Congo less than a week. I had gone from unemployed and homeless with no way to return home, to a training department instructor with flight status and my own apartment. Little of this could have been credited to me. Perhaps my naiveté-based audacity allowed me to believe I could accomplish this goal. But in my heart, I knew "the LORD's hand was on me, and He brought me there."[113]

A Call Home–A Nigerian Rescue

Friday after work the Wigmo van traditionally made the grocery run to town. It was the time most of the guys did their shopping. But Friday afternoons

---

[113] Holy Bible—Ezekiel 40:1 - Holman Christian Standard Bible (HCSB)

were not exclusively for shopping. Many who had tired of their own cooking and company elected to stay after the van went back, consuming a little beer and Belgium food. I decided I should spend some time getting to know downtown Kinshasa, so I agreed to meet the guys at their favorite watering hole, a Belgium owned restaurant called La Barrique which meant barrel in English. My plan was to get my grocery shopping done and place the groceries in the Wigmo van. Then I wanted to go to the main Post Office (Bureau la Poste) to place an international call and buy some stamps for my letters to Karen. But the phone call home was my highest priority. They would be anxiously waiting for any news. They did not yet know I had been hired. Things had moved much too quickly. I had not had time to call them.

Grocery shopping went well. I had bought many more supplies than I had food. I did see several welcomed commodities the little *duka* across from the apartment didn't have. It didn't take long to buy what I needed. I was still in the super frugal mode. I spent far more time familiarizing myself with what was available here in the Congo. If it was not in this modest grocery store…it was not in the Congo. Life as I had known it was headed for some significant accommodating adjustments, none of which troubled me. I was excited and enthusiastic. I placed my groceries in the van and headed for the Bureau du Poste.

The building had once been somewhat stately but was now badly run down in mode of everything post-independence. Everywhere you looked, the rapid decline of neglect and misuse stood as a stark reminder of Congolese independence. The huge main counter was staffed by a significant number of Congolese government postal workers. While the windows were mostly staffed, few were working. Most were reading newspapers or just staring. I watched a couple of foreigners walk up to a window with no line and be directed to another window. I was immediately reminded of the airport terminal at N'Djili. And they wondered why the country was in such bad shape. I got in the line with everybody else. It moved slowly. When it was finally my turn, I managed to tell him what I wanted to do and handed him my father's phone number in the Texas. He immediately demanded a $20 deposit. He told me to wait. When he made the connection, he pointed to a booth for me to go into. I picked up the receiver and heard Daddy's phone ringing. Soon he picked up. I spoke rapidly as I knew the call would be expensive. I told him to get Karen and for her to get a paper and pencil. It was good to hear her voice again. I quickly gave her my mailing address, and the details of my salary. We were both relieved that we would have money coming in again. In less than a month I'd doubled my Southwest School of Aviation flight instructor's salary. I told her the monthly pay would come to the Hamilton National Bank via a wire transfer from Luxemburg. I asked her to tell Daddy to talk to the bank and ask them to call when the transfer arrived. Both Daddy and Karen were excited. I cut the call short to save money and went back to the man at the window to get my change.

When I got to the window the government clerk said I had talked too long and needed to pay him another $5. I told him that was impossible. I had started the timer on my Breitling Navitimer when I picked up the phone in the booth and pushed the stop button when I hung up. I pointed to the timer, which I realized he had no possibility of comprehending, and emphatically told him three minutes…not eleven minutes as he was claiming. It was then that I noticed a movement behind me. The tallest man I'd ever seen in my life pushed ahead of me and spoke in very British English telling the Congolese not to try to cheat me. He was very black and was wearing a long white robe and a little skull cap. His equally tall friend wearing a light blue robe and white skull cap pushed in front of me as well and they were both leaning over the rail towering over the just barely average height Congolese. The Congolese clerk slammed a $10 note on the counter and muttered a long string of unhappy words. I thanked the two men profusely and left. I knew he still had cheated me by three or four dollars, but I decided not to push it. I later learned the two huge Africans were Nigerian Muslims. Apparently they were associated with the Nigerian diplomatic mission in Kinshasa. I mused as I walked down the steps of the Bureau du Poste that life here was going to be very different from life in Hamilton County, Texas. I would never stop learning just how different. I was standing on the periphery of Sheol. *"I said: In the prime of my life I must go to the gates of Sheol."*[114]

With my two immediate priorities, groceries and a phone call home out of the way, I strolled slowly toward the La Barrique, checking out the shops along the way. I was struck by the limited amount of goods for sale considering Kinshasa was the capitol of a large African nation. In every shop without exception, was the ever-present picture of President Mobutu and the country's only political party the MPR.

When I reached the La Barrique, it was packed. I found the Wigmo group sitting at a table in the back. They had saved a place for me. It appeared from their high spirits that there had been little wasted time getting down to some serious drinking. They ordered a beer for me. This was a Belgium owned place and service was good. It didn't take long for me to notice that our table was getting lots of oblique glances. Most of the patrons were dressed for an evening out. Our table was dressed for a day on the FAC flight line. Because I basically worked indoors, I was the only one in long pants but certainly underdressed for where we were. I was a little embarrassed at first, and I felt badly for any who had hoped to have a quiet table and a nice European meal. The Wigmo table had insured that was a pipe dream. However, the manager knew the Wigmo group came often and they spent and tipped well. About an hour or so later I also realized that most in the room viewed us as mercenaries. The heavily Danish accented words of one of my former students came back to me…"you see Jimmy, in some quarters we are considered mercenaries." His words hadn't had that much meaning at the time but now they were becoming perfectly clear. We were, for the most

[114] Holy Bible—Isaiah 38:10 - Holman Christian Standard Bible (HCSB)

part, considered mercenaries. I wasn't sure how I felt about that. I remember initially experiencing considerable uneasiness. At that time the word carried a less than respectable connotation for me. I would later learn the CIA had legions of mercenaries fighting and flying around the world on their behalf. I would learn that they were as much an instrument of U.S. Policy as were the Army, Air Force, Navy, or Marine Corps. Their strategic advantage was being able to deploy under deniable conditions, something the U.S. Air Force could hardly do. A key factor in the cold war was deniability.

I had a good meal and several beers. I had felt a bit uncomfortable about eating such a nice meal and having drinks in a restaurant. It had been years since I felt I could afford that luxury.

The hard core of the group decided to come home whenever the place closed for the night. They would return to the compound via taxi. I was told on the way back that this was normal procedure. They assured me we would all hear them upon their return to the compound. Returning home and slipping quietly into bed apparently violated some Scandinavian cultural tradition. It seemed this was a well-orchestrated operation with the merrymakers already having someone designated to bring their groceries in from the van. I slept well that night. Having secured a paycheck once again allayed untold stress.

Air Congo Visit

I'd decided the previous night that with an entire weekend on my hands and a modest amount of discretionary income, I would go visit some of my students from Southwest School of Aviation who were living here in Kinshasa and flying for Air Congo.

It was nice to awake normally without the demanding summons of my alarm clock. While I was in the shower, a curious thought came to me. I didn't recall seeing any old people. I just credited it to my being preoccupied with calling home then taking in all the sights on Kinshasa's streets. But I did make a mental note to look for them today on my outing.

The Wigmo guys had told me the night before that if I wanted a ride into Kinshasa, just go stand out on the side of the road. They assured me I'd get all kinds of offers. All for compensation, of course, but they said the system worked well. They gave me the going rate and said I should insist I'd be the only passenger, or the Congolese driver would stop every kilometer or so picking up not so nice smelling people. I followed their advice and within a couple of minutes I was in a rickety old car driven by a Congolese man smiling with all five or six of his teeth. I didn't really mind as at least he was smiling. While for the moment I was able to believe he might actually like me a little bit, I was also becoming aware that I was never far from a situation where I could be hacked to death by an excited mob…never far at all.

On my way into Kinshasa I remembered my thought earlier that morning about not seeing any old people. I started watching for them. And I did see some. But not a lot. I decided I'd ask some of my Air Congo friends who had lived here for years…some had grown up here when it was a Belgium colony.

Most of the white Air Congo pilots lived in a large multi-story apartment building just on the other side of downtown Kinshasa. I'd been told to tell the driver I wanted to go to the *ndako na* Air Congo or the house of Air Congo. He immediately knew where I was talking about and shortly after we passed the city center where I'd been the night before, we pulled up to a western-looking apartment building. I had no apartment number, but the white pilot community was small. I just decided to knock on the first door I came to. I did just that. A Belgium lady answered the door. She spoke no English. I heard a man's voice in the background and soon he arrived at the door. It was my student, Jean Caron (pseudonym). He immediately invited me in. I made a mental note that Jean's wife's name was "Sherry." I would later learn when telling another Air Congo pilot about meeting Jean and his wife "Sherry" that her name was really Marie and that "Sherry" was really "*chérie*" meaning darling in French. This gave everybody more than a few laughs for several weeks. While growing up in Hamilton in the 1950s had pretty well assured me I would never hear French spoken, there was absolutely no excuse for my screwing this up. I had heard that before! Sitting in the Texan Theater watching the cartoon staring my favorite character, *Pepe' Le Pew*. The objects of his amorous endeavors were always referred to as "chérie." How stupid could I be! Perhaps as I sat in the theater, I was paying more attention to the girl sitting beside me than I was to the plot on the silver screen. Be that as it may, I realized my French needed some serious work.

Jean immediately went banging on doors and soon his living room was filled with former students and wives. They knew a nice little Belgium café just down the street and they insisted on taking me to lunch. Three of my former students along with their wives came. It was a nice afternoon. We talked of many things. One topic that kept reemerging was the Wigmo/CIA relationship. Apparently, it was not so secret a secret.

One of the pilots at the table, Claude Petit (pseudonym) was born in the Congo. His father had worked for a large Belgium tobacco company. He had grown up in Stanleyville (now called Kisangani). No one at the table had much love for the Congolese. I was a bit disappointed and still view my friends as unjustly racist. However, I could feel the embracing attitude I arrived with rapidly eroding. I asked Claude why I hadn't seen many older people. His answer was…"they all die young." He went on to say that those I saw that I thought were older were probably just in their late forties. Their hard life made them appear much older than they really were. Later, I would understand his remark. The ropes of death were quick to entangle the Congolese. In pre-independence Congo (1950) the percentage of the total population over the age of 65 was 3.8%. This number was never higher and has gradually decreased to its present rate of 2.7%.[115] Their life expectancy at birth is only 55.3 years.[116] All these numbers remain little changed over the past 60 years. While the population has grown over this period, HIV and constant civil war aggressively claim their victims. Having been here less than a week, I could see how these pathetic people had been dealt a cruel hand.

After our truly enjoyable lunch, Jean and Marie offered to drive me back to the Wigmo compound but I had already decided I wanted to explore downtown Kinshasa further, so they dropped me off near the La Barrique where we had eaten the night before. Our lunch had been good. The red wine had been good. The sun, now lower on the horizon, shining gently on my face, worked together with the wine to make the moment perfect. I strolled along the sidewalks looking at the many tourist items offered by the illegal sidewalk venders. All the tourist items for sale, but not many tourists. No tourist in their right mind would come here I thought. I bought some light-weight hand painted air mail stationary and envelopes to use to write home to Karen. I bought a couple of post cards to send to Bill and Mary Wallace at Southwest School of Aviation, and to Camille back in Hamilton. I went back to the post office and purchased some stamps. I still had to fight a little twinge of guilt each time I spent money on anything. It had been a hard couple of years since leaving CENCO. But it was all coming together. I walked out to the side of the road and soon negotiated a ride back home. It had been a great day.

My First FAC Flight

I spent Sunday washing my clothes and my new flight suits (in the kitchen sink). I would have access to the Wigmo houseboys starting Monday. They would handle my washing as well as my dishes and do an extremely cursory cleaning of the apartment. I would later learn this was not just laziness but a blindness to dirt, as most had spent their entire lives living in huts with dirt floors. They simply did not see it. Welcome to the Congo.

I was ready for my alarm Monday morning. I quickly showered, made my lunch, grabbed the duffle bag I had made ready the night before with my flight suit, headset, and mic, and jumped in the Wigmo van. It felt good going to work in the training department. I was the first one to arrive, so I got to use the key they had given me Friday afternoon to let myself in. I went immediately to my desk and began drafting my weight and balance training document. Not too long afterward Felipe and Stan Griffin arrived. Lewis was the last to walk through the door. There was never any sense of urgency about Lewis.

---

[115] Population Division of the United Nations Department of Economic and Social Affairs of the United Nations Secretariat 2010
[116] CIA World Facebook document "2007 edition"

During the morning, Stan and I got to know each other better. He was, to say the very least, stiff. But that was just Stan. He told me he had had some serious disagreements with Romeo Tango and that he would be leaving in a month or so. These differences, according to Stan, stemmed from maintenance policies. Stan wanted things to be like an airline. Romeo Tango just wanted to keep the airplanes in the air and was not averse to taking some short cuts here and there. "Everywhere" would not be hyperbole.

About midmorning the maintenance foreman came and told Felipe a C-54 should be all signed off and ready for a test flight just after lunch. Lewis looked over at me and said…"I don't trust Felipe…why don't you go along and keep an eye on him for me. I've still got a lot of work to do on this report." I smiled so big I thought I heard my cheek muscles rupturing. I asked Felipe if he thought I'd be ok, since I'd never been in a C-54 before. He answered dryly that he flew regularly with an all Congolese crew, therefore he figured he could handle me. I wondered if I was actually floating or if I just felt like I was. I only had around twenty hours of multi-engine time in an old twin engine Piper Apache capable of carrying four passengers. This thing had four huge Pratt & Whitney R-2000 engines. Each was capable of producing 1,450 hp. In its para-configuration it could carry 50 troops 3,900 miles. Although I was still at my desk, I was already airborne. I thanked Lewis profusely and told Felipe I'd do my best not to screw up. Felipe reassured me I'd be just fine. I looked at my watch; it was only 10:30am. How was I ever going to make it till 1:00pm? I was so excited. I went to the training department's huge bookshelf and pulled out the C-54 flight manual. I started studying the cockpit layout diagrams and the normal checklists. I was soon deeply absorbed in my study and my dreams.

At noon I gulped down my sandwich and my regular Mirinda, changed into my flight suit and waited for Felipe. It seemed he was eating in slow motion. Couldn't he see I was ready to go out to the flight line? I was such a novice. I had no idea what a flight test was about. I just assumed it was to see if the airplane would still fly after they put it back together. The LORD graciously looks after fools. About five minutes after 1:00 pm the maintenance supervisor, the lead mechanic for the work they had done, the aircraft's crew chief, and the lead inspector all walked into our office with their clip boards. I wondered what all this was about. I was about to attend my first preflight briefing for a test flight. We all sat down at a round table in the corner and the lead mechanic began to cover the maintenance discrepancies going in, what was found, and the corrective action taken. A signoff sheet was presented to Felipe showing the mechanic's signatures, countersigned by the crew chief's signoff, countersigned again by the inspector. Felipe several times asked for more information on what the pilots had written in their initial "squawk" or maintenance discrepancy entry in the flight log. Felipe wanted to know what the pilots who wrote up the issue had seen so he could look to see if it was gone. He also reviewed the aircraft manufacturer's (Douglas) recommended test flight procedure for the aircraft system involved. I was very impressed. I was suddenly out of my junior birdman world. I silently hoped I wouldn't embarrass myself too badly. In the regular air force you would go to weeks of aircraft systems school, then flight training. I supposed you could say this was flight training. Welcome to Wigmo.

Felipe and the mechanics soon had a plan worked out for checking the systems that had been repaired. We got our clipboards and headsets and headed to the flight line. I was so excited. This was truly a big moment for me. I had never been exposed to systems of such complexity. I was about to climb into the cockpit of the workhorse of the U.S. Air Force during WWII and Korea. I was a bit anxious and certainly anything but overconfident.

The crew chief walked around with Felipe as Felipe checked the items on the preflight inspection form. Many had already been initialed by the crew chief and for those Felipe just gave a quick glance. In about fifteen minutes we were ready to climb onboard via a ladder for use when no air stairs was present.

As soon as I entered the aircraft cabin I was struck by a powerful stench. I asked Felipe, "What in the hell is that disgusting odor?" That, said Felipe, is a smell you will encounter on every flight and never grow accustomed to. It is the smell of our passengers. I said, "don't they ever take a bath?" Of course…occasionally, he said. But soap and water will not take the smell away. The smell comes from their diet. The basic staple for these people is cassava or manioc. They dry the manioc roots in the sun then pound them into flower. They eat it in everything. The smell literally oozes out of their pores. Felipe explained that as it comes from the ground, it could be quite poisonous as it contained cyanide. So the Congolese put the roots in water for three days then let them dry in the sun. While this removes the cyanide, it leaves this horrid smell.

We inspected the fire extinguishers mounted in the cabin, and the emergency window exits to insure they were properly closed. Felipe explained that in this heat, the first thing the mechanics do when they are working inside the aircraft is open the emergency escape windows looking for any relief from the equatorial heat. We checked the cargo doors to insure they were closed properly and moved on as quickly as possible to the cockpit. By the time we reached the cockpit, both Felipe and I were soaking wet with perspiration. I started to close the cockpit door, but Felipe told me to leave it open. With just the two of us onboard, we had no way of knowing what was happening in the back. Smoke, fire, fluid leaks, we needed to have some idea what was going on back there.

I sat down in the right seat and immediately was confronted with a typical military seat belt and shoulder harness configuration. I was embarrassed. I'd never seen anything like that, and Felipe had to show me how to hook them all together. A few minutes ago I was wishing my fellow instructors at Southwest School of Aviation could see me. Now I was glad they could not.

Felipe showed me where to plug in my headset and microphone. We then ran the checklist and proceeded to test some of the cockpit systems before starting the engines. In a couple of minutes we set the brakes and began the engine start procedure. It was all done by checklist. The first engine to be started was number three. I was told three was first because one of the C-54's two hydraulic pumps was powered by the number three engine and a high priority was to get hydraulic pressure to the aircraft's brakes before any additional power was brought online. Felipe told me to count the prop blades as he engaged the engine starter. It was necessary to get some oil moving through the engine before it started running on its own. I was to call "turning–three–six–nine blades." When Felipe heard me say nine blades, he would turn on the ignition and open the fuel cutoff allowing the electric boost pumps to send fuel to the engine. When the right mixture of fuel, air, and fire from the spark plugs was present, the big R-2000 engine's eighteen cylinders would come to life. This would be immediately followed by a significant belch of whitish-blue smoke. That first engine start is as vivid today as it was in 1969. Before the next engine was started, oil, fuel, and hydraulic pressures had to be monitored to insure they had all reached normal. Then the same procedure would begin with number four engine. My heart was pounding. I was euphoric. I wasn't sure how life could possibly get any better than this. I'd forgotten all about the overpowering stench only a few feet behind me.

When all four engines were running, we ran the after starting engines check list and the before taxi check list. Felipe then told me to call and request a taxi clearance. I did and N'Djili ground control responded with the most difficult to understand taxi clearance I'd ever encountered. While it was in English, his accent was so heavy I could scarcely understand what he had just said. He might as well have been speaking Lingala. I did get the runway and the taxi way. I looked over at Felipe who was grinning ear to ear. It seemed he had anticipated my inability to understand the controller. He said we're cleared to taxi. Contact the tower when ready for takeoff. He had given the runway, wind direction and speed, the temperature and the dew point as well as the altimeter setting and taxiways to use. I had gotten the wind and the temperature. And while I was aware that outside the United States the altimeter setting was given in millibars rather than in inches all the new terminology and heavy accent left me a bit overwhelmed. Any cockiness was gone, and I now realized I was a fish out of water and there would be nothing to brag about after this flight. In addition to the controller's accent, he was using the Q-Codes. I'd read about them but never been exposed to them in an operational environment. In the U.S. The controller would have given me the altimeter setting as altimeter 29.92. Here the controller said QNH 1013.2 QFE 1012.4. In the US we didn't even use QFE. We thought it was a good way to get yourself killed. All my book learning was suddenly good for nothing. I was going to have to work very hard to become familiar with all this new stuff. My brain was in overload mode.

At the run-up area Felipe spend considerable time telling me what I would have to do on the takeoff roll. He briefed me on how to advance and retard the props. He showed me the gear and flap handle and briefed me how to do what upon his command. I was already sweating blood, or at least I thought I might be.

Felipe pointed to a V-speed card he had filled out back in the training office. The card had airspeeds penciled in on blanks beside $V_1 - V_r V_2$. He told me to guard the throttles, monitor the oil pressures and manifold pressures of the engines and call the V speeds. On his command retract the gear and flaps. With my head still spinning with all those instructions, Felipe told me to contact the tower and tell them we were ready for takeoff. Then he called for the lineup and takeoff checklist. We were cleared to line up and take off. We completed the checklist and Felipe slowly advanced all four throttles. We checked that each engine was putting out takeoff power, then he gently released the brakes and we started down the runway. Those four R-2000 engines made some real noise. Everything was vibrating. I was in heaven. I checked all four engines, as Felipe was now primarily focused on looking outside to keep us lined up with the centerline of the runway. I called V_1, then V_R. As I called out V_R Felipe began pulling back on the yoke. About the time I called V_2 the aircraft broke ground. The nose wheel first, then the main gears. When we were established in a climb Felipe called "gear up." And I retracted the gear handle. My heart was pounding; my brain euphoric. The gear-in-transit lights immediately came on and the gear began its retraction cycle. There was more aerodynamic and mechanical noise. When all three were locked up in the wheel wells and the gear doors were locked closed, the gear lights went out. Felipe then called for flaps up and I retracted the flap handle. I monitored their progress on the flap position indicator. When they were at zero, I advised Felipe "flaps up." He then called for the after-takeoff checklist. I was literally in heaven. As soon as the checklist was completed, I had a few seconds to look around. Life couldn't possibly get any better than this. I was just sure of it.

We flew about twenty miles from the field in an area clear of arrival and departure traffic and started checking the systems that had been worked on. Everything worked as advertised and soon we were headed back to N'Djili airport.

When we were on five-mile final and had all the checklists completed Felipe asked me if I would like to land the plane. I said "well, I'd sure like to try." He assured me he would be right there if I needed any help and that he would handle the throttles. He dropped the gear and told me to take the controls. If Daddy could only see me now. He had always been there for me during all my screw-ups. "If Only" he could be here now.

Somehow, I managed to get it on the ground in more or less the center of the runway with only the smallest of skips. It was a good landing. I couldn't believe how lucky I'd gotten. I did put the nose wheel down a little too quickly but that wasn't serious. As the aircraft slowed with my very gentle brake applications, Felipe put his feet on the brakes and put his hand on the nose wheel steering and advised he had control of the aircraft. I started pulling up the flaps, opening the engine cowl flaps, moving the mixtures to auto lean, and running the after landing checklist. I had to be the happiest person in the world at that moment. As we entered the military ramp our crew chief martialed the aircraft into its parking spot, insuring we had plenty of wing clearance. Felipe set the parking brake and closed all the mixtures and the four Pratt & Whitney engines sputtered through idle to off. We ran the shutdown checklist and got out of the plane as soon as possible to escape the heavy, overpowering stench coming from the cabin…the same stench I'd forgotten all about just a few short minutes ago. Even the hot equatorial air bouncing off the even hotter tarmac was a relief from what was inside the cabin. We walked through the hanger and into the training department. About five minutes later we were joined by the crew who had come to collect the test flight report and get the debrief.

As soon as the debrief was over I grabbed the C-54 flight manual again and started looking up some of the many things I'd seen on the flight that I had not understood. I asked if I could take it home with me at night if I promised to bring it back each morning. Lewis said that would be fine, so I put it back on the desk and resumed working on the weight and balance course I was writing. Soon it was time to go home. I couldn't believe the day had gone so quickly. When I put my head on the pillow that night it took a while to go to sleep. My head was still filled with all the wonderful events of my first Wigmo flight.

Sudden Tragedy

The next morning I was again the first one to arrive in the training department. I turned on the lights and the air-conditioner and opened my notebook to continue writing my course. I heard the door opening and looked up. Lars Gustafsson (pseudonym), the chief helicopter pilot rushed in. Lars asked where everybody was. I told him nobody else was here yet…that I was it. He said he needed an observer could I come with him. I said sure and started to get into my flight suit. He told me we needed to take off in two or three minutes; get my headset and run to the helicopter pad. I left the training department less than a minute later running for the helicopter. His mechanics were already around it pulling engine covers and pitot tube covers off. I noticed mechanics had stopped working and were standing out on the ramp looking in the direction of the river. When I got to the helicopter pad, I learned that one of our C-46s had experienced landing gear trouble earlier this morning just after takeoff. They had been circling near the airport out over the Congo River Basin while talking to the maintenance department on the radio trying to figure out how to fix the problem. The mechanics said the crew (from Holland) could not get one of the landing gears to retract . . . that one was up but the other was not fully retracted...a very dangerous condition. The crew had tried to pull the emergency landing gear hydraulic dump valve handle but according to their radio transmission, the cable had snapped. In their last call the captain said he was going to get out of his seat and leave the co-pilot at the controls. He planned to see if he could locate where the cable had broken and somehow pull on it in at attempt get the dump valve to open. That was their last transmission. Several minutes later the control tower started receiving telephone calls from cargo companies at the port. They reported a large airplane had just crashed into the river. Boats were en route to the scene, but they were saying the airplane had gone beneath the surface. According to Lars the plane had been down close to 20 minutes now. The ground crew and Lars were shouting back and forth to each other in Swedish. I jumped in along with his crew chief and immediately the helicopter's jet engine began to crank. Within a couple of minutes we were moving toward the river.

This was only my second time in a helicopter, and I was not very relaxed. But there was no time to think about anything. As we approached the wide part of the river (the basin), we noticed a cluster of small fishing boats with more heading from the shore toward the cluster of boats. As we came overhead at what I estimated to be about 200 feet above the water's surface, we could see about three feet of the C-46's vertical stabilizer sticking up out of the water. Its lifeless rotating beacon seemingly proclaiming the fate of everyone onboard. A couple of lifeless bodies were floating face down in the water...an adult male and a small child; like some messengers from Sheol beckoning to the living. There appeared to be no sign of any survivors. The words of David, King of Israel spoken around 1000 BCE flashed through my mind as I tried to visualize the vault of death just below the water's surface. *"For the waves of death engulfed me; the torrents of destruction terrified me. The ropes of Sheol entangled me; the snares of death confronted me."*[117]

The downdraft from our French-made Aerospatiale Alouette's rotor blades was frightening some of the Congolese fishermen and they began jumping out of their boats. So now we had to try to distinguish frightened fishermen flopping around in the crocodile infested river basin from any possible survivors. Of course there were none. My adrenalin was sky high. Had it not been for that, I felt as though I could easily just turn off the switch and block this

[117] Holy Bible—Holman Christian Standard Bible - 2 Samuel 22:5-6

stream of nightmarish images from infecting my brain. Lars began to circle the accident site in increasingly wider circles until we were sure there were no survivors. The helicopter crew chief had thrown a rescue harness and cable in the baggage area as he was climbing in. We climbed to about 1000 feet and headed back to the military ramp. The trip back was surreal. When we touched down and I started to walk back toward the hanger, I realized I was completely drained of energy. As I continued to walk my strength slowly returned.

When I reached the training department, it was empty. Lewis, Felipe, and Stan had all gone up to the radio room. I headed up there as well. There was standing room only as Gus, one of the radio operators was relating the sequence of radio calls he received. In addition, reports were now coming in from the port that a man holding a little child in his arms was seen falling from the sky separately from the aircraft. This would later have serious implications. Romeo Tango said several generals were on their way here to take a helicopter ride to the site. According to him, the newspapers were already starting to call. We were all instructed to say nothing and to return to our departments.

It wasn't long before the Congolese generals in their staff cars and personal Mercedes started arriving. Of course they were too important to park in the parking lot. They drove into the hanger and waited for their MP escorts to open the door for them. Then they strutted to the main office with their "swagger sticks" tucked under their arms or used as pointing devices. To a man they wore Mobutu-style dark sun glasses. Every one of them was grossly overweight. They were truly a ridiculous site. Stan, who had been out in the hanger, came back in and said he had seen a newspaper reporter walking around asking questions and taking pictures. We decided to stay inside and lock the training department door. I resumed work on my weight and balance course.

A Spanish Surprise

Shortly before noon we got the all clear. Journalists were gone…generals all gone. I remember thinking that was logical as it was almost lunch time. As I left the training department, I heard the Alouette's turbine engine starting to crank. I looked out and saw the two Spaniards I'd previously seen working in supply getting ready to climb into the helicopter. They were wearing what was without any doubt, the most expensive scuba equipment and wet suits I'd ever seen. I remember wondering when I first met them why someone had wasted the money to bring two Spaniards who could speak only Spanish, which no one else in supply spoke, all the way from Europe just to have them sweeping and dusting and opening boxes. I now knew. They were in reality highly skilled professional divers. I later learned they had their own little work room where they kept all their tanks and compressors and specialized underwater tools and cameras. The Spanish "gofers" that I'd seen were yet another facet of Wigmo's many talents. This would be just one more of the many times I would see that with Wigmo, all things were not as they appeared. There were many illusions.

The following morning the local French language newspaper would contain a front-page headline about the crash. There was a photo showing a large crane mounted on a barge lifting the crumpled C-46 fuselage from the water to the dock. Dead bodies were everywhere. The crash would take the life of the two Dutch crew, a Congolese FAC loadmaster, and forty-two Congolese military and dependent passengers. The article was hostile toward Wigmo and questioned its safety policies. But as we were studying the article, Lewis was quick to point out that nothing ever, ever appeared in print in this country without Mobutu's approval. Lewis said the relations between Mobutu and the CIA had been growing more strained and this could be a precursor of worse things to come. I took serious note. Lewis said Mobutu came to power with the help of the CIA and he had no intention of leaving power as a result of their "help." Lewis personally believed Mobutu was about to push the CIA out of the picture.

As the wreckage was being examined, and stories from eyewitnesses on the ground were compiled, pictures of what could have been the fatal scenario begin to come together. We knew the captain had left his seat, leaving control of the airplane to the copilot, who had relatively low flight experience. When the cockpit controls were examined, the elevator trim was found all the way nose up indicating there must have been a massive shift in the center of gravity of the aircraft. The only logical explanation for this shift would be that the passengers had all moved forward. The question of why they would have done this began to take on light. The cargo door was ripped from the fuselage. It was found separately from the main fuselage. Many witnesses reported what they thought was a man holding and later dropping a child as they both fell toward the water. If, for whatever reason, the passenger had become so frightened that he tried to leave the aircraft by jumping out the door with his child in his arms, this would explain the door being ripped off and the two bodies we saw on the surface of the water. Speculation was that the captain had previously tried to apply G-force by steeply banking the aircraft, an approved practice in some aircraft, in hopes the gear would free itself and fall. If he had done this and if the passengers had panicked, they could have all rushed forward in an attempt to get away from the open door and the noise that was certainly associated with it. If this happened, most doubt the copilot would have been able to overcome the badly out-of-balance condition. What actually happened that day inside the airplane will never be known.

A Jimmy Jacks Of All Trades

Conditions slowly returned to normal in the Wigmo hanger. After taking several more C-54 flights with Felipe I started learning the C-47 with Stan. While Stan was always stiff, he was nevertheless a nice guy and could be fun.

I enjoyed flying with him. This meant I was now studying both the C-54 flight manual and the C-47. All our C-54 and C-47 aircraft were from the U.S. Air Force and came with the standard air force flight manuals. It was like I was suddenly back in the military. But this time, rather than my green pajamas type scrub suits for surgery I worked in battleship gray flight suits. Not to mention that I was getting paid a heck of a lot more.

Jimmy Joe The *Linguist*

Somehow, during learning two transport category aircraft and finishing teaching my weight and balance course, I found time to take both French and Lingala courses given in-house by Wigmo. I found the Lingala classes more useful than French, as most of the Congolese did not speak French. In addition, the moment I left the Wigmo hanger, I was in their world. Lingala was a primitive language which made word study fascinating. I learned Lingala was from the Bantu family and basically spoken in the northern part of the Congo, Congo Brazzaville, Angola, and the Central African Republic. While Swaheli was spoken in the Eastern Congo and onward toward Kenya and neighboring countries, Lingala was the native language of Mobutu, which made it the official language of the Congo, the military, and the government. The *Force Aérienne Congolaise*, or FAC used it exclusively. There was a real need to learn it quickly. As long as I was a co-pilot, I could lean on the captains who all spoke Lingala to some degree. But someday I hoped I too would be a captain and not speaking Lingala was not an option. I truly enjoyed the Lingala classes. For example, an electric fan was a "machine of the wind." A hearse was "machine of the dead." In some cases, the name for some things was the sound they made. The language was so primitive there were many modern objects for which they had no name...so they put words together to describe it and those words became the name of the object. The electric fan for example, even if you had never heard the word...you knew exactly what they were talking about.

The Demise Of The Training Department

A little learning is a dangerous thing[118]

The bad blood between Lewis and Romeo Tango spilled over onto the training department. I knew from Lewis that he planned to go back to Miami soon. Stan planned to go back to Texas soon as well. One day on a flight I asked Felipe what he thought would happen to the training department after Lewis left. He told me he figured they would close it and merge the pilots into the flight department. This way Romeo Tango would have control over all the pilots, something he didn't have now. And besides, by most accounts he was a control freak. Romeo Tango didn't like me because George Barnes had hired me and therefore, while I showed him due respect, he knew my real allegiance and loyalty were to George.

---
[118] Alexander Pope, an 18th century English poet 1688 - 1744

By the end of my third month there, I was flying several times a week and was copilot qualified on the C-54 and the C-47. My flights were always training department missions but seldom had anything to do with training. These were usually missions coming from the American Embassy or COMISH (United States Military Mission, Congo). Lewis filled out my paperwork and I was officially moved up to pilot's pay rather than dispatcher's pay. This doubled my base pay. I kept the same local living allowance. It was clear to me that Lewis was getting me set up before his departure. I was grateful for his kindness and told him so. While I didn't call home this time about my raise, I did take great pride in my letter. I knew Karen would be relieved and happy but I also knew my father would be in heaven. She always shared my letters with him. My high school years had been a strain on him. I was glad he could now hold his head high when people asked about me.

As I was busy flying and learning the C-54 and C-47, the conditions in Cambodia continued to spiral downward. Sihanouk, worn down by years of overwork and overwhelmed by the ever-increasing complexities of governing his tiny country in the midst of a very hot war in neighboring Vietnam and an ever increasing worldwide cold war, was failing to govern. General Lon Nol and many others were becoming increasing alarmed at the presence of Viet Cong troops operating within Cambodia's borders. Cambodian troops were coming under fire more frequently by the Khmer Rouge forces. Provencial governors were complaining to the central government in Phnom Penh, asking them to do something about the foreign troops and the Khmer Rouge attacks. The frustration of high-ranking conservative officials in Sihanouk's government, including his own cousin Prince Sisowath Sirik Matak was mounting. The situation inside the government became very tense. [119]

An Independence Day *Gift*

Congolese Independence Day was celebrated on 30 June. We had all been advised to stay off the street and out of public places and keep whatever personal protection we relied upon close at hand. All businesses were closed and Wigmo had no flights.

I awoke on the morning of 30 June to find the Wigmo mechanics all in one apartment with the door open. They were huddled around the only decent short-wave radio receiver in the compound. They were flipping back and forth between BBC and VOA. All gave news at the top of the hour. I soon learned that the Christian, pro-western, well-educated Congolese politician Moise Tshombe was dead. He was well respected in his province of Katanga. Elsewhere in the Congo he was widely viewed as the person responsible for the death of Patrice Lumumba.

Tshombe had, shortly after Congolese independence in 1960, declared Katanga province independent and seceded from the Congo. This put him at the heart of a long battle against the government in Kinshasa. Tshombe had the full backing of Belgium and the support of the United States. This put

---

[119] A History of Cambodia (second edition) - David P. Chandler

Belgium and the United States at odds with the United Nations. Tshombe had relied heavily on white mercenaries on more than one occasion. The best known and most controversial of these mercenaries was Thomas Michael (Mad Mike) Hoare. Finally, after a drawn-out conflict, Katanga was defeated and forced back into being part of the Congo. Tshombe fled the country and lived in exile in Spain.

A few months later, he was called back to the Congo to serve as prime minister in a coalition government. But only a few months after that, President Joseph Kasavubu sacked him. Not long after that, Mobutu staged another coup and sacked Kasavubu. Mobutu then filed charges of treason against Tshombe. Not waiting around to see what would happen next, Tshombe once again fled the Congo and returned to Spain. In 1967, while he was still living in Spain, the Congolese government (Mobutu) sentenced Tshombe to death in absentia.

In June of 1967 while on a chartered flight from Ibiza Spain to the Spanish resort island of Mallorca, Tshombe's plane was hijacked and he was kidnapped and brought to Algeria where he was imprisoned. He was later allowed house arrest. While under house arrest, he mysteriously died of a "heart attack" on 29 June 1969, on the eve of Congolese independence. A nice gift to President Mobutu. The Congolese government had unsuccessfully tried to extradite him from Algeria to the Congo where he was to be executed for supposedly murdering a political rival, Patrice Lumumba. His "heart attack" saved Mobutu the trouble of an execution. While his true cause of death was never confirmed, everybody knew he was murdered by agents of Mobutu.

Word on the street years later in Kinshasa was that his pilot had taken a payoff to divert the flight to Algeria and that Tshombe's death was an Independence Day gift. This of course remains unverifiable. One source identifies the two British pilots as conspirators. However they were later released by the Algerian government. Other sources say Francois Bodenan (age 33), a French national, with a criminal record, hijacked Tshombe's flight. Still another account says the famous French mercenary Bob Denard attempted to break Tshombe, his ex-employer, out of prison (or house arrest) in Algeria. Denard failed and lost six or seven mercenaries in the attempt but escaped safely. Again, all unverifiable.

Via radio transmissions from other Wigmo housing units around town we learned the streets were filled with military parades and political party marches. (MPR was the country's sole political party). But this Independence celebration was different. This time they were not just celebrating their country's independence, but the death of Moise Tshombe as well. All agreed it was a good time to stay off the streets. It was Monday and some had been drinking and celebrating since Friday night. The long-held hostility toward the white race that had abused and suppressed them for over eighty years was never far from erupting into dangerous, unpredictable savage violence. Their violent hatred was incapable of differentiating between a white American missionary doctor in the country providing free medical care from a former Belgian colonial oppressor. All white people, men, women, even children were evil and guilty. Any Caucasian who failed to realize this harsh fact was literally playing with death. I stayed in the compound and studied my flight manuals.

My First VIP Flight

A few days later a telex message arrived from the Ministry of Defense requesting a VIP flight for a delegation from the Ministry of Foreign Affairs. The government was hosting a group of Europeans who had been invited by President Mobutu himself to see some of the Congo's most breathtaking sights. They were all in the eastern Congo.

The FAC had an unusual aircraft in its fleet. This was one of the few that was not "on loan" from the United States. This was an old embassy-configured DC-3 (same as C-47 but in VIP configuration). This airplane had been a gift from President Kennedy to President Mobutu. It was horrible-looking both inside and out from neglect. But it was nevertheless a source of pride for the Congolese government. By all accounts, it had been many years since President Mobutu had flown in the plane. Now, anytime he wanted to go anywhere he just commandeered an Air Congo airplane. Air Congo complained bitterly that they were never compensated for any of his presidential missions. But for sure their complaints were not loud enough to reach Mobutu's palace.

This special DC-3 was always flown by the training department. Its registration or tail number bore the initials of President Mobutu, 9T-JDM for Joseph-Desire Mobutu. I'd been in it a couple of times and even helped with a periodic engine run-up and systems check. Now I was going to get a chance to fly it. I was going to fly a piece of history. Lewis assigned the flight to Stan and me. We would leave the following morning. Stan had flown it on several occasions and was familiar with the differences between this VIP configuration and our C-47 military configuration.

But more interesting than getting to fly a piece of history was our destinations. Our passengers were scheduled to see Mount Nyiragongo, a world-famous volcano located in the eastern Congo about 20 miles north of the city of Goma. Goma was almost 1000 miles from Kinshasa and just on the Congo's eastern border with Uganda and Rwanda. We would be staying in the area for several days and this would also give us an opportunity to see Virunga National Park, famous for its wildlife, especially its Gorilla population. We would also see Mai ya Moto, famous for its hot springs and wildlife.

I spent the day flight planning and discussing fuel stop options and alternate airport options. Wigmo did not have station agents in all the airports in the Congo. When we went to an airport where we had no station agent, we had to use the FAC. They were notoriously unreliable. Sometimes they didn't even show up. When they did, sometimes we did not find the fuel they were supposed to have. Often it had been sold on the open market to civilians to run their cars. The C-47 had a range of 1600 miles but in the Congo with usable airports few and far between, it was never wise to allow fuel reserves get anywhere near minimum by flying close to maximum range.

A Look At One Of The Congo's Darkest Moments
Stanleyville

Because the government would be embarrassed if our passengers got a glimpse of the typical FAC incompetence we planned a fuel stop in Kisangani or K-7 where we had a Wigmo station agent. Kisangani was the former Stanleyville; scene of the famous Belgium/U.S, Air Force operation *Dragon Rouge* on 23 November 1964. The operation was led by strafing Wigmo B-26s, Invader fighter-bombers piloted by Cuban-Americans, followed by U.S. Air Force C-130s loaded with Belgium commandos. The purpose was to free a large group of international hostages being held by Simba rebels. The Wigmo B-26s softened up the drop and landing zone. The Belgium para-commandos secured the airport in less than 30 minutes. Not all the hostages made it out alive. This event fostered the famous book "111 Days in Stanleyville" which described the experiences of the hostages during captivity and rescue. I learned virtually within my first hours with Wigmo that we were not to recite history to outsiders.

The refueling stop would not only give us fuel but would provide our passengers a chance to get off and stretch. I was sure that some of our VIP passengers would not want to visit the onboard toilet (honey-bucket) and would prefer to wait till we landed and go inside the terminal. Boy were they going to be in for a surprise. Most of those airport restrooms hadn't been cleaned since independence. Most had had no running water for years. Our VIP passengers would certainly be heading for the bushes or back to the plane with a newly acquired appreciation of our "blue-water" chemical toilet affectionately referred to as "the honey-bucket." Watching all this come down was going to be as much fun as visiting the volcano.

Dispatch notified the passenger contact of the time they would have to be at the Wigmo hanger for us to be able to make the entire day's mission and still land in Goma before dark. The landing lights, as often as not, did not work and there were no other alternative airports. I went home and packed for my first Congo overnight flight. Of course I over packed.

My First Real Mission—The Big Day

Stan had offered to stop by and pick me up. I was ready and out front by 4:45am. Stan was on time. I doubt he had ever been late for anything in his life. Stan had insisted we not wear our flight suits but rather white shirts and dark pants. What a pain with oil dripping from all these large piston engines. Even my flight suits had oil spots. He just never could shake his commuter airline background. I only had three white shirts so I could see I'd be spending my beer drinking time washing uniform shirts. Oh well. I considered myself the luckiest guy in the world and there was no way I was going to complain.

Preflight went well. Fuel tanks were full; oil tanks full; weather was checked as best we could check it. We were ready by 6:00 am. Just after 6:00 am our passengers rolled up in a Force Aérienne Congolaise bus. They were excited and ready. We believed our passengers were part of a government effort to bring European tourists to the Congo. I silently wondered how they were going to do this with half the hotels in the Congo having no water and half the country thought they were still at war. I owed my job to the latter half.

By 6:30 am we taxied out from the military ramp and five minutes later we were airborne. Stan and I settled back for a nice long, hopefully thunderstorm-free flight. Our Congolese loadmaster oversaw taking care of our passengers but apparently somebody forgot to tell him. Fifteen minutes after takeoff he was back on the flight deck asleep at the radio operator's console. Stan & I agreed that it wasn't our problem.

While the Wigmo aircraft were the most complex aircraft I'd ever flown, they were far from being complicated. That simplicity contributed to their success during WWII. It allowed the military to train inexperienced pilots to become reasonably proficient in a minimum time. This same simplicity combined with the Congo's low air traffic volume allowed me to spend most of our flight time looking out the window. Long ago I had developed the habit of a good cockpit instrument scan. So except for scanning the instruments every minute or so, I had little else to do but look out the window. And what I saw was amazing.

The Congo's Magnificent Rainforest

Regardless of all the negative impressions about the place that I'd rapidly acquired since arriving, it was impossible to witness the Congo's majestic beauty and not be impressed. I had never seen anything like it. Within minutes of our departure from Kinshasa, the reddish-brown soil exposed by small subsistence farming plots essentially disappeared. It was replaced by dense jungle…the Congo rainforest; like an enormous lush carpet of green frequently embellished with silver and black traces of rivers and streams. It had to be a hunter and fishermen's paradise. What one had to remember when having such thoughts was that humans were not the top of the food chain down there.

These trees were tall…really tall. The jungle was covered by a green canopy so dense you could see practically nothing of the ground; only hundreds of miles of lush green. The base of the canopy was said to be around 100 to 130 feet above the ground. Occasionally it was possible to get a glimpse of rivers and streams wandering through these dense forests. The streams and rivers were fed by rainfall averaging around seventy inches per year. More than double that of Hamilton County.

Stan Turns Car Salesman

After we'd been in cruise for a while Stan asked me what I was going to do for a car. I told him I hadn't given that much thought yet, as Karen and Jason would not be here for another couple of months. He then asked me how I liked his car. It was a 1968 Volkswagen 1600 Variant station wagon. It was still almost like new. Stan had only driven it to the airport and back plus twice weekly shopping. I dismissed his tactful sales pitch by saying I hadn't saved enough money to buy a car yet, that I'd been sending everything home to get some reserves built up. Stan replied that that was not a problem as Wigmo had a six-month car purchase program where they would lend you the money for a reasonable car purchase and you could repay the interest free loan via six monthly salary deductions. Suddenly the whole car thing started to look more promising. I knew the two-bedroom apartment I'd been waiting for would soon be coming up and I also knew it was not serviced by the Wigmo crew bus. The regular Wigmo pilots all had cars. Many believed the training department would soon be history. I told him I'd like to take a better look at the car when we got back to K-1.

The time flew by and soon we were trying to contact Kisangani tower. We had been making our regular position reports to K-1 via our military HF SSB radio. During one of the calls to Kinshasa call sign, King-1, Kisangani, call sign, King 7, who had been monitoring the frequency, came up and advised he had everything set up for a quick turnaround. Wigmo's station agent was a Swede named George. While he drank a lot, he was nevertheless quite efficient and with his crew of four Congolese, could have an aircraft turned around and airborne in less than thirty minutes. That was a considerable feat considering there was no fuel truck in King 7. Like everything else in the country, the fuel truck had fallen victim to the ravages of war combined with the continuing erosion of neglect.

About twenty minutes out of King 7, I made a radio call to Kisangani tower. That was standard procedure in order to get the weather and runway information plus any other air traffic information. Stan laughed saying not to bother. The control tower's radio only had a range of about 25 miles. He advised me instead to begin making all stations calls giving our position and altitude and that the tower would hear us. When we got close enough, we would be able to hear him. But in the meantime, other aircraft in the area would know our position and exchange info with us. If they were departing, we could even get the airport conditions from them.

On my second blind all-stations call, a departing Air Congo flight responded. He was heading toward Goma so he would not be a traffic factor. He did tell us the wind was calm and the visibility greater than 20 kilometers. Stan and I decided we would plan to enter the airport traffic pattern on a right base for runway 13 if there was no conflicting traffic. We began our decent from 9000 feet at what we estimated to be about 25 miles from the airport based on our tactical VFR aeronautical charts. The airport's VOR and DME navigation aids only worked on occasion and today was apparently not one of those occasions. Most airports in the Congo had no navigation aids at all, so navigating visually using tactical VFR charts was a skill that had to be highly developed. Because the weather was good, we soon had the airport in sight and adjusted our flight path to intercept the final approach course about four miles from the touchdown point. Nonetheless, I couldn't help but wonder what the approach would have been like with a 500 foot overcast ceiling and visibility less than one mile. In the States, you would just fly your instruments. Here, while we had all the onboard instruments, the on-ground transmitters they listened to were inoperative. In the States, flying "by the seat of your pants" was strongly discouraged and labeled unprofessional. Here it was a valued art to be cultivated.

From Rainforest Beauty To Massacre Reminders

As we rolled out on final approach, I noticed the runway was full of potholes. What in the hell is all that I asked Stan? To which Stan replied "Russian and Chinese calling cards…mortar rounds." I was amazed. They were all along the runway. I was thankful for the wide tires the C-47/DC-3 had. They rolled easily over mortar holes. The Fokker F27 Friendship used by Air Congo had to be more careful. Those holes were wide and deep enough to snap off an unlucky landing gear. And God Forbid the government would patch them.

We were cleared to land by Kisangani tower. The runway was long, and we easily made the turnoff leading to the ramp without having to backtrack on the runway. The airport had no parallel taxiways. I supposed with the low traffic volume they really would not have been cost effective to build or maintain. And then I returned to reality. Nothing in the Congo was maintained. I smiled to myself as I acknowledged the tower's clearance to taxi to the ramp.

Immediately the noise from the cabin increased. Obviously they were excited and ready to stretch their legs. I suspected some had been stretching their bladders as well. I couldn't wait to see how that played out. They had been back there almost five hours.

As we turned onto the ramp, I noticed all the buildings, were decorated with pockmarks as well. These could have been calling cards from any number of groups. The Simbas, United Nations forces, the Belgiums, various mercenary units, or even Wigmo's T-28 Trojans or B-26 Marauders.

Wigmo Efficiency

I soon spotted a large red-headed man who was martialing us into a parking spot where 55-gallon (200 liter) fuel drums were waiting on two trailers. One for each side of the aircraft. I could see a hand pump like those used back in Hamilton County by farm tractors with each group of drums. The signature Wigmo military jeep with the infamous and feared Makasi emblem on the side left no doubt the large red-headed man was our station agent. George was all set to give us a quick turn. I would learn later that his Wigmo team could turn an airplane in half the time the Air Congo ground crews required. Their crews were all Congolese. George's team was all Congolese as well. He was the only white face on the ramp. But George had carefully selected his team and they were paid about twice what Air Congo ground crew members made. I later learned George set time limits for fueling each type of aircraft. Some required more fuel. Some required the crew to climb out on the wing from inside the aircraft. These factors all went into George's turnaround time calculations. If they beat George's time, they got a bonus and a cold Primus beer from the little café in the terminal. George had no problem drinking with his Congolese ground crew. George had no problem drinking with anybody. George had no problem drinking on the job. Air Congo crews got nothing. The word was their pay was often two or three months late. George paid in cash every two weeks. George sometimes allowed them to put their family on one of the military flights. So to say George's guys were motivated would not be an embellishment.

Stan carefully explained to our passengers as they were debarking that they must be back at the airplane in fifteen minutes. He explained the necessity of arriving in Goma before sunset. They all scurried off to the terminal just as I had predicted. I could tell by the way some were walking that a restroom call was somewhere between a high priority and critical. I regretted my duties would not allow me to accompany them. Surely it would have been a memorable occasion. But my consolation lay in the fact that I was one hundred percent sure some if not most would not use the so-called restrooms in the terminal and therefore, I could watch the rest of the story unfold. As a matter of fact, I'd already picked out a particularly haughty looking lady that I was certain would soon be back to visit the honey-bucket. By the time they got back to the plane the cabin temperature, amplified by the aluminum fuselage would probably have climbed to somewhere around 110 degrees Fahrenheit. Even though George's crew would have emptied and refilled the honey-bucket with blue-water, the smell inside the tiny closet would make a Hamilton County buzzard puke…worse than being downwind of Seth Moore's rendering plant in August. I loved my new job.

I carefully watched the ground crew fuel the aircraft. When they had finished, I climbed up on the wing and checked the fuel caps to insure they were on tight. I also popped open the engine oil inspection/service access panels and checked each engine oil level and afterword secured its cap. Once my on-the-wing work was done, I went back to the cockpit to put away the last leg's flight plan and flight log. They went into a special place in my flight bag. I would hand them all into dispatch when we returned to K-1. I put the next leg's flight plan on my clipboard, filled out the aircraft's log book, and then called the tower to be sure they had our flight plan. While we were military and technically not required to file anything with them, most of us agreed that if anything went wrong and we ever went missing, we wanted as many people as possible to know about it. But, we knew our only hope would come from Wigmo aircraft and crews. Certainly not from FAC.

As soon as my cockpit chores were done, it was just about time to start engines. But, I wanted to get back to the cabin and see if anything interesting was happening. As soon as I opened the cockpit door leading to the cabin, the whisperings of my evil twin were confirmed. There was a line waiting to get to the honey-bucket. The ladies were clutching their discreet little bags which everyone knew contained their toilet paper. By this time I noticed some of the male passengers had figured out the little mini-drama playing out and were tastefully enjoying the situation along with me. Stan asked in a whispered tone if I thought we should go ahead and start the engines or give them a few more minutes to work through this little emergency. We both knew as soon as the DC-3 started to taxi it would be impossible to stand or walk much less make any serious erodes into the problem at hand. I could just visualize them bouncing off the walls of the tiny little enclosure. We decided to give them a few more minutes. I was pretty sure more than one of them was wishing they were back in Europe right now.

Finally all our passengers found relief and we were soon back in the air. We took off on Runway 13 again as that was virtually a straight-out departure direct toward our destination Goma. Stan had planned to circle the volcano Mount Nyiragongo for the passengers (and ourselves) if we arrived in time. Stan had made this trip several times and from his description, I could hardly wait to see it. I had my cheap little Montgomery Ward video camera in my flight bag and was hoping to get some priceless super 8 video footage before we landed. I had my Petri 35mm purchased from the Navy Exchange in San Diego back in 1960 in my bag as well. I was all set.

This flight segment was much shorter. The distance was only about 300 miles and our flight time was just at two hours. A full thirty minutes before we arrived Stan was pointing to something that to me looked like a tall white cloud. But Stan told me it was the steam rising from the volcano that was causing the cloud. As we came closer, I could see the cone. The lava had piled up around the hole it blew in the earth when it first erupted until it now formed a mountain with a peak at almost 11,500 feet above sea level. I could see the Virunga Mountain Range ahead starting to slope upward. Stan gently moved the props forward followed by the throttles as we were soon going to need to be higher than our present 9000 feet. We would be taking the passengers above the 10,000 feet normally considered to be the highest level for sustained flight without the use of oxygen. But not for long so it would pose no health threat. Stan and I slipped on our oxygen masks as we climbed through 10,000 feet. We leveled at 12,500 feet. The air was now noticeably cooler. Stan told me to get my cameras out and that he would circle the crater keeping it on my side for the first circle. I couldn't imagine life getting any better than this.

As we neared the rim of the crater, I could see the reddish-orange glow of the lava lake. Sporadically you could see the lava stir as a minor upsurge released gas and lava into the air. Occasionally I could get a whiff of the sulfur smell coming from the crater. I could also see a scar going down the side of the mountain indicating the lava's path as it had run down the mountainside toward Goma whenever there was a serious eruption. I slid my cockpit window to the fully open position and was pointing my camera out the window. I didn't dare stick it out into the slipstream, but I had it about as far out as I could without making slipstream contact. I was getting awesome pictures. I'd gone through a roll of 36 exposure 35mm film by the time we finished our first orbit. Stan, who had done this several times offered to shoot my super 8 videos during the orbit to the left. We could hear the passengers in the back. They were excited. I was pretty sure most had completely forgotten about their honey-bucket experience and were overcome as was I with the sheer splendor and majesty of the lake of lava below us.

After the orbit to the left we pointed toward Goma and began our descent. We already had the airport in sight, but we were so high that we had to go out over Lake Kivu and circle to make our descent for landing without hurting the passenger's ears. We were sure they would not mind; Lake Kivu was a spectacular sight. This was truly a highland lake; its surface was 4,800 feet above sea level. The lake was breathtakingly beautiful. I would learn later that night while dining with the Wigmo station agent just how breathtaking.

We made a couple of wide orbits out over the lake, then made a straight-in approach for Runway 36. This was my first landing at a high-altitude airport. I kept thinking we were coming in too hot as the ground was just flying past. But our airspeed was right on the money, perfectly pegged on approach speed. However, while our indicated airspeed was correct, our true airspeed was much higher than indicated. I'd read about this, but this was my first time to experience it. I knew Stan was correct. We fly indicated airspeed and anticipate a high groundspeed at touchdown. The landing went fine. Stan mentioned to me as we were touching down that he was going to have to be very careful with the brake applications in order to keep from overheating them. He did a great job and I was taking careful notice.

The airport was just more reddish-brown dirt and a couple of old stucco buildings pockmarked by bullets. Whoever had been to Kisangani must have been here too.

As soon as the passengers drove away in the van sent by the hotel, Stan and I did a post-flight inspection, finished all the paperwork, secured the airplane, and hopped in the Wigmo jeep with Claus, the German station agent. I stopped to take a picture of the Wigmo water buffalo "Makasi" on the side. In Swahili, Makasi means tough, strong, mean, or not to be messed with.

A Goma Sunset

Before going to the Wigmo safe-house to clean up, Claus asked us if we would like to go watch the sunset and see the sky glow from Mount Nyiragongo. Of course, the answer was a unanimous yes. For some reason Stan had not seen that yet either.

The Wigmo jeep negotiated the steep, pothole-and-large-rock-infested road with ease and soon we were perched atop a little bluff overlooking the city of Goma with Nyiragongo directly in front of us. I got out and sat on the jeep's flat front fender. The sky soon took on a purplish-orange glow and the lights of Goma (what few electric ones there were) started to glow. The kerosene or *pitolo* lights as they are called in Lingala added a soft flicker. It was truly beautiful. I uttered a barely audible "thank you Jesus."

Lake Kivu's "Breathtaking" Beauty

Later that evening Stan and I had dinner with Claus at Goma's best restaurant. It was run by colonial era Belgiums. For whatever reason, the Belgium couple had decided not to leave when all the other Belgiums left with basically the clothes on their backs as the country was exploding from overnight independence. I later learned the few that stayed did so for material reasons, not wanting to lose everything they'd worked so hard to accumulate. I mused that many who made that decision lost not only their property, but their lives as well.

During the meal, which was surprising good for the Congo, I learned that Lake Kivu, at times, had a deadly layer of methane and carbon dioxide hovering over the surface of the water. This was due to the lake water's interaction with a volcano. Claus had been stationed in Goma for several years and had learned from other Europeans living there that Lake Kivu was an exploding lake, one of three in the world. Scientists believe there is evidence of the lake in times long past, having exploded before. They speculate that should this happen again, the methane which normally lies in high concentrations at the bottom of the lake could be released from the water by heat from the volcanic activity. If it ever ignited, an immediate release of carbon dioxide could suffocate everyone nearby. None of this deterred the local fishermen. They were poor and needed their jobs on the large fishing boats. The boats were mostly owned by Greeks who, like the hand full of Belgiums, had stayed on after independence.

After our meal, which wasn't too bad at all, we went back to the Wigmo safehouse and turned in for the night. The air was cool and unlike my apartment in Kinshasa, the bed came with a blanket. I slept well.

Morning Coffee And A Ride In The Park

(Virunga National Park)

The FAC general in charge of the mission in this area had provided a bus large enough to allow Stan and I to accompany the passengers to visit Mai ya Moto. Mai ya Moto means hot water in Lingala and several other local languages. I was soon to learn just how hot.

Claus took us in the Wigmo jeep to the hotel where the passengers were staying. We had breakfast on the outside veranda in the chilly morning air. I was surprised to see such a nice hotel in the Congo. Claus advised it was the best in the entire country at that time. When the early morning clouds began to lift, we could see Mt. Nyiragongo in the background. Not as spectacular as last night but still a majestic view. The coffee we were drinking came from that area. I was told the high elevation and the volcanic soil created ideal conditions for coffee growing. Perhaps it was the coffee combined with the early morning chilled air and the view of Nyiragongo, but it remains today one of the most pleasurable coffee experiences I've had.

Soon the bus arrived, and we started piling onboard for the roughly two hour drive over Congolese highway N2 to Mai ya Moto.

Our route paralleled the Rwandan border on our right for a while. On our left we passed the base of Mount Nyiragongo. There were lakes and streams everywhere. The lakes mostly appeared to be shallow. There were countless impala, antelopes of various types, even some lions. As we moved past the lakes, we saw jabirus, a large stork-looking bird, feeding in the shallows. Their bodies were black and white and their neck and head had orange bands. The bus driver stopped beside the road when we passed the lions. At one point we saw a group of hippos wallowing in the mud. They were huge and the driver told us they could be quite dangerous.

My Stroll In The Park Lands Me In Hot Water

A bit later we arrived at Mai ya Moto. We all got out clutching our cameras. We saw more Hippos and more species of stork-type birds. Some were pink. We made our way down a trail toward a small stream. We could see steam coming from tiny openings in the surface of the ground. I moved away from the group in order to get a better picture of the little holes with the steam coming out. Stan came with me. I found what was certainly a great photo opportunity. But as I took my last step before kneeling to get a good angle, the ground beneath my foot caved in. It had a hard crust on the top and looked perfectly normal. But it was not. Underneath the hard crust was boiling hot mud. I had no idea. As my foot suddenly plunged into the hot mud, which stuck to my foot like wet plaster, I felt a terrible pain all over my foot. I jumped back and immediately began to remove my shoe and sock. When I jerked my sock off, I saw my skin come with it. I was literally being cooked. I fell to the ground. Stan who was now by my side still had a plastic water bottle in his hand. From my Navy medic training I knew I had to cool the surface of my skin or it would continue to "cook." I poured his cold water on my foot. That seemed to produce even more pain. By this time the bus driver was there, and he ran for more cold water. Soon we had all the mud off my foot but the pain I was experiencing was indescribable. For whatever reason, Stan had decided he would grab my super 8 movie camera and document the event. I somehow managed to wave to the camera. I took my knife and cut the bottom of my tee-shirt off to make a bandage. I carefully wrapped my foot and hobbled back to the bus. I hurt like hell but was not going to let my misstep spoil the trip for the rest of the group. I sat in the bus with my foot throbbing for what seemed hours until the rest of the group returned to the bus. Most didn't know anything had happened.

The next item on the agenda was lunch at a little restaurant with a spectacular view. It was primitive but the view was great. I was ready for a Simba beer. The climate here was excellent for growing vegetables so we were treated to artichokes and leeks and strawberries for dessert. All from small local farms. Somehow, despite my pain, I managed to enjoy the meal. We then all piled back in the bus for some more wildlife viewing.

Not far from the restaurant we saw a herd of water buffalo (Makasi), more hippo, and a herd of zebra. Obviously, the driver knew where these park residents hung out. They made great photo opportunities. As we moved along, the driver quickly brought the bus to a slow crawl. There on our right was a small herd of elephants. There were even several young ones in the herd. The male leader was huge. I had no idea they could get that large. His tusks reached almost to the ground. This was my first time to see an elephant in the wild. It was an unforgettable moment.

Mountain Gorillas

By this time it was midafternoon. The driver headed toward the highlight of the trip…the mountain gorillas. My foot was throbbing, and I could tell I was developing a low-grade fever. One of the passengers, a lady with a huge handbag, had a bottle of aspirin in with all her other stuff. I promised myself I'd never again think anything sarcastic about ladies with large handbags. The aspirin made a small dent in my pain but not near what I needed. I knew as soon as we got back to Goma, we had an aircraft first aid box onboard the airplane. I just had to hang on till we made it back. The driver drove around for about twenty minutes and we had spotted nothing. He admitted that sometimes he couldn't find them. But just as it was nearing the time to head back toward Goma, he spotted a group moving through the bushes. We were so incredibly lucky. There was a clearing in the forest, and they came in perfect view. We got to see several adult females and babies. There was a large male, but he never came completely out into the clearing. But still it was a fantastic opportunity. Everybody was well pleased with our sighting. After that the driver headed back to Goma. The roads became unsafe after dark as roaming bands of well-armed bandits preyed on whomever was crazy enough to travel after dark. We were certain it wasn't going to be us.

We arrived back at the hotel just before dark. Claus was already there waiting. As soon as he saw my foot, we headed to the airport to get into the aircraft's first aid kit. When we arrived, it was already dark, but Claus shined the jeep's lights on the door and Stan went onboard and reemerged with the bright red metal kit. We decided we would wait till we got back to the safe-house before opening the kit and treating my foot.

At the safe-house we irrigated my horrible looking raw foot then applied antibiotic burn ointment and this time used a sterile compress to wrap my foot. I searched the medication list and found a suitable pill to help with my pain. Washed the pills down with more Simba and climbed on the bed. Stan and Claus were going back to the hotel to eat and would bring me back some food. I was soon deep asleep. The next thing I knew, they were beside my bed with my meal. It was so hard to wake up, but I knew I needed to eat.

Mercifully the schedule had us in Goma sightseeing for one more day. I spent that time in bed. The burn had left my energy level completely drained. Claus said he was scheduled to get a flight from King 1 the next day and they could send a relief pilot if I wanted. But there was no way short of being in a body bag I would allow that to happen. Stan wanted to call for a relief pilot, but we agreed after reconsidering the facts that Romeo Tango would never forget this little misstep and at this time it was best for me to just hang on. The DC-3 was a simple and forgiving aircraft and Stan could easily manage with me running on something less than all my cylinders. So no call went back to King 1 for a relief pilot.

The next day Stan went back out sightseeing in the park with the group. Claus went to the airport to meet his K1 and K7 flights, and I lay in bed trying to regain my strength. The terrible pain was now manageable as long as I continued to take the pain pills. But for sure it was improving.

Clause had instructed the houseboy to prepare dinner there in the house that night. Claus had managed to teach him well. Besides that, he had spent several years working for a Belgium family. By dinner time, the table was set, and a good-looking meal was waiting for us. I was impressed.

Back To King 1 And More Hot Water

The next morning we headed to the airport at the very civilized hour of 8:30am. King 1 had runway lights that always worked (well almost always) and a VOR navigation aid as well as an NDB. They were usually working because of all the international flights that arrived each week. Our passengers were on time and in high spirits and soon the presidential DC-3 was climbing out of Goma en route to Kisangani (King 7) for another quick fuel stop then on to King 1. Even in my pain, I found time to muse about how our passengers may have acquired some additional appreciation for our lowly honey bucket.

While en enroute back to King 7 and King 1 Stan and I strategized about how I might manage to keep my foot injury from being noticed. But after a few futile sounding plans, we agreed there was no feasible way to conceal it. The best thing to do was hobble off the plane and get out of there in as short a time as possible offering the minimum of explanations. It was a given Romeo Tango and Gold Finger would find out.

Upon arrival back in Kinshasa, we said our goodbyes to our passengers and followed our plan. Stan took all flight documents into dispatch for me. I waited in the car. We were soon out of there and I was soon home. Stan had agreed to come by the following morning and take me to the Presidential Compound where our medical clinic was. I had a couple of additional pain pills with me to help me make it through the night. I noticed I was requiring less medication to control the pain though. This was good.

Cité de l'OUA & A "CIA" Doctor

Stan was waiting outside at the appointed time. I hopped in and off we went. We drove through the city of Kinshasa headed away from the city's central district on the road to Matadi. Soon I saw huge gates. We drove up to the guarded gates. The soldiers guarding the gates snapped to attention and the gates opened immediately. I had not realized it, but Stan's car had diplomatic license plates. All Wigmo employee cars got them. There was a sign that read Cité de l'OUA (OAU village). It was without any doubt the nicest place I'd seen in the Congo. Stan said it was only about two years old and was built when Kinshasa hosted the Organization of African Unity (Organization de l'Unité Africaine in French). Since then it was where visiting foreign dignitaries stayed. It also happened to house President Mobutu's personal doctor and his medical clinic. Stan said it was state of the art.

I'd heard of Mobutu's doctor soon after arriving in the Congo. He was reputed to be working for the CIA. But then everybody said the same thing about us. So what did that mean? I didn't really give all those tales a lot of thought. My later observations led me to believe he didn't really work for them as much as he enjoyed the reputation. I soon learned the CIA would use anyone with access to information they viewed as potentially useful. I believe this was the case with the doctor.

Mobutu's doctor's name was William "Bill" Clark (pseudonym). His medical clinic was one of the first buildings we came to after entering the compound.

When we walked in, the nurses were all American. They asked for my Wigmo ID card. I didn't have mine yet, but I'd been given a temporary paper which I carried. The official ID cards came from the military high command and were signed by General Louis Bobozo, the ANC's chief of staff. The older guys had ID cards signed by Mobutu himself. These were more than regular company ID cards. The guys like to call them "get out of jail cards." The cards carried wording in both French and Lingala which left absolutely no doubt that you were not be detained or hindered in any way and as a matter of fact the police and military were to provide all assistance in expediting our movement. How cool was that! The Wigmo guys had told me that when the police stopped you at a roadblock and they saw that card, their hands started shaking and they started saluting. I wished I had had mine on my first night in country when that SOB jabbed me in the ribs with his FN-49.

There was almost nobody waiting to see the doctor. The nurses took me into a treatment room and removed the dressing I'd put on early that morning. I thought my foot looked pretty good all things considered. There was no visible trace of infection thanks to my numerous painful applications of the antibiotic ointment. But it was still a long way from being healed.

As soon as the nurses had finished cleaning the burn site, Dr. Clark walked in. He was a man with a cold, unfriendly demeanor. I assumed he didn't like my taking up his valuable time. I would later learn he projected this attitude with almost everyone. He asked me what happened. When I told him he shook his head in disapproval again. Like how could I have been so stupid? I must confess I'd had the same thought but I sure as heck didn't need to be hearing it from him right about then.

Clark had come to the Congo in 1960 as a private physician just as the country was escaping from more than seventy-five years of brutal Belgium oppression. By most accounts, Clark had little problem abandoning what ecclesiastical callings he may have had in favor of being in the epicenter of power emanating from Mobutu. He was soon the personal physician of the president as well as the chief surgeon for the Congolese Army (ANC). The CIA lost no time pandering to his feelings of self-worth and soon was influencing Mobutu via Clark in areas strategic to the U.S. Cold war efforts playing out in the region with China and The Soviet Union.

He had the bedside manner and temperament of one of the crocodiles I'd seen a couple of days ago in Virunga National Park. He seemed oblivious to the fact that thousands if not millions of sensitive nerve endings were exposed in the area of my burn. He reapplied an ointment like the one we had in our emergency kit on the airplane, gave me a couple of more tubes, a prescription for some oral antibiotics, a prescription for some mild pain pills, and told me to come back in two weeks. He told me I should not go back to work for a week.

I walked out of the Presidential Clinic in more pain than when I'd walked in. But at least I was relatively assured I would not get an infection, which was my primary concern after pain management.

As we approached the car, Stan asked if I'd given the idea of buying his car any more thought. I said that as a matter of fact I had and asked how much money he would have to have. I knew he had paid for it new and I had figured what I'd be willing to give him for it. Stan replied he'd take $1200 if we did the paperwork now and I'd let him drive it till he left, which he for the first time told me would be in just four weeks. I asked if he would help me with all the paperwork and take me to the Wigmo finance people to set up the six-monthly payments. He said he would. The $1200 was the exact amount I had decided I'd feel comfortable with. It was a fair deal for him and a bargain for me. We shook hands on the deal as we drove away from the clinic.

We stopped for some groceries while we were still in downtown Kinshasa then headed back out to Limete. As I got out of the car, I could see a note stuck on my door. Stan was helping me with my groceries. I opened the note and read it aloud to Stan. Romeo Tango wanted to see me in his office. Oh Bleep! Now nice! Wow I said, it sure didn't take long for the word to get out. Stan thought Dr. Clark might have called him. I didn't really care. Plenty of people had seen me get out of the plane and there was absolutely no possibility I could go unnoticed until I could walk normally. So I concluded that I was going to get my butt chewed out…which I agreed I deserved.

Stan insisted on driving me to the airport. He stored my groceries and headed back to N'Djili. As I walked into Romeo Tango's office, I found Gold Finger there as well. My two biggest fans. But again, I didn't care. I didn't think I was going to get fired and I almost agreed with my stupidity part.

After the butt chewing, I had figured I'd get, I was told to go back home and take care of my foot. I had already determined I'd be back at work in the training department the following day. So as I walked out of the office, I was relieved and looking forward to getting back to work.

As Stan and I were getting ready to leave, a Swedish mechanic named Gus, whom I'd met a week or so before, came up to me and asked if I had a second to talk. He said the apartment I'd been hoping to get would be vacant next week and wanted to know if I was still interested. I said of course and we went into the training department where it was cool and sat down. Gus told me about the monthly rent and the security deposit. It was a large duplex building. The side that was being vacated had two bedrooms, one bathroom plus a "houseboy" bathroom out in the garage, and a very nice patio leading to a garden. Gus handled the dealing with the Congolese landlord. The landlord was a minister or somebody higher up in the government. The house once belonged to Belgiums until the Congolese government took it over. Then, as the way such things went during that period, it was given to some of the inner circle of the new ruling Congolese government. Gus took the rent money to him each month. Money for a house he did not build or buy. Kinda reminded me of when Israel was "given" the promised land. *He would give you—a land with large and beautiful cities that you did not build, houses full of every good thing that you did not fill them with, wells dug that you did not dig, and vineyards and olive groves that you did not plant—and when you eat and are satisfied, be careful not to forget the Lord who brought you out of the land of Egypt, out of the place of slavery.*[120]

I already had some money saved and payday was in three days. Gus said all that would work perfectly. I would give him my rent and deposit on Friday, and I could move in that weekend. Stan said he would help. Things were moving quickly and except for my little misstep, quite well.

I rode the Wigmo bus to work the following morning. My foot was rapidly improving, and I managed to keep busy in the training department writing courses and studying flight manuals and checklists for the aircraft I had already been flying. The rest of the week flew by and soon the weekend was here. Time to move to my new apartment. Just before going home time, a messenger from the administration office arrived with my Wigmo ID card. After signing for it I read it carefully to see if it really said what everybody else's card said. It did…all duly signed by General Bobozo.

As I was being integrated into the Wigmo ranks, U.S B-52s continued a relentless clandestine carpet bombing campaign inside Cambodia. While Nixon and Kissinger receive and deserve most of the blame, the actual secret bombings of Cambodia began back in October of 1965 under President Johnson. Over 2,756,941 tons of bombs were dropped on Cambodia alone via more than 230,516 sorties on 113,716 sites until the bombing halt in August of 1973.[121] *While the purpose of these missions was to destroy the North Vietnamese forces operating from bases inside "neutral" Cambodia, countless thousands of innocent Cambodian villagers were being killed in the process. This drove an enraged Cambodian populous into the arms of the Vietcong and the Khmer Rouge. The Americans became their worst enemy…as well as their own worst enemy. A favorite tactic of the North Vietnamese troops was to hide in the midst of civilians thus using them as human shields.*

Our New Apartment

This was one of the easiest moves I ever made. One load in the back of Stan's little VW Variant station wagon and I was done. I spent more time stocking the much larger kitchen than I did moving my stuff into the apartment. While it was called "furnished," my voice bounced off the plaster walls. But it was going to soon be a home. A place for Karen and Jason.

After the unpacking and kitchen stocking was done, Stan and I sat down to go over the owner's manual and the features of what would soon be "my car." This critter was totally different from anything I'd ever owned before. Its fuel tank held a whopping 10.8 gallons of gas. The engine had a 96.6 cubic inches displacement. I chuckled inside as I remembered the 289 cubic

---

[120] Holy Bible—Holman Christian Standard Bible (HCSB) - Deuteronomy 6:10-12
[121] Bombs Over Cambodia by Taylor Owen and Ben Kierman

inch displacement of our 1964 Ford Mustang. But that was then and there…this was here and now. I was very content. Stan and I agreed that we would go to the finance office Monday and set up the payroll deduction so I could buy his car. The car was spotless inside and out. Stan's meticulous personality was evident in his car just like it was in everything else he did. I liked Stan but I sure as hell was glad I wasn't like him.

Shortly after Stan left Gus came over. He was such a truly nice man. He was very genteel and talked in a very soft quiet voice. Gus was Swedish, from Stockholm. He was an aircraft electrician. Gus wanted to know what I was going to do about a houseboy. He said the family that just moved out had one that at least they were certain was honest. In the Congo where theft was a way of life, that was a considerable attribute. Gus told me that he would be waiting here at my apartment after work on Monday. We could have a "chat" and if I liked him, I could hire him. Gus smiled as he said "have a chat" as he knew my Lingala was still in its infant stages. Gus said he would be here to help me out. So that was that. Before I went to bed that night, I wrote a letter to Karen telling her about our car and our new apartment. It would take a little over a week for the letter to arrive. She'd already told me how my father would sit close to her while she was reading it and wait for her to tell him the news. He always brought the mail home from the post office. For whatever reason, we did not elect to have the postman deliver our mail. For years and years, my father got his mail at P.O. Box 153. It remained that way I supposed until he died.

Free Music

Sleep should have come easily that night, but it didn't. Loud, blaring music which I recognized as the distinctive Congo *soukous* made sleep close to impossible. Soukous was the name of a dance done in all the night clubs as well. It reminded me of a cross between jazz and rumba. If they just hadn't played it so loud, it would be halfway enjoyable. But that night and most subsequent nights, as I lay trying to sleep, the throbbing beats emanating from the nightclub on the street behind my apartment made sure enjoying it would be unlikely. As a footnote, I never went into a Congolese nightclub the entire time I lived there. Not even once. Their hate for us combined with alcohol would be an ugly mix.

Our New Car

On Monday Stan and I went to the finance office as planned and I signed all the paperwork. Stan and I then went up to administration where we met with Wigmo's "fixer." He was an Arab named Victor. He looked like he was right out of a movie. He had a huge hooked nose and one of his eyes was pointed off to the side. Victor's job in Wigmo was to "fix" whatever needed "fixing" which usually meant he would buy whatever license or permit, anybody needed. He could get people anything for a price. Most large companies had someone like Victor, but he was reputed to be the best there was. He could get anything for anybody (for enough money). Victor had all the forms we needed to transfer the car from Stan to me. Stan paid all the fees so all I had to do was sign.

The diplomatic license plate (CD corps diplomatique) remained on the car. My evil twin made me smile as I thought about a group of pilots and mechanics, in most circles referred to as CIA mercenaries driving about in cars with diplomatic license plates. The Wigmo/FAC sticker on the windshield allowing the car on the air force base remained on the car. The sticker number was just transferred from Stan to me. I realized what we were doing in a matter of ten minutes would have taken three days on my own and probably a lot more money. Things were falling into place quickly. I had my own apartment, my own car, my Wigmo ID card and soon Karen and Jason would be here. Now all I needed was for Romeo Tango to forget about my "poached" foot. I realized that was highly unlikely. Oh well. Life was nevertheless very good.

John

Monday after work as I arrived at the apartment Gus was waiting by the back door with a short skinny Congolese. This had to be the houseboy Gus was telling me about. As I got out of the car, they walked over to meet me. I noticed that the potential houseboy walked with a limp. He drug his right foot. He greeted me with the traditional "Mbote patron, mbote mingi." To which I produced some of my improving but still quite basic Lingala with the response "mbote, ozali nini," or hello, who are you. "Nazali John" he replied. Obviously, Gus was impressed. What I was soon to have to confess to him was that we were nearing the limits of my Lingala linguistic ability and I had a cold Primus beer in the refrigerator with his name on it if he would please help me get to know John a little better. Of course Gus agreed. Gus's Lingala was seasoned with a heavy sing-song Swedish accent, but he was nonetheless fluent. I wondered if I would ever speak that well.

After a about thirty minutes of chatting and a liter of Primus, I was convinced John would work just fine. I'd already heard plenty of funny stories and horror stories about the Congolese houseboys, but Gus assured me this was about as good as I could expect. We agreed on John's salary which was based on what Gus told me was the going rate and John headed out the door with the assurance he would be back here in the morning before I left for work. I was wondering about giving him a key to the house when John pointed to one of the kitchen cabinets. He went over and opened one of the cabinet doors and produced a back-door key that had been hidden in the corner. Gus and I laughed and told John I'd see him in the morning.

Mission Accomplished

A couple of days after Stan headed back home to Austin, Lewis called me over to his desk and told me he would be leaving in two weeks as well. He smiled and said his mission here was accomplished. I knew him well enough by this time and respected him enough to not ask "what mission." But Lewis generated a profound aura of confidence and tranquility that left no doubt in my mind Romeo Tango was in serious difficulties…he just didn't know it yet. I smiled at him with all the knowing wisdom my meager twenty-six years could muster up. But in my mind, I was hearing a thunderous applause…we're talking standing ovation quality. Lewis had somehow insured the jerk was going to get what he deserved and with luck I would be around to see it. I was sure of it.

Lewis went on to tell me the training department would be closing, and that Felipe and I would be moving over to flight operations. We would be making regular Force Aérienne Congolaise flights. He went on to say his sources were telling him that Mobutu was getting nervous about the extent of the CIA's control of FAC's operations. Lewis said he would not be surprised to see some major changes soon. I asked him if he thought my job was secure. He smiled and said Mobutu feared those who might replace us more than he feared us and told me not to worry. He told me to keep my head down. Then as somewhat of an afterthought he added "and stay out of hot water." We both laughed.

Later that morning Lewis took me over to flight operations and we went in to see Gold Finger. Lewis and I sat down at his desk. I could feel myself fighting not to gawk at all the obscene gold chains and rings he was wearing. This guy could put some NFL football players to shame. Gold Finger was very jovial and welcomed me back to flight ops…this time as a pilot. I hoped he had forgotten how Lewis snatched me out of his department only a few short months earlier. But who was I kidding? That would never happen.

Lewis explained I was now fully checked out on the C-47 and C-54 and had been studying the T-28 and C-46 systems and could begin checkout in both aircraft at any time. Gold Finger seemed pleased, especially about the T-28s. It also appeared Romeo Tango had forgotten about my foot but deep down inside I knew he would always be waiting for the opportune moment to use it against me. What a jerk. "The evil that men do lives after them; the good is oft interred with their bones."[122] My little misstep would, without any doubt, be around for a while. It would live after me; at least for a while.

While I was learning to fly military airplanes and stay out of hot water, half way around the world in Southeast Asia, Cambodian General Lon Nol and Cambodian Prince Sisowath Sirik Matak were holding very unofficial meetings with the CIA and US military advisors assigned to Cambodia. Their goal was to gauge what support might be expected

---
[122] William Shakespeare

from the US if Prince Sisowath Sirik Matak's cousin and head of state Norodom Sihanouk, Cambodia's former king were deposed.[123]

A Car–Karen & Jason Plus Money In The Bank

In no time at all Karen and Jason had seats booked on Sabena to come to Kinshasa. My C-46 first officer checkout had begun. I was flying almost every day and making a lot of money. As a matter of fact I'd never made so much money in my entire life. Less than five short months ago I was the highest paid flight instructor on Meacham Field making $450 a month. Now my base pay was $1200 plus another $350 living allowance. All in five short months. If I flew more than my base which was 100 hours per month, I'd receive an additional $12 for each flight hour above the first 100. If I flew only 13 days per month, I'd make the 100 flight hour base. I was getting about 120 hours per month and still having a few days off. That meant an additional $240 each month. One month as a first officer I flew 180 hours. Karen was paying off what few bills we had, and we were putting the rest in the bank. I'd never had money in the bank before. Like everybody I knew my age, we were living payday to payday. Suddenly, almost overnight, this changed. It would have been very easy to start congratulating myself. But I refused. Deep down inside I knew this was not by my own hand but rather the hand of God. Pride stalked me like a lion stalks its victim; ready to devour and destroy. I feared pride and I ran from it. *Pride comes before destruction, and an arrogant spirit before a fall.*[124]

I scurried about Kinshasa buying the few things my domestically deficient knowledge knew I had to have before Karen and Jason arrived. I went to the "going home sales" that I found posted on the bulletin board in the grocery store. I got sheets and plates and cheap stainless-steel eating utensils. One of the first sayings I heard upon arriving in the Congo was "if it doesn't fit in your suitcase...don't buy it." I tried hard to follow that. The car was my only exception thus far. Plus Karen would be bringing some things in their checked baggage. I was sure from what I'd seen in the town that Karen, once she got here, could get the rest of what we needed. I just needed to get enough for their first few days.

The last days before Karen and Jason arrived were filled with flying. Gold Finger knew my family was coming and allowed me to fly hard before they came so I could have some days off to meet them at the airport and get them settled into our apartment. They started my C-46 training almost immediately after my transfer into flight operations. I was assigned to fly with the chief pilot, a Columbian named Carlos Cruz (pseudonym). He was diminutive, overweight, and grumpy. His flying proficiency bordered on dangerous. This he apparently knew as he was a real "white knuckle" pilot. He would relax in cruise but during takeoff climb-out, descent and landing he would grab the

---
[123] My War With The CIA by Prince Norodom Sihanouk
[124] Holy Bible—Holman Christian Standard Bible (HCSB) - Proverbs 16:18

yoke with what resembled a stranglehold. I should clarify at this point that "relax" was a bit of a misnomer. What he really did, since he knew I was already proficient at navigation, was to set cruise power, move his seat into the most aft position, recline the back, and go to sleep. I'd been flying with him for over two weeks and had never yet been allowed to touch the controls. Stan and Felipe would give me every other takeoff and landing. I had rapidly become proficient. With the C-46, I knew about the systems because I'd studied them, about fuel management, because I did it while he was asleep. I could tell you about the aircraft's performance because I took meticulous notes. But what the controls felt like…I didn't have a clue. I remember thinking one day somewhere between Kinshasa and Lubumbashi, as I looked across the cockpit and watched the fat little fart sleeping, that he was getting paid an additional $1000 a month on top of his regular captain's pay, just to be chief pilot. Part of the chief pilot's responsibilities was to train. Oh well, this couldn't last forever. Then I'd be one more step toward making captain myself. I was on a roll. I wasn't going to let Carlos Cruz ruin this great experience.

Soon the big day came. I went to the airport and met their flight. I was so happy to see them. They were dead tired. Jason looked dazed. They had been on the airplane for hours. As a matter of fact they had spent 20 hours on three airplanes and had flown 9000 miles. That did not count airport time. Jason was five years old.

I was very happy to see them again and I couldn't wait to show them our new "home." Jason thought our little station wagon was cool. Even though it was night he peered out the window at the Congolese walking and riding bicycles along the side of the road. Soon we were in Limete and at our new home on Begonias street. Karen put Jason straight to bed. Then we unpacked a little and went to bed ourselves. Karen was brave. Heading out with a bunch of bags and a five-year-old to live in the heart of Africa. Unfortunately, I hadn't yet learned to fully appreciate all the organizing and sacrifices and probably anxieties she faced while I was away. "If Only."

Exploring Kinshasa And Adjusting To John

Karen, Jason and I spent a couple of days seeing Kinshasa and shopping for things she knew we needed. Jason was wide-eyed. I also enjoyed watching Karen adjust to working with John. She never lost her cool, but I imagined that it could get frustrating. He was a truly nice person without an unkind bone in his body. But the communication barrier was significant.

A few days later we talked to a friend, another Wigmo pilot, about Jason's schooling. He had young children as well and he put them in the French school. He said it was working out fine. They were Danish and I assumed they spoke no French when they arrived. I was correct but was assured they would pick it up at an amazing speed. Karen and I decided we'd try that as well. The American school was full and reputed to be sub-standard. The French school was by far the biggest and the best in the entire country. Jason was soon enrolled. It wasn't long before he was translating for us when we would go into stores. My French was improving rapidly but his was soon better than mine. As Jason settled into his new school and language, Karen settled into her new home. Soon she and John were a team…well, more or less.

Karen's Lingala Vocabulary

It was fun watching Karen and John. Soon she was learning the backbone of John's linguistic repertoire. Expressions like "mbongo ozail te" (I've got no money) or "matata mingi" (lots of problems) or "eloko ozali te" (there's not any).

It was also easy to feel sorry for John. He was a truly nice person. But he was born into and would die in a life of horrible poverty and disease. My guess about the foot he always had to drag was probably polio. He seemed to have no idea. It was just the way he was. John served as a constant reminder to me of how blessed I was; little of which could be ascribed to my skill or cleverness.

The 1970s–The "Me Decade"

Soon it was the spring of 1970. There were no noticeable seasons to offer any markers in time's passage. Things just went on. I didn't yet have a short-wave radio and we had no TV because the stations all broadcast in horrible French and were filled with Mobutu's self-serving propaganda. World events were moving rapidly but we only watched it via News Week and Time. Their weekly appearance on the news stand was eagerly awaited. Nothing outside the Congo happened in real time for us.

Cambodia's Prince Sihanouk Overthrown In A Bloodless Coup

Cambodia had not yet appeared on my radar screen. But in March of 1970 while Prince Norodom Sihanouk, Cambodia head of state, was touring Europe, China, and Russia, secret meetings intensified between the country's ruling inner circle. The focus of these secret meetings, which had been linked (but never documented) to the CIA and U.S. military representatives stationed in Phnom Penh, was the most effective way to get Sihanouk out of office. Suggestions reportedly ranged from assassination to being deposed via the constitution. The latter prevailed. On 18 March the Cambodian army took up positions around Phnom Penh, the capital city, and a debate was held within the National Assembly. While the vote was held in secret, an almost unanimous result deposed Prince Norodom Sihanouk, Cambodia's head of state.[125]

Prince Sihanouk learned of this as he was in his limo en route to the Moscow airport. He was told by Russia's Premier Aleksei Kosygin. The airport ceremonies continued as

---

[125] The Tragedy of Cambodian History by David P. Chandler

planned and he flew off to Beijing. When this story appeared in News Week I hardly noticed. I barely knew where Cambodia was.

Immediately armored vehicles began to patrol the streets of Phnom Penh and other major cities. The new government was unsure how the population would react. Sihanouk was a god-king to many of Cambodia's less educated. The initial government announcement and Lon Nol's later radio broadcast were subdued for fear of setting off massive public unrest. Within a couple of days government printed posters went up all over the major cities accusing Sihanouk and his wife, Monique of treason.[126] Numerous royal family members were removed from their positions and some placed under house arrest, while others were closely watched. Prince Norodom Phurissara previous Foreign Minister of Cambodia and cousin of Norodom Sihanouk was removed from all responsibility and closely watched. Prince Sisowath Ritharavong, Lt. Col. Cambodian Navy, was placed under house arrest.[127] A few days later, on 23 March, with assistance and encouragement from the Chinese and promise of help from the Vietnamese, Sihanouk in a radio broadcast created a "National Union Government", a "National Liberation Army." He called on Cambodians to disregard the laws and decrees of the Phnom Penh government and to join the resistance. Sihanouk declared war.[128] The population answered his call by the tens of thousands. His cousin Prince Norodom Phurassara joined him a few months later.

I'm sure I read about this in Newsweek or Time magazine but being that it was about some little place over by Vietnam, I failed to take note. I suspect few people outside of the peace activist's circles did.

Of Mice And Men

Just after Karen and Jason arrived I resumed my C-46 so-called training with Carlos. Every few days he would give me a takeoff or a landing. But to say that I was learning anything from him would be inaccurate. I learned things but it was certainly not from him as he slept most of the time.

One day, while Carlos was sleeping, a movement caught my eye down near the bottom of my instrument panel. The C-46 is a somewhat unique aircraft in that its instrument panel is not attached directly to the aircraft. It is suspended. This design leaves a space along the edges of the panel. When I looked, I saw a little brown mouse watching me from behind the instrument panel. Since Karen was now here, I had been getting very nice sandwiches to put in my lunch bag. My evil twin immediately suggested that the little mouse was probably hungry, and I should offer him a bit of my sandwich. I slowly reached over and took my lunch bag out of my open flight bag just to my left. I slowly and quietly opened the bag and tore a little piece of the sandwich bread off and ever so slowly moved it toward the opening. It didn't work...the mouse disappeared. However, I decided to wedge the little piece of bread into the opening and wait. I did, and in a few minutes, the bread

---

[126] The Tragedy of Cambodian History by David P. Chandler
[127] Personal accounts of Norodom Danine daughter of Prince Norodom Phurissara and half-sister of Prince Sisowath Ritharavong
[128] The Tragedy of Cambodian History by David P. Chandler

started wiggling. Then it disappeared. I looked over at Carlos. He was still sleeping. I decided it probably wouldn't be too wise to share this with Carlos.

The following day, after we were in cruise, the little mouse was back. This time he allowed his nose to protrude through the opening. I checked and Carlos was already sleeping. I tore off another piece of bread and started toward the little mouse. This time I was almost at the opening with the bread before he pulled his head back. I wedged the bread in the opening just like on the previous day. It disappeared again; only this time much quicker. This was starting to be fun.

On the third day I had the little critter taking the bread from my hand and nibbling on it before pulling it back inside. How cool was that. But on the fourth day, by some chance occurrence the fat little fart Carlos woke up and found me feeding the mouse. He went ballistic. He went on and on about how they ate the electrical wiring in the airplane (probably true) and how a bite could cause us to die (probably not true if we followed proper first aid procedures which I seriously doubted he knew or remembered). But at any rate, Carlos was the captain and he was always right.

The next day in operations he was complaining to everybody about how I was feeding and encouraging the rats in the airplanes. Most people were looking over at me when Carlos wasn't watching and snickering. Before our departure that morning Gold Finger called me into his office. He was grinning and asked me if that was all I could find to do in the cockpit of the airplane. Then he smiled and told me he didn't need that idiot in his office anymore talking about me feeding any bleeping rats. I couldn't believe it. Gold Finger had a sense of humor. I told him I wouldn't feed the mice anymore. I never saw the little mouse again. The following day maintenance sprayed the aircraft (probably with DDT or Agent Orange) because Carlos had made an entry in the aircraft log which took the form of a maintenance discrepancy. They had to do something. So from then on, I spent my mouse feeding time practicing my navigation skills. Every time I listen to my evil twin I get in trouble.

While Wigmo maintenance was busy killing mice, in Cambodia Nixon and Kissinger were busy killing innocent Cambodian villagers with the B-52 carpet bombing. Thousands of innocent civilians were being killed in an attempt to destroy the Viet Cong's mobile headquarters and camps. Ironically, each non-combatant that died as a result of the indiscriminant bombings, each civilian man, woman, and child killed, created countless recruits for the Khmer Rouge, the same Khmer Rouge Washington and the new puppet government in Phnom Penh were trying to defeat. Washington was defeating itself and couldn't see it. Some CIA analysts were beginning to write this but nobody wanted to listen.[129]

---

[129] Bombs Over Cambodia: New Light on US Air War by Taylor Owen and Ben Kierman

A Monkey Mistake

One day a street vender brought a monkey to the gate. He had it on a leash, and it was riding on his shoulder. I thought what a great pet it would make for Jason, so I bought it. I paid $10 for the little beast. It turned out he had an extremely foul temperament. I named him Gifford (pseudo name) after a high school boyfriend of my sister Camille.

I soon learned that everybody but me apparently knew about their inherent ill-tempered disposition as well as the fact they were virtually impossible to house train. He relieved himself wherever the urge occurred plus he had a propensity toward persistent masturbation. Jason was afraid of him and I detested him. To this day I regret getting Gifford. I regret the anxiety he caused Jason. He soon became history. "If Only"

A Rumor of War[130] and Rumors of Coups

It seemed every couple of months the Belgiums would start talking about rumors of coups against Mobutu. I don't ever remember hearing that from the Congolese. However the rumors were always about some colonel or general wanting to overthrow Mobutu or some military rebellion brewing among the troops out in the provinces. It was a well-known fact the troops were not happy. Only Mobutu's special units seemed to have good morale. And why not, they were always paid on time, always had the best of equipment and living quarters. Most of the Congolese army hadn't been paid in months. Their generals took the payroll funds for themselves. And they wondered why morale was so terrible. Sometimes we would notice roadblocks becoming more frequent. When this would happen some of the Wigmo people would send their families back home. As an American and in Wigmo, I had pretty good sources with COMISH (the US military mission there in the Congo). Most of the time they said they had no reason to believe the stories had any validity. And it was their job, among other things, to know. So at that point Karen and Jason stayed with me. But while the rumors were nebulous, there was very real trouble brewing in the Eastern Congo.

Who Was My Brother's Keeper?

The "cold war" was virtually global at this point. The superpowers were using underdeveloped countries like the Congo and Cambodia as expendable chess pawns in their seemingly unending desire to gain global dominance. The Eastern provinces of the Congo did not escape this cruel fate. The Chinese were in neighboring Tanzania under the pretense of building the Tanzania-Zambia railway.[131] It was no coincidence these same Chinese were arming

---

[130] A 1977 memoir by Philip Caputo
[131] Working On The Railroad: China and the Tanzania-Zambia Railway by George T. Yu—University of California—Berkley Press, Center For Chinese Studies

Congolese rebels in the Congo's Eastern provinces along Lake Tanganyika. The arms would enter through Tanzania's Indian Ocean ports, make their way by land to Lake Tanganyika then by boat across the lake into the hands of the Congolese rebels.

One morning in a briefing given by a guy from the "embassy," we were told that the Congolese navy was failing miserably at interdicting these Chinese arms shipments. As a result the rebels were becoming better armed and more active. We were informed of a significant troop buildup planned to begin immediately. One of Wigmo's main tasks would be supplying the Congolese ANC troops operating in the Eastern Congo. There would be daily flights to Albertville. Mostly these flights were to be C-46 and C-54s due to their lift capability. However C-47s would be based in Albertville for para-commando drops. This operation would begin immediately for an undetermined but extended period. We all viewed this as good news as it would certainly mean many extra flying hours per month for everybody, which translated into more money. The thought did cross my mind that I would be profiting from this increase in hostilities, which would certainly mean more misery and the death of some if not many.

On my walk across the flight line to my aircraft I thought about the aspects of my participation. But quickly decided if I participated or refused to participate some people were going to die. These people had decided to take up arms themselves…although China, Russia, and the United States were certainly offering encouragement. I would be militarily involved on the side of the United States; doing a job the U.S. Air Force was politically prohibited from doing. I would be making double if not more what a U.S. Air Force pilot would be making. I pushed the thought from my mind and walked on toward the plane.

As I got to the plane, rather than the usual hodge-podge of troops, families, animals and furniture, I saw all troops with combat gear. We had an inherent distrust of their military discipline, so we immediately told the officer in charge to insure all magazines were removed and all ejection ports open showing empty. Then we checked.

Fortune was smiling on me. For some mysterious reason, Carlos had signed me off as co-pilot qualified on the C-46. This with no more than five landings and even fewer takeoffs. I was sure he just got tired of me being the first thing he saw when he woke up from his never-ending cockpit napping. The captain I was flying with today was a Belgium named Martin Bertrand (pseudonym) but everybody just called him "Tintin", a French cartoon character. Tintin had a serious limp, the result of a glider accident back in Europe. He was funny, spoke perfect Lingala, and was a truly nice person. He would be the first to tell you his Lingala was a result of his constant string of Congolese girlfriends.

Tintin and I did our preflight inspection. Then we inspected the rifles of the troops, and told them to load their bags and strap in. They were all excited and ready. They broke into a high-spirited chant and boarded in a very military fashion. I'd never seen this side of the ANC before. I was impressed. I did have the thought that I bet this spirit would disappear after a couple of months of no pay and bad living conditions.

Teacher Tintin

Soon we were ready for takeoff. Tintin told me to go ahead and make the takeoff. I respectfully advised him it might not be all that good as I'd only had a handful. To that he laughed and informed me that this airplane was a handful for an experienced C-46 captain and then he asked if I really thought our passengers were going to complain to anybody. I immediately knew Tintin and I were going to be friends. I lined the airplane up with the centerline of the runway and slowly advanced the throttles on the huge R-2800 Pratt & Whitney engines. In a few seconds they were putting out 2000 horsepower each. The airplane started inching toward the left side of the runway. I was trying to move it back with the rudders but without much success. I saw Tintin reach over and make an aileron correction on his yoke (normally an aircraft control reserved for inflight). The plane began moving back to the center line. Around 50 knots airspeed I could feel the rudder beginning to become effective. From then on it was like a huge C-47. I gently pulled and trimmed, and it lifted off the runway. I called gear up and Tintin put the gear handle into the retract position. The huge wheels came up and went into their wheel wells. But unlike the C-47, its tail wheel also retracted. We were flying. I'd just had more fun on that takeoff with Tintin than I'd had in all my flights with Carlos. The C-46 was not quick like the C-47. You rolled in a command and waited for something to happen. This too was fun. Soon we reached our cruise altitude of 9000 feet and Tintin told to me engage the autopilot just like Carlos used to do. But I asked him if it would be OK if I just hand flew the airplane for a while so I could get a better feel for it. He said sure and laughed. After hand flying for about thirty minutes, I finally engaged the autopilot and started recording my engine readings in the aircraft log. Our first checkpoint was coming up as well and I recorded that on my flight log sheet. Tintin was busy reading a French paperback novel. We were flying non-stop so there would be many flight log entries.

Tintin told me I would be making the landing. The airport was right beside the lake (Tanganyika) and there was always a crosswind. The C-46 was notoriously hard to land under normal conditions and infamous in a crosswind. I was very nervous. Tintin told me not to worry that he would get on the controls with me if things started to get seriously out of hand. That helped a little, but I was still quite nervous. He told me to use the ailerons like I'd seen him do on my takeoff roll. He said the rudder would do a good job until the aircraft slowed beyond about 50 knots. Then it would be differential power and aileron. Nothing like the C-47. Even with his assurances, I was nervous.

I lined the plane up on final but was having to keep a pretty good crab (crosswind correction) in order to remained lined up. That was fine and I could do that easily. But at some point, before touchdown that crab was going to have to come out. That's when the problems could begin. The proper technique was to smoothly transition from the crab into a cross-control situation with upwind wing dipped slightly below the horizon and opposite rudder. On touchdown, differential power would have to be used to keep the aircraft's nose (and path) lined up with the runway. While I could walk and chew gum at the same time, this was about ten times worse. Somehow, I got the thing on the runway. Tintin didn't have to take the controls but he sure as heck was giving a lot of genteel instructions. When I finally brought the plane to a slow taxi and relinquished the controls to Tintin, my hands were wet with perspiration. I did not like this airplane very much. I would eventually learn to fly it relatively well, but for sure it would not be my favorite. Kinda like a Hamilton County rattlesnake…fun to look at but must be handled with care.

When we arrived, two large military trucks were waiting to take the ANC troops and their gear to their new base. The Wigmo station agent told us he had received a radio message a few minutes earlier advising our passengers were en route to the airport from a different military base and they were still more than fifty kilometers away. The Wigmo agent suggested we take the jeep and go into town for a nice lunch while he refueled the plane. Tintin and I both thought that sounded like a pretty good idea, so we headed into the center of Albertville which was only a few kilometers away.

Music And Mao Zedong's "Little Red Book"

While we were bouncing along in the jeep Tintin spotted a little roadside market where the Congolese were selling carvings and other trinkets. We stopped and got out to look at what they had to sell. There were primitive yet very interesting ivory carvings, tobacco pipes made from ivory, little box-like musical instruments made from narrow strips of metal, traditional knives and spears, and countless other interesting things. I was ready to skip lunch and stay here but I could see Tintin was hungry. I bought an ivory pipe although I didn't smoke, and a little musical instrument called a *likembe*. It kinda resembled a cigar box with narrow metal strips of varying lengths which when struck with the thumb produced sound. The instrument was played with the thumbs of both hands. It was even making its way into some of the contemporary popular Congolese music bands.

As we were leaving, I spotted several little red books for sale. I initially mistook them to be little pocket New Testament Bibles. I'd had one similar in high school. But when I looked more closely, I realized it was a copy of the famous or should I say infamous Mao Zedong's "Little Red Book." It was in English. Instantly I knew I had to have one. I tried to conceal my excitement in order to keep the little stall owner from jacking up the price. My white face and flight suit were already not helping. I asked him how much he wanted for it. My Lingala was workable, but Lingala was not his first language. We were in the Eastern Congo where Swahili was the primary language. Only the military spoke Lingala. It was then that Tintin stepped in to help me. He was mixing his fluent Lingala with some street Swahili. I was impressed. The merchant must have put out an exploratory offer that was unrealistic. Tintin started in on him with a barrage of insults mixed with smiles. Soon they were both smiling and Tintin handed me the book. I paid a little over a dollar for it. I immediately put it in one on the zipper pockets on the front of my flight suit. My simple, inexperienced, stanchly anti-communist, background was making me feel as though I'd just purchased some piece of pornography. I was afraid someone would see me with it. Looking back years later, it was laughable. I remember even wondering how I was going to smuggle it back into the United States to go into my fledgling library. What if customs found it; would I go to jail? Would I end up on some FBI or even worse CIA "watch list?" Today it still resides in my library.

As we bounced along in the jeep on our way into town, I tried to get some musical sound out of my new likembe. However it didn't take long for me to realize there was more to playing this simple looking thing than first met the eye. This was not a toy. The old guy that sold it to me played it for me as part of his sales pitch. Maybe it would sound better tonight with beer.

My First Combat Casualty Passenger

(Unfortunately, it would not be my last)

Tintin and I had a nice lunch in the restaurant of one of Albertville's few remaining hotels along the lakefront boulevard then headed back to the airport. I'd heard stories about how nice Albertville had been before independence. But that was universal...the same story for the entire Congo.

When we arrived at the airport our passengers were already there. They appeared to have just arrived. I saw two soldiers on liters. As I came closer, I could see serious wounds, one leg and one chest, wrapped in filthy rags. Both looked like they were in plenty of pain. There was another soldier with them who appeared by his insignia to be a medic. I saw no evidence of medical or battlefield wound treatment supplies with him. I wondered why they had bothered to send him. The somewhat grizzly sight would have been much harder for me had it not been for my Navy hospital corpsman training. I turned and climbed into the airplane and made my way through all the cargo, animals, and personal belongings toward the cockpit. I found the sight of the two wounded ANC somewhat unsettling. The "cold war" suddenly didn't look all that cold. Later in cruise as I sat silently staring out the window at the jungle below, I would try to find some justifiable reason for why people were fighting there. But I could find no reasonable reason. Lust for power, control of natural resources, greed, insecurity, and not to be forgotten, the insidious...cold war. Same stuff you read about in the Old Testament...same stuff you read about in world history books. Same stuff you read about in American history books. Hell, the same stuff you read every time you opened Newsweek and Time magazine. It's easy to miss the cold war part in the Bible, but it's there…between the lines.

The guy with the chest wounds died in flight. After some delay waiting for a transport, his lifeless body was taken away in the back of a military truck. Images of a grieving wife and children crept into my mind.

A Congolese Air Force Entrepreneur And Goat Cheese

I glanced over at the huge pile of fresh vegetables in the back of the airplane. It belonged to our Congolese "loadmaster." The loadmasters would buy produce at one location and sell it in another location. I was told they already had customers for all of it. We didn't really mind as we knew most hadn't been paid in a couple of months. As long as they kept it to a reasonable amount none of the Wigmo pilots cared. Sometimes we would order things for ourselves as well. But ours would be ordered over the radio and purchased by the Wigmo station manager so we could be assured of the quality. Today I had ordered some cheese that the Greeks in the Eastern provinces made. It was goat cheese and quite good. We had a little cubbyhole in the cockpit where the cockpit heater didn't reach which served as our own little private refrigerator. I hoped Karen would like my cheese purchase. I had not coordinated the purchase with her as I usually did. I'd heard Tintin ordering his cheese over the radio and on impulse said, "get a kilo for me too." Karen always welcomed my fresh vegetable purchases as well as fresh strawberries, pineapples, and other strange fruits neither of us had ever seen before. But I wasn't so sure about the goat cheese. (It turned out she was delighted.)

Jimmy Joe–Jet Jockey

One day a shiny white Lear Jet 25 taxied onto our military ramp. Two European pilots and a Congolese flight engineer disembarked. Romeo Tango was waiting in the hanger and walked out to meet the crew. We soon learned this airplane had belonged to the Katanga copper mining company Union Minière du Haut Katanga, or Gécamines after Mobutu nationalized the former Belgian company. Word was that Mobutu had "appropriated" the airplane for use by his government ministers and inner circle. This is what happened to anything of significant value after independence. But what was Gécamines' loss would soon be my gain. Wigmo was to crew and maintain the plane. Two captains and two co-pilots were to be trained. I soon learned I had been selected as one of the co-pilots.

The Lear Jet factory in Wichita Kansas sent one of their regular contract instructor pilots to Kinshasa to train us. First, we had ground school for a week, not very thorough but enough. Then the contract pilot started the flight instruction. The emphasis was on training the two captains. When they were done the instructor started with us. After a couple of hours with the instructor, we were put with one of the new Wigmo captains while the instructor rode in the jump-seat. There were a few mistakes but all in all we did well enough. I had thought it would be several more years before I got a chance to fly jets but suddenly one just dropped in out of the sky so to speak. I had done some VIP flying in the presidential C-47 but this would change the whole game. I would now be making some international flights. At the end of the training my pilot's license was endorsed with Lear Jet 25.

The range of the Lear Jet 25 was nothing to envy. It was, in pilot parlance, a "short-legged" airplane. Very few of the neighboring nations' capitols lay within its fuel range. This pretty much limited our flights to airports within the Congo. The domestic flights were in turn limited to only a few airports due to the small size of its wheels and the large size of the mortar and bomb craters still lying unrepaired in most of the country's airport runways. The huge tires on our C-46, C-47, and C-54 aircraft rolled right over them. If the Lear Jet tried to do that, its nose or landing gears would be snapped off like sticks of dry macaroni. As a result, even though I was building some jet time, it was, by comparison to my regular flying, meager.

What's Happening To Our Clothes!

Life was rocking along. Karen and Jason were adapting well. But there were some learning curves for all of us. This was not Texas.

One morning I brought one of my shirts to Karen and ask her if this shirt wasn't supposed to be almost new. The neck was all frayed and the material appeared generally worn out. She asked if I'd ever watched John do the washing; which of course I hadn't. We had no washing machine. Nobody I knew did. The houseboys all washed clothes outside in a specially designed sink. Attached to the sink was a sloping tray often made from cement where the clothing item was laid out and scrubbed with a stiff brush and local detergent just short of "grandma's lye soap." It didn't take long to completely do in anything. From there it was usually passed to the houseboy who would use it for his family or sell it. There was no such thing in the Congo as a favorite shirt…well, at least not for very long.

A "Holy" Worm And Diesel Fuel

One afternoon when I got home from a flight Karen brought Jason to me and showed me his arms. There were several swollen and infected pimple looking places on both arms. John had seen them as well and was chattering away. He was saying something about *mpambó*, and *mazuti*. I knew *mazuti* was diesel fuel. I thought *mpambo* was a worm because I'd heard it referred to associated with fresh fruit. I knew such things were possible but had never run across it before. We were sitting out on the front patio when Gus walked by. He looked at Jason's arm and immediately told us that they were in fact embedded worms and they would have to come out or they would make even worse infections. Gus said the tiny worms lived in the sand waiting for some host to come along. This time Jason was that unlucky host.

Jason was starting to catch on to where this was leading, and he was not at all happy. Gus didn't know anything about the application of diesel fuel but to me it kinda made a little bit of sense. I'd grown up hearing about putting tobacco on wounds but in corps school they told us that wasn't true at all. I wasn't sure about John's diesel idea, but I couldn't think of many serious side effects. John assured us it would work. So I got a little jar of diesel and we rubbed it on one of his wounds. Nothing happened. Karen was sure a needle and gentle pressure would get the worm out. That was the next approach but by this time Jason was 100% involved and his participation was not in the affirmative. He was screaming his head off and was not holding still. After working on the first site for a little while a small maggot looking worm was coaxed out. By this time I realized the diesel John was talking about was in fact working. After a while it was penetrating the enclosure and the worm was getting away from it the easiest way available. Jason became a bit better after the initial fear of the process subsided. He wanted to see each worm that came out. About an hour later we had most of them out. There were still a couple that were too small to do anything with. The only practical approach was to give them time to get a little fatter and then force them out like we had done these. Jason knew all about ticks and chiggers, but this was a first.

April 30, 1970 – President Nixon stuns Americans by announcing U.S. and South Vietnamese incursion into Cambodia .".. not for the purpose of expanding the war into Cambodia but for the purpose of ending the war in Vietnam and winning the just peace we desire." The announcement generates a tidal wave of protest by politicians, the press, students, professors, clergy members, business leaders, and many average Americans against Nixon and the Vietnam War.[132]

Meanwhile, back in Hamilton, my father was watching on the evening news as:

May 1, 1970 – President Nixon calls anti-war students "bums blowing up campuses."

May 2, 1970 – American college campuses erupt in protest over the invasion of Cambodia.

May 4, 1970 – At Kent State University in Ohio, National Guardsmen shoot and kill four student protesters and wound nine. They, too, were protesting the U.S. involvement in Cambodia.

In response to the killings, over 400 colleges and universities across America shut down. In Washington, nearly 100,000 protesters surround various government buildings including the White House and historical monuments. On an impulse, President Nixon exits the White House and pays a late night surprise visit to the Lincoln Memorial and chats with young protesters.[133]

---

[132] The History Place—The Vietnam War
[133] The History Place—The Vietnam War

My Single Engine Airplane Experience Draws Attention

A few weeks later, when I arrived in flight operations to get the paperwork for my flight, I found General Suet A. Ehrabar, a Turkish Air Force general serving as an advisor to Mobutu waiting for me in Gold Finger's office. Although I was not flying with Tintin that day, he was waiting in Gold Finger's office as well. My first reaction was…"this does not look good."

I sat down in the empty chair and waited for somebody to say something. Gold Finger spoke first asking me how many hours of single engine airplane time I had. I wasn't sure but I told them approximately 1600. General Ehrabar spoke next asking me if I had any T-28 time; to which I replied no. The T-28 had an R-1820 engine, a cousin to the C-47's R-1830. I had significant R-1830 experience from flying the C-47. But then they already knew that, so I remained quiet.

General Ehrabar then said "everyone knows the counterinsurgency operation along Lake Tanganyika is not going well. The Congolese Air Force (Wigmo) had been asked to deploy three T-28s in the Eastern Congo, based in Albertville." The pay would be $16.00 per hour not the $12.00 I was making flying as a co-pilot. Since it was not likely that the T-28s would be flying 100 hours per month, they were going to guaranteed we would be paid our base of 100/month. In addition there would be hazardous duty pay. The crew would stay at the Wigmo safe-house and an additional per diem food allowance would be given. General Ehrabar asked if I would be interested.

I took a moment to reply. My mind was already made up…I was trying to be cool. Tintin was smiling; Gold Finger and General Ehrabar were expressionless. I asked what type of missions we would be flying. General Ehrabar replied "patrol and interdict." He went on to say the Congolese Navy had proven ineffectual in curtailing the flow of Chinese arms and ammunition from Tanzania into rebel hands inside the Congo. They wanted T-28 aircraft to patrol up and down the lake at a low enough level to be able to conduct good surveillance. If suspicious vessels were spotted, we were to contact the Congolese Navy trying to set up an interception. If this was not possible and the vessels would not turn around, we were to fire over the bow; if this failed to turn them around, we were to sink the vessels. I asked what kind of vessels these were. The general replied they were usually small 8-10 meter (26-33 foot) wooden cargo boats of the type commonly used between fishing villages along both sides of the lake. The larger cargo boats could only go to the ports due to their size. The smaller wooden boats could go directly into any village. As a result, most of the arms traffic was believed to be moving in these small boats. For whatever reason, they did not believe the smaller boats were going out in the lake to meet the large commercial cargo boats yet. Probably because there was no shortage of boats willing to make to trip across the lake to pick up the cargo. The mission had been explained…all eyes were on me.

I announced I was in. Tintin smiled and shook my hand. It was then I learned he would be the mission commander. I also learned they had already recruited a Swedish co-pilot to round out the team. I was the final member of the group. The Swedish co-pilot, Leif Bergman (pseudonym) was not one of my favorite people but still we got along socially just fine. And besides, I wouldn't be in the same cockpit with him, just talking to him on the radio or looking over at him in his cockpit as we flew in formation. Speaking of formation flying; I had less than zero experience flying in any kind of formation. In flight school, it was against the FAA regulations to get close to another aircraft. Now I was going to be paid to do it. There were no books that I could grab to study up on formation flying techniques. This was going to be very interesting.

So when do we start, I ask? Right now Tintin replied. I can't I said…I have a flight. No you don't Tintin said; Dinger is taking your flight. But how did you know I would agree I asked Tintin. Tintin grinned and replied…I knew. He told me to come with him to supply; I would need a parachute and a helmet. Parachute, I exclaimed; I'm not going to jump out of any damn airplane. You will if it's on fire or you lose your engine. Without its only engine, this thing glides like a footlocker. And if it's on fire…well, how many times have you read about people with no parachute jumping from a tall building to get away from the flames. If you are in trouble that parachute will be your best friend.

Over at stores they brought several helmets for me to try on. I found one that fit perfectly. It had a built-in boom-mic and a tinted visor that pulled down. The parachute part was easy. They just brought me one.

A Return To My Bombing Days
(Minus The Texas Ranger)

I knew Tintin had been flying the T-28 from time to time here but just for practice. He needed to keep current so they would use him for the exercise and maintenance test flights. As we approached the aircraft, I realized for the first time that Tintin would be instructing from behind, not beside me. The T-28 Trojan's two seat configuration was tandem, not side by side like I'd always flown. Communication would be via intercom. There would be no pointing. I was glad I did not have to teach like that back in Southwest School of Aviation.

Tintin went through an in-depth preflight walk-around inspection. He spent time showing me the .50 caliber machinegun mounted on each wing; each wing's 2.25 rocket pot holding 6 rockets and the 500-pound bomb mount on each wing. This little beast could do a lot of damage. The T-28 along with B-26 Marauder were the CIA's aircraft of choice for COIN (counterinsurgency) operations.

Then he spent a lot of time standing on the wing with the canopy open pointing out various aspects inside the cockpit. Throttle, prop, speed brake, instrument panel, gear and flap controls, canopy control. Then he got to the interesting stuff. There was a special panel for armament which we spent a lot of time talking about. He showed me the gun/bomb sight. He then showed me the survival kit which had been substituted for the seat cushion. It strapped onto the bottom of your parachute. He said that most people got rid of the survival kit and used the original soft padded seat bottom. He told me that's what he did and if he was forced to bailout, he would just eat the foam rubber cushion. I laughed but elected to keep my survival kit; at least for now.

While we were finishing up our briefing, two of the Polish armament technicians came out to the plane with a couple of blue practice bombs loaded on a cart and attached them to the bomb mounts. I had learned soon after I arrived that these guys carried British passports and that they had been part of the Polish resistance during WWII. They didn't socialize a lot and mostly kept to themselves. However they were well liked by everybody. They spoke English only when necessary. They came up to us after installing the practice bombs and gave us a scowling warning about how they had better not have to go hunting around in the snake and tick infested bush looking for their bombs. They had damn well better be close to the target. If not…somebody was going to owe them a hell of a lot of beer. They would be driving out to the bombing range later that afternoon to retrieve them. I made a mental note that I'd better not miss.

The engine start was simple. Close to the C-47 in many of its techniques even though the engine was made by Wight, not Pratt & Whitney, and only had one row of 9 cylinders rather than two rows of 9 cylinders like the C-47's engine. They generated about the same power. The first thing I noticed was these engines seemed to run rough. Tintin explained to me that that's just how the 1820 runs; I'd have to get used to it. He laughed and said, "if you think they feel and sound rough now…just wait till you're flying on a dark night." I swallowed hard.

Tintin spent a considerable amount of time once we had the engine running going over all the cockpit flight instruments and engine instruments. We exercised the speed brakes and flight controls, checked the hydraulic system and exercised the cowl flaps. I was feeling confident. We taxied out and just before takeoff Tintin told me to set the rudder trip to six degrees right rudder. "Six degrees…for real?" I asked. I could see Tintin's head nodding in the mirror, so I set the trip at six degrees right rudder. I was having a little trouble remembering to push one of the many buttons on my control stick before speaking. This was the only push to talk intercom I'd flown. Later, the modern jets had a button on the yoke for everything. But that would be years in the future. This was 1970 and this T-28-D model was probably manufactured in the early to mid-1950s then modified for the CIA a few years later. Everything in this airplane appeared to be brand new. Like just out of the factory crate. When they were retrofitted for COIN operations, everything was replaced and updated. I was a minor part of history but didn't realize it at the time.

When I got the tower clearance, I pushed the throttle forward and we immediately started moving down the runway. This was nothing like the lumbering C-46, C-47 or C-54. This was like being shot from a cannon. In a few seconds I realized why the six degrees rudder trim. The torque this thing was producing was unreal. In a matter of just a few seconds I was at rotate and liftoff speed. I was considerably behind the airplane. Things were moving faster than I'd ever experienced in an airplane. Finally I had the presence of mind to pull up the gear and immediately start to get some power off the airplane before I was exceeding any of my structural airspeed limitations. The T-28 D model was not a toy trainer. This was a full featured attack airplane in every sense of the term.

Tintin took control of the radio so I could have time to think and look around the cockpit. This was more fun than anything I could remember. Tintin got us cleared to a block altitude of 5,000 to 10,000 feet. I could practice stalls and steep turns and with Tintin's help some rolls and loops. He had me take it up to attack speed several times and then bring it back to cruise. Then attack speed in a nose-down attitude so I could simulate strafing and bombing configurations. All this went well.

Next, we headed for the bombing range. As we approached, I could hear the Polish armament technician's threats echoing in my ears. I'd better at least get close to the target. We climbed to altitude and Tintin started giving me instructions over the intercom. It was imperative the airplane was trimmed correctly and the "turn coordinator ball was in the center." This would be a "dry run" as we needed to insure the range was clear. The last thing we needed was to club somebody in the head with one of these practice bombs. The dive showed the range was clear. We pulled up hard, advanced the power to max-climb and headed toward the sky at an astounding 4000+ feet per minute. The transport airplanes I'd been flying climbed around 500 feet per minute.

When we reached 10,000 feet, we nosed over; I set the power to Tintin's recommended setting and soon we were at the 255 knot attack speed. I made sure the trim had the ball in the center and then armed the bombs. I found the target in the bomb sight and on Tintin's command I released one of the bombs then pulled up and headed back around for another pass. Tintin said I might not have to buy a beer on that one, but I still missed the target. I think I was more worried about keeping it in the range than I was hitting the target. I could still hear the armament technician's good-natured threats.

The second pass was worse than the first. I think it was because Tintin let me do it all by myself. But nevertheless, still inside the range. I could tell this was going to take some practice. We headed back to the field.

When we landed, I taxied in and Tintin climbed out. He told me to "take it around the patch a few times just to get the feel of things." I made four touch-and-go landings and brought it back in. It was amazing how quickly this thing could reach takeoff speed. To save the brakes, I had not done full stop landings but rather just touch down, configure the airplane on the roll and then apply takeoff power again. On the second touch and go, I started cheating and not applying full power. It was not necessary and besides, I didn't like dealing with all that takeoff power torque. After the final landing I taxied in and walked into operations to meet Tintin.

When I got inside, Tintin told me to be back at 9:00am in the morning for more practice. I was soaking wet with sweat and exhausted. I had a lot to think about on my drive back home.

Jason My T-28 Co-Pilot

When I drove into the drive, Jason heard the car and was waiting outside. His beautiful smile was always such a wonderful welcome. He spotted the helmet the instant I pulled it and my flight bag out of the car. He immediately asked to try it on. He was so cute. He put it on his tiny head and paraded around the house. Karen and I found this very humorous. I had just purchased my first Nikon; a 35mm Nikkormat FTN with a 50mm f2.0 lens. I bought it from a Colombian pilot whom I liked very much and enjoyed flying with. He had had it less than two years and wanted to upgrade. I paid $200 for it. A very fair price at the time considering they were not sold in the Congo. I grabbed the camera and took several shots.

That night Karen and I had a serious talk about my flying the T-28. It seemed I was being driven by some compelling lust for adrenalin. I found myself wanting to go places and do things others around me hadn't done before. That alone might be normal but in me, it was slowly becoming a driving obsession. Of course Karen agreed but I could tell she wasn't excited about my doing this.

The next day was more practice. But this time, all three of us went up. It was my first experience with formation flying. Tintin had his hands full. Leif was not better than I was. But we worked at it and gradually got better. I got my dummy bombs closer to the target as well. We were starting to shape up. I was starting to feel more comfortable in the airplane. In the debrief Tintin announced we would be departing at first light the following morning. Seems General Ehrabar was getting pressure from General Bobozo, the head of all armed forces, to get some COIN assets in the field. COIN or counterinsurgency assets in this case was Wigmo, Tintin, Leif, and me.

While flying the T-28 was what I had wanted, I felt bad about having to go home and tell Karen it was time for me to leave. The drive home from N'Djili to Limete was filled with mixed emotions…a kaleidoscope of desires and responsibilities. My craving for adventure at the expense of my family…my personal version of "live like you were dying." "If Only."

While I was dealing with my demons, President Nixon announced on 7 May 1970 that all U.S. troops would be out of Cambodia by 30 June. On 9 May, a fifty-ship combined U.S.-Vietnamese naval force under Operation Sealords entered Cambodia with the objective of clearing the Mekong River all the way to Phnom Penh. They were temporarily successful.[134]

The Whirlwind Of Chariots

"His chariots are like the whirlwind—to execute His anger with fury and His rebuke with flames of fire."[135]

I held Jason extra-long that morning as I was getting ready to leave. This time in addition to my flight bag I had a large duffle bag. And of course, Jason's favorite, my T-28 helmet. My heart was heavy. I was depressed.

When I got to the airport, I drove out on the flight line this time. A C-47 would be accompanying us with the armament technicians, their toys, a mechanic and an avionics technician, plus some assorted spare parts for the T-28s. There were two "embassy types" going as well. One I recognized to be the information officer for the embassy. The other I'd never seen before. I pulled up to my T-28 and put my flight bag in the back seat. I put my lunch in the front seat and headed for the C-47 with the rest. The two Americans walked over and introduced themselves. None gave their titles. I loaded my stuff on the C-47 and asked one of the mechanics to please offload it for me when they got to Albertville and make sure it got in the Wigmo jeep. He agreed but informed me it could cost me and made the sign of drinking from a bottle. I assumed he was not referring to Mirinda and he would have numerous opportunities to collect. This Wigmo group was different.

I did my walk-around and went over to Tintin who was just finishing up his preflight as well. We chatted about the en route weather which he had on the wing in a dispatch folder. He gave me my copy. This meant I would not have to go back into operations. Leif finished his walk-around and joined us. Our briefing was quick. Our fuel stop would be Mbuji Mayi. It was about half way. With the departure and arrival procedures, and if we used long range cruise, it would take just under three hours. It would also be a pilot pit stop as our tiny cockpit had no "honey bucket." There was a little air force-issued relief bottle in the cockpit, but I just figured I would wait. We parked our cars and headed to the flight line. Gus would drive my car back home for me that night.

---

[134] Cambodia and the Vietnam War—Olive-Drab.com
[135] Holy Bible—Holman Christian Standard Bible (HCSB)

Departure was normal. We all lined up on the runway and took off immediately in trail. By 3000 feet altitude we were joined up in our formation and climbing to our planned altitude of 11,000. We had oxygen should we need to climb higher and the C-47 had extra supplies to keep our supply recharged on the mission, but this seemed fine to everybody.

As we were approaching Kikwit I heard Tintin call me on our discrete frequency (a higher UHF frequency the civilian aircraft did not have) telling me to check my power setting. They were having to slow down. I did and reported it was exactly at cruise. But as I crosschecked my instruments, I noticed my airspeed had dropped by almost 10 knots. No terribly big deal unless you happen to have two other aircraft trying to fly in formation with you. Suddenly Tintin's voice came through the headset embedded in my helmet again. This time he was no so jovial. "Check your *blank blank* (expletive) speedbrake position," he said. "I can see it's extended a little bit." I looked over on the left side of my cockpit and I saw one of the straps on the left arm of my flight suit and gotten tangled up with the speed brake handle. This caused the speed brake to extend ever so slightly but it was enough to induce enough drag to slow my speed thus causing the other two pilots to have to adjust to mine. The noise on our discrete frequency exploded. I was significantly advised I would be buying many, many, beers that night. I figured why not. I already owed the mechanic one. I was glad the beer was cheap in Albertville.

We crossed overhead Mbuji Mayi at max cruise speed and peeled off onto a downwind. We kept our spacing moderately tight, which was how Tintin liked it, and touched down as the aircraft ahead was about to turn off. I was always number two and Tintin was the last to touch down.

As we taxied onto the ramp a contracted agent was waiting. He did not work for Wigmo, which meant we would have to supervise every move his refuelers made. They started on Leif's aircraft first. That meant I was first for the "restroom." I'd never been in this one but held few favorable expectations. I was longing for our aromatic honey bucket but alas it was not here. I was not surprised at what I found and was back out on the ramp in record time.

By the time I got back to the ramp our T-28s had drawn a crowd. The locals did not see many of these type airplanes; and when they did, it was never a good sign. They were ready to start fueling mine. These airplanes did not have the huge fuel tanks the transports had and soon all three planes were fueled and ready. We all did a quick walk-around had got back in and cranked up.

Our final leg to Albertville was just under two hours. We had to dodge a few afternoon cumulonimbus buildups but basically it was a smooth flight. The T-28s didn't have the ultra-long-range radios that the transports had. They weighed too much, and the antennas were too long. But when we crossed over Albertville's airport, we could see the C-47 was not yet on the ground.

Tintin, seeing they were not waiting on us, suggested we make a flyby of downtown Albertville, just to let any of the arms dealers and smugglers or perhaps rebel insurgents know there was a new kid on the block. This time Tintin took the lead. We followed him as he kept descending lower and lower and lining up with Lumumba Boulevard, which ran along the lakeshore. Albertville was 2500 feet above sea level, and I was guessing his altimeter was probably reading about 2550feet. He was literally right in the tops of the palm and eucalyptus trees. If this was an announcement that Wigmo's T-28s were in town, I thought perhaps it could be a bit of an overstatement. But I lowered the nose and inched my throttle and prop forward to keep us with him as we roared down Lumumba Boulevard in the tops of the trees. I remember seeing the Hotel Du Lac go flying by on my left. Tintin was running at attack speed (255 kts). Oh well.

We continued following the road and as we approached the Lukuga River we broke right and followed the lakeshore. The airport was about 10 km north of downtown Albertville. For the first time in my life, I had to climb to land. The T-28's minimum traffic pattern for landing would be around 1500 feet above the ground. We had been flying at about 50 feet.

We deployed our speed brakes to bleed our speed down to landing gear operating speed then dropped the gear. We lowered our flaps as our speed dissipated to each flap setting's speed limitations. Soon we were on the ground. Tintin first, I followed, and Leif was last. As we taxied in, we all opened our canopies to allow some fresh (cooler) air to get in. The Wigmo station agent and his crew were marshaling us to our parking places. The ground crew was excitedly pointing to Leif's engine. As I shut down and climbed out, I found out why. There were small branches and leaves plastered all over the top cylinders of his R-1820 engine. There were also green stains on his prop. Leif obviously had gotten just a tad too low. As we started teasing him about it, he recounted how the overpowering smell of eucalyptus was filling his cockpit. He said he felt like he had just received a giant dose of Tiger Balm. We all laughed. Some of the trees planted along Lumumba Boulevard had just gotten trimmed. The mechanics weren't going to laugh though. When their C-47 landed in just a few minutes, they would have to carefully remove the leaves to keep them from disrupting the air flow around the cylinders and causing hot spots which could lead to uncontrolled detonation and possibly serious piston damage. I could see that Leif would be joining me in buying beer for the mechanics at dinner that night.

While we were still landing some of the Congolese ground crew spotted the C-47 approaching the airport from the west. They were particularly keen in their lookout as that would be the last flight of the day and they could go home. There was no functioning control tower so the C-47's crew just passed overhead to insure the runway was clear and joined a left downwind to land. Soon they were on the ground as well. I already had my belongings from the T-28 loaded into the jeep. The agent had another jeep which he had obtained from the Congolese Air Force for the duration of this operation. With the three of us and the four Wigmo ground support people (two armament technicians and one mechanic and one avionics) we would be needing the extra jeep. Plus, this afternoon we had the additional two Wigmo C-47 pilots. An American from the embassy stationed in Albertville would pick up the other two guys. They had called the Wigmo station agent to get the C-47's arrival time. We were going to have some togetherness on the way to the Wigmo safe-house that night. The station agent had booked the two C-47 pilots' rooms in the Hotel Du Lac as the safe-house could not sleep all of us. They would be going back to K-1 the next day anyway.

As soon as the C-47 landed we got our bags and loaded them in the jeep. We waited while the spares, mechanic's tools, and the armament (bombs, rockets, and 50 caliber rounds) were unloaded and placed in a heavily-reinforced and locked cargo container Wigmo kept at the airport for occasions such as this. I noticed the armament technicians bring three small battleship-gray duffel bags to the jeep. They handed one each to Tintin, Leif, and to me. Then we were off to town and the safe-house. On the way into town I partially unzipped my new duffel bag. I saw a small automatic weapon and three long clips. There were several boxes of military issue ammunition in the bag as well. That explained why the bag had been surprisingly heavy. I zipped the bag back closed and figured I'd deal with this after dinner.

We all rushed through our showers and hurriedly got into some street clothes so we could go downtown and eat. Since the pilots were staying in town at the Hotel Du Lac, we decided we would all eat there. Most of the time we would be eating at the safe-house.

The Wigmo table was large. We had drinks on the terrace and then moved to the inside dining room for dinner. You could still see hints of the hotel's pre-independence splendor…but only dimly as through a mist. Nine years of the neglect that accompanied the "freedom" gained at independence had made its almost-certain indelible mark. With the uncertainty that loomed over the entire Congo, it seemed unlikely anyone would emerge willing to gamble a sizable investment in restoration. The story was the same everywhere in the country, only far more so here with all the rebel activity.

Soon many in our party were in high spirits. I was relieved to see we had the dining room to ourselves. To say the group was noisy bordered on an understatement. I found myself slightly embarrassed. While Wigmo offered classes in French and Lingala for its people, there was obviously no course in social and dining etiquette.

Upon our return, the ground crew and Leif continued drinking from the station's agent's personal stock.

The Mamba Samba

I decided I'd try to get a phone patch through to my father back in Hamilton before going to bed. The radio transmitter and 1000-watt linear amplifier were set up on a desk in a small room. A bed was beside the radio. The bed was used for crew overflow and for rare times when late night radio traffic would demand a continuous radio watch.

The procedure was to go to one of the designated MARS (Military Affiliate Radio System) frequencies and use the call sign assigned to Wigmo. A MARS volunteer would hopefully hear us and answer. If the signal was "patch quality" he would call collect to my father back in Hamilton and I could speak with him. He was always so proud when he got a call. That call would be all his Hamilton coffee drinking buddies would hear about for days.

While I was still tuning the radio, a movement on the floor to my right caught my eye. I looked over just in time to catch a glimpse of the last part of a dark gray snake slithering under the bed. Since the room was well away from the perimeter of the house and had no windows, my first ridiculous conclusion was that the station agent had a pet snake. I walked into the living room where they were still merrily enjoying what appeared to be the last of the agent's stash of alcohol. I asked if he had a pet snake. "Sure," he said…"I keep a couple of pythons around the house for entertainment. If I start missing my wife, they can give me a squeeze. They even remind me of her." Obviously, he was joking. I told him I'd just seen a slender gray looking snake slither under the bed in the radio room. Initially he thought I was kidding. When I convinced him I was not, he came with me to investigate. Of course the entire intoxicated group followed. I looked around the room for something to use against the snake. I saw a cane fishing pole standing up in the corner. I stuck it under the bed and thrashed it around. Within a couple of seconds the snake came out; this time rising into the strike position. It was a dark battleship gray color. Unlike the poisonous snakes I'd know back home in Texas, this one had a narrow head no larger than the rest of its body. The agent let out an expletive and announced in a voice pitched about an octave higher than normal that the snake was a black mamba. I suppose due to the gaggle of drunks in the doorway, the snake had turned toward the wall rather than the door. Now the snake, at least five or six feet long, was between me and the door. I jumped up on the bed, thinking that might offer some separation between me and this terrifying visitor. The agent came back with a baseball bat. However, the length of the snake appeared to be about twice that of the bat. It was then I witnessed one of the most profoundly unwitting acts of my life. The houseboy returned with a can of Shelltox, an aerosol insecticide widely used in the Congo to spray for mosquitoes. Before we could stop him, he approached the snake, lowered himself to almost eye level and gave the snake a dose of insecticide right in the snout. The snake's mouth was wide open at the time showing the famous black mouth from which it draws its name. The snake pulled back, unhurt but now obviously angrier than before.

I used this moment of distraction to leap off the bed and plow directly into the midst of the inebriated spectators blocking the door. I knocked half of them down. Amazing what adrenalin will do. Somebody yanked the houseboy back into the doorway and away from the angry snake. The station agent reemerged with a large and much longer bamboo pole. With this the mamba was finally dispatched. I never fully relaxed in that house again. To this day I can so clearly see what was unquestionably, at least for that night, the luckiest houseboy in Africa. I postponed the call to my father for another day.

Tintin and I decided it was time for bed but thanks to the mamba, sleep now, at least for me, was out of the question. I took time to examine the contents of my gray duffel bag before going to sleep. It was, as I had expected, a machine gun. It looked like an Uzi. On closer inspection, I found the manufacturer's stamp. Yep…that's what it was, an Uzi. This was the closest I'd ever been to one before. I knew some of the highest-ranking ANC's body guards carried them but never thought I'd be carrying one.

I played around with it for a few minutes. I found the semi/full auto mechanism; discovered the magazine release, the grip safety, noticed how the action worked and loaded all three magazines. I put everything back in the bag, zipped it up, and got in bed. I tried not to let my imagination start playing with mamba scenarios. I turned out the bedside light and tried to go to sleep.

Many Thoughts…Little Sleep

Sleep did not come easily. My mind was racing. I thought about the mamba and its possible companions. I thought of the possibility of being called upon to fire the 50-caliber machinegun on each wing or release the 500 pound bombs or 12 rockets against someone who very probably intended me or my country no direct harm. This part was bothering me a lot. Certainly the ones receiving the weapons supplied by the Chinese were doing their best to overthrow Mobutu's pro-western government and replace it with a pro-Russia or pro-China communist one. Certainly this was not in the best interest of the United States. But I was in the Congo, more than 7600 miles from Hamilton Texas. At what point do the political trespasses of these mostly-illiterate bush people motivated by politicians poisoned by Marxism lose their right to life? I was sure 99% had never even heard of America. More to the heart of the matter, at what point did I have the right to take their life. Even when sleep came, it was light and fitful.

Coffee's Caffeine And Sunrise Serotonin

When the alarm sounded, I felt as though I had had no sleep at all. I dressed quickly and went to the living room. Tintin was already having his coffee. Leif emerged a few minutes later looking like he had been beaten with a stick from last night's bout of imbibing. Hopefully he would recover after some coffee.

The station agent said we could not start to the airport until after sunrise. The rebels often closed the road to the airport after about 10:00pm. He said this was done partly to keep the military from traveling but mostly to rob whoever might be imprudent enough to travel well after dark. He said the airport was relatively well secured, but a significant stretch of the 10-kilometer distance from the airport to town was in rebel hands on many nights. He said FAC had no motivation to go out and try to reopen it. They would just wait for sunrise when the rebels melted back into the villages and bush where they hid. It was easy to see why Wigmo had job security. Well, at least for the moment.

I drank my coffee and laughed as the others described my almost soprano voice while dancing around on the bed waiting for my chance to leap to safety.

At first light we were on Lumumba Boulevard heading north toward the airport. My coffee's caffeine, my brain's serotonin, and my adrenaline were all starting to kick in. I was ready to get on with it.

Villagers were already setting up their little stalls beside the road and the shoulders were full of foot and bicycle traffic. Women were walking with incredibly large bundles balanced on their heads. Such a beautiful thing to watch. They walked as though they were gracefully dancing to some inner source of music. They swayed so perfectly in order to keep their load balanced. Truly amazing.

Upon arriving at the airport, we began our walk-around inspection. Our aircraft had been refueled the night before. As we were doing our walk-around, the armament technicians were attaching their loads and arming the machine guns. The plan was for each of us to go out in different directions patrolling a different section. We fully recognized most of the traffic would probably have gone under cover of darkness and we would address that issue later. But today, while we got used to the area and our mission, we would patrol in the daylight.

After finishing our preflight inspections, I asked the station agent if there was an acceptable place to try out my Uzi. Sure, he said. We can take the jeep across the runway to the parameter of the airport. He pointed to a spot. Nobody was close and no people or huts were in the firing trajectory. When Leif heard this, he decided I might have a point. Tintin grumbled that we just wanted to play cowboys. To which I replied that the "king of cowboys who led the low pass down Lumumba the previous afternoon had no right to complain." He picked up his gray duffel bag and hopped in the jeep with us.

Firing My First Machine Gun.

My dry run the previous night gave me familiarity with how the gun operated. That, combined with the fact that as a Texan I had grown up with guns, pretty much made me the group leader. My two European companions were awkward and clueless. I thought to myself that it was interesting that I was the one asking for a few rounds of familiarization. These guys were doing good to distinguish the business end from the stock. We were all hired as pilots...transport pilots...not trained paramilitary ground operations counter-insurgency experts. I remember thinking I was thankful that at least the Israelis had the good sense to put a grip safety on the thing. Leif and Tintin could easily turn this into a dangerous situation. I moved up first, tried my semi then full auto mode, removed my magazine, inspected the chamber, and got back in the jeep. If they were going to shoot somebody accidently, I wanted them to have to work hard to make it me. While I handled the gun with relative proficiency, I was totally amazed at how quickly it fired. I'd never seen anything like that before. I could tell from how the gun handled that the muzzle velocity couldn't possibly be very high. Later I learned it was only around 1300 feet per second. The .22 Long Rifle bullet I hunted with back in Hamilton County fell in the range of around 1100-1500fps. But, my new Uzi, in the stock-collapsed position was only 18.5 inches long. If I wanted more muzzle velocity, I'd be sharing my already cramped cockpit with a long gun. I quickly reasoned that this compact Uzi would be just fine. We drove across the runway and went to our planes. I climbed up on the wing, strapped my Uzi onto my parachute, strapped on my parachute, attached my survival kit, sat down and started latching my seatbelt. I felt like a sardine in a can.

My First Hazardous Pay Mission

I was first to go. I taxied out alone and made my departure from Runway 06 as it was closest to the ramp. It was still early, and the wind was calm. Later, on my return, I could expect a crosswind from the lake. The air was as smooth as velvet. The sun was just above the horizon. It was my favorite time to be flying, before the air had time to get bumpy. My zone for this mission would be the southern third of the lake. Leif had the center third and Tintin had the northern third. I climbed to about 7500 feet and set long range cruise. This would allow me to remain airborne for a longer period. I was about 5000 feet above the surface of the lake. This would allow me a relatively commanding view, yet enough detail to determine what appeared to be suspicious. It was easy to tell the direction of travel of the few boats on the lake by observing their wakes. If they appeared to be heading toward Albertville's port, there was little reason to watch them too closely. I settled into my seat and tried to find a comfortable position. It would be a long time before I could get out and stretch. I had noticed from my extended time in the cockpit the previous day that the firewall and floor near my rudder petals tended to transmit heat radiating from the engine. They were getting warm.

The rest of my body was cool from the outside air temperature which at this altitude was about 18 degrees Fahrenheit cooler than the temperature on the ground. The aircraft's skin had not had time to become cold-soaked yet. Now if only I was sitting on the seat that came from the manufacturer rather than my very hard and somewhat lumpy survival kit… I vowed I'd give this decision some further consideration.

Cat and Mouse
(score: mouse 1 – cat nothing)

About an hour and a half into the mission a small wooden boat caught my attention. I began making wide orbits and watching its course. It was not going to the port at Albertville. But then most small boats didn't. What first caught my eye was he had clearly come from Tanzania's side of the lake. He was now in our side and heading north-westward. His course would take him out of my sector and into Leif's sector. I called Leif on our discrete UHF frequency. Leif apparently didn't want to be bothered with it. I figured he had found a flight course that would keep the sun out of his eyes and was trying to catnap a bit to make up for last night's self-inflicted abuse. A somewhat risky venture being the T-28 had no autopilot. At any rate, regardless of what he was or was not doing, Leif had no interest in becoming involved.

So I followed the boat. I also descended to get a better look. I thought they perhaps had not seen me before as I was 5000 feet above them and was making wide orbits, which would aid in remaining undetected. I made my first pass at about 1000 feet. I could clearly see everybody and for sure they could see the airplane. Everyone onboard was black. There were no women and children; just men. I estimated the boat to be about eight or nine meters long. Secured in the center section underneath a blue, typical United Nations surplus tarpaulin, was their cargo. This probably in itself did not indicate they were smuggling arms. It would be logical they would cover their cargo to protect it from rain or any lake water that might splash in. But when they saw me, they increased their speed. They clearly were afraid of the aircraft.

After the first low pass, I decided I'd get a little closer to them and see if I could get them to change course and go back where they came from. Simple enough…nobody has any problems. So this time I dropped down to about 200 feet above the surface and moved my power up to attack speed. I came thundering down on them. I truly must have looked menacing. Just before passing directly overhead I moved the props fully forward which caused the engine to race. Two jumped out of the boat. This was exactly what I did not want to happen. I pulled up into a sharp climb and banked hard to setup for another pass. As I was climbing and reversing course I could once again see the boat and the two overboard passengers. The boat had stopped, and they were throwing a long rope to the two in the water. I circled to give them time to pull them back into the boat. This would also give me time to figure out what I was going to do next. The last thing I wanted to do was sink the boat as I was not sure that they were in fact smuggling arms. The two jumpers were now hauled back into the boat and the boat resumed it course at full speed for the shore. They were heading for the base of a mountain whose lakeside was a shear stone cliff rising perhaps eight or nine thousand feet straight up. I smiled. I had them. I had my plan. If they continued their present course, they would have to abandon the boat and scramble for cover into the thick mangrove looking bushes growing at the foot of the mountain. There was no other way. The boat could not go into the thick mangroves. They would surely not stay with the boat. When they abandoned the boat, I would strafe and sink the boat without harming anybody. That was the plan. I continued to follow them by making orbiting passes on the boat.

Suddenly when they were about three hundred meters from the base of the cliff, I saw what they were really heading for. There was a crevice in the cliff. Out of the crevice flowed a small stream. The stream appeared only to be about fifteen meters wide. Plenty wide enough for the boat to pass. Absolutely impossible for me to follow. I armed my 50 cals, pushed my prop and throttle to the firewall and felt the T-28 explode with power. I came boring down on the boat but couldn't get them in my gun sight in time. If I continued at this speed trying to get them in my sights, I would hit the side of the stone mountain. I'd die in a ball of flames. The little bastards had outfoxed me. I rolled hard left and pulled back on the stick till I almost blacked out. The powerful T-28 Trojan responded. I kept climbing until most of my airspeed had bled off then I let it hammerhead back into a course parallel with the mountains. I was now clear of danger, but considerably humbler. I'd been outsmarted. It wasn't that they were really that smart. It was just I had failed to notice the little stream coming out of the side of the mountain. Lord knows, such streams are all along the mountain range. I'd vowed that would never happen again. But then, perhaps it was the Lord's hand.

As I headed back south to continue patrolling my sector, I had a lot to think about. Had I done the right thing by trying to give them a chance to escape without their cargo? What if they were just poor village fishermen and I had shot them. But then what if I had just let a load of guns into the Congo that would be in rebel hands by nightfall? I decided to eat my sandwich and drink my Mirinda; this was giving me a headache. Just as I had the first bite of my sandwich in my mouth, the radio call came. It was Leif wanting to know what happened with the boat. I told him they turned out to just be fisherman. Tintin who had been monitoring all this on the frequency laughed and asked…"yes but did you shoot them?" To which I replied…"you're sick." "Yeah Man" he replied. The frequency grew quiet again. Everybody lost in their own thoughts.

We patrolled for about four hours. We reported our fuel remaining to Tintin ever hour. Everybody was getting down to around a quarter of a tank of fuel remaining and probably everybody needed to pee so Tintin announced this was enough for the day. We needed to get back in order to give the mechanics a chance to look at the airplanes. That was more than OK for everybody. I'd had my first combat mission. I'd earned my first combat pay. I'd let some unknown characters with a load of unknown cargo get away. That part I decided I'd keep to myself.

By the time we got back to the airport the crosswind from the lake was gusting across the runway at just about a 90-degree angle. Being 2500 feet above sea level made our true airspeed higher than our indicated airspeed and the crosswind provided no slowing of our groundspeed. This was going to be a tricky landing when we were all three on the runway at the same time. But all went well. We all climbed out of our planes, walked to the edge of the tarmac and took a pee. Tintin quipped that this was our mission debrief. I was fine with that. We hopped in the jeep and headed to the safe-house. The station agent would come in with the mechanics and the armament guys in the other jeep. We promised to call King–1 on the HF radio when we got to the house with our arrival times.

I took a long shower while Tintin was talking to King–1 on the HF radio. I changed into a t-shirt, shorts, and flip-flops and went out on the front porch to sit and enjoy the late afternoon and a cold Simba beer of course. Dinner would be here at the safe-house tonight. I ate and went to bed early. I wondered how Karen and Jason were doing. I knew there was no serious problem or Gus would have passed a message via the Wigmo net. But I still wondered. This night I slept well.

We followed this routine for several days. We encountered nothing sinister enough to shoot at. While the other two were hoping for some excuse to expend a few 50 cals, I was happy to enjoy the missions, draw my hazardous pay, and enjoy the scenery.

A Visit From The General

But things were about to change. We would usually leave for the airport around 2:00pm to be airborne by 3:00pm. Today we would fly after dark. Most of the runway lights did not work so they were going to use the smudge pots. I'd never landed by smudge pots before. Tintin had requested King 1 check the sunset and moon rise and set times and the moon phase for us. He had that information shortly after breakfast. We were fortunate that the moon was going to be almost full. That would make finding the airport easier if there weren't a lot of low clouds. There was only one navigation aid working on the airport…one old unreliable NDB. While that would help, we were going to need to rely, to a large extent, on visual clues. They didn't teach us about this at Southwest School of Aviation.

About 10:00am, as we were lounging around the living room, a black Mercedes drove up. Two military police jumped out and opened the back seat door and the general in charge of our area got out. Even though we were a paramilitary organization, we stood up at attention as he entered. We could see that he appreciated that. He motioned for us to be seated. He had already met Tintin and they immediately began speaking in Lingala. I was truly impressed at Tintin's command of the language. I was able to follow about twenty-five percent of the conversation. Leif was clueless. When the general had finished, Tintin passed the general's message. Simply stated, he advised that the word had been put out a couple of days ago and that as of tonight, only fishermen in designated fishing areas who were obviously fishing (moving around slowly and randomly in the water) could be on the lake. Everybody else could be fired upon. All cross-lake traffic had to be in the daytime. The navy would be out on the lake and he wanted us to be out there as well. Wigmo would be critical, as the navy had already demonstrated they couldn't stop anything. I was glad nobody knew about my "little boat that got away" episode, or they would be saying "the navy and Jimmy couldn't stop anything." Fate is often kind…even to fools. We assured the general we understood completely. He seemed pleased, thanked us, and left.

After the general had driven away, Tintin told us he had also mentioned some villages he wanted strafed. He would be bringing us a tactical map showing the "marked" villages in a couple of days. Tintin was particularly troubled about that. He said often the villages were selected due to tribal reasons and had nothing to do with their giving aid to the rebels. But then, this whole situation was drawn along tribal lines. Minority tribes or tribes not believing they were fairly included in the government could, after years of abuse or neglect, be convinced that the Kinshasa government was their enemy. And, not being from Mobutu's tribe, there would be little or no problem taking up arms against a government more than 1000 miles away that was from a different tribe and spoke a different language. A Congolese had about as much chance changing the color of his skin as he did escaping the real and often brutal effects of tribalism.

"Kill Them All…Let God Sort Them Out"

Tintin said he didn't trust the intelligence the general would be providing. "So, how in the hell do we deal with that," I asked. "I don't know" Tintin replied. We had sandwiches and iced tea for lunch and left for the airport as scheduled.

As we bounced along the semi-paved road to the airport, I recalled a bronze sign on the wall in Gold Finger's office. It read "Kill Them All…Let God Sort Them Out." While the saying was hundreds of years old, I was told the sign had its origin from the early days of Wigmo, in the time when the Congo was torn apart by fighting and filled with mercenaries. On the surface the slogan resounded with machismo, evoking the mercenary images found in books and movies. But upon dissection, its roots ran to the very gates of hell.

Somehow, deep within me, some of the seeds planted while attending the First Baptist Church in Hamilton had survived amidst the human jungle in which I now lived. Not all the Sunday school and Royal Ambassador lessons sowed by Mildred Newson and Beth Spencer and fallen upon rocky soil. Nevertheless, at this time in my life, few of those seeds had sprouted above the surface and become visible. There certainly seemed little results on the surface.

Smudge Pots And Moon Light

When we arrived at the airport, the mechanics were done with their pre-flight, the armament technicians had strapped on their goodies and we were ready to go. The plan was the same. I would take the southern sector, Leif the center, and Tintin the northern sector. We would patrol until about two hours after sunset. Then return to the airport and land by smudge pots. For the night landings, only one airplane on the runway at a time. We were to maintain radio listening watch on both guard (121.5MHz) and our UHF discrete channel for our communications with each other.

I took off and headed south down the lake. Tintin next and headed north. Leif took off last. The air had a light chop and there were still a few cloud buildups remaining but nothing that would hinder our operation. I found if I maintained about 6500 feet, I could stay under most of them and still have good visibility of the lake surface. I set long range cruise and began my patrol. I couldn't believe I was getting paid for this…and hazardous pay as well. I tried not to think about what I would do if I found a suspicious boat. Felipe used to tell me that in the early 1960s when some missions appeared to have too many civilians in the area, many of the Cubans would go out and fire off a few rounds into the jungle to create the illusion they were strafing enemy targets. I started to think that was not such a bad idea. I watched a beautiful sunset.

Soon the lake began to twinkle from the lights of the fishing boats. They were where they were supposed to be. I circled some of the groups just to let them know the government meant business. I did not come close to them as I knew they were truly fishing but I made sure they saw me.

The mission went quickly. The frequency was quiet except for our routine "ops normal" calls. Nobody saw anything. Soon I heard Tintin call for return to base. I was glad to get the call. But now I had to face the unknown of landing by smudge pots. That cranked up the anxiety factor. Tintin called Wigmo on their VHF frequency. They had a handheld radio in the jeep. The mechanics and the station agent were waiting. They got in the jeep and drove down the runway making sure it was clear. The mechanics lit all the smudge pots. That took about 10 minutes.

I arrived first and circled till they had all the pots lit. When they gave the all clear I joined downwind, turned a tight base as I did not want to lose sight of the runway. I could see the pots. They could be described as dim at best. I noticed I didn't have the depth perception that normal landing lights gave. These were not really lights. They were just little twinkles that outlined the sides and ends of the runway. I had never seen what the T-28's landing lights did. I turned them on when I was on about three mile final. They did an adequate job. On short final I could see the surface of the runway. That was all I needed. My touchdown was a little firmer than I would have liked but heck...I was just happy to get on the ground.

As I was turning onto the taxiway, I heard Leif call left downwind. I stopped on the tarmac and positioned my nose so I could watch his final approach and landing. All went well. Tintin was the last to arrive. Leif and been on the ground about five minutes when Tintin called. But he was going for a straight in approach. I suppose he already knew the runway was clear and he could see the smudge pots when he called five mile final. By this time I had shut down and was standing on my wing watching him land. He too made it fine. When Tintin climbed down we were all hungry and ready to go into town for a meal. The station agent and the mechanics had everything done in another fifteen minutes. We piled into our two jeeps and headed into town.

The Diners Club was Annoyed

I had not eaten much that day and was ready for a drink and meal at the Hotel Du Lac. When we pulled up to the hotel, we realized we had a problem. We couldn't leave our flight bags and the Uzis in the jeep. We had no choice but to bring them in with us. I had placed my Uzi in the gray duffel bag it came it; the other two just had theirs slung over their shoulder. We entered the dining room and took a table in the back. The dining room was not large and probably had about ten tables. Three Belgium couples were seated across the dining room already having their meal. It was obviously a planned group dinner. Their gaze followed us as we made our way to our tables. It seemed everybody in our group drug their chair across the floor producing what I considered a loud, annoying and unnecessary noise. Our group was all laughing and talking loudly. The Belgiums were particularly staring at the Uzis slung over Tintin and Leif's shoulders. I figured they had little trouble figuring out what was in my bag as well. We were embarrassingly loud. And of course in their eyes, we were CIA mercenaries.

While waiting on our meal and halfway into the second round of Simba beer, the owner came over to our table. He knew Tintin and they spoke in French. I got enough of the conversation that I didn't need a translation. So did everybody else. Because Tintin was a Belgium and the three couples plus the hotel owner were all Belgiums as well, Tintin made a halfhearted effort to get everyone to tone it down. But in a couple of minutes he was again laughing and swearing loudly with the others. I could see their cold stares. They hurriedly finished their meal and left. Everybody seemed to think that was funny. I understood completely how the Belgiums must have felt. I was becoming uncomfortable with the mission and uncomfortable with my mission mates when out in public together. After the Belgiums left I enjoyed my meal and the conversation.

An Interesting Encounter

At a table in the back of the room, with his back to the wall, facing the door, was a lone diner. Aside from us, he was the only one left in the restaurant. I'd been watching for some time. He didn't seem to be bothered by our noise. He finished off his meal with a couple of glasses of Cognac. He was obviously European. Tintin called out to him and asked if we could buy him a drink; totally in character for Tintin; totally out of character for me. The man accepted our invitation in French. Tintin immediately invited the man to join us. As he drew up a chair, we all introduced ourselves. The conversation gradually turned to the instability of the region. The man also spoke good but heavily accented English. Realizing my faltering French he switched the conversation back to English. Slowly it came to light that he had been one of Tshombe's Belgium mercenaries. He'd come back and was doing some "contract work." No one questioned him further although I'm sure everyone wanted to. Later our talk continued down the line of the present humanitarian situation and how we were all just minor players in a very high stakes game. I mentioned how I sometimes had doubts about being involved in this terrible conflict and how I frequently felt that exposing myself to this unnecessary danger was unfair to my family. He stared off into space and said, "In this line of work it is a given that you risk your life…the only choice is what you risk it for." I don't remember his name, but I carry his words with me always. It was a line that I can keep.

Back at the safe-house, I used the gun cleaning kit I found in the duffel bag and gave the new Uzi a light superficial cleaning. Just the barrel and the chamber. I climbed into bed but again sleep did not come easily. While there had been many things to laugh about at dinner, my brain was finding many things to think about when I should have been sleeping.

Gold For Guns

Things rocked along for the next couple of days in what was settling into a routine. We could honestly say we seemed to have deterred the arms smugglers from making their runs.

In chats with the Wigmo station agent I learned that there were some capitalists in the woodpiles of the Chinese communists. Part of our station agent's job was to cultivate sources and always be on the lookout for new information. This was a very natural outgrowth of his day to day responsibilities. He had been getting stories for some time now about how before the guns could be delivered, the Chinese agents were requiring payment in gold mined by the Congolese rebels. It was gold ore but nevertheless quite valuable. Local sources believed this was not part of the official Chinese policy but merely a creative capitalistic spin applied at the grass roots level. I found this quite amusing; so much for the good Chairman Mao and his "Little Red Book." That's why communism was doomed…Jimmy Joe Jacks could see it…why couldn't Chairman Mao?

Crew Rotation

Gold Finger sent a message saying since I was married, I could rotate out for a week or so and they were sending in another one of the co-pilots to relieve me. He would take his T-28 training here in Albertville and ride observer on missions until he was ready to fly solo. I tried to contain my excitement but Tintin saw it. He told me not to worry, Gold Finger was sending his latest live-in girlfriend here to stay with him for a while. Leif was the only one without a wife or girlfriend and it appeared he was working on improving that situation locally. So all was well. They thought my relief would be here in two or three days.

My Moment Of Truth

The next day we had been given some villages to target. Nobody was very happy about that. I'd already made up my mind that I thought I could scare the living hell out of them with my 50 cals without hurting anybody. I wasn't sure what the others had decided. I didn't really want to know. I did wonder, however, if they had come to the same conclusion I had, but not badly enough to ask them.

We sat around the breakfast table that morning studying the tactical map the general's messenger had delivered. We all brought our maps to the table. This was very serious stuff. We did not want to mark the wrong village on our maps. We were already distrustful of the general's map. It was a relatively easy task as most Congolese did not live in the jungle. Mostly only the pygmies did that. The Bantu lived along the roads and were reputed to be afraid to venture deeply into the jungle. The river and the road provided easy navigation clues. The trick was to find a distinct landmark by or near each village to insure you were looking at the correct village. Most villages were just a tiny dot on our map and, usually did not comprise more than fifteen or twenty little grass huts.

We would fly in formation to the village site then Tintin would lead, Leif would go second, and I would go third. We must all agree that we have the right village before joining into attack formation. We would fly in a high diving circle. After Tintin pulled up Leif, about one mile behind him, would begin firing. When Leif pulled up, I would begin firing. When I pulled up Tintin would be back behind me ready to fire again when I pulled up. Tintin would determine when to break off. Everybody was unusually quiet as we headed to the airport that morning.

I noticed Tintin was walking with a more pronounced limp than he usually had. He always limped due to an aircraft accident he had back in Belgium but today it was worse. When I asked, he told me his feet were starting to get infected from being exposed to the heat generated by the firewall from the T-28's cockpit. He said he was going to need some medicine and probably see a doctor. As a navy corpsman I knew exactly what he needed but wondered if any of it would be available in the pharmacy. I told him I'd go with him to the pharmacy when we got back.

After the strafing run, we would go patrol our areas for a while then call it a day. Tintin's feet could become quite serious if we couldn't find the medication he needed.

Departure was normal and we joined up overhead the field and headed north up the lake. At our checkpoint on the lake we turned heading 295 degrees. We saw National Highway 5 just as we should. We continued the 295 heading and soon the soil started turning reddish brown, just as it should. We saw the dirt foot trails running on the top of the mountain, like they were supposed to do. We saw the dirt trail make a "Y", the sign we were getting close. One of the "Y"s fingers made a "J" and came to an end. Our village was at the end of the "J." From high altitude circling the village appeared to be a small group of reddish-brown mud huts. I wondered what kind of rebel operation or rebel sympathizers these mud huts could be housing. I hoped the general's intelligence sources were better than anything else I had seen associated with the ANC. But by then I didn't care. I'd already decided I was going to shoot to the left of the target. That would allow my rounds to hit the steeply sloping side of the hilltop running into a valley; clear of the huts. I figured that if the villagers started running, they would run down the footpath rather than down the steep hillside. We were about to find out if my plan was going to work.

Tintin gave the command to start the attack…"follow me." I could see him nose over and watched as his cruise speed moved rapidly toward attack speed. Soon Leif followed him down. When I got to the break point, I too lowered my nose and advanced the power to attack setting. I started encountering wake turbulence from both their aircraft so I reduced my descent angle slightly so my path would be above them. When this was accomplished, I pointed my nose back on the target but this time with a steeper angle. I saw Tintin break left. Leif continued then he too broke left. I armed my guns. I had the village in my sights, I then inched my heading about 5 degrees left, waited a second and started firing. As I was firing, I saw people throwing dirt in the air and on their heads. They were terrified. I must have frozen. The next thing I knew I heard Tintin's voice coming over the radio screaming "pull up . . . pull up for *obscenity* sake." I pulled back hard on the yoke and broke left. I had waited far too long to begin my pull up. Tintin's voice came back, "what to *obscenity* were you trying to do…kill them with your prop?" I replied, "I guess I just got carried away." "Keep doing that and they will carry you away from here in the back of a jeep if they can find enough pieces," Tintin said. "I'll be a little less involved next time," I promised.

On our second pass I was more prepared. I refined my plan even more. I even squeezed off a few more rounds than last time; again, in the same place. I was expecting to see blood and carnage, but I didn't. I wondered if their aim was really that bad or they too had picked out their own spot where no one would be hurt. I decided I wouldn't ask. Tintin's voice came back over the radio saying he thought we had delivered the general's message…it was time to head back to our sectors on the lake.

As we patrolled up and down our sectors I wondered if I might find it got easier to shoot on target. I decided I did not want to know the answer to that question. If these people were my enemies, trying to hurt my country, I could be vicious. But they weren't.

Tintin, called saying he had just turned a boat around by firing over their bow. I wished I had some exciting and positive to report. My sector as well as Leif's was quiet. Soon Tintin called an end to the mission and return to base.

My Only Aviation Incident

(in 40 years of flying)

We all arrived at the airport just about the same time. We all had each other in sight. Tintin wanted to make another pass down Lumumba but he had confessed to the general and mentioned that perhaps we should make any future passes out over the water alongside Lumumba rather than trimming the trees along it. So, this time we formed up out over the lake to the south of Albertville and then started our run along the shoreline. We still must have been an awesome sight. Again we pulled up. This time Leif was first, I was second and Tintin last. Tintin wanted to make this a formation landing with everybody on the runway at the same time. Even though we had the typical late afternoon crosswind coming in from over the lake, it would still be fine. Our margins were reduced but still OK.

Leif touched down and was rolling out more slowly than I an anticipated. I slowed to keep a safe distance from him. But then I heard Tintin shouting on the radio for me to hurry up. Apparently, he had been trailing me too closely. I heard him call touchdown and I was a bit concerned but figured he would be able to keep his distance from me like I was from Leif. But such was not the case. Tintin was asking me to speed up when I was trying to slow down so he would not get too close to me. I obliged and gave my aircraft a little nudge of power. Finally Leif cleared the runway and I started breaking heavily in order to get mine stopped before the turnoff. My brakes were fine when I first started applying them. But as I had to apply more and more pressure to get stopped after my acceleration to accommodate Tintin, I found my brakes were becoming less effective. Finally in a move of desperation I was literally standing on them…nothing was happening. They were totally ineffective. It was like I was sliding on ice. I had studied this at Southwest School of Aviation but had never experienced it…a phenomenon known as "brake fade." When the brake disks reach a certain temperature, friction ceases to be generated. Unfortunately such was my case. It was the most helpless feeling I'd ever experienced. I was watching everything in slow motion. I could see the end of the runway coming but there was nothing I could do to stop the airplane. I was for all practical purposes, along for the ride.

A couple of seconds later I felt my nose wheel drop off the end of the runway and sink in the soft sand. The nose strut gave way under the stress and collapsed letting the aircraft's nose lower. This allowed the prop to come in contact with the sand. The aircraft came to a stop. I knew from previous training I had to get out of the aircraft as soon as I could. I shut down the engine, hit the power master off and hopped out on the wing. I wasted no time; with the second hop I was off the wing and sprinting through the sand. I could feel my emergency survival kit slapping my butt as I ran, helmet, parachute, Uzi and all. I didn't know if I was about to catch fire or not. But I was sure if it did, I'd be watching it from a distance.

Probably about fifty meters away I decided I could stop and look backward. There it set, nosed over in the sand; no flames, no hissing rockets. I was safe and the aircraft had only minor damage.

By this time Tintin had cleared the runway and was climbing out of his T-28. He was happy to see I was OK. The first thing he said was "sorry." I was trailing you too close. I smiled and said we were all safe. I did tell him I was visualizing the prop of his aircraft chopping its way through the tail of mine like some monster WeedWacker™ when I goosed the power to speed up. Perhaps my vivid imagination induced a little more power increase than was necessary. However, it would all still have worked had not the brakes faded. What a helpless feeling that was.

The armament technicians were the first to approach the aircraft. One got up on the wing and gave the all clear to the others that the power was off, and nothing was armed. They brought their little cart and started unhooking all their goodies. The mechanics had brought a sawhorse and had some Congolese pulling on the tail so they could slide the sawhorse under the engine cowling. They turned the prop through several times and confirmed the engine was OK. The prop was history as was the nose wheel strut. They confirmed they had everything in spares back in King 1. The parts would be here on the plane that was supposed to rotate me out and bring my replacement in. Deep down inside, I was very happy to be leaving. I would figure out how to tell Gold Finger I didn't want to come back later. But I knew I didn't want any more strafing. While I deep down didn't like these people, they were not my enemies.

While I was battling my own rebel insurgent (my evil twin) over the ethics of taking part in strafing the Congolese rebels, high level Cambodian military officers were acquiring instant wealth. With the United States now picking up the tab for Cambodia's massive military buildup, troop rosters were soon filled with phantom soldiers whose monthly pay created instant wealth for Cambodian commanders. These corrupt commanders soon realized additional wealth could also be made from taking the M-16 rifles provided by the United States and selling them to their new recruits. The new recruits were issued old colonial-era rifles which were no match for the AK-47s carried by the Viet Cong and Khmer Rouge. If they wanted to improve their chances of staying alive, they would have to buy their M-16s. These recruits were mostly from poor rural families. Scraping up the kind of money required to purchase an M-16 meant their families would have to sell a cow or several pigs to purchase the weapon. Corruption, since Sihanouk's ouster, was spreading like a wildfire raging out of control. Ironically, corruption was one of the charges brought against Sihanouk by the Cambodian Congress.[136]

That night I got the first sound night's sleep since arriving in Albertville. The next morning, the air smelled fresher; the coffee's flavor deeper and more complex; my fried eggs, hash browns and salted fish from Lake Tanganyika had never tasted so good. The station agent already had the ETA of the C-47 bringing my relief pilot. The replacement prop and nose gear strut were also onboard along with an extra mechanic specializing in props. Tintin and Leif would be leaving in about an hour to do some more daylight patrols. I would pack and ride to the airport with them to eliminate the need to come back to the safe house for me. I cleaned my Uzi one more time, emptied all my magazines, returning the cartridges to their boxes, and placed everything back in the gray duffel bag. I would miss the Uzi. Shooting it had been fun. And I must confess, carrying it encouraged a little swagger when I walked.

As we bounced along the pothole-filled road to the airport, I was thinking about Jason. I could just see him putting my T-28 helmet back on his tiny little head and running around the living room playing fighter pilot. I was ready to go home. I guess I'd missed Jason more than I had Karen, but I just supposed that was normal. When he was first born, I always wanted Karen to have him all ready for bed when I got home. That way I could play with him for a few minutes and she would put him to bed so the rest of the night would be ours. Now I enjoyed watching him run about playing with his toys and explaining everything under the sun to me. If I could only relive the years I had him sent to bed early…"If Only."

Tintin and Leif's departure was normal. For a few seconds I wished I was going with them; but then the image of the villagers throwing dirt up in the air over their heads flashed back into my mind.

As the relief pilot climbed off the C-47 to greet me he laughed and asked if my T-28 came with brakes. I told him "yes, but don't get them hot or you'll see what I saw and that's hard on your nerves." We all had a big laugh. He

---

[136] The Tragedy of Cambodian History - by David P. Chandler

asked me lots of questions about what the missions were like. I shared my experiences with him while carefully omitting my village strafing experience. I did share my "the one that got away" experience. We had another big laugh. His training was set to begin with Tintin the following day.

Soon the plane was refueled and loaded with passengers (and vegetables of course). I had a lot to think about as the two Pratt & Whitney 1830s droned on and on. We arrived back in King 1 just a little after dark. I picked up my car keys in flight ops and headed for Limete.

Karen and Jason were waiting at the back door as I drove in. I was glad to be home. Jason's trotting around the living room sporting the helmet with its visor pulled down was a wonderful sight. Karen brought me a bottle of Primus. I sipped my beer and listened to both at the same time. I was glad to be home.

Gold Finger's Office Again

The next day I headed for flight operations. I was not on the flight schedule and I needed to somehow convince Gold Finger not to assign me back to the T-28s. I decided the truth, or an abbreviated version of it would be the best approach. When I sat down, he asked some questions about the brakes fading. He had not been aware of the phenomenon before but when word of the incident came back, he heard numerous first hand accounts from some of the older pilots. He mainly wanted to know what it felt like. I told him it was a helpless feeling. He nodded.

I then told him I had some serious questions about the validity of some of our proposed strafing targets. Again he nodded. I told him I was having issues with firing on villagers that might not actually be involved in the conflict. He then laughed and suggested I do what the Cubans used to tell him they did…just go out and spray a few rounds into an empty spot and come back with a tally. I told him I supposed I could do that, but I just felt I'd be doing Wigmo a lot better job flying transports. To my surprise, he smiled again and said he could fix that. Would I be ready to get back on the schedule the next morning…that he was short of copilots. I said I'm ready.

Heavy Flying–New Captains Arrive–More Money

The next several months were filled with heavy flying. I was young, strong, and could stand a diet of seven-day-a-week flying. The overtime was great. I'd rack up 120-150 hours every month. That amounted to around $600 in overtime each month. Each month the Hamilton National Bank would get that strange wire transfer from Lichtenstein. Karen had told me how Daddy would be asked by the ladies working in the Hamilton National Bank where "Lichtenstein" was. Of course that would make him very proud. He had no earthly idea where Lichtenstein was, but he knew enough to say that "it's way over there in Europe." For the first time in our married life, I didn't have to worry about paying the bills. It was a good feeling.

One morning in flight ops I met a couple of new pilots who had just been hired. They were processing in. These pilots were older than our average group. I would later learn they were far more experienced as well. They were also American; something unusual for Wigmo as they normally tried not to look like Americans. Even though all the Wigmo Cubans carried American passports, their appearance always left open the avenue of denial by the U.S.

The new pilots had arrived with a DC-4 or (C-54) Wigmo had purchased in Europe. At first, I assumed they were just ferry pilots, but I soon learned they had been offered jobs. After they left and before I headed for my plane, Gold Finger called me into his office. I was now one of the senior co-pilots and they needed a couple of us to fly with these new guys while they were getting airport and route qualified. I picked the one named Paul whom I'd just finished talking with. We would start flying together as soon as he was all processed in. That's cool I thought…more overtime.

While I was racking up overtime in the Congo, the debriefing of a North Vietnamese defector in October of 1970 revealed a North Vietnamese/Viet Cong Advisory Organization had been set up (in Cambodia?) soon after the coup (Norodom Sihanouk) "to provide key cadre and technical support." Their mission was to "aid the development of a Communist infrastructure in Cambodia by providing experienced cadre to fill the key positions" in the National Front and to "organize and train Cambodian personnel." [137]

Paul Rakisits

Wigmo had a crew house on Dahlias, the street just behind our house. The housing people put Paul and the other pilot, Hank, in that crew house. They were literally just behind our back wall. This made it easy for me to pick Paul up in the morning on the way to the airport, sparing him a ride in whatever crew vehicle they might have. I happily agreed to have Paul ride with me. Two days later our first assignment came. A C-54 flight to Kisangani, Albertville, then back to Kinshasa. A long day. I was happy…a great overtime generator.

I picked Paul up outside the crew house on Dahlias just as the sun was starting to turn the eastern horizon orange. I liked him instantly. Before we had gone five minutes he had his wallet out showing me pictures of his family. He had a beautiful wife named "Marie-Jeanne." She was a former flight attendant. They met while both Paul and Marie-Jeanne were flying charter in Europe. Marie-Jeanne had a son named Claude. Paul and Marie-Jean had a daughter named Natacha. I saw all the pictures and got half their life's story before we got to N'Djili airport. Although I couldn't possibly have realized it at the time, this was the beginning of a friendship that would last till Paul's passing on 9 March 2009…a friendship that would crisscross the world.

---
[137] Pike Archives—How Pol Pot Came To Power by Ben Kiernan

Paul knew his business and I knew mine. We were in and out of flight ops in a matter of minutes. Paul did a meticulous preflight. It was obvious he didn't trust this aircraft, which he'd never flown before, or the mechanics he didn't yet know. Once inside the cockpit he spent an unusual amount of time studying every log book maintenance entry. Paul clearly had had more than his share of crappy airplanes and he had established a habit of working hard at staying alive. I would learn a lot from this man during our hours flying together as well as our countless hours sitting quietly talking.

Paul and I flew together for the next couple of weeks. Operations was making sure he saw all our major airports and routes. Unlike our Colombian chief pilot who slept all the time, Paul never closed his eyes. His instrument scan was tireless. Paul's eyes were like the sweep on a radar screen. They never stopped. He constantly monitored every instrument in the cockpit. He would study the navigational chart and look outside; trying to locate what was depicted on his navigational chart. This was a real professional.

One afternoon, on our last leg of the day, Paul told me to take the left seat. I told him I'd never taxied or made a takeoff in the C-54 from the left seat. On the C-46 or C-47 this would be a non-issue. But the C-54 had nose-wheel steering. I'd never used that before. Paul's response was "get in the left seat and stop making excuses." That was all I needed…"faster than a speeding bullet,"[138] I was over in the left seat; while hardly any "Superman," I was humbled and excited. I could start the engines with my eyes closed, but when it came time to release the parking brake and advance the throttles slightly to taxi out from the ramp, I felt a butterfly or two in my stomach. When it was time for us to make our turn out of our parking space and head for the end of the runway, my butterfly count and increased to level four. But, by the grace of God, the nose wheel steering responded exactly as I had always imagined it would. I took it slowly and cautiously. But it was happening; Jimmy Joe Jacks from Hamilton Texas was taxiing a C-54. Life just couldn't get any better than this. On the taxiway at the end of the runway, I did the before takeoff engine run-up check, Paul read the checklist and I responded to all the challenge items. Paul then advised "before takeoff checklist complete." Paul gave an all stations call on the radio and we both did a visual scan of the traffic pattern and final approach. With no radio response and no visual contact on any traffic, I turned onto the runway, slowly advanced the throttles to takeoff power, we made a final scan of our engine instruments, and I released the brakes. The C-54 started lumbering down the runway. By the time we had reached rudder speed I was back in familiar territory. I rotated and when a positive rate of climb had been established, I called gear up. We were off…flying into the sunset.

When we arrived in Kinshasa a few hours later, I was much more comfortable with the thought of the landing than I had been with taxiing. Felipe had let me land the C-54 many times before and now that I had the fear of the

---

[138] Superman—DC Comics, by Jerry Siegel and Joe Shuster

nose wheel steering behind me…I was ready to give it a go. The landing was uneventful. But as we taxied onto the ramp my friendly butterflies returned. The lead mechanic was marshaling us into the hanger…not to one of the regular C-54 parking spots. He wanted us to nose the airplane into the hanger so they would not have to tug us in. What a fine time to be sitting in the left seat. Paul just smiled. As we neared the entrance to the hanger Paul and I saw General Ehrabar standing in the hanger. Paul smiled again. When we climbed down from the airplane, the general was waiting for us. I was expecting the worse. We saluted and shook hands with the general. Before he could ask any questions, Paul said, General, meet our new C-54 captain (which of course was not true, but Paul figured the general would never know any different). The general said congratulations. I was hoping like hell we would never have to explain this.

"Captain" Jacks

One night as Paul and I were heading into flights ops to hand in the paperwork for that day's flight and check our flight assignment for the following day, we found I was no longer flying with Paul. He was flying with one of the other co-pilots. My name was on the schedule for a C-47 flight with Felipe, but it said "local" which meant takeoff and land in King 1. I assumed it was a test flight. We also noticed Paul's name no longer had a star beside it which meant he was no longer restricted to flying with only senior co-pilots. He was now considered airport and route qualified. In a way I was sad, as I'd really enjoyed my time with Paul. I'd learned a lot from him in those two short weeks. Paul used every situation, every moment, as a teaching opportunity. It had been a great experience.

As I looked in my mail box, I found a note from Gold Finger. My first thought was "this is not good…they're sending me back to Albertville on the T-28s." But when I opened the note, I was pleasantly surprised. Surprised was a gross understatement. I was ecstatic. I was going into captain training on the C-47 beginning the following morning. That explained why I was with Felipe and why our flight was "local." We would probably be doing air work and landings from the left seat. I couldn't wait to get home and tell Karen the good news.

My ride home that night with Paul was quiet but I did tell him how grateful I was to him for all he had shown me in the two short weeks we had flown together.

Over dinner I told Karen about the good news. Most of what we talked about was the extra $400 base pay plus the extra $4 an hour I would be getting after I crossed the 100 flight hour base. It would mean about $600 a month to us. I couldn't wait to send a letter to Daddy telling him the good news.

Local Flying

My next two flights were with Felipe in the C-47. They had two maintenance test flights that needed to be done. So we did one in the morning, came back and had lunch and another in the afternoon. On both flights we practiced maneuvers, including stalls. We also did inflight engine shutdown and restart. That was a first for me. At Southwest School of Aviation it was prohibited to shut down an engine in flight on our twin-engine Piper Apache trainer. We would simulate a shutdown by full power retard then simulate engine feather by advancing the power a tiny bit. But I found my butterflies returning as I retarded the throttle on a perfectly good engine, shut off the mixture control, and feathered the engine. After we were on single engine, Felipe had me do 45-degree bank left and right turns. Then we would restart the engine and shut down the other engine. When we landed after both flights, the back of my flight suit was soaked in perspiration. Felipe gave me quite a workout.

We were finished by 3:30pm which was something I was not accustomed to. I realized I had a little extra time to spend as I liked rather than rushing home to eat and go to bed so I could get up early the next morning and do the same thing again. Being in training had benefits other than the future monetary ones. I decided I'd stop by the crew house on the next street over from our apartment and visit Paul. I had noticed he had a flight segment cancelled so he too was home early.

Captain Robert A. (Bat) Masterson

When I got to the crew house, I found Paul having a gin and tonic with a pilot I hadn't really gotten to know yet. They called him "Bat"...Bat Masterson. Bat had the largest handlebar mustache I'd ever seen. He liked to slowly twist and curl it up into almost a complete ring. I'd said hello merely in passing. I was good to have the opportunity to sit down with Bat and Paul and share a drink.

Since I didn't drink gin or anything else that strong, I was given a beer from their refrigerator and was told to drink it quickly as its owner might return at any time. There were four pilots staying in the crew house at the time. I wasn't sure if they were joking with me or not. But since it was a one-liter bottle, drinking it quickly was out of the question. I just decided if the unknown owner arrived before I had discarded the evidence, I'd offer him a drink, unless of course it was my last swallow.

As with Paul, I liked Bat immediately. I would later find out that he was a highly experienced Air Force fighter-jet test pilot. Bat had flown in all kinds of operations and had just come from a stint in Biafra (the Nigerian civil war). Bat was a devoted family man. I soon learned that like Paul, Bat's family would also soon be arriving in the Congo. But unlike Paul, Bat's family was by some standards considered large. As we visited, I learned that Bat had volunteered to be based in Kisangani. FAC had a lot of missions in that part of the Congo and it was only logical to base an airplane and crew there. Due to the remoteness of Kisangani and the scarcity of everyday supplies, nobody was interested in being based there, even though the company would be providing a nice house. But when they offered it to Bat, he jumped on it. He just wanted to fly his missions, bank his paychecks, enjoy his family and be left alone.

As we continued talking, Paul told Bat I was now in captain training. Paul suggested that Bat take me up there to be based with him while I was getting my line training. Bat said that was fine with him and he'd be happy to train me. That all sounded great except for one issue…what about Karen and Jason. They were just getting settled in. I might be up in Kisangani for five or six weeks. Leaving them alone in Kinshasa, considering the present volatility was out of the question. I asked them not to mention this to anyone yet as I needed to have a talk with Karen.

I finished up my Primus Beer without having been discovered by its rightful owner, placed the evidence in the backyard trash can, and headed home. I had a lot to think about. On one hand, I wanted to do this; on the other, I was dreading the thought. I knew Karen would do whatever I asked but this was bordering on asking too much. I felt depressed as well as guilty as I drove up to the house.

Karen And Jason Go Home

Unlike dinner the previous night when we were considering the extra money we would soon be making, dinner this time was heavy and quiet. Karen knew staying in Kinshasa with Jason while I was away for several weeks was not a good idea. We had been apart for so long. I finally had them here for just a few months and now this. I didn't sleep well that night. Karen probably didn't either. But the decision had been made. If they agreed to send me to Kisangani, they would go home; either to Green Bay where her family lived or back to Hamilton to be with my father. It would be Karen's choice. She never complained but I knew she had to be hurting.

Back at the airport the next morning, before Felipe and I went out for another training session, I went in to talk to Gold Finger about going to Kisangani with Bat. I told him I thought I'd be finished with the local air-work part of my training soon; possibly in time to go up with Bat to avoid a crew rotation. He immediately agreed saying it was a good plan and would save a lot of logistics rotating co-pilots up there every few days. The deal was done.

My flight that morning with Felipe was a review of the previous air-work. I hoped he had not noticed that my mind was somewhere else. When we landed, he said he would sign me off; that I was ready to start my line training. It was then that I told him Bat had agreed to do the en route portion of my training and now that this part was signed off, I would be leaving with Bat for

Kisangani. Felipe looked over at me and asked about my family. "Going home" I replied. "Never good but probably best," he answered. We walked across the ramp, through the hanger, and into flight ops. Both of us lost in our own thoughts. I handed in our flight's paperwork, sincerely thanked Felipe again for being my instructor during the air-work part of my training, and headed home. I would have the next couple of days off while Bat was finishing up his in-processing and getting everything arranged for his move to Kisangani. This would give me time to get Karen and Jason's tickets back to Green Bay. I made yet another depressing drive from N'Djili back home.

I was beginning to see that every time I advanced in my career, there was a price to pay. It was becoming a clearly recognizable pattern. Even with being aware of this treacherous truth whose genesis was straight from hell's doorstep, I doubted I was strong enough to change it. When you are running from your demons while reaching for the stars, the devil will always get his dues. I tried to make believe I could beat the odds and juggle all my obligations without hurting Karen and Jason…but deep inside I knew that, too, was just one more of Satan's lies. "If Only."

The mood at home alternated between Karen's excitement about going home and her sadness about leaving. I welcomed her moments of excitement and shared her down moments as well. This was hard and I just wanted to get their departure behind me. The following morning I went to Wigmo's administration office to arrange their tickets. Admin called to the downtown ticket office and booked them on Pan Am leaving three days later. The fare would be deducted from my next paycheck. The following day I went back to the admin office and picked up their tickets. Another wave of depression came over me as I had their tickets in my hands and read Jason's name on one of them. It was just yesterday Karen and I were driving back from the Naval Hospital in Corpus Christi with our new baby in the back seat of our Mustang. Now I was looking at his name on an international airline ticket. He had his own passport. I wished I'd spent less time away from home with CENCO and less long-hour days at Southwest School of Aviation. "If Only."

The morning of their departure came so quickly. We were all up early. Karen had been packed for a couple of days. She was always organized that way. John was waiting by the door to say his heart-felt goodbye as well. He reminded me of a hotel bellman in ragged shorts, standing there at attention, or as at attention as his lame leg would allow.

We drove to the airport in almost total silence; I felt like my heart was being ripped out. Because of my military ID and airport all-access pass, I accompanied them to the gate. I then walked down on the ramp and watched the Pan Am B-707 push back and taxi out. I saw them waving goodbye through the airplane window. I was relieved when I lost sight of the plane in the climb out. I drove back to Limete to check with Bat on the status of his arrangements. My chest felt like a load of bricks was stacked on it.

Bat poured himself a gin and tonic and we went out and sat down on the back porch. I wanted a beer…I wanted a couple of them…but it was too early. I drank a Miranda and we talked.

I found Bat an exceptionally interesting person. In addition to being an Air Force test pilot, he had also flown in the Nigerian conflict…on the side of the short-lived Republic of Biafra. He was flying transport aircraft while Nigeria's hired mercenaries were trying to shoot him down. Of course on the Nigerian side, Bat and his fellow pilots were considered the mercenaries. I considered myself to be in the company of a living legend. I hung on his every word.

Bat said it would be only a couple of more days until we would leave for Kisangani. He had talked to the station agent on the radio. The Wigmo agent had located a nice house for Bat. It was close to the airport and in a secure area of town. Well, it was as secure as anything in any Congolese city could be.

Bat and I visited for a while longer and then I headed back to my house…a house without Karen and Jason. I'd been looking at it from Bat's back porch as we talked. But now it appeared so different. It looked so empty. Amazing how your mind can play such tricks on you. Last week it was so bright. Now it looked as if it had been covered with some foreboding dark mist.

I was glad when the sun started to set. I was ready to sit in my darkened living room illuminated only by a small kerosene lamp and drink Primus till my depression slowly melted away into mellowness. We had electricity but I liked the dim yellow glow the kerosene lamp produced. I don't guess anybody liked the dark smudge it left on the ceiling. In some ways, it was kinda romantic, like a candle. It reminded me of the cowboy movies I used to watch back in Hamilton at the Texan Theater. It reminded me of the nights we used to spend camping out on the Leon River with our "coal oil" lanterns as the old people (including my father) used to call them. John was gone but he had left my single plate and my meal waiting on the dining table. I stared at the single place setting and visualized their faces. I saw Jason's big eyes looking up in anticipation of telling me some endless tale while we ate. But I was alone. I opened a bottle of Primus took a glass from the cabinet and walked to the living room couch. The greenish blue colored walls now had a weak golden trace from the house's sole light source. I didn't know it at the time, but this kerosene lamp ritual would follow me to Cambodia. Only there, we would have no electricity. Here the dark was voluntary…a place where I sought refuge…an ever-so-slight warmth from the empty house's chill.

Kisangani (King 7)

Bat and I took the C-47 they had assigned to the Kisangani operation loaded with all his belongings and two suitcases for me and flew to our new home. For Bat this would be permanent; for me, my home for several weeks.

George, the Wigmo station agent met us upon arrival. Somehow, we got all our stuff in the jeep headed to the Wigmo safe-house. We would offload our bags and then go check out Bat's new house. For me, the safe-house would be my new home while in Kisangani. If Bat agreed on the house George had found for him, he would move in a day or so. Bat was anxious to get settled in. I was excited as well. The busier I stayed the less time I would have to miss Karen and Jason.

As we drove through town on our way to Bat's new house, the signs of war were everywhere. Almost every downtown building was scarred by machine gun fire. As we drove along, it seems almost every major building and street was the scene of some horrific atrocity of war from the 1964 Simba rebellion. Dark blood stains were still visible in some places.

The house George had found for Bat was quite large with a big front veranda. It was typical French colonial architecture. Bat was quite pleased. George said he would help in finding a houseboy that came recommended. Bat was clearly relieved. We went back to the safe-house and got cleaned up for dinner. George wanted to show us a small restaurant, bar, and casino only about a hundred meters from the safe-house. We would eat there that night.

After everybody had showered and changed, we had a drink on the veranda then headed across the street for dinner. There was a decent crowd of people there, mostly Europeans but also wealthier Congolese. The owner was Greek. We had another drink while waiting for a table. Almost instantly I disliked the place. The music was loud; it was, by my standards, uncomfortably crowded. The food turned out to be only marginally good. The place was also adorned by an assemblage of local ladies of the evening trolling to and fro seeking whom they might ensnare. They all dressed in the local-style wraparound skirt and matching blouse typically worn by Congolese women. On their heads they usually wore a matching headwrap. If they chose to forego the headwrap, they sported a braided hairstyle, tight on the scalp with several tightly wrapped plaits sticking straight out. George had several names for the hairstyles ranging from unflattering racial caricatures to objects from the days of early space exploration.

I had never been in a casino before. I found watching the people playing poker and roulette quite interesting, although I had absolutely no desire to play myself. I found watching their facial expressions fascinating…some animated; some a well-rehearsed expressionless mask. Though this casino was in an old rundown French colonial villa, and the dress code was far from the almost mandatory tuxedos of European casinos, the stakes were often high.

Some games would last 72 hours or more. George told us sometimes entire plantations were lost. I could feel the evil in the air; as heavy as lead.

I handed George money to cover my drink and meal and was getting ready to leave when Bat told me to wait; he was coming too. When Bat had given his share to George, we left the noise and walked slowly down the quiet mostly-dark street. The moon was bright that night and we enjoyed our short walk back to the safe-house. Bat went to his suitcase and produced a bottle of cognac. He offered me a drink, but I passed. I was content to just sit on the veranda and stare out into the neighborhood. The unusually bright moonlight that night provided a panoramic canvas of rundown French colonial houses with no windows or doors, accented by the moon's silver and black brush strokes. The muffled Congolese music coming from the casino and an occasional dog barking made their contributions to the moment. I wondered how Karen and Jason were doing. There was a lot to think about. I looked over at Bat, silently leaning back in his straight back chair, his feet propped up on the railing of the veranda, the orange glow of his cigarette punctuating the darkness, sipping his cognac. We were both lost in our own thoughts. I left Bat alone on the veranda and went to bed.

Gbadolite…A Boomtown In The Jungle

Gbadolite was a small town in the dense jungle located in the northern part of the Congo. The town was about 8 miles south of the Ubangi River which formed the country's border with the Central African Republic. Everything in the Congo was based on tribalism. Mobutu's support came from the military and he made sure the strongest elements of that military were from his tribal region and his tribe, the Ngbandi. While Mobutu was born in Lisala, Gbadolite was his ancestral home. Mobutu had recently embarked on an ambitious building program in and around Gbadolite. He had built a large military training facility there. Recruitment for the military from this area was of strategic importance. Many Belgian paratroopers were based in Gbadolite engaged in training these Congolese recruits. The goal was to turn them into an elite fighting force loyal only to Mobutu.

In addition to the military facility, Mobutu had built a modern hospital and good schools. The building projects in Gbadolite would go on for years and would come to include presidential palaces. Supplies flowed into Gbadolite. Many of them would flow by the C-47 Wigmo just placed in Kisangani. My first flight with Bat out of Kisangani would be to Gbadolite.

George's houseboy had breakfast ready for us the next morning. Then off to the airport. It was not necessary to get up so early every morning here. Most of the airports we would be flying into were only two or three hours away at most and none had working landing lights, including Kisangani. So this was going to be pretty much a daylight operation.

When we arrived at the airport we were met by very professional-looking Belgian para-commandos. Their uniforms looked sharp and they carried themselves with military comportment. They were accompanied by a group of about 15 Congolese para-commandos. They were wearing their paratrooper insignias. I'd never seen any Congolese military forces like these. They were very impressive. When we gave the all clear to board, they grabbed their bags and moved to the aircraft like they were still in basic training. These Belgiums and done a good job. There were plenty of supplies already loaded onboard. Our flight was a short 2 hours 45 minutes. We would have lunch in Gbadolite as guest of the Belgiums, see their base, and then fly back to Kisangani.

It was going to be an easy day. I flew in the left seat and Bat flew in the co-pilot's seat. Bat smoked a lot of cigarettes. I mean a lot. He used a long elegant looking cigarette holder like some English gentleman. Nobody had heard of secondhand cigarette smoke back then. When we had finished the after-takeoff and climb checklist, Bat reached down and opened his "coffee" thermos and poured himself a cup. He lit up a cigarette and slid his seat back and relaxed. I would later learn that his "coffee" was really coffee infused with a generous portion of cognac. As we flew along, Bat, like Paul, would study the map carefully always looking for good emergency landing places. There were no airports; that was a given. So what he was really looking for were good places to make a crash landing. When he would find one, he would mark it on the map. I had never paid that much attention to this aspect of flying before. I was glad he didn't ask me to share my emergency sites with him. I didn't have very many. Only Paul had ever done that with me. I was learning a new aspect of flying. In the US, this was never really an issue because there were airports everywhere. Here there were just hundreds upon hundreds of miles of rainforest.

The landing in Gbadolite was easy. As Congolese airports went, the runway was long and wide with no tall trees at the ends. This town was a showpiece.

As our military cargo was being offloaded, Bat and I went with the Belgium commandos to their base where lunch was waiting. The base was new, neat, clean, and quite modern. After lunch they insisted on driving us around town to see all the new wide streets and street lights. It was hard to believe we were in the Congo.

When we arrived back at the airport, the airplane was already loaded and our military passengers were sitting over in the shade beside a stucco building that served as a terminal. As they were boarding, I hopped up on the wings and checked the engine oil. All was good. Soon we were roaring down the runway enveloped in a cloud of reddish-brown dust. The sky was mostly clear. We received no replies from our all stations blind radio calls. Air Congo served the airport and an occasional single engine missionary aircraft would come but basically, like almost all Congolese airports except Kinshasa, an arriving airplane was an event the locals all stopped to watch.

Our trip back to Kisangani was uneventful. We made our regular HF radio transmissions on the Wigmo's military frequency, reporting our position and expected arrival time for Kisangani. As we joined the traffic pattern, we could see the Wigmo jeep waiting on the ramp. I could already taste my cold Simba beer.

As we were driving back to the safe-house, George told us our mission for tomorrow would be Lisala. George asked me if I'd ever been there before. I answered no. He then said Lisala was an excellent place to buy the popular Congolese hunting spears and the bush knives they used. When the locals heard an airplane landing, the grabbed the spears and knives they'd been buying from those living deeper in the bush and rushed to the plane trying to sell some to the crew and passengers. George said it would be necessary to bargain hard, but it would be worth it. He told us how when he first came to the Congo these spears and knives were cheap and plentiful. He said they were now becoming more difficult to find.

We stopped by Bat's future house to take a look at the progress. They were still painting and cleaning but it would soon be ready. After that we headed to the Wigmo safe-house for a shower, a beer, and dinner.

Lisala

Birthplace of Mobuto

Breakfast the next morning was preceded by coffee on the veranda with Bat. I enjoyed visiting with Bat. He had a certain quiet dignity I found reassuring. George's houseboy had another great meal ready for us. After breakfast, we hopped in the jeep and headed to the airport. As we drove past Bat's house, he was pleased to see the workers already on the job. It wouldn't be long.

At the airport, our passengers were waiting. Some had obviously spent the night at the airport as they had no money for a hotel. This was normal. As I was inspecting the cargo, I noticed our loadmaster had a sack of what appeared to be parcels he was delivering to Lisala. He had established, in addition to his produce business, a parcel delivery service. He had to do something…he often went several months without pay. I thought to myself that I'd bet his general hadn't missed a paycheck. As a matter of fact, he probably had already spent our loadmaster's pay to put fuel in his big shiny black Mercedes.

Lisala, like Kisangani lay on the banks of the Congo River and was linked by the river to Kinshasa. So, most goods went by riverboat rather than by air or truck, but the pilfering via both river and land was reported to be horrendous and the trip took several days. This gave our loadmaster's budding business a definite edge for those with the means to pay.

This time Bat made the takeoff just to keep his considerable skills polished. After takeoff, we switched seats so I could get the practice landing at Lisala. As soon as our seat swap was complete, out came Bat's thermos, his cigarette holder, and his big smile. Bat could enjoy life stranded anywhere if he had his smokes and his little sip.

We circled Lisala so we could get a good look at the airport and so the town would know they had a flight arriving. Like at most airports in the Congo, there was no operating control tower. The terminal was an old rundown abandoned building dating back to pre-independence. The runway at one time had been paved but now was just potholes, the worst of which had been sloppily filled in with gravel.

As we taxied in, I spotted what had to be the spear and knife merchants running to the ramp to get a good position when we opened the door. Some had numerous spears tied together in bundles balanced on their head. I was ready to shed my Wigmo-CIA mercenary image and be a shameless tourist. I had to have some of this stuff for my walls. I'd seen some in Olaf's living room. No Wigmo home should be without a few. This would be a nice surprise for Karen when she returned.

By the time I got down out of the plane, all our passengers and cargo were already on the ramp and our outbound passengers, bags, furniture, chickens and goats, were ready to be loaded. Our loadmaster was busily going over his arriving parcels with what appeared to be one of the local Greeks.

As soon as I appeared in the doorway the spear and knife venders started jumping up and down, waving their arms and spears, and calling out to get our attention. Bat had mentioned he too would perhaps look. So for the next few minutes Bat and I examined and bargained with our new friends. I enjoyed myself and bought several spears and knives in the process. I hauled our loot back to the cockpit while Bat did a walk-around inspection to insure the plane still looked OK.

I started on my paperwork while Bat supervised the loading. This was normally the loadmaster's job but no Wigmo crew expected them to do anything but buy and sell their merchandise. To do otherwise would be courting disaster as they were also known to take money for slipping onboard extra passengers not listed on the FAC manifest. A casual approach would be courting a dangerous overload condition.

Soon we were lined up for takeoff on runway 05. The wind was calm, and this would point us in the direction of Kisangani. Our all stations call went unanswered, meaning there was no traffic in the immediate airport area. During the climb out I made our departure message call to King 1 as Bat flew and lit up a cigarette. By the time we were ready for our descent, all my paperwork was done except for filling in the landing time and remaining fuel. We had no maintenance discrepancies. I'd soon be storing my new Congo treasures in my room and taking a cold shower. Life was good. That night, while sitting on the veranda with my Simba, I wondered how Karen and Jason were doing. I'm sure she was enjoying seeing her mother, brother, and sisters. I wondered what Jason was thinking about all these strange sounding people. He'd grown up only hearing our treasured Texas accent. Those folks talked like they were from an entirely different world. They even teased Karen about her strange Texas accent. I missed them. But while I missed them, I was noticing how I enjoyed my solitude. I found this an uncomfortable thought.

In Cambodia, it was becoming obvious to any citizen with even a minimal degree of political awareness that the ouster of Prince Sihanouk had contributed nothing to peace and stability. Corruption, one of the cornerstones of his accusers, had become far worse under Lon Nol's government. The country had more or less aligned with what the American embassy called the "Democrats" who aligned themselves with General In Tam, and the "Republicans" who were aligned with Prince Sirik Matak. Lon Nol basically remained apolitical. His brother, Lon Non opposed both parties and devoted his efforts to enriching himself, his brother, and their cronies.[139] Inflation was wildly spiraling out of control; shortages of fuel, food, medicine, and basic commodities were pandemic. NVA forces and Viet Cong were operating with impunity within the borders of Cambodia as well as supplying and training Pol Pot's Khmer Rouge. In some instances, they were fighting side by side.[140]

My Captain Checkout

The days literally flew by. I learned to penetrate thunderstorms in the C-47, to make short field landings and takeoffs; use takeoff, landing, and cruise charts, and countless little tricks that I carried with me throughout my flying career. Bat moved into his house and started getting things ready for his large family's arrival. Sometimes I would stay with him rather than at the crew house. It was a good time. I could tell I was getting proficient enough to be released to fly with a co-pilot with less experience. Maybe occasionally even a FAC co-pilot. I was confident I was ready but that was only part of the equation. Bat had to be confident as well. Finally, one day after we had landed, he reached over and shook my hand and told me he thought I would be safe enough to go out and not kill myself. His dry humor. He told me he would go with me to the safe-house and use the radio to send the word to King 1. I thanked him profusely. I think I was almost teary-eyed. This was a big deal. I now, and forever more, would have the title "Captain" before my name. Daddy would be so proud. Although he didn't really understand, he would know it was a big deal. I could just see him sitting in City Drug drinking coffee with all his buddies and telling them the big news.

---

[139] The Tragedy of Cambodian History by David P. Chandler
[140] The Tragedy of Cambodian History by David P. Chandler

Summer was coming to an end, school would be starting soon, I had been checked out a month and it was time for Karen and Jason to return. I made a call via MARS radio back in King 1. A ham radio volunteer in the US put the phone patch through to Karen for me. She was happy about the captain news and happy to be coming back to her home again.

John was happy to see me too. Gus had been paying him for me while I'd been with Bat in Kisangani. And, it was true that with everyone gone he had almost nothing to do. But he nevertheless genuinely welcomed me home. He immediately asked about Karen (*madam*) and Jason (*petite*). A huge smile covered his face when I told him soon…they would be here soon.

Later that evening, after John had left and I was unpacked and washed, I went into the now dark living room, lit my little lamp, got my Primus and went to the couch. Even though I missed Karen and Jason a lot, I still enjoyed my evenings in the darkened room, illuminated only by faint shadows cast from the sole kerosene lamp. I knew this wasn't what "normal" people should be enjoying. I opened my Primus, slowly poured it into my glass, and stared out into the darkness.

Jimmy à Paris

One afternoon after returning from a flight I found a note in my mailbox in dispatch saying I had a meeting in Gold Finger's office the next morning at 9:00am. Other than that I was off the schedule. When I arrived the following morning, I found David Bellows (pseudonym) and the Congolese flight engineer already here. I was on time and they were early.

Gold Finger announced we would be taking the Lear Jet to Paris for a major maintenance inspection. Paris… Jimmy Joe Jacks flying in a private jet to Paris France. How cool was that? The problem was we were scheduled to leave in two days, and we needed to do one hell of a lot of flight planning. This was going to delay Karen's arrival as well.

While I'd studied plenty of jet flight planning back at Southwest School of Aviation, it was all theory and we were using the Boeing 707 as a model. Again at Fowler Flight Engineer School in Los Angeles I'd become even more proficient and even passed my flight engineer FAA written examination. But that was all theory, and this would be for real. I quickly realized I was painfully lacking in experience. The same was true for David, the captain.

We left dispatch with operation's set of hopefully up-to-date charts and approach plates and went into one of the old training department classrooms. There we spread out the charts and started looking for the safest and shortest route to Paris. The Lear 25 had a range of only 1767 miles with a 45 minute reserve. For Africa, that was short.

One major problem was to find airports that lay within our range that would keep us flying generally in the direction of Paris. When flying over central and North Africa, this was a problem. There wasn't an abundance of airports anyway. From the few existing ones, we had to find airports where we could pay for fuel with a company credit card or U.S. dollars cash, and with whom we had diplomatic relations. In Africa, during this time period, that was no easy task.

We finally decided upon Kinshasa to Ft. Lamy (now N'Djamena), and from Ft. Lamy to Tripoli. From Tripoli we would fly to Paris. We were familiar with Ft. Lamy as we used it often flying the C-54's to Belgium and Italy. I'd never landed at Tripoli nor had David, but some of our Cuban pilots had and assured us there would be no problem. Words couldn't express how excited I was about going to Paris. Like London and Rome, I'd heard about Paris all my life. Now I was going. How cool was that!

Unlike the Gulfstreams I would later fly, the Lear's cockpit was cramped…very cramped. With the captain, myself, and the flight engineer, our bags, and all the volumes of out-of-date maintenance records we were transporting, plus the crew's food for the approximately 12-hour trip, the airplane didn't have an abundance of unused cabin space.

Because of the great distance between usable airports in this part of the world, fuel conservation was paramount. Even though the distance between our departure and our destination airport was acceptable, if that airport should become unavailable due to weather or numerous other reasons, we still needed enough fuel to proceed to our alternate airport. In Europe or the United States where good airports were everywhere, this was almost never an issue. Here it was a way of life for our short-legged Lear Jet. In order to maximize our fuel endurance, it would be necessary for us to climb immediately to an altitude like 41,000 or 43,000 feet. Most airliners back in that day would be flying mid-to-low 30,000, levels far below us.

We had one day off to get our personal affairs in order. We were told in the briefing we could easily be in Paris two weeks. I had to force myself to try to look cool, but my excitement was probably obvious to everyone. Two weeks in Paris…WOW.

We had to go draw money from finance. This time we were on a per diem allowance for food and on actual expenses for the hotel. The hotel would be paid with a Wigmo American Express card given to the captain. The European food and incidental allowance was generous. We all got a stack of new $100 bills. Since this was not a mission for "the customer" I figured all this crisp new money did not come from them. Maybe it was from Mabutu's stash. He was rumored to have a substantial one.

Back at home, packing was relatively simple. I dug around and found some of my few non-equatorial clothes and packed them. I told John he could take a week off. Then he was to report here and ask Gus our neighbor if he knew when I would be coming back. If no date, he was to return each day and check. If no news, go back home. I paid him in advance, and we said goodbye.

I had my normal meal by lamplight, washed my own dishes, and went to bed. But sleep did not come easily. On the following day's flight, we would be landing at night in Paris at Le Bourget airport. I'd studied the approach plate. It was complicated; more complicated than any approach I'd ever seen when combined with the arrival. Years later, after countless flights into both Le Bourget and Charles de Gaulle I could almost fly them by memory without looking at the approach plates. But for this flight, I had never flown into Paris before and I was profoundly lacking in experience in the Lear Jet. I was nervous. I was excited. I was going on my first serious jet trip and I was ecstatic about being in Paris for a couple of weeks. I'm sure I must have slept some, but it didn't feel like it. The next morning I was awake and waiting when the alarm went off.

The Flight To Paris

The departure went normal. The flight was to be a short one…less than three hours. About two hours into the flight I noticed how cold the fuselage had become. Any time my arm or leg touched the cockpit's interior, it was like touching ice. We'd been told about this by our instructor, but it was nevertheless a new experience for me. I'd never flown this high before, even as a passenger in an airliner. The outside temperature was reading -52 Celsius or about -62 Fahrenheit. The longer we remained at this altitude the colder the fuselage would become as it became cold soaked. It really wasn't uncomfortable as the aircraft's pressurization system kept the air comfortably warm. It was just an interesting first-time experience. I quickly learned that my can of soda, when placed in the cup holder, would stay cold. No need for ice and a glass.

Our landing at Ft. Lamy went perfectly. It was a nice airport with well-maintained facilities. Chad was previously part of French Equatorial Africa but, like the Congo, soon after gaining independence, civil war broke out. The influence of the French remained everywhere but signs of neglect were becoming visible. Like in the Congo, the president's picture (François Tombalbaye) hung everywhere.

Signs Of The Unquenchable Spirit Of Capitalism
(aka the bribe and human greed)

Refueling was going well. While David and the engineer watched the refueling, I went inside the terminal to the air traffic services office and filed our flight plan and got the latest en route, destination, and alternate airport weather. At both the meteorological office and the Air Traffic Control's flight plan office I was hit up for a slight token of appreciation. Nothing serious, just something working for Wigmo shielded me from. In the Congo they all knew not to mess with us. I didn't think my FAC/Wigmo ID card signed by General Bobozo would get me very far here. So I cheerfully acceded to their "requests" for a little expression of appreciation. It was something like five dollars at each office. I was quite sure that David was being hit up by the fuel driver and his helper for something similar. At the time I thought it to be an "African disease." I would later learn it was pandemic…worldwide; a basic flaw in the human race. In the Congo, in Lingala, the bribe was called "*matabish*", in Arabic it was "*baksheesh*", in Spanish "*mordida*" (the bite), in Cambodia in Khmer it was "*tuk ti*" (tea money). It was as old as humanity. It came with Adam and the fall. It will probably continue until the trumpet blows.

In just over an hour we were airborne and making our way toward 41,000 feet again. About three years later, President François Tombalbaye was killed by units of his own security forces in a coup. New pictures for the walls, new currency notes, and new postage stamps.

The flight to Tripoli would take about 3:30 minutes. Not long after takeoff all green below us had disappeared. It was just yellowish-brown sand occasionally interrupted by what appeared to be black lava from previous volcanic activity. Thousands of miles of barren sand…the Sahara Desert. Thousands of miles of virtually nothing. The change from the lush Congolese rainforests to this was profound.

Virtually everything I knew about Libya came from news articles in News Week and Time magazine. The country was ruled by yet another dictator, a guy named Col. Muammar al-Gaddafi. Gaddafi had overthrown Libya's king and dissolved the monarchy about three years earlier and through his military strong-man tactics was rapidly moving Libya into socialism. He was big on African unity. That's how I figured we got over-flight and landing permission. I was the only American crew member and I wasn't too overjoyed about visiting Libya. I knew Libya's relations with the U.S. were strained at best. There was talk in the news publications of plans to nationalize some of our oil companies. Stanley Griffin the C-47 captain, from whom I'd purchased my car, had worked in Benghazi before coming to the Congo. He liked it. But that was then, and this was now. A call I'd placed to the *customer's* office in the embassy the previous day advised I "should be OK"…typical political double-speak.

When we landed in Tripoli, the airport was modern enough. Military presence was everywhere. They came inside the plane and checked our documents and dug around in our luggage. When I went inside to the flight plan office I was escorted.

As Tombalbaye's picture had been plastered everywhere in Chad, the Libyan leader's picture was on display everywhere here. I remember thinking that this could be counterproductive. This was very possibly the ugliest human face outside of a congenital deformity or terrible trauma I'd ever seen. He had the face only a mother could love, and even then, I'll bet she had to work at it.

I was thinking that perhaps with their new revolutionary socialism, I'd be spared getting hit up for bribes...I was wrong. The official hands of socialism were outstretched everywhere.

I'd read there were still Americans living there. They must have been crazy. Hell, I guess if they were asked, they'd say the same thing about my still being in the Congo. I was glad to get back in the aircraft and get to hell out of Libya.

The captain's "gear up" command and the sound of the landing gear being closed inside the wheel wells was a gratifying sound. I was so ready to see Paris. We were soon out over the water and heading toward Europe; Green, modern (more or less) and civilized Europe. Happiness was Africa in my rear-view mirror...only the Lear didn't have one. But I didn't care. I was happy to be flying at close to eighty percent of the speed of sound toward Paris, *La Ville-Lumière* or the City of Lights. The famed La rue Champs-Élysées would prove to be a long way from the square in Hamilton; although I probably had as much fun on the square...just a different kind of fun.

Francophone Folly

Almost as soon as we entered French airspace, I realized I had a problem. The controllers were speaking English to us, but they spoke very rapidly and their French accented English was so thick they were close to being unintelligible. Routine instructions were OK but when they started clearing us to places with French names, I was lost, literally. The spoken names of these places did not resemble, at least to me, anything that appeared on my chart. Since I was the copilot, radio communication and navigation was my responsibility. I could hear the French controller's irritation building in the tone of their voice. Damn, I thought...if they would just slow down a little bit, I might be able to understand them. But as I learned on this visit to Paris and as would be reinforced on numerous future visits to Paris...the ordinary French didn't particularly like Americans. Much of it I later came to realize was our fault. In any case, I received no mercy from them as we threaded our way in the descent along our arrival route. I was relieved when the last arrival controller handed us over to Le Bourget tower. We shot an ILS approach to runway 07. The approach lighting and runway lighting were good. The landing was uneventful. When we contacted ground control, things got considerably easier as taxiway names are letters and pronounced like A̲lpha, B̲ravo, C̲harlie. By the time we set the parking brake and shut down the engines, I was exhausted.

Customs and immigration officials were the police. They came to the airplane, took our passports, and got back into their car. They checked our documents while sitting in the front seat of their police vehicle and in less than five minutes handed back our passports stamped with French visas. No baggage inspection…no nothing.

An Easter Egg Hunt Without Easter

A representative of the maintenance facility, Transair France, was waiting to take us into what was referred to as a "debrief." We would go over the items we wanted them to do for us (inspections, repairs, etc.) they would make any changes to the work order, and the captain would sign the work order. Countless telex messages had already preceded our arrival agreeing on the basic price and most of the work orders. The big question in our minds and the minds of our people back in Kinshasa was what surprises their inspections would uncover. The airplane had not really been looked after very well after Mobutu "acquired" it. Of course, we realized that the inspection was like an Easter egg hunt to Transair. The more grounding or non-discretionary items the inspectors uncovered, the more money they would make. It was a game as old as aviation itself. Only time would tell how many eggs they would find.

Excitement Trumps Exhaustion

It was now approaching midnight. I should have been exhausted. But I was not. My adrenalin was on the red line, my eyes as big as picnic plates. Jimmy Joe Jacks from Hamilton, Texas, was in Paris. We had rooms booked at the Paris Hilton. It was right down in the thick of everything. Just next to l'Arc de Triomphe, even closer to the Eiffel Tower. The Avenue des Champs-Élysées, the Seine River, famous museums, everything in walking distance.

Nobody Sleeps Here

As our taxi made its way toward the center of Paris, I was amazed at the amount of traffic still on the streets. As we neared the main boulevards, the sidewalks were filled with people. Bars, restaurants, sidewalk cafes…the place was alive with energy which translated into excitement for me. I could see the Eiffel Tower all lit up in the night sky. The Arc de Triomphe was lighted as well. As our taxi pulled up in front of the hotel it became ever more apparent just how close the hotel was to the famous Eiffel Tower.

The Paris Hilton was a wonderful hotel. The lobby was filled with important-looking people, even at this late hour. I felt a bit out of place. It was obvious we were significantly underdressed. But heck, I wasn't going to let a little thing like that ruin my time in Paris.

The professionalism of the bellmen and the people working the reception desk exceeded anything I'd ever experienced. While checking in I asked if my room overlooked the Eiffel Tower. I realized I was coming across like a country bumpkin. The young Frenchman looked at my room number, took back my key, changed an entry on his ledger and handed me a different key.

He smiled and said "yes." I was escorted to my room by a bellman with almost military bearing. As I waked down the hallway toward my room, I found myself dreading the tip I was going to have to turn loose.

Immediately upon entering the room, even before the bellman had my bags on the floor, I shamelessly darted over to the window and pulled the drapes back. Yep…there it was. All lit up in the night sky. What a breathtaking sight. Better than Hamilton's square at Christmas time.

Sadly, a few years later, this flagship of the Hilton Hotel chain fell onto hard times and no longer reflected the magnificence that I was able to see. It was later sold but unfortunately its downward spiral continued.

French Coffee (American Style) Elegantly Dressed People

And Pablo Picasso Eggs

The next morning I was up early. The time difference between Kinshasa and Paris was only one hour. Even if it had been eight hours difference, my excitement was so high nothing could have slowed me down. I was downstairs in the coffee shop before 8:00 am. It was already filled with men in immaculately tailored business suits and tourists wearing super expensive casual wear. The handbags the women carried probably cost more than I made in a month. The safari suit I wore, made by an Indian tailor who owned a shop in downtown Kinshasa looked exactly like what it was. Oh well.

The coffee was world class. Being an American-owned hotel, they understood American style coffee, which differed significantly from the coffee the French preferred to drink (an espresso- like coffee resembling bitter mud). Years later I developed a taste for it.

The typical French breakfast consisted of coffee and orange juice with pastries and jam. A Texan would be in an advanced state of ketosis before noon after such a puny breakfast. However, as I was being led to my table, I had spotted what appeared to be an American business man with a huge serving of eggs benedict in front of him. His breakfast choice was to rescue me from the fate of a "continental breakfast;" of having to survive till noon on something close to bread and water. I would have juice, *coffee American*, and eggs benedict with ham.

When the coffee came, it was so good I was hoping they would not rush with my main course. When my eggs benedict arrived, they came with typical French flair. The plating was done by an artist. The ham caressed the poached eggs, and the heavenly Hollandaise sauce looked like it had been applied by Pablo Picasso himself. My pre-meal prayer included a thank You for my many bountiful blessings. One of these blessings was sitting in the

Paris Hilton in front of this world class breakfast. It would have been easy to be proud; yet I was humbled at the thought. I knew I didn't deserve to be sitting here.

When I walked back into the hotel lobby, I noticed the concierge handing a map of Paris to a couple and pointing out a location to them. When he finished with them, I asked for a map. I would later learn what an absolute treasure trove of information this man was. He told me he had been the working at the Hilton for many years. Ten years later, as a captain for Saudi Arabian Airlines, I would still see him there behind his desk. He had a huge address book with worn-out pages. All good concierges have black books. They are notebooks filled with contacts and telephone numbers. The good ones can produce impossible-to-get tickets to events fully booked for months in advance and reservations at the best restaurants in Paris, even while the restaurants themselves are telling callers they have no more capacity. The best ones are reported to make more money than the hotel managers…mostly from their tips, but also in the form of commissions paid by the establishments for referring a hotel guest to them…all cash and all unreported.

I took my map and found a seat in one of the comfortable lobby chairs. The pilot in me made me stop, study the map, and lay out an orderly route. My evil twin was screaming in my ear…"giddy-up go, Jimmy Joe."

A Towering Experience

I was soon making my way toward the world-famous creation of Gustave Eiffel, the iron lattice tower which bore his name. The feeling of being dwarfed by it increased with each step I took. I must have taken half a roll of Kodachrome 64, 36-exposure film. I wasn't the slightest bit concerned. I had six canisters taped to my Nikon's neck strap (three on each side). All this before I even got to its base. I never imagined myself standing beside it, touching it, much less riding in its elevator. As a matter of fact…I didn't even realize it had an elevator.

On the second observation level I couldn't resist going into the very touristy restaurant and having a coke; a ridiculously expensive Coke, I might add. It would not be my last expensive Coke in Paris. But I just had to say I'd done it. As I sat in the restaurant, slowly drinking my Coke…very, very, slowly, I started reading the little brochure about the Eiffel Tower they had given me when I purchased my elevator ticket. I learned the structure was 1050 feet high. It was built back in 1889 to be part of the World's Fair held in Paris that year. It was the tallest manmade structure in the world until 1930 when the Chrysler Building was erected in New York. It was difficult to believe that I was really sitting in one of the Eiffel Tower's restaurants…drinking a Coke that cost more than two hamburgers, two Dr. Peppers, plus fries at the Dairy Delight run back then by the McFarlands or at Mr. Bobby Stevens' Dairy Kreem out on Hwy 36 North where Storms is today. What would make a semi-reasonably rational person pay this much for a Coke?! Maybe it was something in the air. After I'd milked the drink far past acceptable, I was ready to hit the trail.

More Exploration

I was a shameless wide-eyed wanderer as I headed out from *La Tour Eiffel*, Nikon in hand, for the *Pont d'Iéna*, the nearest of numerous bridges across the Seine River. As I walked over the bridge, I looked down at the water. I had expected it to be some beautiful blue. Instead it was muddier than the Leon River during a rise, with oil slicks from countless diesel-powered tourist boats and barges adding a disgusting sheen. The current was moving rapidly. As I reached the other side, I realized I'd just crossed from the famous left bank or *La Rive Gauche* to the right bank or *Rive Droite*. My already-firmly-established political inclinations told me left anything was not good. However, both my evil twin and I agreed that in this one exceptional case, *La Rive Gauche* was good. I'd already learned from tourist information back in my hotel room that many of the places I wanted to see were on the left bank. This was more than fun, it was interesting. I was going to be walking (and in some cases sitting) in the very spots where famous artists and writers ate, drank, and caroused. I had absolutely no interest in meeting tourists to associate with. The same with the French. I wanted to sit and absorb and savor or more appropriate "*savour*" the Rive Gauche.

Lovers In The Grass

I turned my back on the polluted Seine River and headed for the beautiful Gardens of Trocadéro or *Jardins du Trocadéro* in French. As with the grassy parks at the foot of *La Tour Eiffel*, the beautifully kept lawns surrounding *Jardins du Trocadéro* were also filled with young lovers, talking, and holding hands. Most Parisians are starved for sunlight. During the spring and summer, they flock to the parks just to lie in the grass enjoying the sunshine. Both the gardens associated with the Eiffel Tower and the Gardens of Trocadéro are perfectly aligned; only separated by the Seine and the roads that parallel the river.

While there was a beautiful racetrack shaped garden, I found the water fountains were more spectacular; blew another half roll of film on them. Again, according to the tourist info in my hotel room and on my map, this garden was created as part of the *Palais du Trocadero* and like the Eiffel Tower, was built for the World's Fair held in Paris in 1878. I decided to stop and soak up the moment. I too lay on the grass and watched the beautiful water fountains and the young Parisians. In the park there was a noticeable absence of middle-aged people except for tourists. Most Parisians were the young high school and university-aged students. But I also saw much older men and women sitting on the park benches. Most of the older ones had brought scraps of bread for feeding the pigeons. I found the old equally as interesting as the Parisian youth. As I lay in the grass enjoying the sun just like the others, I wrote notations in a red notebook I carried with me just for recording my thoughts. Life was good…so very good.

Who Was That Man On A Horse?

After writing, watching, and bathing in the sunshine until my soul told me the time was right, I left the garden's green carpet and started making my way toward the Champs-Élysées. As I was leaving, I passed an impressive statue of a military officer on a horse. I learned it was Marshal Ferdinand Foch, once commander of the French forces and later of the Allied Armies during WW1. He was widely respected throughout Allied Europe. I'm afraid I learned most of what I knew about him from the tourist information in my hotel room as well. I'm sure Ted Jones back in my Hamilton High School World History Class tried to teach me about him, but alas, my evil twin wouldn't let me listen.

L'Arc de Triomphe Traffic Jam

Soon I could see the famous Arc de Triomphe. It was massive. It was located in the center of the Place de l'Étoile (later renamed Place Charles de Gaulle). An insane number of major Paris streets (12) all literally collide at this traffic circle. Everybody had the right of way to get on…thus effectively preventing anybody from getting off…insanity. Some years later the situation was improved.

The Arc de Triomphe was built to honor those who fought and died for France in the French Revolution and the Napoleonic Wars. It also is the location of France's unknown solider. I took a lot of photos of it as I approached the circle, spent a few minutes underneath, then headed down the famous Champs-Élysées.

The Champs-Élysées Disenchantment

I was disappointed. It was just a huge commercial, touristy street. Expensive stores and really expensive sidewalk cafes filled with tourists. As an amateur photographer, I could see the street's possibilities at night but as for now, this was a waste of my time. So, I decided I wanted to answer the call of my inner being and for once that agreed with my evil twin's callings. I wanted to go to the arty areas of Paris. For this I would need a taxi.

Montmartre And Moi
(the Bohemian me…the one I keep locked up)

I'd read about a section of Paris where many famous impressionist artists had studios or had lived, worked, and socialized. Famous artists that even I'd heard of before. Artists like Salvador Dalí, Amedeo Modigliani, Claude

Monet, Pablo Picasso, and Vincent van Gogh. Montmartre was also the home for some famous or infamous places for entertainment like the Moulin Rouge (Red Mill or Red Wind Mill), and Le Chat Noi (The Black Cat). Montmartre had been the playground of the Bohemian crowd in the 1880s and 1890s. I decided it would be next on my itinerary for the day.

The Moulin Rouge was the birthplace of the can-can. Aside from the can-can, one of France's most famous entertainers, a man named Joseph Pujo, played the Moulin Rouge in the 1890s. Pujo's stage name was *Le Pétomane* "which translates to "fartomaniac." his profession is also referred to as "flatulist", "farteur," or "fartiste."[141] [142] *Le Pétomane* possessed the rather unusual ability to expel flatulence at will, and in a melodious fashion. His audience included such notables as Edward, Prince of Wales; King Leopold II of the Belgians; and Sigmund Freud.

The Moulin Rouge held an important place in the history of Paris. Even though this modern Moulin Rouge bore little resemblance to the cabaret atmosphere of its predecessor, it was a must do for Jimmy Joe Jacks. I wanted to experience the Moulin Rouge and I had an idea. My newfound friend, the concierge at the Paris Hilton, could get me reservations there for dinner and a show. Sadly, it had become, by his admission, a tourist trap with busloads of foreigners being disgorged in front of its red neon windmill blades each night. On the other hand, I could receive a cheap touristy meal and watch a live "authentic" French cabaret, complete with can-can dancers and imagine I could hear *Le Pétomane*'s performance and see Vincent van Gogh sitting alone at a corner sipping an absinthe, or in deep conversation with one of Montmartre's numerous ladies of the evening. In a couple of days I could say "I did, and I did."

While Van Gogh only painted here for a couple of years of his brief 10-year painting period, it was an extremely productive period. I was particularly drawn to him and his work as my mother kept some books in her library about art of that period. They were filled with prints and I always felt as though his had some almost magnetic attraction. I knew she would have been happy I was doing this. If only she could be here now. "If Only,"

Love At First Sight

As I stepped out of the taxi in the heart of Montmartre, it was love at first sight. The side streets running off the *Boulevard de Clichy* were filled with tiny shops, bars and coffee houses. The sidewalks were filled with "Parisian hippies" and "tourist hippies." I had always secretly admired the carefree, laid-back avant-garde lifestyle the hippies followed, at least for a while. I was never able to do that. Had I done so, my life would almost certainly have been a disaster. But nevertheless I secretly admired them and for this short

---
[141] Le Pétomane 1857-1945 by Jean Nohain and F. Caradec; translated by Warren Tute. Sherbourne Press (1967); republished Dorset Press (1993)
[142] Wikipedia—Le Pétomane

while, I would have the opportunity to be with them; even if only as a "poser."

It was not uncommon to walk through pockets of air heavy with the aroma that I would later learn to associate with the MOAB. The Mbuti's Mother Of All Bongs. Tarot cards were displayed everywhere. They were for sale and there were little store front places where their black art was practiced. Every few yards heavily painted women, usually appearing to be in their late forties and almost exclusively plump, would call out their greeting of allurement. They were so unattractive I pondered how in the world they could be so fat. They must have second jobs or assuredly they would starve to death trying to rely on the world's oldest profession for sustenance.

I soon found a little café that had an ambience right out of an Impressionist's paining. I ordered a coffee knowing full well it would be the typical French (bitter mud) style. It was customary in these little places to pay when the drink arrives. I had my French Francs ready. The price was about a third of what I'd seen posted on the Champs-Élysées. I drank it slowly wishing I could stop the clock freezing this moment in time for a couple of hours. But I had many things yet to cover before the day was over. I forced myself to get up and leave this charming little hole in the wall. As I headed for the famous *Basilique du Sacre-Coeur* (Basilica of the Sacred Heart of Paris) which was only a short walking distance away, I promised I would be back soon…very soon.

Sacre-Coeur
A Time For Meditation And Awe

"My house will be called a house of prayer for all nations."[143]

I'd seen both day and night photos of the magnificent structure. Aside from the Eiffel Tower and the Arch of Triumph, this was probably the most popular image found on post cards. Because it was built on a small hill, it was visible from many parts of Paris when tall buildings did not obstruct the view. The hill was supposed to be the highest spot in the city. Regardless of what I'd seen in the many pictures, I was not ready for what I actually saw. The imposing Basilica sat atop a grassy hill with two long stairs leading up to it.

I had assumed that, like so many other large European cathedrals, *Sacre-Coeur* would be quite old. I was surprised to learn that in reality, it was part of the mammoth building projects that swept Paris in the 1870s through the end of the century. What I almost missed entirely was a much smaller building to the left of *Sacre-Coeur*, known as *Saint Pierre de Montmartre* or Church of Saint Peter of Montmartre. This church claimed its beginning in the third century. It was here that the Society of Jesus founders (Jesuits) reportedly first took their vows in the 1500s. Amazing…I almost missed it.

---

[143] Holman Christian Standard Bible - Isaiah 56:7

I went into both cathedrals. Though I am not Catholic, it was impossible not to be impressed with the overpowering atmosphere of reverence that filled both *Sacre-Coeur* and *Saint Pierre de Montmartre*. In *Sacre-Coeur*, I climbed what seemed endless steps to the top of the dome. When I reached the top of the dome it was possible to see much of the city of Paris. To my amazement, I was alone. Apparently, the long steep stairs appeared too daunting for my fellow tourists. The sun was still bright, and the view was unforgettable. When I descended, I found a place to sit on the massive stone steps and began to record my impressions in my red book again. It was a time of reverence…not excitement. I had much to think about…much to be thankful for, and yes, much to say "if only" over.

Pilgrimage To Harry's "Sank Roo Doe Noo"

But now as the sun started getting closer to the evening horizon, it was time to shift gears. Too much serious thinking could damage my brain. I'd frequently read about the famous Harry's New York Bar located at 5 Rue Daunou, which just happened to be in a perfect direct line from *Sacre-Coeur* to the Paris Hilton. How could I just drive right past it? And of course, the answer was…there was no way.

About fifteen minutes later, I was climbing out of my taxi at 5 *Rue Daunou*. This was a famous expatriate bar where such notables as Sinclair Lewis, Ernest Hemingway, Humphrey Bogart, Rita Hayworth, even the Duke of Windsor and Coco Chanel would gather for a drink and conversation. Of course I was drawn by Ernest Hemingway and Sinclair Lewis. Not that any of these people were role models for my life…obviously, hardly anything but that. I just wanted to experience what they had experienced. I wouldn't have traded places with any of them.

The wood-paneled front gave it character, but it was small; another hole in the wall if you were unaware of its history. Part of that history was their claim to having created the Bloody Mary.

Once inside I fell in love with the place. It was cluttered. The entire ambience was wood paneled clutter. The walls were cluttered with business cards. Currency notes from around the world cluttered another part. University flags, and pictures continued the clutter. They were all covered in a thick layer of nicotinic scum.

The bar, the wall paneling, the benches and chairs, were all made from matching wood. On the mirror over the bar were the words comprehensible to Anglophones "Sank Roo Doe Noo" which would be how an American would say the address of the bar, *5 Rue Daunou* to a taxi driver While many French were visiting the bar now, it was originally created to attract the growing number of Americans coming to Paris in the early 1900s. There was a downstairs bar called the "Ivories" where George Gershwin is reported to have written *An American in Paris*.

Unfortunately, it didn't open 'til later

I was a little early for the business rush, so I was fortunate enough to find a place at the bar. Before my beer was half finished the bar was standing room only and the air was blue with cigarette smoke. Back then everyone in Paris smoked. And not just regular cigarettes…many of the men smoked those horrid Gitanes which were short and came in a blue pack with a picture of what appeared to be a Spanish woman dancing with a tambourine. The cigarettes used a brown colored paper and were absolutely horrible to be around. Smoking back then didn't bother me but those Gitanes were in a class by themselves.

I had a second draft beer just to prolong my ability to sit in my prime location and experience Harry's. This one I sipped slowly as well. Finally I had to face reality…it was time to leave if I planned to have my dinner in one of Paris's famous left bank places. I paid my tab, tipped and thanked the waiter, and stepped out onto the street. I walked a few meters to the closest major street, flagged a taxi and was soon back at the Paris Hilton.

My friend the concierge was still on duty. I'd heard about the many neat eating places in the Latin Quarter, an area popular with the university students. I produced my map and asked what he recommended. I soon had a place along with an address written on a sheet from a Hilton note pad. I scurried up to my room for a quick shower and a fresh change of clothes and I was off again.

Place Saint Michel
A Paris Happening

The Latin Quarter was relatively close to the hotel. As we were almost to the restaurant, I saw this magnificent statue and water fountain with lots of people just sitting and milling around. I knew I could easily find the place where I was going to eat so I told the taxi driver to stop at the statue. I had no idea what it was, but I knew I loved the place. The beautiful statue illuminated in the night, along with the countless people just lounging around was a photographer's dream. I hopped out of the taxi, once again with Nikon in hand, ready to resume my American In Paris experience.

I soon learned this was the famous Place Saint Michel. The statue and fountain were created by French sculptor Davioud in 1860. The statue represents Saint Michel, protector of France, slaying a dragon. While I felt the tourists like myself detracted from the place, I still found plenty of students from the nearby universities using the fountain as a meeting spot. This place was "a happening." I loved it. For more than thirty years I would continue returning to this spot and its countless surrounding Greek restaurants and pizza places. I loved Place Saint Michel and I loved the Left Bank's Latin Quarter.

I'm not sure how long I stayed there, sitting near the base of the fountain where I had a view of both the statue and the people, waiting for the perfect picture. There were many that night. I was there so long I'd begun to wonder if my eating place might have closed. I later learned what a ridiculous thought that was. Many people don't consider eating dinner till around 8:00 pm. Finally I forced myself to leave my perfect spot, pull out my map and head for my restaurant.

A Gastronomic Overdo

Be not among drunkards
or among gluttonous eaters of meat[144]

The restaurant was easy to find. It was located on one of the narrow, pedestrian-only paths in this hundreds-of-years-old section of Paris. My restaurant was a Greek place, filled with both tourists and students. I was lucky still to be able to get a table.

Soon the waiter was handing me a small aperitif menu. Since I'd had Cinzano in Italy, I chose that. The menu was not only Greek but also had a wonderful assortment of other European dishes. The prices were those students could afford. I was in heaven. While I sipped my small glass of Cinzano Rosso, I studied the menu. By the grace of God, the menu included pictures of the plated food. I was excited…great looking food at a price that didn't make me feel guilty.

I ordered Chicken Liver Pâté served on slices of French bread, then a green salad. At that point I bailed out of the French part of the menu and followed my lust after a huge plate of mixed grilled meats prepared in the Greek style. I started to wonder if "my eyes had been bigger than my stomach;" an expression my father used to use.

By the time I'd finished the last of the meat plate, I could hardly hold my eyes open. The waiter insisted I'd feel better if I had a *digestif* to assist in dealing with this ludicrous quantity of food I'd ingested. He told me the after-dinner drink was on the house. I figured the little drink couldn't do much more damage than I'd already done and possible the Europeans were right; I accepted his offer. My evil twin was saying the same thing. As I sipped the *digestif* it became clear the day of physical activity mixed with the excitement and topped off with an absurd amount of food had left me practically comatose. Finally I managed to lift myself from my place at the table. The service had been exceptional, so I tipped generously and headed out for an exploration of the Latin Quarter area in hopes of somehow appeasing the angry demons inside my abdomen.

---

[144] Holy Bible—English Standard Version (ESV) - Proverbs 23:20

As with the area of Montmartre, this place too was love at first sight. The streets were pedestrian traffic only…no cars or motorbikes allowed. The little shops resembled in many ways the shops of Montmartre. But unlike Montmartre, this was an area of eating places. Wonderful food, wonderful prices, wonderful atmosphere. I loved the Left Bank. Here too I would return many times over the next thirty-plus years.

I felt my neck pop several times as I fell off to sleep in the back of the taxi. At last I made it back to the Hilton and went straight to my room. I was in bed in no time and immediately asleep.

The Louvre

"Art washes away from the soul the dust of everyday life."[145]

The following morning when my alarm went off, I decided to doze just a little longer. By the time I managed to climb out of bed, the sun was peeking through the drapes drawn closed by the maid who did the turndown service and placed the little chocolate on my bedside nightstand. I staggered over to the window and pulled the drapes wide open. Sunlight flooded the room. The *La Tour Eiffel* stood majestically as if reminding me that I was in Paris. My mind immediately shifted to the plan of the day (POD in military parlance)…*Musée du Louvre*.

Today I was to see most of the few famous works of art I'd ever heard about. My formal education had not been steeped in art history or art appreciation. Medical and aeronautical subjects displaced any chance of learning about art. From the Dutch Masters through the Picasso, Michelangelo through Warhol, da Vinci through Remington…I was clueless. I'd allocated most of the day for the Louvre.

Downstairs in the restaurant, I had my *coffee American* while I read the Herald Tribune. I was really tempted to repeat the eggs benedict experience from the previous day, but then again, my desire to explore led me to try a combination of fried eggs, bacon, and typical French crêpes. They came with the most exquisite orange marmalade I'd ever tasted. I finished off with fresh juice.

This morning I didn't need the concierge. I told the bellman I wanted to go to the Louvre, and he hailed the next taxi that had been waiting in the hotel taxi queue. In subsequent days, and years, while staying at the Paris Hilton, having become more…shall we say…street smart, I would walk out the front door, smile and wave to bellman, turn right, then turn right again. When out of sight of the hotel bellman I'd stop and wait. Soon a taxi would come along en route to joining the Hilton's taxi queue. He would happily stop for me when I flagged him down, as he would have no wait time to do in the queue and his fellow taxi drivers would not see his bypassing the line. And I would have saved the two or three dollar tip expected by the bellman. Nevertheless,

---

[145] Pablo Picasso

on this morning I had not yet graduated or sunk, whichever way you choose to look at it, to that level, so this morning the bellman got his (my) two bucks.

In no time I was purchasing my ticket. Next, I rented a little headset attached to a tape recorder as my guide. The museum was immense with countless wings filled with various collections. I hardly knew where to start. I'd read an overview of the museum back in my hotel room…about half a page; hardly enough to really show me what to do. So I strapped on my headset and bravely began the seemingly impossible task of seeing and appreciating everything.

However, it seems my evil twin was never far from me. He almost immediately pointed out that if I just sort of ambled aimlessly along appearing to be listening to my headset, I could attach myself, purely by coincidence of course, to one of the tour groups with an English-speaking guide and get a guided tour for free. Appearing to be listening to my headset would be my cover. Heck…with a little practice I might get promoted to CIA operative.

It wasn't long before I'd hitched a ride with a sizable group of tourists from England. The guide had a strong voice that projected even though you were not supposed to speak loudly in the museum. I wormed my way into the group all the while pretending to be engrossed in the message on my tape recorder.

As we moved along, I soon realized she was spending far less time explaining the art than I needed. She probably had to hit several other high points in Paris before mid-afternoon and with such a schedule, detailed explanations were not permitted. I decided I would hang with this group as they covered the museum at a rapid pace, making notes on the places I wanted to go back and revisit. After all, I'd allocated the entire day to seeing the Louve.

About two hours later, just before noon, the tour ended. I decided this would be a good time to break for lunch. I'd seen a restaurant of sorts in the huge complex that comprised the museum proper. My brochure said the rectangular-shaped structure, which initially had been built as a fortress, had over 650,000 square feet of hallways. I would need plenty of time. So I decided to pay what would certainly be its inflated prices and stay on mission rather than waste time leaving to find a cheaper place to eat and return.

I found the restaurant, ate quickly, and resumed my art gazing. My first revisit was, of course, the Mona Lisa, by Leonardo da Vinci. Back then, there was no protective Plexiglas barrier. You could walk right up and lean over the velvet rope keeping the public from actually touching the famous painting and get nose to nose with Mona Lisa. I must have spent fifteen minutes looking at his brush strokes, trying to understand his techniques and reading the plaque that explained a little bit about the work. The excitement and the wonder of the moment was overpowering. Here I was, Jimmy Joe Jacks from Hamilton, Texas, staring nose to nose with Leonardo da Vinci's Mona Lisa.

The Mona Lisa's famous smile was there. Nobody could miss it. Those haunting, beckoning, flirtatious eyes; da Vinci was truly a genius. I could not help but think of my mother and how she would have loved to be here with me. I was so blessed. It was a humbling experience.

Next was the Egyptian collection. It held a special fascination for me. I suppose this was because of the mummies and stone sarcophagi in the collection. My fascination probably dated back to the early 1950s, to the Saturday afternoon matinée movies at the Strand Theater on the square in Hamilton. Silver screen films like "The Mummy" with Boris Karloff would scare the living hell out of us pre-teen kids. I always enjoyed the scary parts because it would sometimes, if I got lucky, afford the opportunity to hold the hand of the girl next to me. Back then, at our age, holding a girl's hand was pretty uncommon and was as exciting as the movie itself. I'd never seen a real "live" mummy before, so I'd probably have to rate that exhibit just behind the Mona Lisa. Also, somehow during all the schooling while I was in the Navy, I'd found time to study about the Rosecrucians. Their metaphysical theories were closely grounded in Egyptology. This probably fueled some of my interest, as I'd actually heard of a couple of the Pharaohs.

The Italian Renaissance was my last stop of the day; not because I planned it that way, but simply because my brain was screaming "no more." I was in sensory overload. It was time for a break.

As I left the colossal collection of the some of the world's most famous art, I was exhausted. I was humbled. I was in a state of reverence. I knew I would return.

Montparnasse

My feet have touched the stones of the narrow passageway known as the Via Doloros in Jerusalem where Jesus is believed by many to have stumbled toward the cross. My feet have touched the narrow streets of Montparnasse where Pablo Picasso and Henri Matisse, Ernest Hemingway and F. Scott Fitzgerald, James Joyce, Vladimir Lenin and Leon Trotsky, along with countless other sculptors, painters, writers, poets and composers have walked. Both were treasured experiences.[146]

Again, as in Montmartre and the Rive Gauche's Latin Quarter, it was love at first sight. The ambiance was literally screaming at me as I stepped out of the taxi. Part of me (my evil twin) was telling me to just send a telex back to Kinshasa saying "I quit…I'm never returning." Of course, my other half was saying, "but what about the aircraft…who will fly it back…what about Karen, and Jason." My evil twin was subdued; at least until a more opportune time.

Montparnasse is a special place for me. On my first trip to Paris I walked its narrow passageways lined with traditional French eating places. Montparnasse has been a haven for artists from around the world since the late 1800s.

---

[146] James Joseph Jacks—circa 2004

Picasso was here just after the turn of the century. Even during and after the great wars, the talented, along with the hangers-on, came to mingle. The crepe restaurants lining its streets today have changed little from when the world's most famous painters, sculptors, and writers flocked here to socialize. Unlike Montmartre, whose primary allure to the art community was debauchery, Montparnasse was a beacon to artists, a place where ideas could be spawned and refined. This is not to imply there was any shortage of "models" on which the artists could work. The narrow streets and cafés, the eating establishments, the entire atmosphere and spirit of the arts exuded from its walkways. The feelings were so strong. Some of my best photography, taken a couple of decades later, was from the streets of Montparnasse by night. Unbelievably I actually managed to sell some of the work via an art printer in Ft. Lauderdale to newly opened offices needing to cover naked walls. Some of these photos hung in the hallways of my office just prior to my retirement and some now hang in my home back in Texas. Montparnasse was special.

I walked its streets, literally engulfed in the spirit of Montparnasse. I was searching for a sidewalk café where I could enjoy a slow drink and a meal while, at the same time, still having an abundance of photo ops. Part of me was getting hungry. The other part didn't want to stop wandering along the sidewalks looking in all the shops, cafés and restaurants. As I walked along, lost in the moment, my head swimming with images, the words of Oscar Wilde interrupted my image stream. "Paradoxically though it may seem, it is none the less true that life imitates art far more than art imitates life." Probably, I was, in light of the undeniable evidence that I was devoid of artistic talent, doing just as he pointed out…attempting to imitate art. I wondered why that was. I decided the answer might come more easily with the assistance of a glass of draft beer from a sidewalk café I'd just spotted. Crepes and cider followed the draft beer. I would remain at the table till almost 10:00pm.

When I got back to my room at the Paris Hilton that night, I was amazed to see I'd shot three rolls of 36 exposure film that afternoon; almost all on the streets and sidewalks of Montparnasse. Later, after they were developed, I was equally amazed to see how uncharacteristically good some were. Years later, I would read the words of the renowned black and white photographer Ansel Adams and acknowledge the truth in his words…"You don't make a photograph just with a camera. You bring to the act of photography all the pictures you have seen, the books you have read, the music you have heard, the people you have loved."

Notre Dame…or Notre Dame de Paris

I rejoiced with those who said to me, "Let us go to the house of the Lord."[147]

The following morning after my coffee, breakfast of champions, and Herald Trib routine, I stopped by the concierge's desk and checked on tickets for the

---
[147] Holman Christian Standard Bible (HCSB) - Psalm 122:1

Moulin Rouge. He smiled and said "of course." I would pick them up upon my return to the hotel. I tried not to choke when he told me the price. I told him I was going alone and only needed one seat. He smiled again and said, "but of course." Oh well…how could I go to Paris and not see it. I signed the ticket order, left him a $5 tip, and headed out the door.

I smiled and waved to the bellman, ducked around the corner, snagged a cab heading for the Hilton's taxi queue, pocketed the bellman's two-dollar tip, and headed toward the famous Notre Dame Cathedral.

As I climbed out of the taxi in front of the famous cathedral, I thought that the Lord must have said to a hell of a lot of people "Let us go to the house of the Lord." Many hundreds were in front and all around the cathedral. There was a sizable line going inside. Endless streams of tour buses were continually regurgitating even more. This was one of the few things in Paris that I'd heard about all my life. Apparently, many of those visiting Paris could say the same thing.

It was old…plenty old. Construction started under Louis VII and was finished over 200 years later in 1345. It was the epitome of French Gothic architecture. What I failed to understand until well into my visit was that I was, for the most part, looking at a restoration. The more than 800-year-old building had not only naturally deteriorated but had received significant damage at the hands of the French themselves during the French Revolution in the 1790s. The more I read as I walked along on my-self guided tour the more I realized how much the building had changed over its 800 years of existence and how little of the original structure remained. During certain periods of the cathedral's history, it had even been used for cult worship such as the Cult of Reason and the Cult of the Supreme Being. Both cults created around the period of the French Revolution in order to turn the people away from any form of Christianity but especially from Catholicism.

While meditatively taking in the ambiance of the cathedral, my focus was drawn to one of the huge columns scattered throughout and supporting the ceilings (and other structural elements I suppose). I, along simultaneously with my evil twin, wondered, considering the fires, bombings, and revolutions, if the column were really made of stone. I knocked on it with my fist and received the resounding reply of metal covered with plaster and cement. My evil twin is a thief, taking joy in robbing my romantic moments. At least I could now coldly and smugly view the cathedral as it truly was rather than how I'd envisioned it to be.

While impressed, especially with the stained glass (most not original) and with the gargoyles, I left Notre Dame de Paris slightly disappointed.

I paused for a few moments in a spot where artists had set up their easels and were sketching the cathedral. I decided this would be a good place for another red book moment. As I tried to organize everything I'd just seen, I found my head filled with swirling images, most contending for prominence. As I sat looking at the main entrance, the northwest facing side, studying the huge belfries, I imagined I could see the contorted frame of Quasimodo moving in and out, ringing the bells. I could almost hear his sorrowful remark to one of the cathedral's gargoyles "Why was I not made of stone like thee?"[148]

The Wisdom Of Chewing Slowly

It was time for lunch; time to go foraging for food amongst the maze of narrow restaurant-lined streets where I'd eaten previously. But this time with the strict understanding that gluttony would not be an option.

From the main entrance of Notre Dame, I could see Place Saint Michel. It was only about four hundred yards away. My stroll down the left bank of the Seine took me past sidewalk sellers of old books. Many were quite old. I was fascinated but since they were mostly in French and I was becoming driven by hunger, I only occasionally slowed to take a quick look.

Soon I was once again in the thick of the little hole in the wall restaurants just off the Rive Gauche. I was lusting for a gyro and this was Greek restaurant heaven. I found a nice place with a shaded sidewalk café and a great view of the left bank foot traffic as well as Place Saint Michel. I realized the view was going to come with a price. But you don't come to Paris to stare at a dirty wall. I happily ordered my expensive gyro and drink. Only about twenty-five yards from here on the little side streets, the prices would be half of this and I planned to revisit those places again soon. I was hopelessly hooked on the Latin Quarter. But for today, I'd found the perfect place to pass an hour or so before moving on to my next spot…Luxembourg Gardens. While sitting there I noticed once again, my rate of mastication was inversely proportional to the price of the food. So was my sipping. Life was good…so very good.

Other than having to be back at the hotel early, my afternoon lay ahead of me in pleasant maze of unhurried tranquility. As long as I got back in time to get cleaned up and be ready in the hotel lobby by 7:30 pm for my tour bus pickup I had an unscripted afternoon. The dinner and show started at 9:00 pm…the afternoon was mine.

Jardin du Luxembourg – Luxembourg Garden

After my lunch I walked the short distance down Blvd. Saint Michel to the beautiful park and garden know as Luxembourg Gardens. The information in my hotel room said it was the second largest park in Paris and consisted of approximately 55 acres of beautifully manicured trees and plants. It is the garden of the Luxembourg Palace which today houses the French Senate. There were many towering shade trees; park benches abounded and countless statues. The park was also filled with countless people; older people were sitting on park benches, young lovers lying in the grass. It was a tranquil,

---
[148] Notre-Dame de Paris—Victor Hugo - 1833

beautiful place. I found an empty park bench with shade and a view of flower gardens. I plopped down just to spend a while taking in the atmosphere of the park.

A French Terrorist Bomb Blast

Suddenly, seeming out of nowhere, I felt something strike my left shoulder with considerable force. I felt something warm on my face and neck. I reached my hand up to see what had hit my shoulder. It was pigeon excrement... an unbelievable quantity of warm pigeon poop all over my shoulder, my left cheek, and my neck. I let out an expletive and began looking around for something to use to wipe it off. I saw a nearby trash can and dug around until I found a well-used napkin I assumed had been used by picnickers. Just then I noticed a policeman, *Police Nationale* walking past. He was chuckling. At first, I gave him a scowl. But then I realized how absolutely ridiculous and yes, actually funny I must have appeared to him. I started to laugh which caused him to laugh even harder. He came over and pointed out a drinking fountain about 100 yards away. He explained to me that this happened all the time...that they'd even "bombed" him. I headed off to try to wash away as much of the damage as I could. He headed off down the pathway. I'm sure he would share the story of the American terrorist victim he met in the park that day.

After a lot of scrubbing I managed to get everything (well...almost everything) off the surface of my shirt and off my neck and cheek. My shirt was still stained but things were a hundred times better than they were a few minutes earlier. I was sure I could still feel the pigeon poop on my neck. I was convinced it was time to bail out of the park and head back to the hotel. I still didn't really feel clean.

A Taste Of French Higher Education
–Académie du Biere

As I left the park, I turned left on Blvd. de Port-Royal. I saw no taxi queues so I decided to just stroll down the sidewalk 'til I could flag one down. I'd only walked a few yards when I spotted a sidewalk café. The sign on the red canvas canopy read *Académie du Biere*. I realized that today I didn't have a lot of time to devote to serious research at the Académie, but I knew I could at least begin work formulating a hypothesis. When the waiter brought me the beer menu...yes, an entire menu devoted to beer. My mind was in message unit overload. I'd never seen so many beers with such exotic names in one place in my life; almost exclusively they were Belgium and abbey ales. I decided I'd walk inside and try to wash myself a little more in their restroom and check out the interior. I lost count of the number of draft beers on tap. On the shelves behind the bar were dozens more. Wow, I was in heaven. Most of the beers back in the Congo were hardly drinkable. I was now standing in a place filled with world class beers. When the waiter returned, I selected a CHIMAY BLANCHE Blonde. Wow it was so good. It was strong with a very distinctive taste. I noticed on the menu that it was 7% alcohol by volume. One would be all I had time for this afternoon. The waiter also pointed out that their primary dish was muscles or *moules*. Again I knew I didn't have time to try them, but I made myself a promise I'd be back here tomorrow for dinner and a few exotic beers.

I liked the waiter…he had been unusually sharing and patient for a Parisian waiter. I left him a nice tip and assured him I'd be back tomorrow evening (not that I thought he really cared). Soon I had a taxi and was heading for the Paris Hilton.

My Near Cardiac Arrest

Upon entering my room, I noticed the shirts, socks and underwear I'd sent out for laundry stacked neatly on my bed. My trousers were hanging in the closet. Per chance my eye caught the total of the laundry bill on the accompanying laundry list. Damn!…this could not possibly be true. I realized the prices were there when I filled out the laundry list but somehow the full impact of the cost had failed to register that morning. I made a rough calculation that the cost to wash my underwear and socks was more than I'd paid for them at Montgomery Ward in Ft. Worth. I figured that after two washes at the hotel, I could pay my Indian tailor back in Kinshasa to make me another pair. I remember seeing a laundry as I was driving along in the taxi that morning, but I couldn't remember where I'd seen it. I vowed I'd find one before I used this one again. The work was very professional and the shirts so carefully folded, but I just couldn't force myself to pay these kinds of prices. Wigmo was paying for my laundry but even with their paying…I could not bring myself to pay this again.

I rushed through my shower, paying particular attention to the left side of my neck and my left cheek. I rushed downstairs and positioned myself where the bellman could easily find me as the tour bus taking us to the Moulin Rouge pulled up in front of the hotel.

Soon the bellman was beckoning to me as well as to another couple. We scurried out and boarded the bus. The bus was quite large, and few people were on it so I figured we would have several more stops at various other hotels picking up tourists destined for the Moulin Rouge. The bus had a lady somewhat like a tour guide who announced various landmarks as we moved through the streets of Paris. I found her very useful as I knew very little about anything I'd not decided to visit or already visited.

Soon the bus was just about filled, and we headed toward *Montmartre* and the famous Moulin Rouge.

Cheap Champaign, Cheap Food, No Place For Elbows On The Table, And A Great Cabaret

The logistics involved in getting us from the bus to seated at the table were carried out with almost military precision, and with about as much feeling. I was soon seated at a long, cramped table, with no place for elbows. There seemed to be hundreds of tourists. But I didn't care. My eyes were scanning the walls where reproductions of the famous posters drawn by Henri de Toulouse-Lautrec and others hung. I imagined him sitting at one of the small tables alongside the wall visiting intimately with artist friends, all the while furiously drawing in his sketchbook. This uncharacteristic knowledge of Henri de Toulouse-Lautrec almost certainly came from the vivid images I still had from the mid-1950s movie Moulin Rouge staring José Ferrer and Zsa Zsa Gabor.

Soon the Champaign came (delivered by waiters with less personality than a cabin attendant on a flight from Newark to Pittsburgh), followed quickly by our meal, which reminded me of the meals served onboard airlines like Sabena or Alitalia. But who cared! I came for the sights, the experience, the moment. I was anything but disappointed. My "Champagne" resembled cheap Chardonnay doused with white wine vinegar with a touch of 7-Up for fizz. But once again…I didn't care. Nothing was going to spoil this captivating event.

The whole episode lasted a little over an hour. We were then herded (literally) out and onboard our waiting busses. Soon we were back at the hotel.

Sleep did not come easy. Vivid images of can-can girls flashing their legs high in the air, Henri de Toulouse-Lautrec…or was it José Ferrer…were there. I saw Théo and Vincent van Gogh. Pissarro, Gaugain, Claude Monet, Degas, and Renoir. In my visions, they were all nursing their small glasses of Absinthe and in my mind certainly discussing how to overthrow the imperialistic art establishment of Paris. They all had their own little tables. When I slept, I dreamed of *"les années folles"* or the crazy years. I wished I could have experienced them for real…not just in my fantasies. I wanted to relive these magic moments as often as I could…and I did. In later years as a jet captain, I often stayed at a hotel which put me within easy walking distance of this magical place.

A Break From Parisian Exploration

Each day I'd managed to exchange notes via the front desk or make an early morning call to David Bellows, my captain, before he left for the airport. He had been so very gracious in allowing me to wander about exploring Paris. However, I was beginning to think at least a courtesy trip with him to the airport was a bit overdue. He'd been going each day. For whatever reason, he seemed to have little interest in the sights of this wonderful city, probably because he was German and had been here many times. While he was a truly nice person, he was totally boring.

The following morning, I scheduled my wakeup call for earlier than normal so I could leave the hotel with him. He was pleased to get my call and we agreed to meet in hotel coffee shop for breakfast later. He informed me he usually did not leave for the airport till around 10:00am, as this would let the morning rush hour traffic dissipate and allow the mechanics at the airport to finish their morning briefings. David and I met in the coffee shop. I had my regular coffee, breakfast and Herald Tribune.

After breakfast we headed for the taxi queue. As we were walking through the lobby, the concierge called out asking how my night at the Moulin Rouge had been. I flashed him a big smile and thumbs up. David just shook his head; I was a shameless tourist.

At the hanger we spent the rest of the morning going over paperwork relating to the inspection and all the ongoing work orders. Most of the cowlings were still open and workers were swarming all over the plane. Even I could realize all these man-hours were going to cost the Congolese government a bundle of money.

We went to lunch just across the street from the hanger where all the French mechanics took their very long lunch break. They ate their lunch, drank wine, and played a game they called baby-*foot* which was some kind of table football (soccer). When they played the game, they get really intense. The ball moved at lightning speed. I was amazed how good they had become at the game. I had tired it once before and did terribly at it. I was also amazed that they could or would drink alcohol during work hours. I later learned this was very acceptable in France during that period.

We stayed at the hanger till about three then headed back into Paris. The idea was once again to beat the rush hour traffic. We came into Paris on the "N2" which was a major highway, joined the loop which the Parisians refer to as the *Périphérique* and looped our way around the city, exiting close to the Paris Hilton.

We talked for a few moments in the hotel lobby then I was off like a streak of greased lightning for my room, a shower, and further courses at the institution of higher learning I'd just discovered…the *Academie du Biere*.

Mulling The Moules Menu

As I hopped out of the taxi, I found there were still a few choice tables left outside. I spotted the same waiter who had taken care of me before. Remarkably he remembered me. I suppose my country-boy-come-to-town demeanor made me stand out a bit from the average French patron. Remarkably, I seemed to be the only tourist there. When he asked what I would like to drink I just told him to pick something for me.

He appeared pleased and soon brought me a bottle and a glass. The beer was a Belgium Witbier, or biere blanche for the French or white for a Texan. The waiter said if I ordered their moule dish prepared using white beer, it would be the perfect pairing. I graciously accepted his recommendations and soon I had a huge plate of *moules à la marinière* with *frites* (French fries). I vowed I would remember his pairing recommendation. Coming from an environment where people drank Pearl Beer, Lone Star Beer, or iced tea, the concept of pairing had never crossed my mind. As adolescents we learned to pair off at a dance or hayride in hopes of getting lucky and maybe getting a kiss or sneaking a feel, but food pairing was a totally foreign concept. Paris France was a long way from Hamilton, or Paris, Texas, for that matter.

I learned from the waiter that I was eating a very traditional French meal. A couple of days earlier I'd learned that crepes and cider was a traditional French meal as well. I noted to myself that I was becoming "worldly," whatever that meant. I wondered if that was good or bad. I later decided it was good if you used it as an opportunity to expand your horizons but bad if it became a component of self-importance or superciliousness. I ordered another beer and tried to learn to open the moules like the French did.

After two beers and according to what my stomach was now accusing me of…a gazillion moules and frites, I tipped my friend the waiter generously and flagged a cab back to the Hilton.

While I explored the joys of Paris, the CIA was struggling to reconcile volumes of conflicting intelligence data, both deductive and empirical, with little success. The Chinese were using the Cambodian port of Sihanoukville as a major transit point from Chinese cargo ships to waiting Chinese truck convoys which would transport the military hardware to the waiting Viet Cong and in some cases the Cambodian Khmer Rouge. Only later would the size of this colossal U.S. intelligence failure become fully known. The CIA through these intelligence failures was significantly misinforming President Nixon and Henry Kissinger. These massive amounts of Chinese arms passing through Sihanoukville's port were significantly facilitated by corrupt Cambodian officials. One name that continued to come up was that of General Lon Nol, who would later become a major player in the coup that deposed then Prince Norodom Sihanouk in March of 1970 and Cambodia's subsequent head of state.[149]

The Opera

The following morning, I settled on a laid back and unhurried agenda. From the list of must-see places found along with all the advertising that inevitably makes its way into Paris hotels, I'd settled on a visit to the famous Paris Opera. Again, how can one come to Paris without visiting The Opera. I

---

[149] Good Questions—Wrong Answers: CIA's Estimates of Arms Traffic Through Sihanoukville During The Vietnam War - Thomas L. Ahern, Jr. - Center For The Study Of Intelligence 2004 - Secret - Declassified 2009

wasn't culturally ready to see an opera performance, but the famous building was a must see.

My foreknowledge of this majestic structure was almost exclusively associated with the 1943 movie Phantom Of The Opera staring Claude Rains. I'd seen it in Hamilton as an adolescent. Claude Rains had the most fascinating voice. I remember after watching the movie wondering why people in Texas couldn't talk like that. Praise God adolescents don't get everything they wish for.

I followed my usual morning routine...coffee, breakfast, the International Herald Tribune and stiff the bellman by flagging a queue bound taxi. I was standing in front of the Opera before 10:00am.

It was my good fortune to arrive at the same time a tour bus arrived; a tour bus full of English-speaking tourists. And best of all...another guide giving her presentation in English. I shamelessly tagged along eavesdropping while maintaining a just barely respectable distance.

The pictures I'd seen didn't begin to do justice to the edifice. The grand staircases, the private boxes, the elaborate paneling, the huge chandelier which in the book and movie crashes into the audience...I was awestruck.

As I gazed at the magnificent chandelier, I imagined I could see Claude Rains, phantom of the opera, sitting in a private box tenderly watching the object of his affections, Christine Dubois, as she performed.

When the tour was over, I went outside and joined many others just sitting on the steps leading to the entrance, enjoying the gentle sun, feverishly scribbling in my little red book, desperately trying to capture the moment. The thrill of experiencing everything I'd encountered in the past few days was indescribable.

When the mood passed, I arose and set out to explore the area. I remembered from studying my map that the famous Galeries Lafayette department store was only a block or two away. This, too was a must see.

Le Grand Hotel

But before I turned the corner, I spotted a place I'd learned about from a fellow hotel guest...the famous Le Grand Hotel. The exterior of the hotel resembled the Opera. I read later they were both designed by the same architect. I was told the coffee served there was the best in the world and the atrium or tea room was lavish. I wanted to see what this place was like inside.

When I entered it was obvious the bellmen knew I didn't belong there. The place was truly opulent. Sunlight was coming through the glass ceiling. I'd never seen anything like it. It made the Paris Hilton look like a Motel 6.

Café de la Paix
Get Ready to Pay

After enjoying the lobby for a few minutes and before I wore out my welcome, I went to the hotel's world-famous Café de la Paix. I braced myself for the price I envisioned I would soon pay for their coveted cup of coffee. But how could I come to Paris and not say I'd had coffee at the Café de la Paix.

The waiter was snooty, totally unlike the wonderful waiter that took such good care of me at the *Academie du Biere*. Regrettably I would learn over the years that this was the norm for Paris. It made me really appreciate the few friendly ones I'd occasionally find.

I ordered only coffee. Of course, the waiter showed distain when I refused to order any pastry to go along with it. The coffee was certainly not disappointing. I wasn't sure how they achieved that wonderful full flavor without the characteristic French bite, but they did. I milked that cup of expensive French coffee for all it was worth; then headed out to the street for more exploring. I had the urge to give the waiter the bird, but I triumphed over my evil twin and didn't.

Galeries Lafayette

When I stepped into Paris' most famous upscale department store, I faced instant sensory overload. There was nothing subtle about Galeries Lafayette…nothing. It was like walking into a gilded birdcage. The center of the building was open with an enormous skylight on the top. Everything was done in ornate gold. There was floor after floor of the ultimate luxury goods. As Le Grand Hotel made the Paris Hilton look like a Motel 6, the Galeries Lafayette made Neiman Marcus look like K-Mart. The place was so famous that many in the store appeared to be tourists. Since I had little interest in these ultra-luxury items other than to marvel that somebody would be willing to pay such astronomical prices for stuff, I soon was ready to move on to something new. I did burn about half a roll of 36 exposure in there before I left, however. I was only about ten minutes from Harry's Bar, but it was far too early to consider that. I could see Place Saint Michel on my map. It appeared to be only about a mile and a half from the Galeries Lafayette where I was. I decided to enjoy the day and just stroll leisurely to the Latin Quarter. There I knew I could find another great sidewalk café or perhaps grab a bite to eat.

Frenchmen Come With Balls Of Steel
To Play *Pétanque* In The Parks Of Paris

As I strolled along, I noticed some men, perhaps of retirement age, playing a game in the park. I'd seen this before from the taxi and wondered what they were doing. The driver told me the name of the game was pétanque (pay tonk). Since the rest of my day was open, I decided to sit on a nearby park bench and watch the old Frenchmen.

They were pitching these obviously heavy metal balls at a much smaller wooden ball. The idea appeared to be making your metal ball land as close as possible to the little wooden ball.

As I sat watching and occasionally snapping a picture, a much older French gentleman came up and sat down beside me on the bench. He immediately began speaking to me in French. He spoke very rapidly. I immediately apologized and explained I was an American. He beamed a big smile and began speaking slowly. I'd learned in just the few days I been in Paris that the older French people, probably the ones who remembered WWII well, seemed to like us a lot more than the middle-aged ones did. The students appeared much friendlier as well. Anyway, I asked my new friend if he would explain what the game was about. He explained the goal was to try to get your metal balls as close as possible to the little one, which he called a *Cochonnet*. He referred to the metal balls as "*boules*." To me, a cochon was the word for pig in French; therefore, cochonnet would probably be a little or baby pig. So, I asked him again to repeat the word. Yep, that's what he said. So, I asked him if it meant "little pig" to which he smiled and replied "*exactement*." I now knew they were playing *Pétanque;* their metal balls were called *boules* and the little ball was called a *Cochonnet*.

Right away I noticed these old guys were taking their game very seriously. They studied each shot and seldom spoke. The old man told me that these players came here several times each week, weather permitting, and almost certainly they would adjourn to a nearby bar after the game.

About then I realized I would be here in this enjoyable park bench moment with this nice old French gentleman for hours if I didn't force myself to move on. I thanked him for his explanations and kindness. It was important to me that he knew I truly enjoyed my time with him. I then resumed my stroll toward Place Saint Michel.

Another Greek Hole-In-The-Wall Restaurant

I had planned to sit on the steps by the fountain at Place Saint Michel for a while and scribble more in my little red book, but hunger got the best of me. Perhaps it could best be described as culinary lust. I found a quaint-looking Greek restaurant; just a hole-in-the-wall among many hole-in-the-wall places. There was a picture of a Greek salad sandwich on their large menu posted outside on the sidewalk that made my mouth water from ten feet away.

The place wasn't particularly busy, so I had a perfect table by the window. I had an inside view and a sidewalk view; the best of both worlds. I ordered a small glass of white house wine and the sandwich which captured my attention.

Soon they both were on the table. Oh my…that sandwich; green salad, chopped olives, anchovies, feta cheese, chopped onions, chopped tomatoes, and sprinkled with olive oil and red-wine vinegar. All this was cradled by hot fresh pita bread. Life was so good. My small glass of white house wine was a French Pinot Grigio. My prayer before I began my wonderful meal contained special thanks for being so fortunate. Congolese in their eastern provinces were starving and being hacked to death during tribal and ethnic fighting. Some even suffered the fate of becoming a meal themselves. I was seated in a wonderful little restaurant on the left bank of the Seine in the Latin Quarter of Paris. I had so much for which to offer thanks.

After my meal, which had tasted as good as it had looked on the menu, I wandered the streets of the Latin Quarter observing the marvelous sights and taking many pictures. The mélange of light and colors, while not surpassing those of Montparnasse, kept my feet moving and my shutter clicking. Everywhere I turned there was an interesting person to photograph, a captivating store front or restaurant, a prefect reflection of light from something. Finally, well after sunset, exhaustion overtook me. I'd taken some great Latin Quarter By Night shots. Dinner that night would be a sandwich and coke in the Hilton's coffee shop. As I went to sleep, my head was still alive with the sights, smells, and sounds of the day. I was so blessed.

Au Revoir Paris

If you are lucky enough to have lived in Paris as a young man, then wherever you go for the rest of your life it stays with you, for Paris is a moveable feast.[150]

My remaining days in Paris were spent, for the most part, revisiting the several areas which held an almost magnetic attraction. I returned daily to the sidewalks, cafes and restaurants of Montparnasse, where I could sit and almost see its famous *années folles* or crazy years residents. La Rive Gauche and the Latin Quarter with its youthful vitality, and ambience beckoned. I returned to the Louvre and to Harry's on "Sank Roo Doe Noo." But *Academie de la Biere* with its wonderful varieties of *moules* and assortment of beers with histories dating back hundreds of years, capped with their typical French fries or *frites* possessed the siren with the greatest allure. I was truly sad when the day finally came. I found the note waiting for me at the front desk of the Hilton. "Test flight at 9:00am. If good depart for K-1 following day."

Over and over I thanked David as we rode in the taxi to Le Bourget airport for allowing me to spend the entire time exploring Paris with the wide eyes of a child. He just smiled, totally in character with his being a man of few words.

---

[150] Ernest Hemingway—From Hemingway's posthumously published Paris memoirs

Our test flight revealed only minor discrepancies which were cleared within two hours of our landing. The payment for the maintenance services had arrived a couple of days earlier. All our log books, and maintenance logs and records were loaded onto the plane. We would plan to depart at 7:30 am the following morning. We had already agreed our route would be the same as when we came. I polished up the return flight plan I'd made while still back in Kinshasa, then spent some time on the phone getting a weather briefing from the French meteorologists.

We left the hotel the following morning at 5:30am. David and the flight mechanic rechecked the aircraft and did the preflight. I went to the Air Traffic Services office and filed the flight plan, picked up all the NOTAMS for our route, picked up the meteorology package they had waiting for us and returned to the plane. The flight engineer had already loaded my bags. Our catering was strapped into a passenger seat. It was time to go.

I made the takeoff. During the busy climb out, I nevertheless managed to sneak one last look at the city I'd learned to enjoy so much. *Au Revoir Paris.*

Marie-Jeanne and Malaria

A couple of days after our uneventful trip back to Kinshasa, I noticed I wasn't feeling normal. I had a dull headache. But as was my custom from as far back as I could remember, I continued on with my normal duties. Since I had the next couple of days off, I headed out to restock the groceries and have things ready for Karen. By the time I'd finished my shopping my headache had gotten much worse and it felt like I might have fever.

On my way back home, I stopped by to visit with Paul. I'd learned his wife, Marie-Jeanne, and his daughter Natacha were here. Marie-Jeanne was a bundle of energy; laughing, running about cleaning the kitchen, and chattering a mile a minute. I liked her immediately...everybody liked her immediately. She was beautiful, charming, and never met a stranger. It was obvious why Paul was so proud of her. And Natacha...was the light of his life. She was Paul's only child. Marie-Jeanne and Natacha were the center of Paul's world.

When Marie-Jeanne found out I wasn't feeling well she insisted on taking my temperature. It was elevated. She gave me a couple of aspirin and after chatting a while, I headed back to the house. While unloading the groceries I started to feel stomach cramps. In spite of the aspirin I could feel my temperature rising. I was getting cold chills and I ached all over. I assumed I was getting the flu. The flu...in my mind a winter illness, here in the Congo...just south of the equator? But whatever it was, I knew I had better get in bed. I decided I would lie down for a while. It was only mid-afternoon. Much too early to go to bed for the night. I lay down on the bed for a rest.

I soon developed severe chills. I began shivering. Waves of chills would pass over me, then subside for a minute or so and then return. Suddenly I felt as though I was going to throw up. I just made it to the bathroom. Out came breakfast and a Miranda. I went back to lay on the bed again. I noticed the place where I'd been lying on the bed was wet with perspiration. This was not good. I tried to sleep but I was too sick.

At some time, I must have slipped off into a fitful sleep. The next thing I knew, I looked up and found Marie-Jeanne sitting on the bed beside me and Paul standing over me. They both looked concerned. Marie-Jeanne had made me some soup realizing I was not well. But when I did not answer the door, they became concerned. I'm glad they did. Marie-Jeanne offered me the soup, but I was too sick to eat it. She said I looked awful. Paul wanted to take me to the Wigmo clinic at Mobutu's OAU center. I did not want to go. Paul prevailed, they loaded me in the car and headed for the OAU compound where President Mobutu's private doctor treated high ranking members of his government and his black sheep (Wigmo). I think that was about the longest ride I can remember. I kept fighting off the urge to throw up while lying in the back seat shivering.

When we arrived at Mobutu's clinic. American nurses took me straight to an ultra-modern treatment room and had me lie down. Soon Dr. Bill Clark (pseudonym) walked in. His bedside manner was cold and uncaring as if he had been interrupted from some important task and I was to blame. He ordered the nurses to start an IV and he actually ordered me to stop shivering. In response, I reached over with my free hand and pinned the arm they were going to use for the IV to the table. I thought if I suddenly had to throw up again, I hoped it went on him.

By now, it was time for the clinic to close. He instructed the nurses to leave me on the treatment table overnight and he would see me in the morning. In some meager defense of the jackass, being left alone in the treatment room of his deserted and locked clinic was probably better than being in any Congolese hospital anywhere in the country.

It was a long night. Several times during the night I had to go throw up in the bathroom across the hall. I removed the IV from the stand and carried it with me. I was too weak to drag the stand. Long ago the fluid had drained out. Being a trained medic, I clamped off the tube. I would have removed the needle myself, but I feared I might need another unit of glucose and water in the morning and the SOB might decide to reinsert the 18 gauge needle himself just for spite. This guy should have stuck to playing CIA informant and left practicing medicine to somebody else. I was relieved when I saw the first rays of dawn through the window.

The nurses were very caring and had all my vital signs ready when Dr. Clark arrived. Without speaking a word to me, he reviewed the chart containing my recent vital signs and instructed one of the nurses to call Wigmo operations and tell them to send a van to pick me up and take me back home. The nurses gave me some pills to take with instructions to keep myself hydrated. I looked at the pills and could tell they were anti-emetics and an anti-malarial medication. They had to kill the infection in my blood that had been introduced by the bite of a female mosquito, probably while I was in Kisangani. I had heard thousands of people, including many infants, died each year in the Congo from malaria. Most of those who died had no access to antimalarial drugs or even the most basic medical treatment. Most people believed the number was far worse than anybody knew due to poor or non-existent communication and record keeping. I was lucky to be alive.

I realized how weak the past 24 hours had left me when I walked from the clinic to the Wigmo van. I climbed into the back seat and told the Congolese driver the Wigmo code name for our apartment complex…"Limete misato" or Limete three. Then I leaned against the window and tried to rest (and not throw up). I had the driver stop by "Limete mibale" or Limete two where Paul and Marie-Jeanne were staying. He brought Paul out to the van. Paul said they would be over very soon to check on me.

By the time I got home I could tell I was starting to recover a bit, but it would be several days before I gained back all the strength that I'd lost in the past twenty-four hours. As I was leaving the clinic, one of the nurses told me there was a high probability I would now experience regular bouts of reoccurring malaria. She said most people did. How nice. Paul and Marie-Jeanne brought me some soup later in the day. She left more for John to feed me later. Soup was about all I could tolerate.

While I was recovering from my bout with malaria in October 1970, the Cambodian legislative assembly adopted a new constitution replacing the kingdom with a republic. The Khmer Republic was declared. Since the coup of 18 March 1970 the country had been entangled in a vicious civil war. Both the coup and the civil war were being supported by the United States which badly needed the Cambodian territories and troops to tie down the North Vietnamese and Viet Cong in order to buy time for the US troop withdrawal in Vietnam. All these events went virtually unnoticed as I supported the CIA's cold war efforts in the Congo.

But the war was not going well for the US interests in Cambodia or anywhere else in Southeast Asia. The poorly-trained, newly-recruited Cambodian army troops were being slaughtered. The high morale the Cambodian armed forces had initially enjoyed quickly disappeared. There were no longer any voluntary enlistments. Cambodia was in chaos.

My First Flight As "Captain Jacks"

Three days after the malaria attack, I was ready to go to flight operations and get back on the schedule. This time, for the first time as Captain Jacks. I was ready to get going. Gold Finger laughed when he saw me and said, "welcome to the Congo." Apparently your first case of malaria was some bizarre rite of passage.

They put me on the schedule for the following day with one of the new copilots. He was from Belgium but had grown up in pre-independence Congo. I'd not yet met him, as he processed in while I was in Kisangani with Bat. We were scheduled for a four-day mission, which included three overnights. My duffle bag would have some extra weight this time. Our mission was Kinshasa to Mbandaka then on to Kisangani where we would remain overnight. The second day would be from Kisangani to Gbadolite with one of the ANC's highest-ranking generals. Our orders were to remain overnight with him in Gbadolite then bring him back to Kisangani, again remaining overnight. The following morning, we would return to Kinshasa. I went home to pack. I stopped by Limete Mibale to tell Paul about my flight. I was excited. I checked out the dinner John had waiting for me on the table, packed my bags, enjoyed a small glass of Primus in the darkened living room, dined by kerosene lamp and went to bed.

I didn't sleep well, probably due to a mild case of anxiety, and welcomed the alarm's harsh ring. I arrived in flight ops ahead of my copilot Jean Jacques. When he arrived, I'd already studied the so-called weather folder, which was basically a waste of paper as the meteorology department was staffed by Congolese who spent most of their time sleeping. Most of the pilots considered them a joke. But, to maintain the appearance of some degree of professionalism, I took a look just to see what they had to say. Our best metrology information came over the radio…pilot to pilot or from our Wigmo station agents at stations where we had one. On this mission I was lucky. We had an agent in Mbandaka and Kisangani. That only left Gbadolite without reliable weather. But we had the Belgium military advisor's HF and VHF frequencies, so at least they could give us an observation over the radio. Besides, they always ran up and down the runway in their jeep to make sure it was clear from animals or tree branches or God knows what. I briefed Jean Jacques and we headed to the plane. I found him a very likable person. We were close to the same age, although my experience far exceeded his. I couldn't help but wonder how he got this job. As we walked across the ramp and along the flight line, I felt the whole world was watching me. More anxiety I suppose. In reality probably nobody took any notice…just two pilots walking to their plane.

At the plane we found our passengers waiting. They were the usual run of people, goats, chickens, furniture, clothing, pots and pans. I'd learned on my first few flights that you had to keep a close eye when you saw the pots and pans. Numerous pilots related instances where they had caught the passengers in the process of building a fire in order to cook a meal in the plane. They had no concept. They cooked inside their houses and huts, why not in the back of the airplane. This Congo was an interesting place.

When we were certain our load was securely tied down, we made our way to the cockpit. Before I even sat down all my anxiety had gone. This was something I was well prepared for. Bat had done a good job. I was ready. I was so ready I told Jean Jacques he could make the takeoff.

Our flight to Mbandaka was easy. We basically were flying north with the Congo River out the left window the entire trip. The sky was still mostly clear as the typical equatorial buildups would not begin to start popping up till around noon. By mid-afternoon, many would sport tops approaching fifty thousand feet, but for the moment the ride was smooth and the view spectacular.

Mbandaka had an interesting history. Discovered by the famous adventurer and explorer Henry Morton Stanley, the city's center lay only about two miles north of the equator. Mbandaka, located on the east bank of the Congo River had been one of the most beautiful and prosperous cities in the Belgium Congo. But it now lay in virtual ruin, with only hints of its pre-independence glory found in crumbling Euro-colonial style architecture. Most parts of the city had no running water and no electricity. The streets were mostly reddish-brown dirt. The city had a fairly decent port to accommodate river freight traffic and several ferries a week connected Mbandaka with Kinshasa. All along the river bank were sunken or half-submerged barges along with hundreds of small wooden Congolese fishing boats. It looked like nobody maintained anything.

Since the airport's control tower was never working, our custom was to make a low circle over the city, then proceed to the airport. Almost immediately after our circle, speeding clouds of dust could be seen making their way from town to the airport a couple of miles east of town. After circling the town, we made a pass down the runway to insure it was clear of livestock. Then we returned and landed on runway 18. There was no terminal, but we went to the rundown area where one had once been. By the time we taxied in, dusty, battleship-gray Land Rovers began to arrive. The British-made Land Rover was the vehicle of choice in the provinces and could go through mud and even flowing streams. They were truly amazing vehicles. After the Land Rovers, some rundown ANC trucks arrived to transport the military passengers and military cargo.

While the aircraft was unloading, I went over to a little stand that was set up under the shade of a tree to get a cold Miranda. Air Congo serviced the airport as well, so vendors found an occasional opportunity to make some money from passengers. As I sat watching Jean Jacques supervise the refueling, a Belgium man walked up to me and started pointing at my Southwest School of Aviation class of 67 ring. Through his broken English and my broken French, he managed to convey to me his son had a ring just like that and asked if it was from Southwest School of Aviation in Texas. I was amazed. Here I was in the heart of the African jungle and the father of one of our graduates walks up to me. It turned out I did in fact know his son. I wrote down my name and my address in Limete for him. He said his son was trying to get hired by Air Congo. Since their pilots were mostly Belgium, I figured out he would have a pretty good chance. Small world.

The passengers were getting ready to board, my Miranda was empty, the airplane was fueled…it was time to get going. I said goodbye to the Belgium and headed back to the C-47. It was already hot as hell and the slight chill of the air at 9000 feet promised welcome relief. As I walked through the cabin, amidst the smiling faces of the passengers, I spotted our loadmaster's pile of personal entrepreneurial cargo. I had wondered during our flight to Mbandaka just what he was going to do for cargo from there to Kisangani. Both were interior cities, both located on the banks of the Congo River. What would be in one city that would not be in the other? I never found out, but obviously there was plenty. Amazing.

I made the takeoff and told Jean Jacques he would make the landing in Kisangani. By that time we were already starting to encounter the afternoon equatorial buildups and were weaving our way through them. Jean Jacques enjoyed this, as it meant we would disengage the autopilot and hand fly.

I was glad when we were lined up on final. It meant I'd soon be visiting with Bat. From our departure message to Wigmo's King 1 and a later contact with King 7, I learned Bat was expected to be on the ground before our arrival. I was looking forward to sharing a beer and my latest adventures with Bat on his veranda.

George was waiting and soon his highly-efficient team was swarming all over our plane. I checked Jean Jacques's paperwork to insure it was all correct, did a thorough walkaround in addition to the one George was doing. Gear pins and chocks were in, control locks installed…it was time to hop in the jeep and head for Bat's house.

As we got out of the jeep, I was so happy that Bat would see me on my first flight as captain. Bat told the others he would bring me to the safe house later…he had bought an old Land Rover in anticipation of his family arriving. Bat and I talked till well after dark then he drove me to the Wigmo safehouse. I ate dinner in my flight suit, then showered and went to bed.

The General

Next morning was another civilized departure time. The general didn't want to leave 'til 10:00am. However, by 8:45 when we arrived at the airport, the place was filled with military units and military police all there to give the general a proper sendoff. What a circus.

Jean Jacque and I did our walk-around and got the plane ready for the flight. Since our plane was in a para configuration, I decided to kick the loadmaster out of the cockpit and let the General have the radio operator/navigator's seat. The military C-47's had provisions for navigators. It would not be all that nice, but a heck of a lot more comfortable than those little metal bucket paratrooper seats in the cabin.

A few minutes after 10:00am the general's motorcade arrived with military jeeps in the lead and in the rear. His black Mercedes sported a Congolese flag on the right side of the hood and an ANC flag of some type on the left side. He looked very stately sitting in the back of his Mercedes. As he got out, I could see that he was huge. He was not only tall but probably weighed over 250 pounds. And of course, no Congolese general could be without his "swagger-stick." But somehow, in spite of all the circus atmosphere, I could see hints of true military bearing.

I met him at the foot of the boarding steps and gave him a smart US Navy salute. He loved that...a white guy saluting him. From that moment on...the general and I were friends. I tried out my best French-Lingala mix and escorted him to the cockpit with us and showed him the navigator's seat. But there was one thing I'd not considered; his huge size. But he grinned, laughed at himself and wiggled in. Once seated it was comfortable and he even had a little desktop area. He was happy. The rest of his delegation filed in and strapped into the paratrooper seats, the loadmaster closed the door, and we were off. There were a few lieutenants in the group, but most were majors and colonels. This was apparently some type of command inspection.

Our flight was relatively short...2 hours fifteen minutes. We called King 1 with our off time. George would also provide them with it when he got back to the safe house. In addition, we called the Belgium detachment in Gbadolite on their military frequency and gave them our ETA. They advised they would notify the ANC command headquarters there in Gbadolite.

As we came into range, we called the Belgiums again on VHF. Most had already left for the airport, but they had radios in their jeeps that would allow them to get the update. Just to be sure, and to give the general a sense of importance we invited him to come up in the cockpit and watch the landing standing up. Totally illegal in the United States but here in the Congo...well...let's just say this was the Congo. We circled the town then as a special favor to the general, circled the military base where he would be going. He took particular interest in the aerial view of the base. He was muttering to himself in Lingala and nodding his head. I was sure I was now the general's favorite white guy. I did not realize it at the time, but this was the beginning of my VIP career that would soon extend to the presidential aircraft and President Mobutu himself.

On final approach we could see a large number of troops lined up in inspection formation. These were the elite of the ANC troops and I have to admit they looked pretty good. At the head was a group of Belgium advisors in their heavily starched commando dress as well.

As we taxied onto the apron, we were marshalled by the Belgium master sergeant who normally guided us in. As we were shutting down our engines, the delegation approached the aircraft. I could see that the governor of the province was probably leading the delegation. All the Congolese wore the same dark gray or black safari-suits, dark glasses and a faux (hopefully) leopard-skin hat. Everybody wanted to dress like the president. I had no idea there were so many black Mercedes in the Congo as I saw lined up beside the ramp. Gbadolite was President Mobutu's showpiece and I had a ringside seat to watch the show.

We shook hands with the general and the loadmaster escorted him to the door. He stepped out first then his delegation debarked. Jean Jacques and I got out last and stood at semi-attention at the foot of the stairs as the general inspected the troops. Then, in a cloud of dust they all drove away leaving the rank and file to climb into their military trucks and head back to their base. I was pretty impressed. I'd never seen this side of the ANC before. Unfortunately, as history would prove, there was a serious shortage of solders of this caliber.

After the delegation left, Jean Jacques completed his paperwork. I inspected the aircraft for any sign of discrepancies. We secured the aircraft, including putting a lock on the door, insured a guard was posted, and went with the Belgiums to our guest quarters. We had just settled in and I'd just gotten out of the shower when the senior Belgium master sergeant came knocking on our door. He said the general had just sent a messenger and that we were invited to have dinner with him that night. The master-sergeant informed us this was a big deal and that not attending was not an option. Damn, I had not packed for this. I found a pair of pants I couldn't even remember why I'd packed that would pass for slacks…actually they were the bottom part of my only safari suite. And I had a short-sleeve white shirt. My shoes were questionable…a cheap rubber imitation of black leather made by Bata and sold by the Indian merchants in Kinshasa. But it was what it was. Nothing could be changed. On the other hand, Jean Jacques, being a European and also newly arrived had a much nicer shirt and pants. I wasn't jealous. I was just happy he didn't look as bad as I did. About 6:00 pm a staff car arrived to take us to dinner. This was going to be interesting.

The General–Jimmy Joe–And The Monkey

We were taken to the house of the governor. As at the airport, the street in front of the house looked like a Mercedes dealership. As we walked into the large garden where the party was, nobody seemed to pay much attention to us. There were a few other white people there including the highest-ranking Belgium military advisor. I thought it best we not go immediately to him, so we just wandered about. We were offered a drink by one of the servers. The general saw us at one point and smiled then went back to his conversations. I noticed a well-managed fire where numerous pieces of meat were being turned on a spit over the flames.

As I walked nearer to get a good look at dinner, the hair on the back of my neck stood up. There were two large monkeys lying in the hot glowing red embers. They looked for all the world like two small children all drawn up into the fetal position. They appeared to be completely intact, their mouths gaping open. Their long tails had been curled up under their stomachs in the direction of their heads. Their skin was charred black and their hair was singed but still visible. I noticed a couple of the Congolese guests joking with one another in reference to our more or less petrified, wide-eyed gapes. I vowed I would not be having any of that. I asked Jean Jacque if he'd ever eaten monkey. He replied he had not but had heard stories about it all his life. I was starting to regret my public relations gestures to the general. If I hadn't given him the VIP treatment, I'd be back enjoying a beer and some of my favorite Congolese dishes of which there were several. I hurried away from the roasting fire and found a place to sit and sip my beer.

There were several well-dressed Congolese women there. I assumed they were wives of the local dignitaries. I noticed one giving me a somewhat more-than-friendly glance. I decided I'd play like I hadn't seen it. I was still worried about having to eat some of that monkey. I sure as hell didn't need any additional excitement right now.

There were long tables set up with white table cloths. This was the first time I'd seen how the insider group of Mobutu's circle lived. About the time I'd finished my first beer, the call to sit down and start dinner was given. The meat had been removed from the spit and carved into smaller pieces and brought to the table. I was afraid to look to see if the monkeys were on the table as well. As the group was moving toward the tables, they were being directed by the general's aid. Jean Jacque and I headed for the most distant table leaving plenty of room for those who outranked us. But we were intercepted by the general's aide and directed to a place at the head table. This apparently was his way of expressing his gratitude for giving him a good flight. I was silently praying his expressions of gratitude would not extend to the two monkeys. We politely stood behind our chairs waiting, as was everyone else, for the general and the governor to be seated. While we were standing there, Jean Jacques whispered something. I thought he had said "I think the monkeys were tame," to which I replied, "who gives a damn if they were tame or not." But Jean Jacques leaned closer and said…"No…I've heard they eat the monkey's brain." My reply was unprintable; my prayer intensified.

We all took our seats at the table. The waiters seemed to have had some degree of European exposure as they began bringing our plates. I was very relieved to see one of my favorite Congolese dishes, chicken mwamba. It was chicken cooked in a peanut and coconut sauce with tiny BB shaped pili-pili peppers adding an aspect to the dish resembling flames from hell. I was still holding out hope the chicken dish would be my escape from the monkey. As the meal began, I started to comprehend any chance of avoiding my destiny was minimal at best. The general, who had been pulling the charred hair and skin from the monkey's shriveled up carcass was now cracking open its skull. My prognostication was growing dimmer by the second. I noticed the governor was looking closely at my face with a hint of amusement. Then the dreaded moment arrived. The general motioned for me to pass him my plate. He was easily within reach. He then placed what I was sure everyone but Jean Jacques and I believed to be a choice piece of the monkey's flesh on my plate. He then took up his spoon and asked if I would like some of the monkey's brains as well. He planned to scoop some of the monkey's brain, looking like partially cooked mush, from the hole he'd made in its skull. I summoned all the pseudo-gratefulness I could muster and declined. To my enduring gratitude the general accepted my decline. Poor Jean Jacques was next.

Everyone waited for the general to begin eating. While waiting, I tried to focus on the chicken mwamba and rice portion of my plate while avoiding looking at the piece of monkey. But sneaking a peak was inevitable. I took a big spoonful of the liquid fire mwamba sauce hoping to anesthetize as many taste buds as possible and put half my portion of monkey in my mouth. The pili-pili immediately went to work. I made a couple of attempts to chew and then swallowed hard. It worked. I imagined I could smell the monkey's flesh but that was probably just psychological trickery. True to my character, I decided to get the other piece out of the way. Another large spoonful of liquid flames from hell and the remaining piece was consumed. I was aware several of the Congolese were watching me. I was struggling with how much counterfeit enjoyment I should embellish upon monkey morsel. I wanted them to believe I had enjoyed it but did not want to cross the line where they would offer me a second helping. My evil twin found amusement watching Jean Jacques deal with his morsels.

A Bedtime Story

Somehow, we made it through the evening and were returned via the same staff car to our guest quarters. As I entered my room, I didn't bother to turn on the light as there was some indirect light from an exterior security light coming through the bedroom window. As I sat down on the edge of the bed to take off my shoes, I heard what sounded like a giggle. I almost jumped out of my skin. I turned toward the sound and saw a tall young Congolese woman dressed in traditional wraparound skirt and blouse sitting on the other bed where I'd unpacked my suitcase. "Mbote" she whispered…"Mbote Mingi" (hello…a big hello to you). "Mbote Na Yo" I somehow managed to utter (and hello to you)…"Sango Nini?" (what is going on). To which she replied that she had just stopped by for a little visit. Still in the semi-dark room I explained that I thought she was very pretty, but I did not want any company that night and that she should leave. She then explained the general had sent her and he would not be happy if she returned before morning. I was beginning to understand the situation. I laughed, she laughed. I moved my bag from the other bed to the floor and motioned for her to sleep on the extra bed. I put my wallet under my pillow and lay down. I was a little uncomfortable having her there with my belongings while I slept but I knew what she had said about the general being unhappy with her was true. Sometime later I fell asleep. As daylight came, I heard my mystery lady closing the front door. When I got up, I checked my belongings. Everything was there.

When I saw Jean Jacques at breakfast, he had a big grin and asked me how I had slept. "You too", I asked. Yes, "me too" he replied. The subject never came up again. We flew the general and his entourage back to where we had picked them up and returned home to King 1.

Karen And Jason Return

With my captain checkout out of the way, I sent a message for Karen and Jason to return. The day of their arrival finally came. I waited anxiously to get my first glimpse of them in the terminal. They were all smiles when I saw them. I knew they had to be tired, but at least for a while their happiness overpowered their exhaustion from their long flight. We stacked the suitcases in the back of our VW Variant station wagon and headed toward Limete. Jason was asleep before we were halfway home.

When we reached the house, I unloaded the bags while Karen took Jason inside. By the time I got all the bags unloaded and back in the house Jason was wandering around reacquainting himself with his room and his toys. It had been several months since he'd seen them. Karen was happy to be home as well…back in a home that was hers.

A Top Secret Order

I was flying almost daily. While I was aware there was a war going on in South East Asia, I knew nothing, as did most of America, about the Nixon administration's secret bombings in Cambodia. *On 17 June 1970, a "Top Secret, Exclusive" cable was sent to General Abrams by the Joint Chiefs to authorize more United States and Vietnamese bombing "in any situation which involves a serious threat to major Cambodian positions, such as a provincial capital whose loss would constitute serious military or psychological blow to the country." The Chiefs ordered Abrams, in accordance with Nixon's instructions, to "conduct the most aggressive U.S. and R.V.N.A.F. [South Vietnamese] air campaign in Cambodia which is feasible…"* [151] As a result of this secret order, tens of thousands of innocent civilians were killed by the indiscriminate and illegal bombings.[152] *From the beginning of the Vietnam War until December 1970, 475,515 tons of ordnance dropped on Cambodia*[153]

---

[151] Sideshow—Kissinger, Nixon and the Destruction of Cambodia by William Shawcross - Simon and Schuster, 1979
[152] Cooper-Church amendment (limiting U.S. Involvement in Cambodia
[153] Bombs Over Cambodia - by Taylor Owen and Ben Kiernan

I Proclaim To You Good News Of Great Joy[154]

Far from South East Asia, life was good. Flying was going well; we were increasing our savings; Jason was learning to speak French like a Frenchman; life was very good. One day Karen announced she thought she might be pregnant. Wow, a chance for a girl! It was soon confirmed…we were going to have a baby. We started imagining what changes would soon be in our midst. It was fun.

The Name Game

We started thinking of names. We (or at least I) did girls names first. But we could not rule out the fifty percent possibility of having another boy. In today's world of computers and the internet, coming up with a multitude of selections would have taken only a few minutes. But in the Congo, our only live time connection with the outside world was via our Montgomery Ward short wave radio. So Karen and I started making handwritten lists. At the top of my list was "Jenny" or Jennifer. I was never able to get that beautiful little song by Brian Hyland, "Ginny Come Lately" out of my head. I first heard it in 1962 while stationed in Corpus Christi. I told myself then that if I ever had a girl her name must be "Jenny Jacks" . . . heck it even sounded good. All I had to do was come up with a "J" middle name and convince Karen. It was Karen who came up with "Joelle." Jennifer Joelle Jacks . . . how cool was that!

Captain Jacks Again

As Karen increased in size, so did the airplanes I flew. They needed me dual-qualified in both the C-47 and the C-54 (DC-4). I had plenty of time in the C-54, and thanks to Paul, I had left-seat time documented by General Ehrabar. It was a simple matter of doing some air-work in the King 1 area for a couple of days practicing emergency procedures, and I was checked out. I was already airport qualified. My pay didn't go up, as Wigmo paid all captains the same and most were dual-qualified, but it meant I was getting even more flight hours. Most months about 160 to 180 flight hours. Bat held the record with 220 but nobody could stand a steady diet of that. That meant about $1000 each month in overtime. Our savings were growing almost as fast as Karen was.

Congolese Craziness

As the size of the planes I flew increased, a bizarre politically-motivated movement emanating from Mobutu's MPR (Mouvement Populaire de la Revolution or Popular Movement of the Revolution) began increasing as well. This movement could hardly be called spontaneous. It was a calculated effort by Mobutu to dissolve any previous identification the Congolese may have

---

[154] Luke 2:10—Holman Christian Standard Bible (HCSB)

had with external political ideologies. His ultimate goal was to consolidate his hold and strengthen his dictatorial powers on the country, beginning with the military.

"Mobutism" as it would later be known, was emerging, but still in a stealth mode, at least to most of the Congolese. Some politicians occasionally briefly entertained objections but they were soon *neutralized*. The situation was always volatile but never quite reached the flash point. However, the exothermic influences were present in most aspects of social and economic life. Large segments of the population were dissatisfied. Total social chaos was never more than a spark away. Somehow, while Karen and I were there, the fatal flash point was never reached.

While Kinshasa was quiet while we were there, the flash point was ever-present on many of my flights. Each day as I walked across the flight line to my aircraft, the number of troops and supplies increased; all heading east. The stability the average Congolese longed for, the simple desire to live in his hut, eat his manioc and chicken and watch his children play in peace without the fear of war seemed to be so far away. The cruel belief that independence from Belgium would bring better conditions appeared to be an illusion. Life for most was worse. Their oppressors before were white. Now many could argue…they were black.

While Mobutu was fashioning ways to solidify his hold on the Congo, the North Vietnamese Army (NVA) and the Viet Cong were operating with virtual impunity within Cambodia. Lon Nol's Cambodian army was no match for the battle-hardened North Vietnamese and Vietcong. In January of 1971 they cut National Route 4, the only land route connecting the nation's capital, Phnom Penh, with its only sea port, Kampong Som (previously Sihanoukville). The capital city of Phnom Penh's population was swelling by the day from the influx of refugees fleeing the fighting in all areas of the countryside. The city was effectively being blockaded by the Khmer Rouge and their North Vietnamese and Viet Cong allies. The North Vietnamese were using vast areas of Cambodia as a conduit for their military supplies and troops into South Vietnam. With the cutting of National Route 4, the Lon Nol government sent an urgent yet very discrete request to the South Vietnamese government for military assistance in clearing and reopening Route 4. The Vietnamese military operation, code named Operation Cuu Lorry 44-02 began on 13 January 1971, as the 4th Armor Brigade with the 12th and 16th Armored Cavalry Regiments, three Ranger battalions, an artillery battalion, and an engineer group, moved 300 kilometers from Can Tho to Ha Tien in fourteen hours. For the next two days, the brigade pushed north along Routes 3 and 4. The NVA and Viet Cong were driven out and the route reopened. After helping the Cambodians set up strongpoints, the 4th Armor Brigade withdrew toward South Vietnam, arriving by 25 January. Due to political embarrassment to the Cambodian government for having to ask for help from an often (?) ethnic enemy, the event went mostly unnoticed. [155] *The event nevertheless showed the fragility and ineffectiveness of the US supplied and funded Cambodian army.*

---

[155] Olive-Drab.com

An Unexpected Visit From A Relative

One day while coming in from an early afternoon test flight, a white DC-6 taxied onto our ramp. My first thought was "how in the hell did the tower allow him to taxi over here on the military ramp." It carried a Nigerian registration and the name on the side read Pan African Airlines. I could see the crew was white. Just as they were shutting down their engines, one of the embassy cars pulled up. I recognized the two guys getting out as two of the CIA (customer) people we dealt with when doing special missions for the T-28s or eastern Congo missions. We also dealt with them when operating down near Angola. One of the mechanics walked up and said the plane belonged to our "sister" company based out of Lagos. I jokingly replied…"I wonder if they are hiring." To which he replied…"get in line."

Soon several other embassy vehicles arrived, offloaded some boxes and crates, and drove away. The Pan African flight fired up a couple of minutes later and taxied out and took off. I never did get to ask them if they were hiring.

Rumors Abound Again

Rumors of coups abounded. Many Air Congo crews were sending families back to Europe. Many married Wigmo personnel were doing the same. The last time all the stories started I sent Karen and Jason home. Last time nothing happened. But this time, she was pregnant, Jason was in school. I held on for a while; but not without abundant uncertainty.

Romeo Tango's Entanglements

Robert Troyes had increasingly become the center of numerous rumors. Word in the hanger was there had been a serious falling out between Romeo Tango and Wigmo's legal owner George Monteiro who maintained an office in London. We all knew that Romeo Tango, along with a few other partners, had purchased a plantation in the area of Isiro. It was, reputedly, a coffee plantation. By any estimate, this was a risky endeavor. But Romeo Tango held one significant trump card other plantation owners lacked. He had free air transportation for his equipment and supplies. Not only was it free, it was "pilfer-free." Nobody was likely to rummage through the cargo on a military aircraft with only one stop between Kinshasa and Isiro. Traveling by road or by river, anything that arrived would be a miracle. I'd never actually seen the plantation, although I'd seen its cargo. But there was no doubt…it existed. His partners inside Wigmo often spoke with excitement of the day when the first crop would finally come in and their investment would be returned. From then on, according to their expectations, it would be easy money. The Bible verse "A greedy man is in a hurry for wealth; he doesn't know that poverty will come to him"[156] came to mind as I listened to them.

---

[156] Holman Christian Standard Bible—Proverbs 28:22

Other Romeo Tango entanglements were starting to trickle out as well. Felipe, who kept close contact with the "embassy" and with the US Military Mission Congo (COMISH) mentioned one Sunday afternoon at a little gathering at his home in Binza that Romeo Tango was no longer in the good graces of the embassy. This could have connections to his alleged misuse of Wigmo aircraft. I considered this above my pay grade and as long as it did not disrupt my earnings, I didn't care what happened to the SOB. The stories only seemed to increase as time went on. I was determined to keep my head down. This was a joke between Paul and me. His favorite parting remark was always "keep your head down Jim." As things later turned out, Paul would have done well to heed his own advice.

Romeo Tango's Demise

Whisperings about Romeo Tango's problems with the Ministry of Defense and the embassy appeared to be escalating. I was becoming pretty certain his days were numbered. Finally it happened. I came to the airport for a flight and found a notice in operations saying Mr. Robert Troyes was no longer with the organization. It was sudden but hardly surprising. There seemed more rejoicing than astonishment amongst the crews. I certainly was in the midst of the many silent revelers. Some weren't exactly silent. Romeo Tango had made few friends and many enemies. One particularly pleasant side note to Romeo Tango being out was that his chief pilot, the fat little fart that didn't like me feeding the mice while he was asleep in the cockpit got the ax as well.

Wigmo Whispers

While the Romeo Tango rumors were finding welcoming ears, stories of discord within the higher echelons of the Armée Nationale Congolaise (ANC) were abounding. It seems every week some high ranking general or minister fell from favor. The ministers were never Mobutu's first self-preservation priority…his generals were. Being a general was a good way to gain almost instant wealth and an equally good way to disappear. More of the Wigmo people were sending their families home.

The CIA Estrangement

Like the nebulous whisperings about Romeo Tango and various ANC generals, so too were stories about disaffection and distrust between the agency and Mobutu. Word was Mobutu was becoming fearful of the CIA's influence and possible ability to precipitate a coup, as they had recently been doing all over the world. Mobutu's plan was to lead the Congo down a middle-of-the-road path of non-alignment; a very understandable goal in the present environment of Cold War super-power strategies. In reality, non-alignment usually meant sliding into the Russian camp. The role of Mobutu's personal physician and unofficial advisor, Dr. Bill Clark, in all this was not evident at the time. But he was said to be experiencing strained relations with the embassy while all this was going on. Felipe was always a good source of embassy rumor mill stories. Sundays at his Binza home were sure to bring political gossip bonanzas. His wife worked there.

Wigmo's Demise

One morning we all came to work to find notices of meetings in the hanger about mid-morning. For those of us going out on flights, we would have to learn what happened at the meetings upon our return. But the rumors were already flying. Wigmo was being replaced by a new Congolese Company. I'd never seen such a frantic frenzy. Some people were already talking about going home even before they heard the official facts. I found this quite amazing.

With nothing solid to base any decisions on, I decided that unless this new Congolese entity was the Devil himself, I would stay and give them a chance. I certainly did not plan to expend much mental energy on this 'til I had all the facts. We fired up our C-54's four Pratt & Whitney R-2000 engines and took off into the first rays of morning sun. I figured I could learn a lot just by monitoring (lurking) Wigmo's long range HF radio frequency 8820 MHz during our eight plus hours of flight time. The words from Psalms 139 came to mind as I watched the sunrise that morning through the windscreen of our C-54…"if I take the wings of the morning."[157] I did a lot of that in the Congo.

We both spent most of the morning glued to our Collins military issue HF radio, either on the 8 Meg and the 17 Meg frequency. The static cracking and popping in our headsets was regularly interrupted that morning by flight crews calling back to King 1 looking for news. But Gus, the radio operator was very guarded with his words. He was speaking on frequencies that could literally be monitored halfway around the world. We did manage to learn mid-morning that Wigmo would be replaced by a Congolese company called "SODEMAC." We were told that was an acronym for Société d'Entretien et de Maintenance d'Avions au Congo. Well, money is money I thought. I would later learn I couldn't have been more wrong.

The Whole Truth

(or at least most of it)

As we taxied in late that afternoon, SODEMAC was the talk of the flight line (and hanger and dispatch, and operations). While we saw nothing in writing, we did learn most of the core details. Wigmo would be out at the end of the month. All employees would be offered a contract with SODEMAC at their same pay. Any not wanting to work for the new Congolese company would have two weeks to arrange their affairs before being required to leave the country. We were already seeing several of the mechanics, mostly those who

[157] Holy Bible—Psalms 139:9 - King Jame Version (KJV Bible)

had been with Wigmo for several years and probably had bulging bank accounts saying they were leaving. With the exception of selling automobiles, most wouldn't need the two weeks.

Then the big blow came. We learned that starting from day one; we would be given half our pay in the local currency which was worthless five feet outside the Congo. Probably five inches would be a more accurate representation of its value. I knew instantly that I could never spend half my pay in the Congo. In the first place, there was nothing to buy. In the second place, the only reason we were all here was for the money. In reality it was like taking a fifty percent pay cut. Most of us lived relatively frugally in order to send the maximum amount of money back home. Besides that…there was nothing to buy in this God-forsaken place. We had no TV, only a cheap eight-track cassette stereo and a cheap Montgomery Ward short wave radio; that was it. We didn't even wear expensive clothes. They would just be beaten to death by John on the cement washboard in the garage. Nothing lasted more than six months. I supposed we could eat a little better, but how much tough Congolese beef can you eat! There was always the black-market money option…many shop owners would sell you dollars but at about half the official rate at which we were getting paid. So about the best we could hope for would be to sell most of our Congolese Francs received on payday to a money changer at the black-market rate, losing fifty percent. Any way I looked at it…the situation was bad. There would be a lot to talk about when I got home tonight. Another thought-filled drive home from the airport.

The New Reality–Life Under SODEMAC

The first of the month came. This month's wire transfer went out as scheduled from Luxemburg. It would be the last. Next month at this time we would be receiving a bag full of Congolese Francs rather than just our usual local living allowance. Many from our group were out-processing. They were, for the most part, excited and ready to go home. Others felt cheated or betrayed. But most had the bad thoughts behind them and were ready to get on the plane back to European civilization.

Paul's Problems

Paul's job with Wigmo wasn't going all that well. Even though I stayed busy flying almost daily I still managed to stop by for a visit a couple of times each week. It was then that I'd pick up disturbing accounts of, at least from Paul's viewpoint, people tampering with items on the aircraft he was scheduled to fly that day. In his mind, he had somehow acquired some serious enemies; in some instances, enemies willing to endanger his life. The experiences he was relating seemed so totally apart from anything I'd previously encountered that I only partially accepted them as reality. I thought he may have been the victim of his own hyperactive imagination, or worse…paranoia. But time would soon to bear out his claims.

The Wrong Hole

One morning as I arrived in dispatch, Gold Finger, having heard my voice, came out of his office to show me a change on the schedule. He almost looked apologetic. He had switched me to fly copilot with Paul on a C-46 flight because the scheduled copilot reported sick late last night. He was quick to assure me I'd be getting captain's pay. I looked at him and smiled saying "I'm getting captain's pay, I'm flying with my good friend…how much do I owe you." He smiled and said thanks. He told me Paul had already gone to the plane and had all the paperwork with him.

As I arrived at the plane, I found Paul, just as I would have expected, going over every inch of the plane's wheel wells and landing gears with his high powered flashlight. I asked if he'd been on the wings yet and he said no. I joked that since he was already an old man, I'd do it. Actually Paul was in incredible shape for someone 46 years old. He had a narrow waist, broad shoulders, and plenty of muscle.

I climbed out on the wing and checked the fuel tanks and the oil tanks. I carried a fuel dipstick and my flashlight. Each wing had three fuel tanks (front, center, and rear). I would open the fuel tank cover and insert the dipstick into the tank. Then pull it up quickly looking for the wet/dry line on the black paint of the stick. The dipstick had white marks and numbers enabling you to find the wet/dry mark and determine how much fuel was in each tank. I would pull a pen from the special pocket on the left sleeve of my flight suit and scribble down the fuel reading which would later be transcribed into the aircraft flight log.

In addition there was a large oil tank (40 gallons) for each engine. The oil tank's cap had its own dip stick attached to the cap. As I checked the oil quantities, I found them both full. I climbed back inside the cabin and secured the window. All looked good. I saw Paul coming up the ladder. He advised he would secure the door. I headed for the cockpit to record the fuel and oil readings and start plugging in my mic and headset, arranging my flight bag for easy access in flight, and finally adjusting my seat and the rudder pedals. Paul was in the left seat making the same adjustments. We read checklists down through engine start. Then Paul gave the command to "clear two" which meant for me to look outside and insure nobody was in the way of the prop and that we had a fire guard posted. I confirmed and counted the prop blades as they turned in response to Paul's engaging the starter. "Three-six-nine-12 blades" I called. Upon hearing twelve Paul moved the fuel mixture to full rich and turned the ignition switch to both. The engine sprang to life and both Paul and I began monitoring the oil pressure. Nothing happened. The needle on the right engine oil pressure gauge did not move. I looked at Paul then out my window to try to figure out why. "Damn!" I said; "Shut it down." There was a huge cloud of what looked like whitish-purple smoke coming from the exhaust. I'd never seen anything like that before.

There was a strong smell of fuel in the air. Paul told me to shut down all electrical and secure the cockpit. He got up and went down to investigate. I followed after the secure checklist was completed.

When we got to the engine, everything appeared to have been misted with fuel. It reminded me of a mosquito spraying machine which fogged or misted its toxic fumes. We were trying to figure out what had gone wrong. Whatever had happened, the problem had come from the exhaust stack. We started examining the oily mist with our hands and nose. Whatever was happening, we seemed to be looking at a mixture of oil and fuel all over the ground and side of the airplane. How did this happen? How could the oil and fuel have become mixed? Paul had an idea.

We climbed back out on the right wing and opened the right engine oil tank. It was still full. Paul was rubbing the "oil" between his fingers and shaking his head. The oil was almost as thin as fuel. Suddenly I remember how the oil had run so quickly down the dip stick. But it was early in the morning…before sunrise and my brain had not reached full operating capacity yet. I should have caught it. The oil was too thin. "Jim…there's fuel mixed in this oil…a lot of fuel." Now it all made sense. When we started cranking the right engine, its oil pump began circulating the ultra-thin oil/fuel mixture. It was so thin that it easily passed past the piston rings and into the combustion part of the cylinders. When the fuel and spark produced ignition the engine began misting the oil/fuel past the rings and out the exhaust stack. The very grave consequence would have been, had we not caught the almost zero oil pressure, that after a minute or two operating without proper lubrication, the engine would have violently seized. We climbed out on the left wing and check. We found the very same thing. Someone had put fuel, not oil in the oil tank; both oil tanks…in the wrong hole. Was it an accident by some new and untrained line service guy or was it an intentional act intended to frighten or harm us? In Paul's mind, there was no doubt. Somebody was out to get him. I was left with much to ponder.

When we got back to operations the cover-up or cover-your-butt operation was already in full swing. Nobody knew anything. But no matter who denied responsibility, a mistake serious enough to destroy an aircraft and all onboard had just happened. Our flight was cancelled as the fuel and oil tanks all had to be drained and the oil filter on the number two engine checked for metal shavings. If shavings were found, an engine inspection would be required. On my way back home, all Paul's words about conspiracy theories began coming back to me; and what about the copilot who called in sick? Could someone have tipped him off? Yes, there was much to ponder.

High Level Storm Clouds (Very High)

I'd been back from the airport about three hours or so when Paul showed up at our place in his little VW Bug. He wanted to buy my lunch downtown at the Memling Hotel. The Memling was about the best eating place Kinshasa had to offer but now only a shadow of its pre-independence glory.

As we sat down at our table, Paul began an interesting story; a story about which I knew nothing. Paul had been a member of the ferry crew that had delivered a DC-4 (C-54) purchased by the Congolese government in Europe. Paul was not involved in the purchase, only the delivery of the pane.

It seems the airplane's airworthiness was questionable. So questionable, that the crew lost an engine just after takeoff while still in Europe and had to remain in Brussels for an extra week waiting for an engine to be ferried from Miami. They then lost a different engine on the last leg of the flight to Kinshasa. But as the story continued, I was surprised to learn that the purchase of a shabby airplane was not the center of the story. The brewing storm was the difference between the money transferred from the Congo to pay for the plane and the actual amount paid for the plane. That and the fact that somebody had apparently bought a "pig in a poke" as folks back in Hamilton would say.

According to Paul, the overage seemed to have disappeared and Paul was being questioned about his possible involvement. In reality, Paul never knew anything about the sale; he was just the ferry pilot. He did have to sign for receipt of the plane, but that was his total involvement. He was now being called to the Ministry of Defense to answer serious questions about the missing money. Paul suspected the involvement of the new head of SODEMAC and the minister himself, but of course they would never hang. Someone else would. Justice was nonexistent in the Congo. Paul was starting to get very concerned.

An Irrational General And A Colt 45

He also mentioned being called into Romeo Tango's office by General Ehrabar. When he walked into the office, he found General Ehrabar sitting behind Romeo Tango desk with a Colt 1911 45 ACP in his lap. According to Paul, the general said. "Paul Rakisits, you are a dangerous man." Paul said he then went on to accuse him of fermenting a "coup d'état." Everybody said General Ehrabar wasn't all there. This seems to confirm it. I asked Paul how in the hell he managed to get out of there. Paul replied that he sat and listened to the general for a while then the general looked at his watch and said he was late…they could talk later. Thankfully, later never came.

Visitors Drop In

One evening as we returned from our flight and were in dispatch checking the next day's schedule, Gold Finger came out and pointed to my name on the schedule for a C-47 flight from King 1 to Bujumbura, the capital of neighboring Burundi. It had a 3:30 am departure which meant we would have a 2:30am report time. What we jokingly called an "O dark thirty departure" in military parlance. I remember thinking that I hoped our passengers or cargo or whatever really needed to arrive there that early. Gold Finger said we would receive our preflight briefing from an ANC officer in the morning. "What's Up" I asked. "They're being pretty tight lipped" was Gold Finger's only reply.

Our fight time would be just under five hours. I was already on overtime, so it was hard to complain. I'd make a little over $160 tomorrow. I thought about the minimum wage back in Hamilton at the time. It was $1.60/per hour. I was getting paid $16/per hour or about 27 cents a minute. I recalled my father's expression when we were talking about my wage. He said, "damn boy...nobody's worth that much money."

The next morning when the alarm went off at 1:45am I fought back the fatigue, climbed out of bed, stumbled into the bathroom, stumbled into my flight suit, and stumbled to the car, hoping to be awake by the time I reached operations.

Whatever fatigue I might have still had disappeared during our briefing by a Lt. Colonel the following morning. We were going to fly to Bujumbura and insert an elite group of Congolese paratroopers. After the drop, we were to land (in theory) on the airport. Their goal was to insure the airport was and would remain secure; I thought my goal was to keep from taking on any ground fire.

I knew how to do drops. I'd trained. I knew the speeds, the flap settings, the light signals and the bell. I could do my part to get them on the ground. I even knew how to read wind indications from the cockpit (rising smoke, ripples on the water, flags, and heck...even windsocks). I knew how to brief the jump master on the wind so he could brief his guys. I could do my job...in a little over five hours we would see how they could do theirs. I asked the colonel about cloud cover contingencies. I could tell by his expression the thought hadn't crossed his mind. I asked about anti-aircraft guns on the airport. His reply was they had none, and they did not know we were coming. He went on to say they did not expect any unfriendlies at the airport. As a matter of fact, he said they expected the airport to be in government hands. Our job was to make sure nobody else thought trying to take the airport was a good idea; just a big show of force. The colonel gave me a seldom-used aeronautical frequency. He said the government forces knew our approximate ETA. If they had control of the airport, they would tune a secondary radio transmitter to that frequency. We were to call using call sign "Makasi Móko" (Makasi 1). Makasi was the word in Lingala for strong or dangerous. It was also their name for the foul-tempered local water buffalo as well as the emblem painted on all the Wigmo jeeps and airplanes. But the irony of it all was that Makasi was the Logo for the now out-of-favor Wigmo...amazing. If the airport was secure, they would reply "Malámu Míngi" (very good) and also fire a purple smoke grenade.

A second C-47 piloted by my friend Olaf and his crew would depart King 1 thirty minutes after us bringing more ground troops and some enhanced firepower. Their mission was to land after we gave the all clear, or if not, divert to Bukavu only 70 miles away and wait for word from us via our long-range high frequency (HF) radio. They would be "Makasi Míbalé" or Makasi 2. The colonel appeared very confident that the airport would be in government hands and this would be a non-event. At several points in the briefing he alluded to the ANC already having mission coordinators in place in Burundi and working closely with the Burundi government.

I'd been following BBC news reports on our short-wave radio about a rebel uprising going on in neighboring Burundi. The news reports had been going on for almost a month now. The rebels had proclaimed a portion of the small country to be independent from Burundi and were calling the new "country" the "Republic of Martyazo."

I didn't recall hearing anything about fighting spilling over into the Congo but every time we flew into Bukavu we saw the refugees and heard horrible stories of tribal atrocities being committed by both the Tutsi and the Hutu. We'd seen plenty of refugees but no fighting.

What I didn't know was that Burundi's president Micombero had just asked President Mobutu for help. The Burundi government appeared pretty confident about their ability to quash this uprising. Apparently, however, they were concerned that meddling, opportunistic neighbors such as Tanzania, encouraged by their Chinese communists' friends might find this time of distraction for the Burundi government a good time to spread their influence.

The colonel went on to say that as we were executing our para-commando drop and show of force, the government forces would be moving out in full force against the insurgents who had already taken over several towns and massacred hundreds of the Tutsi. The rebels were Hutu and according to the colonel were also being armed by the same Chinese communists arming the Congolese rebels in the eastern provinces. The Tutsi made up the majority of the government. The Tutsi and the Hutu hated each other. In my mind, political ideology was a very minor aspect in the dynamics of the situation. It was basically about tribal hatred.

In the months that followed the ill-advised Hutu attack and rebellion, more than 200,000 Hutu would die at the hands of the retaliating Tutsi government forces. As I contemplated the horrible atrocities these people were enduring, the words of Jeremiah in the book of Lamentations kept creeping into my mind…"I am the man who has seen affliction under the rod of God's wrath. He has driven me away and forced me to walk in darkness instead of light."[158] Funny how words spoken 2500 years ago about the Judeans taken into captivity in Babylon after Jerusalem's fall in 586 BC at the hands of the Babylonian army could find such haunting applicability today along Lake Tanganyika. We

---

[158] Holy Bible—Lamentations 3:1-2 - Holman Christian Standard Bible (HCSB)

learn nothing…history repeats itself. "If history repeats itself, and the unexpected always happens, how incapable must Man be of learning from experience."[159]

While I was considering the tragedy at hand and the minor footnote in its history I was about to play, my evil twin was whispering the lyrics of a song by Chubby Checker I used to dance to at the non-commissioned officers (NCO) club at US Naval Air Station in Corpus Christi…"The Wah-Watusi" (another name for the Tutsi tribe). Some of its words kept playing in a loop inside my head . . . "Baby, baby, when you do The Fly, Your arms are wasted wavin' in the sky. Come on and hold me like a lover should, The Watusi makes you feel so good."[160]

In his final words, the colonel said again that the troop insertion we were about to do was just a show of force. It would serve as a warning to any neighboring country possibly entertaining thoughts of getting involved that they would be attacking the Democratic Republic Of The Congo and President Mobutu as well. "I'll make it work" I told him. The briefing was over.

Pre-Mission Adrenalin
Imbued With A Moment of Remorse

As we headed across the flight line, many thoughts were swirling around in my head. It was the last of May, Karen was about six months pregnant with Jenny, and I was looking forward to more overtime, hazardous duty pay, and adrenalin rushes. Where in the hell was my brain?

Our troops were waiting beside the aircraft when we arrived. I went inside and checked to see how well their gear was secured. I was surprised at the amount of equipment and supplies they had considering the size of their back packs. The quality of their life on the ground, for however long their mission called for them to remain, was going to be dependent, to a large degree, on my ability to land after they got boots on the ground and gave the all clear. If I had to go to another airport with all their gear, they would soon find themselves living off the land (probably robbing civilians). But then if they couldn't secure the airport, their supplies onboard my aircraft would rapidly move down their chain of importance; being supplanted by the need to stay alive. All our briefings indicated the airport would be quiet. I hoped for once they were right.

While my co-pilot checked the fuel and oil, I walked around in the darkness with my flashlight checking everything else. Our crew chief was one of the best and assured me the plane was ready. I had the troopers remove their magazines and open the chambers to insure there were no live rounds in the chambers. They would reverse this just before the jump. They were excited,

---
[159] Gearge Bernard Shaw
[160] Wah Watutsi—Words and Music by Dave Appell and Kal Mann

a bit nervous, and very ready to get the show on the road. I signaled to the major in charge and he gave the command for them to board. Our loadmaster secured the door and we started engines. I joked to my co-pilot…"we've kicked the tires, now let's light the fires." Soon we were climbing toward 9,000 feet and awaiting the first hint of orange glow along the eastern horizon indicating dawn. It would have been easy to be tired, but our adrenalin levels insured we were at full alert.

Another C-47 Sunrise

I remember sunrise that morning was particularly beautiful; a glowing red with traces of clouds. It was unusual to see clouds this early in the morning. They would typically start building around 11:00 am as the sun started to warm the earth's surface. What a powerful, and yes, even artistic God that created and controlled this universe…where the wings of dawn come every morning driving away the darkness of night. I wondered if the sign of early morning storm clouds could be some message. I remembered the old rhyme "red skies at night…sailor's delight; red skies at dawn…storm coming on." Certainly I was flying into a humanitarian storm. The pain, fighting, disease, and death taking place in the eastern Congo pushed my ability to comprehend. It was bad…damn bad. I decided to think about something else; like mentally rehearsing the troop insertion I'd soon be taking part in.

The Drop
A Low-Level Insertion

We approached our drop zone a little after 8:00am. It was already daylight, and the eastern sides of the high mountain tops were bathed in golden sunlight. But below the golden tops, the mountains were clothed in clouds. I had purposefully changed course about thirty minutes before our ETA to insure we dropped over the mountains well south of Bujumbura. We would let down over the lake (Tanganyika) then fly up the lake (north) at about 1000 feet off the deck. The jumpmaster was briefed and was happy with a 1000-foot jump. I told him I'd give him 1200 feet if the clouds allowed. He said no…didn't want his guys hanging up there as targets any longer than necessary, just in case somebody started firing. We went over the red and green light and bell drill one more time. Not that he needed to hear it, but so he would know I understood it. They were trained to jump much lower but that cut down their margin of safety in the event something went wrong. The higher we flew, the longer they would be in the air offering themselves as easy targets for small arms fire from the ground. Everybody was happy with 1000 feet. We were fortunate there was no radar. Hopefully there would be no unfriendlies and if so, hopefully they would not see us coming.

As we approached the lake, we could see that the valley around the lake was covered in clouds. I knew the lake well as I'd flown the T-28 up and down it for hours. I was a little uncomfortable not having an accurate altimeter setting but I sure as hell wasn't going to call Bujumbura tower to ask for one. We were the only aircraft on this phase of the mission. Olaf would be coming about 30 minutes behind us. My only hope was while monitoring Bujumbura tower I might hear the tower give some other aircraft the altimeter setting. But that would be mixed blessings. That would mean that another aircraft would be trying to takeoff or land during our operation. I didn't want to contemplate that set of complications.

We began our descent from what is called "VMC on top" which means visual meteorological conditions above an overcast. What that means is we were flying above the clouds but at some time would have to descend into them hoping to "break out" of the clouds in time to be 1000 feet or more above the ground (or lake in this case). We had one of our radios on Bujumbura tower, the other on the frequency the colonel had given us, and our UHF radio tuned to Wigmo's UHF frequency. Going through about 6000 feet while still in the clouds we heard a private airplane approaching Bujumbura ask for the altimeter setting. I got the bonus of the cloud cover ceiling and the wind. It was a small Cessna and would be on the ground long before we dropped our troops. He was probably coming from some large company owned plantation and going into Bujumbura to buy supplies. I couldn't help but chuckle as I tried to visualize his expression when he looked up and saw the sky above the airport full of parachutes. I even got the surface wind at the airport from the transmission. We set our altimeters to the local setting and continued our descent. I was letting down over Burundi territory and I knew it. But I feared the 10,000 foot mountains now towering above us on the Congolese side far more than I did anything in Burundi. I did one short ring on the bell which immediately brought the jump master to the cockpit. I gave him the ceiling, 1600 scattered. But more important, I gave him the wind direction and velocity, which he informed me was well within his comfort level.

We had transmitted our descent message plus the cloud cover information to the Wigmo flight, "Makasi Míbalé" thirty minutes behind us via Wigmo UHF frequency before we dropped below the mountain tops and lost UHF line of sight communications with them. Now it was radio silence. We started to see little glimpses of the lake surface and on some headings a glimpse of green from the cultivated land in Burundi on others. We were descending in a rather tight spiral to insure we did not descend into the mountains on the west side of the lake. Our drop zone was 2585 feet above sea level. So our altimeters needed to read at least 3585 for us to make our ideal drop from 1000 feet. Things were starting to look like we were going to make it all come together. We broke out a little below 4000 feet MSL which gave us three or four hundred feet to play with.

As I turned the plane north toward the drop zone, I spotted a village on the Congo side which I recognized as Baraka. It was one of my T-28 check points. I knew without looking at the map that it was 55 miles south of Bujumbura airport. That was about 20 minutes. Plenty of time for the troops to brief and get ready to jump.

I sent "the 20-minute warning" to the back via our loadmaster. The flight engineer went to the back with him to get the para-door open in preparation for the jump. He, along with the jumpmaster, would check the static lines. They were soon back notifying me the 20-minute check was complete.

I'd noticed the major with a tactical map of the airport discussing it with his troops as we arrived at the airplane that morning. I sent the loadmaster to call him to the cockpit with his map. I explained we would be approaching the airport from the south; if he would like, I could make my first pass almost directly over the ramp giving them a good view of the runway and the grass just west of the runway. The wind was very light and should easily allow them to land on their desired spot. I would then turn to the west and fly along the mountain side climbing to just below the cloud base heading back over the lake south of the airport. As soon as he could get someone to the tower, they were to transmit a message on tower frequency using our call sign Makasi Moko with the message "Malámu Míngi" meaning very good. In lieu of that he could fire two purple smoke grenades. We would not land on just one. I asked him if he was sure they had two purple grenades…to which he replied in French…"Violet est ma couleur préférée " (purple is my favorite color). My gosh…a Congolese with a sense of humor. I was starting to like this guy. He was happy with the plan and headed immediately back to his troops. From that point on we kept the cockpit door open. The loadmaster went over the signal card with the major and all his troops. They had trained with the same checklist. They knew the lights…red - - - six minutes to jump, green and bell - - - jump. Nothing was new. My adrenalin began to rise again. I noticed the palms of my hands were perspiring. I figured theirs were as well. If nothing went wrong, this was going to be a textbook operation.

At my best guess of ten minutes till over the drop zone, I sent the 10-minute announcement back. We used this time to send a quick HF message back to King 1 advising we were 10 minutes to Delta Zulu (drop zone). King 1's reply was "update status when able." They started hooking up to the static line. I could now clearly see the airport and the runway. I could see the terminal. There was a commuter airline on the ramp in front of the terminal, and a fuel truck was moving on the ramp. These were all signs of normal operation. At six minutes the red light went on. My adrenaline was going up. I made the call on the discrete VHF frequency we had gotten in the briefing. Immediately we heard "Malámu Míngi" followed a few seconds later by a purple smoke canister. Then the second one. I sent the word back to the major…"airport reported secure…voice and smoke."

While I wanted to watch the rest of the show, it was time for me to focus on my part of the mission…getting them exactly where they needed to be over the drop zone and at exactly the proper speed. I would give the command; the copilot would turn on the green light and bell.

About two minutes before DZ I slowly reduced the power settings and called for one-quarter flaps. The aircraft pitched ever so gently and settled perfectly into its pitch and speed configuration. I was satisfied with our speed; there would be no more power adjustments. I silently thanked God for the still air and no reported traffic. At one minute till DZ the loadmaster carried the word back and remained in the back with the jumpmaster. We were exactly where we needed to be, I gave the signal and the copilot threw the light switch to green and turned on the bell.

Immediately I could feel the balance of the aircraft change. The CG (center of gravity) was shifting and the speed began to increase. We were losing about 180-200 pounds of payload every two seconds. I gently reduced our power setting and adjusted the pitch trip. I wanted so badly to look out my left side window to see the show, but I dared not. I was there to keep the aircraft exactly on course and stabilized . . . not watch the show out my window. In about a minute the loadmaster returned advising everybody was out and it looked good. I couldn't wait to turn around so I could see what we had just done.

I told the copilot to take the flight controls and hug the side of the mountain cliffs while I tried to reach Olaf on Wigmo UHF. He was there and was still descending through the cloud cover. I reported the estimated cloud bottom and told him we were going to continue orbiting south of the airport. Olaf decided he would orbit about 30 miles north of the airport to be sure we didn't get tangled up with each other.

About 15 minutes after the drop the major gave the airport secure call with his purple smoke canisters. We immediately called Bujumbura tower on its normal frequency, reported 10 miles south at 3500 feet and requested permission to land. His reply, in heavily French-accented English was for me to call on five mile final for runway 35; that I would be number one to land. I swear I could hear a chuckle in his voice. This call along with the major's purple smoke meant no shots had been fired and that we were welcomed by government troops. Immediately our emotions went from tense to euphoric. I took the HF and called King 1 with the news. Gus replied, "you guys get to have all the fun."

I took the checklist and told the copilot that this was his landing. I started reading the approach checklist. As I was finishing up, I heard Olaf call the tower. He'd heard our tower communication. As soon as he'd finished his tower communication, and right in the middle of our landing checklist I heard him calling on UHF saying he was hungry and knew a great place to eat that was only about a five-minute walk from the airport. I finished up the checklist and responded…"me too…let's do it."

Breakfast On A Burundi Colonel

As we taxied in, a military jeep hurried out to meet us. Just in front of the aircraft he did a tight U-turn (the international signal for follow me) and led us to a ramp away from the airline activity. Another jeep came speeding up. I could see our major in the front seat. He was all smiles. We walked over and shook hands. There was a Burundi colonel in the first jeep that had served as our follow me. Our major took me over to him. I saluted him smartly which I could see he appreciated. He was getting a salute from a white mercenary pilot in front of his men. We quickly shut down the aircraft, installed our chocks and gust locks. Just as we were making the final securing, Olaf taxied in. He got no follow me as he had already spotted us and was heading our way.

I took the two lower-ranking officers accompanying the colonel and showed them our cargo. In my best crappy French I told them the C-47 just arriving had even more than I did. They got on their radios and soon a large "deuce and a half" (military parlance for a truck capable of carrying a 2.5 ton payload) came roaring up with some of the Congolese we had just dropped onboard. For a government who was fighting to regain a sizable portion of their country from insurgents, this Burundi military I'd seen up to this point was looking pretty professional. I was sure the farther I got from the airport the more rapidly this would change. But that wasn't my problem.

Olaf's troops piled out in very military fashion and began unloading their equipment and supplies. They then came to our aircraft and in five minutes had it unloaded and on the deuce and a half as well. Olaf asked the Burundi colonel if the little restaurant only a short distance from the airport was still there. He said it was and that he would be most happy to buy breakfast. Since we had been on duty since 2:30am this sounded like a wonderful plan. We headed toward the terminal. The temperature was still cool, so we all elected to walk to the terminal. Our major and their colonel were chattering away. As we strolled along I noted the airport was dotted with Congolese paratroopers busily stowing their parachutes. I'm sure they were relieved that their drop zone had proved friendly. I was upbeat but drained. I would feel better after some breakfast and fresh juice.

An "Informationless" USIS Officer

The Burundi colonel rounded up another jeep and driver. Olaf and I plus our two copilots went in one jeep and our major and the Burundi colonel went in the other jeep. We told our driver that we would drive ourselves which made the short ride more comfortable.

This mountainous area beside the lake was lush with vegetation, fruit and flowers. The roadside had a manicured look; a totally foreign concept in the Congo. As we were piling out in front of the Alps-style restaurant a car heading rapidly in the direction of the airport noticed us. It was a typical American Embassy-looking car. Admittedly, our white faces in military flight suits would have made a rock curious. Two dorky-looking guys that reminded me of refugees from an ivy-league frat house hopped out and headed across the street toward us. They ignored the major and the colonel and headed straight for us. I was the only American in the group and I suppose my posture and haircut heralded the fact. They walked up and introduced themselves as being with the United States Information Service based out of the US Embassy. We shook hands. They gave their names. I said "it's nice to meet you" without introducing myself. They could already tell I wasn't impressed. As for Olaf, even in his best Scandinavian comportment, he was generally only a notch above Eric The Red. This day was no exception; he was true to form. He muttered something in Swedish and continued toward the restaurant. The copilots followed leaving me to deal with the inquisitive "official Americans."

Wigmo 101 was never speak to the press; never speak about missions; never ever. They asked if we had just come from the airport. I replied that we had. "What's going on out there" one of them asked. The obvious leader of the two explained that they had just received reports of aircraft dropping paratroopers onto the airport and that they were on their way out to investigate. "Wow…that's interesting" I said. "I sure hope everything is OK out there." I smiled, said "good luck," turned and walked away. I knew they knew they'd just been blown off. As I rejoined the group at the restaurant entrance, the Burundi colonel smiled and spoke to me in slightly French-accented perfect English, "Captain, I'm not sure they believed you." My gosh…I'd been struggling to communicate with him in my crappy but functional French and now I find the guy spoke English as well as I did. Amazing!

A Roach I Inhaled

Yes, I Suppose I Did Inhale…But Only Half a Roach

The Burundi restaurant staff and manager rushed to welcome the colonel. I was already visualizing our food and service moving up a notch or two. It always helps to visit a restaurant with somebody connected. We were seated at one long table. The Congolese major was sitting next to me; the Burundi colonel next to the major. The colonel recommended the legume omelet with a special sausage made there in Bujumbura in the authentic German style. I was so hungry I could eat from a roadside stand in Limete, I sure as hell could enjoy anything in this place. They had clean white table cloths, new shiny white dishes, and real silverware as opposed to the normal Congolese "tin" forks and spoons that bent when you used them.

Before we could get our napkins in our laps the waiters brought tall glasses of fresh-pressed orange juice. I could see one of the waiters cutting up a huge papaya with a honeydew-looking melon waiting to be next. The little bowls of pili-pili pepper sauce arrived. Then came the legume omelets…huge omelets, covered in wonderful cheese and infused with various vegetables and leeks. I thought the colonel would never pick up his fork. But as soon as his fork hit his omelet, I was digging in as well. Olaf already had a mouth full. Apparently, he wasn't waiting for any Burundi colonel to go first.

The taste was from heaven. The cheese had a bit of salty bite to it and leeks were absolutely my favorite vegetable. Even as hungry as I was, the taste was so good that I was more or less rolling the omelet round in my mouth; savoring each bite. It was then that I felt something scratching my tongue. It was a bit sharp and my thought was that perhaps an inedible piece of one of the vegetables had managed to get into the omelet. But I just chewed and swallowed. It was too good, and I was too hungry to let anything this good go to waste. But as I went for my next bite, I looked down on my plate and saw what had been scratching my tongue. There, barely visible, was the edge of the remaining half of a perfectly dissected cockroach embedded in my uneaten omelet. This was not any wimpy US style roach. This was one of the mammoth size critters so common in the Congo's tropical areas. I couldn't believe it. I was really hungry, and I was determined not to make a spectacle of this, so I began expunging the remaining half of the critter's carcass with my knife and fork. About half way through the process, the Congolese major looked down and saw the remains. Wide-eyed, he looked at me and said "Lompeke ozali wapi" (where is the other part of the roach). "Na kolía" (I ate it) I replied. I thought he was going to throw up. I honestly did. But he too realized the need not to embarrass our Burundi host. But unlike the major, I finished my entire omelet. I left only the most minuscule morsel incarcerating the uneaten portion of the unauthorized ingredient's carcass. The major feigned being full, saying something about how large his omelet had been. He never took another bite. Without much doubt, the major believed he was truly sitting beside some American Neanderthal. While my evil twin laughed, the words of Jesus came to mind…"It's not what goes into the mouth that defiles a man, but what comes out of the mouth, this defiles a man."[161] I chuckled to myself and thought that I must surely be demented.

Compared to the para-drop and the roach I inhaled, the rest of the mission was uneventful. I returned home and began getting Karen ready for her trip back to Hamilton where she and Jason would stay with my father while waiting for Jenny to arrive.

Home Alone…Again

Jason's school was letting out for the summer. My father was excited about having Karen and Jason home again. His life was pretty lonely after my mother's death. He would sit for hours in front of the TV with Sheba (my mother's dog) in his lap. Karen and Jason brought sunlight to the house.

---

[161] Holy Bible—Holman Christian Standard Bible (HCSB) - Matthew 15:11

The tickets were purchased and once again we made the long drive to the airport. Although we'd been through this before, it never seemed to get any easier. I put them on the flight and waited on the ramp as the plane pulled away. I always had that heavy feeling in my stomach as the plane taxied out, made the takeoff and finally disappeared from sight. But this time I'd see them in just three months. Karen was due the last part of August and I'd already arranged my vacation to be there. I would just have to keep busy for the next three months.

I made the short drive to the military end of the airport and checked my schedule. The next day was a rare day off. I could catch up on visiting friends. I hadn't seen Paul in a while and I noticed he was not on the schedule the following day as well. There were plenty of rumors flying around about Paul having problems with the ministry of defense. I wondered how in the heck he had managed to do that.

Paul's Perilous Predicament

Paul and Marie Jeanne had found a nice villa with a beautiful swimming pool only a few blocks from our apartment. In typical fashion, Paul had set out painting and refurbishing the entire place. He resurfaced the pool and installed a circulating pump and filter system. He manicured the yard. They had truly transformed the place. While I could appreciate the beauty, it nonetheless violated one of my basic living-in-the-Congo rules…"if it doesn't fit in your suitcase…don't own it." Paul and I had more than one laugh about that.

The following day, when I arrived at their home, it was mid-afternoon, and the place was filled with activity. Marie Jeanne's mother, Mrs. Peters, had come from Belgium for a visit, along with Claude, Marie Jeanne's son from her previous marriage. Both Mrs. Peters and Marie Jeanne had lived in the Congo back before independence. Marie Jeanne's father had been in the Belgium military and they were stationed there. Mrs. Peters was full of interesting stories about what the place was like years ago. Claude was a strikingly-handsome teenager; somewhat shy and very bright. After taking a tour of Paul's latest renovations, we sat down on the veranda and Paul began his update of the situation.

It was not good and he feared he might be arrested. He and Marie Jeanne were thinking seriously about leaving the country. I thought about all the money they had put into making this villa a stunning place to live. For them to be considering leaving must mean that things were really serious. When I went home that night I had plenty to think about. The main point was how quickly an innocent person could find themselves in unthinkably serious trouble, even up to landing in a Congolese prison. This was a lawless country filled for the most part with people who had grown up learning to hate white people. This was always something that whites living in the war-torn, post-independence Congo should never forget.

A Painful Pay Reality
Plenty of Funny Money

All this Eastern Congo conflict and Tutsi-Hutu problems would mean more money for me. I could see a healthy dose of hazardous duty pay coming my way to sweeten the already sweet overtime pay. For sure it would be needed as SODEMAC would now be giving me half my pay in the Congolese Francs. Next month's wire transfer, while being only half my pay, would still be sizable thanks to the Hutu and the Tutsi. But, even at this early stage, the mounting mountain of Congolese Francs would soon become a problem. You could only buy so much malachite and ivory (still legal to own at the time), only so many spears. The rest would have to be used to purchase dollars at a tremendous discount. Nobody wanted the Congolese Franc. Everybody in the country wanted dollars. This put tremendous pressure on the dollar. Each month it took more and more local currency to buy a dollar. There was a dark cloud appearing on the horizon. But for the moment, a cloud of dollars hung over the Congo's eastern horizon. SODEMAC was still the best deal going. Better than anything back home. I couldn't make this much money flying for Braniff, Pan Am, Delta, or American. And besides, they offered nowhere near the adrenalin high. Continuing to build my bank balance, at least for the moment, looked very alluring.

Back home, my father could sign on our bank account at the Hamilton National Bank. Karen had told me how he would spend hours checking and rechecking the check register and the bank statements. He'd never had this much money in the bank in his entire life. I suppose for me, more important than the money was the fact that I was making him proud after my *asleep at the wheel* high school years. No amount of money could ever erase that, but at least he could hold his head high again.

Discontent Swelled Within SODEMAC
While My Trunks Filled With Artifacts Multiplied

During that summer I flew as hard as I could to keep busy while Karen and Jason were back in Texas. I worked hard at flying and I worked hard at staying out of the internal politics of SODEMAC. As I flew hard and the paydays passed, my stack of Congolese Francs continued to grow. I bought ivory…lots of it. I bought two beautiful matching tusks and another single tusk. I was surprised how heavy they were. When we would fly to Lubumbashi (call sign "green rock") I would buy malachite. I had malachite carvings, malachite ashtrays. I bought Katanga crosses (a cast copper cross once used as a form of currency in Katanga in the 19th and early 20th centuries). Aside from the spears and the ivory, I had two chests filled with serious Congolese artifacts. Often I would request missions to various regions just to find items to buy that would be valuable outside the Congo. I bought masks, and wood fetishes of all types. The Congolese believe spirits could inhabit the items and thus were considered to have mystical or spiritual powers.

While I was trying to see areas of the Congo which lay off the beaten path, and obtain more so-called spirit-inhabited articles, more pilots and mechanics were leaving the company. SODEMAC's new Congolese management was rapidly proving they were clueless about running an aviation operation. They had fancy offices and titles but were never in their office…they hardly ever came to work. The entire finance department was full of the new employees but none of them had any experience.

By the third payday, the wire transfer sending our pay back to our banks was two weeks late. Under Wigmo you could set your watch by it. For almost all of us, this did not create a financial hardship but it sure sowed seeds of anxiety and distrust.

Those living in company-provided houses were informed that SODEMAC was going to start charging them more for the monthly rent. This of course would be taken out of their pay. Most of us figured this money went straight into their pockets. I was lucky. My apartment was part of a two-unit group not associated with SODEMAC and Gus paid directly to the Congolese owner each month. I paid Gus. Although I escaped on that front, the fifty percent in local funny money was starting to become worrisome.

New Jeeps From Disney World™ Arrived
At Least They Were Mickey Mouse™
The Genesis Of An Exit Strategy Emerges

Soon after the new faces arrived in SODEMAC new jeeps made in Spain began arriving. Why jeeps…everybody asked. Nothing's wrong with our old ones. But as soon as they arrived they were sent out to replace the US issue Wigmo jeeps. The new ones proudly displayed the SODEMAC name. The venerable "Makasi" logo was gone. When the new jeeps arrived the old ones were taken by SODEMAC and never seen again. We all figured some of our new "masters" made a bunch on the purchase of these jeeps and then took and sold the perfectly good old ones. Almost immediately after these "toy" jeeps arrived they started having problems. Mickey Mouse was the only way to describe them.

This entire SODEMAC debacle traced its derivation to the growing distrust of Mobutu for the CIA…that and the dependability of the United States as an ally. Mobutu had seen firsthand how the CIA worked when they believe a head of state stood between them and their political goals. We all assumed these stories of infatuation gone south were correct. Mobutu was distancing himself from American control in spectacularly rapid fashion. The CIA, which for years had provided a substantial income to Wigmo's remarkable assemblage of skilled paramilitary personnel, was now the genesis of its demise. While it was not yet my time to leave, I knew leaving was something I should begin seriously evaluating. It was time to begin formulating an exit strategy.

Witchdoctor's Weed
The Toke Of Shamans

While assembling my collection of Congolese artifacts, I began running across various types of pipes; some used for smoking tobacco and others used in ritualistic smoking of a type of locally grown weed or herb. The Congolese believed it induced states where one could communicate with the spirits. This magical plant was also believed to cure various ailments. Warriors smoked it before battle to give them courage. A classic example was the infamous Simba Rebellion in 1964, led by Pierre Mulele. His fighters were told by the local shamans that when they went into battle they would be transformed into "simbas", the Swahili word for lion and that the enemy's bullets would be turned into water. They reportedly got high puffing this magical weed and marched off into battle shouting "Mai Mulele…Mai Mulele" (mai being the word for water and Mulele the name of their leader). I am convinced that one of life's most treacherous and cruel tricks is when men are led to believe what others want them to believe, often with the help of religion.

I was fascinated by the stories I was hearing about these ritualistic practices. To this point in my life I'd never experienced any type of mind-altering substances. I thought this might be a good chance to try it. Whatever this local magic weed was, and I strongly suspected I knew, it was not illegal here in the Congo and probably would be back in the States. So, if I were ever going to find out what the smokers of those long pipes made from gourds were experiencing, the Congo would be the ideal opportunity. I decided I'd speak to John, our houseboy and see if he could get me some to experiment with.

One afternoon, when John was leaving to go home, I asked him about this weed. He smiled from ear to ear and said, "oh yes patron…it's everywhere…I'll bring you some tomorrow." I handed him a five Franc note and told him to keep the change as a little gift. He responded with his predictable smile. I forgot all about the matter as it was now time for my evening beer and my meal.

However, the following morning I was in for the surprise of a lifetime. John, proudly led me out to the garage where he pointed to a huge gunny sack (tow sack for Hamiltonians) filled with the infamous herb (or weed). "Damn John…what the hell is all that" came out before I realized he didn't have a clue what I was saying. I asked him why he had brought me so much. His reply was that he'd purchased four Frank's worth and he'd kept one Franc for himself. I calmed down, thanked him, and told him I'd take a little bit and that he could take the rest back home and sell it. John couldn't believe his good fortune. I opened the bag and stripped off a few handfuls of the still-slightly-moist leaves from their stems and placed them in one of the fruit jars Karen had saved and screwed the lid on. I laced the bag back up and went back into the house. I wasn't completely sure what I was supposed to do with the leaves next. I was pretty sure they should dry out a little more first so I put them in one of the kitchen cabinets. I was kinda glad Karen wasn't there as I had a fairly decent idea that she wouldn't approve of my little social experiment. I promptly forgot about the leaves in the kitchen cabinet; I had a lot going on.

I'd soon be leaving for Texas to be with Karen for Jenny's birth. In addition to that, I'd planned a little diversion on my way home. I had planned to meet Olaf in Stockholm for a day or so on my way to Texas. Some of the Swedish Wigmo employees had already resigned and gone home. Olaf and I planned to get together and visit with them. But things were starting to get complicated. Copenhagen was only a short hop from Stockholm. Some of the Danish guys, when they heard I was going to be so close while they too were home on vacation, insisted that I make the short flight over to Denmark for a night on the town with them as well. I hadn't planned on that extra day but…oh well. Once again…where was my brain; Karen was in her final month of pregnancy and I'm planning to swing by for a short visit with friends in Sweden and Denmark before coming home to Hamilton to be with her. Yet once more I could hear the voice of my terrible evil twin whispering in my ear. I heard the words from a song by Roger Miller…"Dang me, dang me, they oughta take a rope and hang me, high from the highest tree, woman would you weep for me?" I pushed the song from my mind and buried myself in the last remaining days of my flight schedule before leaving for vacation.

A Near Death Experience
Or At Least At The Time I Thought It Was

I was almost all packed. My Nikon, my little super-8 video camera, a few changes of clothes (not too many as I would need the room in my suitcase to bring back new clothes to replace the ones John had beaten to death); I was all set. I was leaving for the airport the first thing in the morning.

John had my meal on the table, the dim glow from the oil lamp was casting its luminance on the walls and ceiling. I opened my beer and slowly sipped it as I thought about going back home. I would soon have a daughter. How cool was that. I would see Karen and Jason again. I'd see my father. But laced with these pleasant thoughts were momentary flashes of guilt about not going straight home.

It was in the midst of this mélange of emotions that the witchdoctor's weed up in the kitchen cabinet came to mind. Somehow, I'd forgotten all about it. I decided that after my beer and before my meal, I'd see if a part of my spirit left my body as the shaman claimed. As I sat on the couch and planned my experiment, I realized I would have to use one of the old Congolese pipes I'd bought for my artifact collection. They had all been smoked before. Most of the old men I'd seen smoking them only had a couple of teeth in their head. I rapidly concluded that if my little psychoactive social investigation was to proceed, any finicky thoughts relating to where the stem of the pipe had been would have to be immediately abandoned.

When I finished my beer, I went to the bedroom and dug through the several pipes already packed in one of my bags till I found what I reasoned to be a suitable instrument for the experiment. As fitting any venerable smoking implement, this one was covered with a gummy film probably owing its origin to smoke byproducts, dust, grime and grunge. I took it to the dining room table and retrieved the fruit jar filled with the now dried plant leaves. Not wanting to get too much of this spell-inducing substance, I only removed a few shreds and placed them in the pipe bowl. I had no experience smoking a pipe, so I failed to realize I didn't have enough to make the smoke flow properly. I tried to light it with a large kitchen match. Nothing happened.

I decided I hadn't used enough flame, so I tore a piece from the page of a Time Magazine and rolled it up lighting it with a kitchen match and moving the blazing Time Magazine page over to the bowl of the pipe and sucked hard. DAMN!! A hot sensation raced down my throat. I must have sucked a six-inch flame through the pipe and down my throat. That Hurt!!

It was now clear that I needed to take a timeout, fall back, and examine more closely the procedure I was trying to use. I formulated some modifications to my experiment. I took more of the magic herb and this time packed it tightly into the bowl of the pipe. No flame would get past that. I was now sure that I could pass the kitchen match flame over the top of the weed packed bowl and gently (with an inordinate stress on gently) suck. Now this should work!

I took a seat at the table, lit the match and moved it in a circular motion above the pipe's bowl, as I'd seen old men back in Hamilton do. I sucked gently on the pipe and waited. Soon molecular breakdown was beginning. The rising carbon atoms began to emit light. Success; my magic weed was now ready to try. I was about to step back in time like the shamans of old and the shamans and witchdoctors of today's Congo. I drew heavily on the pipe and inhaled deeply. I instantly coughed. My lungs did not like that stuff. But I was not about to give up that easily. I took another draw on the pipe and inhaled but this time not as deeply as the first time. I let it remain in my lungs as long as I could stand it counting on the weed's magical makeup to pass through the alveoli walls and into my bloodstream. This stuff had a strange, more or less pungent order; not really offensive, but certainly not in the class with a good

Dutch pipe tobacco. Nothing was happening so I inhaled again…and again…and again.

Suddenly it began to hit me. I realized I'd smoked up the entire contents of the bowl. My head started to feel heavy…very heavy. My arms and legs began to feel heavy as well. I felt like I was going to black out. I realized I needed to get up from the table and try to make it to my bed. I staggered to the bedroom and fell face down on the bed…the room was spinning, and I was starting to lose consciousness. I was terrified. I thought that this stuff was going to relax all my nerves and eventually depress my phrenic nerve and I'd just stop breathing. That was the last thought I recall.

When I awoke, it was morning. I could see the sun's light coming through the curtain. My first thought was I'm alive! I didn't really die after all. My second thought was…did I miss my flight. I frantically looked at the clock beside the bed…praise God it was only about 7:00 am. I slowly sat up and took stock of the situation. I'd spent the night sleeping beside the open suitcase. I was still in my clothes. As I slowly walked into the living room, I saw my lamp burning and my untouched dinner still on the table. I right then decided that I didn't want to be a damn shaman or a witchdoctor and that they could keep their magic weed. I had to finish packing and get to the airport.

Scandinavian Stopover

As my flight touched down in Stockholm, I realized I should be exhausted, but I wasn't. It was already 7:00 pm and the sun was still shining brightly. I was now farther north than Moscow and just about even with St. Petersburg and Alaska. I'd heard how the sun hardly set up here in the summer. Now I could verify it was true.

Customs and immigration were a breeze and soon I was in a taxi on my way to the Grand Hotel. Olaf had recommended the hotel because of its location…just on the waterfront. He had warned me it would be expensive, but I'd decided to treat myself. When the hotel bellman opened the door of the taxi for me, welcomed me to the Grand Hotel, and his assistants already had my bags on the cart, I started wondering if I might be a little bit out of my comfort zone. I was dressed in my best polyester safari suit made by an Indian tailor in downtown Kinshasa. Most people I saw looked like they had just stepped out of Neiman Marcus. It was very safe to say I was the only one in the hotel dressed in a pencil-leg polyester safari suit. Oh well. I handed the doorman a five-dollar bill, which killed me and miffed him, and proceeded to check in. Olaf had remembered to make my reservation. The hotel reception staff was kind not to look down their nose at me. I supposed they had been trained to deal with country bumpkins and refugees from third world tailor shops.

I was soon in my room, which called for parting with another five. I'd have to fly twenty minutes to make that five bucks; really forty minutes as I now had to take half my pay in funny money. The room had a beautiful view of the river. I called Olaf and we agreed on a time when he would pick me up. Then I headed to the shower. Wow…I'll bet Mobutu didn't have a bathroom as nice as this. When I saw the luxurious soap and other toiletries, I decided I'd use the little hand soap bar for my shower and keep the thick perfumed one for my suitcase. I gave the posh bathrobe a close checkout but discovered a little diplomatically worded note saying that since so many of their guests had expressed an interest in having one, we were encouraged to take this one with us and they would gladly put it on our bill. I forget the exact amount, but it approached $100. How about that for class. I chuckled as I envisioned the same situation back in Ft. Worth…"taking this robe is punishable by a fine of $XXXX and up to five years in the state penitentiary" or something like…"take this and you die."

I put on another pencil leg pair of pants from the Indian tailor and headed downstairs. After a couple of beers with Olaf and our other Wigmo Swedish friends I would not care how out of place I looked. Besides they would all probably be wearing something similar. Olaf had just pulled up in an older model Saab. His old car looked as out of place in front of the hotel as I did. But it was obvious from Olaf's big grin he couldn't care less. I decided he was right. I hopped in and he headed for a restaurant were the others were waiting already. This would be a long evening of drinking beer, eating all kinds of Scandinavian traditional dishes and finishing the evening with the national drink, aquavit. aquavit had an alcohol content of around 80-90 proof and tasted slightly like dill or caraway I was going to be way out of my class again. My usual one beer per night had not prepared me for an evening with these hard-drinking Scandinavians.

When we got there it was easy to tell they had not been waiting for Olaf and me to arrive. Everyone was already quite happy. As soon as Olaf and I sat down the waiter started bringing plates of cheese, and all kinds of raw and pickled and marinated herring, a real Scandinavian smorgasbord. Our own private buffet table was just beside our table. I'd never seen so many different kinds of sandwiches in my life. Every imaginable type of bread was used. On most of the breads was smeared a fatty type substance which reminded me of old fashioned lard. The selection of bread and cheese was mind-boggling.

As I looked out the picture-glass window beside our table I could still see the last of the sun's light; it was still twilight. It was already after 9:30pm. When I commented on it, they said if I had come in June, I would see twilight ending just before midnight with the sun coming up again around 3:30am. Less than four hours of darkness. But they were quick to point out that in the winter just the opposite was true. They said some people went into depression and they had abnormally high suicide rates during the long dark winters. This was totally different from the equatorial Congo sunsets. There was virtually no twilight.

The evening was very pleasant with each of the Swedish mechanics taking turns telling funny accounts about their Congo adventures. It was truly a good evening and I was proud I had the opportunity to work with such interesting people. Over the decades I would return to Sweden numerous times, but all of these trips were trumped by memories of this first night of food and friends. "Skoal."

I was up early the next morning. Olaf picked me up and drove me about the city taking in some museums, the Royal Palace, the Vasa Museum where we saw an incredibly well-preserved warship, the Vasa, which sank on its maiden voyage in the middle of Stockholm in 1628. The cold waters had almost perfectly sealed the ship in time. It was a rushed day with hardly enough time to take a breath. We were racing against the clock as my flight de Copenhagen left in mid-afternoon.

Olaf got me to the airport in plenty of time. My flight left on time and an hour and ten minutes later I was in Copenhagen. This time my hotel was the Europa; not nearly as fancy as the Grand had been but again it was centrally located. A Danish pilot was coming to get me and would spend time showing me around the city. Like the previous night, we would have a mini-reunion with Wigmo mechanics who had already bailed out as Wigmo left and SODEMAC came in.

That night was a more or less replay of the previous night. There is intense rivalry between the Swedes and the Danes . . . especially where their food is concerned. The tables were piled high with wonderful Scandinavian food, but I was hard pressed to tell the difference. It was all great; like nothing I'd seen back in Texas. One thing that was the same was that liquid fire they called aquavit . I don't think I'll ever get used to that.

The following day I walked a few meters from my hotel to see their version of Disney Land…Tivoli Gardens. I found it utterly boring. Then I saw the Danish Royal Palace (actually four palaces on the same spot). My flight departed early the next morning, so I was back at the Europa in plenty of time to get a good night sleep.

I was up early the following morning. I'd been a little worried about finding a taxi at that time of day but apparently the taxi drivers knew there would be plenty of people with early flights leaving the hotel then. I easily found one.

I had enjoyed Stockholm more than Copenhagen. As I rode to the airport, I could tell I was ready to get out of Europe and back to Hamilton County. I was probably feeling guilty enjoying myself in Scandinavia with Karen back home only days (hopefully) from Jenny's delivery. I refused to even think of how I'd try to deal with the situation if Jenny decided to come early. It was definitely time for me to get back to Hamilton…before my luck ran out.

The guilt I was experiencing unfortunately would be replayed several times in the future as I was returning to my family in Hamilton. On one subsequent trip, I flew home to Karen and the children via Israel and Greece. On yet another trip, I went home via Rio de Janeiro and San Juan, Puerto Rico. I saw the sights in Rio and laid on the beach in San Juan with one of my Cuban mentors for two days before going on to Hamilton. In moments of rare serious introspection I sincerely believed I was probably beyond redemption. "If Only"

A Gold Watch For Karen

Or

An Appeasement Offering To The Demon Of Guilt

For whatever reason, my flight back to the U.S. routed through Geneva. I had a plane change and a two hour layover before the flight departed for JFK. In Geneva, the process of going to the gate for my next flight led me through a maze of duty free shops. And of course, being Switzerland, an endless assortment of shops selling Swiss watches. I stopped and looked in the ladies' section. Duty-free would save me about fifteen percent on the very same watch if purchased in downtown Geneva. Plus the same watch in the U.S. would cost even more.

I found a beautiful gold ladies dress watch and began to haggle with the owner of the shop on the price. He came down another five percent. Duty free and the negotiated price combined with what was certainly an attack of guilt from having spent the last few days enjoying Scandinavia with friends was enough to guarantee the sale. It was a beautiful watch. Hopefully U.S. Customs in JFK wouldn't hit me with a big tax bill for it. They would already be faced with evaluating the Congolese artifacts I was bringing in. I had carefully listed them all on a separate sheet of paper before leaving Kinshasa. I'd just add the watch at the bottom. Hopefully the customs inspector would have lost interest before reaching the bottom of the list. Anyway, I should be OK if they decided to value the artifacts higher than the price I paid for them. The watch went into my carryon bag and I resumed my stroll to the gate.

Masks–Spears And Swiss Watches

The flight to JFK was just under eight hours. Good flight, good food and an occasional catnap. I was doing OK…all things considered. If we arrived on time and barring any unforeseen delays, I'd make my connecting flight which left from Newark Airport without any problems, even allowing an hour and a half for the ground transportation between airports.

We arrived as advertised. The immigration line moved quickly. It often seemed I got behind somebody with entry problems. This time they had the U.S. citizen line open and things were moving quickly. My bags arrived in one piece and with none missing. The customs officer looked at my list, asked me a couple of questions about the things I had listed, and waved me through. I was going to be in my taxi heading toward Newark airport in no time at all. Rush hour traffic shouldn't be on the road yet…things were looking good.

I had the typical "chatty" New York/New Jersey cab driver. But that was OK. They were pretty entertaining characters, especially for somebody from Hamilton, Texas.

I checked my bags at curbside at Newark and rushed off to the ticket agent to get my boarding pass. Once done, I headed for a pay phone to call Tom Hafford to see if he could pick me up at DFW and take me to his house where I could wait for my father to come pick me up. I reached Tom's wife and she assured me one of them would be at the airport to pick me up. I was invited to spend the night with them which was now looking like a pretty good idea as Daddy didn't like driving in the dark in the Dallas-Ft. Worth area.

I then called home and told them I'd made it back to the States and held my breath as I asked Daddy about Karen. The baby had not come yet; Karen was home and I was soon talking to her. She said she was uncomfortable and that the baby was "shifting downward." The doctor told her any day now. We agreed I'd spend the night with Tom and Daddy would pick me up mid-morning the following day. I sat back and peacefully waited for them to call my flight. I promised myself I'd never push my luck like that again. What if the baby had come while I was out eating smorgasbord, and drinking aquavit with my Wigmo friends? Unfortunately I could hear my evil twin offering convincing alternative options. "Dang me…dang me…they truly should take a rope and hang me."

Tom was waiting for me at the gate. Once again my bags made it. How lucky could a guy get. Soon we were sitting in Tom and Nita's living room. Brad and Jeff, their two boys were running around the living room and I was sharing tales of the Congo. I presented Tom with one of the spears I'd brought back. It was good to see him again. We had been neighbors in Irving while I was working with CENCO. Tom later came to Southwest School of Aviation for a private license. Tom was one of the most intelligent people I'd ever met. My jet lag was starting to show so I retired early. Tomorrow would be a big day. I'd see Daddy, Karen, and Jason. I was so ready to get back to Hamilton.

A Huge Surprise

Daddy got to Tom's just before 10:00am. Tom had left for the office, but Nita and I had a nice visit. Daddy was excited to see me and was full of questions. I was so happy to explain everything he asked about. He was a wonderful father and I was just beginning to see how his personality had influenced mine. The drive from Tom's home in Hurst to Hamilton seemed as though it were only minutes. Daddy was busy telling me about everything going on in Hamilton and all about Jason's exploits. When his car pulled up under the big tree on the northwest corner of the house, Jason and Karen were waiting. Jason had grown in the three months since I'd seen him last. To say that Karen had grown as well would be some gross form of understatement. I'd forgotten how big 9 months pregnant women could be. She was huge. No wonder she said she was a little uncomfortable. I hopped out of the car and caught Jason as he jumped into my arms. I had to pause a second to try to remember how you hug a nine-month pregnant woman. Karen's face was radiant. I'd heard stories about pregnancy doing this to women. It must be true. She looked great.

I lugged my bags into the house and started showing Daddy the artifacts I'd brought back. He was fascinated by them. I had little doubt that he would soon be telling all his coffee drinking buddies all about them. Karen and Jason had seen most of this kind of stuff back in Kinshasa, but that didn't keep Jason from playing with the knives and masks. Karen patiently watched the show.

I'd decided I wouldn't tell her about the watch 'til she had the baby. Besides I wanted to get her initials engraved on the back. I was betting Barnes Jewelry could do that for me. You could buy watches at a couple of places in Hamilton, but Mr. Barnes was a real jeweler. He could work on watches and he did engraving. Now that I was home, I would have plenty of time to get that done. Daddy had a great supper cooked. We ate early as my jet lag was setting in again. My lights went out before it got dark.

Jennifer Joelle Jacks
27 August 1971

When I awoke it was still dark outside. Karen was already up. She said she thought the baby would be coming soon. Now I'm wide awake. She assured me it was not time to go yet but that it was probably going to be today. Since I couldn't sleep anyway, I decided to get up and get dressed.

By mid-morning Karen was ready to go to the hospital. She was calm and I was hyper. We got to the Hamilton County General Hospital and she was admitted right away. By the time they got her into the room, she was already having painful contractions. I'd missed Jason birth, so this was something completely new for me.

She was obviously in pain. I wasn't dealing with her pain very well. I started snapping at the male nurse that was doing her blood pressure. When he left the room Karen, for the first time since we were married snapped at me. She told me I needed to get out of here…that I was just making things worse. I figured this was no time to be quarreling with her, so I said OK, I had some things to do downtown.

I really did. I was going to make a leisurely trip that afternoon down to the square to Barnes Jewelry. I had, for whatever reason, given little thought to the possibility of her going into labor this soon. Once I made it home before the baby came, I went into the relax mode. Now, if I still planned to give her the watch just after she had the baby, I needed to get myself in gear. I told her I'd be back in about an hour and headed home to pick up the watch. I was hoping Mr. Barnes would be there and that the he could do it for me right away. His son had been a classmate, and I was hoping he'd also remember me and do this big favor.

When I walked in the jewelry shop, Mr. Barnes greeted me with "well hello Jimmy Joe." I was sure glad to hear that. I was now sure that I'd get the "KJ" engraved on the back of her watch in time. He took it and examined it carefully. He asked where I got it and when I told him in Geneva, he told me he could buy the main Swiss watch brands. He said because of his low overhead, he could probably special order it for me and beat any price around. I felt really bad that I hadn't thought about his little shop earlier and I sincerely promised him I would in the future. He put the delicate ladies dress watch in a special vice; I selected the font style, and in fifteen minutes he was done. I paid him and was out the door.

I realized I hadn't been gone long enough to negate my little nasty mouth episode orchestrated by my evil twin so I decided I'd just drive around the square, and various parts of town refreshing my memories; seeing what little might have changed. I even stopped by Jordan Pharmacy just to sit at the soda fountain counter again. I knew I couldn't sit there long because the high school crowd would soon arrive, just like they'd been doing for decades. I had an old fashioned fountain drink, chatted with a couple of the older people that remembered me; then headed back to the hospital.

"Ginny Come Lately" Was Not Coming Lately

When I reached the hospital, a nurse stopped me in the hallway as I was making my way to Karen's room. She said Karen was in the delivery room. Already in the delivery room…how could this be? Our soon to be "Little Jenny" wasn't messing around. Wow. The nurse asked me if I wanted to change into scrubs and go in; she remembered I was a surgical tech and had worked with Dr. McCord. I thanked her profusely but declined. I had scrubbed on countless Caesarian Sections, but I didn't know those people. I knew I would not be able to watch Karen in pain. So I headed back to the house. They knew to call me when she came out. Daddy decided to stay at the hospital.

I no sooner got to the house than my jet lag hit me like a ton of bricks. I couldn't keep my eyes open…especially alone in the house. I lay down on the couch and was out like a light. The next thing I remember was the phone ringing. I remember thinking it must have been ringing for a long time before it finally penetrated my consciousness. I staggered to the phone and answered. It was the hospital. They told me we had a baby girl. Then she asked me what we were going to name her. She said she needed to fill out all the paperwork for the doctor to sign. "Jenny" I replied. Yes…"Jenny" I said. "Do you mean Jennifer" she asked. "Yes, that's right . . . Jennifer Joelle" I said. I was still half asleep I was rapidly becoming annoyed by all the questions. "How do you want to spell Jennifer" she asked; "and how do you spell Joelle."

That did it…I still had one foot in the abyss of deep jet lag sleep and she kept badgering me with questions like how do you spell Jennifer. I wanted to say "Jennifer or Jenniffer…pick one and leave me alone." But somehow, despite the very vocal promptings from my evil twin, I suggested she ask Karen. The nurse thanked me and told me I could see the baby any time now. I staggered to the bathroom and washed my face trying to drive back the savage assaults of *desynchronosis*…my temporary but nevertheless brutal battle with the circadian rhythm sleep disorders we'd learned about back in Southwest School of Aviation. But then it was just an interesting section in our flight physiology classes. Now and for the next few days, this was going to be very real. I did clearly realize however that any continued absence from Karen's bedside was not an option. Perhaps I could find some coffee at the hospital.

But as the cold water chased away the veils of sleep, the thoughts of now having a baby girl sent my adrenalin into overdrive. We had a baby girl…how cool is that. I couldn't wait to see Jason and Karen. I got to the car before I realized I'd forgotten the watch. I dashed back inside and got it from the coffee table in the living room. As I drove to the hospital, the lyrics from Brian Hyland's song *Ginny Come Lately* kept playing in my head.

> *"Ginny-Come-Lately, sweet, sweet as can be*
> *You may have come lately but Ginny-Come-Lately*
> *You're the one for me"*
> *"You only had to smile a little smile*
> *Do nothing more than look at me*
> *You only had to smile and in a little while*
> *I was dreamin' recklessly"* [162]

---

[162] Ginny Come Lately written by Gary Geld, Peter Udell

I realized as I was walking into the hospital that I had a lot of remedial relationship reconstruction waiting only a few feet ahead of me. I'd barked at a male nurse, I'd upset Karen, I snapped at the nurse who wanted to know how I wanted to spell Jenny. I'd been a real delinquent on so many varied fronts in such an incredibly short timeframe. What was in my head? But that was then…and this is now. I was going to blow them away with geniality…Mr. Nice…the King of Cordial, the epitome of amiability…Jimmy Jovial Joe Jacks…yes, in a few short feet a truly amazing transformation would take place. No more screw ups.

A nurse met me in the lobby area and took me straight to Karen's room. Every step down that hall was filled with praise and gratitude for the hospital staff. And I truly meant it. I had been a little reluctant about Karen having Jenny in the local hospital but it turned out to be a wonderful choice. It was modern, ultra-clean, and the staff was well trained and caring.

Daddy and Jason were in the room when I got there. I went with them to take my first look at Jenny. Oh my gosh… *"You only had to smile a little smile; Do nothing more than look at me; You only had to smile and in a little while; I was dreamin' recklessly."* She was so beautiful.

We came back to the room, I gave Karen the watch, she tried it on and smiled. She looked pretty tired so we left. I went back and went straight to bed. I did offer a prayer of thanksgiving that all had gone well with the delivery and for the gift of such a beautiful baby girl.

Earlier that day, it was reported in three Soviet newspapers that North Vietnamese pilots are undergoing training in a secret Soviet air base to fly supersonic interceptors against U.S. aircraft. At the time, I failed to even notice.

Hamilton Days

Karen and Jenny were back home in just a few days. I played with the baby, took pictures, spent time fishing with Jason at the Hamilton City Lake and on some of the local creeks. Jason loved to fish, and he was amazingly good for such a young guy. On one trip to the City Lake we had caught a ton of little sun perch. We finally ran out of bait and I was ready to go home. Jason kept begging to stay just a few minutes more. What for I asked…you have no more bait. "I don't need any bait Daddy; I can catch them with just my hook…watch."

The hook was new and was made from a shiny gold-colored metal. He put it where the sun's rays were reflecting off the shiny hook. In no time one of those stupid little sun perch darted out of the shadows and grabbed the empty hook. Amazing, he was hauling in another perch that I would certainly have to clean when we got home. Of course they were not worth cleaning; they were too small, but that wasn't the point. Every young Daniel Boone or Davy Crockett wants to come home and put the fruits of his day of exploring on the table for dinner. I had done the same thing when I was his age, leaving my father to clean the fish. Regardless of what I'd promised before we went, I always managed to disappear when fish cleaning time came. Jason was truly my son.

Jason–The Marksman

"To preserve liberty, it is essential that the whole body of the people always possess arms, and be taught alike, especially when young, how to use them."[163]

While we were spending time fishing, I was thinking about trying to teach Jason how to shoot a rifle. I was thinking about a BB gun. I went to a hardware store and found a Daisy Red Rider BB gun. It looked a bit like a miniature Winchester Model 1894 and for sure was the weapon of choice for Red Rider. It had a lever-action cocking mechanism and a magazine that would hold hundreds of BBs. I got several packages of BBs and headed home. I couldn't wait to start showing him how to use it.

I set up a target on the front porch and used a cardboard box for a backstop. With a muzzle velocity of about 280 feet per second I didn't have to work hard at finding an effective material for arresting the BBs. I used another small box to hold my targets. Jason was so excited. I could tell Daddy was as well. I never had a BB gun per say. My first gun of any type was a Crossman .22 cal. pellet rifle when I was ten. Jason was only seven. Karen didn't say a lot. She was happy to see us spending this quality time together but was worried about his possibly figuring out how to manage some unauthorized use when nobody was around. From the supervised front porch target to unsupervised birds in back yard trees was an easy visualization.

I began by using Dr Pepper cans as targets. Soon they became too easy and we moved downward in size. I spent a lot of time digging in the trash during those early lessons, constantly searching for smaller and smaller targets. Jason struggled with the lever action cocking process for a while, as I had suspected he would, but gradually developed a system for cocking it using his leg.

Within a couple of days and hundreds of BBs we had graduated to not just using the small boxes I found for targets, but specific letters or markings on the box. He was getting pretty good, as well as a bit cocky. And I was getting a little tired of hunting for little boxes. So, I did what my father did with me…I gave him a match stem to shoot at.

I told him when he could hit it, he could brag. Other than that, this was Texas and most young men could shoot well. Jason bet me that I could not hit the match. I took the rifle and hit the match stem with the first shot. I told him when I was a teenager, I could cut a string with a 22 rifle. I watched his expression as he processed my statement. He took the gun and shot; he missed. He shot again and missed again; and again and again.

---

[163] Richard Henry Lee

I decided I would go in the house so I could coo and make silly faces at Jenny. Jason didn't really need me watching every shot. I realize now that I was completely wrong. While my physical presence was not critical to the operation, my physical and emotional presence was needed. Learning to hunt and fish in one's youth is important but is trumped by learning to hunt and fish from one's father. I was a poor learner. In many ways I was a poor father. "If Only"

I'd only been in the house for a few minutes when Jason proudly marched in holding a splintered match stem. "I did it he said. Now it's your turn." I told him how proud I was of him…I really was; we went back out on the front porch for more target practice.

While Jason and I were shooting at matches, Hanoi Radio announces that Deputy Premier Le Thanh Nghi had signed an agreement with Peking whereby the People's Republic of China would provide additional economic and technical aid to North Vietnam.

Back To The Congo

My time in Mayberry came to an end. I said goodbye to Karen and Jason, and looked for a very long time at Jenny. Leaving was hard. It always was, but I'd learned from experience that soon after getting on the plane, my thoughts lay ahead of me…not behind me. I found this disconcerting. I knew it was not particularly healthy.

New York, Rome, Kinshasa. I slept as much as possible to make the flight go quicker. The flight to Rome was not full, so I quickly found three empty seats together, grabbed my pillow and blanket and staked them out before other less experienced travelers realized the opportunity. There were several of us that had the same idea. I'd wake up only to be served a meal then back to sleep. The flight to Kinshasa was full of Congolese…most of whom, regardless of the money they had, would have been more at home in the back of a truck than the airplane cabin. But, I was now accustomed to it. I could sleep through anything as long as I didn't have a screaming kid next to me. Fortune smiled on me…there were no kids.

No Change & Great Change

The apartment looked the same when I got home. Nothing had changed. John had kept it clean. He didn't know exactly when I was coming home so I had to send him to the store for something quick to eat. I unpacked and got ready to fall back into my routine.

The next morning I got in the car and drove to operations to let them know I was back and start hustling flights. As I lounged around operations, then later visiting with the mechanics in the hanger, the talk was all about the political changes taking place in the country and within SODEMAC. Many of the political changes were humorous. Mobutu wanted the country to move away from western influences. The obvious reason was so he could exert more of his own influence. He was trying to revive old customs and Congolese were being pressured to get rid of their Christian names in favor of more authentic names. Most of the whites found this hilarious.

But far from hilarious was the plummeting morale within SODEMAC. Pay had been late again; more and more incompetent Congolese "managers" were being brought in. They never did anything and seldom bothered to come to work but, since they were in charge nothing was done without their approval. Everybody was complaining that paperwork was escalating. Even the simplest tasks now required numerous multi-copied forms. However, the persons responsible for signing the forms never seemed to be in the office. More of our remaining core mechanics were talking of leaving in the immediate future. I resolved I would do my best to not focus on the negative, increase my flying to the limit of my physical ability to save more money, and develop a short-term contingency plan for leaving and a medium-term plan for leaving. The obvious struck me. As Karen, Jason and Jenny were getting ready to return, many families were getting ready to leave.

Long Flights Into Tragedy

Conditions in the Eastern Congo as well as the situation in Burundi were still smoldering, producing untold human suffering. The unthinkable acts of death, maiming, rape and pillage were causing the uprooting of huge segments of the population, mostly along tribal lines. We had several flights a day moving troops and military supplies in and the wounded out. Operations had all the flights I was strong enough to take. It was always a constant struggle trying to balance the money against flight fatigue and the danger of becoming unsafe…too fatigued to safely fly.

When I landed in Goma on my first flight since coming back from the U.S., I found the airport flooded with refugees. Some were from the Congo and some from neighboring Rwanda and Burundi; men and women with all their worldly possessions in large bundles carried on their heads. Children with swollen stomachs indicating malnutrition were the norm.

Conspicuously missing were teenage boys and young men. We were told they were fighting in the bush. The poor would die, the colonels and generals would get rich. This was a scenario that would replay itself in Cambodia in the years to come.

What I saw there was causing me to think in ways I'd never done before…asking myself why this was happening, who and what were behind the tragedies I witnessed almost daily. I reasoned there was much injustice in the world, a thought that never crossed my mind as I was growing up. I supposed that was a good thing. Young men in their teens should spend their time strategizing about whom they hoped next to lavish their affections upon in the back seat of their 1950 Ford…not the brutality and injustice of wars forced upon the masses for the benefit of the few. I was finding there would be ample time for such thoughts later.

The Family's Return

The single most important task I had to accomplish before Karen returned was to find a crib for Jenny. I had reasoned that with all the families going home, surely someone would have a crib for sale. But my heavy flight schedule had prevented my finding one. Karen, along with Jason and Jenny would be here the next day and I had nothing in which Jenny could sleep. I couldn't believe I'd gotten myself into this mess.

When I got back home, it was already dark. They would be here the following afternoon. As I was walking around in Jason's bedroom, I spotted a large unused suitcase. It was deep and hard walled. I got it down and began to examine it. What if I tied the lid open so it would not be able to slam closed? I could pack it with a soft pillow and stuff tee-shirts around the edges to fill in the gaps.

> *Away in the Congo, no crib for a bed*
> *My little Jenny laid down her sweet head*
> *A suitcase with lid held open tight*
> *Was how she would spend her first Congo night*

The neglect I showed here was unpardonable, very out of character for my usual attention to detail. More than forty years later it ranks rather respectably on my "If Only" list. There are numerous far more egregious things on the list, but few epitomize the indefensibly-worthless as does the suitcase for a crib incident.

I met their flight the following day. Jason was excited to get home. Karen was tired. She had just traveled halfway around the world with a seven-year-old and a two-month-old child. I had a real respect for her courage and strength. I still do today.

Karen was very gracious about the no-crib situation. I profusely promised that one way or the other, I would have something in the house the next day. Today I can't remember where I found a crib or some acceptable type of baby bed, but I did.

Congo Craziness
(aka Mobutism)

We (all the whites in SODEMAC) were aware of the true motives behind the rather transparent façade of nationalism or Mobutism. Mobutu desperately feared the super-power influences of the United States, The Soviet Union, and China. He'd seen the effects of their meddling in the affairs of nations around the world. He was experiencing this firsthand with China's meddling in the affairs of his neighbors, Rwanda and Burundi, and at home in his own Eastern provinces. He felt the tightening grip of the U.S and the CIA in his own country. Mobutu needed to unite the peoples of the Congo behind his political party the MPR, behind himself, and steer them away from tribalism. It's doubtful any political doctrine could do this, but he was hell-bent on trying. There were few other options.

We would find out how hell-bent he was on the night of 27 October. I clearly remember the night. I was on a C-47 flight which remained overnight in Kisangani. I'd already visited with Bat. We enjoyed a drink together while Chi Chi, the family's pet chimpanzee, took turns sitting in everybody's lap. From Bat's I had gone to the old Wigmo safe house, now controlled by SODEMAC, where I planned to spend the night with George. After dinner George wanted to walk across the street to the previously Greek owned bar/casino. It, like so many other businesses in the country, had been "nationalized" (a favorite Congolese word for stolen). I would have preferred to sit quietly on the veranda, but I needed to be social, at least to some degree, so I agreed. It was just a few meters from the house as soon as I decided I'd had enough.

We were sitting at the bar; it was noisy and smoke-filled. Suddenly a Greek came in obviously excited. He informed all the whites at the bar that the name of the country had just been changed…from Congo to Zaire. "To what" everybody asked. Zaire. Nobody had ever heard the word and a common question was…"how do you spell it?" to which no one had an answer. The Greek said it had just been announced on the radio in Lingala. He said they were going to change the currency as well. Everybody was in a mild state of shock (and some degree of panic). What about the currency exchange? What else were they about to announce. Most mature observers agreed we were only seeing the tip of the iceberg. Phase I of what?

The following day the newspapers in Lingala and French came out outlining the major changes. The country would be the Republic of Zaire, the army would become Forces Armées Zaïroises—(FAZ), the Congo River would become the Zaire River…the country was in chaos. The air force was now the Force Aerienne Zaïroises. We were hearing that the currency would be changed from the Congolese Franc to a currency called Zaire. Mobutu's picture would be on all the notes. We well understood that we could not be caught laughing or otherwise be interpreted as making fun of the government…but it was so hard to keep from laughing. They were all running around in pure chaos. To begin with, nobody, including us, knew how to spell Zaire. In the back of my mind was what would the value of this new currency be. I already had a huge pile of Congolese Francs thanks to SODEMAC. I would have to exchange them for the new currency…but at what rate. Since there was little I could do about it, I didn't dwell long on that aspect, but I didn't forget about it. Black market exchange rates plummeted. Nobody wanted to get caught holding the old Franc.

When I returned to Kinshasa, I found even more chaos. People were running around painting over the word Congo which was on just about every paintable surface in the country. The absolute funniest thing was the painting over of the word Congolese on the side of all the FAC planes. We were now officially FAZ . . . Force Aerienne Zaïroises. And all over the country, the Congolese were incorrectly spelling the word. It was hilarious.

While the world was laughing at Mobutu, halfway around the world in Cambodia, in November 1971, the Lon Nol government suspended grants of export licenses for major export commodities, such as rice, corn, and cattle in a desperate attempt to mitigate the effects of the stranglehold the Khmer Rouge had on the food supplies of major population centers. War had caused the production of rice to fall to 26.8% of its 1969 level. [164] *With that decline and the control of the major transportation routes by the Khmer Rouge, the major cities, already bloated by the influx of refugees fleeing from the provinces, had no food. Everything had to be flown into the cities by an airlift similar to the one supplying Berlin.*

The Big Zaire Mistake
(what do you mean Zaire is a Portuguese word)

It became even more hilarious when the international weekly magazines hit the press and those on vacation started bringing back what the European press was saying. It turned out that the word "Zaire" wasn't really a Congolese word. It was a Portuguese word. While we were all laughing, for sure it was very quietly in private. You could be expelled from the country in less than 24 hours for making fun of the government. They took such matters very seriously. I didn't recall any Newsweek or Time magazines on the newsstands in Kinshasa that week. Seems like the Zairian government lacked a sense of humor. But the 8 November issue of Time, (overlooked by a careless customs agent at the airport) made it to a secret spot in operations where it was enjoyed by all.

Word soon went out to all the station agents to change the wording on the jeeps from SODEMAC to SODEMAZ. All the new forms that owed their genesis to SODEMAC were now being changed. Pandemonium was the order of the day. All these changes were just adding to everybody's already hyper job insecurity. While the eastern province problems would dictate the necessity of FAC requiring outside help in the form of pilots and mechanics, deep down inside I knew I wouldn't be staying too much longer. The longer I stayed the less chance I figured I'd have of leaving with all the money they would owe me. Payday was now routinely late. I could read the writing on the jeep so to speak. From Makasi to SODEMAC and now SODEMAZ. While I could not plot the exact downward spiral, the eventual outcome was obvious to a cretin. I knew it would not be wise to be the last rat off this ship.

---

[164] The Wartime Economy, 1970-75—Russell R. Ross, edl Cambodia: A Country Study. Washington: GPO for the Library of Congress, 1987

Paul's Sudden Departure

Persona Non Grata

While all this was happening, Paul's problems with the government became more serious. He was worried that he might be arrested. The missing money had to be blamed on somebody…Paul was a likely candidate.

One day when I went to visit with him, he asked me if I wanted to rent his place. He said he would be leaving and wanted to leave quickly and to get rid of as many of the items he'd bought as he possibly could. I told him I didn't really plan on staying that long myself. Then he proposed such a ridiculously low price for everything in the house I couldn't resist. I knew I wouldn't be in the Congo (Zaire) much longer myself, but Paul needed the money to get out of the country and I figured I'd have more time to try to get rid of it myself. He said we would have no trouble transferring the lease agreement. I believed that the owner, a Congolese, certainly knew finding a new tenant would not be easy in this mass exodus environment. While the exodus was not exactly like a herd of stampeding Texas Herefords, it could hold its own with a startled flock of pigeons down at the feed mill in Hamilton. I went home and talked to Karen. She said that this would be fine. I went back over and told Paul. I was worried he might not be around the next time I went looking. He gave me wire instructions for Marie Jeanne's bank account in Brussels, Belgium.

A couple of days later, Paul came by to say they were leaving the next day. I had not expected his departure to be that sudden. He said he was hoping he would not be arrested at the airport when they tried to leave. We completed our basic transaction and he left. I had a flight the following day.

It would be more than two years before I'd see Paul again. Our next meeting would be in Cambodia. In Cambodia, over several beers, he related their departure from the N'Djili airport. Paul said they were extremely worried about his being arrested at the airport. He said as they went through passport control, the police stamped "persona non grata" in his passport and threw it across the table making it land on the floor. Later, in his memoirs *The Adventurous Aviator*, written shortly before his death and completed and published by his daughter Natacha, Paul recounted the intensity of the stress they were under their last few weeks in Zaire and the relief they felt as their flight touched down in Nairobi Kenya. They were so stressed they decided just to spend a couple of weeks there in a nice hotel, relaxing before traveling on to Brussels. But, as he related in our meeting in Phnom Penh, they never made it to Brussels. He was offered a job flying for a diamond mine there in Kenya and they remained there a couple of years.

What Paul's story illustrated was the very real danger of living in a lawless country like the Congo. He could easily have been arrested, thrown into prison, beaten, tortured, and died of disease or malnutrition, all for nothing. He was completely innocent. The Congolese ministers and new SODEMAC officials took the money; Paul took the blame.

Our Life In "Paul's House"

Immediately, Karen and I moved into what we always called "Paul's house." His constant tinkering and remodeling, gardening, and painting, had left his indelible mark on the beautiful house. The yard was perfect, the interior redone, it was nice.

A *Shocking* Experience

There was an aspect to Paul's house with which I was totally unfamiliar…the swimming pool. Soon I managed to let the water get out of pH balance. It quickly turned from turquoise blue to malachite green. Additionally, Paul had purchased a Siemens, German-made, water circulating pump and filter system. For some reason, I had to have it worked on and when I reconnected it, I managed to wire it with an incorrect ground. While putting it back into the pool I stuck one hand in the water while holding onto the metal ladder going into the pool with the other hand. I received a bone-rattling dose of 220 volts of current. I was fortunate I didn't die right on the spot. From that time onward, the pool was not really my favorite part of Paul's house.

Jason and Julia

But in spite of my animosity toward the swimming pool, our family's time there was good. Jason enjoyed playing in the large fenced-in yard with Julia. Julia was a huge Boxer whom we'd had since she was a pup. They had played together at our apartment, but their space was limited. Here they could romp together with seemingly endless space. These were good times. Karen, Jenny, and I would watch from the huge veranda. Life at Paul's house was good.

Mobuto Attacks The Church

In December Mobutu began openly attacking the churches in the country. He feared their Christian influence would stand in the way of his "Africanization" movement. He banned all but three denominations, the Church of Christ in Zaire, the Kimbanguist Church, (a group formed by a Congolese named Simon Kimbangu, a self-proclaimed prophet) and the Roman Catholic Church, with whom he already had a very strained relationship. He mandated all seminaries in the country have a chapter of the JMPR (Mobutu's youth group *Jeunesse du Mouvement Populaire de la Révolution* or Youth of the Popular Revolutionary Movement). The JMPR appeared to be patterned after the infamous "Hitler Youth, League of German Worker Youth"…basically government-sponsored young thugs. Each time I would visit with missionary friends, I'd hear expressions of concern for their work in the country. The country was becoming even more volatile.

More Political Instability
More Craziness
More Coup Rumors

Mobutu's campaign forcing Congolese to change their Christian names to more authentic Congolese names was intensifying. It was becoming difficult for Congolese to find a job in any company if they still had a Christian name. It was becoming difficult to advance in the military, government sector, or government-controlled businesses with a Christian name. On 12 January 1972 Mobutu himself abandoned his Christian name "Joseph-Désiré" and became "Mobutu Sese Seko Kuku Ngbendu wa Za Banga." The translation of his new name was reported to mean "the all-powerful warrior who, because of his endurance and inflexible will to win, will go from conquest to conquest leaving fire in his wake." Few if any of us dreamed the extent to which his extreme paranoia would eventually drive him. But we sure got some good laughs (in private) about his new name.

Our missionary friends were worried; the business community was anxious; black market currency trading was frenzied. Everybody wanted the dollar. Everybody was trying to get every penny of their liquid assets such as cash, jewelry, and anything that would fit in a suitcase, out of the country. Everybody was trying to convert everything they owned that would not fit into a suitcase into portable or liquid assets. Property values were falling, car prices were falling. When I came to the country, finding a good car at a decent price was not easy. Now the market was flooded with underpriced cars, many discounted to more than half their previous value. The bulletin boards in all the shops frequented by foreigners were filled with going-home sale notices. Furniture, refrigerators, barbeque grills…all at radically discounted prices. Everybody was going home.

The high demand for the dollar was putting such pressure on it that its black-market value went up almost daily. The value of my pile of what was now called Zaire fell daily. I had few options. I continued to buy more ivory, malachite, likembeies, various fetishes, and masks; but how much of that stuff, even as authentic and rare as it was, could I reasonably own? I had no choice but to join the hysterical hordes buying dollars on the black market. Each payday I would take my pile of Zaire to my regular Greek merchant, and each month I'd receive fewer dollars. I knew my time to leave could not be far off.

Almost every day there was a new report about some colonel or general planning to overthrow the Mobutu government. Personally, I always figured that if I'd heard about it, Mobutu's secret police had heard about it as well and therefore any such attempt would have little chance of succeeding. But logically or illogically…the rumors took their toll.

Karen, Jason, And Now Jenny Go Home Again

More and more of the original Wigmo people were leaving. SODEMAZ was reportedly advertising in Europe for pilots. The new pilots that were arriving were nowhere near the quality of what was leaving. SODEMAZ seemed, at least outwardly, unfazed by what was happening. All this contributed to the feeling of futility among those of us still remaining. I knew I would soon be following those leaving now. It was like SODEMAZ was somberly marching in a funeral procession to its own grave.

Karen and I discussed what to do. The dangers were obvious. We all understood what a volatile Congolese mob could do when political instability came. The smallest incident could set them off. They had taken to the streets with machetes hacking to death any foreigners they found; no one believed it would be any different when something ignited them again. There was no distinction…men, women, even children. They reverted to some frenzied primeval state. While they hated all whites, they could also easily do the same to fellow Africans from different tribes. The danger was real and present. Karen and I both knew they would be leaving again; this time for good.

Jason was in the American equivalent of the second grade in the French school. His school year was almost over. He could effectively go at any time now. He'd finished most of the school year already. Karen would withdraw him the following week. I began immediately working on the tickets. This time…one-way tickets. They were going back to Hamilton. This time for good.

The following day when I went to the administrative office to order their tickets back home to Texas, the lady who took care of me, the wife of one of the long-time Wigmo mechanics, raised her eyebrow when I handed her the ticket request form containing only one-way routings. "You too" she said in a whispered tone. I nodded. She just shook her head. I knew she and her husband would soon be gone as well. The whole place was coming apart. The once famous Wigmo had been reduced to a footnote in history. I couldn't help but think that Wigmo's fate was a precursor to what lay ahead for the entire country. It seemed as though these poor people were somehow cursed. After emerging from the tyranny of the Belgium colonial era, they rushed headlong into the horrors of endless killings and hardship brought upon them this time by their own people. This place truly was "the heart of darkness." Once again, my drive from the airport back to Limete was filled with heavy thoughts.

Going Home For The Last Time

As always, Karen did her part so well. She withdrew Jason from the French school, she packed, she did it all. I somehow managed to limit my flying so I could spend a little more time with them during their last days. Jason seemed to look forward to going back to Hamilton. Karen stoically moved through her last days in Kinshasa, never complaining.

Their day came. We went to the airport. We all knew the script. Karen and I knew what emotions to expect. I watched for the last time as their plane climbed, banking right, and departed north over the Congo (Zaire) River Basin. I knew I would follow soon. There was a lot to think about. I drove to the military side of the airport, checked my flight schedule and told operations to load me up with flights. I had no need to be in Kinshasa.

The Change

I drove home. The large house was now profoundly empty. Jason's room was empty. The living room was empty. Jenny's crib was empty. Our bedroom was empty. It was mid-afternoon, too early to have a beer and eat dinner. I found the special hand-painted ultra-lightweight blue airmail stationary we used when we wrote letters back home. I wrote a long letter to Karen, addressed the envelope, placed a couple of bright Zaire postage stamps on the envelope, and put it in my flight bag. I'd put it in the outgoing mail box in flight operations in the morning. I opened a Primus beer and went out on the veranda. It was now time to start planning how I'd spend these last months in the Congo.

Strange New Inner Callings

When I walked back into what used to be "our house" the sense of loneliness as well as aloneness was heavy. The aloneness I found strangely appealing, a frighteningly unsettling thought. I felt guilt for even having such contemplations, even if ever so brief. The son of my father was telling me this was not allowed; this was contrary to devotion to one's family. The son of my mother was telling me to take the path less traveled…to experience, to photograph, to write. These things were outside the realm of contemplation when Karen was here. I was clearly experiencing an internal conflict of interest. My dual personalities were dueling.

I had long ago grown accustomed to the whisperings of my evil twin. I knew his beckoning well. I knew how to stuff them back in their hole. But these feelings were different. They came from long-ignored recesses. I started thinking about how I would spend these last months. It was now possible to pursue some of these non-conventional imaginings without experiencing the guilt. There was no one here to leave alone.

The sun was rapidly dropping below the Congo's twilight-less horizon. I got another Primus, returned to my seat on the veranda and stared out into the darkness. I could just hear the muffled noises of the sprawling shanty town of the Congolese in the valley behind and below the house. During the day they were lost in the ambient street noise of Limete but at night the muffled sound of Congolese *soukous* music supplied somewhat of a constant cultural backdrop, an ever-present reminder of where I was. I went to bed without eating that night. The following morning, before leaving for the airport, I put my Nikon and several rolls of film in my flight bag.

A Pygmy Plan Begins Taking Shape

It was hard to think about anything else during my flight that day. I was excited. I had heard missionary friends talking about seeing pygmies in some of the Bantu villages along the roads east of Kisangani. One missionary I met was an etymologist and had recounted seeing pygmies as he drove down a road through the forest. He said he initially thought they were little children but realized some had facial and chest hair. He was currently working on a project to translate the Bible into one of the less prominent dialects spoken in the eastern areas of the country. I was amazed he was still in country…that he had not been told to leave. I suppose because he was not directly involved in the much-feared evangelism of the citizenry, Mobutu's government had passed over his group, Wycliffe Bible Translators, for expulsion…at least for the moment. His name was Phil Hammons (pseudonym). Phil had a PhD in language studies or something like that. I decided I'd make talking with Phil about my idea of visiting the pygmies a high priority.

We landed back in King 1 a little before dark. I went straight to Phil's house. I realized it was probably dinner time for them, but I decided I'd just apologize. I was now a man on a mission.

When I arrived, Phil showed an interest in my idea and even said he might like to come along. He knew I had access to free transportation to Kisangani and I was sure I could secure the use of a jeep from Bat or the station agent in Kisangani for the land-based portion of the trip. We decided we'd set a rough date of three weeks from then. He needed to arrange his work schedule and I needed to put in for some vacation I was going to lose if I left with it still on the books. The days of Wigmo paying you for unused vacation were long gone. We both agreed to make these arrangements and meet again soon to finalize a date. As I was leaving, he gave me a book to read…*The Forest People: A Book About The Pygmies of the Congo*. [165] I started the book that night as soon as I'd finished dinner. I also began a note book in which I'd write down my ideas, concerns, and questions. I was excited.

---

[165] By Colin Turnbull—Chatto & Windus; First Edition edition (1961)

A Change In My Environment

I soon realized not only was "Paul's house" too large for me, but its emptiness just exponentially magnified my loneliness. I put out the word and soon had some non-SODEMAZ Europeans interested in the place. I decided to go back into the old Wigmo bachelor's quarters. But while I was in the process of doing the paperwork, one of the Swedish pilots came to me saying he was going on medical leave for two months and asked if I would be interested in house-sitting his company-provided apartment while he was gone. This would mean living rent free. It was a no-brainer. I happily accepted and moved in the following week.

Goodbye To John

It was clear I would no longer need John. My agreement concerning the place I'd be housesitting was that I would pay the houseboy. I gave John two months' pay in the new funny money and a hug and we said goodbye. I wondered what he would do for work. Houseboy jobs were hard to come by. John wasn't the brightest guy I ever met, but he was pleasant and honest, and he could iron clothes and cook a decent meal. Years later I still laugh when I remember some of his funny expressions.

More Preparations

I went to flight operations and looked at the vacation list. I found an opening in the schedule where I could be gone two weeks without any scheduling difficulties. I quickly filled out the form and walked out with vacation approved. I stopped by and gave this info to Phil. Unfortunately Phil hadn't had time to do anything about arranging an absence from work for himself.

A Flight To Kisangani To Visit Bat (A Jeep And A Junior Partner)

I asked flight ops for the next overnight to Kisangani. Two days later I was sitting in Bat's living room with Chi Chi in my lap. Chi Chi had developed a taste for Simba beer and it was a constant struggle keeping her hairy little lips out of my mug. But it was a good visit. It was always a good visit. Bat assured me I could use their family jeep and he would sponge rides from George in that SODEMAZ "Spanish

piece of crap they call a jeep." I loved Bat. He was so nice, like a cross between an older brother and a father. Bat and Lois's son Jim expressed an interest in going as well. But at that time Jim was not sure exactly when his last day of class for that year was going to be. After drinks with Bat, George and I had dinner at his house. After dinner I continued studying the book about the pygmies and making my notes and plans. The following day I was back in Kinshasa.

Phil Fails Time Off Test

As soon as I got back to Kinshasa, I drove over to Phil's place to find out how he made out arranging his days off. Phil looked a little fidgety. I could tell by his demeanor what he was going to say. It was written all over his face. I later wondered if his wife had swayed his decision. But it really didn't matter. It was now just going to be me and Jim Masterson, and Jim was a maybe.

I watched the schedule for a flight going to Kisangani. I knew if I had to, I could fiddle my vacation schedule a day or so in either direction, but it was always best to avoid owing people favors. We had several flights each week to Kisangani; I was betting I could get one just when I needed it. And sure enough it happened. A couple of days before my vacation was scheduled to begin, I found a note in my mailbox in flight ops. I was listed on the manifest for a flight on a C-54 from King 1 to King 7 on the first day of my vacation…departure time 06:00. It paid to have friends in dispatch and flight ops. It didn't hurt that I was always bringing them little gifts back from the provinces. Little packets of cheese from Albertville, ham from Isiro. Yes, friends were nice to have.

The Little People Of The Forrest

The Mbuti

From my reading and from talking with others, I'd learned we would be almost certain to spot a few pygmies living amongst the Bantu in roadside villages. The Bantu considered the pygmies their "slaves" and "forced" them to do most of the work in their villages. For this they would occasionally pay the pygmies small quantities of cigarettes or other items the Bantu purchased from the small Mhindi-run dukas. Nobody worked very hard and the pygmies didn't really seem to mind their "slave" status.

But according to the book I'd just finished reading, the pygmies, from time to time, would suddenly disappear during the middle of the night and return to their camps deep in the heart of the forest. A place the Bantu feared to go. The interesting twist was that when the pygmies left for the forest, they took with them most of the pots, pans, and metal tools found in the village. When the Bantu awoke the following morning, not only were their "slaves" gone, but also a sizable amount of their personal belongings. According to the studies of one anthropologist, this cycle repeated itself regularly.

Packing For The Pygmy Exploit

The time had finally come. It was time to pack all the things I'd spent days assembling; I vowed I would not pack for my pygmy trip like I packed on my initial trip to the Congo.

My cameras had been ready for days. I was taking my Nikon and my twin lens Yashica Mat. I had a hand-held light meter and my external flash. I packed several sets of batteries for the flash. I had a flashlight with fresh batteries and one set of backup batteries for it. There were countless rolls of 35mm Kodak and Fuji film. I used mostly Kodachrome by Kodak for my slides but occasionally would use Fujichrome when I wanted some contrast and pop to my color. For my Yashica Mat, a medium format camera, I almost exclusively shot 120 black and white film. I had several rolls for it as well. Cameras and film, batteries, and my flashlight took up half of my backpack. I packed a little battery-powered Radio Shack cassette tape recorder which I hoped to use recording some of their speech and if I got really lucky…their music.

In addition to the cameras, I planned to carry my hunting knife, which I normally had in my flight bag or on occasion in my boot. But for this trip I would wear it on my belt. I had learned as a child growing up in Hamilton County that while camping, you needed a knife for something every five minutes.

I also had carefully selected small tins or cans of meat and fish. For dried food I had a small sack of rice, a bag of macaroni, and a small sack of beans. I figured if I couldn't get anything suitable from the Bantu or the pygmies, this would be enough to last me for a week. I'd already spoken with Jim about his food. He was going to do the same. I took a metal pie pan to use for a plate, a skillet, a pot to boil rice, beans, etc. and a fork and spoon. This was going to push my duffle bag to the limit.

I'd gotten a small bottle of water purification tablets from SODEMAZ stores. They used them stocking our emergency survival kits. The stores clerk laughed when he handed them to me. He told me to use them slowly; that when there were gone…there wouldn't be any more. These were from the U.S. Air Force. SODEMAZ would not enjoy Wigmo's privileged status. I commented that I wished this would be the extent of our problems. We both laughed. I told him that I'd be gone before the pills were.

I planned to carry a machete. While it would fit on the back of my pack, I figured for much of the walking time, it would be in my right hand. If we got lucky and managed to get some of the pygmies to take us to their village, we would be walking through dense jungle. I'd purchased it in Limete in one of the small dukas. These were different from the machetes you found in the U.S. in hardware stores or army surplus stores. The ones in the U.S. tended to be very rigid. That rigid type was all I'd ever seen till I got to the Congo. Here the machetes were flexible and lighter in weight. If you worked at it just a little bit, you could get a razor-sharp edge on them. I much preferred these to the ones back home.

I brought the "Boy Scout" type compass I always carried in my flight bag. If for whatever reason, I had to try to make it back out of the jungle on my own, I figured it would be close to impossible without this. Back home, if you ever got lost, you had the sun to tell you which direction to walk. Here, in the rain forest, there was no sun.

For clothes, I packed three tee-shirts and two pair of pants; one long sleeve shirt, and three pairs of underwear and socks. If I was lucky and had access to water, I would be able to fall back to the old system of wear one, wash one. The navy had trained me about the hazards of wearing the same underwear and socks day in and day out. As a medic, I'd seen first-hand the problems that could cause.

For bedding I took an old blanket which we had acquired someplace. I rolled it up tightly and tied it to the outside of the duffle bag.

I took the tactical map we used for navigation out of my flight bag and put it in my backpack. It was laminated. It showed the names of some villages and showed small rivers and streams. Most didn't have names but that really didn't matter. By discerning the patterns in which they fell in relation to each other and to rivers, streams and bridges or river crossings, we could determine our position. It made little difference if we knew the name of the place or not.

My bag was getting full, but I made room for my pre-independence road map published by Mobil Oil. I got my copy from one of the senior Wigmo pilots who had already gone home. These were impossible to find in any of the shops now but were quite common in the mid-1960s. He had laminated the map so it would not become worn from use. The advantage to using the Mobil map was that it contained roads and bridges that no longer existed. So many things had been reclaimed by the jungle when most maintenance stopped after independence. From the air however, faint scars could still be distinguished showing where these roads had been. The Mobil map also named most of the villages whereas the tactical air map did not. It was small when folded, light weight, and could prove useful supplying data for my notes.

I took the Justin work boots (more or less roper style but made of mule skin) that I preferred to fly in rather than the air force issue flight boots Wigmo had provided. I gave them a good coating of mink oil I'd brought back from Texas and laid them out for the following morning. They hadn't been exposed to a lot of the elements while I was flying. Walking through the jungle was going to be a different story.

The last thing I removed from my flight bag and placed in a side pocket was my Beretta 22 auto pistol. It fit perfectly. It didn't offer much of a knockout punch, but it was easy to carry in my flight bag.

One Day In Kisangani
And A Few Revisions To The Plan

It felt strange being out on the ramp and lugging a backpack and a duffle bag rather than my flight bag. I'd decided to wear my flight suit on the trip to Kisangani. I had tennis shorts and a tee-shirt on underneath it. It would be warmer to fly in and could be left with George when we started the drive the following morning. Most of the mechanics and flight crew did not know what I'd planned and were full of questions. Nobody ever went on vacation and stayed in the Congo. Nobody. The idea was to get out of the place as quickly as possible and stay gone as long as possible. They thought I'd lost my mind.

I was in Bat's house a little after noon. It was there I learned that Bat's jeep and been misbehaving. Bat and George had agreed I should take the SODEMAZ jeep since we would be going over 150 km (93 miles) from Kisangani with no major towns in-between and all on rutty dirt roads. I thanked them both.

It was then that I also learned I'd be going in search of the pygmies alone. Jim said he could not afford to take time from his studies. But this held some positive elements as well. Jim would drive with me in the SODEMAZ jeep and then drive the jeep back to Kisangani. He should be able to be back before dark the same day. I could not afford to keep the SODEMAZ jeep for a week. Everybody assured me there was plenty of truck traffic coming from the eastern Congo and Uganda with goods traveling overland to Kisangani. I could easily flag one down and hitch a ride. Probably about five Zaire would make any driver very happy. Happy enough to put me up in the cab with him rather than riding in the back with the cargo like most of the locals did.

Trinkets To Trade With The Natives

There was one item yet to accomplish. I needed to visit one of the dukas and purchase some trinkets to use as gifts to the village people and pygmies. I was going to need their good will. I decided I'd spend twenty or thirty dollars on cheap little gold colored earrings, chains, rings, and other jewelry popular with the village people. I also got several bars of perfumed soap, several small bottles of terrible smelling perfume, and some headscarves.

We went back to the house. I had a very nice visit with Bat, had dinner later that evening with his family and then went to George's house to spend the night.

Red Dirt Roads And "A Spanish Piece Of Crap Jeep"

Early the next morning Jim and I loaded my gear into the SODEMAZ jeep, checked the engine water and oil, checked the extra fuel can and the extra radiator water can, checked the spare tire's inflation, found the jack and tire tool, said goodbye to George and headed east out of Kisangani on highway 4 toward Bunia.

Roadside Beauty

The dry season had just begun so the red dirt road was dusty but thankfully not muddy. The road was relatively narrow, requiring special caution when passing or when approaching opposite direction traffic. The sides of the road almost always were crowded with bicycles and pedestrians. Many walking along the roadside were women with huge loads on their heads and often with small children in hand. The smaller children they rested on one of their hips. The women all wore bright colored clothing. They had a graceful sway to their walk. They could perfectly balance the load on their head, usually without having to steady it with one of their hands. I never tired of watching them.

I was enjoying the drive. Jim was an experienced driver, so I mostly spent my time in the right seat taking occasional pictures as we drove along. Due to the pedestrian traffic, we were only able to drive around 45 km/hr. (28 miles per hour). Around an hour and a half into the trip, we noticed that the engine would occasionally sputter. But it always picked back up again. We both chalked that up to contaminated gas. Most gas in the Congo contained water or other contaminates so this was not out of the ordinary. Fuel filter cleaning was almost a weekly event for everyone. George had placed a small tool bag in the back seat just in case something went wrong. The sputtering began to increase in frequency and finally about two hours after we left, we began to understand that this was not going to go away. We were going to have to get out and try to find the problem.

I was already envisioning myself on my back in the red dust struggling with fuel lines. But when we opened the hood, the problem was evident. The fuel pump was leaking profusely around its seal. Great, I thought. We've found the problem. But where do we find a gasket out in the middle of the jungle. We found the correct socket and extension and soon had the pump removed. We could see the gasket was breaking up. We dared not try to remove the gasket. It would all just crumble. We hoped we could find something to place on top if it just to get down the road. I went back and started digging to the bottom of the tool bag George had put onboard. I was hoping to find tube patching material or anything like that to make a gasket with. No such luck, but I did find some gasket sealer. What were the odds of that! We decided just about our only option other than trying to buy the tube off somebody's bicycle as they rode past was to try to clean and dry what was left of the gasket and pile a bunch of the sealer on top of the gasket, hoping to fill the still-rather-small bad spots. We turned the engine by hand to get the fuel pump cam into the full down position. We then bolted the thing back on; waited a few minutes; then cranked the engine. It started. This was our brand-new Spanish Disneyland jeep.

I hadn't really been worried about the engine starting. I figured it would do that. The big question was would it still be leaking. I was surprised to see it was not. I was really surprised. Even as a teenager working on my own car, I knew not to reuse gaskets. But this time, the great god of gaskets was smiling down upon us. It was dry. I knew it wouldn't hold too long but probably long enough to get back to Kisangani. We hopped back in the jeep and continued on east.

A Pee And A Coconut

A little further on down the road we spotted a little stand selling coconuts. We both needed to take a little break in the bushes and the thought of a refreshing coconut drink finalized the spot. While we were visiting the bushes, the lady was trimming the coconut with her sharp cleaver-like knife. By the time we returned, she had the tops off. The fresh clear coconut water was ready to drink. It was a natural energy drink. After we drank the water, she chopped it up into smaller pieces which we took with us to eat as we bounced down the road.

From time to time we would stop to ask the name of a village. We would then use that information to confirm our position on the map. Years ago, before independence, there were cement kilometer markers all along the highways. They were for the most part, long gone. But surprisingly we were never very far off. I had already marked where I believed we might start to see pygmies in the Bantu villages. We were nearing that area. We began to drive slower as we passed through villages, watching carefully for any unusually small people.

First Pygmy Sighting

As we neared kilometer marker 157, I spotted a man with childlike features. Just like the photos of pygmies I'd seen in the books, he had facial hair. He was standing in the shade of a tree in the Bantu village we were driving through. We slowly pulled the jeep off the road and brought it to a stop under a shade tree. Immediately we were surrounded by swarms of small, Bantu children greeting us with "hujambo…hujambo." To which I replied with one of my seriously few Swahili words…"sijambo." We were now outside the area of Lingala-speaking people and moving into the area where Swahili was spoken. Many of these people primarily spoke a much more limitedly used local dialect but to people from outside their area, they all used Swahili. The farther east you traveled in the Congo, the more prevalent Swahili became. Still, most villages would have someone capable of speaking Lingala due to its conspicuous use by the military and the government. I was hoping this village would have someone.

A middle-aged man approached us, followed by several other adult males. Women's faces began to peer out of mud hut doorways. I was pretty certain the man approaching us was an elder in the village…he turned out to be the chief. As he approached, I greeted him in Swahili with the traditional "hujambo" but immediately transitioned to the Lingala with which I had become significantly more familiar. "O-lob-aka Lingala?" (do you speak Lingala) I asked. "Na-lob-aka Lingala moké" (I speak a little or slowly) he replied. "Malámu, malámu, mingi" (that's good…that's very good) I told him. The adventure was beginning…I had my foot in the door. He invited us to sit with him in the shade. There was a bench type piece of furniture made from wood and split bamboo. As we sat, I introduced myself and Jim. I was quick to point out that I worked for the "Force Aérienne Congolaise" and showed him my ID card signed by General Bobozo." I was hoping if any of them were envisioning thoughts of a shakedown…or worse, this would dissuade them. Soon coconut water arrived. Telling them we'd just had some was never a consideration. "Melesi mingy!" (thank you very much) we said.

As we made small talk, I struggled at not seeming over-preoccupied with what I now realized was not just one but several pygmies in the village. Eventually, however I sensed the moment was right, so I asked him about the "Mbuti" in his village. I asked him if they were "his" or if they worked for him; to which he proudly replied yes. I was starting to allow myself to believe my plan was coming together. I also realized Jim needed to get back to Kisangani before dark…well before dark considering the questionable fuel pump.

Playing to his ego, I asked him if he thought he could get any of his pygmies to agree to take me to into the forest where I could meet other Mbuti. I told him I would reward him with ten Zaire if they agreed. He asked me to wait. He got up and called a conference with them. They were not speaking Swahili and it was not Lingala. While the sound resembled Lingala it clearly was not. Apparently, it was some Bantu dialect that the Mbuti, through their agricultural dependence upon the Bantu had learned to speak.

Soon the chief was back. He brought three adult Mbuti men with him. They all had signs of gray hair, so I was assuming they were senior members of the Mbuti group. The chief said they had agreed and that we could leave first thing in the morning. I decided I would negotiate with the Mbuti later, but definitely before we headed into the jungle. It would not be good to have the United Brotherhood of Pygmy Guides go on strike three or four hours into the forest leaving me to find my way back to the road. While I knew I could do it since I had my compass, it would mean leaving some of my gear behind and involve stress I could well do without. I would settle with them before leaving in the morning.

We unpacked the jeep and I placed my belongings in a hut the chief arranged for me. It was unoccupied. I was afraid to ask why. The roof apparently had some known leaks and needed slight repair. Some teenagers went scurrying into the bush soon returning with armloads of banana leaves which they piled on the roof. I remember thinking what a complex situation this would have been back in Hamilton or even in Kinshasa. Here in fifteen minutes with a handful of teenagers and several arm loads of banana leaves, the problem was resolved. The implications of this were profound and far reaching. I was slowly being changed forever.

Leaving Behind Some Additional Gear

I decided to take more of my gear out and leave it with Jim to take back to Kisangani. I didn't want to have to take it into the forest just in case I had to try to make it back on my own. I gave him the tripod, the tape recorder. This would allow me to keep all the items critical for my making it back to the road on my back. The pygmies could carry the things I could afford to lose if worse came to worse.

Jim and I gave the jeep another inspection. Our main concern was that the fuel pump was not leaking. Thank the Lord it was dry. We checked the oil and water and said our goodbyes. I told him I'd be back in a week or so. I wrote down the kilometer marker just by the village and told him to give it to his father and to George. With that, Jim was off. He would make better time than we did because the last 45 minutes of our trip was spent slowing to a snail's pace each time we drove through a village. This time he could drive normal speed. He should be home before 4:00pm. I returned to my hut and started looking about for my sleeping and cooking arrangements before it became dark.

The village chief offered me one of his chickens for my dinner. I asked him what would be a fair price. He replied about a Zaire. I knew that was too high but agreed to his price as I still needed plenty of goodwill in order to accomplish my mission. His wife quickly killed and plucked the chicken. I asked if he would sell me a little rice since I didn't want to use what I had before I headed out into the jungle. That cost about 50 Makuta. This was more reasonable. I figured if I cut up the chicken and just pan grilled it in my skillet and ate it with rice I would have a more or less decent meal and preserve the food I'd brought for my time in the pygmy's hunting camp   The chief's wife offered me some of her palm oil to use in cooking the chicken but it had a rancid smell and looked worse than it smelled so I politely declined. Normally chicken cooked in palm oil was one of my favorite Congolese dishes. But this stuff was hardly recognizable; its smell was vile.

After ruling out the rancid palm oil, I hoped there would be enough fat on the chicken to keep it from sticking to the pan. But that proved to be a ridiculous thought. Congolese chickens, which run loose in the village and mostly have to forage for food, have almost no fat. The one the chief sold me reminded me of one of those rubber chickens you see for sale in party and toy stores. I had little doubt the texture of the meat would closely resemble that of a rubber chicken as well.

At the last minute I revised my meal preparation plan and elected to roast it over the fire. I would just hack off pieces with my knife and eat them with rice. The idea was to replenish my energy reserve. Enjoying the food would be a peripheral benefit at best. Still that was no excuse not to make the best of it. I readied the small bottles of salt and pepper I'd brought along. The Bantu cultivated garlic and I talked the chief's wife into throwing in a couple of bulbs with the chicken.

I cooked on the chief's wife's fire. I'd never seen anything like it. Back home, I'd been taught to start a good fire of medium size wood, let it burn down to coals, and move the coals around to adjust the heat. What I was looking at was an entirely different concept. The logs were about twice the diameter of a cedar fence post. There were only four of them. They were placed at 90 degrees to each other like the four points of the compass and were only burning on one end. If you wanted to turn up the heat, you pushed the burning ends of the four logs closer together. If you wanted to turn down the heat, you simply pulled the logs further apart. How cool was that. Perfect heat control; once you got the hang of it. Rocks were waiting nearby be arranged if needed to help steady my pot. The rocks could also be used to sit on while cooking.

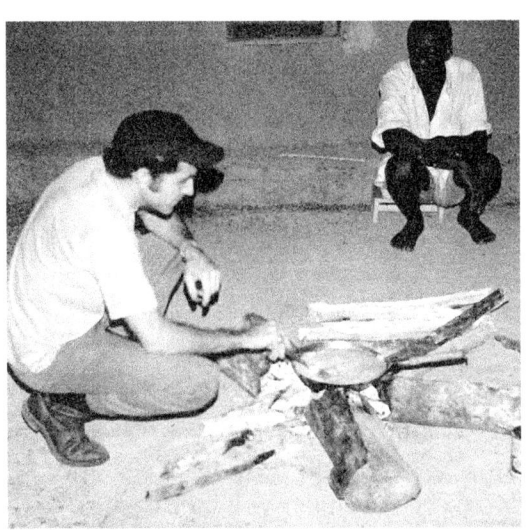

I placed the garlic I got from the Chief's wife in the pan I'd planned to use for the chicken. The plan was to roast the garlic. I wasn't sure exactly how you did this, but I'd seen it in restaurants. I'd also seen little wedges of lemon served with grilled chicken. I saw something that I hoped would turn out to be a lemon and got one of the children to bring one to me. While grilling the chicken and boiling the rice, I spotted several papaya plants growing around the village. I pointed to one and soon little children were bringing several to me...all vying for my attention hoping I would choose theirs and reward them. I picked what I hoped would be a nice one and handed out a few more makuta. I negotiated for a banana to be thrown in with the winning papaya. I was starting to believe I could enjoy this meal, or at the very least, find it palatable. Cooking anything was new to me. My only cooking ever was on camping trips while growing up.

I was surprised how well this operation actually turned out. I used my hunting knife to slice off small pieces of the meat. It did have a bit of a rubbery consistency, but I nevertheless found it enjoyable. I heavily salted the chicken and gave it a generous dose of pepper as well. The lemon looking fruit did in fact turn out to be a lemon or one of its cousins. It had a knobby look but that was OK. I squeezed the juice on the chicken. The roasted garlic was served on the side with the rice. The fact that I was hungry probably influenced my assessment a bit. But considering Karen or John hadn't had a hand in the meal, I was pleased with its outcome...Poulet Français à la Chef Jimmy. Karen would never believe this.

When finished, I took my dishes and headed down to the nearby stream. I washed them with gravel and water. I would hold them over the fire before using them again to kill anything that might possibly still be clinging to the surface. Besides, only God knew what as of yet undiscovered microbes were residing in the stream. I quickly decided this was not a useful line of thought.

Jungle Jim's First Night

Now it was time to turn my attention to sleeping arrangements before it got too dark to see. My hut had a split bamboo elevated platform for use as a bed, table, or community chair. I arranged my bedroll on it. I placed the machete and my flashlight just beside where I would put my head. I placed my bags underneath the sleeping platform and just under where my head would be. My feet were nearest to the door and my head furthest from it. If someone was going to try to steal some of my stuff during the night, they were going to have to get in the hut with me and the machete. I went back outside to enjoy the village social scene before turning in for the night.

Once back outside I found the most popular venue was sitting around a central fire. I noticed many of the huts still had a cooking fire going. Most were waiting for me to come back out so they could learn more about who I was and where I had come from. I had hoped to get a quick bath in the stream before going to bed but I could now see that would have been rude. I took a seat which allowed me to watch the door of my hut. The chief and possibly a handful of others spoke Lingala, but most were speaking something I didn't understand. Phil had already mentioned that within this geographical area many different but often related languages could be found. So I more or less gave up on finding out what it was they were speaking. I was able to use my Lingala with the some of the elders. Just about the entire village gathered around. We had a good time asking each other questions. We talked for about an hour then we all headed off to our huts for the night.

Jimmy And The Night Visitors

I had a difficult time getting to sleep. I would occasionally turn on the flashlight and look at the Breitling Navitimer Little Jimmy had given me as a graduation gift from flight school. It was well after 11:00pm and I was still awake. As I lay there trying to sleep I heard a rustling in the dried banana leaves that made up a substantial part of my hut. I could tell it wasn't a snake as this rustling was rapid. I figured it was a rodent of some type. I slowly reached for my flashlight. I turned quietly in the direction of the noise. It stopped for a second but then resumed. I aimed the flashlight in what I could best determine was the direction of the noise and turned it on. In the periphery of the beam of light I saw two tiny golden shiny eyes. By the shape of the head I could tell it was some rodent. I sat up quickly hoping to scare it away without having to get off the bed. It worked, the rodent disappeared. I lay back down and continued trying to go to sleep.

A few minutes later I heard the little bastard again. This time I decided to just stay quiet and maybe he would give up and go away. That proved a failed strategy. He really didn't seem to be trying to go about his foraging in a stealth mode. Not only did he continue to move about looking for something he could eat, I could tell he was getting closer to my bed. He probably smelled some of the food in my bag. It was then I decided I would try to dispatch him with the machete lying beside my head. I slowly moved my hand till I had it. I then waited as the sounds came closer and closer. Trying to judge where exactly the sound was coming from was not easy. Finally, when I could restrain myself no long, I took a ferocious swing. I could hear the blade's zipping sound as it sliced through the air. The blade buried deep in the dirt floor. I quickly turned on the flashlight hoping to find my little uninvited nocturnal cohabitant in a bisected state. But it turned out this was his lucky night. I put the machete back up by my head, turned off the flashlight and tried to go back to sleep. Sleep did finally come but not before the little assassination exercise repeated itself once more. Hours later I was gradually awakened by the crowing of what seemed to be a disproportionately large number of village roosters. These foul fowls were soon joined by the hushed voices of women beginning their morning choirs (although it was still dark and, in my mind, nowhere near morning). The sound of men's voices soon joined the choirs. Further sleep was clearly out of the question. My only option was to get out of bed. But once my feet were on the ground, I began thinking about the countless photo opportunities waiting just outside my door. I was ready to start my day.

About the time I was dealing with my night visitors, five men were caught breaking into the Watergate Hotel Democratic campaign headquarters.

A few days later, AP photographer Nick Ut took his Pulitzer Prize-winning photograph of 9 year old Phan Thị Kim Phúc, fleeing naked down a road trying to escape a napalm attack by the South Vietnamese Air Force. The pilot mistook them for Viet Cong. The following day the picture ran on the front page of the New York Times.

The Watergate break-in news story I rated as worth following. For the photo that went around the world...I didn't give it a second thought until I was in Cambodia in the midst of the war five months later. Then I understood it all too well.

My Pilgrimage To The Cleansing Stream

I took out clean underwear, socks, and a tee-shirt. I grabbed the little bag that contained my toothbrush, tooth paste, and razor, put on my boots, and headed toward the stream I had hoped to visit last night. By this time the sun was starting to shine through the trees. It looked like half the village was already there. Some were washing pots and dishes, some washing clothes, and some were washing themselves. But for sure, when I arrived, the focus was on me. None had ever seen a white guy (*mondele*) take a bath before.

After I brushed my teeth, I decided it was time to make their day. I carefully removed my clothes insuring they did not get muddy. I took my bar of soap and headed out into the water, being careful to go no more than knee deep. I feared crocodiles could easily be in the deeper water. This apparently was a commonly held fear as nobody was out in the middle. Nobody went any further than knee deep. But even this was no guarantee of safety. I learned soon after arriving in the country that most Congolese killed by the crocks were killed by one hiding in the grass beside the water's edge . . . not one in the water. When their victim got between them and the water, they would race toward the victim at amazing speeds, grab them and drag them out into the deeper water, rolling and pulling them under. Countless Congolese died this way every year. Many were children playing beside the water as their mothers washed clothes.

It seemed that the only ones not snickering or sneaking peaks were the older men. The women and children thought I was the center ring of the circus. Eventually even the older men began to laugh. But they were laughing mostly at the women and children...not so much at me. The water was a pleasant temperature. I quickly washed my hair which felt like it had half the red dirt of yesterday's road trip lodged in it. I soaped and rinsed myself and headed for my clothes. I agilely got into my underwear without getting any of the mud that was on my feet on my underwear. Mastering this move was essential for any young man growing up in Hamilton (who went swimming after school without the permission of his parents). Stock tanks, creeks, and the Leon River banks were muddy. I put on my pants, stood on a rock and washed the mud off my feet again, put on my socks and boots and headed back up the bank toward the camp and breakfast. I doubted any of my many sins had been washed away at the cleansing stream but a hell of a lot of red dirt from yesterday had been.

Our Strategy & Planning Breakfast

For simplicity I decided the night before I would have a breakfast of bananas and papaya. No dishes to wash and no dents in my food supply. I smirked as I wondered what the Paris Hilton would charge for this breakfast. I made it a working breakfast. While eating, the chief and I discussed the logistics of my trip. How many people did I want to go with me, how long did I want to stay, and how much was going to be given to "his" pygmies? The chief and I had already agreed on his payment being ten Zaire the previous afternoon. I told the chief three pygmies would be all I needed and offered them one Zaire each. This would allow the Chief to keep his position of authority. The pygmies asked for two Zaire each, but we agreed on one and a half. A young Bantu would be coming along as well to translate from Lingala into the language of the Mbuti. He would be paid two Zaire. He had accompanied the Mbuti to some of their hunting camps previously. Apparently, this was one Bantu who did not fear the forest. Everybody was happy. The pygmies were excited and ready to get going. I still needed to repack my bags. It was time for me to get moving.

Journey Into The Unknown

Packing my gear only took a couple of minutes. I paused for a quick moment and prayed for protection. In many ways, life itself is a journey through the unknown. We have no assurance of our next breath. However, generally speaking, the vast majority of our life is spent in spheres of relative predictability and familiarity. That being the case, it is still possible to willfully direct your course into areas with higher degrees of unpredictable outcomes and unfamiliar surroundings. I was about to willfully enter one of those areas. I was learning to crave the adrenalin found while in these situations of diminished outcome control and unfamiliarity. Such would be the case when I crossed the red dirt road called National Highway 4 and entered the southern boundaries of The Ituri Forest. I rejoined the group in front of the chief's hut.

We crossed the road and headed north into the forest. I had determined while still in the planning stage back in Kinshasa, that if for any reason I had to get back on my own, all I really needed to do was note which way we left the village. The road ran east and west. If I headed into the forest in a southerly direction from the road, all I would have to do is keep walking north. At some point I would eventually hit the road. From then note the kilometer marker and start walking toward the marker closest to the village which in this case was marker 157. Since we were headed north this morning, all I had to do was walk south till I hit the road. Of course that was a gross oversimplification. There could be rivers and streams to cross which could be deep. There could easily be wild animals and poisonous snakes. While I had a lot of outdoor experience, most of it had not prepared me for this. But I knew all that before I committed to the adventure. The immediate goal now would be always to concentrate on the task at hand and to keep the big picture in focus. I realized I was getting a mild case of the butterflies. I vowed I would keep focused and enjoy this incredible experience.

An Unsolved Mystery

About an hour into the trek I started to notice that the lead man would snap off a tiny branch or leaf and lay it on the ground whenever we came to a fork in the trail. He was clearly laying it in such a way as to indicate which path we took to anyone (or someone) coming behind us. This unnerved me. My mind started rapidly processing scenarios. Who would be coming behind us? Why? Did they mean harm? What could I do to mitigate any dangerous intentions? I did not like the results of my calculations. I was outnumbered, we all had machetes; they even had poison tipped arrows. If any situation led to a physical confrontation, I was certain to lose. Yet their demeanor was not only happy, they were laughing and joking and clearly enjoying themselves. I forced myself to more or less abandon that line of thought. Years later, when considering this mystery, I added an additional scenario…perhaps they were leaving directions for spirits. I'll never know.

We moved along more or less well used paths. The paths were not straight but rather seemed to wind along avoiding difficult areas which would require climbing or excessive hacking with the machetes. As streams were encountered, they had used cut down trees to make little narrow footbridges. Most of the streams we came to were small.

The deeper we went into the forest, the more textbook the rainforest became. Undergrowth was thinning and the canopy was getting taller. While there was plenty of light, it was almost all indirect. It was cool and pleasant. They always kept an eye out for a meal as they walked along. Their poison tipped arrows were never far from hand as they constantly scanned the tree tops and the ground for signs of a meal. They carried little knap-sack bags over their shoulder. These bags appeared to be made from the skin of some animal. Occasionally they would stop and scratch around in the soil. I would learn later that this was usually the work of pygmy women. The men were usually hunters, but these guys did not appear to let so called gender rolls get between them and a meal. At one point along the trail they found some small animal droppings. They quickly abandoned their guide duties and tried to follow the footprints (tiny hoofs) as the droppings appeared to be fresh. For whatever reason, they were unable to locate the small pig or antelope and we resumed our trek down the jungle path.

The Hunting Camp

After about an hour and a half one of the men left the group and started trotting up the trail ahead of us. I was told he was going to announce our arrival. I wasn't expecting any problems, but I considered this a wise move. About fifteen minutes later we arrived at a large clearing with six huts made from sticks and leaves. They were not particularly close together nor did they appear to be in any recognizable order. The entire village rapidly assembled. I was the first white person many had seen up-close. Many wanted to touch my arms. I put down my gear and greeted my new hosts.

Little Laundry To Do Here

Their dress was pretty much as the book and other pictures had portrayed. The men wore only a tiny loin cloth made from some kind of hammered tree bark. The women were topless and wore only a small bark loincloth as well.

My New Digs

Soon I was shown to an empty hut. Like in the Bantu village, I found an empty hut hard to understand. From my studies however I learned that from time to time a family would leave one hunting group and join another. This could have been the case here. Like back in the Bantu village, this hut needed a few minor repairs and soon villagers returned from the forest with the branches and leaves to facilitate the needed reparations.

A Large Rat With Hooves

I stowed my gear inside my new abode and began walking around talking to the villagers and taking pictures. They were both curious and friendly. The women settled back around the fire preparing some kind of plant they planned to eat later on. I saw a small animal roasting on the fire. I recognized the animal from pictures I'd seen as a miniature antelope. They reminded me of a large rat more than an antelope except they had hooves.

The Village *Casino*

Most of the adult men were huddled around a game they were playing. Small stones were being pitched on the ground. It was not only a game of chance, but a bit of friendly wagering seemed to be transpiring as well. The men were drinking what I learned later was palm wine from small gourds and coconut shells. I was offered a sip which I felt obligated to accept. My first mistake was to take a sniff before taking the taste. The predominant scent was of something rotten accompanied by the biting stinging odor of alcohol and acidity in my nostrils. I then realized I was past the point of no return. I swallowed hard. It thankfully did not come back up, but the inside of my mouth was now impregnated with this horrid, rotten taste. I went inside my hut and opened my water canteen. My mouth felt so contaminated I refused to put the canteen to my lips but opened my mouth wide and poured the water in my mouth. I then rinsed my mouth as vigorously as possible. I repeated this procedure several times, and while it lessened the effect, some relentlessly clung on. I wondered if my social sensitivity was worth this rancid residue which at that time seemed permanent. Praise God it finally went away. I rejoined the men at the casino.

Women Returning From Their *"Grocery Shopping"*

As I was heading back toward the men's gathering at the village casino, a group of women was returning from the forest. They were carrying baskets containing roots, berries, and other plants. Since the pygmies were hunter-gatherers, I knew these had been gathered in the forest and not in some nearby garden plot. They were carrying medium sized knives obviously used in digging or cutting the plants. They continued through the village and started down a gentle slope. I followed them at a distance. There was a decent sized stream about 50 meters from the edge of the village. I watched as they went to the water's edge and began washing the plants. I joined them and took a few pictures then returned to join the men as they enjoyed themselves, apparently indifferent to the fact that the women were doing all the work.

The Mother Of All Bongs (MOAB)

When I returned from watching the women at the stream, the men had tired of their game and were preparing to have a little communal smoke. One of the men returned with a pipe made from a long hollowed out cane or large

vine. He packed it with what I at first thought might be locally grown tobacco. Later I realized it was more of the locally grown magic herb. I was looking at the mother of all bongs. This thing had to be at least five feet long. After stuffing the pipe's bowl with the indigenous ingredient, he took a coal from the fire using two small twigs much like one would use a pair of chopsticks; expertly passed the coal over the top of the bowl, while one of the others puffed away to insure self-sustaining combustion had been achieved. The same pungent aroma that I'd experienced that ill-fated night when I carried out my failed ivory pipe experiment was immediately present. I remember thinking that certainly their hunting quota for the day had already been met. They had smitten their brains with that retched palm wine, and now a double dose of mistreatment, the medicine man's magical weed was about to begin its assault. I wondered how any remnant of rational could remain. Soon the smoking congregation was filled with red-eyed, toothless, smiling, and very happy pygmy men. They passed the pipe around the circle in which I found myself included until the bowl was empty. Then some headed toward their huts, some talked, and others dozed away the rest of the afternoon. As I sat watching and occasionally taking a picture, I wondered if they even understood the concept of stress. They had no mortgage payments, no medical bills, no car payments, no college tuitions to worry about. They had no war; no word for war. I could be amid a people in some ways far more advanced than any culture I'd ever experienced. I wrote countless pages in my little red book. My head was filled with images and admiration for these little people of the forest. Finally I too could no longer hold my head upright. I dozed off into the blissful place where the others had gone.

When I awoke the sun's shadows had grown longer. I wondered if some small seeds of contentment had begun to fall on the rocky soil of my mind. If so, I knew these precious seeds would require many favorable growing seasons before any appreciable change germinated…a root that might take hold and someday allow me to be content with my circumstances and subvert my evil twin. Could I learn from these primitive hunter-gatherers? Could they show me how to enjoy living without always having my tachometer pegged out on the red line? That was an interesting thought. I continued writing furiously in my red notebook for some time.

Another Cleansing Stream Experience

I wanted to clean up before dark. I had already planned that my meal tonight would be from the stock I'd brought. I could do that without the light of the sun. However going to the stream in the dark was not something I thought would be a very good idea. I got up and went to my hut and dug out my soap, a fresh underwear and socks and t-shirt and headed toward the stream. I knew the next morning at the stream would be my washing day. Taking care of my dirty clothes.

When I got to the stream, I saw a couple of pygmy women spear fishing in the shallows. I watched them as I made my way to a gravel shoal where I'd planned to have my evening bath. As I started to undress, I heard the sounds of laughter from up on the bank behind me. When I turned to see the source, it appeared half the village was standing up there laughing and joking. Oh well…it was always nice to be appreciated I thought. I'd hate to have one of those little guys mad at me. I read about how long the victim of one of their poison arrows had to live after it nicked you. I looked up at them and grinned. The group immediately exploded in collective laughter. Oh well again…I needed to take a bath and wash my hair. If it was going to be with an audience of pygmies, then it was what it was. I found a dry spot on the gravel bank where my clothes would not get dirty. I put my clean clothes down and then got out of my dirty ones. Like the day before, I took my bar of soap and headed into knee deep water.

The stream was moving gently and the bank and a nice moderate slope. I realized the pygmies probably selected this particular location for their hunting camp because of the favorable characteristics of the streams bank. Additionally, the stream was wide enough here that the sun could easily shine directly through the rainforest canopy. It was as beautiful as any Texas Hill Country Stream I'd ever seen. For a moment I forgot about my washing and the cast of thousands watching from the bank. This was a beautiful place in time.

Evening Meal And Story Telling

After I finished my evening bath, I started getting my meal ready. I planned to get into the provisions I brought from Kinshasa this time. I had waited too late to try and cook my rice so I decided I would try my luck with some of the macaroni. I mooched a spot on one of the women's cooking fires and used some water I got back at the stream. I made sure it was boiling before I added my dried macaroni. When the macaroni looked about ready, I opened one of the small cans of spam and cut it up into bite-size pieces and dumped them into the pot with the macaroni. I added pepper and a bit of salt and I was ready. It would have been better with a spattering of tangy cheese of some kind but still, all in all, it wasn't that bad.

The pygmies had apparently never seen macaroni. By the time I'd finished satisfying their curiosity I'd lost almost half of my meal. The first one to take a bite was a bit cautious but caution soon disappeared and I had to stop the samples, or I would have gone to bed hungry.

They were all chattering away and wanted to learn about me. I could now easily understand how story telling was such a big part of their lives. There was no other entertainment; no radios, no TV, nothing but themselves. I wondered if our society, the generation of my great, great grandfather, Larkin Harrison Jacks had incorporated many of these aspects. Living in the middle of a pine forest in an old board house beside a red dirt road near Star City Arkansas, they too had no electricity, no running water, and no indoor bathroom. They had no TV and no radio. The more I thought about it the more I decided there could have been great similarities.

My Not-So-Bright Bright Idea

As I looked around the campfire at all the smiling pygmy faces, I realized I was experiencing an iconic moment; the perfect photo opportunity. I had trained the Bantu who came with me to look through the viewfinder and push the shutter button on the Nikon. He could do it again.

I went into my hut and got out my camera and my external flash unit. I hooked everything up and went outside to take some pictures. I'd been taking pictures all day, so they were more or less accustomed to the camera. As I approached the group, they were all watching me so I figured this would be a good time to get a great natural looking shot. I focused my 50mm lens and fired. The flash responded as anticipated; the pygmies did not. They jumped up, some of the women screamed, the men shouted, and they disappeared into the surrounding forest faster than cockroaches when you turn on the light. I was alone in the camp.

Several seconds later (it seemed like an eternity) the Bantu slowly and cautiously returned to the camp. I stood in the same spot fidgeting with my camera. The Bantu explained I had seriously frightened them. As best as I could tell, he was saying they thought the flash might have been some kind of powerful god or something. He was using words I did not know the meaning of, but I could tell they had to do with spirits. The pygmy men began slowly returning, the women remained at the edge of the clearing. The men were grumbling. The Bantu told me I had to put the flash up and promise never to bring it out again. I immediately agreed. As a matter of fact, I decided not to push my luck with any more photos that night. I went to my hut and returned without the camera. I apologized to the men and we all sat back down. The women returned to the campfire leading or carrying the children. Slowly the atmosphere returned to normal.

They were filled with questions about my life back in Texas. Because of the road, they knew about big trucks, jeeps, and Land Rovers. I wanted to tell them about television, radio, and movies but I found my Lingala and the level of experience of the Bantu far too limited to even attempt it. I told them about my house, my father, my wife and children; I even told them that I had a dog in Kinshasa and one back in Texas. I told them about telephones. The Bantu had seen a telephone in Kisangani when he went there once so that worked out pretty well. They were fascinated that a human voice could go down a wire. I wished I could have understood what they were saying as each argued his theory of how a voice could travel down something resembling a metal vine. Their explanations were filled with gestures. It would have made this moment even more priceless if only I could have fully understood everything they were saying. After each was finished, they would all laugh.

As the stories and laughter continued, the men once again brought out the long pipe. Once properly lit, it was passed around and all the men took a puff or two. I found I was getting better at not coughing as my turn came around. I laughed to myself as I visualized trying to explain this moment to anybody back home in Hamilton. I concluded that there were probably some things that would be better left unshared. This communal pipe moment would almost certainly be one of them.

More Night Visitors

Gradually storytelling gave way to sleep as one by one the men and their families headed off to their huts. I too was ready for sleep. For my bed, they had fashioned a device similar to the platform I used in the Bantu village. I put my bedroll down on it, slept in my clothes, and quickly fell asleep. During the night I recalled hearing more rustling in my hut but this time, once again recognizing it was not the slithering sound of a snake, decided they probably wouldn't eat all that much. I thought "have a good time…knock yourselves out…I'm going back to sleep." I had stored the rice and macaroni in my metal pot and wedged the skillet on top as a lid.

Washing Away My "Sins" From The Previous Night As Well As My Dirty Clothes

I must have taken my own advice as I didn't recall hearing my little night visitors again that night. When I awoke the sun's light was already coming through the open door of my hut. I could hear the camp starting to come to life. Apparently the pygmies were later sleepers than were the Bantu. I sat up and looked around my hut in a poorly motivated attempt to determine how much my little uninvited critters had eaten. It seemed the containment technique I'd employed to keep my dried food protected had proven successful; it was all there.

I gathered my tooth brush, my razor, my soap and some cheap shaving cream, my clean clothes for today and my dirty clothes and headed for the stream. After brushing my teeth I began trying to shave. Now, for the life of me, I can't now imagine why I thought about shaving. Like who was going to see me? I was miles from anywhere. As I was in the stream shaving, a verse from Leviticus came to mind: "The one who is to be cleansed must wash his clothes, shave off all his hair, and bathe with water; he is clean. Afterward he may enter the camp."[166] I was sure I was completely demented. Why on earth would such an obscure passage from the Bible come to mind? Especially out here in the middle of the jungle. Maybe my MOAB experiences the day before had made me "unclean." Probably it was my evil twin again. I finished scraping my face with the cheap Gillette razor and started washing my clothes with the bar soap I'd just bathed with. Again as I looked up on the bank I found my "Jungle Jim Fan Club" all giggling and pointing. I finished washing myself and my clothes, got dressed and headed back up the slope and into the camp. I spread my clothes out to dry on the sides and top of my hut.

A Light Breakfast

The pygmies' hunting camp did not contain all the array of fresh fruit the Bantu village had. The Bantu cultivated these things. The pygmies just gath-

---

[166] Holy Bible—Holman Christian Standard - Leviticus 14:8

ered what they could find growing in the rainforest. The rainforest, by its very nature, was deprived of sunlight and did not encourage planting many crops. So my morning meal was a bit on the "continental breakfast" side rather than a hearty Texas-style breakfast. I cut up and ate the small papaya I'd stuffed (literally) into my bag before leaving the Bantu village. I chased it down with a mix of stream water and purification tablets. Here it wasn't 9:00 am and I was already looking forward to supper that night. As far as food goes, this was going to be a long day.

A Place Without Time

While I was looking down at my Breitling Navitimer wrist watch, I realized I was looking at the only timepiece in the hunting camp. If I forgot to wind it one day, there would be no indication of time other than the sun's relative position. The more I thought about this the more I became convinced that I'd never in my life been in a situation like that. It was a sobering thought. I promised myself that I'd rethink the matter later over a cold beer and a sunset back at Bat's house.

The Village Goes Hunting (All Together)

The night before, the Bantu told me the pygmies had planned a group hunt for this morning. I'd read about it and now I was going to get to take part. In this activity, the women and even adolescent children are involved. The men coil long nets made from twisted tree bark on their shoulders and move through the forest spreading it much like a fisherman would do. The women and children then advance beating on pots and making lots of noise in an attempt to drive any wild animals, especially the prized miniature antelope into the net. The men wait behind the net with spears and knives or possibly a bow and arrow. When the animal encounters the net the men pounce with whatever means available.

Before long, the men started emerging with their coils of netting. I could feel the energy in the camp pick up. Everyone was in a festive mood. I was pretty certain this festive mood was not for my benefit. I was starting to get a feel for these little people of the forest, and this was just part of their nature. The women were bringing pots to bang on. Hopefully this would force their prey into the net.

As we left the hunting camp and made our way into the forest I was once again impressed with the agility they displayed as they made their way through the forest. This time we were not using any trails. I'm not sure how long we walked, and I forgot to make note of the time. It would have been so easy with my Breitling Navitimer. It was by design a chronograph. All I had to do was push a button to zero it and push another button to start the timer running. Oh well.

I suppose that we had probably made our way for a mile or so through the forest when the men found a place they liked and started setting out their nets. They effortlessly spun the minnow-seine looking nets into a funnel like shape. The women started breaking off branches which they would use to beat the bushes to augment the noise from beating on the pans.

When the net had been positioned the noise and bush beating began. I couldn't help but think about our expression "beating around the bush" which had its origins centuries ago in England when hunters attempted to scare birds into the hunter's waiting nets. I'd read scientists believed the pygmies had been in these forests for nearly 30,000 years. I found little reason to believe they weren't doing something similar to this back then.

Soon a small pig looking animal collided with the net. Almost instantly they pounced on it, quickly dispatching the terrified critter with a wooden club. To my surprise, I found I'd already gone through a full roll of 36 exposure film. I had to stop and load. Thankfully, I'd learned many months ago how to do this reload process with a respectable speed. A few minutes later, one of the miniature antelope became entangled. He met the same club to the head fate as the pig.

The men apparently believed this site had yielded up all it was going to today. They began taking up their nets, coiling them over their shoulders as before. It was time to move to another site.

We walked several more minutes and once again set out the nets. Everyone knew the drill. The women beat the bushes; some of the men helped. Everybody was making a loud noise. It reminded me of a New Year celebration. Except in New Year celebrations, usually nobody gets clubbed in the head. One more pig joined the hunt, so to speak. Shortly afterward the men began to coil their nets back up. It was time to return to the village.

Distribution Of Proceeds

Upon our return to the camp, the women began cleaning the day's catch. Nothing was wasted. If it was edible, it was kept. Each family got a share. I'd learned back in the Bantu village that the Mbuti routinely bartered some of their excess meat for vegetables and other things the Bantu grew in their garden plots.

The men had returned to their casino. I joined them and tried to understand the game they were playing. I could tell that they were wagering. Since they had no money and had no use for money, some were using their arrows as currency. I could tell that the making of an arrow was labor intensive. I had read that after obtaining the various plant extracts with which to make the poisons, often they mixed or compounded them. The process left a dark brown gummy deposit on the tip of the arrow. This was what most of the players were using as "chips."

Time For A Toke

As I continued watching the still unfathomable game of chance, one of the men left for a couple of minutes. He returned with a huge home-rolled cigarette. Rather than paper, he had wrapped the "tobacco" in a leaf. He went to the fire, expertly took out a coal, and lit the thing. Immediately the same smell associated with the mega-bong was present. He contently puffed away on it. This time it was not a communal smoke as last night's super-bong had been. Slowly his eyes began to take on a bloodshot hue. I took several more pictures of the gaming and the happy smoker then decided I could do with a little nap as well. I thought perhaps a nap would take my mind off my empty stomach.

A New Approach To "Bow Hunting"

I found some shade and propped up against a tree to watch the village activities. In addition to collectively watching children, the women were sweeping the dust much like the Bantu women had done, making minor repairs to their huts, and readying food for the evening meal. There seemed to be some type of communal mothering of children. I was never sure which child belonged to which mother.

As I continued leisurely watching the camp activity, the man who had been enjoying his hand-rolled joint passed me with bow in hand. He was heading into the forest. However, he was carrying no arrows. His quiver was empty. I quickly called to the Bantu to ask him where the man was going. The reply was…"he was going hunting." I asked, "where are your arrows?" His reply…"the game ate them." Rather than finding this hilarious, I was overcome with the question "why." Why was he going hunting with no possibility of shooting any game? As he disappeared into the forest, my attention returned to the group still wagering arrows and other types of tokens. Like me, they too had seen him leave with only his bow. But unlike me, they were not giving this event one iota of thought. Probably thirty or forty minutes later the man returned…as he had departed…empty handed. I've recalled this same incident countless times over all these many years. The shroud of mystery remains today as it did then. Why on earth did he do it? Why was there no reaction from the group? I keep coming back to the same vague conclusion…there must be something else to this that I did not understand. Amazing!

Trinkets And Other Gifts

"Many seek a ruler's favor, and everyone is a friend of one who gives gifts."[167]

I made sure soon after arriving in the camp that the pygmies knew I'd come with gifts. Until now, I'd kept them out of sight. But I felt this was going to be a good time to present them. They had shared the village, their hunt, had forgiven my blunder with the flash unit, and even their food. It was clear a bribe wasn't necessary. Their generosity had truly touched my heart. I wanted to share the small trinkets and other items I'd brought along…not cunningly as an instrument of persuasion but from the pure joy of seeing their delight. In the planning stages, I'd figured I would need some motivation to get them to accept me and allow me to stay with them. I had been completely wrong. Back in the Bantu village, it was all about what I would or might give them. With these tiny people of the forest, that greed didn't seem to exist.

I went into my hut and carefully sorted out the little earrings and bracelets, rings, chains, and other shiny things that I thought would help win their favor. I brought out everything I had left.

I walked out with the items wrapped in the largest headscarf. I was concerned that there might be some arguments over who got what when I started handing out the items but that didn't happen. I elected to deal with the male elders first. As I presented the items, the women started to laugh and point and shout with excitement when someone was presented with a gift. It was like they were collectively happy for each other. Since they were of the human species, I knew they certainly must be capable of the darker sides of our nature like greed and anger, but I was blessed on this occasion that I did not see it. As I handed out the soap, I realized that while some had seen soap in the Bantu village, they apparently had never come in contact with perfumed soap. They would sniff the soap while still in the wrapper. We did not have a mirror in the village, so the women had to be content imagining what they looked like wearing earrings by seeing them on the other women.

The Last Supper

(with the pygmies)

It was about time for me to take my evening bath and get ready to put together my meal. I gathered up all my dry clothes and took them inside the hut, selected something to wear after my bath, and headed down to the stream.

---

[167] Holman Christian Standard Bible (HCSB) - Proverbs 19:6

By the time I got to the water several of the women were in the water playing with the perfumed soap. They would lather it on themselves but would not wash it off. They kept sniffing the dried soap on their skin. I walked over and tried to show them that if you washed it off the smell would remain, but they would have no part of it. They made it clear that they were going to use it like they wanted to. I decided I'd better stick to washing myself and leave them to their dried soap sniffing.

Soon I noted that a couple of the women bathers had taken up some spears made from straight tree branches which had been split at one end to form multiple prongs. I could see that the prongs had been shaved to a sharp tip. I had seen them using the spears from a distance the previous day but had failed to take good photos of the business end of them. Before long they had speared a fish; then another and another. They weren't huge but probably seven or eight inches long. One would be plenty good grilled over the fire and served with my rice. But what to do…they had almost no use for money and I had nothing left to offer. My stomach had been scratching my backbone since 10:00 am. I approached them and asked if they would spear one for me. The Bantu wasn't around but apparently my sign language sufficed. They presented me with one from the bank. I was probably more grateful for that fish than they had been for their trinkets. I headed back up the slope of the bank and back into the camp. I gutted the fish on a log and used some green branches to construct a grilling device. I got my pot of rice going and eagerly awaited my meal. My evil twin made me wish for a cold Primus or Simba (beer) while sitting there waiting. He's never far from me.

It seemed the rice took forever. I was hungry. This would not have happened in the Bantu village. I just had some type of disconnect with the Mbuti's food. That was probably because there never seemed to be a supply on hand. Almost everything was acquired on a daily basis. They practiced no agriculture so there was no harvest season. No need to store the harvest. When they were hungry, they went out and foraged or hunted. Apparently this system had been working for them for centuries. But since I did not participate in their hunt and the things they were digging up didn't look all that inviting…I'd found myself feeling awkward about eating any of their food.

Finally my rice reached a consistency remotely resembling Karen's. I decided this was no time to be engaging in any search for culinary excellence. I heaped some on my plate, broke up the fish into small pieces, spread it on top of the rice, added salt and pepper and dug in.

When I had finished, I realized I'd cooked more rice than I could eat. I gave the rest to the lady who had provided me with the fish. She didn't get much of it though as she was mobbed by every child old enough to walk. I left the camp and headed down to the stream to wash my dishes before it got dark. I was accompanied by a gaggle of young children. When we reached the stream most decided upon a spontaneous frolic in the water. As I washed my dishes, I pondered the lifestyle of these little forest people I'd been so privileged to spend time with. Probably nobody in the camp would live to see their sixtieth birthday. But heck, none of us held a guarantee on our next breath. So how did these little people of the forest manage to live like there was no tomorrow? Amazing.

The Last Campfire

I pulled myself from my thoughts, watched a few more seconds of the frolics in the stream, then headed up the bank to stow my gear. After putting my stuff away for the night I returned and took a place beside the fire with one of the elders. The abbreviated Congolese dusk seemed to come even more rapidly in the rainforest.

The customary communal firesides stories and chatter, along with the passing of the bong were about to begin. I knew I didn't have much longer to visit, take notes, make diagrams, and snap pictures. I also recognized there would probably be few things in my life that would top this experience. I didn't want to waste a second. I wanted to savour ever sight, every color, every smell, every sound, every emotion. I wanted to carefully inscribe them on some ineffaceable slate in my mind, immune from the depredations of time; somewhere I could revisit and relive each incredible moment.

The stories and the laughter went on for a long time. It was impossible for me to get most of what was being said. I could tell the Bantu was not getting everything either. They didn't seem to be doing any of this for my benefit. This was their life; the life of their ancestors and hopefully the life of their children.

Eventually someone brought out the long bong. Previously I'd wondered if this was some type of focal point or "facilitation device." It clearly was not. I'd describe it as being more like dessert. To say their mood was unaltered would be a bit misleading as some appeared slightly mellower after partaking. Additionally I feel it's safe to say that everyone inhaled. I would later learn primitive cultures all over the world did this. While enjoying the moment and trying hard to understand all I saw, my evil twin again whispered in my ear. My twin could screw up anything. This time he said that it was a good thing pygmies didn't live in the United States or they would all be in jail.

One by one everybody drifted off to their own huts. I couldn't help but chuckle to myself that here nobody had to turn off the lights when they went to bed. This time I was the last to leave the fire. There was so much to think about. For a while I sat there, lost in my own thoughts, watching the retiring flames from the fire cast shadows on the fronts of the huts. When I got up, I noticed I staggered slightly. Sleep came easily that night.

A Lazy Last Breakfast

I vowed there would be no more days with my backbone scratching my stomach. I grabbed my clothes, my tooth brush, and my pot to bring water back in and headed to the stream. I decided the previous day that the gain from shaving wasn't worth the pain. I washed my face, changed my underwear and socks and put on a fresh t-shirt. I washed yesterday's clothes with bar soap, filled up my pot with water and headed back to camp.

Breakfast was going to be macaroni and a can of sardines. As terrible as that might have sounded to a normal person, my situation was hardly normal, and I found myself actually looking forward to the dish. Chef Jimmy's *cuisine de la camp* you might say. I put the pot of water on the cooking fire I had mooched from the same lady as before. I think she was starting to get used to me. When I went to get the can of sardines, I found they were the kind that came in tomato sauce. Happiness! *Sardines avec la sauce tomate*! Things were looking up for Chef Jimmy. With a little preparatory luck my haute cuisine might rival the remnants of those roasted rodents (miniature antelope) from yesterday's hunt. In addition, to boost my confidence even more, some of the women were starting to pay attention to what would soon be my meal. How cool was that! I was gaining a following.

The macaroni was soon ready. I broke the sardines up into small bite size pieces and spread them on the macaroni; sprinkled liberally with salt and pepper. Voilà!! No kidding…it was good. I have to be perfectly honest, if someone had served me this in a restaurant, I probably would have sent it back. But considering I had minus zero cooking acumen, was in the middle of a Congolese rainforest, and was hungry as hell, this was just fine. I was proud of myself.

I Became A Marked Man

After breakfast and another trip to the stream to wash my dishes, I settled into a shady spot with camera in hand and prepared to spend the morning taking pictures. I had noticed the women working with some grayish-white looking paste over by one of the huts. Before I could get up to take a few pictures, one of the young women came up and took me by the arm and started pulling me toward the women's project. They motioned for me to sit down. Almost immediately most of the men and seeming all the children started crowding around. One of the women began drawing broad grayish-white designs on another girl in the group. At the same time, the grandmother of the group motioned for me to remove my shirt. It was becoming increasingly clear I was soon to be the "canvas" for a collective painting project. They were all giggling. The women had created broad stroked paint brushes by pounding the ends of stems between rocks. They were soon all busily dipping their brushes into the paint and painting each other…and me. They appeared to like circles, crosses, and rings. All the women were topless (as they were most of the time) and were being painted literally from head to toe. When they started to paint my face and chest, the men got involved, pointing and offering design inputs. Although I could not understand them it was pretty clear from the intonations and gestures that the men were being told to go smoke their bong. Before it was all done, just about everyone in the village was covered with designs, including me. But the younger ones, both boys and girls seemed to have the most elaborate designs. I got the Bantu to take a couple of pictures of me being painted. Several months later, back at the Kodak Labs by Dallas Love Field, I would see the results. I was in the picture. It was too bad I didn't have another camera he could use to take pictures of me taking pictures while simultaneously being painted.

A Messenger Arrives

Shortly after the group painting exercise, a pygmy messenger arrived from back at the Bantu village. Soon the Bantu was translating to me that the chief of his village had planned a special ceremony including much traditional dancing. It would be good for me to photograph.

My tactless response, pretty typical for that period in my life, was that I was happy right where I was and that I had not come all this way to take pictures of Bantus living in a village beside a road. I could have done that five kilometers outside of Kisangani. The Bantu nervously explained that the chief had gone to a lot of trouble to arrange this and I must attend.

I was not happy. As a matter of fact, I could already see dollar signs all over this "invitation." The chief knew the pygmies were probably getting lots of loot and that I probably had more. By staging a dance or whatever, he would be opening the opportunity for getting deeper into my pockets.

I had not seen any monetary motivation from the Mbuti. They had a simple childlike charm. To me, the Bantu were the embodiment of everything I detested about the Congo. If I had not had the Bantu with me in the hunting camp, I would have asked the pygmies to lead me back to the road in another day or two. I would then turn west and flag down a ride in a truck to Kisangani, completely bypassing the Bantu village. Flagging down a truck was how I was going to have to get home anyway.

I left the group and walked down to the stream. I wanted to assess my options; evaluate my plusses and my minuses. I realized this was no place to indulge my evil twin by reacting to a situation based on my emotions. It had to be all about which course would produce the most gains with the least amount of losses.

First, I had to realize the Mbuti would not feel slighted if I returned with the Bantu. A couple of them would come along back to the Bantu village as they were staying in that village at the time anyway. As far as I could tell, they were not expecting any more gifts from me.

On the other hand, probably the Bantu chief did have some photo opportunities staged that could prove worthwhile. Without doubt these opportunities were going to cost me some money. I considered the fact that I would be leaving the Congo permanently in a couple of months. I would never have these opportunities again. I could leave with only the pygmies or I could get a Bantu village and the pygmies. Or I could have more pygmy shots.

Farewell To The Mbuti

Putting my emotions behind me, I concluded it was time to say goodbye to the little people of the forest I'd become so fond of and return to the Bantu village. I walked up the slope and back into the center of the hunting camp. The Bantu was nervously awaiting my reply. I said nothing but knelt and crawled in my hut. As I assembled my gear, I looked down at my tee-shirt. I knew I should wear it when we walked (for me often stooping or crouching) through the rain forest. But I decided I would leave the camp and say my goodbyes to my new friends proudly displaying their signatures attesting to my acceptance. I tied the shirt around my waist.

The Mbuti had already concluded I was leaving them. A couple stood ready to leave and help carry my bags. By this time I totally trusted them. I only carried my cameras on my back. I opened my bag and took out my pot and pan. I gave them to the lady who always made room for me as I mooched space over her fire. I gave her all my rice. She reached out and grabbed me. She gave me a hug. One of the younger girls asked if she could have my hunting knife that I wore on my belt. She had been eying it since the first day. I felt terrible but I had to tell her no. Immediately a course of shouts went out teasing the girl about not having been able to get me to turn loose of my knife.

I approached the elders and expressed my sincere thanks in Lingala which was translated by the Bantu. I placed my hand over my heart in the only attempt I could think of to express my gratitude. Their voices rose in excitement and smiles. I turned and we walked away. The men followed for a few meters inside the forest. Possibly some custom of politeness…I didn't know. When I looked back again, they were gone, and the clearing was now out of sight. I figured in a couple of hours at the most we would be back in the

Bantu village beside the road. While I physically left their hunting camp, they never left me.

Mbuti Epilog

In 1972, I was the first white man these Mbuti had ever seen up close. Few people knew anything about them. Their way of life remained undisturbed, protected by the mighty Ituri Forest.

All this has changed since I left the Congo. Beginning shortly after I left in 1972 the country's downward spiral accelerated. In 1996 the conflict in the eastern Congo provinces led to the overthrow of the Mobutu government ending years of chaos. However the resulting breakdown in what little law and order that might have existed under Mobutu's despotic and corrupt rule allowed tribal hostilities to accelerate unrestrained. According to U.S. State Department reports[168] and reports by the United Nations, pygmies were singled out for murder, rape, forced labor, victims of cannibalism, and forced relocation.[169] [170] Significant numbers of pygmies were killed. The rainforest which has been their home for tens of thousands of years is now rapidly being deforested by illegal logging and by mining. The few remaining pygmies often are forced to live in special areas set up for displaced people.

One possibly bright development appears to be that a fledgling tourism industry has sprung up around the few remaining pygmy concentrations.[171] Organized tours now take people to see them in their relatively easily accessible new living areas. From many reports, they have almost been reduced to putting on shows in their new villages to entertain the tourists. Much like a zoo. For this, they receive some small compensations.

Even if the recent atrocities don't return, the Mbuti face new dangers. Their way of live is threatened. They are threatened in direct relationship to their disappearing rainforest. Their culture also directly linked to the rainforest could make them soon extinct; reduced to genetically growth-stunted people living in the cities and towns of the Congo. Here they will certainly continue to face discrimination because of their stature and wrongly perceived inferior intelligence.

The world community can express concern for endangered species. In the United States, entire construction projects can be stopped due to the presence of a species of toad labeled as endangered; freeway construction stopped due to the discovery of endangered spiders; development projects halted when endangered mice were discovered. The European Union (EU) has all-encompassing compilations of legislation protecting endangered species, be it plant or animal. But, with the exception of some muffled outcries from the United

---

[168] 2010 Human Rights Report: Democratic Republic of the Congo
[169] United Nations News Center—21 May 2003
[170] Home Office - UK Border Agency—DRC - 30 June 2009
[171] Okapi Tour and Travel Company—Goma—D.R. Congo

Nations and a handful of NGOs, the annihilation of the endangered Mbuti continues; if not unnoticed, then certainly without meaningful response. Pray for these gentle little people of the forest. "If Only"

Back In The Bantu Village . . . A *Cutting-Edge* Experience

"That's Gotta Hurt"

I knew we were getting close to the village. I heard the sound of a truck passing along the road. Soon, I started to see the brightness of the sun's unfiltered rays ahead of me. We were nearing the cultivated areas where the Bantu had cleared the forest to make room for their garden plots.

As we reached the village, there was much activity. The chief greeted me as we walked into the central area of the village. He explained that the village had decided to schedule a celebration to coincide with my visit. The focal point of the event was the circumcision of several of the village's adolescent males. This was their rite of passage from childhood to manhood. I'd read about and even seen some pictures of these ceremonies but now I would be able to observe it almost first hand.

I also suspected the real focal point was me and how much money they could extract from me by electing to put on this ceremony while I was in their village.

The ceremony was more than just passing from adolescence to manhood; it was an initiation in the brotherhood of Bantu warriors. A fringe benefit was marriage and being considered a man.

Soon after I arrived, the women started dancing. The young initiates probably averaging ten or eleven years of age, were escorted by older men (probably their fathers) to a specially designated hut on the outskirts of the village. They were painted with a white clay paste resembling what the Mbuti had used on me. They wore short grass skirts. They were clearly terrified. A couple of them were physically trembling.

An older man, referred to as "the operator" walked into the hut carrying a wooden handled butcher knife. The chief told me I was not allowed to go in the hut. I thought he really didn't need to tell me that. I was as close to this as I wanted to be. I was snapping photos at a rapid pace. The first young man went into the hut escorted by presumably his father and a couple of other elders. I was assuming they were there to hold the poor little guy down if necessary. The music got louder. I supposed this was to help mask any cries. A few seconds later I heard a muffled cry. A couple of minutes later he emerged from the hut supported by his father. There was bright red blood on both his thighs. He was wearing a device which appeared to be serving as an emergency loin cloth made from what appeared to be banana leaves. The leaves look as if they contained some form of medicine. I spotted blood on his father as well. While the young initiate was weak and needed to be supported, he somehow managed to walk. He was immediately welcomed by shouts from the group. His demeanor, in spite of the trauma he'd just experienced, revealed pride. He knew the village was celebrating his entry into the brotherhood of warriors. My evil twin whispered that was probably the best thought he could be thinking and suggested other less jubilant ones.

The next initiate was led into the hut and a couple of minutes he emerged in like manner as the first. The process repeated itself until all had passed through the initiation process.

When all the candidates had completed the process, they stood together before the village. The women began dancing and the older men shouted support.

After a few minutes of dancing and celebration, the initiates were led away into the jungle. I was told that they would remain in another specially constructed hut where they would receive sacred instruction on the rites and rituals of Bantu manhood. This would continue until they were healed. I had read that the eligible young women from the village would bring food to them during their period of healing and instruction. Some later studies indicated a special bonding took place during their time in this lodge of instruction. The bonds of brotherhood were exceptionally strong for those going through this rite together.

Blood Money

It was still early afternoon and I figured if I could hitch a ride on one of the numerous trucks heading toward Kisangani, I could arrive just about dark. I walked to where my belongings were piled and started to put away my cameras. The chief was watching me intently. I motioned for him to come join me. I knew I had to get this part of the deal over with, so I figured the best way to handle it was directly.

When I was out among the Congolese, I always kept my money in two parts. One in my right-hand front pocket and more in my left. The right pocket was my stash. The left was for show. I reached into my left pocket and pulled out about fifty dollars in the local Zaire currency. I handed it to the chief and expressed my gratitude for his having allowed me to watch this celebration.

The chief's immediate reaction was a loathing scoff. It was at this point that I realized I could have a serious problem on my hands. I tried to reason with him, but he was not in a reasoning state of mind. I then told him OK he could have everything I had in my pocket except five dollars in Zaire that I would need to pay the truck driver. That would make his take for the event about eighty dollars. I never lost sight of the fact that I had my stash but at this point I was starting to get a dog in the fight. He told me he had promised the other families that I would pay good money to photograph this. I told him that the ceremony was very impressive, but I never paid this kind of money to take pictures of anybody. His face was starting to show some real anger.

I did not like where this was going. I could easily find a spear in my back if I were not careful. I had packed my little 22 auto Beretta, but its magazine only held 7 rounds plus one in the chamber. While I had packed it in my bag, I wasn't "packing" it. The old expression never bring a knife to a gun fight suddenly took on a converse meaning. Never bring a 22 auto Beretta to a machete and spear fight held in the heart of a Bantu village. Somehow, I was going to have to talk my way out of this or give the scheming SOB my stash as well.

I finished my packing and slowly reached into my wallet. I took out my "get out of jail card" with General Bobozo's signature boldly on the front. I took everything but my five-dollar truck ride fee and handed it to him. My soft demeanor instantly changed. I coldly told him I worked for the Force Aérienne Congolaise and if he gave me any more problem, I would have General Boboza send troops to his village and they would take him to prison. While I did work for the Force Aérienne Congolaise, I'd met General Bobozo only a couple of times and was sure he would not even remember my name. But my bluff worked. They were terrified of the army due to their frequent atrocities. I stood, returned my card to my wallet, picked up my bags and turned my back on him and started walking. I headed east down the road. I could hear him shouting but the further away the sound of his voice became the more confidence I gained that I might be getting out of this mess.

Fortunately for me, a big Mercedes diesel truck came down the road just at the right moment. I flagged him down. He had cargo piled higher than the sides. I asked him how much to take me to Kisangani. He was a Ugandan and spoke English. He said ten dollars. I countered with five. He opened the door and I jumped in. I piled my gear on the floor under my feet, handed him his money and we were west bound toward Kisangani. I asked him what time we would arrive. Before dark was his answer. Words can hardly express how fortunate I felt to get out of that village without any serious confrontation. All the odds were on the chief's side. I didn't even want to consider what would have happened if my little bluff had failed to work. I did chuckle as I visualized his having to explain to the people in his village when he hadn't gotten the riches from me that he'd promised. The truck driver probably wondered why I was suddenly sporting such a wide grin.

The ride back to Kisangani seemed to go by quickly. I couldn't get the images of the past few days out of my mind. The amazing group of pygmies I'd been so blessed to share time with…those poor little Bantu guys getting circumcised with a butcher knife…the images are as clear today as they were back then.

Without question, my time with the Mbuti was a life-altering experience. To my knowledge, they had no written language…no written record of their history…only stories passed down beside campfires at night. They knew nothing of life outside their forest apart from little glimpses that passed along the red dirt road that left its ugly scar on their ancestral hunting grounds. I had a university education, graduated from a prestigious school of aviation and had seen other parts of the world. Yet, I was certain I learned far more from them than they had learned from me. The Mbuti were a critical part of the genesis of the value system examination I could already feel starting to take place.

While I was bouncing along the road to Kisangani, lost in the memories of my last few days, U.S. President Richard Nixon told his Chief of Staff, H. R. Haldeman, that the FBI should be told to stop further investigation of the Watergate burglary. The conversation was recorded. The recording would later become known as "the smoking gun tape."

After my first decent meal in several days at the casino just down the street from George's house I went to sleep in a real bed. I dreamed of pygmies and bloody butcher knives.

About 2:00 pm the following afternoon, I climbed on a FAC C-54 and headed back to Kinshasa. We arrived just at dark. I checked my schedule, shared some of my pygmy experiences with the dispatcher, and headed for my now very dusty Volkswagen Variant. This time my destination would not be Limete but rather my new housesitting digs in Binza.

Ob-La-Di, Ob-La-Da

I had the following day off. I used the time to unpack and regroup. The apartment complex was anything but quiet. There were eight units. A couple were families, but the rest were loud, hard drinking Polish mechanics and armament technicians mixed with a couple of Brits. But my plan was to stay busy, make as much money as I could and go home by the end of the summer.

The next day I was scheduled to operate a C-47 flight from Kinshasa to Lubumbashi, drop off our passengers, and reposition to Kamina Base then remain overnight (RON). Kamina was in the heart of Katanga Province. It was an old (for all practical purposes abandoned) NATO base built by the

Belgiums before independence. When the civil war began and Katanga broke away from the Congo, NATO troops operated the base. Now that NATO was gone, it was just two super long runways (required due to the 6873 foot MSL elevation) of the airport, and a bunch of deteriorating empty buildings. We were scheduled to remain overnight at Kamina Base then bring a load of troops back to Kinshasa the following day; should have been an easy flight.

When I woke up that morning, I felt a little sluggish but just shrugged it off as still recuperating from sleeping in jungle huts. But by the time we were overhead Mbuji-Mayi I was starting to get a dull headache. As we were offloading our passengers, I started to get chills. The symptoms were all too familiar. I was heading for another bout of malaria. I should have reported sick and spent the night in Lubumbashi which had a very nice company house and Belgium doctors. For whatever reason, I did not. I gave the copilot the leg to Kamina; I just sat in my seat and shivered a couple of times a minute.

Upon our arrival in Kamina Base, the German station agent met us and helped secure the airplane. While we were refueling the agent told us that there was a big Belgium party in town and he was going to take us. I told him I didn't really feel all that well and I just wanted to go to the house and get in bed. He apologized and said he had already given his houseboy the rest of the day off and there was no food for dinner. I was faced with going to bed not only sick but also hungry or going to some damn Belgium party. Looking back, I made a poor decision…I elected to go to the party.

The agent lived on the base which was about 20 kilometers from the town of Kamina. I took a quick shower and got dressed and the three of us headed to town.

When we arrived, the party was already in full swing. There were many families present. The beer was flowing, and the food was about ready to be served. For whatever reason, the entire group was singing the Beatles song *Ob-La-Di, Ob-La-Da* (in French of course). I could tell my temperature was going up and my shivering was increasing. I was too sick to drink a beer. I had a bottle of Mirinda and waited patiently for the server to bring my food; actually I was waiting patiently for the evening to be over and to get into bed.

First the servers (all Congolese) brought the vegetables, boiled potatoes and leaks. When my time finally came, the waiter approached me from behind, with a large tray of steaks resting in a generous portion of a thin oily sauce. He somehow became distracted and failed to notice the tray was tilting downward. It took a couple of seconds for me to realize that this genius was pouring about half the sauce in the tray on my head. I just sat motionless as the steak sauce ran down my forehead. I was truly suffering message unit overload. Between my malaria and my rage, I was incapable of moving or even saying a word. I just sat motionless and stared straight ahead and listened to the exuberant tipsy diners singing Ob-La-Di, Ob-La-Da over and over. The waiter soon realized his mistake. His fellow servers all rushed over and started trying to wipe the top of my head with starched white napkins. I got up and went to the restroom where I tried without measurable success to wash the greasy liquid from my hair and face. By this time it was all over my shirt and running down my neck and back. As I stood trying to wash away at least some of the grease, I looked into the mirror above the lavatory. I don't think I ever saw anything so pathetic. And all the time, they continued to sing "*Ob-La-Di, Ob-La-Da.*"

I returned, and with all the determination I could muster, ate the food that was on my plate. After all, that was the only reason I elected not to go to bed but rather come to town.

The 20-kilometer jeep ride back to the base, with my hair now stiff from the greasy sauce and my shivering getting more violent, seemed like an eternity. Finally we arrived at the company house. I got in the shower and washed and scrubbed myself until all the hot water was gone. Much of the grease and all of the smell remained. I took my malaria pills and aspirin and got in bed. I finally managed to drift off into a fitful sleep punctuated by fits of chills and shivering.

Morning came and I was still weak. The fever seemed lower and the shivering not as bad. I got into my flight suite and went to breakfast. As I sat drinking my coffee, I could still smell that rancid steak sauce. I was very ready to go back to Kinshasa.

Again I gave the copilot the takeoff and landing. I just sat in my seat and tried to be a participating crewmember. I was so glad to hear the wheels chirp on contact with the runway in Kinshasa. I'd survived what at the time seemed to have been the flight from hell.

Mt. Nyiragongo–A Glimpse From On High Into Hell

Therefore hell hath enlarged herself, and opened her mouth without measure: and their glory, and their multitude, and their pomp, and he that rejoiceth, shall descend into it. [172]

On numerus occasions Nyiragongo's lava flows have raced downhill at up to 60 miles per hour (up to 100 km/h). Hundreds have been killed and homes destroyed. After I was long gone, in 2002 it erupted again, this time destroying much of the city of Goma and leaving thousands homeless.

I was keenly aware that my days in the Congo were ending. I could see no possibility of my ever returning. I found myself dreaming of one last big adventure…something on the level of the pygmies.

Previously I'd given a ride on one of my C-47 flights to a couple of young Belgian Alpinists who were heading to Goma for several months of study of the volcano located just a few miles away. I'd jokingly told them that in exchange for the ride, they would have to promise to take me along on one of

[172] Holy Bible - King James Bible (Cambridge Ed.) - Isaiah 5:14

their climbs. They anxiously replied that they would be happy to do so; probably never thinking I'd ever take them up on their offer. But as with my pygmy adventure, I soon found Nyiragongo my center of focus.

One day I used our airborne HF radio to call Goma. When Claus answered our call, I asked him to come up on the back channel (a pre-designated frequency where we could hold non-standard transmissions or requests). Few seconds later I heard him calling us. I asked if the two Belgium Alpinists were still in Goma. "Affirmative" he replied. I asked Claus to contact them and find out when their next climb was to be and if they would still take me along. Claus said he would get in the jeep and drive to where they were staying and get back to me with their answer as soon as he could. I shifted back to our primary HF USB morning channel. When I reported back on frequency, Gus, one of the radio operators commented that I'd been here too long. He had heard my request on the secondary frequency which he always monitored as well. I told him that he was correct and I was about to fix the problem. We both laughed.

A couple of hours later, Goma called us and told us to come up on back channel. When I reported in, he advised they were planning a trip in a couple of weeks. He gave me the exact date. He said they would be happy to have me tag along.

I started planning my trip right there in the cockpit at 9000 feet above sea level. I called King 1 on the HF and asked for a phone patch to dispatch. Again I was told to go to secondary frequency and standby. In a couple of minutes dispatch was online. I asked if they could spare me for about eight days starting in a couple of weeks. Since I was already projected to be on overtime, and they expected to have enough pilots, they gave me the days off I had requested. We terminated the phone patch and I returned to primary frequency and to making my plans for the Mt. Nyiragongo climb.

This time there would be little mental preparation. There was no internet with which to Google™ Mt. Nyiragongo. The one encyclopedia I could find had only a couple of paragraphs. Preparation was just going to be packing my camera, some warm clothes, my T-28 helmet to protect my head during the climb, lots of 35mm film and go. This time I elected to use my Wigmo issue air force flight boots rather than the Justin work boots I picked for the pygmy adventure. At one of the dispatcher's recommendation, I'd asked SODEMAZ stores about sleeping bags. They still had some from the Wigmo era. I was issued one and it was to become an essential part of my gear for the trip. The last thing from the old Wigmo stores was a gas mask. For everything else, Goma had plenty of supplies, so I didn't have to bother with buying my food in Kinshasa.

Claus said the Belgiums told him we would climb to the summit, spend one night on the summit, descend into the crator the following morning, spend the night inside the crater, and ascend the following day and continue down the mountain.

Since there was so little preparation I needed to do, I tried to fly every day to push my flight hours higher. Being off the schedule for a week would cost me some overtime but if I flew hard enough now, the loss wouldn't be so significant…and it was funny money anyway.

I found a C-54 flight going to Goma two days before the scheduled climb and got dispatch to put me on the manifest. The extra day in Goma would allow me to meet with the climbers, go over what supplies I would need, and become familiar with the plan. I knew all this was going to be somewhat mentally taxing as only one of the two spoke some limited English. Almost all our communications would be in French. Although my French had improved considerably during my time there, I still had to concentrate on almost everything I needed to say. It was easier for me to listen than to speak…a concept I found amusing. Still working on that today.

Temporary Insanity

My flight had an early morning departure. I was relieved to find the crew was only the captain, copilot, and loadmaster. They were curious about what I was going to be doing in Goma. When I told them I would be going down inside the crater, all three were certain I had lost my mind. Looking back now, I realize that I often heard the "lost your mind" remarks during my last months in the country. After Karen, Jason, and Jenny had gone back home, it was like another Jimmy had replaced the "normal" Jimmy. It was not necessarily my evil twin, but certainly not the guy who ran my show most of the time. I stowed my gear and sat down at the navigator's station. The drone of the four Pratt & Whitney R-2000 engines was almost hypnotic. I was soon asleep.

Claus met our flight and immediately started the refueling and passenger handling. As soon as the C-54 was airborne on its way back to King 1, we decided to enjoy a sunset. He stopped at a little duka and got four cold Simba beers. He drove me to the top of a hill in Goma. There we parked, sat on the hood of the jeep, drank our beer, and watched the volcano start to impart a soft glow to the evening sky as the sun surrendered to night. It was like a reddish-purple heavenly crown over the mouth of hell. After the breathtaking sunset, we went to the house and had dinner. I went to bed early and slept well.

Two Belgiums And An Aphrodite

Claus had arranged a 9:00 am meeting with the two young Belgiums. They were staying in a small bungalow near the center of town. One of the two Belgiums, Adrien, had climbed Mont Blanc solo at age twelve. He had a live-in Congolese girlfriend. Her name was Léa. She was tall, beautiful, elegant, wore tight jeans and had a figure like a carved black onyx Aphrodite of Milos.

She spoke perfect French and better English than Adrien. Léa obviously was educated. I later learned she was not Congolese but rather a Tutsi from Rwanda. She appeared to have come from an affluent family background. I learned she had fled across the border to Goma, along with her family in order to escape the Hutu-Tutsi violence. It was clear Adrien was developing serious feelings for Léa.

We discussed the overall plan for the trip. I would need no climbing gear. They would provide everything; even the food. They soon understood that not only did I have no climbing experience, but additionally was afraid of heights. Julien, the other Belgium told me not to worry and not to look down. Almost certainly they were not expecting me to have any mountain climbing experience. However the afraid of heights proclamation was an unexpected disclosure.

Next, I was shown the climbing gear…hooks and spikes…just like you see in the movies. As I looked at their equipment, I began to ponder that perhaps I had gotten myself into something over my head. They had ropes, webbings, countless clip devices which I later learned were referred to as carabineers, a hand tool that resembled a cross between an ax and a hammer; and an array of other things I knew nothing about. The frightening thing about my lack of familiarity was that these items would  all be fundamental to our decent into the crater. I pushed that thought out of my mind, asked what supplies I'd need for the trip, and then headed downtown with Claus to shop for them. Julien said they would provide all our camp food and all I would need is snacks…plenty of them to fight the physiological effects of altitude. Our departure would be from their place at 7:00am.

Basically the entire day was spent walking about and looking at the local goods offered for sale in Goma. Being so close to Uganda and Tanzania, and Kenya, there was some significantly different merchandise offered in the shops. I picked up a pair of flip-flops which they recommended for wearing around the camp at night to let my feet rest. I picked up some Band-Aids in case of blisters. I got lots of candy bars, a box of Ritz Cracker knock-offs plus a couple of cans of beans for energy. We had lunch at a nice restaurant, then went to the airport to meet an inbound flight.

On our way from the airport we stopped to look at the various roadside stands setup by the flood of refugees. They offered various handcrafts and services. The refugees' plight was heartbreaking. They had little shelter, little food, had to forage for firewood, and little hope. To make it worse the Zaire government was doing little to help them. Tragedy was everywhere. But as terrible as this was, it would pale to what I would soon experience in Cambodia.

During a sixty-day period encompassing both my Mbuti adventure and the Mt. Nyiragongo experience, U.S. B-52 bombers under orders from President Nixon dropped approximately sixteen thousand tons of ordinance on Cambodia causing untold civilian casualties; most without the knowledge of the U.S. congress.[173] At that time, Cambodia was allied with the United States fighting the Vietcong who were using parts of Cambodia as a sanctuary and for supply routes. I, like the majority of the people in the world, knew almost nothing of the U.S. bombing in Cambodia. Cambodia, Laos, and Thailand were actors in the theater of "the secret war."

The war in Vietnam and the Paris Peace Talks dominated the news stories. However, a news story that captured more attention than Paris occurred on 18 July 1972. Jane Fonda gave her infamous anti-war message on Radio Hanoi.

Rare Air

We pulled up to the Belgiums' bungalow at 7:00am. They were waiting along with all their gear on the front porch. Aphrodite was with them. This time she had shed her jeans and was wearing three-quarter length loose fitting pants like the two Belgiums were wearing. She was wearing a knit stocking cap again as the two Belgiums were wearing. I later learned Léa made all the climbs with them. I had elected to wear my flight suit due to the temperature associated with the high elevation.

We headed north out of Goma on Nation Hwy 2. At the edge of town we stopped and picked up two park rangers. The jeep was full now. The rangers were hanging onto the back of the jeep. Thankfully, the drive was a short one. About 7 miles outside town, we saw a group of Congolese standing beside the road. The park rangers motioned for us to stop. We had reached the point the rangers used to make the ascent. I learned the men beside the road would be our porters. The rangers used these porters whenever they were escorting people up the mountain.

I had not known this previously, but the government strictly controlled who was allowed to make this climb because of the danger. That explained the park rangers. There had been a fatality a few years earlier. The story in Goma was a European was trying to scale the steep wall of the crater, without the proper training or equipment, and fell. When he hit the lava floor of the crater, they said his head exploded like a melon hitting a cement slab.

---

[173] Bombs Over Cambodia—by Taylor Owen and Ben Kiernan

The rangers had a path of sorts from this point to the camp site at the base of the summit. I was glad to see the porters. The spot where we were standing was approximately 5100 feet above sea level. Our base camp was just below the summit which was 11,385 feet above sea level. I needed to be a little over 6000 feet higher than where I presently was standing. I didn't know what exactly to expect but I knew this thin air was going to be physically challenging. I had no idea how challenging.

We piled out and started getting ready for the soon to be steep hike up the mountain side. Claus discussed with the Belgiums about what time we should reach this spot on our way back down in three days. He said he would meet us or have someone else meet us here at this spot. We said goodbye to Claus and started walking up the side of the mountain.

I noticed the Belgiums used a type of walking stick which collapsed and had a sharp pointed end on the bottom and a special hand grip on the top. The Belgiums told the rangers to cut some straight slender tree shoots for Léa and for me. Soon I would understand why.

There was only young vegetation. No tall trees. We were following a lava flow. Everything had been burned when the last major eruption happened. In one aspect, not having to hack a path through the dense vegetation was a blessing but walking on the lava rock required a little getting used to. My air force issue flight boots, while providing ankle support, were not all that well suited for gripping rocks.

About an hour into the climb I could tell my breathing was becoming labored. I wanted to stop and rest frequently, but I pushed myself on not wanting to delay the group. I always considered myself in excellent health compared to the people around me, but I was starting to realize that the Belgiums were in much better shape. The Congolese and Léa didn't seem to notice anything. I reminded myself that they had spent every day of their life above 5000 feet.

There were times I felt the sharp, shooting chest pains I used to experience in high school running the cross country under Coach Ken Scott. I was beginning to hurt a lot. I hoped that, like when running the cross country, I would suddenly experience "runner's high", a massive wave of endorphins and euphoria. I hoped that all the pain I was experiencing would disappear. Those were incredible sensations. But alas the pain reliving wave of endorphins and euphoria never came. I just hurt and ached.

By the second hour into the climb our pace was slowed due to the steepness of the ascent. We were not actually climbing (having to use our hands), but the going was slow and secure footing became important. The staff the porters had cut for me was now indispensable. I used it to steady myself and to more or less pull myself along. The Belgiums were using their devices constantly at this point as well. The Congolese still used nothing for support.

My legs and ankles were starting to ache. I'd get an occasional muscle cramp in my legs. My throat was starting to burn; my breath was labored. I stopped frequently and took a small sip of water from my canteen just to keep my throat from burning. In addition to being thin, the air was also dry. I was starting to wonder if all this discomfort was going to be worth it.

When we stopped for breaks, I had the opportunity to sit down and turn around and look behind me. The view was spectacular. I could look to my right and left and see heavily forested areas that had not been destroyed when the lava rushed down the mountain side. I could look up and see the timberline. Any thoughts about the discomfort outweighing the beauty and grandeur of the climb were dismissed.

The Belgiums pointed out the location where we would spend the night. Unfortunately it was still far above us. The rangers had built several huts just on the timberline. During the night those huts would help fend off the cold. I thanked God for the sleeping bag as well as for the porter carrying it.

Lunch Around Eight Thousand Feet

After what seemed like an eternity we stopped for lunch. There was not really a suitable spot; we just all more or less sat down in the middle of the trail. I'd made a peanut butter and jam sandwich before we left the house. It was now time to enjoy the sandwich and the view. As I sipped the water from my canteen, I was thankful the Belgiums and brought along several plastic jugs full. I was equally thankful the porters were carrying them and not me. It was all I could do to carry myself.

After what seemed like only a couple of short minutes, we resumed our climb. The path was becoming steeper and the air thinner with every step. I was continually looking up at the timberline using it as a goal…something to help me continue and take the next step. Coach Scott had never given us any drills as demanding as this.

We took a few more breaks. The humiliating truth was that the breaks were because of me. The Africans were born in this rare air. The two Belgiums were conditioned and extremely physically fit. My years of almost no physical exercise other than my natural hyperactivity, was now making a painful statement. I was not in shape to be doing this kind of stuff without training. Hardly a startling revelation to anybody other than me.

I found myself continually praying for the strength to continue. I remembered doing the same thing when running cross country races in high school. I recalled this little prayer that I'd once learned in a Sunday school lesson back at the First Baptist Church in Hamilton. It was a prayer said by a long-distance track runner…it went like this: "you pick-em up Lord…I'll put-em down." I would repeat this little prayer over and over using it both to give cadence to my stride and keep my mind off what seemed like an impossible distance to go before crossing the finish line. Here I was, repeating it with each step, high on a mountain side in the heart of Africa; only this time with a cadence appropriate for an ultra-slow-motion video. Amazing. You pick-em up Lord…I'll put-em down.

The Summit

Somehow, by the grace of God (literally), we made it to the summit. The porters and rangers started cleaning up the huts and gathering firewood. The porters had been picking up appropriate pieces of dead wood along the trail for the last hour or so. But it wasn't enough, and they went back down the mountain side for more wood.

We all rested for a moment and then made our way up to the very edge of the crater. While I'd seen the sight from the cockpit, absolutely nothing could equal standing there looking down into the churning sea of red-hot molten rock. The sulfuric smell was very noticeable as we peered down into the crater. The Belgiums explained that the volcanic action came in pulses and when it was experiencing one of the pulses, what potentially could be a lethal belch of gas would often be emitted.

I thanked God and Wigmo for my gas mask. Julien told me the temperature of the churning bright red molten rock was in excess of 400 degrees Celsius. When I commented about how large the crater was, he replied that it was approximately 2 kilometers wide, or 1.2 miles.

We must have sat at the rim of the crater for close to an hour. Just looking, occasionally talking, but mostly lost in our own thoughts. I probably shot a roll of film. After a while Julien announced we needed to go back and start setting up camp before dark and cold set in. I was feeling much better now but noticed the muscles in my ankles and calves were sore. This was almost certainly the result of walking for such a long time at such a relatively steep incline.

The porters already had two fires going; one for them and one for us. They knew the drill. I noticed the t-shirt I'd been wearing under my flight suit was damp from perspiration. I removed it and laid it on the side of my hut to dry.

I put on a fresh one and just wore my jeans and later my wind breaker. I removed my socks and left them to dry with my t-shirt. I put on the flip-flops I had in my equipment bag.

Julien took the lead with the cooking. While I was pretty certain Léa would do well helping with the meal, it appeared she pretty much understood that this was a "man thing" and stayed in the background. Because Julien and Adrien appeared to have this mountain meal preparation down to a fine art, I followed Léa's lead and let them handle the meal. I walked around the camp taking pictures.

The sunset was beautiful to observe from this vantage point. We could watch as parts of the landscape below us became engulfed in the shadows, then darkness, while others clung to their illuminated status for a while longer. It was truly beautiful.

While I was still watching the last of the golden sunlight retreat across the landscape, Adrien pointed back up to the rim of the crater. The steam from inside the crater which was white during daylight was now gently radiating a reddish-orange glow as the moisture droplets reflected the light from the red-hot lava. Again I took up my camera. I decided I'd make my way back up to the summit to look down inside just once more. Even though I knew we would be spending the next night down inside and up close, the attraction was overpowering. I quickly made my way back up to the summit while Julien finished cooking the meal. I was overcome with the majesty and awesome power I witnessed when I reached the top again. I was there probably over a minute before I remembered I was holding my camera. I was lost in the moment. I took several more shots then went back down to the camp.

After our meal, we just sat around the fire; some conversation but mostly just savoring the moment. The Congolese on the other hand were anything but quiet. They were laughing and teasing each other. They provided some wonderful photo ops.

Soon however the chill of the night air at almost 11,000 feet above sea level, started to turn things downright cold. The Congolese retreated to their hut. As we were getting ready to go into our huts, the cry of an elephant echoed through the valley below. Adrien said that was common and told me to remain outside my hut for a few more minutes. In less than a minute, from an entirely different direction, the elephant's trumpeting was answered. Their trumpeting symphony continued throughout the night. It was an unforgettable experience. These huge majestic creatures, probably five thousand feet below us, filled me with an awesome reverence. I'll never forget the moment.

The chill I'd been experiencing no longer seemed important. I huddled close to the fire so I could use its light to record more of my thoughts in my little red journal. I never wanted to forget a single moment of this. I recorded my thoughts about the elephants; I recorded the flickering of the fire light on the sides of the huts. Soon, however the cold became a bit too uncomfortable and I also retreated into my hut, tunneled into my sleeping bag, took a couple of delayed shutter shots of myself in my sleeping bag, and fell asleep. My body was ready for rest.

As I lay sleeping in my hut just below the summit, the high command of the Khmer National Armed Forces (FANK... Forces Armées Nationales Khmères in French) was working frantically with the U.S. Embassy in Phnom Penh and U.S. Military Equipment Delivery Team, Cambodia (MEDTC) based out of the embassy to restructure the fragile and mostly untrained Cambodian military.[174] *For the past two years following the overthrow of Norodom Sihanouk, FANK had been suffering debilitating losses at the hands of North Vietnamese regular army, the Viet Cong, and the Khmer Rouge forces operating inside Cambodia. While the United States government was footing the bill for the military's payroll and supplying all the military hardware, the increasingly unpopular Lon Nol regime was having difficulty finding soldiers. The Lon Nol government was doing its best to conceal its staggering military losses, but the truth was well known on the streets. To replace these losses, the military finally resorted to driving through the streets of the cities with trucks, grabbing young men of military age off the streets and forcibly inducting them into the army. These events were passing largely unnoticed by the outside world with the help of the Nixon administration.*

---

[174] The Khmer Republic at War and the Final Collapse—Lt. Gen. Sak Sutsakhan - U.S. Army Center For Military History—Washington DC

Hi Carb Breakfast, Followed by Pure Terror

When I crawled out of my sleeping bag and emerged from the hut, I realized it was a lot colder than when I'd gone to bed. I made a beeline for the fire.

Julien and Adrien already had a pot of oatmeal going as well as a pot of coffee. I couldn't wait to get my hands on both. For whatever reason I was as hungry as a bear. I thought about my candy bars and my Ritz Cracker knock-offs but decided I should save them for later in the day and for the night inside the crater.

The coffee tasted unusually good. The oatmeal was loaded with sugar; probably Julien loading everybody up to help combat the high altitude. He also had roasted sweet potatoes by placing them in the ashes beside the fire. As I was eating, I realized this was a one utensil meal…a spoon…excluding my hunting knife used to cut open the sweet potato.

When breakfast was finished, Adrien and Julian began assembling the climbing equipment we would use in the decent. I could feel I was starting to get a little apprehensive. Within minutes they both transformed from the two Belgiums I'd met on the plane to for-real mountain climbers. The rapidly increasing difference between us just added to my apprehension. I was considerably outside my environment.

I strapped on my modest backpack containing my meager overnight supplies and my Wigmo issued gas mask, my camera and numerous rolls of film, donned my T-28 helmet and stood waiting. Julien and Adrien loaded all the climbing equipment on their shoulders and harnesses, put the supplies in their backpacks, gave last minute instructions to the porters and rangers and we were off. We made our way back up to the summit.

While I'd been to the summit twice yesterday afternoon and was immersed in its stunning beauty and majesty, I now found the very same place to be threatening…in reality…downright frightening. Julien and Adrien were setting up to begin letting themselves down the almost vertical face of the crater. Every move they made was well rehearsed. I would go down attached to Julien; Léa to Adrien.

As we approached the lip and readied for the decent, I began a string of silent prayers punctuated with strings of expletives for being so stupid and irresponsible as to have gotten myself into this situation. It was entirely my evil twin's idea. But now, that the moment had arrived, I was abandoned…left to face this terrifying situation alone. You'd think, after all these years, I'd have learned how totally irresponsible my evil twin was. I prayed even harder.

Adrien and Léa went over the edge first. Julien and I followed a few seconds later but with a lateral separation. This was to diminish the risk of a dislodged rock from the person above falling on you.

I quickly found that looking down was not a good idea. I just kept looking up at the sky. Words can never do justice to the stark terror I was experiencing. I was hugging the side of that crater wall so closely it was hard for my eyes to focus; I saw just endless black, porous volcanic rock. I didn't feel there was enough room for me to even turn my head from left to right. Most of the time the front of my helmet was in contact with the surface of the wall. Each moment seemed like an hour. Where Julien instructed me to place my foot for each new "step" was only in reality a tiny indentation in the rocks; barely deep enough to get my toes into. The rest of my foot was hanging out in very thin air. Once, I looked at my fingers…their color was a mix of death-white and purple…no circulation. I was clinging to the rocks so hard I'd blocked the blood flow. I tried to release my grip just a little in order to encourage the circulation to return to my fingertips. But relaxing my death grip on the side of the cliff was counterintuitive. I remember praying, "Lord, if you allow me to get out of this alive, I will never, never, ever, ever, do anything this stupid and irresponsible again."

On occasions when I could manage the courage to look obliquely down, I would catch glimpses of Léa as she and Adrien made their way at a surprisingly rapid pace down the cliff. She was like a cross between an elegant ballet dancer and a graceful mountain goat. Léa was going a long way toward erasing a considerable amount of my male-chauvinism.

Much of the delay Julien and I were experiencing was due to his constantly having to tell me where to put my foot next and then coaxing me to find the courage to just put it there and trust him. Again, this was extremely counterintuitive. There was no telling how many times I promised The Lord that if he would just let me get out of this momentary insanity alive, I'd never do anything like this again.

After what seemed like an eternity, I put my foot on a horizontal surface rather than a micro-indentation in the side of the cliff. We had reached what they referred to as a bench. I stopped and sat down; never mind the rope and attachments to Julien. This was a moment of supreme significance. I was once again on level ground; never mind it was almost 11,000 feet above sea level. Thank You Jesus!

I removed my helmet and profusely thanked Julien for getting me to this point alive. We all had a good laugh. I looked at Léa with a new-found respect. I think she realized that.

Inside The Abyss

Since Julien, Adrien, and Léa had all done this before, they were more or less at home in the crater. Julien explained we that we would set up our camp for the night in an area on the bench they'd used before. According to him, they had tried several locations in the past; only having to move during the middle of the night if the lava became too active and the volcano started belching gas.

If the wind currents inside the crater were wrong, they could carry the deadly gas over on you and if you didn't get your mask on quick enough, you could die. Through trial and error, they believed they had found a site that worked favorably. He headed toward that site and started stowing our gear.

The camp site was about half way from the wall of the crater to the end of the first bench. Where the first bench ended there was a drop-off of two or three hundred meters than a second bench. Below the second bench was the hot churning body of lava.

The temperature inside the crater was interesting. The part of your body facing the hot lava was hot. It reminded me of when we sat around the campfire back in Hamilton County. If you sat too close and didn't rotate your body, you would soon feel a stinging on the surface of your skin. It was like your molten lava facing side was hot and needed to be rotated and your back side was cold. Adrien assured me this would become much more pronounced once night set in.

I got out my camera and began walking around the bench looking for different angles from which to take pictures of the lava lake. There were interesting compositions shooting back up toward the lip as well as the limitless shots of the hardened lava rock formations. I was cautioned to not shoot up all my shots now as the night images were far more spectacular.

The day went very quickly. I was more or less left to amuse myself as the two Belgiums were moving around hammering at rocks and writing in their notebooks. They also took pictures but with much less expensive cameras. Léa normally tagged along with Adrien. I was warned to take my mask with me and never let it be out of my reach. Thankfully I didn't need it.

Unlike the descent which seemed endless, the rest of the daylight hours seemed to fly by. In no time at all the sun had gone below the edge of the crater. We could still see the blue sky above us, but the direct sunlight was gone. It was interesting to consider that only a short distance from us, our basecamp was still bathed in golden sunlight. It was a bit like being inside a huge bucket.

There would be no community meal for our dinner as there was no campfire; we had no firewood. As we settled into our camp site for the night, I was able to get great photos of the group. The lava lake was giving off a reddish-orange glow that illuminated their faces. The part not facing the hot lava was dark. There was enough light coming from the lava lake to cast eerie shadows on the walls of the crater. It was a photographer's dream. It was then I realized I'd forgotten about the terror I had experienced only a few hours earlier.

Bean Bombs–Crackers– And Candy

The plan was that my can of beans would serve as my main course. I'd move closer to the edge of the bench where the temperature was just about downright hot, leave the can for a few minutes, run up and turn the can and then go back again and pick up the heated results. I'd open the can with my hunting knife and eat from the can with a spoon. First course…Ritz Crackers…main course…beans direct from the can…dessert candy bar. Amazingly simple…at least at first glance.

However, as with my "mad bomber" affair back in Hamilton High School, I failed to think through the all elements and aspects in my preparation plans. Had I done so, I would have realized I was soon to have another bomb on my hands . . . a *bean bomb*.

As meal time approached, I removed my can of beans from my backpack, and made my way closer to the mouth of the lava lake, all the time testing the temperature of the gravel-like lava pebbles with my hand. I could feel the skin of my face start to sting and itch just as it had when I sat too close for too long to the campfire while growing up back in Hamilton. I quickly set my can of beans down and piled some of the warm lava pebbles up around the sides of the can and made my retreat.

When back at the campsite I opened my first course…the Ritz Crackers. They tasted really good. Looking back I realized I was hungrier than I'd thought and had perhaps savored the hors d'oeuvre course of my meal a bit too long. When I returned for the can I found it warmer than I'd anticipated. There was certainly no need to turn or rotate the can in the hot lava pebbles. I decided it would be wise to allow it to cool before attempting to open the can; this part of the process was good but ominously lacking in scope.

One of many factors I failed to consider was the difference between the atmospheric pressure inside the crater versus the pressure inside the can. The can of beans was probably manufactured and sealed somewhere around sea level where the atmospheric pressure was about 14.7 lbs. per square inch. Our campsite inside the crater was about 10,500 above sea level where the atmospheric pressure had fallen to about 10.13 lbs. per square inch. At sea level the differential pressure between outside and inside pressure was more or less zero. Before I put my can of beans in the warm rocks, the differential pressure had already risen to about 4.5 psi. My can of beans had already gone from a container to a pressure vessel. After heating the air and contents inside the can I can only guess how much more the differential pressure increased; but it is sufficient to say the increase was substantial as I would soon learn.

I got out a couple of my carefully folded sheets of paper towel, my spoon, and my hunting knife which was to serve as the can opener. After allowing the can to cool down, I placed the point of my hunting knife on the top of the can and gave the handle of the knife a firm tap with the palm of my hand. A nanosecond later all hell broke loose, or at least that was my first impression as pulverized bean projectiles accompanied by a significant quantity of the bean sauce came shooting from the can. I could feel the warm contents of the can on my cheeks and dripping off my hand. *Expletive!!#!!* My can of beans had just undergone what is referred to in aeronautics as an explosive decompression. A controlled decompression via a much smaller hole in the can would have allowed the pressure to release at a much more gradual rate; thus avoiding the bean bombs. But a character trait I've suffered with from childhood is the theory that "if a little is good…a lot must be better."

When I recovered from the surprise, I began to assess the loss. My fellow climbers were roaring with laughter. I completed the lid removal process and found a little more than half the can's contents remaining. I was thankful that at least I'd have some of my main course left.

I poured a conservative quantity of water from my canteen on one of the paper towels and wiped as much of the sugary bean sauce and particles off my face and hands as I could. I elected to leave the majority of the mess that landed on my flight suite alone. I didn't want to waste the water. With more than a third of my main course now gone, I chewed slowly trying to make the remainder last as long as possible. I never realized how good canned beans could taste. When I finished, I buried the can in the gravel and returned to the group to enjoy my last course…the candy bar. Later, while chatting with the group I realized I had the only canned food in the camp. They were eating jerky readily available all over Goma as well as some dried fish. I'd eaten both before and found them pretty good. I added canned beans or canned anything to my never-to-do-at-10,000-feet-above-sea-level-list. At least I'd provided the group with a little entertainment.

Nyiragongo Passes Gas

After the excitement of bean bomb entertainment, everyone was ready for sleep. Before crawling in my sleeping bag I used the light coming from the lot lava to illuminate the pages of my red book again. I wanted to be sure I never forgot the sights and sounds I'd experienced. Finally I unrolled my sleeping bag, used my flight suite for a pillow, pulled my camera and my gas mask into the bag with me and got ready to try to sleep. However, it wasn't

long before I realized that my military issue flight bag had the same problem as my skin did. It developed warm spots on the side facing the fire. This required an endless series of rotations and repositions to keep comfortable. All this was diametrically opposed to obtaining a good night's sleep. I kept looking at my Breitling Navitimer to see how much longer till dawn. Sometime in the early morning hours, the volcano decided to expel some of its trapped gas. I heard Julien calling for everyone to get their gas masks on. I quickly sat up, still in my sleeping bag, and dawned my gas mask. As I looked around, I saw Adrien and Léa's heads pop out of one of the bags, Julien was sitting up in his bag wearing his mask. I was waiting to see if they would decide for us to hold in place or quickly relocate until this little flatulent blast episode subsided. It was decided to wait and see how things went. They had already briefed me that usually this kind of event didn't last long. As I looked over at Léa wearing her gas mask, I started to chuckle. Two heads, one white and one chocolate, sticking out of a sleeping bag, both wearing gas masks. How funny was that? More stuff for my red book.

The poisonous air soon moved away; the lava lake went back to is normal boiling and churning; we removed our masks, and I resumed my search for a comfortable position in which to finish out the night and await first light. I'm sure I slept some, but the sleep was so light that it was almost like not sleeping at all.

I could see the sky overhead the mouth of the crater start to turn from dark toward blue. It was some time later however before the sun's rays actually made it into the crater. We could see its golden tones begin to transform the upper portion of the crater's west wall. Gosh it was beautiful.

I was soon out of my bedroll and walking about looking for light and shadows to photograph. Unlike yesterday morning, there would be no coffee this morning. No fire, no firewood. But with all the stunningly beautiful light play all around me, I hardly missed it.

Julien gave me a piece of his beef jerky; I had a candy bar. I shared the last of my Ritz Crackers with the group, and we began to pack up our gear for the ascent. Both Julien and Adrien made some last-minute notations in their notebooks; then we made our way back to the wall.

What Goes Down Must Come Up

They began rigging their climbing gear again. They returned to the same spot where we made the descent. I felt the same apprehension I faced the prior morning as we started our descent. Within minutes we were ready to start back up.

As before, I followed Julien. By the time we had climbed what I would guess to be about fifteen feet, I was once again numb with fear. Over and over I prayed my little "never, never, ever, ever" prayer. My prayers included apologies to Karen, Jason, and Jenny for doing something so irresponsible. "Please Lord, just let me get to the top alive." Like on the descent, I was almost paralyzed with fear. I'd felt this as a child when I would climb a ladder, but this was about one thousand times worse. Each foothold was not really a foothold but more accurately, a toehold. I tried to remember the spots where Julian had put his foot so I could do the same. I remember looking down just once; the rest of the time I stared up at Julian's butt and prayed. It was like time stopped.

Finally I saw Julian's butt disappear over the lip, then his smiling face reappeared. He took hold of the rope and literally hoisted me the last ten feet or so. When I crawled over the edge, I sat on the hard lava rock totally physically and emotionally drained. As I looked up, Adrien and Léa were smiling at me. They beat us to the top. Julian unhooked me but I continued to sit just where I'd plopped down. I needed to acclimate. Gradually my strength and sanity returned. By this time they were all back at the base camp. I slowly got to my feet and headed down to join them.

In the camp we finished packing and took a little rest. Then they announced it was time for us to head down in order to meet Claus at our appointed rendezvous time.

A Blistering Hike Down The Mountain

The porters loaded the gear; I latched on to the staff they'd cut for me on the way up the mountain and we headed down the trail toward the base of the mountain and the road back to Goma.

The pace was far faster than when we'd made the ascent. I found I was having to dig my heels in on each step to keep from stumbling forward. But it wasn't long before I realized this necessary tactic was making my ankle very sore. I feared my flight boots, which I hardly ever wore, were rubbing blisters on my ankles. When we took our first brake, I removed one of my boots and confirmed my suspicion…an ugly raw spot on my heal. The blister had ruptured, and the serum was gone exposing raw flesh. I realized it was going to be a long painful walk to the highway. I laced my boot and we continued down the trail.

Since the walk was all downhill, I was not physically exhausted. Except for my two painful heels, I felt good. I was already getting excited about the numerous rolls of 36 exposure slide film I'd shot on the trip.

When we neared the rendezvous point, I saw Claus's jeep parked under the shade of a tree beside the road. Boy was I going to be glad to sit down and stop rubbing my probably bleeding heels. We all piled in the jeep, Adrien paid the porters, and we said goodbye to them. The rangers would ride most of the way back with us. Adrien paid them as we neared their headquarters.

As we dropped Julien, Adrien, and Léa at their place and said goodbye, I realized our time together had been a unique one. I smiled at Léa as we drove away in the jeep. She had changed the way I thought about a lot of things. I believe she probably knew that.

Claus stopped at a local pharmacy and I picked up some ointment for what was left of the back of my heels. Back at the safe house, I was so ready for a long hot soak in the bath tub. I put on some clean clothes, got a cold beer from the refrigerator and took a seat on the front porch. Claus was still on the radio with King 1.

I was instantly lost in my thoughts; thoughts of the incredible experiences I'd just had. There were thoughts about Julien, Adrien, and Léa, about the elephants I heard in the darkness far below us. I thought of the terror of the descent and ascent and the absolutely unimaginable power residing for the most part, under the surface of this planet we live on. I thought of the people it kills when it decides to break free from its bonds below the earth. I thought about the God that created it all. These were memories I would carry for the rest of my life. I got another Simba beer from the refrigerator and thought about my rapidly approaching departure from this place and my return to Hamilton.

"He is able to humble those who walk in pride." [175]

About noon the following day I climbed onboard a FAC C-54 flight back to Kinshasa. As the engines droned westward toward King 1, I didn't sleep. The images of the Mt. Nyiragongo adventure kept playing in my head. The dominant emotion was not boastful pride at having accomplished something so extraordinary but rather humility coupled with a greater than before realization of mankind's insignificance. Coming face to face with even a small man-

---
[175] Holman Christian Standard Bible (HCSB)—Daniel 4:37

ifestation of the Great Architect Of The Universe's awesome power, such as Mt. Nyiragongo, cannot help but extinguish the ego of any rational human being.

The Final Days

My last weeks in the Congo went by quickly. At my own request, I flew almost every day. My goal was to pile up as much money as I could before leaving. The fact that I would be returning to the U.S. without having made any employment enquiries didn't really frighten me, but I realized it would immediately begin draining our savings.

I took many flights that required staying overnight in the outstations. I used these RON (remain overnight) flights to shop for African artifacts. There were still many rare and authentic items available. I already had two trunks completely filled with rare masks, knives, musical instruments and other fetishes. I had ivory, malachite, Katanga crosses, and a huge bundle of spears. I would receive an extra baggage allowance on my final departure; I planned to use every single kilo of it.

The Big Day

My departure date finally came. I'd been packed for days. The company van picked me up along with all my bags and trunks and took me to the N'Djili airport. There were few goodbyes and little sadness. I would miss a few of the friends I'd made but not many. I'd miss Bat. Paul was already gone. The vast remaining majority were just nice acquaintances.

As the captain advanced the throttles of the B-707 and it began to lumber down the runway, I hit the timer button on my Breitling Navitimer, a habit I'd acquired since starting to fly internationally. I hit the stop button when I felt the nose wheel break ground. Yep we were heavy.

Leaving The Heart Of Darkness

As the Sabena 707 headed toward Brussels, my head was filled with images…of pygmy hunting camps, of communal bongs, the games the pygmies played, of mountains spewing fire, of majestic elephants trumpeting in the night…of the two Alpinists and Aphrodite.

At the other end of the spectrum lay the death, the destruction, and the immeasurable human tragedy, rooted in tribal hate, political ambition, and greed. For those who diligently study the Bible, great parallels exist in Old Testament records dating to the times of Moses, through the Judges, King David, and the Babylonian diaspora. Extra-biblical sources chronicle military campaigns of conquest, almost always ending with the death, torture, and subjection of countless millions.

Today, students of world current events see ethnic or religious hate-driven atrocities like Hitler, Stalin, the Congo, Rwanda and Pol Pot, all forcing genocide on fellow members of their societies. I have concluded that history continues to repeat itself while the human race learns nothing. These experiences, over time, would slowly reshape who I was. I switched my thoughts to Texas, to Karen, Jason, and Jenny.

As we flew north over the Sahara Desert, then later the blue waters of the Alboran and Balearic Seas, I felt relief that I was leaving the dark continent of Africa. I would return for short periods on several occasions as a pilot, though never to the Congo and never at any great length. My overall dark impressions of the Dark Continent remain unchanged.

The Interlude

During an interlude the curtain falls; actors leave the stage; the set is changed; the actors return to the stage; the curtain goes up and the play resumes. My trip home to Texas marked such an interlude.

Early into the long flight I began to sense anxiety. It was nothing specific, just a general sense of unrest. Perhaps I was worried about how I was going to reintegrate into my family; my father, Karen, Jason, and Jenny. I'd experienced this before upon returning…unfortunately this was not a new feeling.

Things seemed to move so much more quickly in the States. I remember having difficulty working a simple cold drink vending machine. I'd see and comment on a car I thought was this years' model. Only to be met with laughter and told the car was four years old. To me, since I'd never seen the car before…it was new. My mind saw no evidence that it had been driven for several years. I was also shocked to see how much more things cost. It was like time had stopped when I left the States, and then suddenly fast forwarded ahead to the present in a single instant upon my return. I would sometimes feel like Washington Irving's character Rip Van Winkle suddenly awaking from a very long sleep.

During the months I'd been living alone, my home environment was basically without sound, save occasional street noises or music that I selected and controlled. I'd seen on previous visits home that I was thrust into a collection of people and objects competing for my attention. I would get very nervous. After a while I decided there was a much more favorable way to spend crossing the Atlantic. I'd start planning fishing trips with Jason.

Tom Hafford–My Old Standby

As with most of my trips home, I'd arranged to stay with Tom for the first night. I could then call Karen and they could come pick me up the following day. It was good to see Tom, his wife and his two boys. Each time I saw them I was amazed at how the boys had grown.

The next day my father drove to Hurst to pick me up. He was full of questions about my life and work in the Congo. I think we talked every second of the way back to Hamilton. While it was so good to see my father again, I was saddened to see how his emphysema had advanced. His every breath was labored. Every step he took exhausted him. His oxygen cylinder was ever present. Yet he hardly complained. It was really hard to see a man who had always been the epitome of physical fitness now in such a state of virtually total disability.

I was excited to see Karen and the children again. I wanted to learn all about what they'd been doing while I was away. I was excited to talk to her about the things I wanted to do. We did talk about the fact that at some point I would need to start looking for a job again, but for the moment, I just wanted to do little fun things with them. Probably the most important thing for me to do was just to listen. Listen to everything they wanted to tell me about.

Each time I came home, I was hit with the sensation that the house looked a little strange. When in reality, it hadn't changed at all. Just funny tricks my mind liked to play. Jason was bubbly with lots of "let's go do" ideas. I loved it. Jenny was simply stunningly beautiful. Her hair looked like spun gold and her eyes like perfectly colored aquamarine. Sometimes I would just sit and stare.

A Trip To "The Lake"

High on my agenda was spending time with my friend Jerry Drake and enjoying Lake Buchanan. We packed up a few days clothing, bought some new fishing gear, and headed south down highway 281 toward Burnet and Lake Buchanan in the beautiful Texas Hill Country.

Jerry's house was right on the water. Jason and I would spend hours fishing with little spinners or sometimes just worms and bobbers from Jerry's back yard. We also would drive a couple of miles to a fishing dock located on Silver Creek. Silver Creek was a finger on the northern part of Lake Buchanan near where the Colorado River flowed into the lake. Generally speaking we had a much better chance to catch more and bigger fish there. They dumped brush into the deep water beside the dock which provided excellent structure where the fish could hang. I always suspected they dropped a little food down amongst the brush from time to time as well. You had to pay a modest fee to fish from the dock, but the cost was reasonable and the joy of watching Jason catch fish was priceless.

Buchanan Dam And Monster Carp

One day we took a drive up to the observatory at Buchanan Dam. This was the dam on the Colorado River which created Lake Buchanan. In those days you could walk on the top of the dam and go down to the water and feed the monster carp that slowly swam up and down the base of the dam. Local legends claimed catfish that could swallow a human lived in the deep waters at the base of the dam. Of course I never missed an opportunity to tell Jason about that. Rather than frighten him, my greatly embellished stories just made him want to go try to catch one. We stayed at the lake visiting with Jerry for a day or so more then returned to Hamilton.

Our New Pontiac Ventura

I'd mentioned to my father that Karen and I wanted to get a car. The last new car we had owned was our 1965 Ford Thunderbird. After entering flight school all we could afford to drive was old (very old) cars. My father had mentioned to Paul Winn Jr. who was running his father's dealership that I might be looking for a car. Paul told my father he had something that we might like.

I went down to take a look. The car he was referring to was a lemon colored 1972 Pontiac Ventura. It was a two door and looked somewhat sporty, but nothing like our 1964 Mustang or the 1965 Thunderbird but better than the old 1955 Buick I drove all through flight school and finally sold to Bobby Wallace for around fifty dollars.

Karen liked the car. Jason was euphoric. Little Jenny didn't care as long as she got to go ride in it with us. While the car's appearance was sporty, there were some hidden hereditary issues. The car's six-cylinder 250 cubic inch engine was adequate power, but it had a two-speed automatic transmission. The first gear was so low and stayed in that first gear for so long that most people thought you were driving around in first gear all the time. For the life of me I'll never understand what possessed Pontiac to build that transmission. Apparently others agreed. That was the last year they made the transmission. We paid about $2800 for our sporty, lemon-colored Ventura with a two-speed transmission.

Jason was getting old enough to begin mastering the art of fishing with artificial bait. Miller–Gunn, a local store and Gulf service station run by Pete Gunn and his wife Elizabeth Miller Gunn always kept a decent assortment of lures, lines, hooks, weights and the like. It was usually necessary to stop by their store before we went fishing to replace the unbelievable number of spinner baits, split shot weights, hooks and bobbers we'd left hanging in trees and buried in submerged stumps along the shores of Hamilton's City Lake or the banks of Pecan Creek, Cowhouse Creek, or the Leon River. While we both left our share hanging in overhead tree branches, for an eight-year-old, he was pretty good. He learned to place his cast close to his target. He had the patience of Job, something I never had. Jason could fish for hours, even if nothing was biting. I, on the other hand, would soon find myself watching the water birds, looking for coon or other animal tracks, or looking for cotton mouth water moccasins. Jason never wavered. The problem was getting him to stop fishing when it was time to go home. We had our favorite spots at

City Lake and every creek in Hamilton County with enough water to fish. Now, forty years later, he never misses an opportunity to fish with his two teenage daughters.

A Distant Call

My summer fishing with Jason soon gave in to fall. He enrolled in Ann Whitney Elementary, where I too had attended. I began thinking about getting back in the air. It was like a voice calling in the distance. I started thinking about going back to Meacham field where I could flight instruct while I filled out airline applications. One of the axioms in aviation is "you must have a flying job to find a flying job."

I could already tell the appeal of an airline career no longer held the allure it had prior to the Congo. Inside Wigmo, I'd gotten a taste of a life beneath the shroud…life inside the secretive CIA proprietary companies scattered around the world…companies few knew existed. In moments of candor I wondered if there was any turning back.

Living Alone Again

I decided to take an apartment in the Dallas–Ft. Worth Metroplex which would position me close to the area's major airports. This way I could take a flying job of some type while looking for the right job. The minor flying job would produce enough income to stop or significantly defray the erosion of our savings until the right job came along. I could come home on the weekends.

The Snooty Fox

On the following Monday morning, with the Sunday edition of the Ft. Worth Star Telegram's in the front seat of our new Pontiac Ventura and a couple of boxes of clothes, a few other household items, pots, pans and dishes, etc., in the trunk, I headed out of town. While I was sad about not seeing Karen, Jason, and Jenny till the following Saturday morning, I was excited about starting a new chapter of my life.

I decided to go via Hico, Glen Rose, and Granbury. While driving north on Highway 281 toward Hico, I stopped for a few moments in Oakwood Cemetery to visit my mother's grave. As I pulled off the highway and turned into the cemetery, I thought about how our relationship had been cut so unnaturally short. Her untimely death in 1965 at the age of fifty-five to ovarian cancer had robbed my father of his beloved wife of almost forty years. It robbed me of a mother I could have known so much better. It robbed Camille of a mother she could only relate to as a teenager. But most of all, death had robbed my mother. She never saw Jason's first step, she never saw Jenny. She missed so much.

I'd visited her grave several times since returning from the Congo, but this morning, it was like I wanted to tell her I was embarking on a new chapter of my life. There was so much she never got to see. I rested under the little oak tree beside her grave. I talked to her for a few minutes, offered a little prayer, and then continued on.

From memory and from a map, I'd already decided Arlington would be a good midpoint location from which to base. I'd searched the classified ads before leaving Hamilton and marked the location of several affordable possibilities. The second one I visited was called the Snooty Fox. I remember thinking it sounded more like an old British pub than an apartment house. I later learned the street that ran just beside the apartments was named Snooty Fox.

When the manager showed me the available units, I immediately settled on a tiny one with a unique floor plan. The bedroom was an open loft. The bottom floor was a small living, a kitchen-dining area combination, and a bathroom. I loved the floor plan and it was the cheapest unit they had. I took it.

It's A Small Small World

My Neighbor–The Widow Of My Childhood Classmate And Friend

While I was filling out the rental agreement, the apartment manager noticed I listed Hamilton Texas as my previous address. She told me that she had a lady living in the apartments who also helped her in the rental office who was the widow of a man from Hamilton. I asked her last name...she replied Vick. My surprise, bordering on shock, was obvious. She asked if I had known the lady's husband. My only reply was "yes."

She was talking about Don Vick, born Jerry Donald Lomax. We had been childhood friends since the fourth grade. I never knew Don's father. Don was an only child and for many years. He and his mom lived together in a small home in Hamilton. Don was one of the smartest kids in the class . . . always. I, on the other hand, had to apply myself to make good grades...until I quit applying. Don was just plain smart; plus he always studied.

While we were in high school his mom finally remarried. She married a well-known and well-liked man named Archie Vick. The Vicks were an old family in Hamilton County. Shortly after his mother married Archie Vick, Don's legal name was changed to Vick. After high school I never saw Don again. Upon finishing college Don joined the army and was sent to flight school. He survived Vietnam but in 1969, prior to his discharge, he was killed in a military plane crash. Now, after so many years of no contact, I was being asked by the apartment manager if I would like to meet Don's widow. Her name was Ruth.

For some absolutely inexcusable reason, I said no. I've looked back on that moment countless times. The only reason I can think of was my obsession with personal privacy. What a selfish thought. I could have shared with her so many of the wonderful moments Don and I had growing up together. How we both learned to swim in stock tanks; how on Saturdays and on week days after school, supposedly without our parent's knowledge, we would swim stark naked in the tanks. How we would grab dried and sometimes not so dried cow pies and chase each other with them. When the looser of the chase was just about to get hit, he would dive underneath the surface and try to swim as far from the other's throwing range as possible before having to come up for air. If the diver miscalculated or his opponent got a lucky shot...the diver would receive a cow pie strike to the head. A strike from one of the fresher varieties found along the water's edge where they were deposited by cows, could easily get in your hair and sometimes even in your ear. There was always great motivation to swim long and hard before emerging for air. What was wrong with me? What on earth was I thinking? I had so much to share which someday she could have in turn share with their child. "If only."

My Friend Solitude Returns

As I unpacked my meager belongings, I felt a sensation of anticipation coming over me. I was once again living alone. There was a cheap TV in the living room, and I'd brought my radio from Hamilton. I had the option of television, rock and roll or doo-wop music from my radio, or silence. These anticipatory thoughts were not healthy, and I knew it. Somehow it didn't seem to matter.

The Job Hunt Begins

I immediately began a daily routine of making the airport rounds checking for flight instructor positions or possibly some charter pilot openings. It didn't take me long to learn that I was overqualified for the local job market and as a result, people were generally reluctant to offer me a job. They feared I would soon be moving on to a better paying position after they had gone to the expense of bringing me in to their organization. I found it hard to disagree. This nevertheless was not helping my situation.

In the evenings I would return and take my best shot at cooking something eatable for my evening meal. Some of my old standby options were macaroni and cheese meals from a box, frozen pizza, hush puppies and fish patties; most usually seemed to turn out only marginably eatable. Many times I'd just give up and go out to a Pizza Hut buffet or McDonalds. I found the mess I made in the kitchen combined with the edibility of my efforts oftentimes produced an inequity.

My Old Friend Toni Page

One of my first stops in the job search circuit was Meacham Field…where I'd attended my flight school. Southwest School of Aviation was still the most prestigious institution in the area if not the country. Most of their students were from other countries, just like when I was a student there.

One of my first stops at the airport was to visit my old friend, editor, publisher, and owner of the Cross-Country News, Toni Page. She was always a ball of energy even in her advanced years. She was one of the early generation female aviators. When they made Toni, they threw away the mold. I'd brought her a couple of spears from the Congo on one of my trips back home. They were proudly displayed in the front office of the newspaper.

Toni and I had a pleasant visit. She kept pushing for an interview, but I told her anything interesting I could tell her about the Congo operations would get me in a lot of trouble. She graciously accepted my decline. After visiting for at least an hour over coffee in the terminal restaurant, I gave her my phone numbers and told her to keep an eye out for me.

More Letters–More Applications

I brought my typewriter with me from Hamilton to the Snooty Fox. I'd had it since my Navy days in San Diego. It reminded me of something Ernest Hemingway would have used. I spent a lot of time up in my bedroom/loft pounding away on letters requesting applications, cover letters for resumes, and networking with colleagues from Wigmo now living back in Europe. I had a phone installed and I spent lots of time on the phone as well.

Just before going to the Congo I'd contacted Air America, a sister CIA proprietary company. At that time they told me they had no immediate openings but would keep me on file. I almost immediately left for the Congo and never followed up again. I'd brought their letter with me from Hamilton and decided to send them another request even though I didn't hold out a lot of hope.

The reason for my lack of enthusiasm about Air America stemmed from an interesting coincidence. Wigmo and Air America had shared a common HF (high frequency) long range radio frequency. It was one of our lower band frequencies and we normally never heard each other. We knew they were there but with the huge time differences and the frequencies propagation characteristics we usually never got in each other's way. They were mostly in Vietnam and Laos, we were in Africa. However, late one afternoon, while we were on the ground in Goma talking to King 1, we heard them drifting in on our frequency. We immediately exchanged greetings. This had happened enough that we knew who they were, and they knew who we were. Of course with all aviation people, worldwide, almost immediately the subject of employment opportunities arose. They had stated Air America was winding down significant aspects of their operation in South East Asia due to some unfortunate media attention that stimulated the equally unwanted attention of U.S. Congress. They wanted to know if we were hiring. We told them that in fact we were but that was due to all the rats leaving the ship…that we were in the process of sinking. I nevertheless wrote them a note referencing my previous contact with them and updating my significant qualifications since our last contact.

Weekends In Hamilton

On Friday evenings or Saturday mornings I'd make the drive back to Hamilton. It was good to see Karen and the kids and good to eat her cooking or that of my father. My Snooty Fox cooking endeavors were poor at best and in my father's home we ate very well. But by each Sunday, I was ready for Monday and my return to the solitude of the Snooty Fox. Part of me hated what I was becoming.

As the last of summer slipped toward fall, Jason and I fished away those precious few lazy weekends. I had fun playing with Jenny, but I could tell I was having to work at finding something to talk with Karen about. I knew the problem was inside me and related probably to my growing passion for solitude. Karen was always trying to make my time with the family restful and pleasant.

But while Hamilton County's final days of summer were slow, in Paris, Washington, Saigon, and Hanoi movement was taking place. Kissinger was busy selling out the South Vietnamese in a frantic effort to produce some results in the war situation that would help Nixon get reelected. Our allies, our principles, nothing mattered…only Nixon's reelection and Kissinger's own shot at the Nobel Peace Prize. I failed, however, to notice anything but the boldest of headlines.

The Cambodian Call

One weekend, while I was in Hamilton, I went to visit Jerry Drake who had a home on Lake Buchanan. While there I got a call from my father saying someone had called the house looking for me. The man had said it was about a flying job in Cambodia. My father had meticulously written down the man's name…Ford…Roger M. Ford. He gave me his phone number. I recognized the number as being in the Ft. Worth area.

Heck, I wasn't even sure where Cambodia was. I thought it was someplace near Thailand and Vietnam. You never heard much about Thailand, but Vietnam was in every newspaper you picked up and on every six o'clock news program. I immediately realized that if this Cambodian operation had any connection to the conflict going on over in Vietnam, it held the potential for some serious money…another "Wigmo" operation. I picked up the phone and dialed the number.

The number turned out to be that of a hotel. I asked to be connected with Mr. Roger Ford. To my surprise, my call was immediately put through. A man answered. It was Ford. He asked me a few questions about my work in the Congo. I could tell by the nature of some of the questions, he was fishing to see if I was for real. After less than five minutes he asked me to come up to Ft. Worth on Monday to have lunch with him. I told him I would see him on Monday. I spent the rest of the afternoon visiting with Jerry and drove back to Hamilton.

Karen was always supportive but I could tell she was somewhat disappointed that I was not being offered a job back home somewhere in the United States. Roger had told me the company was owned by an American. That's about all he was willing to give up on the phone. He said he would explain more when we met on Monday. I was starting to like the sound of this already.

Monday…My Macedonian Call

The Monday morning drive back to my Snooty Fox abode was filled with excitement. More than the money…the excitement was about more adventure. I wondered how the interview would go; what kind of questions Ford would ask. How my qualifications would match with their requirements.

I arrived at the hotel a few minutes before noon. Roger had said for me to call him from the lobby. He said the hotel had a very nice buffet and we could start our meeting over lunch. I did as he had instructed and soon a huge man, stepped out of the elevator. I'd told him on the phone what I was wearing; he walked straight to me and offered his mammoth bear-paw hand. Not only was Roger's frame huge, he was also fat. I would later learn he was on his college wrestling team.

As we talked over our meal I was impressed at his ultra-low-key demeanor. His voice was quiet, and he spoke mostly in a low monotone voice with the exception of an occasional muffled laugh. During our conversation I learned he was ex-army, a major, and a pilot. I would later learn he was specially discharged from the army to take part in this operation. He continued asking me about my role within Wigmo's organization. I could tell without asking he already knew who they were. I made certain, even as our conversation became friendlier and more casual, that no reference to the CIA would pass across my lips…:not even a hint. He would occasionally plant opportunities in what I was sure were inducements, but I ignored them all. While we were eating, he got up several times to completely refill his plate to the brim. I was quite sure I'd never seen anyone eat that much.

After our meal, which for him also included several helpings of desserts of various types, we went up to his room. There he explained more in depth about the nature of the operation. He gave me the company's name, TRI-9 Corporation. He said they were not involved in any offensive operations only air transport. However, he did dwell at length on my T-28 experience in

Wigmo's counterinsurgency operations. When I asked if these "air transport" operations ever encountered any hostile fire, he quietly chuckled, smiled, and replied "occasionally." When I asked about casualties, his reply was "rarely." When he explained the pay, it was almost to the dollar what Wigmo had paid; all in U.S. dollars in country or via wire transfers "depending on one's personal tax situation"…again with his muffled little chuckle. He asked if I was interested and I told him yes. He asked me when I could start; I asked if three weeks from now would be OK and he replied that would be fine. During this process my twisted evil twin pulled a Bible verse from an obscure cobwebbed corner of my brain and dragged it across my cognizant mind much like a banner towing aircraft would parade an advertisement across the sky over a large gathering of people…"A Macedonian man was standing and pleading with him, Cross over to Macedonia and help us."[176] My Cambodian calling was nothing like Paul's Macedonian Call and I'll be quite lucky if I'm not reminded of that while standing before the judgment seat.

I signed a commitment statement, a letter of agreement (LOA) as well as a confidentiality agreement and was told I would receive my tickets shortly. Roger said I would first receive a ticket to Bangkok. He told me to get a visa only for Thailand; that my visa into Phnom Penh would be arranged for me from Thailand. My immediate suspicion was they were avoiding clearly traceable travel. He told me he was leaving for Cambodia (also via Thailand) in a couple of days and that he would see me in Phnom Penh.

As I drove away from the hotel my head was swirling. I was filled with excitement. But along with the excitement was the unsettling feeling about Karen, Jason, and Jenny. They would not be coming with me. It was becoming very clear to me that I was enjoying the part of my life apart from them more than I was my part with them. As I was experiencing extreme guilt for these feelings, as I well should have been, the Apostle Paul's words came to mind…"I don't understand what I am doing. For I don't practice what I want to do, but instead do what I hate." [177]

When I reached the Snooty Fox I called Karen with the news. I was sure I heard anxiety in her voice…but it may have just been my own demons. I told her I would stay here until I got the tickets just in case something fell through. She said OK as she always did.

As I wrestled with telling Karen what this really meant, the Paris Peace Talks appeared to be making progress. President Nixon suspended Operation Linebacker, Kissinger flew to Vietnam and met with President Nguyen Van Thieu to discuss the peace agreement. But our South Vietnamese allies believed we were selling them out and refused to buy into what Kissinger had worked out with the North Vietnamese. Kissinger, frantically trying to come up with anything that will get Nixon elected, declares "we believe peace is at hand." Nothing could have been farther from the truth.

---

[176] Holy Bible—Holman Christian Standard Bible (HCSB) - Acts 16:9
[177] Holy Bible—International Standard Version (©2012) - Romans 7:15

As the time of my departure approached, I was beginning to think something might have fallen through as the tickets had not arrived. I called the number Roger had given me, and it turned out there had been an administrative mess up…the guy responsible for doing my tickets had been on vacation. They gave me my confirmation numbers, sent a telegram, and told me to report to the airline ticket desk with the telegram on a specific date. It also gave me the hotel where I should stay in Bangkok and a telephone number to call upon arrival for my visa and ticket to Phnom Penh. I hurriedly packed my things, spent half a day cleaning the apartment, retrieved my deposit and headed for Hamilton.

Our Last Trip Together

The nearest Thai embassy was in Washington DC. I decided I would take Karen along. She arranged for someone to watch Jenny. I got two tickets to Washington and we were off. We spent a couple of days there while I was getting my visa for Thailand then returned to Hamilton. The visa process went well, but soon it was time to leave. While we were in Washington, I snapped a black and white photo of Karen in her fur coat which I always thought was the best picture she ever took. It would be the last picture I would take of her as my wife.

Cambodia – Trail of Tears

Bangkok

From the airport, I went straight to the Nana Hotel where I was instructed to stay. When I presented my passport at the front desk, the beautiful young lady handling my check-in process took my passport and went into an adjoining office. She returned with a man who introduced himself as the manager. He said he would have a special car and driver waiting for me the first thing in the morning that would "take me to my destination." He assured me Mr. Ford had already given the driver thorough instructions and I need not worry about anything. He told me he would have a wakeup call for 7:00 am in case I was not already up. The bellman took my bags and showed me to my room.

It was still early afternoon and far too soon for me to try to sleep even though my body was now twelve hours "ahead" of Hamilton Texas time.

The Nana Coffee Shop–A Wide Menu

I took a shower and went down to the hotel coffee shop for a bite to eat. To my amazement it was filled with Americans. After my Wigmo time these guys were easy to spot. They were mostly U.S. Air Force types on assignments requiring civilian clothes (civies) or they were stationed at small clandestine bases deep in the rural areas of northern and eastern Thailand bordering on Laos and extremely close to China. But regardless of where they were stationed, they wore civilian clothes. The military personnel generally fit a mostly squeaky-clean mold with distinguishing military haircuts. There was another group of older, less squeaky guys with haircuts ranging from shaved to shoulder-length. They were the Continental Air Service and Air America group, and mostly based in Laos.

The immediate impression upon entering the coffee shop was the disproportionate number of suggestively clad, mostly young, heavily painted and unaccompanied women. I'd come down to get something to eat and quickly found the coffee shop was offering more than meals. Roger Ford had neglected to mention this.

I ordered a burger and a Coke and tried to eat, but most of my time was spent saying "no thank you." The food wasn't half bad…something the Congo had a hard time saying. The Thais had quickly learned to master middle-class American food preferences and were well tapped into the vast sums of money this sizable force of clandestine visitors had to spend. I finished my meal and headed back upstairs. In spite of my excitement, I managed somehow to get to sleep.

A Rainy Drive—A Shadowy Visa

The next morning, I enjoyed a first-class American style breakfast and was waiting for the driver in the lobby as instructed. At the stroke of 9:00 am the bellman came and advised my car and driver were waiting outside. As I walked out, I saw a late model Toyota with dark tented windows in front. The driver got out and introduced himself. His name was Kim. I would use Kim many times over the next several years. Kim spoke good English albeit with a heavy accent. Almost immediately after we pulled away from the Nana, it began to rain. As we drove through the city, I could see standing water everywhere. Kim explained that this was normal during the rainy season and that we were now in the final weeks of it. I did not directly ask Kim where we were going. I only asked if we were going to get my visa to which he replied yes.

After about thirty minutes' drive in Bangkok's impossible traffic exacerbated by the falling rain, we arrived at a nondescript building. There was a typical drainage ditch running parallel to the street which I had to cross via a makeshift and wobbly wooden bridge. Actually "bridge" was flattery. At any rate, Kim and I made it across. Kim knocked on the door. An Asian man dressed in Chinese style pajamas answered. Kim spoke to him in Chinese and the man took my passport. He instructed us to wait. One thing I was sure of…this was not the visa section of the Cambodian Embassy. We sat on an unpainted wooden bench under the shelter of the porch. In a few minutes the man returned with my passport. He showed me the visa and advised there was a $20 fee. I checked and there was a very official looking visa. I'd already been told the "company" was paying for the visa, so I was sure this was just another of the countless forms of corruption one has to deal with in this line of work. I handed the man a twenty dollar note. Then Kim drove me on to the ticket office of Air Vietnam where I presented the confirmation number I'd previously received. A few minutes later I was handed my ticket. My departure for the forty-five-minute flight from Bangkok to Phnom Penh left at 10:30 am the following morning.

Kim graciously told me he had been engaged by my employer for the entire day and said he would be happy to show me some of the famous tourist attractions in the city. I accepted his offer and spent the remainder of the day in some kind of wide-eyed trance. This was the most exotic city I'd ever seen. Paris was exciting in a sophisticated European way, but Bangkok was the perfect mix of exotic and mysterious.

First, I toured the royal palace; then the floating market. After that we went to Old Town. Kim cautioned me about eating from the little shops along the street selling all kinds of food but to no avail. I loved Thai food at first sight and sniff. Wigmo's training courses had taught to learn to live off the land as soon as we arrived. Start building the local bacteria colonies in your stomach while you are still close to the best medical care that will be available to you.

Then when you find yourself where eating choices are less than desirable you won't have trouble finding things you can tolerate. In the Congo this was a bit of a chore…here it was a gastronomic pleasure. I faithfully and enthusiastically followed Wigmo's advice. Yum! Kim dropped me off at the hotel around 7:30pm. I happily gave Kim a generous tip, told him I'd see him at 6:45 in the morning, and headed to the hotel bar for a drink before going up to my room.

While I was exploring Bangkok, President Nixon was re-elected and more U.S. troops departed Vietnam as part of our troop withdrawal. I did not vote. On the radio, Nights In White Satin by The Moody Blues, I Can See Clearly Now by Johnny Nash, and Ben by Michael Jackson were playing, for our troops on American Forces Radio Saigon.

The Nana Hotel Bar–Another Planet

Nothing I'd previously experienced prepared me for the bar in the Nana Hotel…nothing. Heavily painted and revealingly clad young as well as not quite so young women were standing and sitting everywhere. Many of them were sitting at the bar but managed to populate a large percent of the tables as well. Since I didn't relish the inevitable besiegement that having my drink at the congested bar would trigger, I elected to take a small table for two over against the wall. The bar was dark…like really dark, except for the proliferation of ultraviolet (UV-A or "black") light sources. The UV-A light distorted the colors in the room, especially the copious quantities of lipstick these fallen angels wore. They looked surreal. It reminded me of some kind of alien planet. Most of them walked with a ridiculously exaggerated swish. About the time my butt hit the chair I was wishing I'd simply ordered a beer with the meal I had just finished at the little mom and pop sidewalk Thai restaurant.

Soon a waitress was asking for my order. I'd already learned that Singha Beer was Thailand's version of Budweiser. Many of the American expats living there would argue Singha was far better. My beer was not immediately forthcoming. Before my beer arrived I had politely returned the smiles of several *angels flying too close to the ground* and with equal politeness repeated my "no thank you." By the time I'd had my first few sips I'd become quite impressed with the telepathy or angel-intercom used to signal who was a player and who wasn't. It didn't take long before I was collectively identified as a no-player and was able to finish my drink in peace. When I'd finished my drink and was making my way toward the door, a couple of die-hard angels gave me one last shot. I went up to my room alone and tried to get a good night's sleep. But sleep didn't come easy that night…I was too excited.

My alarm sounded and the backup wakeup call came at 5:30am. I did not want to miss my flight due to Bangkok's notorious gridlock traffic. The bellman was at my door almost immediately after my call. Each floor had a bellman-security person. My call to the front desk was immediately relayed back up to my floor via walkie-talkie. He placed my bags in the holding area and by a couple of minutes after 6:00am, I was sitting in the Nana Coffee Shop. To my surprise, several Americans were already having morning coffee and breakfast. Some were still accompanied by their fiancée of the previous evening. This was definitely a long way from anything I'd ever known…this was not Texas.

Kim was waiting and as soon as the bellman saw me, he moved my bags to Kim's car. I quickly paid my bill and walked briskly to the waiting car. Fully one hour later, I was making my way to Air Vietnam's check-in.

Descending Into Cambodia
A Land of Wonder–A Land of Tears

I strained to get my first glimpse of Cambodia from the Boeing 727's window as we descended through the clouds. I could see forest covered foothills in the distance, but it was mostly flat flooded rice fields dotted with palm trees. As we taxied off the runway and toward the terminal, I was struck by how small the terminal was and how old all the airplanes were. I could see several Convairs on the ramp. This was the airplane I'd been told I'd be flying. They were far more modern than any of the piston airplanes I'd flown in the Congo. They were still in use by airlines in the United States. There were also plenty of C-46 and C-47 (DC-3) aircraft. I looked across the ramp as I was making my way from the plane to Phnom Penh's outdoor terminal. On the other side of the airport, the ramp was filled with C-130, C-47, AC-47, T-28, plus OV1 and OV10 (military observer or spotter aircraft) planes. The civilian ramp had military personnel with new M-16s everywhere. While the physical features of the Cambodians appeared similar to the Thais, it was obvious this was not Thailand. Cambodia was a country at war.

I was one of only a handful of Americans on the plane. I was met midway across the ramp by an American asking me if I was Jimmy Jacks. When I replied yes, he introduced himself as Josh Oates, (pseudonym) asked for my passport and escorted me across the ramp and directly to the head of the immigration checkpoint line. I could hear numerous French voices grumbling in line behind me. I didn't bother to turn around. I was immediately stamped into the country and taken to the baggage collection area. When I had my two bags, they were given to a Cambodian in an airline uniform who was told to take them to the Tri-9 office. My escort "shook hands" with the customs agent and my customs formalities were instantly finished.

Josh was Tri-9's director of maintenance. He told me Roger Ford, Tri-9's chief pilot and director of flight operations would be landing shortly and wanted me to accompany him on his next flight which was scheduled to be a quick turn after landing. We walked over to a little restaurant in the arrival and departure area and ordered a cold drink. I had some kind of Cambodian cola knockoff. No sooner had they brought our drink than Roger's flight landed. Josh's men were meeting the plane. I spotted Roger walking toward the terminal. He stood easily head and shoulders above all the Cambodians. He joined us, virtually inhaled an orange soft drink, immediately got up and told me to come along; he would give me an indoctrination flight.

My First Tri-9 Flight

When we arrived at the plane I looked around and didn't see his copilot. When I asked where he was, Roger said..."you're it." He had given the copilot the rest of the afternoon off. Roger said they were shorthanded, and everybody had been flying a little too much. I casually mentioned I'd never seen the cockpit of a Convair 440 before, to which he replied..."don't worry...you'll be seeing plenty of them." I also was not accustomed to flying in an airline operation. While we were in the middle of a war and the U.S. government was underwriting our operations with fuel and contracts to the Cambodian airline companies, the deceptive airline mantle was our ability to be in the country without being in violation of congress's edicts.

Roger and the three cabin attendants were all in uniform. I was wearing one of my pencil-legged safari suites made by the Indian tailor back in Kinshasa. To say I looked a bit out of place would have been an understatement. I noticed the cabin crew curiously watching me. I hopped in the right seat, adjusted the seatbelt and got the mic and called for a clearance. Like in my initial Congo flights, I had trouble understanding the controller's English. I jotted down the clearance, and immediately we started running the checklist. I had never heard of half the things on the checklist and likewise had little idea where they were located. By the time we were ready for the before takeoff checklist I was stressed, and the back of my shirt was wet in spite of the fact that the Convair had air-conditioning and pressurization. Thankfully, the before takeoff checklist was short and soon we were roaring down the runway.

My first in-aircraft opinion of Roger was heading south rapidly. This was cowboy...this was not Wigmo...this was not professional. I had had no training on the aircraft and this sure as hell was not how to learn. This was a far more modern cockpit than our Wigmo planes and I didn't even know where the emergency checklists were, much less how to execute them. I was definitely not professionally impressed. Roger, however had this type of personality that made just about everybody like him...including me.

Within what seemed no time at all, we were approaching Battambang. The first thing I noticed about the decent to landing was it was not initiated till we were within about five miles of the airport. When the descent began, we started going down like a brick falling from the sky. It was steep. When I asked Roger about the steep descent, he smiled and said it was better than pulling a SAM 7 out of our butt. I knew enough about SAM 7 missiles to know most encounters were fatal. I asked him if the bad guys were really that close to the airport. Again that Roger Ford smile accompanying an almost inaudible…"oh yes."

The rapid decent scared some of our passengers but for others, it appeared to be the high point of the flight.

Our return passengers were all waiting as we taxied in. We had fueled in Phnom Penh for the return leg so within about ten minutes we were ready to start engines. I did much better with the check list this time as I'd used the brief flight to Battambang to hunt around and locate as many of the switches and other controls as possible.

When we reached the end of the runway Roger told me to make the takeoff. As I smoothly moved the throttles forward to the takeoff position, I was impressed with the power these huge R-2800 engines with alcohol injection were putting out. WOW! If my father could see me now.

As we approached Phnom Penh's Pochentong airport Roger asked me if I was ready to try a landing. My answer, of course, was "of course." He assured me that the Convair didn't have any serious landing idiosyncrasies and that I'd be just fine. He advised the steep decent we executed in Battambang would not be necessary here in Phnom Penh…at least not yet. That was a relief. I made a normal approach and a smooth landing. I'd never flown an aircraft with thrust reversers before but that worked just fine as well. As we taxied in, I noted my back was a little wet again. Even though it had been fun, it was obviously stressful as well. I was ready to head home, wherever home was going to be.

Josh and his crew met the flight to see if we had any maintenance issues. The plane was clean (clear of "squawks" or maintenance discrepancies) so we all headed to the Tri-9 office. The mechanics secured the aircraft, I grabbed my bags and we got in the crew cars. I rode with Roger. Josh and the mechanics rode in a jeep. I learned I'd be staying with Roger that night; that he had a large company provided villa and plenty of empty bedrooms. He said he had an apartment all set up for me that was fully furnished and already had a maid. He told me we would fly again first thing the following morning but for only a half day. From there he would take me to the Tri-9 administration office, process me in, get me an ID card, then take me to get some uniforms made and show me my new apartment. Roger, for all his apparent lack of cockpit discipline, managed to make things move quickly. I was very satisfied with how my first day had gone. I woke up in the Nana hotel, drove through Bangkok traffic, flew to Phnom Penh, and had taken my first Convair 440 flight and my first flight with Tri-9.

The houseboy, husband of the cook, carried my bags to the room where I'd be sleeping. I sat down in the large living room and had a beer while Roger drank another orange soda…I learned Roger did not drink. As a matter of fact, he was a Seven Day Adventist. I would later learn he was a rather liberated Adventist.

The Vietnamese cook had prepared a great meal. Roger and I ate alone at the large table. He had to get up a couple of times to take phone calls related to flight operations; some came from the embassy. While we ate, I noticed two teenage girls and a younger girl peeking around the corner at us and giggling. Roger explained that they were the daughters of his cook. He smiled and said, "they like you." I replied, "I wasn't going to like anybody but my bed tonight." He smiled and our conversation moved on to how flight operations worked. When the meal was finished, we both went upstairs. He showed me my room, the bathroom associated with my room, told me what time breakfast was and we said goodnight.

New Faces–New Names–New Places

The following morning at breakfast Roger once again demonstrated his incredible capacity to pack away food. Amazing! Breakfast went quickly and we were soon off to the airport. It was not yet 7:00 am and the airport was buzzing with passengers and crew. Roger pointed to an area where some passengers had slept the night before in order to be near the head of the check-in line. He explained that a ticket didn't mean a lot here as the ticket agents regularly took bribes to place people on the passenger manifest. I immediately made the connection with the Congolese loadmasters. I noticed many passengers in military uniform in the line.

Roger and I went to the Tri-9 office (nothing more than a single small room), got our manifest, a copy of the weather, a copy of the flight plan, and a security briefing provided by the Khmer Air Force on the condition around Pochentong and our destination Kompong Som (Sihanoukville). Mortar rounds had hit Kompong Som the night before but did no damage. Nobody seemed to take much notice of mortar attacks. We were carrying large amounts of cargo in addition to the passengers' bags. The cargo was mostly food going to merchants in Kompong Som. Roger explained the Khmer Rouge were managing to keep a stranglehold on many major cities forcing critical supplies to be airlifted in.

As I was doing my walk-around preflight inspection with Roger, I noticed more money changing hands at the foot of the air-stair door. Roger mentioned that the air force sergeant and 1st lieutenant taking the money probably had not been paid in a couple of months because their colonel and general had pocketed it. Memories of the Congo again flashed through my mind. The mechanics briefed us on minor repairs they had made, handed us a flight release, and we climbed into the cockpit.

Departure was normal and soon we were heading southwest, loosely paralleling National Highway 4 which was hopelessly cut by the Khmer Rouge forces. Anything moving on the road was a target and as a result, not much moved. On today's flight, there were few rice paddies like there had been yesterday on the flight to Battambang. We were flying over beautiful forest covered mountains. Rivers and waterfalls were visible in the mountain forest below. The forest and mountains were part of the Cardamom mountain range. Their beauty was breathtaking. Roger pointed out deserted rubber plantations. The Khmer Rouge made sure nothing was operating that could benefit the enemy (us).

The flight was short; only about 35 minutes. Soon I could see the Gulf of Thailand out the left window. We would be landing at a Cambodian Air Force Base named Ream. Ream was still eleven miles from the town of Kompong Som or Sihanoukville as it was called before the coup in 1970 which deposed the head of state Norodom Sihanouk. The road was only passable during daylight hours. At night the Khmer Rouge would move out from the cover of the mountain forest and take control of the road. Travel even during the day was risky and required a heavily armed military convoy escort. So for our passengers and cargo, reaching Ream was only part of their journey. The road trip to and from the airport was the dangerous part.

Roger's Oops

We contacted the military air traffic controller and were advised the runway in use was 21. Both Roger and I had visual contact on the airport. Roger advised this was going to be another steep approach. The extended centerline of runway 21 ran directly into the mountains. The approach would have been a bit steep under normal conditions. But according to Roger, the mountain range just north east of the runway was KR territory and frequently used by them to shell the airport. So we would need to keep it high. The KR were most commonly armed with Chinese manufactured AK-47s which had a maximum "effective" range of about 400 meters or about 1300 feet but were capable of doing serious damage well over that distance. If they chose to use a SAM 7 that day, you were pretty well screwed. The Russians were making sure there was an abundant supply of SAM 7 missiles available to the Khmer Rouge. This factor normally resulted in the pilots requesting to land the other direction, on runway 03 which would allow for a normal or even slightly lower profile landing (carrier landing). But for whatever reason…probably because it was a straight-in approach requiring less time, Roger accepted runway 21 without questioning it and I didn't yet know the difference. Our briefing did mention that no reports of SAM 7 launches in the vicinity of that airport had been received recently. We all knew that meant nothing if the KR decided to make you their first.

The use of a steep approach like we had done the day before in Battambang normally would have been OK except for one thing…the runway here was only 4200 feet long. This was short for any transport aircraft…really short. But when making a steep approach like we would be doing, the lack of landing distance removed almost all the cushion. There was close to zero margin for error. We set up on an almost straight in approach and when we finally were clear of the last mountain on final, Roger set up a decent rate that was pushing 2000 feet per minute. A normal sink for this final stage of the approach in this airplane would have been around 500 feet per minute. At some point very close to the end of the runway, we were going to have to trade all that sink for a normal decent rate or prang the runway at a destructive sink rate. Roger had kept his speed pretty close to normal which would have been good if we were on a normal approach, but we were not…we were on a tactical approach. At some point Roger was going to need to trade some airspeed for some lift to reduce the sink. Even though I was not familiar with the performance characteristics of the Convair 440 I could tell he did not have the airspeed to trade. In order to break the excessive decent rate…with the airspeed he had, we were going to need an increase in power. I asked if he wanted some more power which I could have given him. He said no. He managed to break the sink rate but in doing so our airspeed fell significantly below our target speed. As if that were not enough, he was now setup to land a couple of yards short of the runway. Again I asked if he wanted power…again he said no.

The runway was built up above the terrain to keep it from flooding during the heavy monsoon rains. We struck the earthen mound about three feet before the asphalt runway. The touchdown made a loud noise as we slammed the ground just short of the runway threshold. We then continued onto the runway. I could hear some of the passengers in the back screaming.

Roger appeared a little shaken and quite embarrassed. When we parked on the ramp, we both went out to inspect the damage. We both went to the wheel wells of the main landing gears. The left main wheel had a slight but distinguishable ripple in the metal. If we had been in the States, the aircraft would have been grounded until a ferry permit could have been issued allowing it to fly without passengers to an advanced maintenance facility where all types of metallurgy testing could be conducted. As we looked at the damage, our passengers were boarding. Roger and I climbed back in the cockpit and flew back to Phnom Penh.

When we arrived back in Phnom Penh and taxied onto the ramp, I noticed the crew chief, a Filipino in his late fifties pointing at our airplane attempting to show the other Filipino mechanics something. When we parked, they were all swarming around the aft section of the fuselage. I made myself busy completing the flight's paperwork. I was going to let Roger deal with this. Roger left the plane first. When I finished all the paperwork and finally came down the air-stair, the crew chief asked me what in the world happened and pointed to a ripple in the sheet metal on the side of the fuselage. "I don't know…better ask Roger I replied" and headed toward the terminal. Mercifully the flying day was over and we were heading to Tri-9's main office to start my in-processing. On the way to the office Roger commented that it might be best if we don't mention the little landing incident. I nodded in agreement.

The Tri-9 Office

We soon arrived at a building used by Tri-9 as its administrative center. Roger took me immediately to meet the owner of the organization, an American named John Zoeller (pseudonym). As we chatted, I learned John had been in the aviation business for many years and that he often based out of Singapore. While we were chatting his wife, a Korean named Joy (pseudonym) walked into the office. She came across as formal and business like. I later learned that she more or less ran everything while John nursed a serious drinking problem. After a short visit, Roger took me over to where all the paperwork was handled. I went into a small office where another Filipino sat. His name was Abe and he was in charge of all administration. He handed me a stack of forms. One was for my ID, another for my contract and salary with bank instructions, another for next of kin, and finally an expense reimbursement form for hotel and meals in Bangkok. Of course he made the usual photo copies of my passport, pilot's licenses, radio license, medical certificate, etc. There was also a form for a two-week salary advance to be withheld from my first month's pay. This would be offset by a local living allowance in lieu of my not electing to live in a company provided hotel room.

Abe had an irritating quirk of insisting every "i" was dotted and every "t" crossed. But then, how could such non-skilled people ever justify their existence without such useless and inconsequential little regiments. I played his game. I needed an ID card and an expense reimbursement not to mention a paycheck.

While I was busy humoring Abe another Korean walked in. His name was Johnny Yum (pseudonym). Roger introduced Johnny as Joy's brother. Johnny handled all the higher-level contacts in town. Johnny struck me as exceptionally hyper. He had a serious burn scar on his face which I later learned was allegedly from napalm in the Korean war. Apparently he had been a child and was a civilian casualty. I would later learn that both Johnny and his sister Joy carried American passports; almost certainly thanks to John.

After what seemed like an eternity, I completed all the paperwork to Abe's satisfaction (not really...I just wore him down). Next stop was the tailor.

As Roger and I drove through Phnom Penh I frequently noticed crude obviously political caricatures on billboards. I asked who the villain in the caricatures was. "That is the former head of state, the former king, now Prince Norodom Sihanouk who was deposed by the present government a couple of years ago" was Roger's answer. "The royal family is...what you might say...on the outs right now", Roger added.

The tailor's shop was a modest place, but he had several men sewing on suits, safari suits, shirts and pants. Roger was well known there so we were looked after immediately. After the customary cup of hot tea, I was measured for trousers and shirts.

My "Ike-cut" Uniform Shirts

The shirt of choice was white cotton, short sleeve, with shoulder straps to accommodate our epaulettes. They had fold-over pockets to keep our whiz wheels (CR-4 flight computers) from falling out. The pocket flap had a special opening for our pen. But these were different than others I'd seen. They were referred to as "Eisenhower" cuts. The body of the shirt was short, really short and only came to just below my belt line. The sleeves were short. The waist area was patterned after the famous WWII Ike jacket. When I asked why they decided to go with this design I was told it wasn't mandatory, but most guys liked the ventilation provided by not having a shirttail tucked in. Then, in typical Roger fashion, he added, "plus, some guys like the ability to reach under it quickly." Although I failed to understand the remark at the time, I would soon understand well. In less than fifteen minutes, I was measured, told to come back the next afternoon for a fitting, and we were on to our next stop…my new apartment.

My "Fully Furnished" Apartment

On the way over to where I was going to spend the next few months, Roger got around to telling me the story behind the apartment. Seems Tri-9's previous maintenance director had developed some psychological issues. I'd learned from the Congo that such developments weren't all that uncommon in this line of work. But in this case, the presenting symptoms became significant enough that repatriation and therapy were deemed necessary. The rent for his apartment was two weeks past due. I also learned that not only was his maid living there but also his girlfriend or now ex-girlfriend. With my evil twin's penchant for privacy and solitude red flags went up all around. I explained to Roger that I didn't like overcomplicated living environments and if it became necessary, I'd pick my own girlfriend. Roger, in turn pointed out that if I just sent the maid to the apartment owner with the two weeks rent plus the next month's rent, I wouldn't have to come up with the normal security deposit. The owner of the apartment would think the original tenant was still there. I wasn't really enamored with the idea but being it was almost 4:00 pm I decided that whatever I decided to do…it would be later when I was more familiar with the situation. In the meantime I told him this arrangement would be fine.

Yat–The Maid

We rang the bell and soon…God Forgive Me…what was probably the ugliest woman I'd ever seen in my entire life opened the door. Not only had she been shortchanged in the area of physical attractiveness, but on top of that, she had one of the worst cases of acne I'd ever seen. Roger, obviously reading my shock, assured me she would keep the two-bedroom apartment spotlessly clean and that she was a halfway decent cook. Again I agreed reasoning I could correct everything at a later date. I moved my bags to the master bedroom and returned to the living room to finish my visit with Roger.

Sokha–The Ex-Girlfriend

While Roger was showing me around the apartment, the ex-girlfriend arrived. Roger knew her well and introduced us. Her name was Sokha (pseudonym). She was attractive and spoke relatively good English. Yat spoke none.

Roger told me Sokha could finish showing me the place. He told me we would be flying together again tomorrow morning early but that this time the crew car would be here for me and should be ready at 6:30am. Roger said he still had to go by to have a short visit with the air attaché before finally going home. I thanked him for all his help, and he left.

Sokha and I had to have a serious talk quickly. I had noticed there was no food in the refrigerator and no meal had been prepared. I had only seen some already cooked white rice on the counter and a tiny quantity of some kind of something that I was sure I was not yet ready to learn to eat. It was definitely some kind of peasant Khmer food. Since I needed to have dinner and I also needed to have a serious talk with Sokha about our future relationship (or lack thereof) I asked her if there was someplace close where we could go eat. She replied yes…less than five minutes from here. Good food and good price she said. I told her I'd buy her dinner if she showed me the restaurant. She was pleased and we left.

It turned out the place was less than five minutes away. It was less than 100 meters from the apartment entrance.

The temperature was pleasant and the walk interesting. It was my first time to be out walking in Cambodia. Sokha was very good at explaining things. The restaurant was basically Chinese. We managed to get a quiet table. The waiters and the owner all knew Sokha. Apparently, she and her former boyfriend had eaten here frequently.

As we ate, she told me she was very sad when he left Cambodia and that she was still hoping he would come back to get her. How tragic, I thought, but kept that to myself. This did however make what I needed to tell her easier. I told her that she would have to move…that I felt it would be too crowded with three of us living there. I explained I realized it might be difficult for her to try to find a place to stay right away and that she could stay in the apartment until the first of next month but that she would have to move into the bedroom with Yat. I could see the relief on her face. She had not been expecting to see anyone move into the apartment and coming home and finding me was a bit of a shock although she must surely have known that something like this was eventually inevitable. We had an enjoyable meal with her asking me many questions about my life in the United States.

Immediately upon our return to the apartment she moved her clothes into the maid's bedroom. We then sat for a minute while she volunteered to help me manage the maid and the ordering of groceries until I got settled in. This was a tremendous help as the maid spoke zero English. She told me about how much it would cost to buy food for the next three or four days. I gave her the amount she said she needed and we said goodnight.

The Cambodian Crew Car

At 6:30 am I was standing out on the sidewalk in front of my apartment when I spotted the most ridiculous looking car I'd ever seen in my life coming down the street. It's hard to describe something the reader can't identify with. With the exception of possibly something a circus clown might use as a prop, I can't think of anything that would come close to relating. Not only was the front half of this car a different color from the back…the two halves were from different make and model cars. I would later see more of these hybrid vehicles, but the Tri-9 crew car was my first. Obviously the two originals had met with some type of terminal damage either front-ended or rear-ended. Some resourceful Cambodian body shop had somehow figured out how to weld the salvageable remaining pieces into a whole while still keeping the engine, powertrain, and other significant subsystems in some state of functionality. As it approached, I realized This Was Our Crew Car! I saw two pilots in the front and two already in the back. I'd seen a couple of them at the airport. When they saw my disbelief, they all began laughing…recalling their first encounters. "It's not as bad as it looks" they retorted. "You'll get used to it."

In the front seat I could see a long homemade stick shift protruding up out of the floorboard. The transmission was quite loud and warm…probably because we were sitting right on top of it. The seats were comfortable enough though they too were from different vehicles. Most of the in-dash instruments did not work and looked like they were also orphans from yet another collision.

More Airport Enterprises

When we arrived at the airport, I went with the other crew members to the Tri-9 office. We gathered our paperwork and started going over the manifest. Since Roger was not yet there, I took the paperwork and went on to the plane. The crew chief, another middle-aged Filipino met me at the plane and went over the aircraft log with me. I then started the walk-around. Roger joined me as I was finishing up. He went over the log book entries, paying special attention to the previous crew's write-ups. As we were still doing this, our passengers began boarding. I checked the baggage compartments to examine the cargo load…full to the max. I was sure we were significantly heavier than the manifest showed. Roger had told me about that on the first day. It was the same in Wigmo. The loadmasters had to feed their families. Here various station agents and ramp supervisors had "business partners" in the outstations. They would slip their un-manifested cargo onboard and their "partner" would remove it on the other end. A merchant was standing by to receive the un-manifested goods and quickly pay a handsome sum just to have something to sell to the commodity starved market in the outlaying cities. Many people were profiting from the war. Even with all the pain, the misery, and the suffering being inflicted, there would always be an element that could find a way to profit from the tragedy. It was the same in The Congo. The story was as old as recorded history; supply and demand; greed trumping compassion. I sighed and climbed the air-stair and went into the cockpit. As Roger sat down in the left seat, he looked over at me and asked "well…how was your night?" I smiled and said, "I slept very well thank you." Roger brandished an all-knowing smile.

Sihanoukville–Land of Opportunity

My second flight to Ream Air Force Base and the nearby city of Sihanoukville or Kompong Som as it was now called after the coup that toppled Prince Sihanouk, was every bit as breathtaking as it had been the previous day. The mountains and streams reminded me of Colorado.

When we contacted the tower this time, the runway in use was 03, the approach that was made out over the Gulf of Thailand rather than over the Khmer Rouge infested Cardamom Mountain range. This was good as it allowed me to experience the other approach to the airport. In the future, many approaches to this airport would be in heavy monsoon rainstorms. It was essential to be proficient and thunderstorms were no place to acquire airport proficiency.

Roger apologized for not giving me the landing, but the airport's runway was much too short for my Convair 440 landing experience level. I wholeheartedly agreed. Besides, after yesterday, it looked to me like Roger could use a little more practice.

As we taxied in, I noticed a black Mercedes waiting on the ramp. When we parked it drove up and stopped just by the cargo door of the aircraft. An enlisted Khmer Air Force man got out of the Mercedes opened the trunk and walked over to the aircraft's cargo compartment door. A Khmer Air Force colonel remained in the back seat keeping the cargo compartment in full view. As I was watching, I heard Roger telling me not to pay too much attention to what was going on. When the Khmer Akas Airline ground personnel opened the cargo door, the driver stepped forwarded, removed a small suitcase, placed it in the trunk of the Mercedes, got back in and drove away. "What in the hell was all that about", I asked. "What do you think paid for that Mercedes and the gold Rolex the Colonel was wearing plus the villa and the Hong Kong bank account you can't see," Roger said with a smile. "I suppose the less I know the better off I am," I said. Roger's only response was another smile.

This time a badly wounded Khmer army enlisted man and his wife and small child were among our passengers back to Phnom Penh. I was told he had been injured in a rocket attack the night before. The wife looked frightened…her husband's face had lost all color…probably from excessive blood loss. They just stretched him out on the floor. He had an IV running. The war was beginning to take on real dimensions for me. The flight back to Phnom Penh was normal. I made the takeoff out of Ream and the landing in Pochentong.

A New Captain And A New Friend

When we taxied onto the ramp in Pochentong, Roger told me he would be getting off and I'd be flying with another captain. He had administrative duties to attend to back at the Tri-9 office. He reminded me of my tailor appointment and told me the crew driver would take me there after dropping off the other pilot.

Out of courtesy and protocol I walked over and introduced myself to the captain. He was an American from Florida. This was his first overseas job. His name was Bob Faith. He was tall and well built. I estimated his age to be around fifty. He gave me an obvious head to toe scan as if to see what in the hell had just been dumped on him. His way of speech was slightly Yankee and leaned toward sarcasm and surliness. He had a long cigarette hanging from his mouth. My first impression of him was the epitome of unsociability.

I noticed he spent much more time on the walkaround than Roger did. When we entered to cockpit, I got a big lecture on what I was to touch and what I was not to touch. Then he called for the checklist. He had a specific way to do everything…his way…and he made it clear that that's how things would be done. I thought to myself that this was going to be a very long flight.

This flight was to Battambang. After takeoff when the cabin attendant came in the cockpit to see what we wanted to drink, it was the male chief cabin attendant. With Roger, it had always been the females. I learned from Bob that he had standing orders only the male chief cabin attendant would enter the cockpit. He declared the females "an unnecessary distraction." That was too bad as I had found them kind of interesting.

In cruise, rather than putting the airplane on autopilot, Bob wanted me to hand fly the plane. He said that was the only way to learn how to fly it. In his words…"an idiot can sit there and let George do it"; George being slang for the autopilot. I supposed he was right…but that really didn't matter…"the captain is always right."

As we approached Battambang and the top of the descent, he took over the flight controls. Right away I noticed how smoothly he maneuvered the aircraft. He briefed me on the approach…something Roger never did, and then called for the checklist. A beautiful approach and landing.

The CIA Out Of Gas

As we were parking, I noticed a military jeep with what appeared to be an American behind the wheel pulling up under the right engine. "What in the hell is that" I asked. "One of the CIA guys stationed here" Bob replied. "He's having trouble getting gas for his jeep…the stuff available here on the street causes all kinds of problems. He comes up regularly and takes two jerrycans full…nice guy…you'll like him."

Since this was far from being my first face to face with an employee of the CIA it was a non-event. But Bob was right…I did find him likable. What I found more interesting than the CIA agent was how quickly the fuel came out of that fuel drain. I'd never seen anything like that on any other plane I'd flown. Both jerrycans were filled in no time at all.

Since the passengers were experiencing a slight delay in the terminal, I used the time to wonder around in the back of the airplane and examine the galley area. The three cabin attendants were in the galley setting up their service for the flight back to Phnom Penh. I introduced myself. The two female attendants were quite attractive. As a matter of fact…close to beautiful.

Jerks Are Jerks

Still no passengers so I wondered down on the ramp. As I approached Bob, he was ranting about some "VIP government asshole holding up the flight because he had not arrived at the airport yet and the military police who ultimately control the airport were not going to let us depart until 'his excellency' arrived." As I watched Bob, I couldn't help but think that he wouldn't have lasted a week in the Congo. I was well conditioned for this kind of thing.

Finally "his excellency" arrived. His car came straight onto the ramp. His body guards jumped out and opened the door for him. Like the Congolese, this full-of-himself little jerk carried a swagger stick. I made the mental note that jerks are jerks no matter where in the world you find them, and many appeared to have an affinity or fetish for swagger sticks.

Bob gave me the takeoff and I hand flew the plane all the way back to Phnom Penh. He told me to make the approach and landing as well. I made a smooth landing and gently applied the thrust reversers. Bob just grunted and told me I wouldn't make a pimple on a good pilot's butt. I thanked him for letting me fly.

We did a quick turn and flew to Kompong Som. Bob gave me the takeoff. We had two U.S. Military officers onboard…both wearing civilian clothes. They were part of Military Equipment Delivery Team, Cambodia (MEDTEC). Bob allowed them to ride in the cockpit with us. I quickly made friends with them both and learned they regularly went to Kompong Som inspecting the delivery of U.S. provided military hardware and supplies as well as trying to spot or uncover information on Russian and Chinese provided military hardware and supplies going through the port destined for the North Vietnamese Regular Army Forces (NVA) and the Viet Cong guerrillas (VC). The Cambodian government vehemently denied the enemy was being supplied through the Sihanoukville port, but intelligence had long ago made this a well-documented fact.[178] Key members of the government we were supporting were selling arms to their own enemies and in the process becoming filthy rich.

The passenger boarding went well and we managed a quick turnaround. This time we had two seriously wounded Khmer Army soldiers onboard. We radioed ahead to the military requesting ambulances. Bob again gave me the takeoff.

After landing Bob and I debriefed the crew chief, then made our way across the ramp to the Tri-9 office to hand in our paperwork. As we left the plane, I noticed there was no waiting ambulance and both critically wounded soldiers, trying to hold their attached and running IVs were laying on the tarmac under the airplane. At least they were out of the direct sunlight. I wondered if they would have to bribe somebody to give them a ride into Phnom Penh to the hospital.

After handing in all our paperwork at the Tri-9 office, Bob and I walked to the sidewalk in front of the airport. The Tri-9 driver had been waiting in the shade of a tree with a handful of other drivers. He scurried to our special Tri-9 hybrid conveyance contraption and soon we were heading into town. As we made our way along the road into town, I did notice the car appeared to have a little crab to the left. Not too serious, but I was sure it ate up tires at a pretty good rate.

On our way into town I noticed even more of the political satire caricature billboards demonizing deposed head of state Prince Norodom Sihanouk. I remarked that somebody must have really been scared that his supporters would rise up. Bob appeared to know next to nothing about the local politics. He just sat there puffing away on his cigarette.

The driver dropped Bob off at large three-bedroom apartment he shared with two other Tri-9 pilots. Bob invited me to stay and visit for a while but I needed to get to the tailor, so I told him I'd come in another day.

---

[178] Good Questions—Wrong Answers, CIA's Estimate of Arms Traffic Throught Sihanoukville During The Vietnam War—Thomas L. Ahern, Jr.—Center for the Study of Intelligence - Feb. 2004—Secret—Declassified

When I reached the tailor my shirts and uniform pants fit perfectly. I was able to take them without coming back for any minor corrections. I'd had a full day and was ready to go back to my apartment.

My First Letter Home

It was close to dark when I arrived back at my apartment. Yat had dinner ready. I'd already told Sokha she would be welcome to eat the evening meal with me until she moved out. I figured I could use the time to ask her things about life in Cambodia. Many of the mechanics and pilots appeared to have little interest in the people or the customs. Sokha could prove useful. When I got to the apartment Sokha had apparently just arrived from her job. I had intended to ask her where she worked but I'd forgotten. It was some kind of office job. I took a quick shower and we sat down to eat.

After our meal and interesting conversation, I told her I needed to write letters. She left for her bedroom. I didn't see her again till the next morning.

I'd purchased some cheap writing paper and envelopes from one of the little shops close to the apartment. Tri-9 would mail our letters for us. All I had to do was give it to the driver in the morning.

I sat at the dining room table, illuminated only by the kerosene lamp. Most of the time there was no electricity due to the fuel shortage caused by the Khmer Rouge stranglehold on all the land traffic. As I started the letter, I realized I had so much I could write about…the people, the sights. I knew a husband should miss his wife…and I did miss Karen. I missed my children…but still nothing wanted to come out. It was like the pen wouldn't move. Finally I managed to get a couple of pages done. My heart wasn't in it. I felt so empty. I was drawing comfort from my old friend, the kerosene lamp. I was getting to the point the dim yellow light bouncing off the walls of my Congo and now Cambodia dining rooms was my comfort zone. What was wrong with me? While Yat and Sokha were in the house with me, I couldn't see them; only the dimly lit room. Could it be a significant part of me didn't want to see anything else? As I sat in the flickering lamp light, my senses starting to feel the mellowing influences of the beer I'd been drinking, my mind flashed back to Bat's front veranda in Kisangani. As we sat staring out into the darkness together during one of our many long veranda chats, I had been telling him about my confusing feelings for Karen verses my desires to be alone. He had sighed and as he continued staring out into the darkness, he said…"if life were that simple…we'd all live in the past." I understood well…very well.

The next morning Yat had breakfast waiting for me. Sokha had waited for me to finish my shower before coming out of the bedroom. She smiled and said good morning. I got my flight bag and headed downstairs to wait for the crew car.

Merchants Of Death
The CIA's Colossal Miscalculation

My first flight of the day was to Sihanoukville or Kompong Som. As I walked toward the plane, I noticed the usual pre-departure flurry of commerce, bribes by passengers to get onboard, bribes to get excessive baggage onboard; the secretive packages placed on board by the station agents. It was all there. It was always there.

As we cruised toward Sihanoukville's Ream Air Force Base, I realized the petty, entrepreneurial, even excusable enterprises I'd just seen flourishing at Pochentong airport, were in the grand scope of things nothing compared to what was happening on a daily (and nightly) basis just a few miles ahead of us. The mega-million-dollar, merchant of death, treasonous transactions taking place on a regular basis on the docks of the seaport in Kompong Som made the transactions I'd just witnessed back on the ramp pale in comparison.

According to Cambodian nationals, working for the CIA and embedded in the Cambodian armed forces and in Cambodian "trading companies" operating on and around the port, the U.S. intelligence sources had been drastically underestimating the arms traffic flowing to the Vietcong via Sihanoukville's port. According to Cambodian CIA operatives, not only was the port used to offload munitions bound from China for the Vietcong; the port was used to store them until they were needed. They then would move from Cambodia to the South Vietnam border via a Cambodian owned trucking company.

A major result of this colossal intelligence failure was the devastating consequences to U.S. troops in South Vietnam. The official position and therefore the central focus of munitions interdiction was the so-called Hồ Chí Minh trail. Lives were lost and forces expended in these interdiction efforts while the arms traffic coming through Sihanoukville's port, equally if not more important, went, for the most part, unhindered. This arms traffic was facilitated by the highest levels in Cambodia's government and armed forces making various individuals mega fortunes in "port fees" paid to them by the Chinese. I would later meet more than one of these benefactors of the "port fees." It was hard to look at the miserable bastards without showing open contempt.

More Maimed Soldiers

As we taxied up to the terminal at Ream, I saw a military ambulance waiting on the tarmac. I wondered what new mockery of humanity was inside. As soon as the passengers were off the plane a captain in the Cambodian Air Force made his way up to the cockpit. He was carrying a document signed by somebody ordering us to take two seriously wounded soldiers to Phnom

Penh. Since we would have somehow made room for them anyway, I wondered if the document was merely an ego exercise by the signer.

I walked over to the ambulance and looked inside. It was not airconditioned. The back door was wide open in a futile attempt to make the temperature inside more tolerable. One soldier had only a bloody stump for his right leg. The other and an abdominal wound of some type. A blood-soaked winding of once white gauze was probably holding his intestines in. Both had lost all color. I wondered how either could be alive when we landed back in Phnom Penh.

When the passengers were all boarded, they brought the two stretchers and placed them in the isle. We closed the door and cranked up. As I felt the pressurization and air-conditioner kick in I wondered if it would make any difference to either of them. I was glad to get back in the air and point the plane toward Phnom Penh. About midway through the flight the cabin attendant came to the cockpit and advised that the passengers believed one of the solders had died. I got up and went back to check. He was dead. Like the ones I'd seen in the Congo…lifeless. I returned to the cockpit and advised the captain. We flew on in silence toward Pochentong Airport. They offloaded the dead body and placed it in the waiting military ambulance beside the poor bastard with only one leg. They drove away in a self-important rush. I wondered if the rush would make any difference. I was starting to wonder if anything made any difference.

Our next leg was to Battambang. I didn't have much to say on the flight. I thought about the soldier who died. I thought about the solider with one leg. I wondered if he had a family. I wondered if he would live long enough to see a doctor's face. I wondered what humanity had learned in all these centuries of war and bloodshed. I wondered what I was doing here. *"I have seen all the things that are done under the sun and have found everything to be futile, a pursuit of the wind."* [179]

I was ready to get back to my apartment that evening. I was ready for a beer and quiet time watching the kerosene lamp light flicker on the walls of my living room.

When I arrived home it was almost dark. Sokha was already home. She had changed into pants and a blouse and her hair was down. She actually looked pretty. I knew she was testing the water. I smiled and told her I'd had a rough day. She was welcome to sit with me, but I was not in the mood to talk. I drank two beers and sat in the darkness watching the shadows play. I wished I had some music, but I hadn't had time to arrange a player of any type yet. Sokha patiently respected my need for quiet. After a while we got up and ate dinner which was waiting on the table. After dinner she went to her room…I to mine.

---

[179] Holman Christian Standard Bible (HCSB) Ecclesiastes 1:14 Solomon, King of Israel

A New Face–A New Friend

The next morning I saw Roger in flight operations. He told me an old friend of his was coming in to join us; that they had flown together in the army. Roger said he was sure I was going to like him; said his name was Cecil Wroten and that he was a retired army colonel. As I walked across the ramp the thought came to me that I hope he was not like other retired colonels I'd flow with.

I was flying with Bob Faith again that day. Once we were in cruise Bob departed from his stiff demeanor and started telling me about his local love life, or perhaps it should be better referred to as his domestic love life. Seems some ephemeral amorous feelings had arisen for his maid. He shook his head and told me that soon after their relationship blossomed her requests began. She began by explaining that it was very improper for someone in her situation not to have someone under her doing most of the work…that her job was to supervise and manage the house. So he said he hired another maid…a maid for his maid so to speak. He said that was soon followed by a request for tuition money so she could attend secretarial school. Bob was shaking his head in disbelief at his own stupidity and proceeded to warn me not to make the same mistake. He said next would probably be a request for a motorbike (moto) so she wouldn't have to ride a cyclo (a bicycle powered rickshaw) to school. I was struggling not to laugh. My image of this icy, stern, navy carrier pilot was rapidly dissolving. What a hoot.

The rest of the day went about normal, or normal for this war-torn place. We arrived back in Phnom Penh after our second trip to Battambang more or less on time. We arrived in mid-afternoon. I was fortunate that Bob was ready to get home, so we were in the crew car less than ten minutes after we shut down our engine, but not before Roger came up and introduced us both to Cy Wroten. Cy was about my height with salt and pepper hair and a pencil-point nose. He had large blue eyes and what appeared to be a newly started yet already nicotine stained beard. Cy was from West Virginia. He had resigned a position with Collins Radio to come be part of this special operation. I instantly liked him. We talked for only a couple of minutes as Cy and Roger appeared busy…apparently with Cy's indoctrination.

I was planning to use the rest of the afternoon to go to the large market in the center of Phnom Penh. I'd heard a lot about it. All the foreigners called it Central Market, but the locals called it *Phsar Thmey* or *Phsar Thom Thmey* meaning new market or grand or big new market. Roger told me about it on my first day in country and I'd been anxious to see it. Today I wanted to wonder around before everything closed. Since leaving Hamilton I'd developed a love for wondering around the sidewalks of strange new cities and Phnom Penh appeared to be far more exotic than anything I'd ever seen…even more than Paris. I'd been too busy to do any exploring up till now. I was more than ready to start.

In addition to today's little outing, my schedule showed I would have the upcoming Saturday off and I'd already planned to ask Sokha if she would show me some of the sights. Our sightseeing would be limited to the city proper as nobody ventured far outside the city unless they were in an armed convoy and even then, it was a risk. Travel after sunset was only for tactical missions. I looked toward Saturday with anticipation. I was ready to start a life outside the cockpit.

Affordable Dentistry

I quickly changed clothes, grabbed my Nikon along with the four rolls of 35mm film in film cans which I had taped to my camera strap and headed out the door. This was my first real outing since arriving.

My apartment was on Monivong Street, named for King Sisowath Monivong, the King of Cambodia from 1927 until his death in 1941. Monivong was lined with small interesting shops and eating places, mostly owned by the merchant class Chinese ethnic minority. All the shops were open front, so it was easy to stop and look or walk in. Everyone was extremely welcoming. Politeness was a basic pillar of Cambodian society.

As I neared the vicinity of Psar Thmey I turned right on a side street that fed into the huge market area. The scene changed immediately. After walking only a few feet I noticed an unusual cart-vendor sitting on the side walk on a stool beside his cart. Inside his clear glass sided pushcart was an array of dentures and crowns plus some primitive dental instruments, files and pliers. Sitting on the sidewalk beside his stool was the patient, mouth wide open grimacing in pain. I couldn't believe what I was seeing. I was somewhat embarrassed, but the rarity of this photographic moment outweighed my embarrassment. I snapped several frames, nodded politely and moved on.

Dante's *Inferno*

As I inched my way along the side street leading to Psar Thmey I was confronted by a steady barrage of panhandlers, vagrants, beggars, merchants of *kachha* (marijuana), and people missing limbs. Those missing hands, arms, and legs were not just men of military age; no one was excluded…old men, women, children…they were all there.

The amputees were the victims of land mines; their stumps vivid reminders of who really was bearing the burden of the Russian, Chinese, and American chess game being played out in Cambodia, Laos, and Vietnam. Equally unfortunate…many of the pawns in the game were America's sons and daughters. I never saw a general missing an arm or a leg; nor a colonel or major. These gruesome injuries were mostly the domain of the privates, the sergeants, and the village non-combatants on their way to their rice fields. The country was covered with incalculable numbers of landmines seeded by all the warring parties. It seemed every inch of the country was mined; the

Americans provided the M14 mine or "toe popper," the Chinese and Russians provided the deadlier POMZ-2M. Everybody rushed to Cambodia to contribute their version of these true "weapons of mass destruction" as they are sarcastically referred to. The estimated number of landmines covering Cambodia would eventually climb to 10,000,000 or expressed differently, 143 per square mile.[180]

Most of these street hustlers soliciting my attention and hopefully my favor were truly in need. I was confronted with an endless parade of humanity's most unfortunate; like a cast of characters from Dante's *Inferno*. My head was spinning like some centrifuge trying to separate reality from fantasy. In most cases I had no neat classification . . . no explanation; at least no humanly acceptable explanation. These people were the victims of madness; the madness of the war.

I was becoming overwhelmed. My mind was experiencing message unit overload. I needed to sit down and unplug for a moment. I needed to sort through everything I'd just seen. I turned into a sidewalk café, took a seat on a plastic chair at a plastic table and ordered a Coke. When it arrived, I was sure it was a Cambodian bottled knockoff, but I didn't care; I'd learned to believe they were normal while I was In the Congo. I watched as the waiter pored it over ice that I was sure was loaded with microbes as yet unknown to the medical establishment. But again, as I'd learned to do in the Congo…I ignored normal impulses and swallowed.

Within a few seconds I realized the mental timeout I'd hoped to find was merely make-believe. In front of my table were child beggars, teenage mothers clutching their babies, more amputees, all with outstretched hands hoping for contributions. Again like in Dante's Inferno, calling and reaching out to me from their hell. I snapped a few hurried shots with my Nikon but because they kept pushing in so close to me hoping to get some pocket change, I was unable to get any decent shots.

Within a nanosecond of my first contribution of alms hitting the first outstretched palm, more came swarming from all directions. The owner of the café came out and tried to shoo them away but to no avail. They were driven by desperation and could give a damn less what he said. Finally a policeman came over and threatened to kick them. Apparently his threat presented itself as credible; they cursed and scowled and withdrew to across the street. With my next sip of Coke came a shabbily dressed and street-dirty girl appearing to be in her early teens…having hardly begun to develop breasts, offered to go someplace with me for a short time. In exasperation, I gave up on my coke, paid the waiter, and headed for the entrance to the Psar Thmey. I could see military police guarding the entrance so I figured they might be able to keep the street people away. I was followed every step of the way by the crowd of them, some hobbling, desperately trying to keep up, still holding out hope of a

---

[180] United Nations—UNICEF—The State of The World's Children - 1996

small token of sympathy. The horrid sensation of turning my back on these desperate creatures was sobered by the reality that all my paycheck would not change anything. These people were truthfully beyond hope. Fortunately, they fell away as I neared the marketplace entrance.

The Merchants of Psar Thmey

The inside of the market was huge. A large well-ventilated dome fed by four long halls for even more vendor stalls. The structure was designed by the famous French architect Louis Chauchon and built in 1937 and at the time was billed as "Asia's largest market." Immediately upon entering the main area (the dome) I found gold, diamonds, precious stones of all types, money changers, wrist watch merchants, and merchants selling reading and sun glasses. There were real stones and fake stones, Rolex watches and fake Rolex watches. Police armed with AK-47s were patrolling everywhere. No robber in his right mind would contemplate robbing this place. I later learned that most of the authentic high-end watches, ruby, sapphire, and diamond merchants were across the street in the gold market but for sure there was no shortage of them here.

As I moved away from the center area the camera and electronic merchants had their stalls. Toward the end extremities of the four feeders were the clothing merchants and the fruit, fish and meat vendors, and the fresh vegetable vendors. Most of them had closed down shop for the day as they did not want to end up with perishable fresh merchandise on hand overnight. I wondered about just trying to take in the sights and smells. I took what I expected to be wonderful photos of the meat and vegetable market. The gold and jewelry merchants were not too enthusiastic about being photographed.

I wondered about the market until they started to pull the bars and shutters over their shops and the jewelry merchants began locking their merchandise in their safes.

Dancing Lights—Uneasy Nights

As I left the market the sun had already fallen below the buildings. I'd had enough of the sidewalks of Phnom Penh…at least for this day. I made my way briskly toward my apartment, my beer, and the lights of the lamp dancing on my living room wall. My small Montgomery Ward radio was tuned to AFVN" (American Forces Vietnam Network) Saigon. Home of the famous "Gooooood Morning Vietnam." As I watched the shadows dance, I saw the outstretched arms of all those poor creatures I'd encountered that afternoon; arms outstretched, pleading for help. I knew how Virgil and Dante felt in Gustave Doré's painting, *The Styx*. I would later relate U.S. B-52 Bombings of Cambodia to the *Inferno* as well. The music Saigon was playing wasn't particularly helping matters; *The First Time Ever I Saw Your Face*, *Alone Again (Nat-*

urally), *Vincent / Castles In The Air*. I wondered if I would try again to write Karen. I didn't.

Sleep failed to come easily…the images I'd seen refused to leave my head. It would be easy to blame the Cambodians for not taking care of their own…or perhaps better put, the mess others made. But the truth was, they were overwhelmed, their government and social structure were coming apart at the seams. I wondered what kind of a god could permit such injustice. The answer…our God…*Yahweh*. I didn't like my conclusion.

As I lay struggling with sleep, I heard a loud explosion. It was not the sound I associated with the nightly inbound rockets. I didn't know what it was but since it did not sound particularly close, I ignored it.

Sleep finally came, but not the deep sleep I needed. The noises through the open window from the alley below, the images in my head, everything was clashing…nothing was rhyming.

The next morning I learned the Khmer Rouge had sent "frogmen" into Phnom Penh's port where what few barges that made it up the Mekong were unloaded. They had blown up The Bright Star, a fully loaded vessel with much needed supplies. The Khmer Rouge were able to control long stretches of the Mekong River bank thus making passage up the river to Phnom Penh with the critically needed supplies almost impossible. Now they were slipping into Phnom Penh's port.

Kissinger & Nixon, Paris Peace Talks & Christmas

The days melted into weeks. We were all flying hard…at least 100 hours per month. Cecil Wroten had arrived in country with a new DC-4 type rating but in reality, had almost no time in the aircraft. Because I had command time in the DC-4 I was assigned to fly with Cy for a while until he got comfortable in the airplane. As we flew together, we became friends. I enjoyed flying with Cy.

Another pilot I liked instantly was a newly arrived Cuban pilot named Hugo Vega (pseudonym). Hugo was a very experienced Convair pilot. He was from Miami and he knew almost all of the Cuban pilots I'd flown with in the Congo. Hugo was so funny. He always made me laugh. Hugo and Bob Faith shared a house together. Hugo was a bit of a Casanova. He liked to flirt with the cabin attendants though as far as I could tell nothing ever came from it. I learned a lot from Hugo, as I did from Bob, but Hugo was much more fun to fly with. Hugo kept trying to "hook me up" with the cabin attendants but I just couldn't get interested.

As Christmas approached the Paris Peace Talks faltered. For us, peace seemed such an extraneous term. Everyday somebody came home with a new 7.62 bullet hole in their fuselage; sometimes striking somebody inside…occasionally critically. Almost every flight transported some wounded. The city took rocket fire every night. There was a curfew past 8:00 pm in an order to try to catch the Khmer Rouge sappers who regularly slipped into the city and detonated their satchel packs filled with explosives. Most nights my sleep was interrupted by the sound of Soviet/Chinese 122mm rockets or its little brother, the Chinese 107mm. Both dispensed incendiary and anti-personnel shrapnel. Though notoriously inaccurate, when fired at a city, death and devastation were virtually assured. It was designed to create terror amongst urban populations. By all accounts, it was a success. Rarely did they land close to my apartment but most mornings, while enroute to the airport, we would see new signs of the previous night's strikes. Crowds of gawking people on their way to work were a sure sign of a rocket strike. For the dead, often the bodies still lay where they fell. Picking up the night's dead didn't appear to be a high government priority. The airport was a favored target.

Each and every day more refugees poured into Phnom Penh from the countryside. They slept in makeshift camps or if they were lucky with family or friends. Life in the camps was terrible. Every day I would see more signs of the exploding population. Relief agencies were pouring into Phnom Penh along with the refugees; providing or attempting to provide medical care and relief supplies. Every time I left my apartment, I saw some new human tragedy. I realized that here I was much closer to the horror of war than I'd been in the Congo. In the Congo I had to fly five hours to see it. Here, if I walked five minutes, I saw it, I smelled it, I touched it.

Sokha had found an apartment and moved out. It was just me and Yat. I didn't really like her, but I needed her and didn't want to go through the hassle of finding a new maid and the waiting-to-see-if-she-works-out period. I would attend an occasional party held by Roger at the company villa or one held by the U.S. Air Attaché from whom came much of our security briefings. At Roger's parties there were always plenty of anxious young ladies from nice families hoping to snag a path to American citizenship. I attended few and paid little attention to the waiting damsels or more properly damsels in distress.

Deck The Halls

Phnom Penh, in spite of being under constant rocket attack and staggering under the burden of tens of thousands of refugees pouring in from the countryside, food, fuel, and electricity shortages, overwhelmed hospitals, and souring inflation, started decorating for Christmas. Most of the population was Buddhist but Cambodians loved holidays and festivities, plus, Christmas was good for business. So every day on my way home from the airport, I watched as Christmas trees, wreaths of holly, and Santa Clause decorations appeared.

Linebacker Two–The Christmas Bombings
A Present From President Nixon And Henry Kissinger

The Paris negotiations were going nowhere. Newly elected President Nixon was under pressure to bring the troops home with honor. So, by order of the president, in hope of jarring the North Vietnamese out of their stalwart position, a new bombing campaign started against the North Vietnamese; Operation Linebacker Two. It lasted for 12 days, including a three-day bombing period making use of up to 120 B-52s. Strategic surgical strikes were carried out on fighter airfields, transport targets and supply depots in and around Hanoi and Haiphong. U.S. aircraft dropped more than 20,000 tons of bombs in this operation. Twenty-six U.S. plane were lost, and 93 airmen were killed, captured or missing; The North Vietnam admitted to between 1,300 and 1,600 dead. [181] We had unofficial notifications of some large upcoming bombing campaign against the North but mostly our news came from BBC (British Broadcasting Corp.) and VOA (Voice Of America).

A Case Of Mistaken Identity

One day as I sat back in the cabin of the Convair 440, relaxing before the passengers boarded, Roger came walking out to the plane with one of the most popular air hostesses. She was very pretty as well as being popular. Obviously she wasn't going to be on our flight, so I wondered what he was up to. As Roger and the hostess walked into the cabin, Roger was all smiles. The hostess was giggling shyly and covering her mouth in typical Asian fashion. I still thought little about it till Roger said…"look what I brought you." She spoke English so I knew I had to really be careful. I stood and greeted her. We had flown together before. Roger excused himself and returned to the flight operations office; she remained. I tried to keep our conversation devoid of pregnant pauses, but it was difficult. I was saved by the approaching hoard of boarding passengers. I politely excused myself, gave the traditional *sathoouk* (hands pressed together as in prayer and raised just above the chin level with head slightly bowed) and rushed off into the cockpit. Boy was I going to have a word with Roger when we got back!

On my return as I walked into flight ops, Roger was beaming ear to ear and asked…"well?" "Well what?" I replied. "I brought you the one you said was kinda nice," Roger replied. I suddenly recalled a conversation we'd had recently on a flight; a conversation where Roger was asking me why I hadn't been going out with any of the girls. My reply was I didn't really see anything all that interesting and besides I was still married. "Yes," he replied, "but you told me yourself you hadn't written home in a month." He continued with saying that it was impossible for me not to have seen anything interesting. Then I recalled the casual statement I'd made about one that I thought was unique but always looked so sad. Roger had thought I was referring to the

---
[181] BBC News—24 December 2012

one he brought out to the aircraft in a disastrous attempt to play cupid…I was not.

That night Sokha stopped by the house for a visit. I related the incident to her. She asked me to describe the one I was really mentioning to Roger. When I did, she smiled and told me to forget it. Sokha said she was a royal family member whose uncle owned the airline. She said they were high school classmates. Further, that she never dated anybody and a "white skin" like me would be out of the question…her family would never allow it. I smiled and replied that at least I had good taste. We went out to dinner together that night…just a couple of blocks down the street. As we walked along the sidewalk, the sounds of B-52s carpet bombing seemed to be coming from just across the river. I wondered how many innocent people were dying. *"As when one plows and breaks up the soil, turning up rocks, so our bones have been scattered at the mouth of Sheol"*[182] Each day more refugees poured into the city. Most were not running from the Khmer Rouge; they were running from American B-52 bombers.

Merry ~~Texas~~ Cambodian Christmas You All

We were flying every day…even Christmas. While the Americans paused the bombing of Hanoi on Christmas day, nothing paused in Cambodia. Cambodian T-28s dropped their napalm; by most accounts on more non-Khmer Rouge than on the enemy. [183] The airports were full of the wounded and the fleeing. I flew; I made money; I got my adrenalin high; I went where none from Hamilton Texas had gone before. I bought my little roll of tickets; I paid to go inside; I paid to dance. But the cost of the tickets was high…so very high. I would be paying for each dance for many years to come.

I was scarcely aware it was Christmas. Had it not been for the guilt pangs when I got out of bed on Christmas morning, guilt for not being home on Christmas for Jason and Jenny, it would have been just another day of max weight takeoffs and dodging ground fire.

That night, alone in my apartment, with the exception of Yat, who didn't really exist for me, my guilt returned. While it was Christmas night for me, it was Christmas morning for them. Karen and my father would be sitting in the living room around the tree watching Jason and my sweet Jenny open and play with their gifts. There were moments when I considered hating myself. These turpitudes were far too grave to blame on my evil twin. I retreated back into the dim light, accompanied by my old friend, the lamp's dancing shadows, and lulled by the buzz from the San Miguel beer in my hand…delivered courtesy of U.S. Air Force C-130s from U-Tapao Air Force Base in Thailand.

---

[182] Holy Bible - Holman Christian Standard Bible (HCSB)—Psalms 141:7
[183] American Bombardment of Kampuchea—Ben Kiernan—ref British Journalist William Shacross

I went to bed early. I prayed sleep would come quickly. I longed for the simpler times, for the nights when my father would come listen to my bedtime prayers…"Now I lay me down to sleep; I pray the Lord my soul to keep; watch and guard me through the night; and wake me with the morning light."

Jakarta Junket

As I walked into operations Cy motioned for me to step outside with him. Cy at times tended to be a bit dramatic and this was one of those times. He said we had secured some aircraft with a lot of official assistance and we needed to go to Jakarta, inspect them, and ferry them back to Phnom Penh. He said this was a bit of a hush-hush mission as there was a lot of opposition to the war around Asia and Europe, to say nothing of back home, and there might be some who would like to block these aircraft from leaving Indonesia to join the war effort in Cambodia. He asked if I'd like to be part of the mission. The answer was "of course…when do we leave?" "Tomorrow" Cy said with a smile and another caution not to talk about the mission. Cy had already changed my schedule in anticipation of my affirmative response. My schedule for today was only half a day followed by days off for an unspecified time. Cy had already mentioned I was to go to the administration office upon my return to draw my per diem and other travel expenses. He also said I would not lose money; that I would be paid just like I was here flying. I needed to clear my head and Jakarta sounded like a pretty good place to try.

Drawing my per diem and other travel funds didn't take long. They had my airline ticket ready as well. Packing my clothes that night didn't take long…I didn't bring a lot with we when I came to Cambodia.

The next morning Cy had the driver swing by to get me. On the way to the airport Cy asked me if I'd heard all the B-52s rattling the ground last night. "Yep," I replied, "shook my bed as well. Sounded like they were just across the river." "I wonder how many poor bastards died last night that never even laid eyes on a Khmer Rouge?" My thoughts went back to the ignorant peace-niks we were talking about the previous morning. There are no bomb racks, no rocket pods, and no 50 caliber machine guns under the wings of the planes we are going to get. My part of "the war effort" is saving lives, feeding the refugees, transporting the wounded . . . not killing people. Of course the Congo was slightly different. One could of course claim that we were in fact "prolonging the war effort" and thereby should be stopped. But for me, the way to stop the war was to stop both sides from killing each other…not leaving one side to be massacred by the other. There were no good answers. I decided to think about Jakarta. I'd never been there and this should be fun.

Jakarta…Land of Lights (Night Lights That Is)

Our flight didn't take long. We were soon checked into our rooms at the Intercontinental Hotel before dark. This was a real break from my apartment in Phnom Penh or the Nana Hotel in Bangkok. My father would have told me I was in "high cotton." I wondered where the budget for our rooms was coming from…I wondered where the money for these planes was coming from. Tri-9 didn't seem to have this kind of funds. But such thoughts were a waste of my brain power…I had an appointment with Cy in a few minutes downstairs in the hotel bar and later a promise to go out looking for a unique and fun place to eat. I could hear my father telling me "Boy don't look a gift horse in the mouth."

The bar was elegant and the drinks expensive. Needless to say both Cy and I sipped slowly. The bar was filled with stylishly dressed ladies whom I suspected of being ladies of the evening. But they were light years ahead of Bangkok's Nana Hotel crowd. After one drink Cy and I decided it was time to go foraging for food.

Outside the hotel but a respectful distance from the drive where the taxi and limos pulled up was a line of *becaks*, the Indonesian version of a cyclo. You ride in the front of the little rickshaw type device and the driver sits behind and peddles. When the drivers saw we were looking their way, they began calling out and waving in an attempt to be selected from the group. Of course, like in Phnom Penh, a spirited negotiating process precedes the final selection. Since they only seat one person comfortably we elected to take two and were soon in the sidewalk and mom and pop restaurant district of Jakarta. Apparently fares were had to find for the drivers. They volunteered to wait for us for no charge if we would use them to get back to the hotel.

My Indonesia Near-Death Experience

After a good meal, as Cy and I were preparing to head back to our hotel, Cy had what seemed at the time to be a fun idea…let's race back to the hotel. Sounded harmless enough…the loser pays both fares. I don't usually wager on anything but with my pockets loaded with newly drawn travel advance money I jumped on the offer.

My driver was the faster of the two and for the first part of the race, I was somewhat comfortably in the lead. But suddenly Cy's becak pulled up beside me. Cy was grinning from ear to ear and as his becak took the lead, He shouted back to me that he had promised his driver five dollars extra if he won. I could see our hotel about two blocks away, but it was on the opposite of the boulevard. We would have to go past the hotel to a point where we could make a U-turn and go back. So, not to be outdone, I waved five dollars over my head so my driver sitting behind me could see it. I felt an immediate surge of power and heard a cackling laugh from just behind my head. I started to think I might not be paying for both fares after all…I had a real chance of winning this race. But then, the fun, at least for me, suddenly changed to stark terror. Just in front of me, Cy's driver made an insane swerve through a little pedestrian crossing and started up the boulevard in the wrong direction…in the face of an opposite direction stream of headlights. Within a few seconds my driver had followed. "Oh Lord…I've survived the Congo…the daily dance of dodging AK-47 7.62mm rounds, the hand fired 50 cal incendiary rounds, the threat of SAM 7 missiles…only to die on the streets of Jakarta, going against speeding, horn-blowing cars, in an insane becak race! Lord Jesus, where is my brain?"

Cy's driver arrived first. I paid both drivers and tipped mine the five dollars I'd promised him if he had won…even though he lost. I wanted to fall down and kiss the ground just to be safe again…but I didn't; it looked pretty dirty.

We Check The New Aircraft–The Media Checks Us

The next morning we met Roger and went to inspect the aircraft. We made use of a small private office. Once inside, Roger said we may have a little problem. A news reporter had called him and had been snooping around the airport and the airplanes. Thankfully there were guards around ours. But the guards alone were enough to tell the reporter he might be on to something. We spent the morning going over the maintenance history of the two planes that were ready. The records looked pretty good as they were both previously owned by Garuda, the national airline. But as all three of us knew…paper often doesn't tell the entire story. It was going to be up to us to walk, crawl, and peer with flashlights into ever part of that plane. While we were still in the office an American in a suit…the typical embassy type entered the little office we were using. Roger nodded that it was OK to talk in front of us. He said the press was trying to put together a story…a story saying these aircraft were destined for the war effort in Cambodia. If the story made it to the streets, he could almost guarantee the government would be forced to block the export of the aircraft. He mentioned someone else was working to facilitate the expeditious processing of the deregistration paperwork (before the aircraft could become U.S. registered, they must first be deregistered in Indonesia). My guess was, but never confirmed, that this was a CIA employee with a briefcase full of money he did not have to give strict accounting for. He must have been successful as by mid-afternoon we were handed the new U.S. registration temporary certificate. We were told we should have the aircraft out of the country early the next morning and Roger needed to get another crew here to take the remaining one out by tomorrow night.

We worked feverishly to inspect the aircraft, no longer to insure the aircraft was accurately represented, but merely inspecting to be sure it appeared safe for us to fly over water. I didn't like taking an airplane I knew nothing about and heading out over the Gulf of Thailand. Thankfully most of the trip would be overland. We returned to the same area for dinner where we had eaten the night before and at dawn's first light, we departed Jakarta.

A New Year

The day after we arrived back with the new aircraft Roger held a New Year's party at his company villa. Partly out of boredom and partly because it would look too bad to add his New Year's party to the sizable list of other gatherings I'd failed to attend, I went. Because Sokha had been the girlfriend of our previous maintenance director, she was invited. There were a couple of U.S. military officers from the material delivery team and a couple from the Air Attaché office there that night. I noticed one of them was paying overt attention to Sokha. I suppose she had started to give up on her boyfriend ever coming back to get her as she was tastefully acknowledging his attention. The air hostess whom I'd mentioned to Roger was there as well.

Later that night Roger asked me if I realized the girls at the party did not know I was married. "Your joking" was my reply. "Not at all," Roger said. "Why on earth would they think that," I asked. "You're not wearing a ring," he said. "Of course I am," I said, and held up my right hand with my wedding ring worn inside my flight school ring. To that Roger replied that he'd never noticed it either. "Maybe that explains all the smiles I've been getting from them I thought.

During the evening the housekeeper came and spoke with Roger. He left and returned a couple of minutes later and whispered to Cy and me that a telex just came in confirming the crew had departed Jakarta with our other aircraft and without being foiled by the press. I'd learned, some time ago that the press doesn't give up on a story they think will get them a good byline. It would only be a matter of time.

Phnom Penh's Pochentong Airport Takes Another Hit

The enemy were inching their way toward Phnom Penh. Rocket and mortar attacks were becoming almost an everyday occurrence. On 7 January, a Sunday, the Phnom Penh airport took three separate mortar attacks. The max range of most mortars used by the enemy was less than 2000 meters. That was about the length of the airport's runway. That meant the bastards were watching us move around. I had to be crazy for getting out of bed and going to work. I made a note of it in my journal.

Ho Was Getting Low On Ammo

As the new year began, rumors of a movement in the Paris Peace Accord started making the rounds. The peace talks resumed in Paris on 8 January 1973. After the Christmas Bombing which blew Hanoi almost off the map, the North Vietnamese discovered new negotiating flexibility…amazing what

20,000 tons of bombs can do to enhance a spirit of peace and cooperation. An agreement was reached shortly.

In Washington, on 15 January, President Nixon announced a halt to all U.S. bombing of North Vietnam. But in the skies over Cambodia, not much changed. If there was one good thing that came from the pounding we gave Hanoi, it was that our flights were taking less ground fire. That was because those 20,000[184] tons of bombs had significantly damaged the NVA reserves of ammunition. As a result, they were only taking what they considered the sure shots. But each night from about six miles overhead Cambodia's rice fields, villages, schools and orphanages, the unrelenting waves of B-52s continued delivering their payload of death and destruction. Unfortunately though, by journalists and Khmer military accounts, the bombs seldom fell on the Khmer Rouge. By most journalistic accounts, from those correspondents who actually ventured outside the relative safety of Phnom Penh to see firsthand the carnage the B52's had left, the targeting or "boxing" appeared indiscriminate.

Intelligence sources and journalists, as well as Khmer Army officers were saying the people in the countryside were being driven into the arms of the Khmer Rouge by fear and hatred caused by the American bombings. [185] Most of the people dying were not Khmer Rouge. There was no winning the hearts and minds of these poor souls.

How Low Can You Go?

Meanwhile, during the daylight hours, the F-111 fighters were screaming across the country flying just off the deck, dropping their payloads of cluster bombs, concussion bombs and napalm. The human suffering was unimaginable. By night or by day, many were destined to pay.

One morning returning to Phnom Penh from Battambang, we got a call from "Disco," an air force AWACS EC-121 (Lockheed Constellation) advising to be on the lookout for an F-111 below us. These *Connies*, as they were affectionately called, were basically orbiting radar control stations. They were also engaged in (SIGINT) or radio signal intelligence gathering. This morning they called us on the guard frequency to advise we were about to fly through a strike zone, but that all the action would be several thousand feet below us. "Traffic will be coming from left to right low" was the controller's traffic advisory. It was only a matter of seconds later that we saw the traffic…it was indeed low…like inches off the deck. I assumed the pilot was using terrain-following radar or ground hugging technology. I knew that I was glad I was up in my cockpit rather than down there in his. He was certainly below all ground-based radar. His speed was incredibly fast. Thankfully our friends up in Disco could see him. He went screaming underneath us then just off our

---

[184] The Columbia History of the Vietnam War - David L. Anderson - Columbia University Press

[185] The American Bombardment of Kampuchea 1969-1973—Ben Kiernan referencing William Shawcross

right wing released his payload. We saw the flash and a few seconds later our entire airplane was lifted up by the shock waves from the bombs he released. It was like flying into a thunder cloud. I watched the orange flames explode outward and upward. I wondered how many poor non-combatant villagers had just been taken away by this *chariot of fire*. *"As they continued walking and talking, a chariot of fire with horses of fire suddenly appeared and separated the two of them."*[186]

I pushed the thought of what it must be like on the ground rapidly out of my head. It was rumored many bomb victims never had a scratch on them…that they were killed by the concussion. On very rare occasions when I would join some of the journalists who hung out at the Café de la Poste just across from the post office in Phnom Penh, I would hear them talking about a relatively new weapon called a thermobaric bomb. These weapons were initially being used against known areas of VC tunnel networks; later their use became more widespread. These bombs burned the oxygen from the surrounding air and created tremendous pressures in tunnels or other shelters. Those far enough away from the center of the blast would sometimes appear to be unmarked. In reality, the sudden vacuum created after the explosion passed would collapse their lungs. The reporters' stories echoed a briefing we had received from the air force. This was probably as terrifying to the Cambodian people as the death raining from the unseen and unheard B-52s. My head was starting to get far too many negative message units. I was starting to need a break.

Running On Empty

Sokha and I, along with some of her friends, would on occasion go out in the early evening for dinner. Dinner by necessity had to begin early and end early due to the curfew. She regularly encouraged me to get to know some of her friends a little better, but nothing ever clicked. I knew I felt so empty inside but none of them appeared to offer any serious remedy. At night as I would go to sleep, I felt as though a deep empty well was in my chest. I started hugging a pillow when I slept. As a child I was never allowed to use a pillow…"it would make my spine crooked;" now I had trouble sleeping without one…not under my head but tucked against my chest. I knew this couldn't be a good sign, but I was powerless to do anything. I could go home and remove all these terrible images from my sight though not from my head. I could feel this war starting to get personal. I was starting to, as the old men back in Hamilton County would say…*have a dog in the fight*; I was getting emotionally involved. This was new to me. I never experienced such feelings in the Congo. I was deeply troubled by what I saw in the Congo's eastern provinces but never to the point where I felt like I wanted to run out and get involved. To make things even worse…I had stopped writing Karen. I had no desire to share what I was going through. I was starting to grow accustomed to that idea. I didn't like it, but it was what it was. On top of everything else…I'd started smoking again; Dunhills.

---
[186] Holy Bible - Holman Christian Standard Bible (HCSB) - 2 Kings 2:11

A Flight With Mystery Lady

One morning as I was preparing for a flight to Kompong Som, I discovered the cabin attendant I'd asked Sokha about, the royal family member whose uncle owned the airline we were supporting, was scheduled to operate the flight with me. I wasn't even sure of her name as the airline schedules just used nicknames. She was listed as "Nine." I would later learn that was short for Danine.

After takeoff she was the one to serve the cockpit. I tried to engage her in some trivial conversation but got no place fast. That night I asked Sokha if she could help arrange some meeting after work with her. She shook her head, told me I was wasting my time, but agreed to try. The next day I had my answer…NO. Sokha explained that it would be impossible for someone in her position to be seen in public with me. Immediately seeing the possibilities…I advised it did not necessarily have to be in public. Again the following day, the response was No.

New Year Again–Chinese That Is
Year Of The Ox–3 February 1973

I had started to notice a proliferation of everything red all over Phnom Penh. Red paper lanterns, red and gold decorations, red shirts, if it could be made red, it was. I learned Chinese New Year was approaching. This was a big thing where all the Chinese shops closed, they exchanged fruit baskets and had huge parties. It lasted several days. The Chinese all thoroughly cleaned their houses in a ceremony which was supposed to sweep away any bad luck and make room for good luck. Symbols representing good health, good luck, long life, and happiness were plastered all over their doors and windows. Every Chinese doorway had food in front of it, usually on trays sitting on the ground. They left it for evil spirits to eat hoping the spirit would go away rather than go into their house. They exchanged gifts of money in small narrow red envelopes conveniently the size of currency notes. I found all this interesting and a welcome diversion to the war.

Captain Jacks Again

The heavy flying continued; the shelling of the city continued; the influx of refugees continued; the tragedy and suffering multiplied; the empty well in my chest grew deeper.

While I was already an experienced captain in the DC-3 and DC-4 the real need for pilots was in the Convair 440 aircraft we were acquiring. One afternoon, after my last flight, I had a note in my box saying Roger wanted to see me in his office downtown. When I got there, I found Cy and Roger waiting for me.

They wanted me to travel to the U.S. and take my Convair 440 type rating training. This would allow me to fly the Convair 240-340-and 440 as pilot in command (captain). They told me the class would begin in just over a month and asked if I wanted to accept. This would mean a lot more money, so I readily agreed.

As the days of heavy flying turned into weeks, I would occasionally be on the same flight with Nine. She was beginning to at least acknowledge my presence.

One day when I arrived back to my apartment, Sokha was waiting for me in the living room. She informed me that I owed her big time; that Nine was willing to come for a short visit to my apartment if we were not alone. I owe you was my reply.

A Change In Direction

The day of Nine's visit came. My schedule was for only two flights therefore I was home by 3:00pm. Yat had already been instructed to have a nice meal ready. I was a little anxious.

When she arrived, we sat for a few minutes. I asked her about her family. I was terribly ignorant of Cambodia's history. She was somewhat surprised that I knew so little. I did assume that she was closely related to the guy whose picture I'd seen in political caricatures, King Norodom Sihanouk; she was. I asked her about her father. Her eyes became moist, and she looked down toward the floor. "He's gone to the forest," was her reply. I had already learned what that term meant. It meant he had left Phnom Penh under cover of darkness to join up with King Sihanouk and his resistance fighters in Cambodia's jungle. They were fighting the Lon Nol regime, the very people I was there supporting. Like his cousin King Sihanouk, Prince Phurissara was now an enemy of the people. By default, this put them fighting as allies with the Khmer Rouge. All the lucrative contracts that funded our operations were for the purpose of keeping Lon Nol and his government in power. I asked if her mother was still alive, she said that she was but that she was seriously ill and not expected to live much longer. I'd heard many of the royal family married their relatives, so I asked if her mother was a Norodom. "No," she replied…"she is a Sisowath." "There was a King Sisowath," I commented; "is he your mother's relative?" "Yes," she replied…he was her grandfather. "So your father's grandfather was King Norodom and your mother's grandfather was King Sisowath?" I asked. That's right she answered…still looking at the floor. I then uttered the most preposterous thing: "then your great-grandfathers on both sides of your family were kings." She didn't bother to answer.

I realized this was not exactly how you begin a happy first evening together, so I pointed toward the table and we sat down to a dinner by kerosene lamp and music from Armed Forces Radio Saigon.

After dinner she began to keep an eye on her watch. Shortly before 8:00 pm she said she needed to go watch from the balcony for her ride. Soon a small car with several people inside pulled up and stopped in front of our apartment building. She explained it was her cousin and some friends coming to take her home; that her family did not know about her visit. I took her hand and asked if I could see her again. "Yes," she replied as she hurried out the door. I walked her down the stairway but not out onto the street. It was seriously forbidden for her to be seen in public with me. That night sleep did not come easily. I knew I wanted to see her again.

A Grease Gun For My Flight Bag

The battle raged on in the provinces; the smaller provincial airports became more of a security threat. The Khmer Rouge were literally watching every move we made via spies planted in civilian clothes. We suspected some were even employed as baggage handlers. Some of the guys were starting to complain about personal safety after hours in Phnom Penh, Battambang, and Kompong Som as well. Others were taking matters into their own hands and procuring their own personal protection from the very active local open market. If we provided it to the Khmer military, it could be purchased on the streets. To that end, one day an embassy jeep drove up to Roger's villa while I happen to be there. It was carrying a huge cache of weapons. There were Thompson submachine guns, M-79 grenade launchers, 12-gauge Winchester Model 1897 pumps (the old ones with a hammer), several cases of M61 grenades, Smith & Wesson snub nose (2in barrel) .38 Specials, AK47s, a couple of M2-A carbines, and a couple of M3-A submachine guns (grease guns). Since I was first on the scene and I knew they wouldn't last long, I picked a grease gun, a M2 carbine, and one of the 12-gauge pumps. I already had an AK-47 courtesy of Roger. I also grabbed six or seven of the grenades.

I liked the Smith & Wesson .38 Special because it could easily be carried and concealed but its firepower paled upon coming face to face with an AK-47. We frequently joked that "you never bring a knife to a gun fight." This fairly approximated the usefulness of the .38 special in a serious confrontation. Since I already had carried a Colt Cobra 38 special I passed. The Colt I had acquired via another well connected source.

I liked the grease gun because one of the Army's delivery team members had one. It could be disassembled down small enough to fit easily in my flight bag or brief case and reassembled in about ten seconds. I used to practice remaining extremely proficient in taking it from my flight bag and putting it back into fire-ready condition. Its metal hand grip also served as an oil reservoir to keep the slide action lubricated and for protection from overheating. It even had a tiny dipstick to check its oil level.

The delivery team guy who brought the cache warned us about buying AK-47 7.62 rounds off the local market. He cautioned us only to draw our ammunition from the embassy as the CIA had let a huge contract to manufacture "spiked" (explode on firing) 7.62 ammunition and had insured it fell into the hands of the Khmer Rouge and the VC. The VC and KR would sometimes sell some of this spiked ammo to arms dealers for cash without ever knowing they had just "dodged the bullet." If we got one of those it would be "taps" he said. I gathered up my haul and headed for my apartment before anybody else got there and accused me of hording…which would have been true.

A couple of days later, Cy and I went to a little shop that made leather shoes. Cy had made a sketch of a holster design and asked if I would like to have one made as well. The second I saw his design I loved it. My Colt Cobra would hang inverted under my left arm. Under my right arm would hang a pouch containing two sections; each section holding 12 rounds. The rounds hung inverted as well. When the cover for one of the two ammunition pockets, which was positioned at the bottom, was opened, shells would fall by force of gravity, one at a time into your open hand. The inverted .38 under my left arm and the ammo pouch under my right arm were connected by straps that crossed on my back. Nothing was visible from the front which would have been fine if we were wearing jackets, but we were not; it was too hot. I now completely understood the open at the bottom Eisenhower blouses we used for uniform shirts. If required, your right hand could easily slip up under the blouse and retrieve the snub-nose 38 hanging inverted under your left arm. As it cleared your blouse it was ready to fire. But here again we found ourselves back to bringing a knife to a gun fight scenario. It was without question better than being unarmed, but just barely.

Quiet In The Center Of The Storm

Nine started to come regularly. I found her easy to be around. We could never go out into public, but she brought peace. I would tell her about the things I'd seen each day. She would quietly listen.

At times she would tell me about how she missed her father and how the government's orchestrated hate campaigns toward the royal family hurt her so deeply. It was as if her life turned upside down on 18 March 1970, when General Lon Nol and the National Assembly deposed King Norodom Sihanouk. To make things even worse, one of her uncles on her mother's side, Prince Sisowath Sirik Matak, helped orchestrate the coup. It was shortly after the coup that her father, HRH Prince Norodom Phurassara, left to join his cousin King Norodom Sihanouk in the fight against the Lon Nol and Sisowath Sirik Matak regime. She told me about the endless radio and television propaganda directed against the royal family. This was necessary because the king was deeply loved by the Cambodian people and the fragile and paranoid new Lon Nol–Sirik Matak regime feared the people would rise up against it. She told me how middle-class people who were easily influenced by the government's propaganda often made rude remarks to her face. But at the airport, the peasant baggage loaders worshipped her. She was a *Cinderella Princess* to them. And she truly loved them. I was amazed when I watched her move about the airport stopping so frequently to talk to the lowest laborers. She was always strong…she never allowed the government to make her ashamed of who she was. She was Her Highness Princess Norodom Danine and she would never allow the government to take that away from her.

Al Rockoff–War Photographer–The Best Of The Best

Meanwhile the storm outside my apartment walls raged on. More wounded…more refugees more widows and orphans. Part of me didn't want to look; the other part told me had to look and try to understand.

By this time I'd become an advanced amateur photographer. But I took few pictures during my time in Cambodia. Cambodia was my silent period. Somehow, I felt it was obscene to photograph all this misery. Yet, on the other hand, I understood the need for some, who were called into the photojournalism field, to document this tragedy in all its shocking, sickening, horror and gore.

Perhaps the person most successful at fulfilling this call to document the war was a man I saw on occasion when I'd go out at night…Al Rockoff. Al was a U.S. Army combat photographer who came to Cambodia as a civilian photojournalist. He, at great risk of losing his own life, took some of the most iconic images of the conflict in Cambodia. He was seriously wounded on more than one occasion in his single-focused drive to show the war as it was. Al's lens looked into the very soul of the Cambodian people and their suffering; he received numerous acclaims. Al often came off as a little bit strange and many people found him hard to like. I guess just because of that and his stunning images of something that had become a deep part of me…I liked Al Rockoff. Al was portrayed, in the famous movie "The Killing Fields." As most who know Al would say the portrayal was unfair…bordering on slanderous. Later, as Phnom fell to the Khmer Rouge, Al would stay behind refusing to be evacuated to document the horrible carnage

A Photo Opportunity Versus Respect And Compassion Earned Me A Trip To The Embassy

One day on a flight from Kampong Chhnang back to Phnom Penh the military had a seriously wounded solider and his young wife waiting to be transported back. As usual, we boarded the passengers first then, just before we were ready to close the door we brought in the wounded solider and laid him out on his blood-soaked stretcher in the isle. His wife sat on the floor in the isle. He looked really bad. His face had lost all color…almost like that of a person already dead. I checked his pulse; it was weak and thready; his skin was clammy; he was barely conscious. From my Navy Corpsman and surgical technician training I knew he was experiencing hypovolemic shock…he didn't have enough blood to go around. I could tell he wasn't going to be around very long…possibly not long enough to reach Phnom Penh. I muttered an expletive, patted his terrified wife's hand and stood up to leave. A European passenger complained about his having paid for a passenger seat not a seat with a bloody soldier at his feet. As I stood to go into the cockpit I pointed my finger in his face and gave him a look that silenced him instantly, then turned and went into the cockpit. The click of the door closing was a reprieve from the tragedy unfolding in the cabin. The whole world was mad- completely *obscenity* mad.

While we were still in the climb, I heard the dreaded sound of the cockpit door being opened. The male purser advised the solider was dead. I didn't bother to go back and check for sure. There was no need. I called ahead on the military frequency and advised we had a wounded solider onboard. I knew he was already dead, but I also knew they would probably not put much emphasis on getting there on time if they knew this.

As the plane was still taxiing in, I got up and went to the back. I was going to make sure no impatient, irreverent SOB stepped over the solider. I told the purser (male cabin attendant) to stand behind the body and block the aisle. He made an announcement that all were to remain seated until the body and the soldier's wife had deplaned. I could see some were not happy about being inconvenienced but they could also tell by my menacing glare that testing the purser's order was not a good idea.

The ambulance was waiting on the ramp. The medics came toward the plane. As we shut down the engines and opened the door, they came into the cabin to get him. They immediately discovered he was dead. When the body and the wife were off the plane, I returned to the cockpit to complete my paperwork.

I took much longer than normal to complete the flight log. It was my last flight of the day, I was drained, and what was the hurry anyway. As I opened the cockpit door, I saw a significant pool of blood on the carpet in the aisle where the stretcher had been. I hoped they could remove it all. I sure as *obscenity* didn't want to see it every time I came onboard this plane.

As I got to the foot of the air-stair, I saw the dead soldier's body underneath the wing beside the landing gear; his widow squatting in typical peasant manner crying; constantly wiping his face as if to comfort him in some way. Just in front of them was a guy with a camera, crouching down to be at her eye level, clicking rapidly and fanning his film advance lever. He must have been some photojournalist who had talked his way onto the ramp to get up close to what he obviously regarded as a photo opportunity. But this was no Al Rockoff. His clothes were new and well pressed. He looked like he'd just walked out of Abercrombie & Fitch. I exploded. It was not my intention to scream. My intention was to order him in no uncertain terms to get the *obscenity* out of her face and to hand me his *obscenity* camera. He ignored me continuing to click away. I grabbed the camera which was attached to a strap around his neck and jerked with all my might. He fell backwards and one of the clips that held the camera to the strap broke. The camera went flying to the ground. He started to push himself up, but I kicked his arms out from under him. By this time the two military police who guarded the gate to the ramp came running over. I had already started for the snub-nose .38 under my blouse but the two M16s the MP had made that bad move unnecessary. I picked up the camera and because it was a Nikon, I expertly flipped the back open in one quick snap of my wrists. I jerked his 35mm film out and ripped it off its spool. I made sure every last fame was soaked in light. Then I threw it at him. He kept shouting over and over that I'd broken his camera. I told him he was *obscenity* lucky I hadn't broken his *obscenity* skull. I took his camera and gave it to the military police and in mixed Khmer-English suggested the MP's impound his camera as there were supposed to be no photos taken on the ramp. I could tell by the hint of a smile on the first-lieutenant face that we had had a meeting of the minds. Before sunset that camera would be for sale in a no-questions-asked downtown camera shop.

The soldier's widow was sobbing more now. The commotion had frightened her. As the MPs escorted the Abercrombie & Fitch would-be war correspondent off the airport, I knelt down and patted her hand again. I took out a huge wad of Khmer currency and handed it to her. It was probably worth about thirty dollars…probably about two month's pay for her husband, assuming he had been paid which was probably a bad assumption. She raised her hands in the traditional gesture of reverence and thanks while still bowing her head toward the face of her dead husband. I touched her still gesturing hands gently enclosing them in my hands, rose and walked away. As I drove away in the crew car, I saw the jackass would-be war correspondent haggling with a taxi for a ride back into town. He did not have his camera.

That night I asked Nine to hold me particularly close…longing for shelter from all that I'd seen.

The next day, at the airport, as I was checking into dispatch, I found I had been rescheduled for a later flight. They had a call from the U.S. Air Attaché that I needed to report to the embassy. I thought…oh crap…I bet I know what this is about. That little wuss was probably some *obscenity* senator's son…or worse…the ambassador's son or nephew. Oh well…I'd do it all over again so with zero remorse, I climbed into the waiting company car and headed to the embassy.

My first question after walking into the heavily secure air attaché's office was…"well, who was the little bastard?" They gave me his name which I have long since forgotten and informed me he was not the ambassador's son or nephew and apparently not related to any member of congress. "Well, that's good news…now what's the bad news," I asked. The assistant air attaché said the bad news was that the ambassador was pissed…that he was trying to run a war and did not need to be distracted by things like this. I saw this as a good way out, so I said I agreed wholeheartedly and promised not to start anything if I ever ran into him again. They replied that that was highly unlikely as the MPs wrote a report about how he had broken security and how he had failed to respect Khmer sensitivities; the latter being far more serious and likely to get him a ticket out of here. The assistant air attaché asked if I had just issued a sincere apology along with a promise my name would not come across the ambassador's desk again. "Why of course," I replied and headed back to the airport.

The Return Of Bat Masterson

Back in operations Cy asked me if I still kept up with any of the experienced DC-4 captains I'd flown with in the Congo. "Why yes," I replied, "I just got a letter from one of the most experienced yesterday. He's in Malta and looking for work." Cy asked if I had a contact number for him. I pulled his letter from my flight bag and copied the address for him. I headed to the plane. When I returned two and a half hours later, Cy met me with a smile and said that Bat would be here within two weeks. "Do you know any more?" he asked. I went to my flight bag again; this time for my friend Paul Rakisits. I told Cy he was going to owe me an employment agency fee.

Flight Training And Divorce

My type rating ground school and flight training was to be in Arlington Texas. A retired FAA inspector would be giving us the training. He had been specially arranged I was told. I would have some time to see Karen, Jason, and Jenny. I was looking forward to seeing the children. I was dreading having to tell Karen I wanted a divorce. While I still loved her, we had, over time, drifted apart. I was sure she already knew this, but that didn't make it any easier. My flight back to Texas was probably the longest flight of my life. I tried to sleep but sleep would not come. Images of our good times of closeness kept passing through my mind. So did all the empty times. I knew things had gradually changed and would never return. I felt guilty while still knowing I had to save my life. There were no winners here.

I had arranged to arrive a few days before my class began. I'd shared with Cy what I had planned to do. He understood. From Dallas Love Field I went straight to Hamilton. Karen knew something was wrong. I told her the next day. I told her I only wanted my clothes and if she didn't mind my African artifact collection; she agreed, but of course with pain. I left the African artifacts in her care. Basically I left with my memories. I returned to Dallas to get ready for training. I saw an attorney in Ft. Worth two days before my class started. The entire process took less than an hour. It was like cutting off my arm with a dull knife. There was no feeling of freedom; only a dull, deep depression. I'd left Karen with two children and a chain of broken dreams. A grossly futile attempt to live out a reality only found in children's nursery rhymes…a world view with a zero base in reality.

The words of David, King of Israel, kept coming to me. *"Be gracious to me, God, according to Your faithful love; according to Your abundant compassion, blot out my rebellion. Wash away my guilt and cleanse me from my sin. For I am conscious of my rebellion, and my sin is always before me."*[187]

Training went well. I got my Convair type rating allowing me to fly as pilot in command on the Convair. While preparing to return I did some shopping for things I would need to make my life a little more amicable back in Cambodia…some music cassettes, a better radio with more short-wave bands, another Swiss Army Knife, really basic stuff. Looking back now upon what I thought was worthwhile to buy, it's easy to see how rudimentary some aspects of my life had become. In some ways it was fundamental; in others it was a tangle of confusion. While trying to live each moment in order to experience the all-out adrenalin rush, leaving no emotion unsampled, I was, in the process, pushing perilously close to the redline; the point beyond which no sane person should venture. Whether or not I actually crossed that I suppose I'll never know, but now, more than forty years later, I can testify that if not crossed…I came damn close; close enough to suffer damage.

Starting Over

As soon as I got back, I was put in captain's line training. It was only a formality but since we were technically working under the FAA's regulations, or at least whenever it was practical, it was necessary to fly with a senior captain and have him certify I was airport and route qualified…a foregone conclusion. Within a couple of days I was duly signed off and my paycheck moved up again.

Nine was happy to see me again. I was happy to see her as well. Her visits continued. Her mother wasn't doing well at all. Nine was spending more and more time at the hospital with her. Her brothers and her sister all knew the end was not far away. They believed she knew this as well. So far, I'd met none of her family.

Some Steroids For The Khmer Air Force

While I was settling back into life in Cambodia and the slightly increased responsibilities of being pilot-in-command again, the Khmer Air Force began receiving significant amounts of aircraft and support equipment courtesy of the winding-down U.S. involvement in South Vietnam. I wondered if the U.S. really gave a damn about the Cambodians or if providing them with all this military hardware (which they did not have the trained manpower to operate) was simply cheaper than shipping it back home. I wondered if they ever gave any thought to what would happen to all that equipment if the Khmer Rouge overran the country; a possibility I was beginning to assign more weight to with each passing day.

---

[187] Holy Bible - Holman Christian Standard Bible (HCSB) - Psalms 51:1-3

I knew Washington cared about Cambodia…they did not want the country to fall into Communist hands. But care about the Cambodian people…I was sure Washington did not; only those of us who were here, who knew and loved the country cared; to that extent, we were pawns just as were the Khmer people; expendable little pawns on the vast chessboard of global politics. *Obscenity*!

A Visitor To The Presidential Palace

To complicate the Khmer Air Force's situation, a son-in-law of deposed King Norodom Sihanouk, serving in the KAF as a T-28 pilot, took off from Pochentong airport, flew to the Presidential Palace about three minutes away, circled a couple of times, then began bombing the place. Reports said 43 were killed and 35 more were injured. Fortunately for President Lon Nol, he was not in the building at the time. The entire air force was immediately grounded for a few days until an investigation revealed he acted alone. It was soon back to business as normal. In many ways, the ground war was completely dependent on the KAF.

The KAF had many brave, dedicated, and well-trained men, but not nearly enough. The ground war was progressing poorly for Lon Nol's army (FANK or Forces Armées Nationales Khmères). The country was overrun with North Vietnam Army troops as well as Khmer Rouge; the poorly trained FANK troops were no match for these battle-harden troops. In most cases, the only way they could keep from being massacred was by calling in air support. T-28s were joining U.S. Air Force fighters in providing this critical air support. But all knew that after the congressionally mandated bombing halt on 15 August 1973, only a few short months away, there would be no more U.S. air support; the KAF would be on its own.

In addition to the demands on the KAF fighter pilots, the helicopter pilots were facing round-the-clock missions moving in replacements for the increasing number of FANK casualties. Had the KAF forces been five times what they were, it still would not have been enough. None of this was the fault of the brave men of the KAF…it was the result of years if not decades of governmental neglect.

The U.S. began a massive training effort in Thailand in an attempt to train more pilots and technicians, but no matter how many instructors and how much money they threw on the project, pilot and mechanic trainees could not be created out of thin air. Dark clouds were looming on Cambodia's horizon; the undeniable facts did not bode well. These things weighed heavily on my heart. Many were unquestionably destined to die.

This Time There Would Be No Radio Call From Tintin

Not long after this, Roger called me to the office. He said the embassy had asked if we had any T-28 qualified people who would be willing to very unofficially fly some of these planes on "ferry flights only" to a U.S. maintenance facility in Bangkok. Roger said the implication was that the scope of the missions would be far wider ranging than "ferry flights." He clearly indicated if something went wrong, we would be on our own as this was a very gray area which could be construed as U.S. citizens flying in the air force of another country…exactly what I was doing in the Congo with Wigmo. The only problem was the Congo was officially a "cold war." Cambodia was a very "hot war" with tremendous press and hostile congressional scrutiny. It took me about a micro-second to say no. I was already hearing from reporters how some of the T-28 bombings were accidentally killing innocent not-combatants, not their intended Khmer Rouge targets. This invariably happens in large scale bombing campaigns. I did not want to become a part of this. I was already seeing more of the war than I wanted…I didn't need to be looking at it through a bombsight. I still heard Tintin's radio call in my dreams, "pull up…pull up for *obscenity* sake."

A New Kid On The Block

By mid-March the Khmer Rouge had most roads leading in and out of Phnom Penh blocked.[188] Civilian aircraft piloted by civilian pilots were commencing the biggest airlift since Berlin. Robert and Cy had landed a contract on their own . . . outside of Tri-9. The company would be called South East Asia Air Transport or SEAAT. They asked if I wanted to come fly with them. It didn't take long to answer yes.

Some pilots were not asked to join SEAAT. Some turned down the offer and remained with Tri-9. Both Tri-9 and SEAAT began extensive pilot searches back in the States. We had some success in finding furloughed Air America and Continental Air Services (another proprietary airline) pilots from Laos. They were combat experienced and knew the area. This group of pilots were our highest recruiting priority. We also found a few pilots back in the U.S. that had never flown in this type of environment before. They were a mixed bag. Some hit the ground like they were born to do this…others returned home (either voluntarily or involuntarily). Work became a constant stream of new faces. Most who decided to stay did in fact stay…most to the very tragic end. The place had a way of surreptitiously enslaving you; once it had you it seldom relinquished its death grip.

Another Congo Comrade

Right about this time my old friend and mentor Paul Rakisits arrived. He had been flying in Tanzania for a mining company after leaving the Congo, but the job played out. He'd sent word to Bat asking if there were openings here. Bat got Paul a spot with SEAAT. Paul arrived in country while I was back in

---

[188] Air America in Cambodia—LMAT and the Khmer Air Force - Dr. Joe F. Leeker - University of Texas at Dallas - 2008, updated 2010

Texas. It was good to see him again. This time his wife Marie Jeanne did not come.

New Kids In The Neighborhood

Due to the severity of the food shortages and the increasing effectiveness of the Khmer Rouge blockade, the demand for airlift capacity far overshadowed our ability to provide that lift capacity. More Thailand based U.S. Air Force C-130 cargo flights were initiated; Bird Air, another proprietary or *special customer* airline started flying. Bird Air received U.S. Air Force C-130 aircraft under what was reported as very favorable conditions. Others said the airplanes always belonged to the Air Force. I had little time to worry about the validity of such things.

Almost overnight, small operations with ancient airplanes began arriving in country. These planes and crews (mostly Taiwan Chinese) were operated under several newly formed Cambodian airlines. The Phnom Penh Airlift had begun.

Nine's Brother HH Prince Sisowath Duong Khara

I'm not sure how long it had been known, but one day it came to my attention that I was no longer a secret to Nine's family. Being "no longer a secret" was a far reach from having approval status, however. A few weeks later her oldest brother Duong Khara (17 years her senior and the de facto head of family) and I had lunch. It was a pleasant but serious conversation. He was of course very keen to learn my thoughts about his little sister. I liked him instantly; I liked him a lot. Nine loved "Bong Hut" (big brother Hut in English) as he was called inside the family; outside the family he was "Macha Hut" (prince Hut in English). Being seventeen years older than his little sister Nine, he was both big brother and often surrogate father in periods when her father was away.

I learned Nine's mother had been married twice. Her first husband was a Sisowath; he died early in life leaving her a young widow with two sons, Duong Khara (Hut) and Ritharavong (Hen). She then married Prince Norodom Phurissara (Tong). Tong was Nine's father.

Big Airplanes...Little Runways

The stranglehold the KR had on the country's roads, railways, and airports was increasingly taking its toll on the population. Food and fuel shortages began to cause riots in various parts of the country. Even in areas where good rice crops had escaped the pillaging of the Khmer Rouge, it could not reach Phnom Penh and the other cities because all the roads were cut. Virtually every major city was cut off... no food, no fuel, no medicine; everything was sealed off. Human suffering was high. You never really think about how useful a road is until you no longer have it.

The need to transport these critical commodities effectively could only be met with larger airplanes. This was the embassy's highest priority…keeping the population lined up behind Lon Nol's increasingly unpopular regime. Key to doing this was keeping them fed and supplied. The embassy was sparing no expense in keeping their newly found Cambodian friends fed and enlisting in Lon Nol's army.

In order to resupply the numerous key cities, large airplanes like the DC-4 and Convair would have to land on short (unsafe) and in some cases non-paved runways. My Congo skill placed me close to leader of the pack status in this new small airport arena. In the Congo I'd learned to fly large transport aircraft as one would fly a small airplane. While I constantly tried to hone my airline skills, I prided myself in my previously lesser used cowboy skills. Cowboy flying began taking on a dominant role in our day to day operations. The excitement level and the danger level advanced hand in hand.

A New Kind Of Runway

The Khmer Rouge had long controlled National Highway 5 running northwest out of Phnom Penh toward the rice growing areas of Battambang. Highway 5 also ran through the strategic town of Kompong Chhnang. Kompong Chhnang was located on the shores of the fish rich Tonle Sap Lake. The Khmer Rouge had not yet managed to interdict the supply of fish coming from the lake, but they held complete control of Highway five running south out of Kompong Chhnang toward Phnom Penh. Phnom Penh's food supplies were at critically low levels while Kompong Chhnang had enough fresh and dried fish to feed the city. The problem was transporting it to Phnom Penh. Route 5 was not an option.

The runway at Kompong Chhnang was a short unpaved strip which turned into mud in the rainy season. The engineers who designed the Convair made it as an airliner for modern airports. Never in their wildest dreams did they visualize it operating in an environment such as Kompong Chhnang, therefore it was poorly suited for the job. Its mighty engines augmented by water-alcohol injection gave it significant lift capability, but its runway suitability sucked.

Because of the strategic importance of the city to Phnom Penh's food crisis, the U.S. had installed what is referred to as a steel mat runway on top of the dirt strip. The proper term of this steel mat was Pierced Steel Plank or PSP Mat. It had its origins back at the beginning of WWII. Basically they were steel planks ten feet long by 15 inches wide which could be rapidly clipped together to form a runway surface. I'd read about and seen pictures of them while in flight school but had no training on how to land on one. Cy and Bat had experience in landing on them, so I decided I'd go along with one of them first before I tried it on my own. I had no concern about them when it was dry, but the rainy season was coming on. When it was wet it was slick as glass. When it was dry the tires contacting the steel produced a screaming sound.

After my PSP mat checkout I was scheduled to operate on my own. My checkout with Bat was uneventful...of course it was dry that day. On my first flight, the military controller on the ground advised over the radio that it had just rained and while no longer raining, the runway was wet. How nice...just what I needed; a new copilot and a wet steel mat runway. There was a slight crosswind on final. I yawed the crab out in the flair in order to be longitudinally aligned with the runway. I had my approach speed as low as I dared configured with high drag/lift and high power; basically landing with lots of power on and just above a stall speed. I scared the crap out of the copilot who'd never seen that type of approach before. After touchdown the remainder of the landing was uneventful. All that remained was to load the cargo and get airborne before dark when the Khmer Rouge came out.

My Kompong Chhnang Near Death Experience

Loading of the cargo and passengers was organized and didn't take unusually long. The problem was it was almost dark, and the mother of all black rain clouds was moving straight toward the departure end of the runway. Our flight back to Phnom Penh would only take about 25 minutes and the military controllers would hold the airport open for me.

Finally we were loaded. I allowed the purser, whom I knew I could trust, to close the entrance door. The copilot and I were already seated in the cockpit with the right engine running. As the air-stair door started closing I began cranking the left engine. It lit immediately and stabilized at the preset 1000 rpm. We immediately took the runway lined up. The black cloud was now literally right on the departure end of the runway. If I didn't take off, we would be stuck here overnight. I'd already been warned that any aircraft left overnight at most of the outstations would be another statistic by sunrise. We advanced the power, turned on the anti-detonation system which allowed the alcohol injection system to kick in and took the power up to takeoff power. As we released the brakes the aircraft lurched forward. Somewhere around 70 knots I felt the aircraft start to weathervane into the crosswind putting our longitudinal alignment at a slight variance to our path over the ground. I was able to fight it back with aggressive aileron and rudder. Finally we broke ground. I called gear up and brought back the throttles to max climb power. Almost immediately we flew into a torrent of rain. The sound of the rain pounding on the fuselage was deafening. I felt the airplane lose lift. The torrents of water hitting the wing were destroying the lift on top of the wing. As heavy as we were, I needed every last ounce of power these engines could generate, I looked at my ADI quantity, only about 25% remaining. The cylinder head temperatures were rapidly starting to fall from the almost solid sheets of water spilling over them. Running at these power settings, I needed the heads to remain hot, not start cooling off rapidly. I ordered the cowl flaps closed in an attempt to keep the temperature from falling any lower. We were barely climbing…perhaps 300 feet per minute. We should be climbing almost 1000 feet per minute. I knew I needed the extra power the ADI was giving me, but I could see it was almost gone. We continued to move away from the airport but still only barely climbing; we were about to be sitting ducks for Khmer Rouge with 50 cals or even AK-47s. I could not afford to bank left back over the Tonle Sap as the horizontal lift component used to make the turn would be taken from the vertical lift component I needed to get above the ground. For a few seconds, that seemed like an eternity, we were in very bad circumstances…dire straits.

Then, as suddenly as it had begun, it was over. With one last bounce of turbulence, we broke out of the black cloud and into the clear. I immediately reduced power back to the normal climb setting, turned off the ADI, and started opening the cowl flaps. Thank you, Jesus…literally.

Wars And Dreams Of Wars

My nights were never peaceful. Once Nine left to go back home, the assault would begin; either the shaking of my apartment's floor from the nearby B-52 bombings just across the river or from terrifying dreams of being captured by the Khmer Rouge or the VC. The dreams came several times each week. The B-52's came every night. The bombing halt was coming in August. By order of President Nixon, bombing had already ceased in Vietnam. The air assets previously in Vietnam were now redirected toward Cambodia. It was like they wanted to be sure they wouldn't have any bombs left by the August 15th bombing halt. Comings in groups of three, each B-52 would drop 108 five hundred-pound bombs; thousands of innocent Cambodian civilians were being killed. It was hard to find anybody who cared. Ironically, all this firepower…the strike fighters, the FACs, and the AC-130 gunships employed in the Vietnam War were suddenly available for the Khmer forces.[189] All this death raining down from the sky on hapless Khmer peasant farmers and villagers was sanitized and reclassified as "air assists." If only these "assists" were hitting the Khmer Rouge…but so frequently…they were assisting the Khmer Rouge.[190] "If only"

My dreams always seemed to center on my being chased or my taking shelter inside some type of parameter defense while the enemy advanced toward my position. They would be coming over the walls and my gun would jam. I was never out of ammo, but rather for some reason, I couldn't unjam or feed in another magazine. The terror would mount as they continued to advance closer and closer. I never succeed in these dreams. I would awake just as they were coming over the walls only feet from me. I would sit straight up in bed, covered in perspiration my heart pounding. I would be literally terrified. When I would realize it was just a dream, I'd lie back in bed and try to go

---

[189] Berent, Mark (2012-04-26). To War in Style (Short Story) (Kindle Locations 32-33
[190] American Bombardment Of Kampuchea 1969-1973—Ben Kiernan PhD

back to sleep. Sometimes the dream would return and sometimes it wouldn't. I learned that if I tried to stay awake for a while, I had a better chance of the dream not returning. Spending my nights in the arms of a nightmare had become my new normalcy. I longed for the times back in Hamilton, in my bedroom in our house at the top of the hill, when I would be awakened in the peace of the early morning still, by my father's large, gentle hands lovingly massaging my back.

All kinds of amateur shrinks have told me these dreams had all kinds of meanings from sexual impotence to repressed rage and hostility toward something I was powerless to change. I knew I could rule the first theory out, so I allowed them to humor themselves by acquiescence.

With beer and my magic herb I would routinely mellow out. But this allowed me to reflect and reflection often produced remorse and guilt over all the things in my life I wished I could go back and do differently. The Bible says "reflections of the heart belong to man"[191] but at that point in my life…reflection sucked.

My Old Acquaintance Anopheles Returns

About half way through my first flight of the morning I started to feel like I was coming down with the flu. I had headache and fever; I started shivering. I'd seen these symptoms since soon after arriving in the Congo…this wasn't the flu…it was malaria. I carried the parasitic microorganism received from the bite of an Anopheles mosquito in my blood. Some of the guys took a chloroquine-based prophylactic in hopes of warding off the disease but I had elected not to use it. A known side effect…dizziness or blurred vision caused my eyes to experience spasms so serious that at times I had trouble seeing the runway. I made the decision that I would probably live longer continuing to experience the reoccurrences than I would struggling to see the runway on short final. I dragged through the rest of that day's flights; we had no extra pilots to step in for me.

Nine was supposed to come for a visit that night. When I got to the apartment she was already there waiting. She could see I was sick. I took a shower and tried to sit, talk, and have dinner. It was impossible. I got in bed. She instructed Yat to keep plenty of water and watch me. But as the evening went on, I got worse…my temp was over 40 degrees Celsius which was 104 degrees Fahrenheit. I would drift off to sleep but never for long. When Bong Hut came to get her, she went down and told him she wanted to stay with me that night. He decided to come up and check on me. I was having one of my Khmer Rouge nightmares when he walked into my bedroom…the first time he had ever been to my apartment. I was told later that I sat up in bed screaming and pointing at him saying he was a Khmer Rouge. When I awoke the following morning I found Nine lying on the side of my bed wide awake

---

[191] Holy Bible - Holman Christian Standard Bible - Proverbs 16:1

watching me. I was very weak, but the crisis had passed. Nine went back home early that morning. I missed a day's work. I was starting to realize how important Nine was to me.

Happy Birthday

My thirtieth birthday passed uncelebrated…there was nothing to celebrate; I flew all day. My life was becoming irrevocably interwoven into the fabric of these suffering people and the outcome of the war. The enemy was within rocket and mortar range of the outskirts of Phnom Penh; several embassies had evacuated non-essential personnel; the U.S. Embassy evacuated its dependents.

During the month of April alone, the Khmer Rouge's stranglehold on the Mekong River Supply Route for Phnom Penh was able to destroy one POL (Petroleum, Oil, Lubricants) ship, one munitions barge, two cargo ships, and damage eight other ships. The danger was so great that one crew refused to sail and had to be replaced.[192]

So, after flying all day, I went back to my apartment, had dinner, and sat alone drinking San Miguel Beer…courtesy of a U.S. C-130 crew from Thailand. As the shadows from my kerosene lamp danced on the walls and ceiling, I cleaned my AK-47, and listened to The Tracks Of My Tears on AFVN Radio–Saigon. I went to bed early hoping the nightmares would not return. On the night of his 30th birthday, Jimmy Joe Jacks was a long way from Hamilton Texas.

Our Communication Network

Soon after arrival we were given AN-PRC 25 VHF FM combat-net radio transceiver. AN stood for Army-Navy. The PRC meant Portable, Radio, Communication. But since that was such a mouthful, they were just called "Prick 25s." We didn't use these very often but when rocket attacks were coming in more heavily than usual, we all monitored the embassy frequency. They were extremely short range like about 8 kilometers or five miles. They were best used just for listening to the more powerful command stations. We could, however, from my apartment and later my villa, reach the embassy although that was discouraged. Because they were so heavy, even though they were designed to be a backpack type radio, mine rarely left the house.

Later we were issued "black bricks," hand held Motorola VHF walkie-talkies. In addition to the embassy frequencies we also had access to Air America's net operated from a small rented upper story room on Monivong Street. When we received our "black bricks", most everyone abandoned their "Prick 25s."

---

[192] The Khmer Republic at War and the Final Collapse

HH Princess Sisowath Darameth 1913-1973
Nine's Mother Goes

It was late afternoon. I was back from my flights and had just finished my shower. Yat answered the knock at the door. It was Nine. She was with some older women I'd never seen. They were wearing black sampots and white blouses. I instantly assumed Nine's mother was dying or was already dead. Nine spoke softly saying her mother had died that afternoon and that I needed to get dressed quickly in a pair of my black slacks and a white shirt. They sat on the couch and waited for me to change. Nine made it clear that I was not to dawdle.

When I came out of the bedroom, they all stood and moved toward the door. They were discretely watching me closely. This was the first time anyone from her family other than Bong Hut had seen me. Nine's demeanor toward me was noticeably different. She was about to show me to her world. There was no "boyfriend" about this moment. Any allusion of a secret relationship was, from this moment forward, a thing of the past. Though she was experiencing the loss of her mother, and while she clearly looked to me for some measure of comfort, she was strong and resolute. Her every move for the next several days was rigidly scripted by her family's protocol…this included how she responded to me. Things became very formal. Visions of "Guess Who's Coming To Dinner" were ricocheting around inside my head.

We drove to the home of her next oldest brother Bong Hen. Although Nine's mother had lived with her oldest son, Bong Hut, his new villa was not completed yet. The doctors had informed the family she would not live much longer. It was decided she would not die in the hospital but at home. Bong Hen had a large villa with a large first-floor salon. She left the hospital in the morning. She died about 3:00pm that same afternoon.

When we arrived at Bong Hen's villa, we entered a large room; her mother's body was on a waist-high platform draped in golden silk and surrounded by white flowers and flowers carved from sandalwood. Funeral music was playing. It is impossible to adequately describe the effect of the wailing flutes except to say the hair on the back of my neck was standing up. Almost everyone in the room was far too polite to stare but many were stealing discrete glances.

Her oldest brother, Bong Hut, took me and introduced me to family members mostly in order of their rank and age. While they mostly spoke in Khmer, they used the French term, Nine's *fiancé*, when referring to me. Nine left me with her brother and I did not speak to her again until it was time for me to go back to my apartment. Most of the men were sitting in chairs out on the veranda. In Cambodian culture, the men tended to leave all the religious stuff to the ladies. The women mostly remained in the main room beside the body.

While we were talking on the veranda, Bong Hut used some of this time to explain to me how the funeral ritual would be observed. Immediately following her death, her body was washed by older female family members. Her face and arms were then ceremonially washed by her children. Then the female elders in the family dressed her in the finest quality silk sampot (traditional Cambodian skirt) and blouse.

As with our funeral customs when I was growing up back in Hamilton, the body was never left alone. Her children and grandchildren and an *achar* or priest would remain with the body, even sleeping beside the body.

Several times each day until the cremation ceremony Buddhist monks would come and recite chants meant to comfort her spirit. They believed her spirit was hovering near her body and would hear the chanting and be led across into the next life by the sound of the chanting. Bong Hut said her cremation service would be in five days.

Caskets And Coins

On the second day of the ceremony the body was placed in beautiful but unadorned rosewood casket. Before the lid was closed, the *achar*, accompanied by Bong Hut and Bong Hen placed a gold coin in their mother's mouth. After the cremation, when the family members and close family servants go to gather the ashes, the gold coin would be found…symbolizing that she could not take it with her into the next life. Not altogether unlike the Christian belief "Naked came I out of my mother's womb, and naked shall I return thither: the Lord gave, and the Lord hath taken away; blessed be the name of the Lord."[193]

From Darkness Into Light

I went to the ceremony each day after work. By the third day I was no longer a curiosity…well perhaps an exaggeration…I suppose "less of a curiosity" would be more accurate.

As the days of the funeral ceremony progressed, more of Nine's colleagues from work came to pay respects. They saw me there and the word spread around the airport like a wildfire; all now knew what only some had suspected.

Car Of The Dead

The day of the funeral came. I had the entire day off the flight schedule. I was up early. By 6:30 am we were all assembled at Bong Hen's villa. This was a huge funeral. Several hundred people were there already.

---

[193] Holy Bible—King James Version—Job 1:21

In Cambodia, the body is taken to the pagoda or in the case of a very large funeral, which this was, to a suitable place near the pagoda where the huge funeral pyre would be. The casket was moved from the house to a waiting *lon duc sop* (car of the dead) which somewhat resembled a large parade float profusely garlanded with white jasmine blossoms.

As the body emerged from the house the *achar* signaled the musicians to begin. The eerie, unnerving, wail of the flutes once again caused the hair on my neck to stand straight up. This sensation was so strong I wondered if it was visible to those around me. The casket was placed on the *lon duc sop* and draped in a large sheet of white silk. The silk had subdued traces of gold on it.

Nine, like all her brothers and sister, was dressed from head to toe in white. Both male and female direct family members wore the traditional *sampot chang kben*, a type of very long skirt with the trailing portion twisted into a large strand and tucked between their legs and secured in the center of their back. Normally these would be made of colorful hand-woven Khmer silk but for this occasion, they were all white. Both male and female royal family members wore the colorful sampot chang kben on extremely formal religious and state occasions. Ordinary Khmer wore them in their wedding ceremony. Nine, because of certain duties she had to perform at the ceremony also had her head covered with a long white krama (a traditional Khmer scarf usually brightly colored). Her brothers all shaved their heads the night before. I, like all other non-family members, wore black pants and white shirt.

The immediate family walked directly behind the *lon duc sop*. The others walked in mass behind the family members.

The Pyre

"Death is a mirror in which the entire meaning of life is reflected."[194]

The funeral procession moved through the streets and toward the Botum Wathei Pagoda. The pagoda was directly south of the Royal Palace and was associated with the palace. The stupas of many royal family members and high-ranking politicians were there. The stupas (A stupa (Sanskrit: "heap") is a mound-like or hemispherical structure containing relics (such as śarīra–typically the remains of Buddhist monks or nuns,) that is used as a place of meditation.[2]. of both Nine's grandparents (her mother's father and her father's father) were there. The stupas of great grandparents on both her mother's side and her father's side, King Norodom and King Sisowath were only a few meters away inside the palace. Her mother was truly coming home.

All the time the procession moved through the streets the music never ceased. The wailing of the flutes no longer sounded eerie to me. It was almost soothing. The procession was escorted both by military police due to

---

[194] The Tibetan Book of Living and Dying

Bong Hen's position in the military and civilian police. Several high-ranking politicians attended. Nine's father had held several ministerial level posts including that of foreign minister. Interestingly even Prince Sisowath Sirik Matak, who engineered the coupe that deposed King Sihanouk, went to the house to pay respects during the funeral and his wife, Princess Norodom Kethneari attended the actual cremation.

When we arrived in the park just opposite the pagoda, I was astounded at the size of the huge pile of wood about to be burned. This was going to be one huge fire.

I was being escorted or watched after by the husband of one of Nine's mother's sisters. He was not going to be directly involved in the cremation ceremony itself, so he was assigned to be with me and to explain things. He spoke good English. I felt very out of place there. I had spoken no more than a couple of sentences to Nine that morning. As the cremation began, she was probably fifty yards away.

The ceremonial fire was placed on the pyre by an uncle of King Sihanouk, a brother of Queen Kossomak, HRH Samdeck Sisowath Monireth. Within a few short minutes, the flames were leaping into the sky.

As the fire started to burn, I was told by one of Nine's aunts that I should not watch the fire and to turn toward the east because my birthday was too close to the date of her mother's death and the date of the cremation. There was another person there who also did not look for the same reason.

I left as the fire was burning down but still glowing hot. Several hours later but before dark, when the *achar* had ascertained that only small fragments of bones and teeth remained, the family returned, prayed and poured water on the ashes to cool them down and picked up bone fragments and ashes to put in the silver urn where they would remain. The gold coin would also be retrieved at this time. A custom was for sons, if they chose, to keep one of the teeth and have it incased in gold and worn around the neck. Bong Hut did this. I'm not sure about the others. I did not participate in this last part which was only for immediate family.

As the embers from Princess Sisowath Darameth's funeral pyre cooled, the flames from the Watergate scandal had reached 1600 Pennsylvania Avenue; Nixon aides H.R. Haldeman and John Ehrlichman resigned.

The next time I saw Nine, she was wearing all black. She would do this for six months.

Acquaintances From The Underworld

The longer I stayed in Cambodia, the more I became aware of an element in the aviation field that rivaled anything from the underworld of Greek mythology. Perhaps the best non-Asian example was an American named Steven

Brooks (pseudonym). He was a nice looking super likable, used car salesman type. Steven epitomized the proverbial fast-talking eternal optimist. He would take any shortcut available to him, regardless of the risk to human life in order to make a profit. He ran engines far beyond their scheduled overhaul, falsified maintenance and overhaul records, log books, even pilot's licenses. According to press reports, he and another pilot who had flown with him in Cambodia died in a plane crash a few years after Cambodia fell. The plane was full of marijuana having a street value of more than two million dollars.

But Steven was not alone. Numerous Chinese were bringing in old run-out DC-3 aircraft and operating them in the numerous new startup airlines. I can't count the times I heard them do an engine run-up at the end of the runway before takeoff…their engines sputtering so loudly nobody in their right mind would takeoff. They would turn onto the runway, advance the power, and go sputtering and smoking down the runway. Most of the time they made it; sometimes they didn't.

The most infamous of these junk airplane owner/operators was a Chinese named Johnny Lee (pseudonym) and perhaps the most amazing of these Chinese junkers was a Boeing 307. The B-307 was an adaptation from Boeing's B-17 bomber. It had four engines (the same engines used by the DC-3), was pressurized, and required a flight engineer. Pan Am and TWA were the first airlines to put them into service. Most of us had never heard of a Boeing 307. It was poorly maintained like most of the Chinese operated airplanes and on 27 June 1974, shortly after takeoff from Battambang, three of its four engines failed. It crashed in a rice field killing 19 of its 33 passengers.

Government corruption was so bad that no amount of malpractice, no amount of lives lost, could ground these anything-for-profit operators. The same operator crashed a DC-3 (C-47) 19 May 1973 in Svay Rieng claiming the lives of eleven.

On 2 October 1972 the same operator had crashed a DC-3 in Kampot, this time killing only 9 passengers. In July of 1972, in Kompong Som he crashed another DC, fortunately this time killing no one.

No matter how many people this unscrupulous aircraft operator killed, no matter how much grief and suffering he caused, he just paid off more officials and continued spreading his death and destruction.

The demons in hell are waiting for Johnny Lee along with all the miserable bastards he bribed so he could continue flying and killing people. Johnny Lee was the reincarnation of Charon, the underworld evil spirit who ferried the dead across the streams of Acheron into Hades. Charon's fee was a gold coin placed in the mouth of the dead before leaving on their journey into the underworld. This heartless SOB took his fee from the living as well as from the dead. There was no place on earth like Cambodia during the Phnom Penh airlift.

My Pochentong Near Death Experience

It was my last flight of the day. We were returning to home base from Battambang. I never descended early. There was no need. My plane was pressurized I could remain high and descend rapidly just before reaching the airport without hurting the passenger's ears. In my decent, no more than six miles from the airport we heard a loud bang, the aircraft yawed, and the left engine immediately began running rough. I checked my instruments and could see we were losing power on the left engine. I looked out the window and the left engine cowling was covered with oil. We were heavy, plenty heavy but well within the aircraft's normal capability. My first concern was to try to save the engine from doing extensive damage to itself. I immediately began the engine shutdown procedure. I looked again out the window at the left engine. This time, in addition to lots of oil, more oil than I'd ever seen coming from any engine, I thought I could see a slight deformity in the cowling.

I knew that if I didn't shut the engine down right then, it could cause serious damage. The aircraft had an auto-feather system, but we always kept it turned off except during takeoff. There was no time for the engine shutdown checklist. I pulled the power back on the left engine, ordered the co-pilot to retard the prop, I shut off the left mixture control, and initiated engine feather. The prop started moving toward the feather position but then stopped. The engine was no longer running but it was still turning. This condition is called windmilling.

Something had stopped the prop from going all the way into the feather position thereby allowing the airflow to turn the prop much as the wind turns a windmill pumping water. As the prop continued to cause the engine to turn, more oil was being pumped out. Now, in addition to the cowling and now a large area of the wing being covered with oil, I could see a large bump starting to appear at the one o'clock position on the cowling. The cowling was being pounded by something. Seconds later the bump on the cowling ruptured; we could see one of the cylinders had come off and was being moved up and down by the piston. Because the prop would not feather, the engine was now being turned by the prop rather than the prop by the engine.

I asked the co-pilot to check the left engine feather pump circuit breakers. When he replied they were popped a short-lived surge of optimism swept over us. With luck, we could reset the blown circuit breakers and resume the feathering process. He reset them and I hit the feather button again. Almost immediately they blew a second time.

"Hold the bastards in by hand" I instructed. "I'll fry the feather pump before I let it fry us." When the copilot was in position and physically holding the circuit breakers in by hand I pushed and held the feather button in. I saw the amp meters move toward full scale. I could see the prop was not moving. Then I saw the amp meters drop back to normal. I had fried the feather pump to the point it burned some wires or something. Whatever had happened, the normal amp reading was telling me the circuit to the feather pump was now open and the feather pump was no longer an option. What that really meant was the prop blade position was going to remain where it was, which meant it would continue turning the engine which would in turn continue shucking itself. Our circumstances were going to hell in a hand basket…rapidly.

I had already moved the remaining engine up to max cruise power and had to open the cowl flaps to help cool it. In spite of this we were continuing to lose altitude. We were about five miles out and I was already starting to have serious reservations about making the runway. While we were five miles from the airport, I was not lined up on final approach. I was almost 90 degrees from the final approach course. In order to put myself on even a short final, my track miles needed to be at least six. We were continuing to lose altitude and I knew even with max continuous power on the good engine we would not be able to hold altitude. It was a fact that from our present position to touchdown, the best I could hope for was a descent rate that might make the runway.

I changed our heading 15 degrees to the left which would place us intercepting the final approach course on less than a two-mile final. The maneuver onto final would require a much steeper bank that what was normally considered safe on short final, never mind being on single engine. The bank would also rob some of my lift, taking it from my vertical lift component and using it for horizontal lift. There were no options…only a few critical decisions as to when to initiate the required actions. I called for max continuous power. The co-pilot moved the throttle up to the max continuous setting. We opened the cowl flaps more trying to keep our remaining engine temperature from exceeding limits. I told the co-pilot to advise the control tower we were declaring an emergency and were requesting landing priority. He did and we received our clearance to land immediately; all other traffic was diverted or sent into holding patterns. The tower asked if we wanted the fire trucks beside the runway. I advised that that was affirmative. Have them positioned in place.

We continued to lose altitude at a rate that made our reaching the runway very questionable. I looked desperately for a place to put the plane down in an emergency landing; there was nothing but houses and villages below us. The cylinder head temperatures on the right engine continued to rise. We opened the cowl flaps all the way.

I ordered the co-pilot to turn on the alcohol injection. We were not scheduled to make another takeoff so our ADI (anti-detonation injection) fluid was low. The engine surged as the ADI injection began. The co-pilot inched the power toward takeoff power. We did not want to apply full takeoff power until absolutely necessary. The added power helped slow our descent rate, but we could not arrest it. We selected the flaps to their first setting which would produce some much-needed lift.

I knew that at some point we would have to drop the landing gear. I did not know the extent to which it would increase our drag and our descent rate, but I knew it would be horrendously detrimental. I knew that we must delay extending the gear until the very last possible second if we were to have any chance of reaching the end of the runway. What I did not know was how long it would take the gear to go down in our present hydraulic configuration. It would certainly be slower than normal. If I miscalculated, only by a fraction, we would all parish in a ball of flames. I paused for a couple of seconds and prayed *"Yea, though I walk through the valley of the shadow of death, I will fear no evil: for thou art with me; thy rod and thy staff they comfort me."*[195]

Approaching interception of our final approach course, I banked the aircraft hard to the right and commanded takeoff power on the right engine. I was pushing on the rudder peddle with all my might. As anticipated, our descent rate increased due to the steep bank. As soon as we rolled out on final, I called for gear down. I backed this up with a call for emergency gear extension (pneumatically plowing open the uplocks). I heard the gear doors open and the gear begin to extend. An eternity passed before the red gear in transit lights went out and the green gear down and locked lights came on.

Our airspeed was dangerously low. I was using every extra knot to provide lift…not forward speed. Heightening the tension was the ever-present awareness that I was not only dangerously close to a stall but also equally dangerously close to being unable to control the aircraft (VMCA), a speed below which one cannot maintain directional control in the air with max power applied. I'd never been more focused in my life. By the grace of and with the help of God, we touched down literally inches after the start of the runway. Later, when I viewed our touchdown tire marks on the runway from our SEAAT jeep, they were less than two feet from where the runway surface began…about one second from landing short.

After landing, sitting in a sweat soaked shirt with my legs still shaking, the crew chief came onboard and told me he had seen the left engine stop turning only a few hundred feet before the end of the runway. The engine had finally seized. The seizing of the engine allowed the prop to stop turning, which reduced the drag and without question allowed us to reach the end of the runway. Till today, I believe the hand of the LORD seized the engine to save our lives…the lives of five crew and 52 passengers.

---

[195] Holy Bible - King James Version—Psalms 23:4 attributed to David, King of Israel circa 1000 BC

By the time I stopped shaking, signed all the flight's paperwork and got down from the plane a large crowd of airport MPs, mechanics, and airline employees were gathered around the oil drenched cowling the mechanics had just removed from our left engine. They were pointing to a large bullet hole in the side of my cowling. My guess was it was a 50-caliber antiaircraft round. The investigation later confirmed it was in fact a 50-caliber round. Some of our briefings had reported AA sites in other parts of the country but I hadn't heard of one this close to Phnom Penh before. I was sure the air attaché would have plenty of questions about just where I took this little jewel.

The mechanics had already determined that the 50-caliber round had penetrated the engine cowling and the cylinder wall. Once inside the cylinder the piston was instantly shattered. From there the piston began the destruction of the cylinder, breaking it loose from the engine case and finally pushing the cylinder partially through the cowling.

The cylinders on large radial engines such as the Pratt & Whitney R-2800 were external rather than being inside a block. Probably within a few seconds from the bullet strike the cylinder was separated from engine case. The mechanics advised the engine was scrap metal. Only some externally mounted accessories like generators and starters, magnetos, coils, etc., could be saved. They weren't sure why the prop wouldn't feather but said it was probably due to massive metal chip contamination throughout the entire oil system. As was their normal custom, they had already written on the cowling with a magic marker "From Charlie With Love." I walked away from the aircraft very thankful to be alive. I took a picture. It was left behind when I was evacuated.

From The Pagoda Arose More Than Chants

I learned early on that a sure way to get on your crew chief's s-list was to continually be coming in with bullet holes in "his" airplane. Being probably the most cautious of the SEAT pilots augmented by the fact that the planes I flew were pressurized allowing me to stay high longer and get hit less, I managed to stay pretty close to the bottom of their list. However, as just recounted, I was not immune to taking a round now and then.

One day on departure from Battambang heading back to Phnom Penh, we heard three tap…tap…tap sounds come from the back of the plane. Our pressurization hiccupped then returned to normal. Almost immediately the senior cabin attendant entered the cockpit advising we had bullet holes in the fuselage back in the galley. He said nobody in the back was hit. I sent the copilot back to take a look instructing him to look for damage to hydraulic lines or flight controls. He returned a couple of minutes later saying they appeared to have missed the critical stuff. We checked all our quantity and pressure indicators, which appeared normal and continued on to Phnom Penh. He said they did not appear to be AA (antiaircraft) but rather 7.62mm

(AK-47). With luck the crew chief could just tape over them with speed tape after certifying nothing critical had been struck. We carefully marked the location on the map where we believe we took the rounds. The position was suspiciously close to a large pagoda sitting on a small hill about three miles from the airport. The embassy had briefed us that the pagodas had been put off limits to airstrikes and that probably meant they would become sanctuaries. I couldn't help but muse that normally sanctuaries were where birds and other wildlife went to get away from hunters. In this case, it appears the hunters went there to hunt the birds (us). We called Disco, the AWAC and advised them we had taken small arms fire and gave them the coordinates. I called flight ops and gave the good news to the crew chief. He was guaranteed be waiting with a scowl and a roll of 210 mile per hour speed tape. I looked at the co-pilot, smiled, and said, "just another day in paradise." The rest of the flight was uneventful.

The Orphanage

One day, while talking to some American missionaries working in Cambodia I per chance learned about a young Korean Christian man who was struggling to shelter and feed a bunch of orphaned Khmer kids. The government was overwhelmed and unable to make even a small dent in caring for the hundreds upon hundreds of children being orphaned as a result of the war. These missionaries were from the same group I'd met in the Congo; the Christian and Missionary Alliance or CAMA. Here they were called CAMA Cambodia.

I asked one of the missionary couples I had recently met, Merle and Louisa Graven, if they could take me to see the orphanage. They readily agreed. I went straight to their house after my final flight of the day and they drove me to a neighborhood of water filled muddy streets and wooden houses. There, down a narrow footpath, we came to a wooden and tin structure. I could hear the chatter and the laugher of innumerable small children inside. A slim and very pleasant young Asian man met us at the doorway. He said his name was Jimmy (pseudonym). He spoke pretty good English. He showed us around the place. There was no furniture, only mosquito nets and mats for the children to sleep on. I saw a large blackboard where he apparently was attempting to provide some schooling as well. There was a young Cambodian lady with him. She too was a Christian I was told.

I asked how I could help. Jimmy quickly replied that feeding them was the most pressing need. With the food shortages, especially rice which would be their basic diet, this was a daily escalating problem. He was receiving no organized support. Just occasional donation from anyone he could persuade. I decided I could help. I had an idea, but the plan would take a day or two to put into action. In the meantime, I took all the money I had on me, probably about $20, and gave it to him. He was very thankful. I told him I would see him again soon.

My Fishy Idea Flopped

The following day I had a flight to one of my favorite airports…Kompong Chhnang. As usual, the wholesale fish merchants were overseeing the loading of their baskets of fish and haggling with us to carry more than our contract called for. I almost always said no, but today I had come with an idea. I planned to help Jimmy feed his orphans. So I told him I would carry five extra baskets of fish in exchange for one basket. He immediately started trying to convince me to take money rather than his fish as he figured I did not know the value of the fish (which I didn't) and he could get a better deal by giving me money. I held firm on my demand and soon was the proud owner of a basket of live, flopping, 12-13-inch-long catfish which I had placed in the cockpit. I made him give me some extra ice to help them make the thirty-minute flight back to Phnom Penh. I was pretty sure the co-pilot would rather have seen me take the money rather than a basket of dripping, flopping, fish. When he made captain, the call would be his, but today we would be flying with the orphan's fish.

After the flight I had the driver drop me and my fish at the orphanage. Jimmy was surprised to see me so soon and even more surprised to see the fish. He did appear a little reluctant about the fish, but I insisted the children would really enjoy something nice for a change…not just rice gruel. I stayed a few minutes playing with the little children then headed back to my apartment.

The next morning, I found a note from Merle Graven, saying Jimmy had come to him saying many of the children had come down with diarrhea because of the fish. Apparently, they were too rich for their system after only eating rice and some occasional green vegetables in their soup. So much for my fish idea.

Rice And Green Vegetables

My New Contraband

But I was far from defeated. I knew I could persuade a couple of the more soft-hearted pilots to put the bite on the wholesalers for fresh vegetables and rice. I smiled as I reviewed my plan; I should have been a mobster.

By the end of the day Bat was enthusiastically on board and he promised he would not see me again before he had enlisted Paul Rakisits as well. The plan was coming together. I wasn't exactly sure how the missionaries and the other Christians associated with the orphanage would view my plan in light of their Christian sensitivities; I decided it would be best they not find out. The operation was classified "SECRET." Besides, God used all kinds of unsavory people in the Bible to accomplish his goals. Matthew was a tax collector. Rahab, a prostitute, was not only the great-great-grandmother of King David but also an ancestor of Jesus. The first person saved through belief in Jesus was a thief dying with Jesus on the cross. I elected to believe that God would turn his All-Seeing-Eyes in another direction. The plan worked; the missionaries and Jimmy never found the source of their gifts of food for the children; the children went to bed each night with stomachs satisfied.

Espionnage Affaire

Hank (pseudonym) was one of the assistant air attachés. I liked Hank immediately; I'd liked anybody who wore cowboy boots in Cambodia. Sometimes, on the ground in Phnom Penh while our aircraft was being loaded, I'd go over and sit in the U.S. Air force's bunker; partly because I enjoyed their company and partly because it had lots of sandbags piled up all around it. It could withstand just about anything the Khmer Rouge had short of a direct hit.

One day as I sat in the bunker chatting with one of the enlisted men whose job it was to supervise the quick unloading of the U.S. C-130 supply flights, Hank came in. He was obviously mad about something. My casual "hey man…what's up" unleashed the whole story. In a narrative heavily laced with expletives I learned that Hank and been "seeing" a certain, very attractive Swiss or German (most people weren't sure) travel agent named Valérie (pseudonym). She and the man she lived with…whom I had thought was her husband up until this point, ran a travel agency in Phnom Penh. It seems some embassy official had learned of what I later discovered was their not-so-discrete liaison and made an issue out of it, telling Hank she was an East German agent and he was compromising our operations. I could tell by his total loss of cool that Hank already *had a dog in the fight* as the old timers back in Hamilton used to say. He was told that if he didn't break it off immediately, he would be out of Cambodia on the next flight taking with him a serious blotch on his military record that would guarantee him no further promotions, if not a discharge. I kinda felt sorry for him, and yet I had to wonder how he could have thought that relationship would not come back to bite him…as it just had. A couple of months later Hank was gone. I never asked if he broke off the little affair. Never bothered to ask if she was the reason he left. It is said that "love is blind." I believe it's fair to say that both love and lust are blind.

The Kompong Chhnang Toll Road

One day we landed in Kompong Chhnang just about lunch time. The loading of our aircraft was going to take about 45 minutes. The lieutenant in charge of the airport at the time suggested we try a restaurant he recommended about three miles away in the center of town. Upon hearing that, one of our regular fish shippers who had received some merchandise from Phnom Penh on our flight offered to let us ride into town with the cargo we just brought in for him. It sounded like a pretty good idea. After dark it would have been suicidal but for the moment, FANK (the Cambodian Army) had the road open.

The truck we were riding in was stopped by the military police at the gate leading off the airport. They were talking to the driver. They began to argue...money changed hands, and we moved forward. The shipper explained to me if his driver had not paid, they would have made him unload all the cargo from the truck so they could "inspect" it.

I swear we hadn't gone another couple of minutes, and we came to another road block. These guys were from a different military unit. Again the driver shucked out money. All in all, this happened four times before reaching the restaurant where we hopped out. As I was thanking the shipper for the ride, I asked if this happened all the time. "All the time," was his reply. "It's just part of the cost of doing business." We enjoyed a nice traditional meal of soup and rice and headed back to the airport via a *motodop* (motorbike taxi). The check points never acknowledged our presence; we drove right through them. In spite of these blatant exercises in corruption, I found it hard to think too badly of them. Most probably were paid only sporadically while their colonels and generals drove about in luxury cars, eating in the best restaurants, accompanied by their harems. Sometimes a guy's gotta do what a guy's gotta do.

My Nightly Visitors

Scarcely a day passed that I didn't see some horror of war that would return later in a bad dream. While I wasn't concerned about my sanity...I started to dread going to sleep at night. Several times each week I would awake an hour or so after falling asleep, my heart pounding from fright. When talking to other pilots, some would recount the same experience. Years later I learned this was a common symptom of Post-Traumatic Stress Disorder or PTSD. Unfortunately for us, it would be seven more years, in 1980, before it was officially recognized as a disorder. [196] Many of us knew we had lots of bad dreams, almost all of us jumped at sudden or loud noises, some of us would see something which would trigger some playback in our head. Most of us were up tight all the time and losing one's cool was a frequent occurrence...but hell...we all just thought that was normal.

For the waves of death engulfed me; the torrents of destruction terrified me. The ropes of Sheol entangled me; the snares of death confronted me.[197]

A Family Outing

My relationship with Nine was starting to move out of the closet. One night she told me that her family had planned a dinner at a well-known Chinese restaurant and all the family would be there. She explained this was a signal to the general public that the family had accepted our relationship. Needless

---

[196] The United States Department of Veterans Affairs - PTSD History and Overview - Matthew J. Friedman, MD, PhD
[197] Holy Bible - Holman Christian Standard Bible - 2 Samuel 22:5-6

to say, I was just a bit apprehensive. Except for her eldest brother, Bong Hut, I'd only seen her family at the funeral.

On the night of the dinner, Nine came early. She wanted to spend a few minutes briefing me on little family nuances I should be aware of. Seems while they all more or less got along, there were, nevertheless, some areas of sensitivity into which I should not stumble. I was going to have a hard enough time learning all their names, much less subtleties in interrelationships.

Bong Hut and his wife came to pick us up. He drove a large late model Mercedes. We chatted about politics and how the war was going all the way to the restaurant.

At the main entrance, we were escorted to a private dining room. On the way, the owner of the restaurant met us and greeted Bong Hut. Apparently, he was more of a VIP than I'd initially assumed. The owner kept bowing and *satouking* (classic greeting and sign of respect where the hands are pressed together as if praying and brought up touching the mouth). As we entered the private dining room most of the family was already seated around a huge circular table. In the center of the table was a smaller circular, rotating table resembling a lazy-Susan.

Soon after we were seated, they began serving hot tea from tea pots. There were at least three servers for our table; sometimes as many as five. We drank the tea from small porcelain tea cups which had no handles. The tea still had pieces of the tea leaves floating in it. I figured this was not a mistake but rather by design. I could smell the scent of jasmine. I'd had jasmine tea in Cambodia before but never in such an elegant environment.

Next, they brought in the starter dishes. There were so many different varieties; each on its own plate. There were plates of roasted peanuts, boiled peanuts, plates of cold meats like pork and duck and stuff I didn't have a clue what it was. There were plates of cold vegetables, some pickled; most I'd never seen before…all carved into artistic shapes.

Before leaving the apartment Nine had told me it would be necessary to pace myself by eating only little bits of each thing as there would be many courses. She had warned there might possibly be up to nine. At the time I thought that would be easy enough to handle but when I saw all those wonderful and exotic appetizers, I realized pacing myself was indeed going to be a problem. I could have made a meal out of each one. Inside my head Nine and my evil twin were engaged in a shouting match…Nine's soft voice whispering "pace yourself" and my evil's twin's persuasive response…"just one more bite." Somehow, I managed to contain my wolf-it-all-up impulse and nibble like a cottontail on a carrot top. But even when I paused for a break, I kept eying my favorite ones. Midway through the snacks several bottles of Chinese beer were placed on the table. By this time I was more than ready for a glass.

As all the nibbling foods were removed from the table in anticipation of the full array of main dishes, I noticed there were still a few of my favorites left uneaten…my eyes followed them all the way out the door. I could hear my father's voice telling me to eat all the food on my plate, reminding me of all the hungry children in the world who were starving. I could just see one of those waiters stuffing them in his mouth as he was heading down the hall to toward the kitchen…and they sure as hell weren't starving.

The main courses began to arrive. There was one plate with a Peking Duck, one with an entire fish, including the head (it looked like some kind of carp and probably weighted five pounds), a plate of roast pork, and a dish of chicken. Small rice bowls were at each place setting along with a porcelain Chinese soup spoon, a silver western style soup spoon, and of course our chopsticks. I had already learned the entire spoon and chopstick drill…all the dos and don'ts concerning my spoon and chopsticks.

The servers put rice in each of our small rice bowls. There were large bowls of soup, plus bowls of shrimp and squid carved in various shapes and mixed with vegetables and simmered in some kind of sauce. There was a plate with a bunch of round deep-fried balls with some kind of spike sticking out. I was told the spike was the claw of a crab and that it had shrimp paste molded around it then was deep fried. There was another dish of sea food with a rich cream sauce placed on top of a plate of dried noodles. Everything looked like a complete meal in itself. I now fully understood Nine's pace yourself instructions.

Along with all this food, a bottle containing some kind of clear alcohol drink was placed on the table. I was told it was rice wine and seeing my curiosity, one of the servers poured a small quantity into a small specially-designed porcelain cup. It was slightly warm and tasted like liquid fire. I politely smiled. Everyone was watching to see my reaction. I felt the warming effect of the drink making its way to my stomach. I quickly moved on to rice and tea hoping to extinguish the fire; all the time I continued to smile. I figured I could go the rest of my life without missing that stuff. While I'd never had moonshine, I reckoned I'd just come pretty damn close.

Chinese "Soul Food" Experience

(my evil twin made me say it)

The main courses were wonderful. Probably some of the most enjoyable food I'd ever had…with one exception. As my eyes explored the incredible array of delicacies spread before me, they came to rest on a dish of braised chicken parts…parts as not in wings and necks…parts as in heads and feet; a plate piled high with braised chicken heads and feet. They came complete with beaks and claws. I later learned The Chinese and Cambodians considered this some of the best meat on the chicken…the meat close to the bone.

Well, this country boy from Hamilton Texas had an unequivocally dissimilar interpretation of that pile of parts. I'd seen the feet of countless chickens as they scratched and pecked their way around in a chicken coup filled with chicken poo. I'd seen the amalgamation of poo and feathers clinging to their feet. As for the chicken heads…most of the feathers were gone but an occasional quill was left standing like the occasional surviving mesquite after a grass fire moves across a Central Texas cow pasture.

Nine's older sister (her only sister) Princess Norodom Ronida was seated directly opposite me. She was as totally focused on me as she could be without being rude. Soon I noticed most of those seated at the table were as well. The single collective thought of all at the entire table was…would he or wouldn't he. I'd eaten monkey in the Congo, and various others questionable things since I left Hamilton…I could eat one of those chicken feet. I smiled, picked one out of the plate with my serving spoon, placed it on my plate, grabbed it with my chopsticks and bit off the big toe in the center. I chewed it up, bone, claw and all, all the while grinning like a monkey eating cockleburs as my father used to say. As I chomped down on the bones, I was sure everybody at the table could hear the cracking and crunching. I pushed the images of Hamilton County chicken coups out of my mind. I kept telling myself to just imagine this was Vivian Drake's Sunday dinner fried chicken. The sweet and hot sauce was very good. This helped me get through the ordeal. The following day Nine told me you didn't eat the bone, you only stripped the meat from the bone. I had to laugh, and still do some forty years later, when I realize how ridiculous I must have looked to her family.

By the time the evening was over, I was so full I was physically uncomfortable. But the experience was worth it. I'd met her brothers, her sister and her family, and more importantly…this obligatory public appearance with her family was now behind me. We were officially out of the closet.

As we left our private dining room, the owner met us bowing all the way to the door. Every eye in the restaurant was on our group. Bong Hut stopped and acknowledged a couple of the diners. Phnom Penh, even though the nation's capital, was still, at the upper levels, a small village where everybody knew everybody…as well as their business.

When I got in bed that night, I had a new understanding of "kings and vagabonds." These were interesting times. I pulled my pillow into my chest, said my prayers, and hoped my night visitors would not once again return to terrify me.

Some Gave All

The morning began like all the others…crew car ride to the airport, morning briefing on the latest hotspots (usually worthless), and the usual micro-economy underneath the aircraft as passengers, smugglers, and cargo all vied and bribed for the precious space aboard the flight.

Our flight to Kompong Som was good; the aircraft was running well, the crew chief who was onboard running scans with the engine analyzer attempting to determine how long he could continue to run our spark plugs said all looked well. We didn't take any rounds during the climb-out or decent...*just another day in Paradise.*

We loaded our passengers, the usual array of businessmen, families, and military (both the well and the wounded), plus large quantities of fish fresh from the fishing boats that had been out on the Gulf of Thailand all night. This cargo of fish was vital to the airlift of food into the blockaded capital of Phnom Penh.

Ream Airbase was right on the water's edge. The temperature was still cool, and we had a gentle breeze coming off the water which allowed us to put on a few extra containers of fish. The mountains to our north and the bay to the south looked like something straight out of a tourist brochure. But this Tuesday morning 5 June 1973 picturesque setting would soon morph into the flames of hell.

We had adjusted our track so we would join a right base for Runway 23 at Phnom Penh's Pochentong Airport. As we entered right base, we heard a U.S. Air Force OV-10 (Bronco), call sign *Nail 42*, call for takeoff. I looked down and saw the battleship gray OV-10 at the holding point on the main taxiway leading from the military ramp. The tower cleared him onto the runway and to takeoff. The air traffic controllers were terribly inept during this period. The pilot saw us and asked if we were going to be OK, meaning would we have enough separation being I was already by this time on final with our gear down and legally had the right of way. Of course I jokingly replied...I get paid by the hour. He laughed and started his takeoff roll. I pulled back our power a little bit and continued our approach. This was wartime and we operated on close separation regularly. As I watched him go down the runway, suddenly, just as I was expecting him to lift off, he began what appeared to be a max effort abort. Stories from other Nail pilots vary as to exactly what his intentions were later judged to have been, but I could see him suddenly decelerating and sparks started coming from the aircraft's belly tank (centerline mounted 230-gallon fuel drop tank) which appeared to be grinding on the runway. The sparks almost immediately turned to flames as the fuel leaking from the now ruptured tank ignited.

We immediately called a missed approach which I'm sure nobody heard at that point. But rather than breaking off, I continued at low level down the right side of the runway keeping the now fully-engulfed OV-10 in my cockpit left window. I could see the pilot in the cockpit. He appeared to be getting ready to leave the aircraft.

He was soon behind us and out of my line of sight. I gave the flight controls to the co-pilot and told him to bring up the landing gear, put the flaps to approach setting, maintain this low altitude and approach speed and to circle back onto final again. While he was doing this, I grabbed my 35mm Nikon from my flight bag and started taking pictures; this time out the right window over the co-pilot's shoulder. I'd taken about three or four frames and ran out of film. I quickly dug in my flight bag and pulled out another roll. Over several years of practice I'd gotten pretty fast at reloading film. By the time we were back on final approach the OV-10 was completely engulfed in flames. I tried to see if the pilot was still in the cockpit; it appeared he was not. I looked but I couldn't see him standing on the runway anywhere…which wouldn't have been a good idea as his rockets were already spewing and skipping along the runway. We finished our low pass; I shot up the entire new roll of film and circled back around for a landing.

Other aircraft were starting to arrive. Most were low on fuel. We made a short landing, stopping short of the burning aircraft, turned around on the runway and taxied onto the ramp. I asked the tower if the pilot made it out safely. He replied that he did not.

While they were refueling us for the next flight, I walked over to the U.S. Air Force loadmaster's heavily sandbagged operations center and gave him my two rolls of film with instructions to pass it to the Air Attaché. He immediately rang the embassy on the field radio. They told him Lt. Col. Mark Berent (radio call sign Papa Wolf) was already on his way and should arrive any minute. The sergeant said he would give the film to him. As I walked slowly back to the airplane, I wondered if I would be next. First Lieutenant Dick Gray, pilot of Nail 42 was listed as Killed In Action…military terminology which sterilizes or dehumanizes the real tragedy. "All gave some"; that day 1st Lt. Dick Gray, "gave all." Rest In Peace Dick Gray.

When The Americans Stop Bombing…What Then?

The 15 August 1973 congressionally mandated bombing halt in Cambodia would mean relief to the apolitical Cambodian peasant farmers who were suffering from the U.S. Air Force bombings. Unfortunately, it would provide equal relief to the Khmer Rouge whose full goals were yet unknown both to the people of Cambodia and to the rest of the world. It was clear, even to the least astute political pundit, that the Lon Nol government would be unlikely to withstand the almost certain all-out military assault on Phnom Penh which would follow the bombing halt.

The Khmer Rouge was basically a shadowy group to the outside world, but the Cambodia people already well understood their brutality and cruelty. By design, knowledge of their terror tactics had long ago reached Phnom Penh and the other major capitals that were not already in Khmer Rouge hands. These hordes of demons clad in black enjoyed killing.

"A day of darkness and gloom, a day of clouds and dense overcast, like the dawn spreading over the mountains; a great and strong people appears, such as never existed in ages past and never will again in all the generations to come." [198]

All believed the American backed government of Lon Nol would fall; it would only be a matter of time. That timeframe was the subject of constant speculation among both the Cambodians and the expatriate community. This fearful speculation and the constant proliferation of rumors fueled previously unimagined devaluation to Cambodia's local currency, the Riel and to the entire spectrum of what was left of the economy.

The prices of basic commodities such as chicken, pork, fish, and rice were rapidly climbing beyond the reach of the poorer segments of the population. The Americans were flying in tons upon tons of rice as aid to help stabilize the price, but the corruption of government officials insured most of the direct benefit did not reach those who needed it the most.

Chronic fuel shortages, caused by the Khmer Rouge's ability to seriously restrict the flow of barge traffic up and down the Mekong, was resulting in power outages lasting most of the day. Many businesses were basically unable to function. The ability to preserve meats, medicines, and other commodities requiring refrigeration was critically hindered. Rumor became more of an influence on the free market that fact itself.

The Economics Of Hard Times

The blockade of Phnom Penh and other major cities restricted the flow of goods. The more transportable a valuable commodity was, the more in demand it became.

For example, in normal times, a Mercedes car, a beautiful villa, and a diamond were valuable commodities. However in times of extreme uncertainty where the free flow of goods was restricted, such as during the blockade, only the goods that were easily transportable had value. As time progressed, this became more pronounced. Those with the ability and means to leave the country were doing so. They were trying to sell their beautiful homes but there were no buyers. Nobody believed in the future. You could not put a home in your suitcase. While the Mercedes was in fact normally transportable, with the Khmer Rouge controlling all the major routes into and out of the country, the luxury automobile was no longer transportable. It would have to remain in Phnom Penh when the Khmer Rouge took over…thus you could buy them for pennies on the dollar with few takers.

On the other hand, a diamond, unlike a luxury home and automobile, was extremely portable, as was gold. It would not only fit in your suitcase, it would fit in your handbag or be stitched into the lining of your pants. The price of diamonds went through the roof…as did the price of gold. The

---
[198] Holy Bible - Holman Christian Standard Bible (HCSB) - Joel 2:2

Cambodian Riel was worthless outside the borders of Cambodia. Everyone wanted to get rid of their riels and get into dollars. This demand on the dollar drove up its value while the great number of riels on the market made them worthless. This scenario worsened day after day. Again, those at the lowest strata of the Cambodian society suffered the most.

While this was horrible for the local population, the pilots, who were paid in dollars benefitted immensely. Rent for my apartment when I moved in was $100 in riels. Six months later its dollar equivalent was forty.

As all this was happening, we started to hear the journalists telling how the newly arrived refugees streaming into Phnom Penh from all over the countryside were reporting the confiscation of their private property and all property was being placed into a communal system controlled by the Khmer Rouge central committee. If any still held out hope that these murderous monsters in black pajamas could be better than the corrupt government of Lon Nol, this seemed to drive a stake into the heart of that fallacy.

Temple Rubbings Versus Temple Robbings

The Khmer Rouge controlled the area of the country bordering Thailand where most of the world-renowned temples were located. However there were other well-known archeological sites located all over the country which were left unguarded due to enemy action. Now when going to the shops which sold the traditional tourist replicas of 1000 year old statues and "temple rubbings" made from impressions taken from the walls of these famous temples, it was possible to acquire authentic heads and hands broken off these priceless artifacts. While I could not be sure of their authenticity, a journalist I knew told me some European antique dealers were making lots of money in this illegal trade. Just another way this insane war was hurting the country.

The Bombing Halt–Possible Evacuation

Time marched unrelentingly toward what at times seemed like the edge of some cliff overlooking the gates of hell. I was starting to have flashbacks during waking hours…often during flights, of what fate would befall those left behind when all the Americans, Europeans, and other foreigners left Phnom Penh. These were horrid images, often composites of the malnutrition, maiming, death and sorrow that seemed an inescapable daily occurrence . . . like standing before the open gates of hell, unable to turn away. I saw a sign above the gate… *"Ye who enter, abandon all hope."* [199] I cursed myself for thinking too much. A trait inherited without doubt from my mother.

The embassy was already drafting and reviewing evacuation plans. We received regular updates. It was officially called Contingency Plan 5060C, but locally referred to as "Operation Eagle Pull." It was based on three basic options ranging from civilized to gutsy. Civilized was leaving from Pochen-

---

[199] Dante Alighieri, Inferno

tong airport via chartered aircraft (Bird Air and others). That plan of course could only work if the airport was still in our hands or not under attack. Gutsy was sending in the Marines to secure LZs (landing zones) inside the city then bringing in CH-53 helicopters (Jolly Green Giants) and landing in open field LZs near the embassy and in other strategic locations. We were briefed on the signals which would announce the beginning of the operation and proceed to our assigned LZ. Things were starting to take on a previously unseen tone of urgency. At the forefront of all this was Nine…what if we got the call to go. While I had decided that I loved her, we weren't married. She was still wearing black. How could I get her out? Visas at this time were not easy to come by and half of Phnom Penh was waiting in line to get one. I knew I had some pull at the embassy; this would be the ultimate measurement of it. I decided I needed to go have a talk with my friend Jack McCarthy the U.S. Consul.

"Then She's Yours–Take Her"

As usual, Jack's desk was piled high with papers, but he smiled and welcomed me into his small office. He knew Nine and I had a relationship. Hell, by this time it appeared all of Phnom Penh knew. Phnom Penh was just a small village with what was estimated to be over a half million refugee population.

I had expected to have to make a long and difficult case. But to my amazement, Jack asked if I were going to marry her. When I answered yes, he replied "then she's yours…take her. Bring me her passport; I'll put the visa in it as soon as I get it." While his statement sounded a bit chauvinistic, we both clearly understood it meant as far as the U.S. Embassy was concerned, she was my responsibility…just as though she had been my wife.

I left his office with the weight of the world lifted from my shoulders. That night I told Nine to have the driver bring her passport when he returned to take her home. The following day Nine had a U.S. Visa in her passport. Jack had put an entry on the visa noting "Mrs. James Jacks." That entry would later prove to be priceless.

Phnom Penh back then was the Wild West and the embassy has some real red-blooded cowboys. I'm glad Jack McCarthy was one of them. The next time I saw Bong Hut, I could tell he was genuinely impressed and proud. His little sister had a visa to the United States in less than 24 hours; in reality, in about thirty minutes. I also could tell he was relieved. If anybody was harboring any reservations about my intentions, they were now baseless.

Spiraling

As the economy was spiraling downward and black-market prices were spiraling upward, I too found myself spiraling up and down. By June of 1973 the Khmer Rouge controlled areas as close as ten miles from the center of Phnom Penh, putting a normal climb and descent well within range of their

SAM-7 missiles and in some cases within AK-47 range. As a result, after takeoff we would spiral overhead the airport until reaching 5000 feet before leaving the airport traffic pattern. We did the same when landing. We would plan our flight to arrive overhead the airport at 5000 feet then spiral down. This made the airport traffic pattern a very interesting place, especially in times of poor visibility. The air traffic controllers had no radar, so it was pretty much up to each pilot to maintain visual separation. Semi-coordinated chaos was about the kindest thing one could say about the situation. The bright side of this was I was getting paid by the hour and this precaution added about five minutes on each end of the leg so a flight from Phnom Penh to Battambang would now earn me and extra 20 minutes flight time.

The Pol Pot Weight Loss Program

As the flying continued at a relentless pace and the enemy continued tightening their stranglehold, the day to day stress started to take its toll. To the conscious mind, it was hardly perceivable, yet from the moment you rolled out of bed and put your feet on the floor, it was all around. Each day you drove to the airport wondering what hideous atrocity you would see or hear about from the previous night's rocket attacks. Each day as you walked on the tarmac of the airport you wondered if today one of the numerous rockets that landed on the airport almost daily would have your name on it. Each time you advance the throttles, released the brakes, and started the takeoff roll, you wondered if during the previous night some KR had infiltrated the airport's security perimeter and lay in hiding with a shoulder fired Surface To Air Missile (SAM) that would lock on to your glowing exhaust and send you off into eternity in a yellowish-orange ball of flames.

The constant exposure to this low-level almost hidden stress gradually began to resemble normalcy, but our subconscious mind was recognizing this as untrue. Our physical bodies began to follow the lead of our unconscious mind. We all lost weight. Slowly over a gradual period of time, we all became almost gaunt. This was not just with the pilots, I saw it in the journalists as well. Strangely, I did not notice it in the Cambodians although I'm sure it had to be present, at least in some of them. I called it my Pol Pot Weight Loss Program.

In addition to the weight loss, we all were hypersensitive to sudden movement or loud noise. The insides of our arms and hands were covered with small clear blisters which then ruptured leaving our hands and arms as rough as sandpaper. We later learned it had a name…stress rash or hives

Personally I was smoking like a chimney. I even began modifying my Dunhill cigarette tobacco with a special blend of my own; a mixture of fifty percent Dunhill tobacco and fifty percent local magical weed or herb quite similar to that used by the Mbuti of the Congo. Nine voiced strong disapproval of my experimentations in this black art of blending but I ignored her displeasure.

How To Insure The Eagle Pulled Nine

The stability of the country was deteriorating by the day. The embassy continued to refine Eagle Pull. We started talking about evacuation calls that might come in the middle of the night and songs played over and over on Radio Saigon which would be our signal to go to our pre-determined LZ or if not accessible to the closest LZ. All during these discussions, I kept wondering…if it happens in the middle of the night, how do I get to Nine? If it happens while I'm flying, who will get her? Moving in with me without the traditional social ceremonies was not an option. Nine was still wearing black and within the Buddhist mandated mourning period.

I'd become personal friends with the Air Attaché Colonel David Howard Opfer. Dave had assured me he would send someone for her or personally put her on the evacuation flight if it came down while I was flying. He knew Nine well as she and I had been to his home on several occasions.

The plan we settled on was somewhat of a hybrid. We would not move in together but…every night rather than going home, she would stay with me. She would leave early in the morning and go home to her family. The plan involved my moving out of the apartment on busy Monivong Boulevard and finding a house reasonably accessible to one or more of the LZs.

There was little objection from her family as by this time, especially after the "outing"…there was no turning back. Within a few days Nine, while I was busy flying, had found a two-story villa with high walls in a safe neighborhood and centrally located to the LZs. She took me to see it. I'd already had an embassy OK that it was a suitable area. She showed Bong Hut and her sister. They all agreed. A couple of days later I signed the contract.

The villa was located just off Monivong and close to the police headquarters for our area. It was a small two-story structure. Downstairs there was a large living room and dining room on the bottom floor. The top floor had two large bedrooms and two baths. The second bedroom and bath were never used. There was an attached carport. In typical Cambodian fashion, adjoining the back side of the house was a large kitchen with adjoining maid's quarters. A covered walkway led between the house and the kitchen/maid's quarters. It had a yard and flower beds. The part I liked the most was the upstairs bedroom had a large area for a salon as well as a large veranda. There were chairs and benches on the veranda where we would later spend much time before dinner.

The distance from villa to LZ Hotel was 2.3 kilometers or just under 1.5 miles. I worked it out that in moderate traffic which was most of the time since fuel was in such critical supply, we could be at LZ Hotel in less than five minutes. That would work.

Decorating Our Home

While Nine was busy adding her special touches to the rented villa, I was busy adding mine. In our bedroom wardrobe I put several little U.S. issue cardboard cylinders containing M61 fragmentation grenades. I stacked them neatly on the bottom shelf of the wardrobe just next to her shoes. What was I thinking? She found them the next day and about the most understated thing I can say is she lost her composure. At that stage in my life, it was necessary for me to struggle with understanding her lack of understanding. After all, I hadn't put them on the nightstand. They were U.S. Army issue certifiably safe. I did note that I needed to work on my sensitivity.

On the other side of the wardrobe I had propped my AK-47. Under my side of the bed, yet still easily in reach I stashed my M2 carbine. I truly loved that little gun. It was cuddly like a carbine should be yet packed a decent punch somewhat similar to a 30-30. I never felt like I could hit much of anything with the AK-47. When I held the M2, my accuracy was close to what I had at age 16 back in Hamilton with my 22 rifle. Plus, with its 30-shot magazine, I could compensate for some of the accuracy that had slowly slipped away over the subsequent 14 years.

Downstairs in the dining room I modified the dining table. On the underside of the tabletop I attached a little shelf where I could rest my Colt 1911 45 ACP. If intruded upon while still sitting at the dining table, since my mother had never allowed me to eat with my elbows on the table, my hands would be in my lap and my right hand could ever so undetectably caress the most perfect handgun design known to man, silently slip its safety off with my right thumb, and begin pumping 230gr full metal jacket rounds into the intruder's crotch.

The only meal we ate at home was our evening meal. I generally ate wearing my Colt Cobra 38 Special in its shoulder holster accompanied by its 24 round ammo pouch.

I realized that to someone coming into our home from outside the area of conflict, my living conditions, as well as the homes, apartments, and hotel rooms of everybody I flew with, would look like some doomsday survivalist nut's place of last stand. But that would only be to the untrained eye. Each weapon was specific to its purpose. The grenades were specific to clearing the stairwell if our house was being stormed. A fragmentation grenade tossed down the stairwell would stun and maim anybody within 15 yards. Another tossed into the living room from the first or second step from the top would clear the living room. Then by immediately running down the stairway with the AK-47 on full auto, taking full advantage of the shock produced by the two grenades, I could more or less insure everything that didn't belong in the house was eliminated or in serious hurt. Of course if faced by overwhelming numbers, all I would do was make a sizable dent in their numbers before I died.

The M2 Carbine was for defending the house if the intruders were not yet inside the walls and gate. If I could see them, I could hit them. Unfortunately it had a substantial muzzle flash which would provide them with a beacon in hitting me as well.

A Winchester Model 97 12-gauge shotgun was downstairs under the stairwell along with a mattress. In case of rocket attacks the stairwell would serve as our bunker. Nine and I would spend many a night huddled under the heavy terrazzo stairs, listening to the airstrike and artillery radio traffic on the PRC 25, with our two maids huddled at our feet like scared puppies. As soon as the rockets started falling or the inbound artillery started coming in, those two little chipmunks would be out of their maids' quarters and into the house as fast as greased lightning, standing at the foot of the stairs waiting for Nine and I to come down, pillows and PRC 25 in hand. They would light the kerosene lamp and keep it turned down low. I soon learned to sleep with the PRC 25's receiver tucked under my head cracking in my left ear. While I was getting some very low level of rest, I could also track what was going on.

My M3A (grease gun) submachine gun, for the most part remained unassembled and in my flight bag. It was not as well suited as the survival aids.

Our transition from my apartment to living together in our villa went unnoticed to most people. She arrived discretely shortly before I would come in from my flight or orphanage run. She would leave discretely the following morning and go back to her family. We leased a Mercedes and driver which allowed her to come and go more freely. The gates to the house were closed. When the car honked, one of the maids would open the gate, the car would drive in, the gates would close then she would get out.

The Move–My Personal Transition Scoreboard:

Physical Transition 10—Psychological Transition

Near Zero

I was, like all with whom I worked, a literal bundle of raw nerves. We were all showing signs of the 24/7 stress we lived under. The curious thing was, at the time, almost nobody realized the extent or how serious this was. In my case, "Almost nobody" except Nine, the maids, the driver, and others who had to live in close proximity with me.

I was smoking two packs of cigarettes a day…some laced with the magic herb I'd discovered in the Congo. As soon as I got home and had a shower, I drank at least two beers. I jumped at any loud or sudden noise. A car backfiring, a door slammed by the wind, something falling and breaking, any sudden movement; all these produced sudden defensive actions. Late one afternoon, while sitting out on our veranda, a shadow caused by the sun and a leaf from a nearby tree moved across the floor just in front of me. My reaction was that of a frightened animal. While I barely remember it now…forty years later it is still vivid to Nine.

The slightest little thing that did not go perfectly produced anger. There was almost zero tolerance of anything. Nine suffered the most. Each time any of the household staff didn't perform perfectly, she was the first line…she had to bear the brunt of my displeasure. I was truly a terrible person, living without compassion for the ones closest to me.

Yet interestingly, while I could show deep compassion for the orphans, I saw but hardly knew, I failed miserably in seeing the hell I was imposing on Nine and others around me. For years I have prayed for and asked for forgiveness for the countless thoughtless acts during that period of my life. Back then there was no such acronym as PTSD, no counseling for it, nothing to read to help you cope. I suppose help was in the Bible as the missionaries I knew didn't seem to be experiencing what we pilots were, but back then I didn't read my Bible very much. Perhaps the words of a Judean itinerant preacher speaking to the masses on a mountain side offered some clues to my unenviable state: *"Blessed (happy) are the meek, for they will inherit the earth. Blessed (happy) are the pure in heart, for they will see God. Blessed (happy) are the peacemakers, for they will be called children of God."*[200] I was not meek; I was anything but pure in heart; I could hardly be called a peacemaker and back then I was seldom happy.

Our *Senprane* Ceremony

While I still had the apartment our cohabitation retained some degree of deniability; the apartment was mine. With the advent of the villa, our margin of deniability diminished to near zero; the villa was ours. For cultural and social reasons, some expression of formal family approval of our relationship was sorely needed.

By Buddhist traditions Nine, and by extension I, were in a one-hundred-day period of deep mourning. No celebration of any type could take place. This period of mourning would be less restrictive after the one-hundred-day phase passed but would continue for a full year.

To salvage Nine's reputation…what portion might remain after committing to marry not only an American, but also a CIA proprietary company pilot, some official family recognition of our relationship needed to take place soon. The 12 August congressionally mandated bombing halt was almost upon us. Rumors abounded that within days of the bombing halt, the Lon Nol government would fall, and the Khmer Rouge would take over the country. Operation Eagle Pull was already in the planning stage. This statement of family recognition needed to get on a fast track very soon.

---

[200] Holy Bible - New International Version—Matthew Chapter 5.

Bong Hut, with the mostly unneeded help of several of Nine's aunts, started arranging a ceremony referred to as *Senprane*. In my eyes as well as in Bong Hut's, you just pick a day convenient to the majority of the family and start setting things up. Matters soon proved far more complex. The aunts were insisting Buddhist monk fortunetellers had to determine the date by using astrology. Bong Hut was about as thrilled with this as I was. I later learned he had gently suggested to the monks that any date they picked would be acceptable to us…"as long as it was before the 12 August bombing halt." And sure enough, the astrological forces all came into perfect alignment on August 2, 1973…ten days before the bombing halt. Nine's mother and aunt as well as Bong Hut had always taken very good care of the monks from this particular pagoda which was just next to the Royal Palace. It was the pagoda used by most of the Royal Family; the pagoda where Nine's mother's cremation had taken place. Bong Hut had assured me their astrological readings would be congruent with our needs. I loved Bong Hut!

Nine invited none of her friends. I invited none of the pilots I worked with. It was basically a religious ceremony whose purpose was to inform Nine's dead ancestors of our intention to marry as well as a statement to the living that these plans had the family's approval. Since her mother was dead and her father in political exile, only her mother's sisters and other close family attended. It was a very small group. The only other non-Cambodian attending the ceremony was my friend, the Air Attaché Colonel David Howard Opfer. Bong Hut had sent word via clandestine sources to Nine's father that the ceremony was taking place. We never received confirmation that he got the message, but we chose to believe that he did.

Nine's family provided the food. I had Olympia and San Miguel Beer flown in on an Air Force C-130 from Thailand. Because of the recent death of her mother, the occasion was not really festive. Thoughts of her mother were heavy on Nine's mind. Plus one of her aunts and a distant relative were getting on her nerves pretty bad. The entire event lasted only half a day. I was back in the cockpit the following day. While not a real wedding, it would turn out to be the only "wedding" we would ever have.

Out Of Gas

One evening, not long after sunset, Nine and I were just getting ready to go down for dinner. I got a call on the radio saying one of the Air Attaché cars would soon be at my house. Could I please go down to open the gate? I wondered why one of Dave Opfer's embassy beasts would be stopping by my place. I figured somebody must need a ride someplace the next morning and they had forgotten to make arrangements for tickets. They did this frequently as they knew they could always ride in the cockpit's jump-seat with us. Nine had barely alerted the maids when I heard the iron gate creaking open. I hurried down to greet whoever was coming. As I walked out on the front porch, I spotted an Air Force major whom I knew well and who shall remain nameless. He was accompanied by about five or six neighborhood young men pushing the colossal bullet-proof glass and armor-plated Ford beast through my gate. Our Mercedes was already in the garage. We barely had room to close the front gate. The major was profusely apologizing. Seems he had headed out for a quick bite at a local restaurant without first bothering to check the fuel gauge. He said there was absolutely no extra automobile gas at the embassy…only diesel. He said he'd already arranged to get gas by 6:00 am tomorrow morning; would it please be OK if they left the car in my driveway overnight. He said Dave had recommended my place when he learned where the car was stranded. I told him of course that would be fine…that I wasn't really trying to keep a low profile in my neighborhood anyway (sarcasm from my evil twin). I invited him in for a beer.

Within a matter of minutes, embassy drivers were out front to pick up the major and take him back. I explained I had to leave for the airport a little after six the following morning and did not need to be out on the street recruiting half the neighborhood to move this mega-ton monster out of my drive. He assured me it would be gone. I told him this favor was going to cost him…like more American beer from Thailand via one of the C-130. He said I could consider it done. Nine appeared to find all this amusing after having to endure my lectures about the need for us to keep a low profile in the neighborhood for security reasons. She was kind enough not to mention it. The following morning the car was gone on time as promised and a couple of days later I had four cases of Olympia beer. Not really all that good but compared to what we had locally, it was stellar. Apparently, Olympia had a large Base Exchange contract with the military so that was the beer of the day for a while.

How We Lost The War

On one of the afternoons when I finished flying early, I stopped by the MEDTC house where several members of the team (Military Equipment Delivery Team) lived. As I walked into the living room the conversation was lively to say the least. It seems one of the army majors had just contracted gonorrhea. He was the object of a very lively and light-hearted group condemnation. He was not being adjudicated by a panel of his peers for the minor social *faux pas* of acquiring a sexually transmitted disease; no, he was being enthusiastically condemned for acquiring it twice…twice from the same girl. When an explanation was demanded, his feeble but sincere reply was…"she was just so good I couldn't help it;" Amazing.

The Neak Luong Tragedy

Before daylight on the morning of 6 August 1973, the small town of Neak Luong, on the Mekong River about 38 miles southeast of Phnom Penh was changed forever. An American B-52 flying almost six miles overhead unloaded its payload of bombs on the towns sleeping population. The town was friendly…not enemy. The bombs killed almost 400 people. The strike severely damaged an orphanage and a hospital. No known enemy was killed. The carnage was beyond comprehension. Abaddo…place of destruction, dwelling place of the dead. New York Times correspondent Sydney Schanberg described the carnage like this: *"A woman's scalp sways on a clump of tall grass. A bloody pillow here, a shred of a sarong caught on a barbed wire there. A large bloodstain on the brown earth. A pair of infant's rubber sandals among some unexploded military shells."*[201] This tragic mistake came only six days before the bombing halt. The woman whose scalp swayed on the clump of grass never knew what hit her; she never had time to run for cover. She was probably sleeping in her bed with husband and children around her. *"Time is filled with swift transition, naught of earth unmoved can stand, build your hopes on things eternal, hold to God's unchanging hand."*[202] I struggled futilely to find God in any of this carnage. I don't believe He was there.

My good friend Col. Dave Opfer, who loved the Cambodian people as few others I've known, was tragically misquoted by the press as he struggled to find some way to explain this unpardonable tragedy. Over and over my mind kept replaying the same loop…if they were not sure of their target why were they dropping bombs; why was the release button pushed. I learned three weeks later, the crew of the B-52 had made a procedural mistake. My mind kept wondering if this error could ever have happened over someplace other than Southeast Asia? I doubted it. *"They are smashed to pieces from dawn to dusk; they perish forever while no one notices."*[203]

In an ensuing investigation into the incident, three crew members received official letters of reprimand and a navigator received a $700 fine. [204] I conjectured that worked out to about $2 for each person who was killed, maimed, and disfigured.

The mission was supposed to be an "offset target" where the target was seven miles offset to the direct course. It came out in the hearings that the navigator neglected to activate the offset switch; therefore, the aircraft flew directly to the radio beacon which was in the center of the town.[205] I have personally used navigation equipment capable of offset navigation. While the procedure is much more complicated than normal navigation, I have never made a navigational error using the technique. We made our calculations and had other crew members double check our work. Then we followed written procedures and another pilot verified the procedures were correctly followed. Why did no one see the offset navigation mode had not been activated? Where were their standard procedures?

---

[201] Pulitzer Prize and a Sigma Delta Chi Award winning journalist Sydney Schanberg quoted in Melvin Mencher News Reporting and Writing, 11th edition.
[202] Hold to God's Unchanging Hand - Jennie Wilson - Public Domain
[203] Holy Bible - Holman Christian Standard Bible—Job 4:20
[204] UP via S. F. Chronicle—28 August 1973
[205] UP via S. F. Chronicle—28 August 1973

Neak Luong was not an isolated incident. Scholars have well documented this widespread pattern of tragedy. While I felt anger toward the pilots, I could also imagine the misgivings they must have experienced. How could they not have wondered about the certainty of their mission planners concerning the hostile nature of their targets? Finally, some pilots begin to question and refuse their orders to fly the missions. I'm not certain how I would have responded. My deepest insights lead me to believe I would have probably, as almost all did, follow my orders and accepted the mission. I'm glad I was not a B-52 pilot assigned to those first clandestine and later headline making bombing missions over Cambodia. *War does not determine who is right–only who is left.*[206]

The Neak Luong Tragedy was the talk on the streets from Phnom Penh to Paris as well as on the campuses of the United States. I was starting to question my values. I found it hard to look my Cambodian friends in the eye as they came, not to condemn…but searching for some thread of reason in this tragedy…"why?"…they kept asking why. I had no answers.

The War Back At Home

As the Air Force and President Nixon continued trying to defend the U.S. involvement in South East Asia, especially in light of the Leak Luong Tragedy, another battle was heating up for the Nixon administration…Watergate. On 15 August, Nixon took to the airways to fire some artillery rounds of his own at the growing ranks of his accusers. I picked up pieces of it on my shortwave radio. *"But as the weeks have gone by, it has become clear that both the hearings themselves and some of the commentaries on them have become increasingly absorbed in an effort to implicate the President personally in the illegal activities that took place.*

Because the abuses occurred during my Administration, and in the campaign for my reelection, I accept full responsibility for them. I regret that these events took place, and I do not question the right of a Senate committee to investigate charges made against the President to the extent that this is relevant to legislative duties.

However, it is my constitutional responsibility to defend the integrity of this great office against false charges. I also believe that it is important to address the overriding question of what we as a nation can learn from this experience and what we should now do. I intend to discuss both of these subjects tonight."[207] And that he did. He was guilty as sin; I knew it; the nation knew it; the world knew it.

Some Bad Press

I stepped out of the backseat of our Mercedes and headed into the terminal for my first flight of the day. The driver pulled away and headed back to the house to get Nine and take her so she could go with her family to have break-

---
[206] Bertrand Russell
[207] Richard M. Nixon - Address to the Nation About the Watergare Investigations August 15, 1973

fast and do the daily grocery shopping. It was our daily routine. It was what all better off women in Phnom Penh did. It was something Nine had grown up doing. Nothing should have been different; yet something was. I noticed the airport workers were following me with their eyes. Because I was an American, they always did this. But today, something was different. As I stepped into operations, the lead dispatcher handed me a note. I was to call the embassy. I recognized the number as one belonging to the air attaché.

When I called, one of the air force majors answered. He began talking in a hushed voice. He asked if I'd seen this morning's edition of Phnom Penh's leading French language newspaper. When I replied that I had not, he commenced briefing me on an article that was in today's edition. The article was about Nine and her father. The article identified Nine by name and said she was married to an American CIA pilot. "*Expletive*" I responded. "Don't these *obscenity* idiots have anything better to *expletive* write about!"

My first thought was for Nine. She and her sister and sister-in-law plus an aunt or two would soon be out eating breakfast then going into the most public market in Phnom Penh. I asked the major for the embassy assessment of any immediate personal danger to her. He replied that while it was impossible to say with certainty, this was guaranteed to be a government sanctioned article; part of their continuing campaign of attacks against Sihanouk, and by extension, the royal family. The government feared the Cambodian masses, whose majority still loved the king and worshiped him as almost a god-king. The war was not going well for the Lon Nol government and they needed something to take the people's minds off the war Lon Nol and his supporters had dragged the country into.

The car was already headed back to town. I'd meant to get a two-way radio for the driver but that was just one of several things I never seemed to get around to taking care of. I could always call the embassy back and have somebody go quickly to the house and tell her to stay home. But then that would just cause more stress for her. I was sure that she would soon find out from her family about the article. Her brother Bong Hut and her second brother Bong Hen, a high-ranking officer in the Navy with even higher-ranking friends, would already be accessing the situation and she would be told by them what was or was not deemed safe. I pushed my fear for her safety out of my mind and took the flight dispatch information, studied it for a moment and walked to the plane. The co-pilot was already doing the pre-flight inspection. I was only scheduled for two flights that day so I would be home early. I could talk to Bong Hut and get a realistic assessment of the situation. I could think of nothing else during those two flights.

That night, Bong Hut told me the same thing the major had; that this reporter was notorious for kissing up to the Lon Nol régime and that things had been much worse immediately following the coup that ousted Sihanouk and again when her father had defected to join Sihanouk. While these words were somewhat consoling, I nevertheless remained anxious about her for several weeks.

The Red Mist

"Yes, every mortal man is only a vapor"[208]

I no longer remember why I was not flying that day, but for some reason, I was off the schedule. It was getting close to noon. I'd been over at the SEAAT office taking care of something. While I was there, we heard several loud explosions; the unmistakable sound a rocket makes when it slams into its target. It was very loud; like a Chinese/Russian 122mm rocket. Cy, Roger, and I had become astonishingly callused to the sounds these devices of destruction made. Such sounds were inevitably followed by images of the rocket's indiscriminate destruction. The more this scene repeated, the more vivid my visualizations became.

As we were driving home, I had already dismissed the rocket attack from my mind. However, about a half a mile from our office I noticed a large crowd of people, some running toward and some running away from one of the entrances to a refugee encampment. Heavy black smoke was rapidly rising into the sky. As I approached, I could see that almost half the camp was already ablaze. There was a strong breeze that day and the breeze was fanning the fire into an unbelievable intensity. I told the driver to pull over. I grabbed my camera and rushed down the embankment and into the camp. My goal at that time was to capture this surreal experience on film.

The camp was a mass of cardboard and scrap-wood shanties. These peasants were streaming into Phnom Penh daily, fleeing from the war and the verified indiscriminate bombings by the B-52s. They arrived penniless. They tried to construct shelter with anything they could find. But "finding" was already a problem. The endless streams of refugees descending upon Phnom Penh daily like invading swarms of locust had long ago stripped away anything usable...with or without permission. They were literally living on the ground, many under the open sky.

By the time I reached the area where the burning shelters were, the light was reduced to what one would encounter just before dusk. The sky had turned black. There was no visible blue sky...only black and gray. The sun appeared as a dim red ball I could easily look at directly. Screams of agony and screams of fear pierced the loud sounds of people calling out for loved ones or calling out for help; the scene was surreal.

As I moved forward, I came to one of the rocket impact spots. There was a large crater in the ground. A couple of shanties had once stood where the crater was; blood and body parts were everywhere. Clothing was scattered everywhere. Bodies were everywhere; children, men, women, arms, legs,

---

[208] Holy Bible - Holman Christian Standard Bible (HCSB) - Psalm 39:5

pieces of chest cavities. The carnage was so great; the images so shocking, that evidently my mind started throwing up some type of filter. I could feel my emotions shutting down. My mind was still recording the sights, sounds and smells; it was recording them in full high definition. But they seemed distant…like I was seated in an audience watching the scene play out far away up on a stage. My mind was demonstrating some remarkable form of self-preservation.

More and more of the shanties were catching fire; the blaze was spreading rapidly. It was evident the entire encampment would soon be in flames. My skin was beginning to tingle from the radiant energy coming from the fire. The wind shifted directions frequently. When it shifted the wrong direction, I started to inhale smoke. Everyone now was running out, not back into the camp. People who were able to walk were carrying babies and belongings and fleeing away from the flames and carnage. Police and military were beginning to arrive, but they could do little. Many remained outside the area. I took a few more photos but soon realized I needed to be offering help not documenting this living hell.

I let my Nikon hang around my neck. I took a child from a woman's arms so she could carry her other infant and a bundle filled with what was probably her sole remaining possessions. We started up a steep path that led out of the indention where the camp had sprung up. As we made our way up the steep trail, I noticed people ahead of me on the trail were slowing. As I came nearer, I saw why. What minutes before was a human being, a woman, was now literally splattered all over a partly standing wall.

I'd already learned that when a strong blast such as from one of these rockets or a bomb explodes in close proximity to someone, a significant part of the body just vaporizes into a red mist; with notable exception…teeth and hair. They seem always to remain. The wall looked like it had been spray painted with her blood. On the wall's still damp coat of blood were plastered huge chunks of her hair. Her chest cavity was empty; its contents somewhere in the red mist on the wall and dripping from the surrounding plants. Her left arm was still attached. At the end of her arm was her gray, bloodless charred hand. Holding that hand and screaming in fear and confusion was a naked baby girl. She was probably around eighteen months old. How she was not killed by the blast that killed what probably was her mother remains an enigma forty years later.

People continued to slow down and look at the scene straight from Dante's Inferno's Seventh Circle (Violence). I knew I could not continue to stand there…my mind felt like it was coming apart at the seams; I could feel the mother of the child in my arms pushing on my back in an effort to get me to move forward. I responded and continued on toward the top.

The words of Job while expressing his frustration toward God were streaming through my mind. *"When disaster brings sudden death, He* (God) *mocks the despair of the innocent. The earth is handed over to the wicked; He blindfolds its judges. If it isn't, He, then who is it?"* [209] Yes, where in the hell was God? I was pretty sure He wasn't behind me in that smoking inferno of death and agony. Nor was he on the launching end of those 122mm Russian rockets. If God was really omnipresent how could he just stand idly by? It was equally hard not to wonder where He was when the B-52 bombing mission planners were "boxing" their targets.

By this time relief agency people (Red Cross, World Vision, Catholic Relief Service, etc.) were arriving. I pulled a World Vision aid worker I knew aside and handed the child I was carrying to her and asked her to help the child's mother. I then turned and headed back against the flow of fleeing refugees…back down into the huge pit.

It was now getting difficult to breathe. By this time there were easily several hundred refugees standing on the top looking down into what had previously been their camp…now they were looking into the mouth of hell. When I got to where the young girl had been crying and clinging to the lifeless arm of her mother, only the body parts remained. Someone had mercifully removed the child. Relieved, I realized my mind had reached its message unit overload point and was starting to enter an additional level of shutdown. I had to get out; for many reasons, I had to get out. The wind and the thermal currents from the fire had started to throw sparks onto the shelters not adjacent to the advancing fire. New fires were starting all around me. It was time to go. As I climbed the steep incline, I could tell I was starting to breathe in too much smoke. Sparks and embers were landing on me. I held my shirt over my nose. Once again, my mind turned to the book of Job; *"But mankind is born for trouble, as surely as sparks fly upward."* [210]

As I was making my way back to the car, I ran into one of the photojournalists I'd gotten to know. He did good work and unlike many, risked his skin to get the real story. He asked me what it was like down there; said that he had arrived too late to get any good shots from inside.

By this time my mind was in such a shutdown state that it was like I was looking at the journalist, knowing what he was saying, but not able to hear his voice; only his lips moving and the awareness of what he was saying…a very strange experience. He told me that even though he had no good shots down inside, there were countless stories here from the survivors he could use. He was a good journalist. Most would have just gone for the byline shots that had a chance of making the front page of some paper back stateside…one containing a photo credit that was sure to boost their portfolio. This guy was different. I rewound the roll of film I had in my camera and gave it to him along with the first roll I'd shot. I told him he owed me a beer…no need for any photo credit.

---

[209] Holy Bible - Holman Christian Standard Bible (HCSB)—Job: 23-24
[210] Holy Bible - Holman Christian Standard Bible (HCSB)—Job 5:7

I turned, walked back to my car and headed home. I didn't ever want to see those images again. I did; I saw one of my shots a couple of days later in the Herald Tribune. His accompanying story was one I would have been proud to have written. I was glad I'd given him the pictures.

It was much later that evening before I tried to share even a tiny fraction of what I'd seen that morning with Nine. Gradually, over a period of many years, I've slowly surrendered some of those horrible frames so indelibly burned into my mind. This is the first time some have been retold.

As I lay in bed that night, I wondered if the architects of this crazy war back in Washington and Hanoi knew that teeth and hair were so difficult do destroy. Probably Hanoi did. I wished someone would force the Washington war architects to come sees this; to have this lady's vaporized blood and tissue cover them from head to toe. Fortunately, some grotesque evidence always remains behind, hopefully to testify against them…against them all.

That night was another "please hold me very tight" night. Her gentle arms *"Wiping out the traces of the people and the places that I've been"*[211]…she held me till the fear inside finally subsided.

As I lay beside her in the bed, waiting for sleep to come, I wondered how I could have come so far from Hamilton's endless summer days; Hamilton, my Mayberry, where warm golden sunlight bathed everything. How did I get here…to this land of tragedy and tears…to this land of the red mist?

Beelzebub

On my way home from the airport the following day, I had the driver take me back to the burned-out refugee camp, just to see the final chapter. I left my Nikon in the car. As I descended into the pit, large areas were still smoldering. Body parts still remained. Flies had come to feast on the flesh and now dried blood. Flies always seemed to find opportunity in death. Truly Beelzebub…"Lord of The Flies" and "the prince of demons"[212] was in that pit. I could feel him.

My heart was empty. That spirit that lived in me and from time to time inspired or perhaps drove me to take pictures and seek new experiences so passionately in the Congo was now gone. I was too close to these people. I could more easily go to the funeral of a friend and take pictures than continue documenting this misery.

As I walked back to the car, I wondered how we, as human beings, could commit such atrocious carnage against fellow human beings. How could the Khmer Rouge release those 122mm indiscriminate devices of death and destruction on what they certainly knew was a non-combatant population. What had these innocent peasants ever done to them? The people the

[211] Loving Her Was Easier - Kris Kristofferson - 1971
[212] Holy Bible—NIV—Matthew 12:24

Khmer Rouge were shelling were the very people they were claiming to be liberating. My conclusion...it was done over divergent socioeconomic viewpoints. I then concluded the Americans were no different; our B-52 payloads dwarfed the random 122mm rockets. Like the Khmer Rouge, our bomb damage assessments (BDAs) had long been reporting not only were many of those killed, wounded, or made homeless by our attacks friendly...they were non-combatants as well. My conclusion for what motivated the Americans was the same...divergent socioeconomic views; a pitiful lot...the entire human race.

I sank back into the rear seat of the Mercedes, told the driver to take me home, took out one of my specially blended Dunhill cigarettes, lit up, and inhaled deeply. A passage from the book of Job came to mind as the effects of my deep inhale began to reach my brain; the part where God questions Job with "Have the gates of death been revealed to you? Have you seen the gates of deep darkness?"[213] Without any *expletive* question...I'd seen them. Years later looking back on all these experiences, I wonder how any trace of tenderness inside me ever managed to survive. God is indeed merciful. I'm living proof.

More Pig Pilot Tales

On the rare occasions when I would be together with the DC-3 (C-47) pilots in a non-work environment, I would find myself laughing to the point of tears at their stories from the airports I could never fly into. Because I flew the Convair which was too large to get into most of the provincial unpaved landing strips, I missed an entire dimension of the war. They, like me, flew food and wounded into Phnom Penh. But the airports I flew into were more sterile, less provincial. Their everyday routine was like a cross between a nightmare and a comedy. The villagers in the province were devoid of even the basic understanding of life in the larger cities and their antics could fill volumes. These rare get-togethers were always a time of joy in the midst of the tragedy. Years later, when we would sometimes meet, it was always the stories of the DC-3 "pig pilots" which brought the most smiles.

One More Pig Tale

One day, one of the Chinese shippers with a lucrative contract to supply pork for Phnom Penh's refugee swollen, half-starved, population offered me a cute little pig if I would take a little extra weight onboard. My orphanage was well stocked at the moment, so I decided I'd take him up on his offer. It was kinda a cute little critter anyway. I had figured I would give it to somebody back in Phnom Penh but by the time I was ready to head for the house, I'd started to like the little guy. So, over the driver's objection, I dumped him in the trunk of the Mercedes and off we went. All the way home I would could hear him thrashing around back there and squealing his head off. I was more

---

[213] Holman Christian Standard Bible (HCSB)—Job 38:17

than a little concerned about what his other end might be doing but obviously not enough to have engendered a little common sense. I was relieved to only find a little Pig pee in the back upon arrival back at the house. As I let him out, he raced around the yard and started smelling the maids. Nine and both maids how joined the driver in being unhappy with me. But I thought having a pet pig would be a hoot, so I was more or less oblivious to their displeasure.

Within a day or do he would run to the gate when he heard the Mercedes diesel engine clattering outside. He couldn't wait for me to get out of the car. Unfortunately, along with the pig, were both maids telling me about all the mischief the little guy had gotten into since I left.

Finally, after about a month of enjoying his frolicking I was met upon my return by a quite unhappy Nine and the two maids. Nine told me they had said either the pig went or they did. It seems during the day, the little guy had gotten into their flowerbed and eaten or trampled the entire thing. I probably could have talked them out of that, but it seems the little bastard went into their bedroom with his muddy feet fresh from their flower bed and gotten up on one of their beds. They always kept their quarters spotless. It was apparent that I was going to have to admit defeat and let the little guy meet his fate amongst the city's starving population. The following day, he was "given" to somebody. But for a while, if only a short while, I had a pet pig.

A New Group Of Copilots Brings A Round Of Applause

In the midst of the horrors of war historically its participants manage to find or create levity. One of those moments which lives on decades after the war was when a new group of copilots arrived from California. They came on a DC-4 which SEAAT brought from the States. They were part of the ferry crew.

For some reason which I no longer remember, probably either maintenance or delays getting the importation clearance from the Cambodian government, the aircraft remained in the Philippines for several days. During this interlude, these naughty newcomers to Southeast Asia immersed themselves in the debaucheries of Philippine nightlife. It seems they placed particular emphasis on the damsels of the dusk. Several days later, upon their arrival in Phnom Penh, it appeared more than one had been less cautious than prudence would dictate.

Our tainted new crewmembers joined most of the other single SEAAT pilots living in the Sokhalay Hotel. The presence of the pilots had naturally attracted a significant group of Phnom Penh's ladies of the evening or ladies in waiting so to speak. Each evening there was a grand convocation in the Sokhalay bar just about the time happy hour was celebrated. Our rash newcomers, exercising their usual abandonment of caution commenced immediately to spread their infectious joy throughout the entire hotel harem where monogamy was an unknown concept. A few days later SEAAT flight operations had a pandemic of social disease on their hands so to speak. It would be months before these junior birdmen were forgiven by those higher on the seniority list for this social transgression. Though long ago forgiven it appears it shall never be forgotten.

We Get A "Security Director"

One day while accompanying our crew chief on the inspection he always performed while the plane was being loaded, he asked me if I'd noticed the new guy who had been hanging around the airport restaurant for the last couple of days. Of course, I said no as Nine always sent my food to the airport with the driver. The food in the airport restaurant, and I use the term "restaurant" very loosely, was close to inedible. The pilots joked that eating the beef in there was like eating one Hồ Chí Minh's sandals, which were known to be made from old truck tires. The chicken they served reminded me of those toy rubber chickens children play with.

Our crew chief went on to say everybody was speculating he must be some kind of FAA (Federal Aviation Agency) inspector spying out how we were conducting our operation or perhaps part of military CID (Criminal Investigation Division or Command). Everybody ruled out CIA as we knew most of them and they sure as heck did not have the time to be sitting around the airport restaurant. I personally ruled out the FAA as we had it from very reliable sources that they had been told to stay away from our operation. CID of course was a possibility, but they normally would just plant somebody inside the operation for a couple of months, gather their facts, and then move the guy out. I just shrugged and told him I didn't have a clue.

When we landed back in Phnom Penh after our Battambang flight even more scuttlebutt was floating around. I decided I'd go over to the little airport restaurant, have a Mirinda before I went home, and see if I could spot this mysterious guy responsible for all the gossip.

I took a table near the rear of the place with my back to the wall and near the rear entrance. This was the preferred place to sit for most of us as we could watch both entrances; a practice acquired soon after arriving in Cambodia. Immediately I spotted the guy I was sure was the source of all the scuttlebutt. He was short, well built, wore a tight black t-shirt with an obviously unnecessary short sleeve shirt layered on top and black military type pants. His hair was close cut in a typical military style. Instantly I could see he was "printing" (the bulge made by a concealed weapon) from underneath the outer shirt. The print was so obvious that I couldn't help but wonder if it wasn't done for effect. My Eisenhower pilot blouse was perfect for concealing the snub-nose 38 special which always hung just underneath my left armpit. This guy needed a lesson on how to carry an under-arm concealed firearm. While most people knew we carried, most of us did not print. This guy was just too obvious. He kept constantly scanning the room. In my judgment this scanning was about as intentional as his printing. On top of that, he kept "adjusting." No real professional continually adjusts the position of his supposedly concealed weapon. He was indeed an interesting character. One thing I could be certain of…this was no undercover CID operation. He was so obvious he would flunk out of the first week of CID initial training.

I purposefully allowed him to catch me watching him. Before long two other pilots plus a crew chief came and joined me at the table. It was obvious we were all watching mystery guy. This did seem to bug him as he soon paid for his drink, got up, and left.

As he was walking out the door, I noticed he was printing from the back as well. He had what I was sure was a pair of num-chuks (a traditional Okinawan martial arts weapon consisting of two sticks connected at one end by a short chain or rope) stuck in his right hip pocket and covered by his black t-shirt. But, to my amazement, I was pretty sure I could see the print a 45 would make if it were placed in the small of his back, again underneath his t-shirt and his outer shirt. This one I wasn't totally sure about. The small of the back was a highly favored position for many who carried the Colt 45 auto concealed. But what was this guy expecting to encounter that would justify his carrying all this stuff around? Cambodia wasn't Hollywood. Any serious problem would come from grenades, and AK-47s. All the crap he was carrying brought to mind the old Special Forces or SOG (Special Operations Group) joke that "you never bring a knife to a gun fight." Since I had the best embassy contacts in the company, aside from Roger and Cy, everybody was looking at me for a comment. All I could do was shrug. I told them I didn't have a clue who he might be but that he was sure one strange dude.

We adjourned our little conference and got ready to go home for the day. Nine had our car and driver waiting for me in the parking lot. He pulled up to the curb to get me as soon as he saw me coming out. As I was getting in the car, I spotted our mystery man sitting at the wheel of a Mercedes parked in the parking lot. He was in a position which gave a good view of the terminal entrance. I was pretty sure the car belonged to SEAAT. I wondered what all this could mean. Usually Roger was very sharing with our internal happenings. But maybe I was mistaken; maybe it was not one of our company cars. It would not be long before I found out. The next morning a notice was on the flight operations bulletin board advising of a 7:00 pm meeting the following night at the company villa. Attendance was mandatory.

The living room of the villa was crowded with all the pilots and mechanics. As soon as I walked in, I spotted our mystery man. He was standing in the back of the room. Basically, with the exception of everyone's casual glances, he was being ignored. No one went up to introduce themselves. Like me, they probably figured we were all owed an explanation. Cy was seated at the table next to Roger. Cy did not look particularly happy.

Roger began the meeting with a few short statements about the status of what we all hoped would soon be more embassy contracts, statements about new spare parts and spare engines; the usual routine stuff.

But it wasn't long before he got to the real purpose of the meeting. Roger told us he would like to introduce our new "security director." The room immediately was filled with murmuring. Murmurings usually have a tone…either happy or unhappy. I failed to detect any happy intonations. Everybody had already identified the man as the strange guy we'd seen at the airport over the past few days. Now the mystery was removed…or at least part of it was.

Roger called him to the front and presented him to us. His name was Donald Aaron Samson III (pseudonym). He supposedly had been a Special Forces type in Vietnam, then went to Laos as a civilian. Roger had hired him from Laos where Air America and Continental Air Service (CAS) were being forced to wind down their operations due to slashed funding from Washington. So now all the *dogs of war* or *Canes Bellatores* appeared headed for Phnom Penh, the new O.K. Corral.

Roger went on to tell us what an expert Mr. Samson was in the area of personal and corporate security. I kept waiting for someone to question this decision, but nothing came, just cold faces. So, at the next pause, I asked Roger with a big smile, if he cared to share with us what new factors we might all need to be watching for concerning our personal security…obviously it must be something serious to justify the expense of a position solely devoted to security. I could see Roger was not particularly overjoyed with my question but he could see everyone else was so he tried as best he could to make a case for the new position.

Roger, in my mind, took a big risk and asked Donald to share with us the many security issues we faced daily both as individuals and as a company. Donald spent a few very lame minutes failing to make any points or friends. Finally, I asked Donald if he could provide any local empirical evidence supporting our supposed security risks. His doubly lame reply was he'd only been here a couple of days but in South East Asia, the risk was always present. The murmurings were beginning to increase. Since his hiring was not a negotiable item, I decided to let the issue drop by saying I looked forward to working with him in the future. Some of the other pilots were far less kind.

SEAAT's Hiring Spree

The Cambodian war effort was picking up dramatically. The U.S. needed to keep Cambodia from falling until it could get all its troops out of Vietnam and reinforce the South Vietnamese Army, so they had a chance of holding off the North Vietnam Regular Army. We all knew Washington didn't really give a damn what happened to Cambodia outside of its Vietnam objectives.

The embassy was talking about much larger contracts which SEAAT hoped to secure, but in order to do that we had to have the lift capability. In light of this, Roger went on a hiring spree. He hired a manager of administration, and a finance manager named Romeo Roberts (pseudonym) from California who had zero experience in aviation. At least the administration guy came from Air America's Laos operation.

The bright side of the hiring spree is he got several highly experienced CAS and Air America pilots from Laos. Some of the pilots he hired from the States with little or no paramilitary experience worked out well. Many did not. This was a time of expansion but a time when SEAAT lacked the capital to divert from its daily operations budget for the new equipment and crews needed for the possible embassy contracts. About this time our paydays began getting less punctual.

The Misadventures Of Sampson—Our Security Superhero

Love Bug In A Tree

One of the pilots Roger acquired from Laos, Elliot Walton (pseudonym) brought his wife and teenage daughter Juliette (pseudonym) with him. Elliot's daughter was fairly attractive. Almost immediately our new California finance guru kindled a romantic relationship with Juliette. Samson from the beginning did not like Romeo. I suspected he thought our Romeo was in a prime place to misdirect funds, but our Superhero lacked the accounting acumen to know how to catch him.

Since Romeo and the pilot's family were temporarily staying in the SEAAT villa, it wasn't long before the fair young damsel found her way down the second story hall and into the bedroom and waiting arms of Romeo. Our Security Superhero tried to make it his business to know about all such imprudence and straightaway set out to document it. The more sensitive information he had on someone, the more control he could exert.

One day, while Romeo was downstairs in his office, Security Superhero placed a miniature microphone bugging device under the nightstand beside the bed. Unfortunately for our Superhero, the device was not of a professional grade (probably purchased in Singapore) and lacked the range to facilitate surveillance with anywhere near prudent distance from the target. This range shortcoming forced Superhero to climb a tree just outside Romeo's bedroom window to await the action.

While we will never know for sure all the elements of this misadventure, the crucial ones are these. In the midst of Romeo and Juliette's mutual expressions of clandestine amour, it began to rain. Whether or not the branch upon which Superhero was perched would have continued to withstand his weight or whether it was the added weight of his now wet clothes which caused it to snap we shall never know, but the branch indeed did snap. According to someone still downstairs, it snapped quite loudly. After the snapping of the initial branch, there followed a couple of additional snaps as our Superhero broke every branch between him and the ground. Then came the thud as he hit the ground. According to eye witnesses, all the lights in the villa came on and everyone started trying to find out what was going on. Superhero was found half dazed in the mud underneath the tree still clutching the miniature transmitter's receiver. Poor Juliette failed to make it back to her room in time to avoid detection. And poor Romeo was caught with his proverbial pants down so to speak. Much loud shouting was attributed to Juliette's father Elliot.

The Kill Instinct

One afternoon following my final flight of the day I stopped by the SEAAT villa for some now forgotten reason. In the front yard, underneath the same tree from which he had fallen during his calamitous "love bug" episode I found Donald working out doing bench presses. He gave me his usual calculated scowl and continued pumping his iron. As I was nearing his bench, his expression suddenly changed, he let his barbell down quickly to their support and grabbed a pellet pistol lying beside his head, pointed up into the tree branches, took a quick aim and fired. A second later a small now lifeless bird hit the ground beside us with a thump. "What the *expletive* did you do that for" I asked. "To keep my kill instinct up Jacks" was his reply. I just shook my head and continued on into the living room. Donald Aaron Samson was one strange dude.

Donald's "Got You" Game

One afternoon, on my way home from the airport, I was sitting in the back of the Mercedes reading some company notices and other business documents, I became aware of a car on the right side of our car. I always sat in the back seat on the right side so I could more easily talk to the driver. This car to our right was uncommonly close. As I looked up, I found myself staring directly into the barrel of a Colt 45 automatic. From my perspective I felt like I was staring down the barrel of a 155mm howitzer. Just behind the barrel was the grinning face of Donald. I lowered my window and was greeted by "got you Jacks…see how easy it is." He was actually smiling…the first time I'd ever seen Donald smile. He then pulled away abruptly and sped away. I immediately understood his remark. He was referencing my comment in the meeting asking if there was any firsthand evidence that we as individuals were in danger.

I suppose a normal person would have been somewhere between annoyed and furious at having had a gun pointed at his head. I just shook my head with mild amusement. I thought I might be starting to appreciate this guy. In his own way I could see he did have a sense of humor, albeit somewhat twisted.

An Awakening

Nine and I began attending church. It was a non-denominational church which offered services in English each Sunday evening. I'm not sure if it was the recent passing of my grandmother Grace Rogers Aldredge Tyner, my awareness that Nine had no understanding of Christianity, or, the Christian and Missionary Alliance missionaries I knew…I'm not certain, but I began to feel the need to get my life closer to God. Getting closer to God wasn't all that hard as I could have hardly been any farther from Him.

Serious questions had slowly grown up in the weed filled maze of my religious beliefs since leaving the First Baptist Church in Hamilton. Being exposed to no religious teachings for the past 13 years combined with undisciplined studies in mysticism and philosophy, had pretty much left my understanding of God and salvation a works-based disaster. I was painfully aware I was a sinner and equally painfully aware that my efforts to save myself were falling seriously short. I bombarded my friend, Christian and Missionary Alliance (CAMA) missionary Rev. Merle Graven with many hard questions stemming from deep welled cynicism. Grace was a concept that had somehow pretty much eluded me. Nine, on the other hand, approached the subject of salvation with the simplicity of a child; I should have taken notes.

Nine Accepts Christ

One afternoon we were visiting other missionary friends, Dr. Dean Kroh and his wife Esther. They had been a doctor and nurse, husband and wife missionary team for CAMA in the Congo while I was there. While I was talking to Dean, Esther and Nine were sitting in the other corner of the living room talking quietly. Then Dean and I noticed they got up and left and went into a bedroom. Looking back now I suspect Dean had been keenly aware of their conversation from the beginning. When they returned from their time alone, Esther announced that Nine had accepted the Lord. Nine was a Christian. Thirty years later Nine and I would visit with Dean and Esther and Rev. Merle Graven and his wife Louisa.

Missionaries–Mercenaries–And Machine Guns

One afternoon Nine and I were visiting Dean and Esther in their home in Toul Kork, a suburb of Phnom Penh. Dean and Ester's children were home for a short visit from the school in Kuala Lumpur, Malaysia that all the missionary children attended. Once, on a previous visit, I'd left my briefcase (the one in which I carried the M3-A grease gun) lying on their living room couch. Dean picked it up to move it to the floor to make more sitting room on the couch. He immediately noticed how heavy it was and asked, "what do you have in there…lead," meaning it for a joke. I smiled and replied, "why yes, as a matter of fact…thirty pieces of lead," meaning it as a joking reference to the Biblical thirty pieces of silver. Of course, being a missionary Dean got the thirty pieces of silver part but being a missionary, he failed to get the allusion to the thirty round magazine containing 45 caliber ACP rounds. I had to open the briefcase to explain my very poorly thoughtout humor.

Apparently, Dean had told his children that he and their mother had a friend who carried a machine gun in his briefcase. Their curiosity overcame them, and they asked their father if he would ask me to show it to them. I obliged but all the while wishing the Lord would hasten to bind my sarcastic tongue.

SEAAT Gets A Troubadour

One day as I was coming out of flight operations, I saw a passenger heading into baggage claim. He was long (6'4" tall) lanky, clad in western shirt and jeans, wearing boots, and carrying a guitar case. What in the hell is that I asked? God only knows was the reply.

Later that day I heard about the new copilot we had…a guy who liked to dress in jeans and boots and played the guitar. He soon claimed a place of prominence in the Sokhalay night scene and served well as a copilot quickly learning the art of wartime flying. He later became Captain David Nowlen of Southwest Airlines with some degree of notoriety in his adopted home town of Nashville. Dave went on to write Broken Wing the song made famous by LeAnn Rimes. After retiring from Southwest, Dave returned to South East Asia, has visited Cambodia many times, has built two schools in the provinces, and now lives in Thailand.

From Tacos To Turtle Eggs

You're A Long Way From Texas Jimmy Jacks

One day while on a flight to Battambang we encountered a delay due to a disabled aircraft with a blown tire on the airport's only runway. It became evident we were going to be stranded for a while. The crew decided to spend the delay time in the airport's restaurant. The purser ordered turtle eggs from the menu. He insisted I try some, so he ordered a few extra. I was anything but overjoyed about the prospect of eating a turtle's egg. But, while in the Congo I'd eaten things in order not to offend the host; I figured this was going to be another of those times.

When the dish arrived, I was surprised and disheartened at the quantity. I didn't count them but there was a hell of a lot on that dish. One was more than I was looking for. Since we were on duty, ordering a beer to help wash them down was not an option; I figured my best strategy was to pray, don't breathe lest I smell them, gulp quickly and chase with Coke. I looked up as I brought them from the plate toward my mouth; fully half the people in the restaurant had their eyes on those eggs and my mouth. I can't remember now what it tasted like…probably because it went down so quickly. Everyone at the table laughed. I think half the restaurant laughed. I took a big sip of coke and tried to inconspicuously swish it around in my mouth. Years later I learned many species of Cambodia's turtles had become endangered, mostly due to the centuries old practice of eating their eggs.

They finally managed to get the runway cleared and a few minutes later we were cranking up our engines for the flight back to Phnom Penh. I was in a little bit of a hurry and in the process of foolishly trying to make up for some of the time we had lost, I only spiraled twice before taking up our course to Pochentong. That put me too low over the pagoda we'd been warned not to fly low over. Just overhead the pagoda I heard the unmistakable sound of an AK47 round striking the fuselage. When the copilot got back to the cockpit reporting nobody was hit and that the round hadn't struck anything critical, I joked that it was God thumping me for being impatient and taking a shortcut. I can also now wonder if it was His thumping me for eating the egg of a now endangered species. When we landed back in Phnom Penh the crew chief thumped me as well for getting a hole in his beloved aircraft.

My Moon-Eating Dragon

Nightmares were an unwavering occurrence; as surely as the sun rose in the eastern sky, my night terrors were summoned dutifully with the evening. Normally these terrible dreams were the kind that left me sitting up in bed with my heart pounding and drenched in perspiration. The worst kinds were the ones that returned after you managed to get back to sleep.

One night however I had a dream employing a different script. I saw a huge full silver moon racing in slow motion across the night sky being chased by "Puff The Magic Dragon," the U.S. Air Force's close air support C-47 (actually an AC-47) retrofitted with three General Electric mini-guns. The aircraft, also called "ole Spooky" could fire between 50 to 100 rounds of 7.62mm rounds per second. The guns fired so fast that by the time the sound reached the ground, our ears only heard a long uninterrupted BURRRRRRRP. We often watched from our second-floor bedroom balcony as its tracer rounds (every 5th round) raced through the night sky toward their target. But this night, "Puff" was chasing the moon; Puff's tracer rounds viciously trying to shatter the moon's silver form. I kept wishing the moon would go faster and escape.

When I awoke, I was not in the normal terrified state I usually found myself in upon awaking. I was excited but not frightened; I wanted the moon to win…to get away; I wanted the moon to escape from Puff The Magic Dragon's dreadful fire-breathing attack. The moon and Puff, like my usual disturbing recurring dreams, had to have its geneses in the sights that pummeled our minds almost daily.

If I was in the air force, I would have no choice…I would have to stay here and finish my assignment. But I was not. My contractual obligation was long ago finished. I could walk away at any time. It was like I'd bought a ticket to some house of horrors and I was determined to make it all the way through to the end; like I was determined to get my money's worth, to see every last gory scene.

Why So Hard Jimmy?

On this particular afternoon, I'd managed to get home early. Nine was still out with her nieces. She had been to Bong Hut's house to visit his two daughters, Nip and Voy, who were almost like younger sisters to her. I had gone out on our bedroom balcony to drink a beer and smoke one of my special-blend Dunhills and pick my 5-string banjo I'd brought back from Hamilton. As I sat relaxing, I saw Bong Hut's Mercedes pulling up. His driver had brought Nine back. Nip and Voy plus Bong Hut's youngest daughter Dede, just out of diapers, had decided to take the opportunity to go for a little drive. They waved from the car as it pulled away.

Soon Nine was upstairs and joining me on the balcony. I continued singing and playing but noticed concern on her face, I stopped, and she gently posed the question…"Jimmy, why so hard?" I hadn't realized it, but I'd been flailing the banjo with unusual force. "Why so hard" indeed. I just shrugged but her question lingered. I began to realize there were few things I did with a gentle touch anymore.

Letters And Pictures

Karen was good about writing and sending news and pictures. Even though we were divorced she would send news about my father, and updates on Jason and Jenny plus pictures. When I saw their pictures, I frequently had moist eyes. I was always happy to get her letters. Jenny's growth was the most noticeable. With every picture came something new. I could always feel her care for me, and later on for Nine. Karen had a loving heart. Our relation continued until she died many years later. When people would refer to Karen as my "ex-wife" I would politely reply "no…she is my first wife."

The Saturday Night Massacre

While I battled my night terrors and the daily horrors of the war, halfway around the world, an increasingly embattled Richard Nixon was becoming more desperate. On 20 October 1973 in what immediately became known as The Saturday Night Massacre, Nixon fired Archibald Cox and abolishes the office of the special prosecutor. Attorney General Richardson and Deputy Attorney General William D. Ruckelshaus resigned. Pressure for impeachment continued to mount in Congress. Amazingly I paid scant attention.

Departed Spirits—Mediums And Machetes

On one of my rare days off, Nine's eldest brother Bong Hut stopped by the house. He remembered my asking him about the Cambodian's view concerning mediums and spirits. He told me about a ceremony that would be that afternoon at the home of someone he knew and asked if I would like to go and watch. He said it would be OK for me to take pictures. My answer was an enthusiastic "yes."

We arrived at the home and Bong Hut introduced me. We chatted for a few minutes then Bong Hut left me there as he had an important meeting he could not get out of. People were already arriving; probably around twenty in all. Soon two people arrived; a man and a woman. I believed the man, because of his dress, was an achar, somewhat of a cross between a lay monk and a master of ceremonies. The lady looked pretty unkempt. She was obviously *kru boromey* or literally "teacher of spiritual beings or more accurately translated but less accurate in connotation, teacher of the ten attributes which enable the attainment of nirvana. In the common Cambodian rather abbreviated view…she called, identified, and talked with the spirits…asking them questions in behalf of the living.[214] She was a medium.

The people began taking seats on mats on the ground out in the yard under the shade of some very large trees. Unfortunately, with Bong Hut gone, there was no one to explain what was happening. I could feel the tension in the group growing. I could feel myself growing tense as well.

Soon the achar began speaking to the group. Then he began beating on a traditional drum. Almost immediately the expression on the face of the woman who accompanied him began to change. Her eyes became fixed in space not looking directly at anyone but rather almost through people and her facial muscles appeared to grow tense. She was going into a trance. I'd seen it in the Congo…the drums followed by the trance state; I was seeing the same thing here . . . halfway around the world from the Congo.

From as far back as I could remember, I'd had a strong curiosity about the spirit world. I knew it existed. There was just too much evidence. Even the Bible clearly states its existence. I always wondered why so many people refused to recognize it. The Bible does clearly state that we should not engage these spirits, but rather steer well clear. But for today I was quite willing to set aside all the Biblical warnings I'd heard and anxiously awaited a peek into the dark world of these departed spirit entities.

The Cambodians believe in ghosts called *knouch* (pronounced *kmout*). Certain mediums can call these knouch up from the spirit world and can ask them questions in behalf of the living. A biblical example parallel would be when King Saul called up Samuel by using a medium or witch. According to Khmer belief, they are tormented by hunger and thirst and are allowed out of

---
[214] Philip Coggan—Cambodia expert and author of *Hotel Cambodia*

hell (Sheol) once each year to be fed by their families during a special time called Pchum Ben. Pchum Ben is one of the most sacred periods in the Cambodian year.

After some chanting and drum beats it appeared the woman entered a trance. She held a machete which she began to swing just above our heads as she jumped about. To me it seemed the machete was only inches above my head. The noise it made as she sliced the air was scaring the hell out of me. She began shrieking. I was told she was communicating with spirits. This First Baptist Church boy from Hamilton Texas was now very sure he was someplace he did not need to be. By the Grace of God the ceremony ended without anyone being decapitated although a couple appeared to become temporarily "possessed" by one or more or the "spirits." I vowed I would never do this again.

38 Specials Threats And Bedpans

The fact that it happened so gradually combined with my normal acute focus on work resulted in my failing to recognize I'd suffered a serious loss of strength. Finally, one day as I was boarding the aircraft, I had to stop and rest before reaching the top of the air stair. I wondered if I had the strength to make it all the way up the stairs. Somehow I managed to make it to the cockpit but by then I was totally exhausted. I collapsed in the captain's seat and needed to wait another couple of minutes before I could begin my cockpit flow and call for the checklist. I knew right then that this was my last flight till I could find out what was wrong and get my strength back.

By the time we landed back in Phnom Penh I was much worse. I needed help getting from the plane to the car. When I got home, I had no appetite. I went to bed but had wall to wall bad dreams. It was a relief to hear the first roosters starting to crow a little after 3:00am.

The next morning Nine took me to the clinic her family used. It was owned by a French doctor; many considered him the most qualified in the city. Nine stayed with me during the doctor's visit. The doctor, in typical French medical form poked around on me then wanted to give me an IV treatment of vitamins. He said when that was finished, I should go home and stay in bed. He wanted me to return the following day for the results of my blood work.

The IV treatment was going to take over an hour so Nine decided she would leave me and go to the market for that day's food. The driver took her to the market while I stayed behind getting the treatment.

When the IV was finished, I went to the office to pay the bill. Nine had not yet returned. While I was standing at the window waiting to get my receipt, I passed out. The next thing I remembered was people standing around me trying to put me up on a gurney. They took me to a room and put me in a bed. I was feeling a little stronger by this time, so I helped them remove my pants and my shirt. This of course exposed the little problem of my shoulder holster, 38 special, and ammo pouch. They reached to take it like they had my pants and shirt. I wasn't sure where they had put them…in the night stand perhaps. But I knew my 38 wasn't going anywhere. I slung it over the bed post at the head of my bed in a manner that allowed it to hang just to the right of my head. I hung it inverted as I wore it so it would be easy to reach, then I lay back in the bed.

It wasn't long before a big beefy Vietnamese nurse with a neck bigger than most of those sow pigs we flew barged into the room with what was close to being the largest syringe I'd ever seen. There was what I estimated to be a 12-gauge needle on the syringe. She was heading straight for me with the bedside demeanor of a charging rhino. I swear that 12-gauge needle from my position in the bed as it rushed toward me looked bigger than the barrel of a 12-gauge shotgun. I shouted "stop at the top of my lungs but she continued her advance telling me to roll over…the doctor had ordered this. I shouted at her again, but she continued her advance with seemingly even more determination. In desperation I grabbed the bedpan from the bedside stand and threatened her with it. She gave me a defiant look and started pulling on the sheet. I slung it at her with all my might. That got her attention. Fortunately for the old wench my aim had been affected by my condition, so it missed her, but not by much. She was now onboard; we had had a meeting of the minds. She retreated rapidly as I reached for my Colt Cobra 38 Special. Of course I would not have shot her but she sure as hell did not know that. I could see a group of whispering nurses peeking into the room from the hallway.

Nine said the nurses rushed to meet her as she came through the clinic's main door beseeching her to please help them with me. I'm sure they were wondering how she could live with such a beast. Nine came to my bed and told me she was thoroughly embarrassed. She asked me if I'd really thrown something at one of the nurses. "Yes" I replied and pointed proudly to the bedpan on the floor on the other side of the room. I could see she was not impressed. By now some of the nurses were starting to inch they way back into the room…in absolute wonder at how she was controlling me. Nine explained that the doctor was worried about me and I really needed to take this shot. I demanded to know what it was and to look closely at the syringe and needle (Cambodia did not yet have disposable syringes and needles and there were horror stories everywhere of their "serialization" techniques. The head nurse came and explained everything to Nine. I've long since forgotten what she said the injection was. I obediently and without further protest submitted with the stipulation it would not be from the same old wench that I'd thrown the bedpan at. They promised she would never come in my room again…probably because she refused. Anyway, I took the shot and fell asleep. When I awoke, I was told my lab results confirmed the doctor's suspicions; I had typhoid.

Back in school in the Navy I'd studied about typhoid, but I couldn't ever recall seeing a case. Largely, in the United States, the disease had been eradicated. I had the low white blood cell count, and the doctor's continued poking at my stomach had confirmed tenderness. Nine insured our maid always washed all fresh vegetables in disinfectant but I was not so scrupulous about what I ate when I went out with the crew on flights. Looking back, I should have diagnosed myself, but I had just been so focused on other things that I failed to see what was happening to me.

The doctor was very concerned about my stomach wall being perforated so he put me on an almost soup and very soft food diet and he started giving me valium injections to calm some of the agitation that came along with the disease. I'd been running a low-grade fever which I'd also incredibly allowed to go undetected. Amazing.

After about two weeks of complete bed rest, I was allowed to return home. During this time in the hospital my life significantly changed. I was not flying; I was not running full speed ahead from the moment my feet left the bed and hit the terrazzo floor; I saw no terrible scenes of war and carnage. The valium kept me in a rested and relaxed state. I gained weight. For the first time in my life I weighed what others did.

Addicted!

When I left the hospital, the doctor wanted me to rest an additional week to 10 days before resuming normal flight duty. He gave me a prescription for valium tablets. In Cambodia, no prescriptions as we know them in the United States were required. The doctor simply wrote on a piece of paper the name of the medication, the dosage, and how many times a day. If you could spell it, you could buy it. No doctor's order necessary.

When I'd completed my days of home rest and my valium regiment and returned to flight status, I found I missed the tranquil cocoon I'd been peacefully residing in for the past month. I found myself having trouble sleeping; even the slightest thing irritated me, I was tense and clinched my fists and my teeth. By the second day back on the flight schedule I knew I was an accident waiting to happen. On the way back home that evening I had the driver stop by the pharmacy. I bought thirty tablets. I took one as soon as I got home. Every time I felt them wearing off, I took another one. I did not like being without it's mellowing effect.

One afternoon, as I walked into the pharmacy to buy another bottle of these pills I'd become so attached to, the young pharmacist who owned the shop looked sincerely into my face and asked "why would such a young, intelligent, man as you, with such a wonderful life, want to take these terrible pills. You can easily become addicted to them." He stopped short of telling me I already was addicted. His words jolted me like a bolt of lightning. I instantly knew he was right. I supposed I'd already begin to suspect that I might be. I stopped in the middle of the transaction, slowly replied "baht" or yes, "Akun" or thank you, and "Khnum yol," I understand. I turned and walked out of the pharmacy without the precious valium I'd gone in to get.

The next few days were difficult. The withdrawal symptoms were terrible and got worse before finally starting to subside. I simply employed the iron will I'd inherited from my father and endured. Slowly the withdrawal symptoms left me completely and I returned to normal while all the while continuing with my flights

That dreadful medication has never touched my lips since. Years later I learned millions had become addicted to it. I was lucky to have survived its destructive clutch. I will forever be grateful to the young pharmacist who cared enough to challenge me rather than staying quiet and taking my money.

Another Cambodian Christmas

We had some meager Christmas decorations, but there were no presents under the tree, no Jason or Jenny to watch open them, no Christmas cards, it was almost surreal. I knew it was Christmas, the stores in Phnom Penh all had Christmas decorations. Christmas cards had been replaced with News Week and Time reports of the war in Vietnam with occasional references to the equally real war going on in Cambodia. The magazines usually managed to have some hint of a Christmas theme but past the front page, it was depressing as hell. Back home, the entire nation was obsessed with ending the war. The White House was providing comic relief to the hell that was the Vietnam War and its illegitimate child, the war going on here in Cambodia.

I drank more, smoked more specially blended Dunhills, played my banjo more, and listened to Armed Forces Radio Saigon more. I'd sit close and listen as the sound came through the crappy little speaker on my radio primarily designed for short wave news reception. Every song they played seemed to lead me in the wrong direction…someplace I didn't want to go. I looked eagerly toward January and a new year.

A Hole In Three
Four Anti-Aircraft Rounds In Number Three Engine That Is

It was 20 January of 1974. I was scheduled for only a half day that day so the mechanics could have the time to do some routine preventative maintenance on the engines. As I walked by the chief pilot's office, I saw my good friend Paul Rakisits sitting at his desk. I stuck my head in the door just to say hello. He asked if I was done for the day and I said yes. He asked if I wanted to fly to Battambang with him on the Carvair. The Carvair was a converted C-54 that looked for all the world like a mini-747 with propellers. It was developed for flying large oversized cargo. The nose of the aircraft opened outward allowing automobiles and other oversized cargo to be loaded. I'd only flown one a couple of times so I thought this would be a hoot…a good time to fly and visit with my old friend and mentor.

Strolling out to the airplane with Paul was just like old times back in the Congo. It was a nice afternoon, the weather was good, no rockets were falling on the airport; this would be a good time to visit.

Our flight to Battambang was routine. We relived the same old stories we'd shared a hundred times, and we spent time catching up on how our families were doing. The flight went perfectly until we were on the decent back into Phnom Penh. Around four thousand feet we were hit by ground fire. The number three engine started sputtering and shaking. We quickly agreed we had to shut it down. Paul looked over at me and grinned and said…"you know the drill. I'll fly, you shut her down." I grinned back and said…"just like old times."

Paul stopped our decent as we didn't want to get any closer to whoever was shooting at us. This was supposed to be friendly held territory beneath us. After all it was only about five miles from the airport. The oil pressure on number three had fallen to almost zero. Hopefully we could get it feathered. When I looked out the right window there was oil all over the cowling and starting to move back onto the wing. The mechanics were going to be pissed about having to not only change an engine but also having to clean the oil off the right side of the aircraft as well. I ran through the engine failure and secure checklist with a little grin on my face as I visualized their group of scowling faces looking up at us from underneath the engine. I suspected this, though clearly not our fault, was going to require some beer to get us back in their good graces once again. They would claim we started our decent too soon because we were in a hurry to finish the flight and get home. Aircraft mechanics were seldom gifted with a sense of humor that was intelligible to pilots.

Paul made a steep approach and a perfect landing. The Carvair taxiing in with its right side all covered in oil was guaranteed to draw a crowd. As we shutdown they scurried over and were examining the cowling. I knew they would be looking at the bullet hole, but this was a little more interest than normal. When we climbed down and took a look for ourselves, we found that we had not taken one round, but four. A Khmer Air Force lieutenant was walking briskly toward us with his clipboard. He was obviously going to want to know our best guess as to where the ground fire came from. T-28 would almost certainly soon be dispatched to the estimated location. Without question, the Khmer Rouge who fired the shots were hiding in the midst of a friendly village. The villagers were terrified of these black pajama clad little teenage bastards. They would just as soon kill you as look at you. That means the villagers were twice the losers…once by having these killers in their village and second when the T-28s came and strafed and bombed their village.

No wonder they were abandoning their homes and rice fields and crowding into Phnom Penh. There all they had to worry about was the Khmer Rouge rockets…not the T-28s and B-52s. What a *expletive-ed* up war!

They soon had the cowling removed. It appeared the engine case had been cracked as well. That engine was toast…history. Paul pulled a black ink felt tip marker from his flight bag and inscribed on the cowling near the bullet holes "Rakisits/Jacks . . . January 20, 1974 . . . Phnom Penh." As we walked back to the terminal together, he looked over at me with his famous Paul Rakisits grin and said…"all in a day's work." "Yes," I replied…"just another day in paradise." I was glad I'd joined him that day; it had been a good flight.

Haey Neak Ta

About two weeks after the second of the three new year celebrations celebrated in Cambodia (the Jan 1st new year, the Chinese New Year, around February and then the Cambodian New Year, around April) I watched what was probably the most bizarre celebration I'd ever seen. It was called Haey Neak Ta. A neak ta is a spirit which hangs around after death. Some are believed benevolent, some mischievous, and some downright evil, but all are believed to be very powerful and from time to time get actively involved in the affairs of the livings. This particular ceremony is deeply rooted in Chinese religious practice, but the Cambodians were happy to accept it as well.

During Haey Neak Ta, shamans enter a trance state and invite these spirits to possess them. After the spirit enters the shaman, he (or sometimes she) is able to be subjected to several kinds of self-mutilation which would normally produce unimaginable pain without apparently feeling anything. I saw these shamans being paraded through the streets on platforms carried by devotees of this practice. Large crowds gathered to watch the procession. Some of the shamans had long metal skewers (like those used in grilling shish kebabs back in our backyards in Hamilton) driven through both cheeks with no apparent bleeding or pain. Others were cutting their tongues with razor sharp knives. This would cause bleeding and the blood was smeared on small pieces of paper and handed out to eager spectators in the crowd. This was supposed to bring good fortune in the new Chinese year. Some would spray the blood onto people and on business fronts to bring good luck, drive away evil spirits, and bring prosperity to the business. There was a guy on a bed of nails being paraded around as well. Both shamans and devotees were dressed in bright red clothing trimmed often in gold. The same colors seen around Chinese New Year. This was truly an amazing display.

Frankly I was more than a little uncomfortable with the whole scene. I'd seen things somewhat similar while I was in the Congo, but nothing as dramatic as this. I was sure the air was filled with evil and I was very happy to get the heck out of there…but only after I had taken a few pictures which were subsequently lost when I had to evacuate. I had a lot to think about that night.

Airports–Attachés And Agents

My friend Col. Opfer's assignment was coming to an end. He would return to the U.S. and soon retire. Nine and I, along with several from the embassy were going to the airport to say goodbye at a little ceremony in the departure lounge. Nine had bought a beautiful ruby pendent as a gift for his wife.

There were probably twenty people in the departure lounge for the occasion. There were several other Cambodians and foreigners also there waiting for their flight's departure. Some were taking pictures. While Nine and I were saying our personal farewell, I saw a Cambodian take a picture. All my bells instantly went off. I stared hard at the man who gave me an apologetic "Sohm toh" or sorry. In order not to embarrass Dave or create an incident I turned away from him and resumed my conversation with Dave. But deep inside, my instincts were telling me something was very wrong. I seemed to be the only one of that opinion as they kept taking pictures supposedly of each other but always with some of our group in the background. I had to forced myself to let it go. Although over the years I'd speak with Dave a few times, that was the last time I saw him. Several months later I stumbled on the photos in my file at the 12th Bureau (Cambodia's version of the CIA). Nine and I were clearly persons of interest.

A Happy Song Amidst This Melancholy Opera

One welcome bright note in the midst of the tragedy playing out every day was the song birds. I discovered Cambodia had birds capable of producing the most beautiful sounds. I would sometimes go out on the veranda just to sit and listen to them. I never thought I could think such a thought, but their music far exceeded the beauty of our mocking bird. God provided blessings even in the midst of all this heartbreak. I was sure the birds singing these heartwarming songs were familiar with the line in Psalm 98:4 "Make a joyful noise unto the Lord."[215]

The Haze

For many months each year Cambodia was plagued with an incessant haze. Back in Hamilton County you could easily see the hills many miles away. In the oil fields of Loco Hills New Mexico you could almost see forever. Cambodia, like the war, was a constant haze. I often mused that there must be a haze back home on Capitol Hill was well. What a mess I managed to get myself in the midst of.

Political Fog

Meanwhile, as pigs and tales of pig pilots and beautiful songbirds provided a bit of relief from the weight of the war, the legitimacy of the Lon Nol government which we were struggling to keep in power was in question just about everywhere in the world except Phnom

---

[215] Holy Bible—King James Version—Psalm 98:4

Penh and Washington D.C. Prince (former king) Norodom Sihanouk's government in exile, known as the Royal Government of National Union of Cambodia (RGNUC), headquartered in Peking, controlled, according to informed estimates, 60 percent of the territory of Cambodia and 40 percent of the country's population, excluding most major provincial capitals.[216] This "control" was in reality reinforced by the brutal Khmer Rouge.

In the spring of 1974, Prince Sihanouk and the party's "deputy" prime minister Khieu Samphan who only recently had emerged from the shadows of Cambodia's Khmer Rouge jungle strongholds, embarked on an eleven nation tour (orchestrated by China). The tour included Hanoi, Peking, Africa, and Europe. During this tour, the hard-line communists in Cambodia and their sponsors in China and Hanoi, could be clearly seen distancing themselves from Prince Sihanouk and promoting the much more hardline communists. On this trip, Khieu Samphan was introduced as "head of the delegation and member of the Political Bureau of the NUFC or National United Front of Cambodia (yet another unheard-of political party). Not only was Prince Sihanouk being abandoned by the hard-line Chinese and Vietnamese, but his party was being sidelined by the newly Peking blessed NUFC.

I didn't really spend a lot of time trying to see through this political fog, but when I did, I found the lines becoming blurred...the lines of why we (including me) were here. Sometimes it just didn't pay to think too much.

Nixon's Noose Tightens

While the drama of who Cambodia's legitimate ruler was or should be played out in Southeast Asia, the noose was tightening around President Richard Nixon's neck. The democrats in congress smelled blood and presidential dishonesty (hardly anything new) and would not get off the trail. As a result, on April 30, 1974, the White House was forced to release more than 1,200 pages of edited transcripts of the Nixon tapes to the House Judiciary Committee. But the committee insists that the tapes themselves must be turned over. Most of us were watching this more than we were trying to decipher the murky maze of Cambodia's new political acronyms and who was really behind them. It required less thought.

The Vietnamese Army Comes To Cambodia

For a few days at the end of April and beginning of May 1974, while Richard Nixon clung desperately to his disintegrating presidency, the South Vietnamese Army mounted an operation on North Vietnamese and Viet Cong forces operating inside Cambodia. This operation (the Battle of Svay Rieng) penetrated at least 16km inside Cambodia's border. The Viet Cong and North Vietnamese had long been known to have supply bases and troops inside Cambodia around the area of Svay Rieng. Obviously, the Khmer Rouge weren't Cambodia's only worry. This caught the attention of everyone. The Cambodian's animosity toward the Vietnamese was never far from sight and uninvited Vietnamese troops on their soil stirred their passion.

[216] Cambodia 1974: Governments on Trial - Donald Kirk - University of California Press

The barstool generals of the Sokhalay Hotel had several scenarios on the implications of the Battle of Svay Rieng as well. Would they go back into South Vietnam? Would they continue to push deeper into Cambodia? Would the North Vietnamese send more regular troops to join the Viet Cong already here in Cambodia? What would the Khmer Rouge do?

It seemed nothing anywhere around me ended on a positive note. Nine was the only positive thing I could reach out and touch. Still, life wasn't all that bad…if you didn't pause to think too much. I dealt with it by drinking a lot, inhaling deeply, and holding Nine tightly. However, something good was about to come into the picture; something I could reach out and touch.

Jason Comes To Cambodia

We had another airplane coming. It would be ferried all the way from the States. It would be coming via the Atlantic and Europe then the Middle East. Cy Wroten was planning to bring his family onboard. I had a perfect way to get Jason to Cambodia…only one little issue…Karen. I was sure she would never allow him to fly across the Atlantic in a WWII airplane associated with a CIA proprietary company and land in the middle of a war zone.

But, SHE DID! I couldn't believe my eyes when I read the letter. I'd promised to fly Karen along with Jason to Florida where he would meet up with Cy and Cy's family. I will remain eternally grateful to Karen for allowing Jason to join me in Cambodia.

My son, still only nine years old, onboard a C-54 lumbering across the Atlantic Ocean, sleeping in a sleeping bag, eating box lunches, hopping from Gander to Shannon, then Italy, the middle east, India, and finally Thailand; going to a country and a war that was now in the headlines and six o'clock evening news daily. Looking back now, it is a truly mindboggling thought. Back then, it appeared perfectly normal. What was I thinking?

The plane had been delayed in Bangkok for several days waiting for diplomatic clearance to come into the country. They hung out at the Nana Hotel, a R&R (rest and recreation) hotel used by the Americans working in the war effort in Thailand, Laos, Vietnam, and Cambodia. They enjoyed the swimming pool while Cy struggled with the embassy to get all the clearances we needed. While we were totally supported by the U.S. Government, there were aspects of our operation that were shaded in gray and required sensitive handling. But then the whole war was shaded in gray.

Finally, the big day came. Our flight schedule was critical as well as our pilot roster. I asked Nine to meet the flight and told her I'd be home about an hour later. She was apprehensive about meeting Jason for the first time but, at the same time she was determined he was going to be a significant part of her life. She went to the airport and met the flight.

Cy mentioned to Nine that Jason had at times not been the most genial traveling companion. Cy noted that he was probably under a lot of stress entering this new environment. That was without question a significant understatement.

When I arrived home, he was already exploring the place. I was so glad to see him. Nine was trying hard to be accepted. Jason had determined this acceptance would be on his own terms; but that too was fine.

Jason And French Bread

Sometimes when I had the car, Nine and Jason would ride around in a cyclo. He had acquired a taste for the French style bread in the Congo. Nine would buy some for our evening meal only to find that Jason had eaten half of it in the cyclo on the way home. It was super fresh, just out of the oven and Jason literally found it irresistible.

Jason And Our Home Defense System

Jason was fascinated by the somewhat interesting spectrum of weaponry deployed throughout the house. He discovered the M-2 Carbine beneath the bed and promptly took it downstairs to explain to the driver how he should use it to defend the house. He remembered his gun safety lessons and his countless hours of target practice with his BB gun. Nine told him he should take it back upstairs as his father would not be very pleased to learn he had taken it out of its place under the bed. He gave her a scowl but took it back upstairs. He did get a little scolding when I came home, but deep down inside, although I could not allow him to be doing something as dangerous as playing with that gun, especially without any training on the M-2, I totally understood his fascination. I was proud he understood the concept of safeguarding the house and its occupants in my absence. I'd worked hard over the years to instill this sense of obligation.

Swimming At The Country Club

Nine would take Jason almost daily to the Cercle Sportif. Completed in 1929, it stood as a monument to the lifestyle of the French and Cambodian elite during Cambodia's French Colonial period. There were tennis courts and a swimming pool. At the poolside tables and restaurant were found the families of Cambodia's nouveau riche, created almost overnight by the grand-scale corruption ushered in by the American war involvement immediately following the CIA orchestrated coup that ousted Prince (former king) Norodom Sihanouk. Nine would sit for hours watching as Jason played with his new friends, mostly French or the children of diplomats. At that time Jason still retained some of his fluency in French. Nine didn't really enjoy the place but was happy to take Jason. He would always want to stop by the French bakery and pick up more fresh bread most of which he would eat before they got back home.

While Jason played with international friends in the Cercle Sportif, back in Washington the presidency of Richard Nixon was coming unraveled. On 24 July, the Supreme Court ruled unanimously that Nixon must turn over the tape recordings of 64 White House conversations, rejecting the president's claims of executive privilege. Three days later on 27 July the House Judiciary Committee passed the first of three articles of impeachment, charging obstruction of justice. Though Jason probably had no clue about any of this, even the usually politically deaf pig pilots were starting to take notice. Nine and I talked about it; everyone in Phnom Penh was talking about it. It became a hotter topic than the war.

Gerald Who?

We all heard the news that President Nixon would resign. Some said they would stay up and listen to VOA or BBC for the confirmation. They already had heard his speech announcing he would resign. I decided that the outcome was pretty much determined. The time of resignation announced. I decided I would go to bed at my normal hour and learn about it tomorrow from the short-wave radio.

When I awoke the following morning, we had a new president. Nobody knew anything about him. He was not elected. He became vice president when Spiro Agnew resigned. Later that day when I talked with some of my friends in the Air Attachés office they were laughing. There was a critical shortage of pictures of the new president which were supposed to be displayed all over the place. People were running around trying to make copies of copies. It was a hoot.

Disneyland And Deadlines

Karen had made it very clear that under no circumstances was Jason to be late for school opening in September. Clearly, being late was not an option. I made arrangements for tickets for the three of us.

Our tickets were routed Phnom Penh, Singapore, Hawaii, Los Angeles. We did not plan any sightseeing till we got to Los Angeles. This would allow us to get Jason home just in time for his birthday and school. I was scheduled to fly till the very last day. Not only did Nine have to pack, she had to go pick up the tickets.

After finishing my final flight of the day, I had a note in my box saying Cy wanted me to stop by his place before going home. When I met him, he asked if I would be interested in checking on the new airplane we had in Ft. Lauderdale. It had already been there for some time going through a U.S. registration process. Everybody felt like it should be going much faster. However since we had not left anybody there overseeing the work, it was a little like giving the fox the keys to the hen house. Cy said SEAAT would pay all our expenses and keep me on basic monthly flying guarantee while I was with the plane. I required no persuasion. This would be a good chance for

Nine to see another part of the U.S. Nine was excited about that, yet anxious about meeting my father and friends for the first time.

Nine's Arrest Warrant

As we were getting ready for our departure, one of Nine's family friends came to her and cautioned her about leaving. He said the Minister of Interior had issued an order saying she should be arrested if she tried to leave the country. Through Bong Hut's connections we soon obtained a copy of the order…written in French, saying just that. If she tried to leave the country…seize her. There was no question, it was because of her father who had already joined Sihanouk's party in the jungle to take part in the resistance movement. I thought it rather unfair to extend this sanction to Prince Phurissara's twenty-four-year-old daughter. Like whose side did they think she was on? The newspaper article was slandering her because she was married to an "American CIA pilot." Now they are accusing her of being a communist sympathizer! Childish logic…but then that's how the entire war was run. Why should I be surprised?

Another Trip To The Embassy

Armed with a copy of the arrest warrant, I headed to the embassy. First to see my friend Jack McCarthy again. Nine was starting to get famous at the embassy…or perhaps infamous. Jack took one look at the paper and just shook his head. "This is over my pay grade" he remarked and picked up the phone. He called the ambassador's office. They told him the ambassador had a few minutes between appointments and could see us. Jack took me up to his office. He was newly arrived and had only been there three or four months. His name was John Dean. He was polite but not overly friendly. He didn't need anyone to translate it for him. It was obvious this was a distraction he did not need. He picked up the phone, called H.E. SU Sonn, Le Directeur General de la Police Nationale. He was put right through. In a less than pleasant tone of voice he told SU Sonn that he was to rescind that order immediately, and she was to be allowed to leave the country. He thanked him and hung up. Ambassador Dean then turned to me and said he had better never see her face in this country again. I replied…Mr. Ambassador, I can assure you, you will not. Nine and I kept my word to Ambassador Dean. She returned thirty-three years later in 2007.

As we walked back to Jack's office I said, "well it appears I owe you again." He just smiled.

Few Goodbyes

Though not yet having a plan on how we would get around the issue of bringing Nine back into Cambodia, we planned to try to bring her back. Like everyone else, we did not comprehend the brutality that would come upon Cambodia when the inevitable fall of Lon Nol's regime came. We believed she would return relatively soon. With this in mind, Nine did not want to unnecessarily upset her family with a big tearful goodbye scene. Without any doubt, Bong Hut was happy to see her getting out of there. Although he, like almost everyone else, was convinced the U.S. backed Lon Nol regime would fall and be replaced by some form of socialism-communism based government, none correctly comprehended how brutal the Khmer Rouge would be. This miscalculation eventually cost him and his siblings their lives. Nine would be the sole exception.

Nine said the minimum number of goodbyes and we headed for the airport. We were both very concerned what would happen when we went through immigration control at the airport. Jack McCarty had asked me if I wanted him to come along but I'd said no, that we should be OK. There was a U.S. Air Force master-sergeant with a radio link to the Air Attaché's office on alert if things started to go south but praise God, we didn't need it.

Few takeoffs have brought such relief. I kept discretely looking out the window hoping not to see a jeep pulling up to block the plane before we could get airborne. When I heard the gear come up and the gear doors finally close, I breathed a huge sigh of relief.

Welcome To America & Happy 10th Birthday

We were in California. We stayed at a hotel near Disney Land and rented a convertible. I wanted to get Jason a birthday gift and he had expressed some interest in a guitar. We went to a pawnshop just off Hollywood Boulevard that had a sizable inventory of guitars. Each guitar probably a testimony to once aspiring musicians with hope of becoming a star in tensile town. Jason settled on a Fender Mustang.

We drove up and down Hollywood Boulevard in the convertible, Nine & Jason eating strawberries and checking out all the characters parading up and down the sidewalks. To say this sidewalk cast of characters was unusual would be kind. I wondered what the people in Hamilton would think if some of them went walking about the square on a Saturday afternoon. You could sell tickets to watch that I mused.

Our visit to Disneyland was fun. Nine and I enjoyed it as much as Jason. I did have an embarrassing moment however late in the evening. Unknown to me, they had a fireworks show each evening. I was not facing the direction of the display when it began. A very loud explosion accompanied the rockets pyrotechnics. I dropped to the ground instinctively. People all around us must have thought I'd lost my mind. It seemed I'd brought Cambodia along on our vacation. I would carry it around for many years.

Nine's First Hamilton Experience

We made it back to Hamilton in time for school. Nine met my father, some of my friends who were still around Hamilton, many of my father's friends and she met Karen.

I could tell all of this was a little overwhelming for Nine. While she was raised in an aristocratic home, this was nevertheless culture shock. Hamilton still had real cowboys…well ranchers and ranch hands. She may have thought they only existed in the movies.

The view from the other side of the window must have been equally strange. People found themselves face to face with a real Cambodian. Some had never seen an Asian except in the movies. Almost all of them only had a general idea where Cambodia was, and of course some were clueless. I found it particularly trying while at the same time amusing when we would be somewhere together and someone I knew would walk up and introduce themselves to her. But when they had a question for her…they would turn and ask me. I had to swallow my impulse to semi-sarcastically tell them "why don't you ask her…she can talk…she speaks English, French, and her own language Khmer." But I didn't because I knew and understood them…in my innermost being, I was them.

A Letter From Cy

While we were in Hamilton a letter from Cy arrived. The situation was getting even more desperate back in Cambodia. The blockage of land routes was tightening. The rainy season would soon be over, and the fighting would intensify as troops could move about more easily. Things would almost certainly get even worse. The embassy was letting more contracts. According to Cy, another proprietary airline, Bird Air, had just landed a very lucrative contract flying C-130s into Phnom Penh trying to keep the swelling population fed. Cy wanted me to get out to Ft. Lauderdale and push to get our C-54 out of maintenance and back to Cambodia. Nine and I would leave Hamilton a few days later heading to Florida.

A Deal On Wheels

I knew I did not want to fly to Florida. While Cy and asked me to hurry, I wanted Nine to have the experience of seeing the eastern half of the United States from the road rather than from thirty-five thousand feet. I would use the same ploy I'd used when I left for the Congo the first time. I would drive somebody's car so they could fly. The trick would be finding one that needed to go to Ft. Lauderdale.

Fortune shown upon us and we found one wanting to go to Pompano Beach only 25 miles north of Ft. Lauderdale airport. Nine and I were excited. The contract allowed us five days to deliver the car which was more than enough time. We packed our meager wardrobes picked up our car, another convertible, and headed toward Florida.

The Scenic Route

Gas was cheap, we were young and in love, and for the first time in recent memory, the depressing, brutal fog of war was not all-encompassing. I was a new person. I was happy; the sun was golden; the grass was green; the breeze was gentle. I was not going to waste a second of this. We turned south toward Houston and from there all the way through Louisiana, Mississippi, Alabama and deep into Florida exploring the old South via Highway 90 enjoying each and every stoplight.

Somewhere not too far from the Louisiana Texas state line, Nine saw sugar cane for sale at a roadside stand. She made me stop and get her some. She showed me how to strip it with my teeth. She chewed on its sweet fiber for hours. We enjoyed the old southern mansions and huge, stately, moss draped oaks, the bejeweled magnolias, the lagoons and bayous. This was healing my soul. God knows I needed it.

Ft. Lauderdale

We dropped the convertible off at the owner's house, picked up a cheap, by the week rate subcompact rental car and started looking for an affordable motel close to the airport. We found just the perfect spot on U.S. 1 in Dania Beach just a couple of miles south of the airport. The snow birds had not arrived yet from Canada, so the summer rates were still going. The room was small, clean, with a little kitchenette. There was a pool and shuffleboard of all things just outside our door. I was an entirely different person away from the war. Nine was still adapting to our western culture but she enjoyed seeing me in a more relaxed mode even more.

The Airplane

We purposefully had not told the maintenance facility that we would have someone arriving to check on the plane. I carried a letter on SEAAT letterhead signed by Roger saying I was authorized to act for the company.

Nine and I took a drive around the airport as soon as we got unpacked. I found the maintenance facility and spotted our DC-4 (C-54) sitting outside on the ramp. I knew enough about airports and maintenance facilities to know it had not been touched in a while. I got out and went up to the fence to get a closer look. Basically it was just gathering dust.

The following morning I went to the maintenance facility and introduced myself to the owner whose name I'd gotten from Cy and to whom the letter was addressed. He was a pushy rude New Yorker. There was an almost instant animosity. I hated situations like that as it almost guarantees there will be no meaningful cooperation. However, he already knew he had a problem. He had taken a sizable prepayment for the work he was supposed to be doing and then as soon as Cy had left, he pushed our aircraft to the back and started taking in new business to get fresh money.

By halfway through the afternoon, I'd already learned by walking around the hanger floor and talking to his mechanics that there were serious money and morale issues. I'd ascertained the work package was roughly only sixty percent complete. The owner was saying he needed us to pay him even more money before he could start seriously working on the plane again. I sent a telegram back to Cy late that afternoon. I was still working my way through all the signed off maintenance tasks and it was obvious he had been padding the man-hours. My initial assessment was we could easily find ourselves in a difficult situation if in fact we were not already there. He was demanding more money before serious resumption of the work. Would that be throwing good money after bad? I was glad this was not my call. I waited for my instructions. While waiting, Nine and I explored Ft. Lauderdale and Hollywood. It was a bit touristy but still quite nice. We were both enjoying our time there.

Money And The FAA Arrive

One morning when I got to the airport two men wearing J.C. Penney short sleeve polyester shirts with ties to match were out at the airplane. A mechanic was bringing a ladder up to the number two engine for them. This could only be the FAA I thought. As I approached their matching name badges confirmed my suspicion.

After I'd stood there watching for a while and after one had climbed up on the ladder and with the help of a flashlight had read the serial number from the engine's data plate to his associate on the ground. They were checking to see if the engine on the airplane matched what the engine log showed. Apparently, they matched. Then they turned to me and asked if I was with this airplane. "Well, that depends on what you find" I said with a smile. The other guy replied "I don't suspect we'll be finding much…it seems you guys have some friends in pretty high places. We got a call saying go easy." "Well, that's very interesting" I replied.

The conversation then shifted to what it was like flying over there. I replied that that was interesting as well. They asked if we ever got shot at like in Vietnam, to which I replied, "every once in a while." They then asked where we got our major maintenance done. I gave them the name of our primary facility in Bangkok and our backup facility in Taiwan. They jotted both places down in their notes. They left soon afterwards. As they were walking away, I decided I liked them better than I did the owner of the maintenance facility.

A couple of days later they stopped back by the hanger. Apparently, they had a pretty light schedule. The one who had asked the maintenance facility question commented that he had looked the places up in their directory. He mentioned that nobody had ever heard of them, but they had the highest levels of FAA certification and that there was just about nothing they were not licensed to work on. I answered that I believed they were owned by this friend in high places. This time they laughed.

Locked Gates And Security Guards

The work dragged on at a snail's pace. I was constantly hearing they were having trouble finding parts for the plane. I asked where everybody else was getting them which was not well received. The complaints from the mechanics on the hanger floor were becoming more intense. They indicated their pay was late. I was pretty sure we weren't getting our parts because they weren't being ordered because they had no money to pay for them. I sent another Western Union to Cy telling him I was very concerned.

A couple of days later when I drove up to the hanger, the gates were closed and chained. Security guards were guarding the gate. I walked up to them and said I needed in, that we had an aircraft inside. They said there was a court order…nobody was allowed in and nothing…repeat absolutely nothing…not even a sheet of paper was coming out. A bank had foreclosed and was going to dispose of the assets. I went to the bank and was directed to one of their officers. He confirmed that they had foreclosed and that I may or may not be able to get our airplane back but that would not be until court proceedings and advised me that probably would not be anytime soon. He was very nice but very specific and sure of their legal rights…at least as he understood them. I left him the phone number of our motel.

This time I called Cy. He said he hadn't trusted the owner of that company since the first day he met him but had few other options. Cy said he would contact "the customer" and let them take care of it. "The customer" was slang for the agency.

A couple of days later the banker called me back and told me I could remove the aircraft. Cy had given me the name of a man on the airport who would let me park the aircraft there. I contacted the man and he had a tug go over to the maintenance facility and tow the airplane over to his ramp.

I called Cy and told him the aircraft was safe on the ramp and asked what I should do now. He said go back home to Texas and return here as soon as you can. I asked if I could stay Christmas at home then return. Of course, he agreed. Nine and I checked out of our little place and headed back home to Texas.

A Texas Christmas

Nine and I spent Christmas with my father, Jason, and Jenny then Camille and her husband Travis. Seeing them in the Christmas environment was both joyful and sad. Yet it beat the hell out of another Christmas in Cambodia.

Right after Christmas I left for Cambodia. Nine stayed back in Hamilton with my father. This would be an ineffaceable period in both our memories.

The Dry-Season Offensive
The Beginning Of The End

Like every year, the rains had stopped in October. They would not return till sometime in April. The winds picked up and quickly dried the ground facilitating troop and equipment movements. Rockets rather than rain now fell on Phnom Penh.

The Khmer Rouge had been planning and preparing for their dry-season offensive for months. Phnom Penh had long been in their stranglehold. They planned for this massive dry-season offensive operation to be the final blow that would bring the Lon Nol government to its knees. By the time I arrived back in Phnom Penh, it was evident the Khmer Rouge offensive was in full swing.

For practical purposes, the Khmer Rouge controlled the banks of the Mekong which at this time was significantly less wide due to no rain. This rendered the civilian convoys, even with military escorts, much easier targets, almost sitting ducks. The convoys would form up in Vietnam at the mouth of the Mekong to make their run up the river to Phnom Penh. Many convoys never made it. Some operators refused to risk their boats and crews, some had to turn back, and some were sunk due to enemy fire and mines.

For practical purposes the Khmer rouge controlled all the highways in Cambodia. Virtually nothing could reach Phnom Penh by road. What rice crops remained in the country were rapidly falling into the hands of the Khmer Rouge.

Food and fuel were in critical supply. The local airlines were operating from dawn to dusk into every airport still open. Many were comparing the situation to the Berlin Airlift. The U.S. was pouring aid money into the airlift but even with the infusion of money, not enough food was moving into Phnom Penh. The only thing that seemed to be reaching the city in significant quantities was refugees; the population fleeing the fighting. It was like they were running from the edge of the target directly to the bull's-eye.

Phnom Penh—City Of Sorrow

I was not prepared for what I saw when I stepped off the plane at Phnom Penh's Pochentong airport. It looked like half the aircraft on the ramp were not flyable; many of the non-flyable ones appeared to be damaged by rockets.

Tension at the airport was high. Nobody strolled across the ramp anymore; everybody scurried. Many of the pilots were now wearing flak jackets and some wore helmets. I expected things to be worse, but nothing like this.

As I walked into flight operations it was lit only by a small Colman type light. No power; generators had been redirected to more critical areas. I chatted with one of the pilots for a few minutes. He related how things had deteriorated in the four months I'd been gone.

I bummed a ride to the SEAAT office from with one of the mechanics. Roger's father had come to Cambodia to help out. I'd never met him, but we'd heard all about each other. He immediately handed me a stack of $100 notes which Roger had instructed him to give me as a payment on some of my expenses while I was in the states. Roger was out of country trying to get more airplanes, but lessors willing to allow their aircraft to fly into Cambodia were apparently few and far between. He said that the only insurance we could get was through Lloyds of London and our coverage was for one week at a time renewable at their option on a weekly basis…a significant indicator of the risk level they believed existed for airplanes and those in them. Roger's dad advised that flying had been a little slow for the moment and they had more pilots than they had airplanes to fly. He assured me my seniority would guarantee me flight hours as long as we could keep the planes flying. They were just getting shot up and hit by rockets faster than they could be repaired or replaced. I told him I'd need a couple of days to get my personal affairs organized and I'd be ready. He called the SEAAT car to take me home. While waiting for the car I asked about Cy. Was he still here? Roger's dad said Cy was away in Bangkok doing the same thing as Roger…looking for airplanes. He said SEAAT had unofficially setup an office in BKK, operating more or less out of the Nana Hotel. This put him close to the embassy guys that were calling the shots for our operation here in Phnom Penh.

Our Villa

The driver remembered where I lived. As we moved through downtown Phnom Penh, there were noticeably fewer cars. As a matter of fact, mostly motos and bicycles. All along the sides of the road people were selling gasoline and diesel fuel in one-liter bottles. There were long lines at what few gas stations remained open. Many had closed due to the inability to get fuel and the corruption money required to get the delivery. I found it amazing that micro-economies were managing to flourish in the midst of these shortages and skyrocketing prices. At one roadside stand I saw several one-liter bottles filled with the distinctive 140 octane aviation fuel our Convairs required. It could only have come from the airport. Theft of the precious fuel had been a problem long before I left for the states. I imagined the problem must be tenfold now.

As the driver turned off Monivong Street and onto the street where our villa was, I could feel waves of depression washing over me. This was our home…now it was an empty villa. We had gone leaving two maids with operating funds for about six weeks. That was four months ago. I wondered if anyone would still be there. The driver honked as we approached the gate. In a few seconds, while I was still trying to get the gate to open, I heard the sound of flip-flops scurrying down the driveway. Wow, somebody was still here.

In a few seconds I saw the big eyes and semi-toothless mouth of Ien, one of our maids. She was so excited to see me. She had tears…I hoped they were tears of joy.

I started dragging my bags from the trunk of the Mercedes. She insisted on carrying the heaviest one herself. As we made our way into the living room, I saw it was spotless. Perfectly swept and dusted; everything in place just as when we had left. Upstairs in our salon-bedroom, everything was just as we'd left it. There too spotlessly clean.

I asked her where the younger maid Yaran was. She informed me that Yaran's husband had been sent to another district with the army and as with so many poor military families, she had followed him. I asked her if she had run out of money. She replied that she had but that she had gone to Bong Hut's house and they had given her money to buy food and keep the electric bill paid…which should have been almost nothing since we never had electricity anymore anyway.

I had no idea how much Nine and paid her every month I handed her one of the $100 bills and asked her to go buy food for a couple of days and keep the rest as her salary. She didn't want to take the money but when I insisted, she pressed her hands together in the traditional *sampeah* gesture of respect then hurried off to get something for me to eat. At this time of the day, I figured it would come from some street-side restaurant where the poorer locals ate. I didn't mind.

I went back upstairs and began to unpack. Ien soon returned with two large bottles of San Miguel in a plastic bucket filled with ice and a glass. She was so proud of herself. She then hurried back down to the outdoor kitchen to start setting up my meal. She knew I would tell her when I was ready to come down and eat.

I took the two San Miguel beers and went out on the upstairs veranda. That too was spotless. I walked over to the edge of the veranda to survey the neighborhood. As I was standing there, a Volkswagen Beetle was driving past. In it I recognized my friend Allen Green (pseudonym) with World Vision. He saw me at the same time. He stopped, backed up and turned into the drive. I went down to meet him.

Allen was late to an engagement but stayed long enough to tell me that he and his wife had divorced, and he was back in country alone still working on the World Vision hospital construction project. I told him that I'd left Nine back in the states with my father and I'd only been back in the house about thirty minutes. Allen immediately asked me what I was going to do living in this big house all alone. I told him I hadn't really given that any thought, but that it was something I would need to address in the very near future. He told me he was living alone in a large three story house himself and asked me if I'd like to come stay with him. He said if I'd like to share half the food costs, he would be very happy to have the company. The house was provided as part of his World Vision contract anyway. I told him I was interested and maybe we could talk more about it tomorrow. He said that would be perfect and he'd be by to pick me up the following afternoon.

We said goodbye and I went back up on the veranda to finish my beer and watch it get dark. I brought my banjo out of the bedroom. It felt strange in my hands. Enormous sadness came over me as I visualized Nine sitting beside me listening to me play. I stared at the place where she used to sit and wondered why I'd come back. I wished I had one of my special blend Dunhills, but I didn't.

I called down from the bedroom's back window to the kitchen below telling Ien I was ready to eat. Five minutes later I sat down at the dining table. I ran my hand underneath the table to insure the 45 was still there; it was. While I ate the rather decent impromptu meal Ien had put together I stared at the empty chair directly across from me where Nine always sat. This place sucked and I knew I needed to get out of it at the earliest possible moment.

After my meal I returned back upstairs. Ien had the kerosene lamp lit and sitting in its usual place. I tuned the FM radio to Armed Forces Radio Saigon and finished my remaining San Miguel, watching the sometimes-flickering light of the lamp dance on the walls and ceiling.

Later, after the news and more music, I got into the bed beside the empty spot where Nine always slept. As I drifted off to sleep, I questioned why I'd come back. It was now clear to me and almost everyone else here that we would soon lose this war. Why did I feel I needed to be a part of finishing a war we were clearly destined to lose? Could I possibly influence the outcome, even in a small way…No. Could I help any of the Cambodian people suffering so terribly…No, at least not in the grand scope of things…perhaps momentarily, but I could contribute nothing of lasting value. So, why was I here? I pulled the sheet around me (not because I was cold but as some protection from the mosquitoes) and prayed for sleep without the terrifying dreams. Sleep was light as it always had been; inbound rockets and outbound artillery plus the sound of exploding 500-pound bombs being dropped from Cambodian Air Force T-28s punctuated the night. The next-door rooster's 4:30am crowing heralded the end of that night's battle with sleep.

The World Vision House

The next morning, I went to pay the back rent owed on the villa. I paid only up through the end of the month. I wasn't yet sure about moving in with Allen, but I was sure I could not continue to live in the villa without Nine. I also knew I would not be happy in the frolicking atmosphere of the Sokhalay Hotel where all the bachelor status pilots stayed. I was pretty sure I could go stay with Nine's family, but I didn't want to do that either. My presence there would be a security liability.

In the middle of the afternoon Allen arrived. I was glad to see him. As we drove to his place, he continuously pointed out new rocket strikes and new shantytowns populated with newly-arrived refugees from the provinces. No work, no food, surviving on the handouts of relief organizations, these tragic victims had lost their past and could see no future. Life for them was frozen in the terrible endless moment.

As we approached the gate of the World Vision villa, Allen honked the horn and soon the iron gate swung open. Cambodia's automatic gate-openers needed no batteries…who said this was a backward country. A middle-aged man had opened it. Allen explained he was the husband of the cook and maid. He served as a gardener and also helped with the housecleaning. Allen said they were Christians. World Vision was a Christian relief organization and their policy was to hire Christians where they could.

The house was nice with a large living room and dining room. Upstairs were several bedrooms. Allen occupied one…the others were empty. Unlike my villa where the kitchen was outside with the maid's quarters, the kitchen here was inside. The cook/maid was a plump middle aged very pleasant lady. She was busy cooking on a kerosene stove. I was immediately uncomfortable with that as my childhood memories hosted several incidents where kerosene cook stoves had exploded seriously injuring or killing people and burning down houses. Life here was a calculated risk; just here the acceptable level of risk was off the scale by normal standards. I figured the odds here higher that I'd be unlucky enough to be were a rocket landed rather than beside that stove when it blew up.

Allen showed me the rest of the house. My mind was made up. It was relatively close to the SEAAT office and on the way to the airport. Plus, Nine's memories weren't tied to everything in the place. I told Allen I would be so happy to take his offer. He asked me if I wanted to go get my stuff and come back that night, but I said no, I need to work things out with Ien first but the day after that would be fine. Allen drove me back to the Villa.

Saying Goodbye To Our Cambodia Home

Ien met me at the gate and we walked together to the house. I really felt bad for her as I knew she seriously needed this job. We walked into the living room and I asked her to sit down with me. But by Cambodian tradition, she refused and remained standing in front of me. I explained to her that I would be moving in with Mr. Allen and I would be closing the villa. I told her that I could not take her with me as Mr. Allen already had a maid. She had tears in her eyes. I felt terrible as well. I gave her an additional fifty dollars which was probably almost two months pay and gave her a little hug. I asked if she had cold beer and my special Dunhills for me and she smiled, wiped her eyes, nodded yes and scurried away.

As I walked upstairs, I felt like I was betraying those close to me. It was like I was trying to write a song about my life, and nothing was rhyming…nothing. I couldn't see any useful purpose in anything I was doing. Had I come to love the Cambodian people…yes. Was I doing good here…yes. But in the end, would any of it make any difference? From my present vantage point I couldn't see that it would.

I took solace knowing that in a few minutes I'd be on the upstairs veranda, beer and banjo in hand. My special blend Dunhills helping turn this jumble of thoughts into lyrics with powerful, structured meter; at least till the rooster crowed and morning's light returned exposing the tear-stained blank page.

My New House–My New Roommate

I was up early, I was completely packed before 9:00am. There was little to pack. The kitchen stuff that belonged to us I gave to Ien. Nine's personal clothing I packed in some of our unused suitcases. All my "home defense hardware" I packed into a couple of duffle bags and dribbled it downstairs. Allen sent a World Vision pickup to the house and I loaded it all up. I took all my military radio equipment but had to leave an antenna up on the roof as I simply wasn't in the mood to climb up on the roof to retrieve it. I could easily get another with all the coax from the Air Force guys. I had failed to mention to Allen the extent of my "hardware." Due to the fact that Allen worked for a Christian relief agency, he was seen in the eyes of many as a missionary, albeit a bit of a cowboy one. He had already proven he had a propensity toward adventure from some of his Vietnam stories so I figured he wouldn't really have a problem with my stuff as long as I kept them in relatively low profile.

Just being in the new surroundings had an immediate uplifting experience. I didn't see Nine around everything in this house as I had back in our villa. I did not see her in the bed beside me. The empty hole in my chest was larger and ached more than anytime previously. But Allen provided some relief. He was genuinely funny and we got along well.

My First Flight Gets Cancelled

A couple of days later I was on the schedule to make my first flight since returning back in country. When I arrived at the airport the operations manager met me saying they had been trying to call me on the radio to stop me from coming. That our plane took shrapnel from a rocket attack the previous night and was not flyable. Well, the radio they had been trying to get to answer was still in a box in the corner of my new bedroom. When I asked how badly, they replied it was quite serious. They said it would take several days to finish if they could get all the parts.

When I walked out on the ramp...without flak-jacket, I saw we were not the only casualties. It got some stuff on the military ramp and another C-47 on our side. It was hard to tell the fresh casualties from all the other collection of damaged aircraft increasingly collecting on the ramp. The enemy was within three miles of the airport and according to many sources could send squads onto the airport at night anytime they wanted.

I decided to go back to the SEAAT office and have a talk with Roger's dad. As I walked into the office his face did not have its usual beaming smile. While I'd known the one that took the rocket hit last night was our last Convair, I did not know how bleak the outlook was for the new ones which were supposed to be coming any day. We could get the embassy contracts...we simply could not get the airplanes. The only ones coming into country were pure junk and were uninsured. SEAAT was not going to play that game.

The situation was obvious, but I asked the question anyway. "So, how does this affect me?" Roger's dad replied, they could buy my ticket back home if I wanted to go back now, or I could wait on standby with only housing and food allowance with no pay to see if more aircraft came. I told him I'd tell him in a day or so, thanked him sincerely, and headed back to the World Vision house. But before I left, I used the phone and called the embassy and arranged another antenna and coax for my radio. This was no time to be without communication.

An Employment Offer From World Vision

I was busy unpacking my military issue PRC radio and the amplified CB radio which I used to communicate with some groups when Allen came in for lunch. The hospital project was just about three minutes away on motorbike, so he generally just rode the moto to the jobsite and left the VW in the drive. When I told him about the Convair taking a rocket the night before and my immediate flying prospects on hold, he smiled and said that that was quite a coincidence as he had just been talking to his country manager about me and his boss had asked if I would be interested in helping with the hospital project. He said he had money in the budget and could hire me immediately as Allen's assistant and the number two man on the project. I remember my immediate thought being...God has a plan. At the very moment my aviation employment appeared to be ending, a job opening in my military specialty fell into my lap. I was truly amazed at this turn of events. I asked when I could start; Allen replied...how about tomorrow morning. We shook hands and headed for the kitchen table for lunch.

After lunch Allen took me up on the roof. This house, like many Cambodian villas, had a large flat roof with about a one-meter high wall all the way around; perfect for sitting on. As we were walking about, I noticed there was another bedroom. It was probably intended as some type of maid's quarters. I opened the door and looked in. It had large windows on both sides providing a good airflow. Most of the time there was no air-conditioning anyway because fuel for the diesel generator was rightfully being diverted to World Vision's Enfant Rehydration Center in Toul Kork. I asked Allen if I could sleep up there rather than in the bedroom. He said pick your poison; there'll be plenty of mosquitoes in either one. I said I'd like to try out the rooftop suite first. We had a good laugh.

The rooftop provided a view of the World Vision Hospital construction site. The surrounding area was not built-up at that time so you could look out onto rice paddies. I immediately liked the rooftop and decided that would be my replacement for the balcony at our villa. But just thinking about that made me miss Nine.

A Visit To Bong Hut's

After I'd finished unpacking and setting up my PRC-25 radio, my CB base station with amplifier and putting my "black brick" on charge, I took a shower, hopped on the moto and headed to Nine's oldest brother's house. Allan had said to consider the moto mine and if I needed the car just ask. Setting up the radios had been much easier than I'd originally envisioned as being on the rooftop, all I had to do was climb up on top of my bedroom and strap the antennas in place with wire. I let the coax hang down the wall and threaded them through the window screen. My rooftop palace was complete.

I was happy to see Nine's family and of course they were excited to learn all about how she was doing and see the small handful of pictures I'd brought back. Bong Hut and I soon moved away from the mass of chattering women and launched into hushed conversation about how the war was going and the pathetic state of the government.

Night of Carnage

A couple of days later, around 10:30 at night, Allen and I were up on the roof after dinner watching the AC-130 gunships as they targeted Khmer Rouge positions probably no more than four or five miles from our house. Suddenly my radio started going off. It was one of the guys from the Air Attaché's office. They knew I'd moved in with Allen (since I'd just put the bite on them for a new antenna and coax cable). They said that the airport had been hit a few minutes ago with a barrage of 122s (Chinese and/or Russian made rockets used by the Khmer Rouge) and there had been a lot of casualties. Some of the Cambodian Air Force medics had loaded a couple that were still alive but critically wounded into a jeep and rushed them to the World Vision Pediatric Rehydration Center, located in Toul Kork, which was the closest medical facility to the airport. They obviously didn't understand the facility was for treating infants. They saw the European nurses and figured this would do. Dropped them in the driveway and rushed back to the airport. I've forgotten how, but they knew I was a navy trained medic. They wanted us to go out and try to get them on into Phnom Penh and to Calmette Hospital…at the time the largest medical facility in the country. Allen and I headed for the World Vision pickup. We paused to grab our emergency bags (for personal use) then headed for the Rehydration Center.

When we arrived two World Vision nurses had just arrived as well. We quickly loaded the blood soaked two soldiers into the back of the pickup. Allen drove and I rode in the back with the two nurses. One had a sucking chest wound where shrapnel had ripped a huge hole. His color was ashen, and I wondered how the wound was still sucking…he looked like he was dead already. He lay in a huge pool or blood. One of the nurses was trying to cover the hole with a compress.

The other soldier had his leg barely attached by tissue just above his knee. Blood was spurting from everywhere. The second terrified nurse was frantically and mindlessly digging around in the emergency supplies trying to get an IV bottle and an IV set. My evil twin barked at her that if she didn't control the *obscenity* bleeding there would be no need for the *obscenity* IV she was trying to start. Stop the *obscenity* bleeding!!! I realized a few seconds later that she was a pediatric nurse assigned to the pediatric rehydration center, not a trauma nurse or a trained surgical technician like I was. I then realized if I didn't try immediately to stabilize her, I'd be trying to save this poor guy alone. I reached over and patted her hand as the pickup lunged forward into the dark Toul Kork street. I ask her to get some hemostats out of the bag, the largest ones she could find, and some gauze called sponges. I instructed her to sponge the site where the blood was spurting then quickly remove the sponge and I would clamp. After about the third or fourth bleeder we were functioning as a team. I could see her relaxing. But we were going to lose the guy if we didn't get the bleeding stopped. He looked at me and said in Khmer "aoh hayoy choeung khyom"…my leg is gone. I reassured him in my best Khmer he was not going to die, although I didn't believe it. Three or four minutes later we had the bleeding slowed enough that she could start the IV. How she miraculously managed to find a vein in the back of that pickup bouncing over gravel roads slipping and sliding in the blood-soaked pickup bed is beyond me. But God was with her and she did.

Somehow, we arrived at the hospital with both solders still alive. I was not prepared for the sight that awaited us as we pulled up to Calmett's emergency room. The hall leading to the surgical suites was full of gurneys. They must have run out of gurneys because dead and dying solders were lying all over the floor in pools of blood. The doctors, I was later told, hadn't slept in two days. It was obvious that more would-be patients were dying waiting to see a doctor than were being saved. There were no units of blood…no nothing. My head was reeling…my mind was going into message unit overload again. My first thought was to stay and try to help…but there was no more space to work and no more instruments or supplies…no more sterilized instruments, no more units of blood, no more treatment rooms, no more nurses, no more doctors. No *obscenity* nothing. I left the building walking like a zombie and went and sat down on the front seat of the pickup. My blood-soaked clothing leaving marks like the strokes of some Absinthe crazed artist's blood red paint strokes all over the World Vision pickup seats. I see it today as clearly as I saw it then. The nurse squeezed in beside me. She was gentle, offering what comfort she could. I could tell by the look in her eyes this could go beyond comfort. Allen and I dropped them off at their house. I wasn't in the mood to be comforted. Allen and I drove home in silence. The soldier's blood was starting to make my pants and shirt stick to my skin. I needed a very long shower. Somehow, I knew that all the water in the world wasn't going to wash the feeling of his drying blood off my skin. Shakespeare's words from Macbeth flashed through my mind with typical Jacks sarcasm…"out damned spot." When I left the shower, I wrapped my blood-soaked clothes in a newspaper I found in the kitchen and buried them as deeply as I could in the kitchen trash can. How did I *obscenity* get to this *obscenity* state. Images of the night were fast-forwarding through my mind. An *Inferno* of my own creation; a hell even Dante could not have imagined…all without coercion from others…save that demon within…never experiencing satisfaction…always demanding more. I could have been back in Hamilton with Nine. I wondered at what point, after he had finished with me, Satan or his demon would discard me to my own destruction. In the shower that night…my very long shower…I prayed.

Final Flight Of The Phnom Penh Pig Pilots

This, now famous band of merry men, while not disbanding, reluctantly receded into their own footnote in history. Usually in now declassified documents gathering dust in university libraries devoted to the Vietnam War effort.

It was the end of March 1975. Although the spirit of the courageous band of brothers who self-effacingly referred to themselves as Phnom Penh Pig Pilots was still unbroken, for them the war was lost. There were no more planes to fly; no more airports in which to operate. All had been destroyed by the Khmer Rouge. The American Embassy started putting pressure on all "non-essential" Americans to leave the country to lessen the burden of the evacuation which by now was a foregone conclusion. This once vital bunch of aviation misfits and heroes had now been reduced to "non-essential." The plans for Operation Eagle Pull had been drawn up and rehearsed countless times. Everyone knew their part. The time had come for those, no longer essential in maintaining the official U.S. presence in Cambodia to leave the country. That last ignominious moment was imminent, looming over every aspect of our lives.

All had come to love Cambodia. Many had come to love Cambodian women. In most cases, reality would dictate they leave both behind.

One by one they said their goodbyes and made their way back to where they planned to await the next war. Many went to Bangkok, many stayed in South East Asia. A few went back to the U.S. The famous *dogs of war*, or *canis bellatorus* faded into the mist until summoned again. All leaving significant pieces of themselves behind, mostly lost forever.

In the final moments as Operation Eagle Pull began, there would be a handful, who by personal miscalculations, would miss Eagle Pull and be left behind.

All the Pig Pilots and other ground support people who missed the evacuation eventually made it to safety. One, reportedly walked through the jungle all the way to Thailand. He later told reporters the trek took a month. Two others took refuge in the Le Royal Hotel and were among those few foreigners released by the Khmer Rouge. They found safety in Thailand. One of those two was our great protector Donald Aaron Samson III (pseudonym) who had purposefully stayed behind to bobby-trap our offices and reek other forms of havoc. He later told me he had also bobby-trapped the toilets. Ironically…most of the KR had never seen an indoor toilet. These two who took refuge in the Le Royal Hotel would later see their experience portrayed in the 1984 movie, The Killing Fields.

Dancing With The Devil…Fiddling While Rome Burned

The Khmer Rouge had Phnom Penh surrounded. The highways into and out of Phnom Penh were blocked; the Mekong was totally blockaded; all that came in and went out of Phnom Penh came by military airlift. Phnom Penh was the only airport in the country not controlled by the Khmer Rouge, and by night many would say they controlled Phnom Penh's airport as well. The Pig Pilots were gone. U.S. Air Force C-130 transports were the sole source. The Khmer Rouge were only minutes outside Phnom Penh's center. Day and night rockets rained down on the city. Civilians were the targets. Their strategy…to terrorize the civilian population in order to use them as yet another weapon to bring down the government. My mind was scarcely able to comprehend all the carnage. I could feel my mind temporarily taking time-outs when the sights became too much. The timeouts were starting to become more frequent. I knew the time for me to go was approaching.

And yet in the midst of all this…the night clubs and bars were filled with revelers. Admittedly only a tiny fraction of the population of the city but nonetheless enough to pack them every night. It was impossible for those in such places not to know the evil that waited just outside the city; everyone knew. It was impossible for them not to see the death and destruction I saw every day. Some of the nocturnal revelers had even taken the Christmas song "Santa Clause Is Coming To Town and inserted the name of one of the bloodiest of the Khmer Rouge leaders as if to mock the reality of what was about to transpire. Each night they returned to inhale the smoke and cheap perfume the cities night clubs and bars offered; as if the alcohol and the arms of a bar girl would make reality go away. And who's to say, perhaps for some it did; at least until the dawn's first light.

To be perfectly honest, there was little difference between them and me, only modality. They sought refuge in the night clubs and bars, I, in solitude, the yellow dancing light of my old friend the kerosene lamp, beer, and magic herb. In rare moments, I would manage few a few lifeless strums on my faithful banjo. But there were no joyous licks like when Nine and I sat out on our balcony. Now just a few joyless cords, usually minor cords, which were very rare in five-string bluegrass type music. It was safe to say at this point I was semi-functional or probably more accurately expressed, basically dysfunctional. In order to protect what remained of my normal identity, I was progressively turning down the volume on what remained of my external senses. I knew I was messed up, but it would be many months, and in some cases years before I realized how far from normal I had gone.

My Departure Nears

On the morning of 6 April, I got a call on my black brick (Motorola walkie-talkie) saying to monitor the frequency closely. I knew what that meant. Our time was near. That came directly from the Air Attaché office. Later in the morning the World Vision country manager came by and said we would go out the following morning on a special embassy flight. We would be going to Bangkok. Pack light but bring out all critical papers, etc.; we would not be coming back.

Agonizing Goodbyes

I went to Bong Hut's house, Villa Darameth, at noon as I knew he would be coming home for his regular lunch and nap. My body and mind were numb. It was like I could see everybody's lips moving but there was no sound…like somebody had turned the volume all the way down.

I told him I had to go. We both knew this was the moment he and I had privately talked about for weeks. He asked me to take care of Nine. Tears were streaming down my face. I tried to regain my composure and go back out in the living room where everyone else was politely waiting. I explained that I would be going out in the morning but that this was just a precautionary move and we would all be back as soon as the situation got better. Everyone pretended they believed what I was saying. That was one of the most traumatic moments of my life. It will always remain so. I still remember it as if it were yesterday.

From Bong Hut's house I went to Srey Touch's house. This was Nine's only sister. When I walked in, she knew this was the day. I was wearing my flak jacket and carrying my black brick. She had only seen my flak jacket someplace on the floor or the back seat of our Mercedes, but this was the first time she'd seen me wearing it. Nine had left all the things she had from her mother with Srey Touch. I had come to take what I could. Her husband had asked if I could take her and the children with me on the flight but by this time there were no extra seats…none. I looked at all the silver vases and bowls, and countless other things. I took the jewelry, and a couple of silver bowls and vases that could fit in a pillow case. I had no idea Nine had all that stuff.

Srey Touch was recovering from a serious attack of malaria and had just come out of the hospital. She was still weak but was standing quietly sometimes politely looking at me when we spoke but mostly looking down toward the floor. My heart was breaking. Her three beautiful little children were standing beside her. I clasped my hands together in the traditional som pas and lowered my head slightly…she did the same. We both had tears in our eyes. She looked down in order not to show too much emotion. I gently kissed the top of her head, turned and walked out. Again tears streaming down my face. I got in the World Vision pickup and headed back to our house. My world was crashing down on me.

When I got to the house, I dragged Nine's things up the stairs and plopped them on the bed. I now had to try to go through all the things we had (most still in boxes on the floor) and figure out what we had to try to salvage. Like when your house is on fire and you have only seconds to grab the important things. But this time, I spent hours. It was like time stood still. Turning papers page by page, each document pulling my memories back to someplace in time.

Finally, I realized I was having a hard time seeing what I was doing. It was dark. I hadn't realized the time was passing. I walked down stairs in the dark. My meal was set out on the table by the maid before she had left; all covered with the little device they used to keep flies off food. I wasn't hungry. I just left it there. She could eat it in the morning herself. I went to the ice chest and got two cold beers and made my way back up to the roof. I stopped by the bedroom to get my black brick. I took the PRC25 with me. It should really be full of chatter this night. It was then that I realized I hadn't heard my radio in hours. It was now chattering and crackling like it always did. It must have been doing that while I was up in the room going through our personal belongings. I'd just been in such a state of shutdown I hadn't heard it.

Up on the roof, it was the usual night show of magnesium flares turning darkness to daylight, 50 cal tracers, and the burp of Puff The Magic Dragon and the AC130 gunships. But tonight was different. I dared to hope that in a few days this would be over, and the poor people of Cambodia would finally get relief from all their suffering. This was a view commonly held on the streets and even within the embassy. Even Bong Hut believed the suffering would end. They knew there would be reprisals for those higher up in the government who had contributed to the Lon Nol government's resistance. It was impossible for anyone to foresee the horror that was to come. We all could not have been more mistaken. But for that night…my last night in Cambodia until 2007 some thirty-two years later, I believed their horrible ordeal might almost be over. How terribly wrong we all were. After I tired of the show, I tried sleep. No sleep came that night.

7 April 1975–Special Embassy Flight Out

I have no recollection of how I got to the airport. I remember walking through the open-air terminal and past all those who still worked there, mostly military. I had overwhelming feelings of shame, guilt, and embarrassment; I was leaving them behind…behind to face the almost certain bloodbath resulting from the conflict we started. We were abandoning them. Many wished me a safe journey. Others stared silently as I walked toward the specially chartered Continental Air Service C-46.

A couple from the Air Attaché's office were there. Other embassy staff were there as well. They were being sent out now to lessen the burden when Eagle Pull came. Plenty of U.S. Air Force enlisted men providing ground handling and support. The two World Vision nurses from the bloody night in the back of the pickup were there as well, along with other WV third-country nationals (mostly Australian and Filipino). I didn't speak to anyone. My jaws were clenched tight.

As I stood in the small crowd waiting to board the flight, the rocket warning siren went off. I knew the sound well. People started shouting for everyone to get on the ground. I was already on the ground before the first shout. My reflexes were well conditioned. A few seconds later I heard the familiar explosion. I could tell the sound had come from the Cambodian Air Force side of the airport. After the traditional wait, I got up and walked to the nose of the aircraft. I could see smoke coming from an area on the Cambodian Air Force Ramp. It didn't look like they'd hit anything critical. Actually, almost everything critical over there had already been hit. As I stood looking at the smoke rising, I noticed a huge black oil stain on the leg of my best safari suit. Ruined! *Expletive!!* It was like the sorry bastards had given me one last thump as I was leaving. I opened my flak jacket and pulled out one of my Dunhill *special blends* and lit up. A few deep inhales later I heard the loadmaster calling for boarding. I crushed out most of the cigarette and started for the plane. As I walked, I pulled out the box of Dunhills in the front pocket of my safari suit jacket, threw it to the ground, and smashed it with my shoe. I never smoked again…tobacco or otherwise; no quit smoking books, no substitutes, no rock candy, no hypnosis courses, no nothing. I just turned and walked away.

The airplane was hot and filled with worried wives and more non-essential embassy staff. I was relieved to hear first the number two followed a few seconds later by the number one Curtis Wright R-2800 engines come sputtering to life, accompanied by their customary cloud of blue smoke. I knew, God Willing, we would soon be airborne and the close to unbearable heat inside the aircraft's cabin would soon be gone. I was praying not for a safe flight but that nobody would throw up.

My last glimpse of Cambodia was through tears and unimaginable heaviness in my heart. Tears were streaming down my cheeks. I didn't give damn who saw them. Looking back now it was partly the reality that so many so close to me would soon be facing incalculable hardship. I could never have imagined how horrific it would, in actuality, turn out to be. I knew, even then, that I was living in a monumental moment, something much bigger than me. I felt as though some cruel fist was thrust into my chest and my heart was being ripped out. At the time I was only thinking of my world and the world of Nine and her family, whom I'd come to love. Today, it is clear that this marked the first chapter in the unparallel human tragedy of Pol Pot's Khmer Rouge's Killing Fields. Millions would die at the hands of these brutal bastards.

Bangkok – The Final Curtain Begins To Close

As we left the aircraft, I was on autopilot, almost zombie like. I remember seeing a huge cardboard box in the middle of the walkway leading to customs and immigration. Two U.S. Embassy guys were standing by it asking all of us if we had anything we would like to put in the box before we went through customs. I looked in and saw some black bricks (walkie talkies) and various other semi-government stuff, mostly from the "non-critical" embassy staff. My brand new, state-of-the-art government issue black brick was about to become the prize of the pile. I gestured to it with the two embassy guys. One immediately walked over and snatched it up. A kinda "dubs on that one" move. We both smiled. Then with a much more serious look, I reached into my carry-on duffle bag and pulled out my 38 special and shoulder holster with my traditional 14 rounds in the twin ammo pouches. The 38 was usually nestled under my left armpit. I had it neatly wrapped in an old krama. The embassy guy and I bent over into the box together and I handed him the bundle. The way he handled it I knew he wasn't a diplomat. He carefully wrapped it back up and put it in a pouch his companion was carrying. Sure as hell didn't need that on me if Thai customs happened to be in a curious mood. But, in reality, the Thai were a very willing host to the entire operation in Laos and Cambodia. But why take the chance.

My mental haze was beginning to clear as I walked out into the main airport entrance. A couple of World Vision Thailand were herding us into vans for the trip to the hotel. I remember nothing of the drive from the airport. I vaguely remember the check-in. It was a beautiful Intercontinental. We were briefed before going to our rooms that our hotel and meals were covered by World Vision and that there would be a debrief and devotional at 3:00 pm in special room reserved by World Vision. Dr. Steven Moody, pseudonym. I remember thinking I needed a drink…not a *expletive* devotional. Anyway, I got to the room, piled my baggage on the floor in the corner, set the alarm for 2:00pm and lay down on the bed. I immediately fell into a deep sleep. The next thing I remember was the alarm calling me from beyond the dead. I got up, took a shower and headed to the debrief/devotional.

Christian Abandonment

Carry each other's burdens, and in this way, you will fulfill the law of Christ.[217]

"Beware of false prophets who come to you in sheep's clothing but inwardly are ravaging wolves. You'll recognize them by their fruit. Are grapes gathered from thorn bushes or figs from thistles? In the same way, every good tree produces good fruit, but a bad tree produces bad fruit. A good tree can't produce bad fruit; neither can a bad tree produce good fruit.[218]

The room was full of chairs. I found a seat and waited for the meeting to begin. Dr. Steven Moore leader of the entire World Vision organization was waiting up front.

Dr. Moore began with prayer. Then he explained that they were all grateful for our brave service and that we could stay in the hotel for a couple of more days resting before returning to our homes (some in US, some Australia, some to the Philippians). I was just half listening but when they started handing out tickets, I saw mine was to Dallas Texas and I said a silent "Thank You Jesus."

Dr. Moore then suggested we end with a time of silent prayer. Apparently, this was some drill Christian NGO's were accustomed to. Everyone slid out of their chairs turned, got on their knees with their head and shoulders resting on the seat of the chair and began praying (at least that's what I assumed they were doing). I had no trouble with this as my soul was deeply destressed. Probably more than ever in my life. More than at the loss of my mother back in 1965. My soul was in such pain and was crying out to what I supposed was God. Almost immediately I broke out in uncontrollable sobs…like nothing I'd ever experienced before. I knew others in the room could almost certainly hear me, but I didn't give a damn. My soul was in such horrible pain. I'd walked off and left my second family alone to face the dangers of the Khmer Rouge. I'd abandoned my Khmer friends. They had been so naïve and trusting. We certainly repaid them well. At that time, I had no idea of the unimaginable horrors that awaited them, but I knew it was going to be really, really bad. In retrospect, I could never have imagined how bad.

I have no idea how long I had been praying. The seat of the chair was wet with my tears. I raised my head to see if others were still praying. The freaking room was empty. Even Dr. Moore was gone. Later, I confronted him about what I viewed as their unthinkable abandonment. He brushed it off by

---

[217] Galatians 6:2, Holy Bible, NIV Version
[218] Matthew 7:15-18, Holy Bible, Holman Christian Standard Bible (HCSB)

saying they thought I just needed some time alone to pray through whatever it was that bothered me. Where in the Bible did it say that?!

Babies In Baskets—One Last Mission Before Going Legit

While still grieving for those I'd left behind, My energy level was coming back. Cy was supposed to be here in Bangkok. I left the hotel after breakfast (on World Vision) and headed out for the Nana Hotel which was only a short distance away. There I'd hoped to find Cy and get an update on the situation. I was now officially unemployed. Not having a job for any extended period was not an option.

When I got to the Nana, it was like a reunion. I knew all the girls behind the desk and the bellmen and drivers waiting for a tourist client. This had served as our R&R (military slang for rest and recreation) base since 1972. I asked the girls at the desk if Mr. Cy was here. They immediately gave me his room number. But as I was walking to the elevator, the bellman told me he was in the restaurant having breakfast. I found him, just as the bellman had said. He was sitting with another man I didn't know. I was reluctant to interrupt but when Cy saw me, he immediately motioned for me to come over. He was genuinely glad to see me. In a few minutes I would find out why.

Cy had been contacted by the US Military Mission in Bangkok (JUSMAGTHAI) who coordinated all the US Military missions in Cambodia. They had an urgent appeal from the Embassy in Phnom Penh. World Vision had a rehydration center in Phnom Penh full of babies who were extremely weak and would never survive after World Vision pulled out, the electricity from the generator stopped, and the IV solutions they needed to stay alive were all gone. For the most part, the babies had been abandoned by their frightened, bewildered, peasant mothers. Most of the men were in the military or already killed in the fighting. I'd seen these infants countless times when I went, usually with Allen, in the middle of the night to get the diesel generator running again. Always not due to mechanical failures, but due to the staff forgetting to check the fuel supply and letting it run dry.

The man sitting with Cy had purchased a Convair 240 somewhere and was trying to find a place to put it to work in Cambodia. However, after he acquired it, the conditions became impossible in Cambodia. No airports remaining to operate into and from and nobody willing to insure the aircraft. I had an instant distrust of the guy. It turns out Cy did too. The man had a pilot's license which showed he was qualified to operate it as pilot in command. Cy suspected, since it was a temporary license, that it was forged. He wanted Cy to be his co-pilot. Cy was already an experienced pilot in command, but he did not want to get in the right seat with a guy who might not be able to fly the airplane in any type of emergency. Cy was demanding that they take me along. The guy needed money and did not want this opportunity to get away as it would pay several thousand dollars, so he readily agreed for me to join the flight.

They were discussing the best way to handle the turnaround on the ground in Phnom Penh as the airport now was under almost constant shelling. Together we designed a plan. I was amazed as I could instantly see in my head how the operation could work. The aircraft was in a cargo configuration. This made the situation easy to manage. We took four eye-screws and attached strong wire cable through the eye. We made two. They were screwed into the aft section of the cargo compartment. We then attached a quick disconnect (quick draw) device to the other end of the two wire cables. We then screwed the final two eye-screws into the floor at the forward end of the cargo compartment. With this setup, we could quickly undo the line from the forward eye-screws thus opening the setup to allow baskets to be threaded on the wire. Now all we needed to do was buy the equipment (easily found in most Thai hardware stores) and go do the installation out at the airport. The only remaining element was a basket for each infant. This would have to come from Phnom Penh as there would be no time to secure them in the baskets while we were on the ground at the airport.

We called JUSTMAG and asked if they could have a phone patch with World Vision PNH at 1:00 pm. They called us back and advised it was set up. At 1:30 pm we were waiting in the communications room (radio room) at JUSTMAG. We were back in my old familiar environment, Collins KWM2 HF transceivers powered by 1000w linear amplifiers. Amazingly, Cy was equally at home. After retirement as a full bird colonel from the US Army, Cy had gone to work for Collins. His market was the US military. The aircraft owner was far out of his league, a duck out of water.

We told World Vision they needed to go to the Central Market in Phnom Penh and buy big wicker baskets, one for each baby. They were told to insure the babies had plenty of blankets to keep warm and to insure the babies were securely strapped in the baskets. They were to have everything ready. As we approached PNH and ready to commence our steep decent to avoid Khmer Rouge ground fire, we would call on a discrete VHF frequency. Normally we would have used UHF, but this aircraft did not have any military radios. The US Military would then send message (not via radio) to the control tower. We would be a radio silence operation.

That evening I joined Cy at the Nana for a few beers and to celebrate what we hoped would be a perfect mission the following day.

Lord, teach us to pray, just as John also taught his disciples.[219]

When Cy and I got to the airport the following morning, we went straight to the hanger where the plane was kept. They already had it sitting out on the

---
[219] Luke 11:1-13 Holy Bible - Holman Christian Standard Bible (HCSB)

ramp. The owner was there doing an external inspection (walk around). Neither Cy nor I trusted his professionalism and proficiency on the Convair. All looked OK so we moved into the aircraft and started our interior inspection than moving to the cockpit check.

Soon a van moved up to the aircraft. I saw Dr. Moore was among the group. We soon learned the group was his own media team along with a couple of nurses. His expression was priceless when he saw me. He had no idea what I had done before I joined his team as a local hire for the hospital project. Anyway, he immediately gravitated toward me to be his liaison with the pilots. It was doubly sweet when he asked if I knew how to fly this airplane and I got to respond with "Of Course."

I was relieved to see how easily the engines started and how smoothly they ran. Our takeoff was normal. My agreement with Cy, I rode in the cockpit in the jump-seat, just in case something happened. My role quickly changed as we were about to start descent. I worked the radio and talked with the US Air Force personnel on the ground. The crew was maintaining radio silence. As I remember, it was about 11:00am. Soon the Air Force came back that the tower was ready, we would be number two to land and we could expect to be the only one in the traffic pattern when it was time to land. Our parking was arranged, and a US Air Force Sargeant would marshal us in. We would shut down #2 engine and our "cargo handlers" would come from the terminal in almost a run around the front of the aircraft staying clear of #1 engine which was still running. The Air Force ground handlers would take the babies from the nurses and hand them up to our nurses through the right-side utility door. The airport had not had any inbound in over an hour. All looked pretty good…if you didn't stop to think about everything that could go wrong. Our biggest fear was being hit by inbound rockets while we were on the ground or taking some AA or ground to air fire on the climb out. Cy started the stop watch as we shut down #2.

The World Vision nurses (all Cambodian) came running out to the aircraft with their precious cargo all strapped into their baskets. They arrived at the nose of the aircraft just as the prop stopped spinning. Our World Vision crew in the airplane were ready. The babies came into the plane through the utility door and were immediately handed to a nurse who ran with the basket to the back of the aircraft and threaded it on the cable. It was beautiful to watch. The plan was coming together just as I had envisioned. In what seemed like only an instant the last basket was threaded on the cables and the two latches were clicked onto the forward eyes. We were done. I signaled the cockpit as the door was closing and I heard the familiar "clear #2" call. Number two engine was running in seconds and we immediately started to taxi. I rushed to the cockpit and silently ran the checklist that the flight crew normally ran. I announced "before takeoff checklist complete" as we were approaching the takeoff end of the runway. The crew slowed down from the taxi speed just enough to keep from skidding and throwing everybody in the back on the deck as they rounded the turn and took the runway. The throttles were up to takeoff power immediately. The takeoff run was unusually short as we were very light and had not taken a lot of fuel so we would be light for the takeoff. With throttles full, and alcohol injection on, the Convair climbed like a homesick angel. I'd never been in a Convair that light during takeoff. We were usually seriously overloaded with troops and injured and critical supplies. Our climb angle must have looked spectacular for those watching back on the tarmac. I hoped they were praying for us.

Immediately after the flight crew reduced the climb angle enough for me to be able to walk, which was after we were out of range of SAM-7 heat seeking missiles, I got up and went back to check on our precious cargo. I was hoping our system worked and they were all just as they were when we snapped the two cables into place. I was relieved to see they were all in place and nurses keeping a close eye on them. Some had their eyes open. Most appeared to be sleeping. I was relieved.

I was not ready for what I saw from Dr. Moore. He was on his knees praying to the camera. He was determined to milk the last ounce of Public Relations out of these babies. I warned the nurses not being used as stage props that this was not a regular passenger aircraft…it had been modified for cargo and as such could easily become quite cold. They were to watch and if the babies started to get seriously cold, they were to come tell me and we could try to adjust the temperature with what was left of the climate control system after the cargo conversion. The flight was going to be short…less than an hour. By the grace of God, the temperature remained tolerable. Soon it was time for descent.

I wondered what Dr. Moore had planned upon our arrival. In my mind, considering the sensitive nature of our "cargo" I would have planned something extremely low key…almost clandestine.

As we opened the door, there was a small group of people out on the ramp waiting along with several vans. Most looked like embassy type. Dr. Moore's onboard PR crew darted down the air stair and positioned to be ready for Dr. Moore, the nurses and the babies. I stayed in the cockpit away from the eyes of the press.

After they all left, in vans for God knows where, I came down, helped with the post flight inspection then rode to the Nana Hotel with Cy. Time for a tall drink. The following day there were articles in the press. Most asking why these babies were about to be shipped off to the United States where they would grow up with nobody looking like them. Nobody to identify with. Everywhere I turned I saw the United States making horrible messes in South East Asia. As I sipped my super cold Singha beer there in the Nana bar with Cy, I mused that "with friends like America, one would never need enemies." A few days later I flew back to Hamilton to join my father and Nine. It would be more than thirty years before Nine and I would return to Cambodia.

Epilogue

Mayberry Today

While Hamilton's population is just about the same as it was in the 1950s, much has changed. The tiny jail that existed back then is now large and frequently used. The weekly Hamilton Herald News's front page, while valiantly struggling to find positive images and stories, is forced to report stories of crime and criminals along with the traditional news. Hamilton is no longer a "dry county" and alcohol is sold everywhere. Many stores are now open on Sunday. Much has changed. *Sic transit gloria mundi*. Hamilton's change appears to a large degree to mirror the change transpiring across the United States.

The Congo

Today, in the Eastern Congo where I flew countless missions, nothing has changed. The same people are still fighting each other. It is conservatively estimated more than 4 million Congolese have died.[220] The outside influences of the cold war era have diminished. Disease, poverty, corruption, the rape of the country's resources by its leaders continues unabated. Again, history repeats itself.

Cambodia Post Pol Pot

Cambodia fell to the Khmer Rouge on 17 April 1975 when the Khmer Rouge troops, clad in black pajama type uniforms marched into Phnom Penh. They ordered the mass evacuation of the entire city into the provinces where they would be executed or die of starvation. This began the reign of terror by the Communist Party of Kampuchea (CPK) or Khmer Rouge. Under the murderous rule of its highly secret party leadership, headed by Pol Pot, they systematically eliminated almost all the educated, even semi-educated population. They burned all the money. Cambodia was the only country in the entire world with no currency. Everything was bartered or owned and controlled by the government.

[220] Widipedia 2018

Beneath The Shroud

Anyone that could be identified as associated with previous government, business sector, school teachers, etc. all were ruthlessly murdered. If they wore glasses . . . they were killed. In their satanic twisted worldview, glasses meant you could read; therefore, you were not a true peasant. Their two favorite methods for murdering their victims…smashing their skulls with a hoe handle or slitting their throats with the saw-tooth, razor sharp leaf from a palm tree. The most conservative estimates say two million were killed. The more likely estimates of those who were murdered or died of starvation range closer to four million. The total population of

Cambodia when the Khmer Rouge began their reign of terror in 1975 was estimated to be 7.3 million.[221] It was a genocide unparalleled since the Jews under Hitler. The brutality of the Khmer Rouge was unparalleled in modern history. They controlled the population through fear and starvation.

In the aftermath of the Khmer Rouge, Cambodia has struggled valiantly to recover from the deep and deadly wounds inflected by Pol Pot's Khmer Rouge. There is no family left untouched by their brutality.

These murderous Khmer Rouge bastards killed

---

[221] Population Division of the Department of Economic and Social Affairs of the United Nations Secretariat, World Population Prospects: The 2010 Revision

Nine's father, HRH Prince Norodom Phurissara, her brother Prince Sisowath Doung Khara, her brother Prince Sisowath Ritharavong, her sister Princess Norodom Ronida, her sister's husband and three precious little children, her brother Prince Norodom Vondera, his wife and two children, her brother Prince Norodom Vinsady, and her brother Prince Norodom Thanarath. Only Princess Norodom Danine, my wife, was left. Only she survived because she was safe in

Hamilton with my father. She escaped the terrible slaughter. There is no way to grasp the depth of her survivor's guilt; even today. There were times when

the spirits of those we betrayed and left behind weighed so heavily upon me I felt I could hardly breathe. How can spirits be heavy, you might ask. They can produce unimaginable weight. I recall as a child often hearing the older men saying, "I wish I didn't know now what I didn't know then." I remember thinking how can anybody say that. Now I clearly see they were correct. "If Only."

It is easy to overlook those who equally share in the guilt of this tragic period in history. Those responsible for the overthrow of the Cambodian government and its replacement with a puppet regime under the complete control of the U.S. government should not be overlooked. Their guilt is great; the blood on their hands immeasurable. The voices of innocent non-combatant Cambodian peasants killed or maimed physically as well as mentally as tens of thousands of US bombs rained down from US Air Force B-52 bombers from 35,000 feet above their

village in the middle of the night, cry out for justice, for at least recognition. Although history is now clearly beginning to see their guilt, it is unlikely those responsible will ever acknowledge the travesty.

In September of 2007 after I retired, we returned to Cambodia for the first time. A few distant relatives and friends remained. All others, gone without a trace, lying in unmarked graves they had been forced to dig before their throats were cut or their skulls smashed. There will be a special place in hell reserved for those satanic demons. The greatest guilt and tragedy of all this, which equals or exceeds the guilt of the Khmer rouge, is that of the United States and its principal architects of this senseless slaughter, Richard Nixon and Henry Kissinger. who used and discarded these poor insignificant brown pawns in their cold-war chess game with China and Russia. Volumes have been written on the cold war strategies; the genocide carried out by the Khmer Rouge is scarcely a footnote in history. The story of Cambodia is stored away in the monstrous archives of failed American foreign policy.

Today Cambodia is prospering on the surface, with sustained economic growth of 7.5%.[222] They are slowly developing a capable democratic government and leadership. It did not come quickly or easily but there is progress. There is hope.

"The guns and the bombs, the rockets and the warships, are all symbols of human failure." [223]

The Rebirth

In June of 1975, after returning home to Texas from Cambodia, I experienced what psychologists refer to as a Religious Crisis, Spiritual Crisis, or Spiritual Emergency. My external awareness or mental peripheral vision had been reduced to a tiny circle consisting of my wife, my sister, and my father. My mind was almost in total shutdown. Any loud sudden noise produced a significant physical reaction. I could not perform even the simplest mental tasks. I had no help. There was sympathy from my family but no help. They did not understand and had no idea what to do. I did my best to hide it from the outside world. PTSD was unknown at that time. I knew something was wrong and I didn't want anyone else to find out.

---

[222] World Bank 2018
[223] President Lyndon Baines Johnson, 36th President Of The United States—1963—1969 Vietnam Era

It was during this ordeal that I had my *road to Damascus*. It was then that God drove me to my knees and demanded I start following Him and allow Him to direct my path. I was changed forever. The overnight change was intense. My gradual healing began immediately.. The process, closely resembling Paul's *Roman Road*, is still ongoing. I'm now at peace with myself about all I've seen and done. I've now forgiven myself for all the missteps, all the failures, all the "*If Only*" times in my life. I've apologized to all I consciously remember hurting, some in person, some in prayer. I've apologized in prayer to all those I left behind in April of 1975. The Jimmy Joe Jacks from Hamilton Texas who always viewed life as short and followed his motto, *carpe diem*, no longer exists.

God has provided unwarranted grace and mercy. Now, some 40 plus years after Cambodia, I have children and grandchildren, and soon, God Willing, great grandchildren. My PTSD has retreated deep within my being and is seldom triggered. Nine and I have been married more than 45 years. We maintain a home in Texas and spend most of our time in Cambodia. Yet, not a single day goes by that we do not remember those who were left behind.

INDEX

122mm, 400, 457, 459–461
281 Drive In, 21
50 cals, 196–197, 202, 423
7.62, 114, 399, 411–412

A Low-Level Insertion, 274
A.C. and Cleo Hays, 16
A.G. Thompson, 15
Air Force, 12, 47, 56, 78, 85, 93, 104, 107, 115, 121–123, 125, 129, 133, 136, 140, 147, 151, 167, 175, 179, 182, 190, 211, 214, 300, 310–311, 320, 345, 349, 375, 381–382, 388, 393, 402, 407–408, 417–420, 437, 442–443, 452, 455–456, 470–471, 477, 485, 493, 495, 497, 500, 503, 508, 513
AK-47, 405, 411, 425, 435, 447, 449
Albertville, 175, 177–178, 182, 187–190, 194–195, 202, 204, 206, 208, 210, 309
ANC, 122, 127–128, 131–132, 163, 175–178, 192, 203, 254–255, 257–258, 265, 271–272
Ann Whitney, 11, 14, 20, 366
Archie Vick, 367

B-26, 50, 85, 154, 183
B-52, 173, 348, 398, 402, 423, 453–455, 459, 461, 513
Bantu, 147, 202, 307, 309–310, 314–315, 317, 321, 323, 326–334, 336–342
Bat Masterson, 211, 416
Battambang, 379–380, 382, 389–390, 394–395, 407, 411, 421, 430–431, 434, 447, 463, 469, 476–477
Bay of Pigs, 33, 47, 49, 52, 69
Belgium, 26, 30, 35, 46, 50, 53, 83, 85, 92, 94, 102, 113–114, 117, 134–135, 137, 148–149, 151, 158, 161, 163, 175, 200–201, 203, 217, 222, 242, 246, 254–258, 263, 281, 302, 305, 343, 345, 347
Ben Kiernan, 208, 261, 348, 402, 407, 423
Ben Linton, 10–11, 14
Benjamin Linton, 10
Bert and Fay Schrank, 11–12, 14
Bert Schrank, 88
Bill Wallace, 92, 105
Bob & Evelyn Jones, 17
Bobby Newman, 27
Bobby Stevens, 228
Bobby Swinson, 18
Bobby Wallace, 106, 365

INDEX

Brigade 2506, 50
Bujumbura, 270–271, 274–277, 279
Burundi., 270, 272, 275

C-46, 131–132, 144, 146, 168–170, 172, 175–176, 180, 185, 209, 268, 378, 503
C-47, 122, 127, 132, 146–148, 150–151, 154, 168, 176, 180, 182, 184–185, 187–190, 206, 209–211, 215–216, 220, 224, 256–257, 262, 270, 272, 274, 278, 300, 342, 344, 378, 430, 461, 470, 496
C-54, 129, 132, 139, 143, 146–148, 168, 180, 185, 208–210, 222, 262, 266, 270, 309, 342, 346, 361, 476, 481, 486–487
Cambodia, 3–4, 6, 12, 21–22, 30, 54, 57, 65, 71, 73–74, 76, 78, 90, 92–93, 97, 99, 101, 103–105, 110, 114, 120–121, 148, 165, 168–169, 171–174, 181, 187, 206, 208, 214, 220, 224, 246, 253, 261, 263, 298, 301–302, 320, 348, 353, 370, 372, 378, 386, 391–393, 396–398, 402–403, 405, 407, 410, 413, 417–419, 423, 428–431, 435, 437, 439, 443–445, 455, 463–465, 469–470, 472, 474–476, 478–482, 484–486, 489–491, 494, 499, 502–504, 506, 509, 511–512, 514–515
Camille, 9, 15, 32, 39, 45, 78, 87–88, 90, 138, 174, 366, 489
Carvair, 476–477
CENCO, 80–82, 84–85, 92–94, 102, 107, 125, 138, 213, 291
Central Intelligence Agency, 6
Central Scientific Company, 80
China, 12, 30, 78, 104, 163, 171, 174–175, 192, 297, 299, 375, 393, 480, 514
Chinese, 78, 97, 154, 172, 174–175, 182, 192, 201–202, 246, 272, 376, 382, 386, 391, 393, 396–397, 400, 409, 420, 430, 438–440, 457, 461, 478, 480, 497
Christmas, 45–46, 69, 77, 125, 227, 399–402, 406, 476, 489–490, 500
CIA, 6–7, 26, 33, 35, 39, 46–47, 49–50, 52, 54, 74–75, 78, 83, 85, 92, 103–105, 123–125, 130, 133, 136–138, 146, 162–163, 167–169, 171, 173, 178, 183–184, 200, 219, 237, 246, 252–253, 264–265, 283, 300, 366, 369, 371, 390–391, 393, 405, 412, 451, 456, 463, 479, 481–482, 484

INDEX

Cindy Robinson, 14, 17
Clyde L. Weatherby, 18
COIN, 183, 185–186, 427, 429–430
Cold War, 3, 136, 148, 163, 174, 178–179, 253, 265, 419, 511, 514
Commandos, 85, 151, 217
Congo, 3, 22, 26, 30, 35, 39, 46–47, 50, 53, 56, 73, 75, 78, 83, 85, 92–93, 100, 102–106, 110, 113–114, 117–120, 125, 127–128, 131, 133–134, 136–138, 144, 147–152, 154–155, 158–159, 162–163, 166, 169, 171, 174–175, 178, 180, 182, 186, 190–192, 196, 198, 208, 211–212, 216–220, 223–225, 242, 251, 253–258, 262–267, 270, 272–275, 278, 280–284, 286, 289, 291, 297–302, 306–307, 310–313, 315, 336–338, 343–344, 362–364, 366–367, 369, 371, 375, 377–379, 381, 385, 388, 390, 392, 394, 397, 399–400, 403, 405, 408, 416, 419, 421, 424, 435, 441, 447, 450, 460, 468–469, 472, 477–478, 482, 486, 511
Congolese Air Force, 78, 104, 125, 179, 182, 190
Continental Air Service, 375, 465, 503
Corpus Christi, 58–60, 62–63, 72, 78–80, 82–83, 213, 262, 273
Cuba, 33, 49, 52, 64–66, 69

Daddy, 35, 58, 77, 86–87, 90, 99, 104, 133–134, 143, 207, 210, 220, 291–292, 294–296
David Nowlen, 469
David P. Chandler, 71–72, 74, 76, 78, 92, 97, 101, 104, 115, 148, 171–172, 206, 220
Deputy Premier Le Thanh Nghi, 297
Diem, 9–10, 15, 17, 45, 53, 73–74, 76, 182, 222, 403, 515
Don Vick, 367
Dr. McCord, 64, 293
Dr. Robert A. Kooken, 14

Eagle Pull, 445, 448, 451, 499–500, 503
East Boynton Street, 11, 14
East Hill, 10, 12, 14
East Ward Elementary School, 10
Eastern provinces, 174–175, 179, 250, 272, 300, 408
Elvis, 13–16, 18

F-111, 407
FAC, 126–127, 131–132, 135, 138, 146–147, 150–151, 156, 159, 167–168, 193, 212, 219–220, 224, 301, 342,

INDEX

361
Fay Schrank, 11–12, 14, 87
FBI, 105, 178, 342
First Baptist Church, 7,
  12–13, 23, 33, 90, 110, 199,
  351, 468, 473
First Lieutenant Dick Gray,
  443
Florida, 49, 105, 389, 481,
  486–487
Force Aérienne Congolaise,
  78, 104, 121, 125, 127, 131,
  147, 152, 168, 315, 341
Fred Fetty, 9
Fred's Café, 9

Gécamines, 179
George Barnes, 115, 119–121,
  123, 131, 147
Ginny Come Lately, 66, 262,
  294
Goma, 131, 150–151,
  154–158, 160–162, 298,
  338, 344–348, 358, 360,
  369

Hamilton, 4, 6–7, 9–12,
  14–18, 20, 23, 25–26, 28,
  30–35, 39–40, 42–43, 45,
  47, 54, 58, 64, 77, 82,
  85–90, 93–96, 98–99,
  101–102, 104, 106–107,
  109–110, 117, 128, 134–135,
  137–138, 153, 155, 177, 181,
  191–192, 194, 199, 207,
  209, 212, 214, 225–227,
  230, 237–238, 246–247,
  270–271, 280, 282,
  285–286, 289–292, 295,
  302, 305–306, 310, 316,
  320, 327, 351, 356–357,
  361, 364–371, 373, 375,
  395, 402, 408, 416,
  424–425, 427, 437, 441,
  449, 460, 468, 471, 473,
  478–479, 485–486, 490,
  499, 509, 511, 513, 515
Hamilton Bulldogs, 9, 104
Hamilton City Lake, 15, 42,
  295
Hamilton County, 6, 9–11,
  17–18, 25, 32–33, 77, 90,
  96, 99, 110, 117, 128, 135,
  153, 155, 177, 194, 289,
  292, 310, 356, 366–367,
  370, 408, 441, 479
Hamilton County General
  Hospital, 10, 25, 90, 292
Hamilton High School, 26,
  40, 47, 82, 102, 230, 357
Hamilton National Bank, 82,
  93, 134, 207, 282
Hardy Morgan, 17, 27
Harry's, 233–234, 248, 250
Haskell Harelik, 16
Hattie Newman, 27–28
Henry Kissinger, 101, 105,
  246, 401, 514
HF, 125, 132, 153, 197, 218,
  254, 266, 272, 276–277,
  345, 369, 507
Ho Chi Minh Trail, 21
Hutu, 272, 282, 347

INDEX

If Only, 40, 46, 69, 78, 87–90, 107, 110, 143, 170, 174, 187, 195, 206, 213, 231–233, 290, 297, 299, 327, 339, 368, 423, 462, 513, 515
incursion, 181

Jakarta, 403–406
James J. Jacks, 38
James Joseph Jacks, 1–2, 238
James McDonald, 10, 19
Jason, 84–85, 87, 90, 98, 102, 104–106, 110, 153, 165, 167, 169–172, 174, 180–181, 186–187, 197, 206–207, 212–216, 220–221, 238, 261–262, 264, 280, 282, 285, 291–292, 294–299, 303, 305–306, 346, 360, 363–366, 370, 372, 402, 416, 471, 476, 481–483, 485, 489
Jason Jerome Jacks, 84
Jennifer Joelle Jacks, 262, 292
Jenny, 66, 262, 273, 280, 285, 289–290, 293–295, 297–299, 303, 305–306, 346, 360, 363–366, 370, 372–373, 402, 416, 471, 476, 489
Jerry Donald Lomax, 367
Jerry Drake, 23, 107, 119, 364, 370
Jimmie, 9, 19, 88–90

Jimmie and Lois Jacks, 19
Jimmie Jacks, 9
Jimmy, 6, 10–11, 18–21, 24–25, 34, 58, 64, 66, 85, 88, 91, 94–96, 100, 106, 109–110, 116, 135, 146–147, 179, 198, 202, 209, 221, 226, 228, 231, 237, 258, 293, 295, 318–319, 335, 346, 378, 425, 435–437, 469, 471, 515
Jimmy Joe Jacks, 6, 34, 95–96, 110, 202, 209, 221, 226, 231, 237, 425, 515
Joe Ruben Register, 21–22
John and Blanch Morgan, 18
John F. Kennedy, 45, 47, 49, 76
Joseph Desiré Mobutu, 39

K-7, 151
Karen, 72–74, 77–88, 90–94, 98, 100, 102, 104–107, 119, 134, 138, 148, 153, 165–167, 169–172, 174, 179–181, 186–187, 197, 206–207, 210, 212–216, 219–221, 238, 251, 261–264, 273, 280–282, 285, 289–299, 302–303, 305–306, 318, 333, 346, 360, 363–366, 370–373, 392, 399, 402, 408, 416, 471, 481, 483, 486
Katanga, 30, 46, 53, 73, 148–149, 179, 282, 342–343, 362
KCLW, 18, 45
Khmer Rouge, 5, 73, 148, 165,

173, 206, 220, 246, 263,
    301, 353, 381–382, 388,
    392, 399–400, 402–403,
    407, 410–413, 417–425,
    437, 443–446, 451,
    460–461, 477–478,
    480–481, 485, 490, 497,
    499–500, 504–505, 507,
    511–512, 514
King 1, 131, 161–162, 197,
    205, 207, 210, 219–221,
    256–257, 261–262, 266,
    270, 272, 276–277, 307,
    309, 345–346, 361, 369
King 7, 153, 162, 215, 256, 309
King Norodom Sihanouk, 12,
    30, 410, 412, 418
King Norodom Suramarit, 30
Kinshasa, 105–106, 110,
    116–117, 119, 127–128, 131,
    134–138, 148–150,
    152–153, 159, 162, 164,
    169–170, 179, 198,
    208–209, 212, 218, 222,
    226–227, 238, 243, 251,
    254–255, 258, 263–264,
    270, 287, 290, 292, 297,
    301, 306, 309, 316, 321,
    326–327, 342–345, 361,
    379
Kisangani, 137, 151, 153–154,
    157, 162, 208, 212–219,
    221, 253–254, 256, 300,
    307–309, 312–316, 327,
    336, 340–342, 392
Kissinger, 101, 104–105, 165,
    173, 246, 261, 370, 372,
    399, 401, 514
Kompong Chhnang,
    421–422, 436–437
Kompong Som, 381–382,
    388, 391, 393, 409, 411,
    430, 442

Lake Kivu, 157–158
Laos, 6, 12, 21, 46, 54, 56–57,
    62, 105, 348, 369, 375, 396,
    419, 465–466, 481, 504
Leila Craddock;, 16
Leon River, 9, 15, 23, 214,
    229, 320, 365
Liechtenstein, 85, 105, 123
Lieutenant Commander Don
    L. McCord, 61
Linebacker Two, 401
Little Jimmy, 10–11, 18–20,
    24–25, 91, 106, 109–110,
    116, 319
Loco Hills New Mexico,
    30–31, 479
Lois, 9, 19, 86, 89–90, 104,
    309
Lois Jacks, 19
Lon Nol, 71, 94, 120, 148,
    168, 172, 220, 246, 263,
    301, 353, 410, 412, 418,
    421, 443–445, 451, 456,
    479, 484–485, 490, 503
Lon Non, 220
Long Beach, 39–40, 42,
    44–45, 48
Lumumba, 26, 30, 39, 46, 50,
    121, 128, 148–149, 189,
    193, 204

INDEX

M-16, 206
Mao Zedong, 177
MARS, 115, 191, 221
Masterson, 211, 309, 416
Meacham Field, 92, 94, 99, 101, 123, 169, 366, 369
Mercenaries, 50, 56, 93, 135–136, 149, 167, 198, 200–201, 214, 468
Michal, 5, 17–19, 31
Michal Jones, 5, 17
Milano, 106–110, 113, 116
Mildred Newson, 199
Milton Harelik, 16
Mobutu, 26, 39, 90, 92, 100, 131, 135, 145–147, 149–150, 162–163, 168, 171, 174, 179, 182, 192, 198, 216, 226, 252, 257–259, 262–263, 265, 272–273, 283, 288, 297, 299–301, 303–304, 307, 338
Moise Tshombe, 30, 53, 100, 148–149
Monkey, 15, 59, 174, 258–260, 441
MPR, 131, 135, 149, 262, 300
Mr. Linton, 10–11

Nana, 375–378, 380, 404, 481, 491, 506–507, 509
Neak Luong, 453, 455
New Year, 18, 46, 69, 330, 406, 409, 476, 478
Ngo Dinh Diem, 15, 45, 53, 73–74
Nicholson Street, 10

Nixon, 45, 104, 114, 165, 173, 181, 187, 246, 261, 342, 348, 353, 370, 372, 377, 399, 401, 407, 423, 429, 455, 471, 480, 483, 514
Norodom Sihanouk, 12, 30, 65, 71, 74, 90, 92, 99, 114, 169, 171–172, 208, 246, 353, 382, 384, 391, 410, 412, 418, 480, 482
North Vietnamese, 21, 97, 105, 114, 165, 208, 253, 263, 295, 353, 372, 391, 401, 406, 480–481
NVA, 101, 220, 263, 391, 407

Operation Linebacker, 372, 401
Otto Lengefeld, 13, 15
OV1, 378
OV-10, 442–443

Paris, 110, 221–223, 225–241, 243–251, 321, 348, 370, 372, 376, 395, 399, 401, 406, 455
Patrice Lumumba, 26, 30, 39, 46, 50, 148–149
Paul, 23, 73, 208–212, 217, 251–254, 262, 265, 267–270, 281, 302–303, 308, 362, 365, 372, 416, 419, 436, 476–478, 515
Paul Rakisits, 208, 270, 416, 419, 436, 476, 478
Perry Country Club, 29
Phnom Penh, 73, 92, 148,

INDEX

171–173, 187, 263, 302, 353, 372–373, 376, 378, 380, 383–384, 389–391, 394–395, 398–400, 403–404, 406–411, 413–414, 419–422, 425, 431, 434, 436–437, 441–447, 453, 455–457, 461–463, 465, 468, 470, 473, 476–478, 483, 486, 490–491, 498–500, 506–507, 511
Phurissara, 5, 172, 410, 420, 484, 513
Pierre Mulele, 78, 284
Pig Pilot, 461
Pochentong, 380–381, 389, 393–394, 406, 418, 431, 442, 470, 490
Pol Pot, 71–73, 115, 208, 220, 363, 447, 504, 511–512
Pottsville, 24, 29
Priddy, 29
Prince Norodom Phurissara, 5, 172, 420, 513
Prince Sihanouk, 30, 101, 103, 120, 171, 220, 388, 480
Prince Sisowath Sirik Matak, 120, 148, 168–169, 412, 429
Prof. Rodney Love, 28

Randy, 14, 16, 19–20, 29
Randy Hays, 14, 20, 29
Ream Air Force Base, 388, 393
Red SAM, 65
Riley's Funeral Home, 9

Rock House Baptist Church, 23
Roy Orbison, 18, 63–64
Russia, 12, 72, 104, 171, 175, 192, 514
Russian, 78, 154, 265, 391, 396, 457, 459, 497

SA-2, 64–65
SAM-7, 447, 509
San Diego High School, 48, 50, 54–56
SEAAT, 419, 433, 457, 462, 464–467, 469, 483, 487, 491, 494, 496
Secret War, 6, 54, 348
Seth Moore, 155
Sihanoukville, 104, 246, 263, 381–382, 388, 391, 393
Sisowath Darameth, 426, 429
SODEMAC, 266–267, 270, 282–283, 289, 297–301, 303
SOG, 99, 101, 464
South Vietnam, 15, 21, 53–54, 56–57, 65, 69, 73–75, 97, 99, 121, 263, 393, 417, 481
Southwest School of Aviation, 92–94, 106, 123, 126, 130, 134, 136, 138, 141, 183, 197, 205, 211, 213, 221, 255, 291, 294, 369
Soviet, 35, 46, 64–65, 163, 295, 299, 400
Soviet Union, 64, 163, 299
Special Forces, 47, 54–55, 464–465

INDEX

St. Thomas Catholic Church, 10–11, 14
Stanleyville, 50, 56, 83, 85, 137, 151
Strand Theater, 10, 17, 238

T-28, 85, 154, 168, 182–187, 189, 195–196, 200, 202–203, 205–206, 274–275, 345, 354, 371, 378, 418–419, 477
Tanzania, 174–175, 182, 195, 272, 347, 419
Texan Theater, 17, 137, 214
Texas Rangers, 28–29
Thailand, 6, 56, 62, 65, 348, 370, 372–373, 375, 377–378, 382, 388, 402, 405, 418, 420, 425, 442, 445, 452–453, 469, 481, 500, 504
Thomas Addis Emmett, 13
Travis Cozby, 15–16, 20, 23
Tri-9, 371, 378–381, 383–385, 387, 389, 391–392, 404, 419
Tutsi., 272, 282

UHF, 188, 195, 199, 275, 277, 507
Union Minière du Haut Katanga, 179
United States Naval Training Center, 37, 39
USS Los Angeles, 39–41, 43–48
Uzi, 192–194, 200–201, 205–206

VHF, 199, 254, 257, 276, 425, 507
Viet Cong, 21, 26, 53, 57, 60, 79, 83, 101, 104–105, 114, 148, 173, 206, 208, 220, 246, 253, 263, 320, 353, 391, 480–481
Vietnam, 5–6, 12, 15, 17, 21, 26, 45–47, 53–54, 56–57, 60, 65, 69, 73–75, 79, 83, 92, 97, 99–100, 104–105, 114, 121, 148, 172, 181, 187, 246, 253, 261, 263, 297, 348, 367, 369–370, 372, 376–378, 391, 393, 396, 398, 401, 407, 417–418, 423, 465, 476, 481, 488, 490, 495, 499, 514
Vivian Drake, 23, 25, 91, 441
Volcano, 150–151, 156, 158, 344, 346, 356, 359

Wigmo, 85, 103–105, 114–116, 123, 125, 127–128, 130–138, 140, 143, 146–159, 162–167, 170, 173–175, 177, 179–180, 182, 186–191, 193, 197–199, 201, 207–208, 213–216, 218–219, 222, 224, 243, 252–254, 256, 262, 264–267, 271, 275, 277, 279, 283, 285, 288–289, 291, 300, 305, 307–308, 310–311, 345, 351, 354,

366, 369–372, 375–377, 379, 388, 419
William L. "Billy" Hamilton, 93
Wolfman Jack, 20
World Vision, 459, 492–499, 501–508

Zaire, 300–304, 306, 312, 315–316, 321, 340–341, 348

www.ingramcontent.com/pod-product-compliance
Lightning Source LLC
Chambersburg PA
CBHW060048230426

43661CB00004B/707